Motion Picture Performers:
A Bibliography of Magazine and Periodical Articles, 1900-1969

compiled by
MEL SCHUSTER

The Scarecrow Press, Inc.
Metuchen, N.J.   1971

ISBN 0-8108-0407-7

Library of Congress Catalog Card Number 70-154300

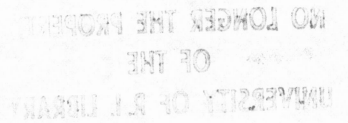

Contents

iii

INTRODUCTION

This Bibliography is intended as a guide and time-saving device for biographical or career-oriented research on Motion Picture Performers. It does not claim to be definitive, as the sources of research material are vast and the number of motion picture performers seemingly inexhaustible. Furthermore, the completeness of this work is closely related to the dictates, conditions and scope of the collection at the Library & Museum of the Performing Arts, the New York Public Library at Lincoln Center. The strengths and weaknesses of this work closely align those of that collection. The degree of the collection's completeness is manifested in this work by the following conditions:

1. The selection of magazines and periodicals perused issue-by-issue was primarily dependent on availability within this collection.

2. The incompleteness of a run of any given magazine may be a result of unavailability of back issues, an occasionally missed/misplaced issue, or bound but damaged issues. Also, the internal routines of the library sometimes make issues immediately unavailable, i.e., being bound, temporarily misplaced, on loan, on exhibition, etc.

Selection of Publications

The selection of magazines and periodicals documented was geared to appropriateness of content. Advice from librarians in the Theatre Collection was obtained to confirm and broaden a prepared list of English language publications to be included. The only critical judgment made regarding qualitative value of publications was the decision not to include "fan" magazines which have evolved a style of reporting not wholly suited to the purpose of this work. A reversal of this decision may ultimately be made for a future supplement to this volume. Exceptions were made in the case of fan magazines during the teens and twenties. These publications were more inclined to produce useful biographical data. Also, material on motion picture performers is scarce in general magazines prior to the mid-to-late thirties, increasing the

v

value of the early fan publications. The entire run of Photo-play Magazine is documented; although the earlier issues are the most useful it would have been an arbitrary decision to select a cut-off date in its documentation.

Newspapers are not included because of the overwhelming output of that industry. Certain newspapers' magazine editions are included, however; namely The New York Times Magazine, the Christian Science Monitor Magazine, the New York Times Book Review, and the Herald Tribune Book Review.

The content of articles sought for this work was biographical, career-oriented, analytical or critical. Reviews of performances or vehicles are not generally included. Likewise, picture spreads with minimal annotation were omitted. There are exceptions in both cases; but it is assumed that any disfavor will be aimed at what is missing rather than the lagniappe of material included beyond the established boundaries of this work.

For various reasons certain publications were not documented. These and any others on which attention focuses will be covered in a supplementary issue. Records of omitted publications as well as missing issues of included publications have been kept and will serve as a guide to obligatory inclusion in the future.

The entire runs of Readers' Guide and Biography Index were consulted for data from the publications they cover. Though the time span of this work is generalized as 1900 through 1969, the cut-off dates of these two major research sources vary:

Readers' Guide: February, 1969
Biography Index: August, 1969

Selection of Performers

Establishing criteria for selection of performers to be included invited an unending list of exceptions. Instead, research was started without focus on any performers. Magazines and periodicals examined by issue yielded a list augmented by various sources chosen for their representativeness and thoroughness. Those sources include:

1. Blum, Daniel. A Pictorial History of The Silent
    Screen. N. Y. : Grosset & Dunlap, 1953. (Any star
    mentioned four times in this book was included.
    Four mentions was an arbitrary number, but
    selected as being representative of the magnitude
    of the star.)

2. Blum, Daniel & Willis, John. Screen World. N. Y. :
    Crown Publishers, Volumes 12 through 20, 1961-
    1969. (These annuals were used as reminders of
    names representative of the movies during the
    1960's).

3. Cameron, Ian and Elisabeth. Dames. N. Y. :
    Frederick A. Praeger, Inc. , 1969.

4. Cameron, Ian & Elisabeth. The Heavies. N. Y. :
    Frederick A. Praeger, Inc. , 1969.

5. Everson, William K. The Bad Guys. N. Y. : The
    Citadel Press, 1964.

6. Meyers, Warren B. Who Is That? N. Y. : Personal-
    ity Posters, Inc. , 1965.

7. Osborne Robert. Academy Awards Illustrated.
    Marvin Miller Enterprises, Hollywood, Calif. , 1965.

8. Twomey, Alfred E. & McClure, Arthur F. The Vers-
    atiles. South Brunswick and N. Y. : A. S. Barnes
    and Company, 1969.

9. _____. Who's Who in Hollywood. N. Y. : Dell
    Publishing Co. , Vol 1-3, 1948; Vol. 1-4, 1949;
    Vol. 1-12, 1957; Vol. 1-20, 1965; Vol. 1-22, 1967.

Since the end of the regime of the major motion picture studios with their stable of contract players, performers
have moved more freely from medium to medium, making it
difficult to substantiate a claim that a performer is a star of
a given medium. This career flexibility broadened already
loose inclusion criteria, as well as necessitating the explora-
tion of stage, television and radio publications.

There are numerous performers included who might
more properly be described as other than motion picture
performers, e. g. , stage, TV, radio performers, politicians,
directors, producers, businessmen, models, sports figures,

etc. However, once motion picture acting merited articles on that phase of a performer's career, he/she was included without further definition. As the material sought was biographical, no editing was effected as to articles on a given performer. Thus, in many cases there is a great deal of material on non-performing aspects of a performer's career.

Users of this volume are requested to call attention to omitted performers or publications, as well as to errors that may have found their way into this volume. A supplementary volume will not only correct these situations, but will also update the contained material as well as keep abreast of emerging performers.

Special attention is drawn to the following list of performers who were researched but are not otherwise included because no material on them was found.

As this bibliography is focused on performers, it is constructed alphabetically by performer. No other indexing was felt necessary.

Cross referencing has been kept to a minimum. If an article concerned more than one performer, it was entered under each performer. In the case of teams (Laurel & Hardy, Martin & Lewis, Burns & Allen), groups (Andrews Sisters) or families (Redgrave Family, Nelson Family) there is a combined entry if the article applied to the combination of people. If the article applied to a performer individually rather than within the group, entry is made under the name of the applicable performer. In such cases cross referencing has been utilized.

Gratitude is hereby expressed to the various employees at the Lincoln Center Library who, through their job capacities, were called upon to help, either with knowing advice or by carting piles of old magazines to and from storage places. Gratitude is also extended to friends who patiently tolerated moods ranging from enthusiasm to boredom, and especially to Richard Jackson who was subjected to those moods on a day-to-day basis but remained loyally encouraging.

PERFORMERS NOT INCLUDED
IN THE BIBLIOGRAPHY

No articles were found on these listed performers. However, there is a vast amount of material on genre movies, periods of movie-making, studios, motion picture acting and actors (in general), etc. which might produce useful information on these people.

Abbott, John
Addy, Wesley
Adrian, Iris
Agnew, Robert
Ahn, Phillip
Ainsworth, Sidney
Akins, Claude
Alexander, John
Allen, Corey
Ames, Ramsey
Ames, Robert
Anderson, Herbert
Anderson, Michael Jr.
Anderson, Richard
Andersson, Harriet
Ankrum, Morris
Arletty
Arno, Sig
Arnt, Charles
Arthur, Johnny
Arthur, Robert
Arvidson, Linda
Aubrey, Jimmy

Bachelor, Stephanie
Bacon, Irving
Baldwin, Peter
Baldwin, Walter
Barbier, George
Bardette, Trevor
Barnett, Chester
Barnett, Griff

Barrie, James
Barrie, Mona
Barrie, Nigel
Barry, Wesley
Bartok, Eva
Bary, Leon
Barzell, Wolfe
Bassett, Russell
Baxter, Alan
Beddoe, Don
Bedoya, Alphonso
Belasco, Leon
Bell, Tom
Benham, Harry
Bennett, Belle
Bennett, Bruce
Bennett, Marjorie
Best, James
Best, Willie
Bettger, Lyle
Bevans, Clem
Biberman, Abner
Bissell, Whit
Blake, Gladys
Blake, Marie
Blanchard, Mari
Blane, Sally
Blue, Ben
Bochner, Lloyd
Bonanova, Fortunio
Borchers, Cornell
Boros, Ferike

Bowers, Kenny
Bowery Boys
Boyd, Mary
Bradley, Grace
Breck, Peter
Bremer, Lucille
Bressart, Felix
Brissac, Virginia
Brodie, Steve
Bronson, Charles
Bronson, Lillian
Brooke, Hillary
Brooks, Hazel
Brooks, Leslie
Brooks, Phyllis
Brown, Barbara
Brown, Charles D.
Brown, Pamela
Brunetti, Argentina
Bryant, Nana
Buetel, Jack
Buka, Donald
Burke, Walter
Burns, Paul E.

Cabot, Susan
Cady, Frank
Cahill, Marie
Calleia, Joseph
Campbell, Webster
Campeau, Frank
Campos, Rafael
Canty, Marietta
Carey, Harry Jr.
Carey, Timothy
Carleton, Claire
Carmen, Jewel
Carmichael, Ian
Carter, Ann
Caruso, Anthony
Cass, Maurice
Cassel, Seymour
Cassinelli, Dolores
Castiglioni, Iphogenie
Castle, Peggy
Cavanagh, Paul
Cavanaugh, Hobart
Chamberlin, Howard

Chambers, Wheaton
Chaney, Lon Jr.
Cheshire, Harry
Chong, Peter
Ciolli, Augusta
Clark, Andy
Clary, Charles
Clements, Stanley
Clute, Chester
Coe, Barry
Collins, Cora Sue
Conlin, Jimmy
Connelly, Bobby
Conrad, William
Cook, Elisha, Jr.
Cook, Marianne
Cooper, Melville
Corby, Ellen
Corcoran, Kevin
Corday, Mara
Cornell, Lillian
Corrigan, Lloyd
Cortese, Valentina
Cossart, Ernest
Courtleigh, William Jr.
Courtney, Inez
Cowan, Jerome
Coxen, Ed
Craig, Alec
Culver, Lillian
Culver, Roland
Cunningham, Cecil
Curtis, Willia Pearl

Dandridge, Ruby
Dano, Royal
Danova, Cesare
Dante, Michael
Danton, Ray
Darby, Kim
Darcel, Denise
Darvi, Bella
Da Silva, Howard
Davidson, William B.
Davis, Boyd
Davis, Mildred
Day, Marceline
Dearing, Edgar

x

De Banzie, Brenda
De Briac, Jean
De Corsia, Ted
Dehner, John
Delevanti, Cyril
Dell, Myra
De Mille, Katherine
De Putti, Lya
Devon, Richard
Dexter, Brad
Dexter, Elliot
Dick, Douglas
Dierkes, John
Dominguez, Joe
Donaldson, Ted
Donnelly, Ruth
Dowling, Constance
Dowling, Doris
Drake, Charles
Driscoll, Bobby
Dubbins, Don
Dubov, Paul
Dudley, Robert
Dugan, Tom
Dumbrille, Douglas
Dumke, Ralph
Dunn, Emma
Duvall, Robert

Eagles, Jeanne
Edeson, Robert
Edmunds, William
Edwards, Sarah
Elliot, Dick
Elliott, Denholm
Ellison, James
Elsom, Isobel
Emhardt, Robert
Emmett, Fern
Ericson, John
Esmond, Carl
Estabrook, Howard
Evans, Barry
Everett, Chad
Eyeton, Bessie

Fadden, Thomas
Faire, Virginia Brown

Farrar, David
Feld, Fritz
Ferguson, Frank
Field, Virginia
Filauri, Antonio
Finch, Flora
Finlay, Frank
Fischer, Margarita
Fitzroy, Emily
Fix, Paul
Flavin, James
Flowers, Bess
Flynn, Maurice
Fong, Benson
Fong, Harold
Foo, Wing
Forbes, Mary
Forrest, Steve
Foster, Norman
Fowley, Douglas
Fox, Sidney
Francen, Victor
Francis, Alec B.
Franz, Arthur
Fraser, John
Frazee, Jane
Frazer, Robert
Freeman, Kathleen
Fuller, Lance
Fung, Willie

Gaines, Richard
Galindo, Nacho
Garde, Betty
Gargan, Edward
Garralaga, Martin
Gates, Maxine
Gateson, Marjorie
Geray, Steven
Gilchrist, Connie
Gillingwater, Claude
Gillis, Ann
Girardot, Annie
Givney, Kathryn
Glass, Ned
Gleason, Lucile
Glendon, J. Frank
Gombell, Minna

xi

Ruysdael, Basil
Ryan, Irene
Ryan, Sheila
Ryan, Tim

St. John, Betta
St. John, Howard
Salmi, Albert
Salter, Harry
Sanford, Erskine
Sanford, Ralph
San Juan, Olga
Sawyer, Joseph
Schafer, Natalie
Schilling, Gus
Scott, Gordon
Sessions, Almira
Shannon, Harry
Shaughnessy, Mickey
Shay, William
Sheffield, Johnny
Sherry, J. Barney
Shigeta, James
Shimada, Teru
Shoemaker, Ann
Short, Antrim
Siletti, Mario
Sills, Milton
Silva, Henry
Silvera, Frank
Silverheels, Jay
Simmons, Beverly Sue
Simms, Larry
Skala, Lelia
Smalley, Phillips
Smith, Kent
Sorel, Jean
Sothern, Jean
Sparv, Camilla
Stanley, Forrest
Stanton, Paul
Stedman, Myrtle
Steel, Anthony
Steel, Bob
Sterling, Ford
Stevens, Emily
Stevens, K. T.
Stevens, Warren

Stewart, Martha
Stewart, Paul
Stockwell, Guy
Stone, Harold J.
Stossel, Ludwig
Stowell, William
Strode, Woody
Strudwick, Shepperd
Sully, Frank
Sundberg, Clinton
Suratt, Valeska

Taeger, Ralph
Taka, Miiko
Talmadge, Natalie
Taylor, Don
Taylor, Kent
Taylor, Libby
Teal, Ray
Teasdale, Veree
Tennant, Barbara
Thimig, Helene
Thompson, Carlos
Thompson, Rex
Tilbury, Zeffie
Tiller, Nadia
Tindall, Loren
Tomack, Sid
Tombes, Andrew
Tong, Kam
Torn, Rip
Torvay, Jose
Travers, Bill
Travers, Richard
Tremayne, Les
Trevor, Norman
Triesault, Ivan
Tryon, Tom
Tsiang, H. T.
Tuttle, Lurene
Tyler, Beverly
Tyler, Leon
Tyne, George

Vague, Vera
Vallone, Raf
Van, Bobby
Van der Vlis, Diana

xv

Van Eyck, Peter
Van Rooten, Luis
Van Zandt, Philip
Varconi, Victor
Varden, Norma
Vaughn, Dorothy
Vermilyea, Harold
Vernon, Bobby
Vickers, Martha
Vignon, Jean-Paul
Vincent, June
Vinson, Helen
Vitale, Milly
Vivian, Percival
Voight, Jon
Vye, Murvyn

Walker, Charlotte
Walker, Nella
Waller, Eddie
Walsh, George
Ward, James
Warde, Frederick
Warren, Katherine
Warrick, Ruth
Washbourne, Mona
Watkin, Pierre
Wattis, Richard
Weaver, Marjorie
Webber, Robert
Welch, Niles
Weldon, Ben
Wellman, William Jr.
Werbiseck, Gisela
Westman, Nydia
Whelan, Arlene
Whipper, Leigh
White, Jesse
White, Wilfred Hyde
Whitehead, O. Z.
Whitney, Claire
Whittell, Josephine
Wickes, Mary
Wild, Jack
Wilke, Robert J.
Williams, Adam
Williams, John

Williams, Rhys
Wilson, Ernest
Wilson, Janis
Windsor, Claire
Winwood, Estelle
Witherspoon, Cora
Wolfe, Ian
Wong, Jean
Wood, Douglas
Wright, Will

Yaconelli, Frank
Young, James
Young, Mary
Young, Polly Ann
Yowlachie, Chief

Zucco, George

HOW TO READ THE ENTRIES

The entries are arranged chronologically, permitting a researcher to start at the earliest published material and follow through progressively.

The sequence of the individual article entry is outlined below:

1. The writer's name, where applicable.
2. Title of the article.
3. Name of publication.
4. Publication volume.
5. Number within volume, where applicable.
6. Page number.
7. Date.

Example: Hamilton, S. Wedding day.   Photop 33-2:38 Jl '48

An article entitled "Wedding Day" written by S. Hamilton may be found in Photoplay Magazine on page 38 of Volume 33, number 2, dated July 1948.

Abbreviations used within entries.

Ap	April
Ag	August
cur	current
D	December
ed	editor; edited
F	February
filmog.	filmography
inc.	including
intv.	interview
Ja	January
Je	June
Jl	July
Mr	March
My	May
N	November
n. d.	not dated
O	October
p	Page
S	September
sup	Supplement

ABBREVIATIONS FOR PUBLICATIONS

This is not a complete list of all publications referred to.

Adv & Sell	Advertising and Sales Management
Am Ann	Americana Annual
Am Artist	American Artist
Am Cinematographer	American Cinematographer
Am City	The American City
Am For	American Forests
Am Heritage	American Heritage
Am Home	The American Home
Am Mag	American Magazine
Am Mer	American Mercury
Am Rec G	The American Record Guide
Am Scand R	American Scandinavian Review
Arts & Dec	Arts and Decoration
Atlan	The Atlantic
Bet Hom & Gard	Better Homes and Gardens
Bookm	Bookman
Brit Bk Yr	Britannica Book of the Year
Bsns W	Business Week
C S Mon Mag	Christian Science Monitor Magazine
CTA J	CTA Journal
Can Art	Canadian Art
Canad Forum	Canadian Forum
Carnegie Mag	Carnegie Magazine
Cath World	The Catholic World
Cent	Century
Christian Cent	The Christian Century
Colliers	Collier's
Colliers Yrbk	Collier's Yearbook
Contemp R	Contemporary Review
Cosmop	Cosmopolitan
Cur Bio	Current Biography
Cur Bio Yrbk	Current Biography Yearbook
Cur Hist	Current History
Cur Lit	Current Literature
Cur Opinion	Current Opinion
D Aus B	Dictionary of Australian Biography
DAB	Dictionary of American Biography
DNB	Dictionary of National Biography
Dance Mag	Dance Magazine

Delin	Delineator
Drama & Theatre	Drama and Theatre
Duns R	Dun's Review
Ed & Pub	Editor & Publisher
Educ Screen	The Educational Screen
Educ Vict	Education for Victory
Era	The Era
Etude	The Etude
Everybodys	Everybody's Magazine
Film Fan Mo	Film Fan Monthly
Film Q	Film Quarterly
Film Society R	Film Society Review
Films & Filming	Films and Filming
Freeman	The Freeman
Good H	Good Housekeeping
Harper	Harper's Magazine
Harper Baz	Harper's Bazaar
Hi Fi	High Fidelity
Hollywood Q	Hollywood Quarterly
Horn Bk	The Horn Book Magazine
House & Gard	House & Garden
House B	House Beautiful
Illus Lond N	Illustrated London News
Illus World	Illustrated World
Ind	Independent and Weekly Review
Ind Woman	Independent Woman
Instructor	The Instructor
Inter Am	Inter-American
L. Angeles Mus Q.	Los Angeles County Museum Quarterly
Ladies Home J	Ladies' Home Journal
Lib J	Library Journal
Lippinc	Lippincott's Magazine
Lit Digest	Literary Digest
Liv Age	Living Age
Liv for Young Hom	Living for Young Homemakers
Mag Art	Magazine of Art
McCalls	McCall's
McClure	McClure's Magazine
Midland Sch	Midland Schools
Mlle	Mademoiselle
Motor B	Motor Boating
Mumsey	Mumsey's Magazine
Mus Am	Musical America
Music J	Music Journal
N. Am R	North American Review
NCAB	National Cyclopaedia of American Biography

N. Y. Her Trib Bk R	New York Herald Tribune Book Review
N. Y. Times Bk R	New York Times Book Review
N. Y. Times Mag	New York Times Magazine
Nat Educ Assn J	Journal of the National Education Association
Nat Parent Teacher	National Parent-Teacher
Nat R	National Review
Nations Bus	Nation's Business
Negro Hist Bul	The Negro History Bulletin
New Repub	New Republic
New Statesm	New Statesman and Nation
New Yorker	The New Yorker
Numis	Numismatic News
Overland	Overland Monthly
PTA Mag	The PTA Magazine
Parents Mag	Parents' Magazine
Parks & Rec	Parks & Recreation
Photop	Photoplay
Pict R	Pictorial Review
Plays & Players	Plays and Players
Pop Mech	Popular Mechanics Magazine
Pop Phot	Popular Photography
Pop Sci	Popular Science Monthly
Ptr Ink	Printers' Ink
Pub W	Publishers' Weekly
Putnams	Putnam's Magazine
Q J Speech Ed	Quarterly Journal of Speech Education
Q of Film, Radio & Television	Quarterly of Film, Radio and Television
R of Rs	Review of Reviews, American
Radio & TV News	Radio & Television News
Ramp Mag	Ramparts Magazine
Read Digest	Reader's Digest
Redbook	Redbook Magazine
Rev	Review
Roy Soc Arts J	Royal Society of Arts Journal
S. Atlan Q	South Atlantic Quarterly
Sales Mgt	Sales Management
Sat Eve Post	Saturday Evening Post
Sat R	Saturday Review
Sch & Soc	School and Society
Sci Am	Scientific American
Sci Digest	Science Digest
Sci N L	Science News Letter
Scrib Com	Scribner's Commentator
Scrib Mag	Scribner's Magazine
Sight & Sound	Sight and Sound
Spectator (Lond)	Spectator (London)

Sports Illus	Sports Illustrated
Sr Schol	Senior Scholastic
St N	St. Nicholas
Strand	The Strand Magazine
TV Personalities	TV Personalities Biographical Sketch Book
Tech World	Technical World Magazine
Todays Health	Today's Health
Tulane Drama R	Tulane Drama Review
20th Cent	Twentieth Century
U. N. Bul	United Nations Bulletin
U. N. Rev	United Nations Review
U. N. World	United Nations World
U. S. Camera	U. S. Camera and Travel
U. S. Dept State Bul	United States Department of State Bulletin
U. S. News	U. S. News and World Report
Vital Speeches	Vital Speeches of the Day
Wilson Lib Bul	Wilson Library Bulletin
Windsor	The Windsor Magazine
Woman Cit	Woman Citizen
Womans H C	Woman's Home Companion
Womans J	Woman's Journal
Writer	The Writer

BIBLIOGRAPHY OF PERFORMERS

ABBOTT, BUD
Biography. Cur Bio 1941
Nugent, F. S. Loco boy makes good. N. Y. Times Mag
  p8 Ag 24 '41
Crichton, L. Up from the rank. Colliers 108:42
  O 25 '41
Eddy, D. $5,000,000 belly laugh. Am Mag 135:42 Ja '43
Frank, S. Gold-plated corn. Colliers 120:24 N 8 '47
When the tax collector takes everything. U. S. News
  46:121 Je 15 '59
(See also: ABBOTT AND COSTELLO)

ABBOTT AND COSTELLO
Zeitlin, I. Clamor boys. Photop 19-6:42 N '41
Reese, H. A. Older the gag, the louder the laugh; how
  Abbott and Costello have proved it. Sat Eve Post
  214:19 Ap 25 '42
Bud, Lou and the kids; Lou Costello Jr. Youth Foundation.
  Newsweek 30:25 D 15 '47
The strange partnership of Abbott and Costello. TV Guide
  6-3:6 Ja 16 '53
(See also: ABBOTT, BUD; COSTELLO, LOU)

ABEL, WALTER
Actors, characters, exciting new theatres. New York
  State Community Theatre Journal. 4-3:9 Jl '64.

ADAMS, EDIE
Bracker, M. Up and coming. N. Y. Times Mag p74
  Ap 26 '53
Bracker, M. Sister Eileen. Sr Schol 62:6 My 25 '53
Growing girl. Theatre Arts 37:12 N '53
Biography. Cur Bio 15:3 F '54
  Same. Cur Bio Yrbk 1954:9 '54
Laughing Lady. TV Guide 3-27:8 Jl 2 '55
Goldberg, H. Edie is a lady. Cosmop 139:26 D '55
Jill-of-all-trades. Newsweek 47:56 Ap 2 '56
Edie Adams and Ernie Kovacs. Sat Eve Post D 28 '57

Wood, C. TV personalities biographical sketch book.
  TV Personalities p38 '57
Torre, M. Edie Adams: how I survived. Redbook 119:46
  S '62
Tiger time for Edie Adams. TV Guide 10-52:10 D 29 '62
Tax missionary. Time 81:46 Mr 1 '63
Bunzel, P. Edie wins a big one. Life 54:95 Ap 5 '63
Lewis, R. W. Year in the life of Edie Adams. Sat Eve
  Post 236:24 Ap 13 '63
Amory, C. Celebrity register. McCalls 90:122 Je '63
Adams, E. Strangers kept me from dying. Photop 64-5:72
  N '63

ADAMS, JULIE
  (also known as Julia Adams)
  Julia in jeopardy. Life 36:105 Ap 19 '54

ADAMS, KATHRYN
  Obit. Screen World 11:215 '60

ADAMS, NICK
  Adams, N. The day a star was born. Photop 50-6:52
    D '56
  Jones, C. & Adams, N. Don't be difficult. Photop 54-1:65
    Jl '58
  March, B. Mom, I'm sorry I lied to you. Photop 55-4:44
    Ap '59
  Adams, N. Marriage is swell! Photop 56-2:62 Ag '59
  Nick from Nanticoke. TV Guide 8-3:12 Ja 16 '60
  Borie, M. Does she really want a divorce? Photop 57-4:
    36 Ap ' 60
  Cohen, M. A lot to learn about girls. Photop 57-6:44 Je '60
  Nichols, M. Brash Bantam. Coronet 48:20 My '60
  Reed, M. Why he exposed his private hell Photop 67-4:14
    Ap '65
  Obit. Newsweek 71:81 F 19 '68
    Screen World 20:231 '69
  Terry, P. Little man with a big heart. Photop 73-5:72
    My '68

ADDAMS, DAWN
  Dawn's early light.   Life 33:129 N 17 '52
  On stardom's stairway. Coronet 35:50 Ja '54
  Once upon a time: Dawn Addams marries Prince of
    Roccasecca de' Volsci. Life 36:131 My 17 '54
  Lane, J. F. My life as Chaplin's leading lady. Films &
    Filming 3-11:12 Ag '57

Gals and gauls. Time 80:52 D 21 '62

ADLER, LUTHER
  Nolan, J. E. Five tv heavies. Film Fan Mo 92:15 F '69

ADOREE, RENEE
  Wilson, H. The genius enchanting. Photop 30-1:63 Je '26
  Albert, K. The girl who just missed stardom. Photop 37-2:48 Ja '30
  Uselton, R. A. Renee Adoree, inc. filmog. Films In Review 19-6:345 Je/Jl '68

AGAR, JOHN
  Waterbury, R. The love story of Shirley Temple and her sergeant. Photop 27-2:56 Jl '45
  Waterbury, R. Shirley, Lohengrin and happiness. Photop 28-1:28 D '45
  Temple, S. The Shirley I know. Photop 31-6:64 N '47
  Downing, H. Talk about John Agar. Photop 33-6:44 N '48
  McElroy, J. Breakfast in Hollywood. Photop 36-3:58 Ag '49
  Parsons, L. O. What happened to the Temple marriage. Photop 36-7:32 D '49
  Maxwell, E. This you must understand. Photop 37-2:34 F '50
  Parsons, L. O. The John Agar puzzle. Photop 39-5:44 My '51

AHERNE, BRIAN
  Taviner, R. Who is Brian Aherne? Photop 44-2:36 Jl '33
  Roberts, K. He likes to fly. Colliers 100:11 O 2 '37
  Zeitlin, I. How Olivia sees her sister's romance. Photop 53-11:27 N '39
  Fletcher, A. W. Hollywood at home. Photop 54-7:18 Jl '40
  Interesting people at home. House & Gard 82:36 Ag '42
  Sharpe, H. Categorically speaking. Photop 23-6:50 N '43
  Bentley, J. And now goodbye. Photop 25-1:27 Je '44
  Cold shoulder. Am Mag 140:55 Ag '45
  I learned about flying from that! Flying 43:44 N '48
  Two by two across the USA. Life 47:61 D 21 '59
  Biography. Cur Bio 21:3 F '60
  Same. Cur Bio Yrbk 1960:3 '61

ALBERGHETTI, ANNA MARIA
  Angel from paradise. Time 55:57 My 8 '50
  Italy's Anna Maria Alberghetti. Life 28:36 My 29 '50
  Diva at 14. Newsweek 36:78 Jl 10 '50

Ford, E.   Maid in waiting.   Photop 44-3:72 S '53
Anna Maria, happy in the rain.   Life 37:65 Ag 30 '54
Biography.   Cur Bio 16:3 Ja '55
   Same.   Cur Bio Yrbk 1955:3 '56
Wood, C.   TV personalities biographical sketchbook.
   TV Personalities p96 '57
March, B.   I'm scared of marriage.   Photop 56-1:44 Jl
   '59
Waif on Broadway.   N. Y. Times Mag p16 Ap 23 '61
Martin, P.   Backstage with Anna Maria.   Sat Eve Post
   234:96 N 25 '61

ALBERNI, LUIS
   Obit.   Screen World 14:221 '63

ALBERS, HANS
   Obit.   Screen World 12:219 '61
   Lundquist, G.   Hans Albers, inc. filmog.   Films In Re-
   view 16-3:150 Mr '65

ALBERT, EDDIE
   Zeitlin, I.   Funny face.   Photop 53-12:31 D '39
   Crichton, K.   Amazing Albert.   Colliers 108:14 Jl 5 '41
   Biography.   Cur Bio 15:5 Ja '54
   Same.   Cur Bio Yrbk 1954:14 '54
   Virtue of nightclubs.   Time 63:47 My 3 '54
   New husband and wife hit.   Look 18:74 Jl 13 '54
   Zolotow, M.   Eddie Albert.   Cosmop 137:26 Ag '54
   Wood, C.   TV personalities biographical sketchbook.
   TV Personalities. p15 '54
   Hollywood hobbyists.   Woman's H C 83:45 O '56
   Whitney, D.   It's about the atavistic urge.   TV Guide
   14-2:16 Ja 8 '66
   Raddatz, L.   What keeps Eddie Albert busy, happy and
   rich?   TV Guide   17-36:16 S 6 '69

ALBERTSON, Frank
   Gray, B.   Filmography.   Films In Review 15-4:254
   Ap '64
   Obit.   Screen World 16:219 '65

ALBERTSON, MABEL
   Raker, A.   Filmography.   Films In Review 19-8:521
   O '68

ALBRIGHT, HARDIE
   Hamilton, S.   We should have known.   Photop 41-2:60 Ja '32

ALBRIGHT, LOLA
Camera shy. Am Mag 150:59 Jl '50
Have Gunn, will travel. TV Guide 7-1:18 Ja 3 '59
What Lola wants Lola gets. Look 23:69 F 17 '59
Men look twice. Time 74:64 S 14 '59
What it's like to be Lola. TV Guide 9-6:9 F 11 '61
Nichols, M. Gunn's girl. Coronet 50:16 My '61
Lewis, R. W. When Lola came to town. TV Guide 14-
   2:22 Ja 8 '66

ALDA, ALAN
Owl and the pussycat. Ebony 20:98 F '65
Why am I playing quarterback for the Detroit Lions?
   Sat Eve Post 241:56 N 16 '68

ALDA, ROBERT
Eaton, H. Discovery in "blue." Photop 28-2:60 Ja '46
Wood, C. TV personalities biographical sketchbook.
   TV Personalities p117 '57

ALDEN, MARY
Winship, M. A recamier of the films. Photop 21-3:77
   F '22
Alden, M. How to lose your husband. Photop 25-6:28
   My '24
Don, V. J. I'm tired of smother roles. Photop 35-1:37
   D '28

ALEXANDER, BEN
Wood, C. TV personalities biographical sketchbook.
   TV Personalities p82 '54

ALLASIO, MARISA
Person of promise. Films & Filming 4-3:31 D '57

ALLBRITTON, LOUISE
Holliday, K. All for Allbritton. Photop 26-3:50 F '45
Marshall, J. Tall, torrid and Texas. Colliers 115:17
   Ap 28 '45
McClelland, D. Louise Allbritton, inc. filmog. Screen
   Facts 18:45 n. d.

ALLEN, GRACIE
Pic-ings. Pict R 37:34 Ap '36
Menken, H. Laughs from the ladies. Delin 129:64 Ag
   '36
Albert, D. Her adopted children remade Gracie Allen's

life.   Photop 51-4:45 Ap '37
Candidette.   Time 35:36 Mr 18 '40
Burns, G.   Gracie Allen as I know her.   Ind Woman
   19:198 Jl '40
Biography.   Cur Bio '40
Foster, I. W.   Gracie isn't so dumb off the air.   Ind
   Woman 26:292 O '47
Biography.   Cur Bio Mr '51
   Same Cur Bio Yrbk 1951:75 '52
Gracie Allen's own story; inside me, ed by J. K. Morris.
   Womans H C 80:40 Mr '53
Seldes, G.   Comical gentlewoman.   Sat R 36:37 My 2 '53
Gould, J.   TV's top comediennes.   N. Y. Times Mag
   p16 D 27 '53
How Gracie gets that way.   TV Guide 3-41:13 O 8 '55
Burns, G.   I love her, that's why! excerpt.   Coronet
   39:82 Ap '56
She's tired of being Gracie Allen.   TV Guide 6-24:28 Je
   14 '58
Amory, C.   Celebrity register.   McCalls 90:136 My '63
Obit.   Cur Bio 25:3 O '64
   Cur Bio Yrbk 1964:3 '64
   Time 84:87 S 4 '64
   Illus Lond N 245:345 S 5 '64
   Newsweek 64:59 S 7 '64
   Screen World 16:219 '65
(See also: BURNS AND ALLEN)

ALLEN, JOSEPH JR.
Obit.   Screen World 14:221 '63

ALLGOOD, SARA
Obit.   Newsweek 36:63 S 25 '50
   Time 56:94 S 25 '50

ALLISON, MAY
Durand, E.   Winsome May Allison.   Feature Movie
   4-1:31 O 10 '15
Manners, M.   May Allison is back.   Photop 14-4:95 S '18
Winship, M.   The tale of a tear.   Photop 19-2:71 Ja '21
Winship, M.   The girl on the cover.   Photop 24-6:80 N
   '23

ALLYSON, JUNE
Two girls.   Life 17:63 Jl 17 '44
Holliday, K.   Sweet and lively - June Allyson.   Photop
   25-5:56 O '44

Crichton, K.   Up and coming.   Colliers 114:24 N 11 '44
St. Johns, A. R.   Girl of the moment.   Photop 26-1:30
   D '44; 26-2:32 Ja '45
Allyson in wonderland.   Am Mag 139:124 F '45
Allyson, J.   I'm like this.   Photop 26-5:34 Ap '45
Parsons, L. O.   Ask me no questions.   Photop 27-1:32
   Je '45
Allyson, J.   The Van Johnson I know.   Photop 27-4:36
   S '45
June Allyson overcomes a twisted back to dance and climb
   to stardom.   Life 19:87 O 1 '45
Waterbury, R.   They're Mr. and Mrs. Dick Powell.
   Photop 27-6:32 N '45
Sailor takes a wife.   Time 47:94 Mr 11 '46
St. Johns, E.   Corner on happiness.   Photop 28-6:38
   My '46
Howe, H.   June days.   Photop 29-3:54 Ag '46
Walker, N.   Two girls and a friendship.   Photop 29-6:
   50 N '46
Mamlok, M.   Sunshine in her hands.   Photop 30-4:43
   Mr '47
St. Johns, A. R.   How June Allyson is learning to be
   happy.   Photop 30-6:36 My '47
Perkins, L.   Photolife of June Allyson.   Photop 32-5:56
   Ap '48
Edwards, R.   Play truth or consequences with June Ally-
   son.   Photop 32-6:62 My '48
Copeland, J.   Early June.   Photop 33-2:64 Jl '48
Scott, D.   Sunny side up.   Photop 34-4:44 Mr '49
Allyson, J.   Lady with a past.   Photop 36-1:46 My '49
Powell, D.   Mr. and Mrs. Mike.   Photop 36-4:48 S '49
Allyson, J.   My prayer.   Photop 37-1:32 Ja '50
Shore, D.   Pamela makes it perfect.   Photop 37-3:36
   Mr '50
Dreier, H.   Welcome home.   Photop 37-5:60 My '50
Arnold, M.   The best years of our lives.   Photop 38-1:
   44 Jl '50
Arnold, M.   The happy heart.   Photop 38-5:36 N '50
Engstead, J.   I was there.   Photop 38-6:36 D '50
Martin, P.   Hollywood's child bride.   Sat Eve Post 223:
   34 Ja 20 '51
Zeitlin, I.   Hollywood's first family.   Photop 40-5:46
   N '51
Biography.   Cur Bio 13:3 Ja '52
   Same.   Cur Bio Yrbk 1952:13 '53
Downing, H.   The heart grows up.   Photop 41-6:52 Je '52
Hopper, H.   Is June Allyson retiring?   Photop 42-4:38

O '52
Leon, R.   Lovely weather for June.   Photop 44-4:56 O
    '53
Voight, R. D.   June Allyson says: Our adopted child
    taught us family love.   Womans H C 81:18 F '54
Allyson, J.   What's a girl to do?   Photop 45-5:22 My '54
Allyson, J.   Mothers are for loving.   Photop 45-6:50
    Je '54
Hall, G.   She's nobody's baby now!   Photop 46-3:48
    S '54
Allyson, J.   Mother's little dividends.   Photop 47-1:38
    Ja '55
Maynard, J.   She was a prisoner of fear.   Photop 47-3:
    59 Mr '55
Balling, F. D.   So you think vacations are fun?   Photop
    48-1:37 Jl '55
Are you a shrike?   Womans H C   82:34 Jl '55
Hubler, R. G.   All about Allyson.   Coronet 38:158 O '55
Ott, B.   Rumor's targets.   Photop 48-6:50 D '55
Whitcomb, J.   On location with The opposite sex.   Cosmop
    141:68 O '56
Phillips, D.   She couldn't say yes.   She couldn't say no.
    Photop 50-5:48 N '56
Hartung, P. T.   All-American.   Commonweal 65:312 D
    21 '56
Harrison, J.   The three weeks we'd like to forget.
    Photop 52-1:48 Jl '57
Maynard, J.   Let's be frank about me.   Sat Eve Post
    230:17 D '14; 20 D 21 '57
The girl next door gets the glamor treatment.   TV Guide
    7-40:9 O 3 '59
Miss Allyson was not amused.   TV Guide 8-38:17 S 17 '60
Tornabene, L.   Lunch date with June Allyson and Dick
    Powell.   Cosmop 150:11 Ja '61
Dinter, C.   Divorce.   Photop 59-4:38 Ap '61
Wilkie, J.   You don't sound like mommy.   Photop 60-4:
    54 O '61
Morre, M.   Much-mended marriage of Dick Powell and
    June Allyson.   McCalls 89:94 Je '62
Maynard, J.   June says "I do" to barber.   Photop 65-
    1:60 Ja '64
It never had a chance.   Photop 65-6:54 Je '64
Young, C.   June Allyson, inc. filmog.   Films In Review
    19-9:535 N '68

ALVARDO, DON
    Obit.   Screen World 19:228 '68

AMECHE, DON

Taviner, R.   Love is good luck to Don Ameche.   Photop
50-6:60 D '36

Sharpe, H.   Happy hellion.   Photop 52-3:15 Mr; 52-4:30
Ap; 52-5:62 My '38

Maxwell, J.   Don Ameche's wife talks about his clothes.
Womans H C 66:63 Ja '39

Street, J.   The saint is a sinner.   Radio Guide p2 Mr
29 '39

Hayes, B.   What I plan for my son in today's troubled
world.   Photop 54-1:66 Ja '40

Waterbury, R.   Don, Alice and Ty.   Photop 54-4:14 Ap
'40

Zarat, I.   How Don Ameche lives.   Photop 19-3:30 Ag
'41

Ameche, D.   My commandments for my children.
Photop 25-2:45 Jl '44

Ameche, D.   What I notice about women.   TV Guide 5-6:
5 F 8 '52

Ameche's ascent.   New Yorker 31:32 Ap 2 '55

Considine, B.   Many lives of Don Ameche.   Cosmop 139:
22 Jl '55

Ringmaster.   TV Guide 10-51:6 D 22 '62

He has moved out of the center ring.   TV Guide 13-17:
24 Ap 24 '65

Biography.   Cur Bio 26:3 My '65

Same.   Cur Bio Yrbk 1965:13 '65

Meehan, T.   Goodbye Sam Spade, hello Stephen Foster.
Sat Eve Post 239:18 Mr 12 '66

AMES, ADRIENNE

Stevens, G.   Divorce taught them how truly they were
married.   Photop 48-7:50 D '35

AMES, LEON

Gehman, R.   The world's luckiest father.   TV Guide 10-
20:22 My 19 '62

ANDERS, MERRY

Wood, C.   TV personalities biographical sketchbook.
TV Personalities p13 '56

ANDERSON, CLAIRE

Obit.   Screen World 16:219 '65

ANDERSON, DONNA

Person of promise.   Films & Filming 6-12:17 S '60

ANDERSON, EDDIE "ROCHESTER"
  Keen, H.   Rochester, Skippy Smith & Co; production that
    knows no color line.   Survey   31:379 S '42
  Muir, F.   What's that, boss?   How Rochester parlayed a
    cement-mixer voice into fame and fortune.   Sat Eve
    Post 215:15 Je 19 '43
  Jack Benny's man Rochester.   TV Guide 3-35:20 Ag 27
    '55

ANDERSON, G. M. (BRONCHO BILLY)
  Cary, H.   Bad man of the movies.   Tech World 28:480
    Je '15
  Where are they now?   Newsweek 62:12 Ag 19 '63

ANDERSON, JUDITH
  Roberts, K.   Assorted roles.   Colliers 88:22 Ag 1 '31
  They stand out from the crowd.   Lit Digest 119:12 Mr 2
    '35
  Biography.   Cur Bio '41
  Three-star classic.   Time 40:45 D 21 '42
  Wallsten, R.   Shakespeare on the jungle circuit.   Colliers
    114:23 D 9 '44
  Brown, J. M.   Genuine virtuosity.   Sat R 30:24 N 22 '47
  Gilder, R.   Actors all: Judith Anderson's Media.
    Theatre Arts 31:10 D '47
  My current reading.   Sat R 31:6 Ja 17 '48
  Myers, P.   Three first ladies.   Dramatics p14 O '51
  Harvey, E.   John Brown's Body hits the road.   Colliers
    130:24 D 6 '52
  Lady Hamlet.   Newsweek 46:55 Jl 18 '55
  Personality of the month.   Plays & Players 7-12:3 S '60
  Biography.   Cur Bio 22:3 F '61
    Same.   Cur Bio Yrbk 1961:9 '62
  Whitney, D.   Every inch a queen.   TV Guide 16-4:12 Ja
    27 '68
  Redinger, E. L.   Interview.   Drama & Theatre 7-2:93
    Win '68/69
  People.   Time 93:32 Ja 3 '69

ANDERSON, MARY
  Kingsley, G.   Mary Anderson of the films.   Photop 12-
    1:80 Je '17

ANDERSON, MIGNON
  Holmes, H.   The little "Dresden China girl."   Photop
    4-6:59 N '13

ANDERSON, WARNER
  Wood, C.   TV personalities biographical sketchbook.
    TV Personalities p139 '54

ANDERSSON, BIBI
  Burnevich, J.   Bibi Andersson.   Sequences 12-48:32
    F '67

ANDES, KEITH
  He always has the last laugh.   TV Guide 8-32:8 Ag 6 '60

ANDRE, GWILI
  Obit.   Screen World 11:215 '60

ANDRESS, URSULA
  Hamilton, J.   Ursula Andress of Dr. No: Beauty finds
    its way.   Look 26:72 D 31 '62
  Hamilton, J.   Ursula Andress: success story of a lazy
    beauty.   Look 27:54 N 5 '63
  Ursula major.   Newsweek 64:79B Jl 20 '64
  Ursula Andress and her hidden persuader.   Esquire 65:
    80 Ja '66
  Ursula.   U. S. Camera 29:64 Ag '66

ANDREWS, DANA
  Sharpe, H.   The remarkable Andrews.   Photop 22-5:44
    Ap '43
  Steele, J. H.   Portrait of a minister's son.   Photop
    25-2:54 Jl '44
  Chapman, J.   The man who loved Laura.   Photop 26-4:
    36 Mr '45
  Perkins, L.   Photolife of Dana Andrews.   Photop 28-3:
    54 F '46
  Harris, E.   D is for Dana.   Photop 28-5:40 Ap '46
  Deere, D.   Runaway.   Photop 29-2:41 Jl '46
  Downing, H.   The low road.   Photop 30-3:59 F '47
  Harris, E.   Dana Andrews faces east.   Photop 30-6:44
    My '47
  Howe, H.   A man of distinction.   Photop 32-5:68 Ap '48
  Biography.   Cur Bio 20:4 O '59
  Same.   Cur Bio Yrbk 1959:11 '60

ANDREWS, EDWARD
  TV's button-down actor.   TV Guide 12-47:15 N 21 '64

ANDREWS, HARRY
  Harry Andrews.   Plays & Players 9-7:5 Ap '62

ANDREWS, JULIE
People are talking about . . . Vogue 124:124 O 1 '54
Young and happy. New Yorker 30:36 N 20 '54
Markel, H.   Girl friend. N. Y. Times Mag p33 N 21 '54
I predict these will be the bright new stars of 1955.
    Look 19:16 Ja 11 '55
Theatre Arts gallery.   Theatre Arts 39:29 F '55
New musical in Manhattan.   Time 67:89 Mr 26 '56
Biography.   Time 67:89 Mr 26 '56
Millstein, G.   Flowering of a fair lady. N. Y. Times
    Mag p24 Ap 1 '56
Julie Andrews, My fair lady.   Newsweek 47:63 My 7 '56
Biography.   Cur Bio 17:3 Jl '56
    Same.   Cur Bio Yrbk 1956:16 '57
Robinson, S.   Loverly Julie.   McCalls 84:42 O '56
Markel, H.   Eliza's year; it's been loverly. N. Y. Times
    Mag p14 Mr 10 '57
Britain is smitten by Fair lady.   Life 44:20 My 12 '58
Eliza into Cinderella. N. Y. Times Mag p62 Mr 24 '57
Once upon a time.   TV Guide 5-13:10 Mr 30 '57
Co-stars kiss.   Life 52:78 Ja 5 '62
Stars at rehearsal.   Newsweek 55:78 F 1 '60
Kelly, V.   Julie Andrews and Carol Burnett; a wacky
    TV caper.   Look 26:80 Je 19 '62
Gordon, S.   Julie Andrews goes to Hollywood.   Look 27:
    123 N 19 '63
Burnett, C. ed. by H. Markel.   My friend Julie Andrews.
    Good H 157:34 N '63
Hamill, P.   My fair Julie.   Sat Eve Post 236:68 D 21
    '63
Once and future queen.   Time 84:42 O 9 '64
Julie for Emily.   Newsweek 64:96 N 2 '64
Biography.   Newsweek 64:96 N 2 '64
Zeitlin, D.   At last Hollywood discovers the toast of
    Broadway: Julie.   Life 57:117 N 13 '64
Poppy, J.   Julie Andrews' star rises higher with The
    sound of music.   Look 29:38 Ja 26 '65
A star is born.   Photop 67-1:42 Ja '65
Premiere ordains her a queen.   Life 58:61 Mr 12 '65
Joyous Julie and her Sound of music.   Life 58:52 Mr 12
    '65
Steinem, G.   Julie Andrews.   Vogue 145:124 Mr 15 '65
Miller, E.   Bird in her nest.   Seventeen 24:134 Mr '65
Hano, A.   Julie Andrews: her magic, her moods.
    Good H 160:90 My '65
York, C.   The woman who broke up her home.   Photop
    68-2:20 Ag '65

Morgan, T. B. Julie, baby. Look 29:47 D 28 '65
Smith, G. Someday it will all be just wonderful. Sat
    Eve Post 239:34 Ja 29 '66
Christy, G. All the things I love most. Good H 162:
    90 Mr '66
Newquist, R. Julie Andrews: intv. McCalls 93:83 Mr
    '66
Shipman, D. The all-conquering governess. Films &
    Filming 12-11:16 Ag '66
Poppy, J. Hawaii. Look 30:54 S 6 '66
Ronan, M. Lively arts; intv. Sr Schol 89:22 D 2 '66
Now and future queen. Time 88:53 D 23 '66
Lerman, L. International movie report. Mlle 64:119
    F '67
Robinson, S. My London; intv. McCalls 94:46 Ap '67
Long-winded lady; movie-making in Algonquin Hotel.
    New Yorker 43:21 Je 17 '67
Zill, J. A. Julie plays Gertie. Look 31:63 S 19 '67
Wells, T. My daughter, Julie Andrews. Good H 166:
    98 Mr '68
Ellis, E. Her secret rendezvous. Photop 73-4:54 Ap
    '68
Frankel, J. Sound of more music; filming of Star!
    Sat Eve Post 241:28 Je 29 '68
Kerr, M. Why she lives alone. Photop 73-6:56 Je '68
Arkadin. Film clips. Sight & Sound 37-4:211 Aut '68
O'Brien, F. Won't marry man she lives with. Photop
    74-5:46 N '68
Valentine, L. Their songs of love. Photop 75-1:35 Ja
    '69
Lawrenson, H. Sweet Julie. Esquire 71:62 Ja '69
Rose, L. I wonder about sex. Photop 75-3:59 Mr '69

ANDREWS, LaVERNE
    Obit. Screen World 19:228 '68
    (See also: ANDREWS SISTERS)

ANDREWS, LOIS
    Obit. Screen World 20:231 '69

ANDREWS, MAXENE
    (See: ANDRES SIS

ANDREWS, PATTY
    (See: ANDREWS SISTERS)

ANDREWS SISTERS (Patty, Maxene, LaVerne)
    Crichton, K. Sweet and hot. Colliers 104:16 O 28 '39

Juke-box divas. Time 38:36 D 1 '41
Three zombies of swing. Newsweek 24:94 S 18 '44
(See also: ANDREWS, LaVERNE)

ANGELI, PIER
New star from Italy. Life 30:77 Mr 19 '51
Strauss, T. Hollywood natural. Colliers 129:52 Ap 26
'52
Roberts, W. Zing went the strings of his heart.
Photop 42-3:44 S '52
Armstrong, G. Is it really love? Photop 43-3:68 Mr
'53
Angeli, P. Saludos Amiga. Photop 44-3:38 S '53
Gould, H. Ready for love. Photop 44-4:44 O '53
Flight of fancy. Life 37:68 Jl 12 '54
Hall, G. Sleeping beauty wakes up. Photop 46-2:36 Ag
'54
Watson, E. M. D. Italy's twin sisters. Cosmop 137:28
S '54
Pierangeli, Mrs. I. My daughter was ready for marriage.
Photop 47-2:37 F '55
Ott, B. Honeymoon on the heavenly side. Photop 47-3:
33 Mr '55
Block, M. What are angels made of? Photop 47-6:44
Je '55
Booth, M. Heaven in their arms. Photop 49-2:47 F '56
Fine part for Pier. Life 41:41 Jl 30 '56
Lane, L. Behold - this is my beloved. Photop 50-4:
54 O '56
Townsend, P. Laughter chases the blues. Photop 51-4:
64 Ap '57
Schuyler, D. Three against a storm. Photop 54-1:38
Jl '58
Tuneful transformation of a wistful movie waif. Life 45:
67 D 15 '58
Aelion, A. A little boy lost. Photop 56-3:42 S '59
Holtzer, J. Can a man ever forget the woman he loved?
Photop 58-4:48 O '60
Carpozi, G. Pier won't take my son. Photop 67-1:40
Ja '65
Marzoni, E. Perry belongs with me. Photop 67-1:41
Ja '65

ANKA, PAUL
Pair of songbirds. Newsweek 56:82 Jl 4 '60
Prideaux, T. Paul Anka, kids' wonder singer. Life

49:67 Ag 29 '60
Nichols, M.   Canada's teenage Croesus.   Coronet 50:10
   My '61
Davidson, B.   Bobby Darin and Paul Anka; boy wonders,
   but why?   McCalls 89:110 O '61
Paul the comforter.   Time 78:62 N 3 '61
The baby-faced Midas of rock 'n roll.   TV Guide 10-24:
   19 Je 16 '62
Biography.   Cur Bio 25:3 F '64
Same.   Cur Bio Yrbk 1964:3 '64
Miller, E.   Paul in Poland.   Seventeen 23:160 Ap '64

ANKERS, EVELYN
McClelland, D.   Evelyn Ankers: queen of horrors, inc.
   filmog.   Film Fan Mo 88:3 O '68

ANNABELLA
Roberts, K.   From hen house to Hollywood.   Colliers
   101:12 Ja 22 '38
Reid, S.   Mrs. Tyrone Power.   Photop 53-8:24 Ag '39
Hall, G.   The Tyrone Powers fight it out.   Photop 19-
   2:38 Jl '41

ANN-MARGRET
Britten, R.   Kissing strangers can be fun.   Photop 60-5:
   48 N '61
Henderson, B.   Little girl with the big urge.   Photop
   61-2:54 F '62
Setting fire to Texas.   Life 52:49 Ap 20 '62
When she hit the beat.   TV Guide 10-31:15 Ag 4 '62
Barber, R.   New star in the west.   Show 2-9:68 S '62
Somers, A.   You can't play with love.   Photop 62-3:60
   S '62
Corbin, J.   Why I prefer divorced men.   Photop 62-5:57
   N '62
Watch the birdie and see Ann-Margret soar.   Life 54:60
   Ja 11 '63
Ann-Margret tries new hair styles.   Seventeen 23:156 Ap
   '63
DeBlasio, E.   Ann-Margret's life story.   Photop 63-4:60
   Ap; 63-5:59 My '63
Jennings, D.   Ann-Margret.   Sat Eve Post 236:70 My 4
   '63
Sight & Sound; on location of Viva Las Vegas.   McCalls
   91:12 N '63
Miller, E.   I did that.   Seventeen 24:138 F '65
Tornabene, L.   Tomorrow's stars.   Good H 160:26 Mr '65

Allen, W.   Attention.   See Europe with the king of the international set (me).   Esquire 65:55 F '66
Reynolds, L.   How she got Roger Smith.   Photop 72-2:
   58 Ag '67
What to wear?   TV Guide 17-44:10 N 1 '69

ANSARA, MICHAEL
   The slings and (broken) arrows of outrageous (TV) fortune.
      TV Guide 5-13:28 Mr 30 '57
   He was bored with looking noble.   TV Guide 8-18:28 Ap
      30 '60
   Wood, C.   TV personalities biographical sketchbook
      TV Personalities p60 '57

ANSON, LURA
   Obit.   Screen World 20:231 '69

ANTRIM, HARRY
   Obit.   Screen World 19:228 '68

AOKI, TSURU
   Scher, L.   A flower of Japan.   Photop 10-1:110 Je '16

ARBUCKLE, ROSCOE "FATTY"
   Owen, K.   Heavyweight athletics.   Photop 8-3:35 Ag '15
   Bartlett, R.   Why aren't we killed?   Photop 9-5:81 Ap '16
   Fatty Arbuckle off the screen.   Lit Digest 55:40 Jl 14 '17
   Cohn, A. A.   He never laughs on Sunday.   Photop 16-1:
      58 Je '19
   Arbuckle, R.   Love confessions of a fat man.   Photop
      20-4:22 S '21
   Affront to public decency.   Outlook 133:17 Ja 3 '23
   Arbuckle's plea for another chance.   Lit Digest 76:33 Ja
      13 '23
   Bigelow, W. F.   N. E. A. calls Will Hayes to account.
      Good H 76:8 Mr '23
   Ellis, T.   Just let me work.   Photop 39-4:65 Mr '31
   Quirk, J. R.   Give Arbuckle a chance.   Photop 40-2:57
      Jl '31

ARDEN, EVE
   Davis, L. & Cleveland, J.   Mistress wisecrack.   Colliers
      109:17 F 14 '42
   Carlile, T.   Eve Arden, teacher's pet.   Colliers 129:20
      Ja 5 '52
   No competition.   Time 60:88 O 13 '52
   Eve Arden.   TV Guide 6-2:7 Ja 9 '53

Teacher's pet.   TV Guide 1-5:17 My 1 '53
Goldberg, H.   Our Miss Brooks, America's favorite
  schoolmarm.   Cosmop 134:70 Je '53
A stands for Arden.   Am Mag 156:59 Jl '53
Biography.   Cur Bio 14:16 S '53
  Same.   Cur Bio Yrbk 1953:31 '53
Best, K. & Hillyer, K.   Story of Eve Arden.   McCalls
  81:42 N '53
Gould, J.   TV's top comediennes.   N.Y. Times Mag p17
  D 27 '53
She's a one-man woman.   TV Guide 2-14:5 Ap 2 '54
Our new Miss Brooks.   TV Guide 3-46:8 N 12 '55
Goodbye Miss Brooks?   TV Guide 4-17:13 Ap 28 '56
Wood, C.   TV personalities biographical sketch book
  TV Personalities p124 '56
It give me great pleasure.   TV Guide 5-48:14 N 30 '57
Fessier, M. Jr.   Mrs. West of the succhini patch.
  TV Guide 15-49:16 D 9 '67

ARKIN, ALAN
Child of the city.   Newsweek 68:96 Jl 18 '66
Alan Arkin is coming.   Life 61:33 Jl 22 '66
Schisgal, M.   I'm interviewing you.   TV Guide 14-36:12
  S 3 '66
Gussow, M.   Alan Arkin: matchless maskmaker.   Holi-
  day 40:91 O '66
Weinraub, B.   Alan Arkin talks about what its like to be
  a star.   N.Y. Times Mag p30 Mr 12 '67
Biography.   Brit Bk Yr 1967:143 '67
Biography.   Cur Bio 28:3 O '67
  Same.   Cur Bio Yrbk 1967:11 '68
Austin, D.   After Alan Arkin.   Films & Filming 14-2:4
  N '67
Inspector Clouseau and The heart is a lonely hunter.
  Time 92:82 Ag 9 '68

ARLEN, RICHARD
Albert, K.   One star is enough.   Photop 35-5:72 Ap '27
LeStrange, R.   Dick Arlen, sky rider.   Photop 26-6:53
  My '45

ARLISS, GEORGE
Mephistophelian genius of Arliss.   Cur Lit 51:552 N '11
Eaton, W. P.   Arliss as an actor.   Am Mag 73:361 Ja
  '12
Cather, W. S.   New types of acting: the character actor
  displaces the star.   McClure 42:41 F '14

Moses, M. J. Portrait acting of George Arliss. Bell-
    man 23:457 O 27 '17
Arliss augmentation of the films; a real raja and a film
    devil. Arts & Dec 14:369 Mr '21
Sumner, K. Story of a great actor. Am Mag 92:18 D
    '21
Realism on the stage. Atlan 131:433 Ap '23
Just dying to go on the stage. Colliers 76:16 Jl 11 '25
Behind the scenes. Colliers 76:14 Ag 29 '25
Up the years from Bloomsbury; autob. Ladies Home J
    44:10 Ja; 17 F; 33 Mr; 35 Ap; 47 My '27
Newfoundland dog, as remembered by George Arliss.
    Outlook 148:390 Mr 7 '28
Disraeli speaks. Lit Digest 105:19 Ap 12 '30
Marble, A. L. George Arliss and the merger of stage
    and screen. Photo-Era 65:178 S '30
Mr. Arliss makes a speech. Atlan 147:145 F '31
Lang, H. He has two bosses. Photop 39-6:39 My '31
Skinner, R. D. Alexander Hamilton. Commonweal 14:
    525 S 30 '31
It's like the lawns of England. Womans H C 59:19 Ag '32
Powell, S. M. George Arliss. Cinema Digest 1-13:14
    O 31 '32
Biery, R. Arliss puts his foot down. Photop 44-1:47
    Je '33
Martin, H. George Arliss. Cinema Digest 3-3:13 Ap 3
    '33
Melcher, E. Ann Harding and George Arliss. Cinema
    Digest 3-7:11 My 1 '33
Schallert, E. Actors don't grow old. Photop 46-2:60 Jl
    '34
Iron Duke Arliss doesn't fall off his horse. Newsweek
    5:32 F 2 '35
Londoner looks at Hollywood. Cur Hist 51:39 Mr '40
Where authors become writers. Sat R 21:14 Mr 30 '40
Obit. Newsweek 27:97 F 18 '46
    Time 47:79 F 18 '46
    Roy Soc Arts J 94:228 Mr 1 '46
    Cur Bio 7:7 Mr '46
    Wilson Lib Bul 20:568 Ap '46
    Cur Bio Yrbk 1946:16 '47

ARMENDARIZ, PEDRO
    Obit. Screen World 15:219 '64

ARNE, PETER
    Person of promise. Films & Filming 3-1:17 O '56

ARNESS, JAMES
  Wood, C. TV personalities biographical sketchbook.
    TV Personalities p23 '56
  Marshal from Minneapolis. TV Guide 5-19:24 My 11 '57
  Hero of Gunsmoke. Look 21:115 O 29 '57
  DeRoos, R. Private life of Gunsmoke's star.
    Sat Eve Post Ap 12 '58
  Hamilton, S. Gunnin' for a shy guy. Photop 54-3:60 S
    '58
  Hoffman, J. I simply couldn't give enough. Photop 56-
    1:46 Jl '59
  Tall in the saddle and on the ground too. TV Guide 9-
    47:6 N 25; 9-48:22 D 2 '61

ARNOLD, EDWARD
  Darnton, C. Diamond Jim comes back. Photop 48-2:
    30 Jl '35
  Biographical sketch. Time 26:32 Ag 12 '35
  Proctor, K. From pauper to prince. Photop 49-5:78
    My '36
  Crichton, K. Top heavy. Colliers 98:17 S 26 '36
  Biography. NCAB 45:392 '62
  Obit. Am Ann 1957: 56 '57
    Brit Bk Yr 1957:570 '57
    Illus Lond N 228:456 My 5 '56
    Newsweek 47:73 My 7 '56
    Screen World 8:221 '57
    Time 67:106 My 7 '56

ARNOLD, PHIL
  Obit. Screen World 20:231 '69

ARTHUR, GEORGE K.
  Tozzi, R. George K. Arthur, inc. filmog. Films In
    Review 13-3:151 Mr '62

ARTHUR, JEAN
  Stuart, M. Did she steal Clara's picture? Photop 37-3:
    43 F '30
  Ryan, D. Jean Arthur charms men. Photop 48-7:44
    D '35
  Pettit, G. Now you'll understand Jean Arthur. Photop
    51-2:56 F '37
  Fletcher, A. W. Hidden heritage. Photop 51-8:31 Ag
    '37
  Hartley, K. Play truth or consequences with Jean Arthur.
    Photop 53-2:14 F '39

Condon, F. Leave the lady be. Colliers 106:24 Jl 27
  '40
French, W. F. What Hollywood thinks of Jean Arthur.
  Photop 21-4:49 S '42
Parsons, L. O. The art of being Arthur. Photop 24-6:
  30 My '44
Biography. Cur Bio Mr '45
Student. Newsweek 29:56 Ap 21 '47
Peter Pan. Time 55:49 My 8 '50
Harris, E. Actress nobody knows. Colliers 126:22 O
  7 '50
Parsons, L. O. Disappearing Jean Arthur. Cosmop
  134:6 My '53
Seclusive Jean Arthur in her California home. Life 8:59
  Mr 11 '60
Vermilye, J. Jean Arthur, inc. filmog. Films In Re-
  view 17-6:329 Je/Jl '66
The houses that Jean built. TV Guide 14-46:30 N 12 '66
DeRoos, A. It's back to Carmel--for now. TV Guide
  14-48:12 N 26 '66

ASHER, MAX
  Obit. Screen World 9:221 '58

ASTAIRE, FRED
  Leamy, H. Ascending Astaires; intv. Colliers 81:12
    Mr 31 '28
  Janney, J. Brother and sister who never quarrel. Am
    Mag 112:30 D '31
  Hayden, K. Star news from London. Photop 45-4:76
    Mr '34
  Baskett, K. I'd just love to dance with Fred Astaire.
    Photop 47-5:30 Ap '35
  Hall, L. That cute Astaire. Delin 127:68 D '35
  Lewis, F. The private life of Fred Astaire. Photop 48-
    7:26 D '35; 49-1:34 Ja '36
  Burnet, D. Watching his step. Pict R 37:10 Ja '36
  Holdom, C. One step at a time. C S Mon Mag p3 Mr
    4 '36
  Fred Astaire's dancing. Theatre Arts 20:409 Je '36
  Follow the feet. Am Mag 121:40 Je '36
  Jacobs, M. Why fame can't spoil Fred Astaire. Photop
    49-6:21 Je '36
  Portrait. Time 28:38 Ag 31 '36
  Dancing with Astaire and Rogers. Lit Digest 122:20 D
    12 '36
  Eustis, M. Actor-dancer attacks his part. Theatre

Arts 21:371 My '37

Green, J. Fred is fun. Photop 51-7:58 Jl '37

Hartley, K. Play truth or consequences with Fred Astaire. Photop 53-5:26 My '39

Murphy, G. as told to Jerry Asher. My friend Fred. Photop 54-3:32 Mr '40

Fred Astaire plots out new routines. Life 9:36 D 30 '40

Barnett, L. Fred Astaire is the number 1 exponent of America's only native and original dance form. Life 11:72 Ag 25 '41

Biography. Cur Bio S '45

Astaire's last dance. Life 19:54 D 31 '45

Forty years a hoofer. N. Y. Times Mag p32 S 8 '46

Dancing feat. Time 49:88 Mr 17 '47

This is the way to teach your child to dance. Parents Mag 23:40 Ag '48

Howe, H. Tap happy. Photop 33-5:52 O '48

Shipp, C. How to dance like four antelopes. Colliers 123:14 Ja 8 '49

Fred Astaire and . . . N. Y. Times Mag p40 Mr 12 '50

Astaire in air. Life 30:156 Mr 26 '51

Simon, B. Fred Astaire, slow and intimate; recordings. Sat R 36:79 F 28 '53

Finklea and Austerlitz, alias Charisse and Astaire. Newsweek 42:48 Jl 6 '53

Knight, A. Hommage a Fred Astaire. Sat R 36:28 Jl 25 '53

Triple trouble. Colliers 132:44 Jl 25 '53

Jamison, B. B. Ageless Astaire. N. Y. Times Mag p20 Ag 2 '53

Fearless Fred on a fire escape. Life 35:79 Ag 10 '53

Pratley, G. Fred Astaire, inc. filmog. Films In Review 8-1:12 Ja '57

Looking at the star. Newsweek 49:106 Ap 1 '57

Nichols, M. Ageless Astaire. Coronet 42:8 My '57

Knight, A. Choreography for camera; Fred Astaire. Dance Mag 31:16 My '57

Ginger and old dad. Newsweek 52:62 S 15 '58

Now for the dance bash. TV Guide 6-41:12 O 11 '58

Famous pair's new partners. Life 45:44 O 20 '58

One of the finest hours. Newsweek 52:88 O 27 '58

Fred Astaire. Vogue 133:14 F 1 '59

Astaire, F. Steps in Time, condensation. McCalls 86: 40 Ap '59

Lerman, L. Point of departure. Mlle 49:104 S '59

Astaire tries for a topper. Life 47:61 O 26 '59

An evening with Fred Astaire and Gene Kelly.   TV Guide
    7-44:8 O 31 '59
Astaire, F.   My early years; excerpt from Steps in Time.
    Dance Mag 33:50 Ag; 28 S; 47 O; 48 N '59
Davidson, B.   Fred Astaire; the five women in his life.
    Look 23:36 N 10; 23:80 N 24 '59
Conrad, D.   Two feet in the air.   Films & Filming 6-3:
    11 D '59
Dance Magazine 1959 award winner.   Dance Mag 34:28
    Mr '60
O'Hara, J.   There's no one quite like him.   Show 2-10:
    75 O '62
Biography.   Cur Bio 25:5 Ap '64
    Same.   Cur Bio Yrbk 1964:13 '64
Zeitlin, D.   Old dog's new tricks at 66; intv.   Life 59:
    89 O 29 '65
Talks to teens.   Seventeen 25:154 O '66
Swisher, V. H   Special for the special.   Dance Mag 42:
    24 Ja '68
Ardmore, J.   Loneliness of a dancer.   Photop 73-3:64
    Mr '68

ASTHER, NILS
    Albert, K.   Something about myself.   Photop 35-3:32 F;
        35-4:57 Mr '29

ASTOR, MARY
    Biery, R.   The secred wedding of Mary Astor.   Photop
        40-6:28 N '31
    Baskett, K.   Her face was her misfortune.   Photop 46-1:
        68 Je '34
    Diary: Hollywood goes white over Mary Astor's purple
        ink.   Newsweek 8:17 Ag 22 '36
    Thorpe v. Astor.   Time 28:42 Ag 17; 28:30 Ag 24 '36
    Astor, M.   Will he want to come home?   Photop 26-6:48
        My '45
    It's candidly Mary Astor.   Newsweek 53:88 Ja 12 '59
    Alpert, H.   Siren in search of serenity.   Sat R 42:65 Ja
        17 '59
    Serebnick , J.   New creative writers.   Lib J 85:2201 Je
        1 '60
    Biography.   Cur Bio 22:3 N '61
        Same.   Cur Bio Yrbk 1961:16 '62
    Meeting Mary Astor.   Sight & Sound 33-2:73 Spg '64

ATES, ROSCOE
    Obit.   Screen World 14:221 '63

ATTENBOROUGH, RICHARD
Talk with a producer. Newsweek 56-57 D 26 '60
Attenborough, R. Two in harmony. Films & Filming
7-12:9 S '61
Ratcliffe, M. Richard Attenborough. Films & Filming
9-11:15 Ag '63
Ratcliffe, M. The public image and the private eyes of
Richard Attenborough. Films & Filming 9-11:15 Ag
'63
Gow, G. Elements of truth. Richard Attenborough talks
about his new role as director. Films & Filming 15-
8:4 Je '69
Musel, R. Join us, Richard, I'm going to be interviewed.
TV Guide 17-41:14 O 11 '69

ATWILL, LIONEL
Daggett, W. P. Stage and better speech; Lionel Atwill in
Deburau. Q. J. Speech Ed 7:318 N '21
Gray, B. Letter. FIR 14-8:510 O '63

AUER, MISCHA
Zeitlin, I. One man Auer. Photop 52-12:68 D '38
Obit. Illus Lond N 250:13 Mr 11 '67
Time 89:10 Mr 17 '67
Newsweek 69:78 Mr 20 '67
Screen World 19:228 '68

AUGUST, EDWIN
Wallis, R. Edwin August--writer, producer, actor.
Photop 5-2:44 Ja '14
Photoplays and chickens. Photop 7-2:82 Ja '15

AUMONT, JEAN PIERRE
Montez, M. The man I love. Photop 23-6:52 N '43
Hall, G. Overseas report on Jean Pierre Aumont.
Photop 24-6:54 My '44
Hall, G. Reunion of Maria Montez and Jean Pierre Au-
mont. Photop 27-2:27 Jl '45
Marshall, J. Strange embarrassment of Madame Aumont.
Colliers 119-12 Je 28 '47
Montez, M. This is my husband. Photop 31-3:64 Ag '47
Grace's Riviera romance. Life 38:14 My 30 '55
Jones, M. W. An afternoon with Madame Aumont.
Photop 52-2:38 Ag '57

AUTRY, GENE
Baskette, K. Playboy of the western world. Photop 52-

1:61 Ja '38

Johnston, A.   Tenor on horseback.   Sat Eve Post 212:18
   S 2 '39

Chase, F.   Radio's richest cowboy.   Radio Guide p4 N 17
   '39

Double mint ranch.   Time 35:47 Ja 15 '40

Rhea, M.   We are pals.   Photop 20-5:43 Ap '42

Sour note.   Am Mag 143:60 Ap '47

Cowboy in clover.   Time 50:89 Ag 18 '47

Biography.   Cur Bio D '47

Knauth, P.   Gene Autry Inc.   Life 24:88 Je 28 '48

Same, abridged.   Read Digest 53:84 D '48

Arentz, B.   Gene Autry, businessman, pilot.   Flying
   45:30 D '49

Mr. Harper.   After hours; falling idol.   Harper 200:99
   Ja '50

Autry's comin' this away.   TV Guide 3-29:13 Jl 22 '50

Hughes, C.   Gene Autry rides back to the top.   Coronet
   30:89 Je '51

Autry, G.   My partner, Champion.   TV Guide 4-37:16 S
   14 '51

The inside story of Gene Autry.   TV Guide 5-20:4 My 16
   '52

Gene Autry's unusual collection.   TV Guide 6-2:52 Ja 9
   '53

Gene Autry's cowboy dictionary.   TV Guide 1-27:8 O 2
   '53

Meanwhile, back at their ranches . . .   TV Guide 7-32:
   17 Ag 8 '59

Cowboy tycoon.   Newsweek 63:57 Ja 6 '64

Cocchi, J.   Filmography.   Screen Facts 5:56   n. d.

AVALON, FRANKIE

Christy, G.   I feel sort of shy and all alone.   Photop
   55-5:54 My '59

Lyle, J.   Something was wrong . . . terribly wrong.
   Photop 57-2:60 F '60

Hoffman, J.   Why Frankie won't talk about his secret
   bride.   Photop 57-5:47 My '60

Now you know how it feels to be a daddy.   Photop 58-2:
   42 Ag '60

Jaffe, G.   This is how it all began.   Photop 60-2:56 Ag
   '61

Hoffman, J.   Come on in . . . I need you!   Photop 60-
   5:36 N '61

Ardmore, J.   We have his wedding album.   Photop 63-4:
   43 Ap '63

Corbin, J.   Presenting Frankie Jr.   Photop 65-2:66 F
'64

AYRES, AGNES
Evans, D.   One of Anatol's affairs.   Photop 20-3:21 Ag
'21
Bahn, C. B.   Quoting Agnes Ayres.   Cinema Digest 4-2:
10 My 22 '33

AYRES, LEW
Gordon, G.   Lonely Lew.   Photop 37-6:71 My '30
Brayton, P.   Lew stares at stars.   Photop 39-4:66 Mr
'31
Grant, J.   Lew wants another chance.   Photop 42-6:82
N '32
Early, D.   Lew Ayres' own story of the break-up of his
and Ginger Rogers marriage.   Photop 50-1:22 Jl '36
Steele, J. H.   Portrait of a man who came back.   Photop
53-9:27 S '39
Objector Ayres.   Newsweek 19:30 Ap 13 '42
Pacifist.   New Repub 106:525 Ap 20 '42
Fletcher, A. W.   The strange case of Lew Ayres.
Photop 21-2:29 Jl '42
St. Johns, A. R.   Letter from Lew Ayres.   Photop 27-
1:28 Je '45
Leonard H.   Present and accounted for.   Sight & Sound
15-59:86 Aut '46
Wallace, I.   Amazing comeback of Lew Ayres.   Coronet
25:131 N '48
Waterbury, R.   This is a love story.   Photop 34-4:64
Mr '49
Look applauds.   Look 20:24 My 15 '56
Dalmas, H.   Lew Ayres: Hollywood's ambassador of
faith.   Coronet 41:117 D '56
Where are they now?   Newsweek 71:20 Ap 15 '58
Dissenter of another war.   Newsweek 71:20 Ap 15 '68

BABY LeROY

Hamilton, S. So I'm a movie star. Photop 43-6:60 My '33

BACALL, LAUREN

Debut in To have and have not. Life 17:77 O 16 '44
Crichton, K. Watch for Bacall. Colliers 114:64 O 21 '44
Talents and tailoring. Time 44:92 O 23 '44
Hall, G. The life of "The look." Photop 26-5:56 Ap '45
Wickware, F. S. Lauren Bacall. Life 18:100 My 7 '45
Bacall, L. I'm like this. Photop 27-1:54 Je '45
Delehanty, T. Bogie and his "slim." Photop 27-2:32 Jl '45
Ashland, J. Bogart and Bacall. Photop 27-5:40 O '45
Bogart, H. In defense of my wife. Photop 29-1:39 Je '46
Maternity clothes. Life 25:99 O 4 '48
Bogart, H. The most unforgiveable character I've met. Photop 36-2:48 Jl '49
Siren without sequins. Life 34:65 Ap 27 '53
I hate young men. Look 17:36 N 3 '53
Know not the face of fear. Photop 51-4:50 Ap '57
Harris, R. The big rumor. Photop 52-6:21 D '57
Talk with a star. Newsweek 51:110 Mr 10 '58
Advance notice. Vogue 134:142 S 15 '59
Young American legend. Vogue 134:106 N 15 '59
Harris, R. It isn't easy to kill a memory. Photop 58-2:66 Ag '60
Markel, H. What is a man? Redbook 119:12 Jl '62
Hagen, R. Lauren Bacall, inc. filmog. Films In Review 15-4:217 Ap '64
New baby. Time 87:68 Ja 7 '66
Nurse Bacall gets unstarched. Life 60:35 F 11 '66
Zimmermann, G. Bacall comes back big. Look 30:95 Mr 22 '66
Meehan, T. She travels by roller coaster. Sat Eve Post 239:34 My 21 '66
Command generation. Time 88:50 Jl 29 '66
Lauren Bacall talks about Bogart, Sinatra and her new life. McCalls 93:24 Jl '66
Redbook readers talk with Lauren Bacall. Redbook 127:45 Jl '66
We orbit around; intv. Mlle 63:348 Ag '66

Frankel, H. Tough guy and the jet set. Sat R 49:33 S
  24 '66
Hepburn, K. Lauren Bacall. McCalls 94:104 O '66
Middle age: the command generation. Read Digest 89:
  201 O '66

BACKUS, JIM
  The man in the $150 suit. TV Guide 1-31:17 O 30 '53
  Wood, C. TV personalities biographical sketchbook.
  TV Personalities p149 '54
  Backus, J. I feel I have a right. TV Guide 5-30:6 Jl
    27 '57
  Man in the lampshade. Time 72:52 D 15 '58
  Pursued by Magoo. TV Guide 9-21:14 My 27 '61
  Lewis, J. D. This is Jim Backus? TV Guide 13-7:20
    F 13 '65

BACLANOVA, OLGA
  Dawson, E. Baclanova. Photop 34-3:65 Ag '28

BADDELEY, HERMIONE
  The perfect barmaid. Plays & Players 1-5:6 F '54
  Oliver, E. Off broadway; performance of I only want an
  answer. New Yorker 43:101 F 17 '68

BADHAM, MARY
  Mary Badham, small star from Alabama. Vogue 140:122
    Ag 1 '62

BAGGOT, KING
  Barry, J. King Baggot--chronic president. Photop 4-6:
    52 N '13

BAILEY, PEARL
  Lazy singing. Newsweek 25:104 Je 25 '45
  Carnival in St. Louis. Newsweek 27:84 Ap 15 '46
  Just crazy, we're happy. Life 33:89 D 1 '52
  Biography. Cur Bio 16:11 Je '55
    Same. Cur Bio Yrbk 1955:34 '56
  Watt, D. Tables for two. New Yorker 33:113 Ja 25 '58
  Dolly rediviva. Time 90:56 N 24 '67
  Pearl in the raw. Newsweek 70:110 D 4 '67
  Prideaux, T. Big new deal for Dolly--hello Pearl.
    Life 63:128 D 8 '67
  Lantz, R. Hello, Dolly! Ebony 23:83 Ja '68
  Two hands and a point of view. Vogue 151:118 Ap 15 '68

BAINTER, FAY
Schmidt, K. Star of tomorrow. Everybodys 39:106 Ag
'18
Story of an actress--myself. Forum 61:590 My '19
Barrington, A. L. Fay Bainter at home; a delightful a-
partment in one of New York's remodeled brownstone
houses. House B 46:318 N '19
Only 26, but on the stage 21 years. Am Mag 89:34 Ap
'20
Roberts, K. It takes experience; intv. Colliers 95:16
Ja 12 '35
Stein, J. Fay Bainter, inc. filmog. Films In Review
16-1:27 Ja '65
Obit. Newsweek 71:62 Ap 29 '68
Time 91:90 Ap 26 '68
Screen World 20:231 '69

BAIRD, LEAH
Kegler, E. Leah Baird--believer in dreams. Photop
5-1:43 D '13
Winship, M. She's a regular trooper. Photop 25-4:64
Mr '24

BAKER, CARROLL
Girl on the eve of a triumph. Life 40:111 Je 11 '56
Nichols, M. Grown-up baby doll. Coronet 40:11 N '56
Carroll Baker. Look 20:95 D 25 '56
Ryan, T. C. Baby doll. Colliers 139:51 Ja 4 '57
Hall, G. The rebel and the lady. Photop 51-1:42 Ja '57
Gehman, R. I feel bad about Baby doll. Photop 51-6:
70 Je '57
Baby doll grows up. Newsweek 50:87 S 2 '57
Love story of Carroll Baker. Look 23:128 N 24 '59
Practice for an actress. Life 49:41 N 28 '60
Millstein, G. Talk with Carroll Baker, ex-baby doll.
N. Y. Times Mag p18 D 17 '61
LaBadie, D. W. Free agent. Show 1-3:60 D '61
Barber, S. How it feels to act in the nude. Photop
64-2:55 Ag '63
Lewis, R. W. Baby doll grows up. Sat Eve Post 236:
63 N 2 '63
Carroll cavorts in Kenya. Life 57:76 Jl 17 '64
Housewife in Houriland. Time 84:74 S 18 '64
Lint, J. E. Why she acts without clothes. Photop 66-6:
33 D '64
Lewis, R. W. Lady was a tramp. Sat Eve Post 239:
37 F 27 '65

Baby doll grows up.   Newsweek 65:94 Ap 26 '65
Is she carrying sex too far?   Photop 67-4:29 Ap '65
Put your clothes on.   Photop 68-1:57 Jl '65

BAKER, DIANE
Barclay, C.   If only I'd listened to my mom.   Photop
57-3:34 Mr '60
She has a firm grip on reality.   TV Guide 8-34:24 Ag 20
'60
Ehrlich, H.   Diane Baker, Peck's good girl.   Look 29:
56 Mr 23 '65

BAKER, STANLEY
Personality of the month.   Films & Filming 6-2:5 N '59

BALIN, INA
She who got slapped.   Life 46:73 F 23 '59
Talk with a star.   Newsweek 56:88 Jl 18 '60
Fun in the sun for a future star.   Life 49:107 Jl 18 '60
What makes a woman interesting?   Photop 58-2:60 Ag '60

BALL, LUCILLE
Crichton, K.   Three loves has she.   Colliers 108:16 Ag
16 '41
Gilmore, H.   Stop crying!   Photop 20-3:58 F '42
Lucille Ball wins first chance as a big-time star.   Life
13:116 O 5 '42
Technicolor Tessie.   Life 15:65 Ag 9 '43
Hamilton, S.   Riotous redhead.   Photop 24-4:52 Mr '44
Peters, S.   My Hollywood friends.   Photop 28-4:52 Mr
'46
Nugent, F.   The bouncing Ball.   Photop 29-4:60 S '46
Howe, H.   The lady that's known as Lucy.   Photop 30-4:
56 Mr '47
Arnaz, D.   I love Lucy.   TV Guide 5-4:4 Ja 25 '52
TV team; I love Locy.   Newsweek 39:67 F 18 '52
Unaverage situation.   Time 59:73 F 18 '52
Beauty into buffoon.   Life 32:93 F 18 '52
Ace, G.   Invisible men of TV.   Sat R 35:33 Mr 8 '52
Sassafrassa, the queen.   Time 59:62 My 26 '52
Desi Arnaz and Lucille Ball could never be happy together.
TV Guide 5-23:4 Je 6 '52
Sher, J. & M.   Cuban and the redhead.   Am Mag 154:26
S '52
Biography.   Cur Bio 13:9 S '52
Same.   Cur Bio Yrbk 1952:34 '53
Desilu formula for top TV: brains, beauty, now a baby.

Newsweek 41:56 Ja 19 '53
Birth of a memo: I love Lucy. Time 61:50 Ja 26 '53
Arnaz, D. Why I love Lucy; as told by E. Harris.
    McCalls 80:24 Ja '53
Morehead, A. Lucy Ball. Cosmop 134:15 Ja '53
What the script ordered. Life 34:29 F 2 '53
Gould, J. Why millions love Lucy. N. Y. Times Mag
    p16 Mr 1 '53
Lucy's boys; I love Lucy. Life 34:89 Ap 6 '53
Oppenheimer, J. Lucy's two babies. Look 17:20 Ap 21
    '53
Seldes, G. Comical gentlewoman. Sat R 36:37 My 2 '53
Ball, L. as told to C. Shipp. Our babies will be happy.
    Womans H C 80:41 My '53
Morris, J. K. We love little Desi. Parents Mag 28:39
    Je '53
Roll out the red carpet. TV Guide 1-16:4 Jl 17 '53
Johnson, J. What's the secret of I love Lucy? Coronet
    34:36 Jl '53
My favorite redhead. Newsweek 42:31 S 21 '53
Grandpa's girl. Time 62:28 S 21 '53
Lucille Ball denounced as a red. New Repub 129:4 S 28
    '53
Big bad bishop and the strawberry blonde. Christian
    Cent 70:1100 S 30 '53
The Lucille Ball-Communist probe story. TV Guide 1-27:
    13 O 2 '53
He loves Lucy. Reporter 9:4 O 13 '53
Gould, J. TV's top comediennes. N. Y. Times Mag p17
    D 27 '53
From show girl to mother hen. TV Guide 2-17:5 Ap 23
    '54
Harris, E. Real story of Lucille Ball; abridged. Read
    Digest My '54
Lucy and the gifted child. Time 63:59 Je 28 '54
Arnaz, D. Who's quitting! TV Guide 2-31:3 Jl 31 '54
Lucy goes shopping. Look 18:10 D 28 '54
Biography. Colliers Yrbk 1954:445 '54
Wood, C. TV personalities biographical sketchbook.
    TV Personalities p 62 '54
Perils of Lucy. Look 19:57 N 15 '55
Lucy goes home again. Look 20:108 Ap 17 '56
Berquist, L. Desi and Lucy. Look 20:74 D 25 '56
Executive session. TV Guide 5-2:17 Ja 12 '57
Sharnik, J. Is Lucy still loveable? House & Gard 111:
    32 My '57
You can't stand still. TV Guide 5-44:8 N 2 '57

New tycoon. Time 72:69 Ap 7 '58
Agar, C. Desilu; or, From rags to riches. N.Y.
     Times Mag p32 Ap 20 '58
Martin, P. I call on Lucy and Desi. Sat Eve Post 230:
     32 My 31 '58
Is it true what they say about Lucy? TV Guide 6-28:8
     Jl 12 '58
$30 million Desilu gamble. Life 45:24 O 6 '58
Why Lucy loves Desilu. Bsns W p98 N 22 '58
Scott, J. A. How to be a success in show business.
     Cosmop 145:67 N '58
Lucy the lecturer. TV Guide 7-44:6 O 31 '59
Christian, F. Lucille Ball's serious life with Desi Arnaz.
     Cosmop 148:69 Ja '60
Dinter, C. I just couldn't take any more. Photop 57-6:
     56 Je '60
A visit with Lucille Ball. TV Guide 8-29:17 Jl 16 '60
Calamity Lucy. Newsweek 56:86 Ag 22 '60
Lucy leaves TV for Broadway. Look 24:32 S 27 '60
Ball, L. as told to L. Slater. Way it happened.
     McCalls 87:106 S '60
Gehman, R. Theatre arts gallery. Theatre Arts 44:18
     D '60
Gelman, M. Lucille Ball. Theatre 2-12:19 D '60
Sexy eyes over Hope's shoulder. Life 50:107 Mr 17 '61
Dinter, C. Divorce. Photop 59-4:38 Ap '61
Lusty return for Lucy. Life 52:74 Ja 5 '62
Efron, E. Lucy clowns again. TV Guide 10-39:6 S 29
     '62
Lucy: a new outlook. Look 26:88 O 9 '62
Millstein, G. Lucy becomes president. N. Y. Times
     Mag p36 D 9 '62
Don't laugh when you call me president. McCalls 90:51
     Mr '63
Jenkins, D. Madame president. TV Guide 11-14:22 Ap
     6 '63
Ace, G. That same wax of Ball again. Sat R 47:14 My
     16 '64
Gehman, R. They still call her Lucy. TV Guide 12-36:
     18 S 5 '64
Searle, R. The real Ball. TV Guide 14-18:19 Ap 30 '66
O'Brien, F. My biggest mistake as a mother. Photop
     71-6:52 Je '67
Whitney, D. The president wore a dress to the stock-
     holder's meeting. TV Guide 15-28:16 Jl 15 '67
Defining Lucy: the realist who really cares. Broadcast-
     ing 73:117 Jl 31 '67

Hobson, D.   Four days with the remarkable Mrs. Morton.
   TV Guide 16-13:23 Mr 30 '68
$54,000,000 bonanza: Lucille Ball.   Vogue 151:216 My
   '68
Thomas, B.   Lady millionaire, Hollywood style.   Good H
   166:50 Je '68
Balling, F.   What she was afraid to tell.   Photop 75-2:
   53 F '69
David, M.   Son turns on older women.   Photop 76-6:74
   D '69

BALL, SUSAN
   Morris, T.   Susan Ball's great decision.   McCalls 82:46
      F '55
   Obit.   Newsweek 46:63 Ag 15 '55
      Time 66:73 Ag 15 '55
      Brit Bk Yr 1956:508 '56
      Screen World 7:221 '56

BALLIN, MABEL
   Obit.   Screen World 10:221 '59

BALSAM, MARTIN
   Phelan, D.   Martin Balsam.   Films In Review 15-7:454
      Ag/S '64

BANCROFT, ANNE
   The lady has a complaint.   TV Guide 5-9:28 Mr 2 '57
   Biography.   Time 71:88 Ja 27 '58
   Millstein, G.   Seesaw saga of an actress.   N.Y. Times
      Mag p22 F 9 '58
   Anne's emotional replenishment.   Life 44:98 F 17 '58
   Three remarkable young actresses.   Vogue 131:144 Mr 1
      '58
   Three for the stars.   Mlle 47:84 Je '58
   Theatre.   Mlle 48:41 Ja '59
   Who is Stanislavsky.   Time 74:46 D 21 '59
   Nichols, M.   Stardom bound.   Coronet 47:63 Ja '60
   Harrity, R.   Annie Sullivan lives again.   Cosmop 148:8
      F '60
   Biography.   Cur Bio 21:3 Je '60
      Same.   Cur Bio Yrbk 1960:14 '61
   Biography.   Am Ann 1961:74 '61
   Another miracle.   Newsweek 58:72 Jl 24 '61
   Bancroft, A.   I was always able to say okay, here I am,
      mold me.   Show 1-1:92 O '61
   Moris, J. A.   Second-chance actress. Sat Eve Post 234:

38 D 9 '61

Drury, M. She may be the most exciting actress of the century. McCalls 89:113 My '62

Redbook dialogue. Redbook 121:56 Jl '63

Ebert, A. What did you want most at seventeen? Seventeen 22:131 S '63

McClelland, D. Bancroft and Bergen. Films In Review 14-9:573 N '63

Battling Bancroft. Life 57:133 N 20 '64

Biography. Am Ann 1964:449 '64

Lemon, R. Anne Bancroft: hey, ma, I can do that. Sat Eve Post 238:87 N 20 '65

BANCROFT, GEORGE

Lang, H. Good old George. Photop 38-5:35 O '30

Lang, H. George comes to earth. Photop 40-4:40 S '31

Obit. Screen World 8:221 '57

BANKHEAD, TALLULAH

Denten, F. Here comes Tallulah. Photop 39-6:46 My '31

Bay, M. B. Ends of fashion; intv. Colliers 88:17 S 19 '31

Heffernan, H. Tallulah Bankhead. Cinema Digest 1-11:11 O 3 '32

Bell, N. B. Tallulah Bankhead. Cinema Digest 1-13:15 O 31 '32

Miss Bankhead shines in Dark victory. Newsweek 4:26 N 17 '34

Somerset Maugham stands corrected; Tallulah Bankhead gives an exciting, arresting performance in Rain. Lit Digest 119:20 F 23 '35

Ramsey, E. Double helping of fame; children of famous people. Delin 130:11 Ja '37

Reflecting glory; in her home town Tallulah Bankhead makes good. Lit Digest 123:22 My 29 '37

Eustis, M. Footlight parade. Theatre Arts 23:718 O '39

Meade, J. R. Girlhood of a star. Womans H C 67:23 Ag '40

Biography. Cur Bio '41

Hughes, C. Leading and vibrant ladies. N.Y. Times Mag p10 Ja 4 '42

Frazier, G. Broadway's brightest star. Life 14:46 F 15 '43

Berger, M. Tallulah. N.Y. Times Mag p19 F 27 '44

Tallulah the great. N.Y. Times Mag p28 Mr 18 '45

Comment on the citronella circuit. N.Y. Times Mag p16

Jl 21 '46

Krutch, J. W.   Drama. Nation 164:403 Ap 5 '47

Brown, J. M.   Grounded eagle.   Sat R 30:40 Ap 12 '47

Zolotow, M.   Alabama tornado.   Sat Eve Post 219:15 Ap
    12; 30 Ap 19; 28 Ap 26 '47

Shane, T.   Tallulah, to you.   Colliers 119:22 Ap 16 '47

Bankhead, T.   Why I love the Giants.   N. Y. Times Mag
    p14 Je 29 '47

It's not the road, it's detours. N. Y. Times Mag p20 S
    26 '48

One woman show.   Time 52:76 N 22 '48

Tallulah tantrums in current revival of Noel Coward's
    Private lives.   Life 25:64 D 27 '48

Name of Tallulah.   Nation 168:347 Mr 26 '49

Tallulah the actress vs. Tallulah the tube.   Life 26:36
    Mr 28 '49

Two Tallulahs?   Newsweek 33:56 Mr 28 '49

Sound of a bell.   New Yorker 25:25 Ap 2 '49

Tallulah sings.   Newsweek 36:86 D 18 '50

Tallulah looted.   Newsweek 37:24 Ja 15 '51

Talking about Tallulah.   Read Digest 58:53 Ap '51

Tallulah on Tallulah.   Life 30:90 Je 25 '51

Woman at work.   Time 58:51 S 17 '51

Lardner, J.   Tallulah goes to the ballgame.   Womans
    H C 78:26 S '51

Sutton, H.   Tallulah the tourist.   Sat R 34:36 N 24 '51

Benchley, N.   Offstage.   Theatre Arts 35:50 N '51

My life with father.   Coronet 31:56 N '51

Tallu hullabaloo.   Newsweek 38:22 D 24 '51

Trial by stage whisper.   Time 58:17 D 24 '51

Bankhead's banking.   Newsweek 38:17 D 31 '51

Et tu Tallulah?   Life 32:101 My 12 '52

She tells all?   Sat R 35:11 S 27 '51

There's only one Tallulah.   TV Guide 5-41:34 O 10 '52

Hit and a miss.   Newsweek 40:114 O 20 '52

Hoffman, T.   We like Tallulah.   New Repub 127:30 N 17
    '52

Spelvin, G.   Basket of pomegranates for Tallulah!
    Theatre Arts 36:25 N '52

Carroll, J.   Miss Bankhead brought to book.   Theatre
    Arts 36:8 N '52

Clark, T.   Female Falstaff.   Am Mer 75:110 D '52

Would that it were so; Tallulah as manager of the Giants.
    Colliers 131:70 Ja 10 '53

Biography.   Cur Bio 14:3 Ja '53
    Same.   Cur Bio Yrbk 1953:41 '53

Tallulah's five lives.   Look 17:83 F 24 '53

Bankhead, T.   Reply to Would that it were so; Tallulah
   as manager of the Giants.   Colliers 131:6 Mr 14 '53
Best seller in a night club.   Theatre Arts 37:17 Ap '53
Biography.   Colliers Yrbk 1953:68 '53
Lioness in the living room.   Time 63:70 Ja 18 '54
Not three-d, but no-t.   N. Y. Times Mag p14 Ja 31 '54
It's Tallulah, Dahlings.   TV Guide 2-7:17 F 12 '54
Bankhead, Tallulah as told to H. LaCossitt.   My daughter,
   Barbara.   Cosmop 136:79 Ap '54
What is so rare as a Willie Mays?   Look 18:52 S 21 '54
Bankhead's return.   Newsweek 44:60 S 27 '54
Bankhead, T.   Caught with my facts down.   Theatre Arts
   38:22 S '54
Brown, J. M.   Seeing things.   Sat R 37:40 O 2 '54
Tallulah's three lovers.   Life 37:105 O 4 '54
Miss Bankhead.   New Yorker 30:31 N 13 '54
Biography.   Colliers Yrbk 1955:467 '55
Hewes, H.   Broadway postscript.   Sat R 39:22 Mr 3 '56
Sobering thoughts?   Theatre Arts 40:11 Je '56
Hayes, R.   Miss Bankhead vs. Henry James.   Common-
   weal 65:638 Mr 22 '57
Don't say I called you 'Darling'!   TV Guide 5-49:8 D 7
   '57
Your daughter really ought to be an actress darling!
   Good H 146:94 Mr '58
Mehling, H.   Living legends.   Todays Helath 37:58 My
   '59
Lardner, J.   Air; big party.   New Yorker 35:122 N 21 '59
Gelman, M.   Tallulah Bankhead.   Theatre 2-8:15 Ag '60
Where are they now?   Newsweek 71:14 Mr 18 '68
Obit.   Time 92:60 D 20 '68
   Newsweek 72:91 D 23 '68
   Cur Bio 30:48 F '69
   Screen World 20:231 '69
Tallulah.   Newsweek 72:80 D 23 '68
Ace, G.   Darling is hushed.   Sat R 52:12 Ja 11 '69
Koll, D.   Tallulah.   Film Fan Mo 91:22 Ja '69
Vermilye, J.   Tallulah, inc. filmog.   Film Fan Mo 93:1
   Mr '69
Haven, S.   A light goes out.   Photop 75-3:16 Mr '69
Roman, R. C.   Honey-haired, cello voiced, mercurial
   Tallulah, that's me.   After Dark 11-4:24 Ag '69

BANKY, VILMA
   Howe, H.   Hot dickety-dog.   Photop 29-1:37 D '25
   Lieber, E.   Vilma and Rod.   Photop 42-2:34 Jl '32

BANNEN, IAN
   Person of promise.   Films & Filming 5-9:17 Je '59

BARA, THEDA
   Franklin, W.   Purgatory's ivory angel; intv.   Photop 8-4:
      68 S '15
   Evans, D.   Does Theda Bara believe her own press-
      agent.   Photop 8-6:62 My '18
   How I became a film vampire.   Forum 61:715 Je; 62:83
      Jl '19
   Mullett, M. B.   Theda Bara, queen of the vampires.
      Am Mag 90:34 S '20
   Perelman, S. J.   Cloudland revisited.   New Yorker 28:
      34 O 18 '52
   Obit.   Newsweek 45:71 Ap 18 '55
      Time 65:104 Ap 18 '55
      Am Ann   1956:75 '56
      Brit Bk Yr 1956:508 '56
      Screen World 7:221 '56
   Bodeen, D.   Theda Bara, inc. filmog.   Films In Review
      19-5:266 My '68

BARCROFT, ROY
   Danard, D.   Roy Barcroft.   Films In Review 12-6:381
      Je/Jl '61
   Barbour, A. G.   Roy Barcroft.   Screen Facts 1-1:31 n. d.

BARDOT, BRIGITTE
   Nichols, M.   Foreign accent in starlets.   Coronet 40:44
      Ag '56
   Brigitte Bardot.   Time 70:120 N 11 '57
   U. S. geta a look at Brigitte.   Life 48:83 N 18 '57
   Peck's bad girl.   Newsweek 51:68 Ja 6 '58
   Bardot conquers America.   Look 22:63 Ja 7 '58
   People are talking about . . .   Vogue 131:86 Mr 15 '58
   Schneider, P. E.   France's fabulous young five.   N. Y.
      Times Mag p12 Mr 30 '58
   Bardot and the ad-men.   America 99:188 My 10 '58
   Howard, T.   Bad little bad girl.   Sat Eve Post 230:32
      Je 14 '58
   Charged charms of Brigitte.   Life 44:51 Je 30 '58
   Lot more than meets the eye.   Life 44:57 Je 30 '58
   Zing go the strings of Bardot's heart.   Life 45:45 S 8 '58
   Whitcomb, J.   Brigitte Bardot.   Cosmop 145:73 N '58
   Explaining herself.   Newsweek 53:100 F 16 '59
   Flight from the sexy?   Newsweek 53:100 F 16 '59
   Which is which?   Look 23:62 Mr 31 '59

In the news.   Dance Mag 33:47 Mr '59
Brigitte's mentor.   New Yorker 35:34 My 2 '59
Baby-faced new beau for Bardot.   Life 46:59 My 18 '59
Famous bride's small wedding.   Life 46:145 Je 29 '59
Gardner, M.   Brigitte's my sister.   Photop 56-1:38 Jl
   '59
Bardolatrie in Paris.   Life 47:14 Ag 10 '59
Frenchmen at work.   Time 75:55 Ja 25 '60
Famous BB has a bebe.   Life 48:82 Ja 25 '60
Biography.   Cur Bio 21:3 Ja '60
   Same.   Cur Bio Yrbk 1960:17 '61
Blake, E.   To think . . . I didn't want the baby.   Photop
   57-5:38 My '60
Morgan, J. B.   Brigitte Bardot; problem child.   Look 24:
   81 Ag 16 '60
Gill, B.   Current cinema.   New Yorker 36:205 N 12 '60
No meow.   Newsweek 56:90 N 28 '60
Genet.   Letter from Paris.   New Yorker 148:50 D 10 '60
Suicide!   Photop 58-6:71 D '60
France's far-out sex siren.   Look 51:84 Jl 28 '61
Lyle, J.   Two Bardots--which one is lying?   Photop 61-
   1:56 Ja '62
Slater, L.   Brigitte Bardot.   McCalls 89:97 Ap '62
Bardot, B.   Alone at the top.   20th Cent 171:85 Spg '62
Be good boys; Brigitte Bardot's new year's gift on radio-
   diffusion-television française.   Newsweek 61:66 Ja 14
   '63
Durgnat, R.   BB.   Films & Filming 9-4:16 Ja '63
Robbins, F.   An interview he waited for.   Photop 64-4:
   40 O '63
Grenier, R. P.   Mlle. Sagan; intv.   Ladies Home J 82:
   42 Ja '65
Duras, M.   Bardot-Bardot.   Vogue 145:170 Ap 1 '65
Les girls in Mexico.   Life 58:53 Ap 2 '65
Brossard, C.   On the set with Moreau and Bardot.   Look
   29:64 My 4 '65
Hamill, P.   No place left to hide.   Sat Eve Post 238:41
   My 8 '65
Mon dieu!   hoo boy!   U. S. visit.   Newsweek 67:54 Ja 3
   '66
Fun couples.   Newsweek 68:58 Jl 25 '66
Genet.   Letter from Paris; Brigitte Bardot on color TV.
   New Yorker 43:96 Ja 20 '68
Discontented countess.   Life 64:85 My 3 '68
Brigitte Bardot sets a fashion in Spain.   Holiday 44:46
   Ag '68
Musel, R.   Brigitte Bardot tries TV.   TV Guide 16-48:

31 N 30 '68

BARI, LYNN
My unfinished love story.   Photop 23-4:60 S '43
Bari, L.   Three wonderful weeks.   Photop 26-1:29 D '44
She's the apple of his private eye.   TV Guide 3-29:16 Jl
22 '50

BARKER, JESS
Waterbury, R.   This is Susan Hayward.   Photop 39-5:
52 My '51
Zeitlin, I.   Three loves has Susan Hayward.   Photop 42-
5:41 N '52
Corwin, J.   Smash up.   Photop 44-5:36 N '53

BARKER, LEX
Waterbury, R.   The lady said yes.   Photop 44-6:48 D '53

BARNES, BINNIE
Baskette, K.   Binnie with a grin.   Photop 46-5:67 O '34

BARNES, JOANNA
The studious type.   TV Guide 5-12:12 Je 1 '57
Jane with a brain for Tarzan.   Life 47:70 N 16 '59

BARRIE, WENDY
Taviner, R.   The third merry wife of Windsor.   Photop
47-6:57 My '35
Really pet.   Newsweek 34:54 S 19 '49
Wendy Barrie--penthouse lady with fireside charm.
TeleVision Guide p20 O 22 '49
Barrie, W.   There's moonlight on those mimeographs.
TV Guide 3-26:20 Jl 1 '50
Sly art of scene stealing.   Life 29:87 S 25 '50

BARRISCALE, BESSIE
Peltret, E.   Bessie Barriscale's nemesis.   Photop 13-4:
37 Mr '18
Obit.   Screen World 17:233 '66

BARRY, DON "RED"
Curiosity draws the crowd.   Radio & TV News 42:41 S
'49

BARRY, GENE
Wood, C.   TV personalities biographical sketchbook.
TV Personalities p155 '56

Nichols, M. Depressed by success. Coronet 47:12 Mr
 '60
Dandiest gun in the west. TV Guide 8-21:17 My 21 '60
Hano, A. Beauties make the best suspects. TV Guide
 11-47:8 N 23 '63
Bogdanovich, P. Everything's new but the car. TV
 Guide 13-32:8 Ag 7 '65

BARRYMORE, DIANA
Sobol, L. Baby Barrymore. Am Mag 131:20 Je '41
Barrymores meet. Life 12:35 Mr 9 '42
Riley, N. Barrymore brat. Colliers 110:48 O 3 '42
Biographical sketch. Time 40:84 O 5 '42
Barrymore, D. & Frank, G. Too much, too soon; a-
 bridged. Look 21:113 Mr 5; 76 Mr 19; 119 Ap 2; 57
 Ap 16 '57
Churchill, A. Beautiful but damned. Sat R 40:17 Ap 6
 '57
Dolbier, M. Top billing for Miss Diana Barrymore.
 N.Y. Her Trib Bk R p2 Ap 14 '57
E-lu-lu . . . baby. Time 69:126 Ap 15 '57
Bewildered, lost. Newsweek 55:42 F 8 '60
Obit. Newsweek 55:42 F 8 '60
 Time 75:94 F 8 '60
 Brit Bk Yr 1961:511 '61
 Screen World 12:219 '61
(See also: BARRYMORE, ETHEL; BARRYMORE, JOHN;
 BARRYMORE, JOHN DREW; BARRYMORE, LIONEL;
 BARRYMORE FAMILY)

BARRYMORE, ETHEL
Career. Mumsey 22:889 Mr '00
Kobbee, G. Girlishness of Barrymore. Ladies Home J
 20:3 Je '03
Young girl and the stage. Harper 40:998 N '06
 Same abridged. Cur Lit 41:661 D '06
Laughlin, C. E. How Ethel Barrymore thinks a young
 girl should dress. Ladies Home J 25:13 My '08
Seven ages of Ethel Barrymore. Womans H C 37:21
 Ja '10
How can I be a great actress? Ladies Home J 28:6 Mr
 15 '11
Gray, D. Ethel Barrymore's little son. Ladies Home J
 28:13 Ap 1 '11
Dale, A. Star of the Barrymores. Cosmop 52:693 Ap
 '12
Why I want to play Emma McChesney. Am Mag 80:40

N '15

Actors' strike.   Outlook 123:11 S 3 '19

Moses, M. J.   Miss Barrymore to our girls; intv. Delin
    96:5 My '20

My reminiscences.   Delin 103:6 S; 12 O; 8 N; 14 D '23;
    104:16 Ja; 12 F '24

Wood, P. E.   Ethel Barrymore had stage fright; intv.
    Delin 109:8 Ag '26

Porter, K.   Our changing stage; intv.   World's Work 56:
    220 Je '28

Miss Barrymore in the Kingdom of God.   Lit Digest 100:
    21 Ja 12 '29

DeCasseres, B.   School for scandal.   Arts & Dec 36:68
    Ja '32

Anthony, S. B. II.   Woman's next step; intv.   N. Y.
    Times Mag p11 Ja 12 '41

Career.   Ind Woman 20:1 Ja '41

Biography.   Cur Bio '41

Hughes, C.   Leading and vibrant ladies.   N. Y. Times
    Mag p10 Ja 4 '42

Heylbut, R.   Adventures in music.   Etude 60:79 F '42

St. Johns, A. R.   Ethel Barrymore, queen once more.
    Read Digest 43:17 N '43

Hutchins, J. K.   Her name in lights since 1901.   N. Y.
    Times Mag p14 S 24 '44

New Barrymore play; Embezzled heaven.   N. Y. Times
    Mag p24 O 22 '44

Bankhead, T.   My friend, Miss Barrymore.   Colliers
    123:13 Ap 23 '49

Brady, T.   Miss Barrymore at 70.   N. Y. Times Mag
    p22 Ag 14 '49

Kirkland, A.   Matterhorn at twilight.   Theatre Arts 33:
    26 N '49

About Miss Barrymore.   N. Y. Times Mag p18 Ja 23 '52

Jamison, B. B.   Ethel Barrymore in mid-career at 75.
    N. Y. Times Mag p25 Ag 15 '54

Wilson, J. S.   Queen of the American stage.   Theatre
    Arts 38:28 D '54

Barrymore, E.   Memories; an autobiography; abridged.
    Ladies Home J 72:42 F; 64 Mr; 78 Ap; 80 My '55

Freedley, G.   Theatre's dowager.   Sat R 38:28 Ap 9 '55

Royalty of the theater.   Newsweek 45:114 Ap 11 '55

Stage darkened.   Newsweek 53:28 Je 29 '59

That's all there is.   Life 46:116 Je 29 '59

That's all there is.   Time 73:53 Je 29 '59

Obit.   Cur Bio 20:4 S '59
    Cur Bio Yrbk 1959:25 '60

Am Ann 1960:80 '60
Brit Bk Yr 1960:505 '60
Colliers Yrbk 1960:719 '60
Screen World 11:215 '60
Gray, B. An Ethel Barrymore index. Films In Review
14-6:357 Je/Jl '63
(See also: BARRYMORE, DIANA; BARRYMORE, JOHN;
BARRYMORE, JOHN DREW; BARRYMORE, LIONEL;
BARRYMORE FAMILY)

BARRYMORE, JOHN
Boyesen, H. H. John Barrymore's work. Cosmop 32:
305 Ja '02
John Barrymore arrives--a great man. Everybodys 35:
122 Jl '16
Hartley, M. John Barrymore's Ibbetson. Dial 64:227
Mr 14 '18
Johnson, J. The art of John Barrymore. Photop 15-3:
54 F '19
Sumner, K. Hidden talents of Jack Barrymore. Am Mag
87:36 Je '19
Merritt, P. John and Lionel. Everybodys 41:31 Ag '19
Hackett, F. John Barrymore as Richard III. New Repub
22:122 Mr 24 '20
Firkins, O. W. John Barrymore in Richard III. Rev
2:312 Mr 27 '20
Lewisohn, L. Life and death of Richard III. Nation 110:
403 Mr 27 '20
Barrymore's bout with Richard. Lit Digest 65:36 Ap 3
'20
Woollcott, A. Two Barrymores. Everybodys 42:31 Je
'20
Patterson, A. John Barrymore's romance. Photop 18-6:
32 N '20
Why aren't the pictures better? Ladies Home J 39:7 Ag
'22
Young, S. Hamlet. New Repub 33:45 D 6 '22
Lewisohn, L. Hamlet himself. Nation 115:646 D 6 '22
Wright, C. Mr. Barrymore's Hamlet. Freeman 6:400
Ja 3 '23
John Barrymore's new idea of Hamlet. Lit Digest 76:30
Ja 6 '23
Eaton, W. P. Mr. Barrymore's Hamlet. Freeman 6:
424 Ja 10 '23
Furness, H. H. Hamlet of John Barrymore. Drama 13:
207 Mr '23
John Barrymore stirs London; Hamlet becomes a subject

of discussion. Lit Digest 84:29 Mr 28 '25
Smith, A. Mr. Barrymore pays his annual visit. Photop
    28-3:65 Ag '25
Gabriel, G. W. John Barrymore as Hamlet. World's
    Work 50:498 S '25
Confessions of an actor. Ladies Home J 42:30 O; 12 N;
    14 D '25; 43:12 Ja; 17 F '26
Reniers, P. Shadow stage. Ind 118:469 Ap 30 '27
Hamlet in Hollywood. Ladies Home J 44:6 Je; 17 Jl '27
Young, S. Terrible thing. New Repub 52:98 S 14 '27
Up against it in Hollywood. Ladies Home J 45:15 Ja '28
Waterbury, R. Barrymore ballyhoo. Photop 34-3:72 Ag
    '28
Lardner, R. Onward and upward; or Jack Barrymore's
    revenge. Colliers 83:18 F 16 '29
Collins, F. L. John Barrymore's successor. Womans H
    C 56:10 Ap '29
Skinner, R. D. When John Barrymore talks. Common-
    weal 11:659 Ap 9 '30
Barrymore chases the whale again. Lit Digest 106:15
    Ag 30 '30
Lang, H. This odd chap Barrymore. Photop 39-4:31
    Mr '31
Those incredible Barrymores. Am Mag 115:11 F; 20 Mr
    '33
Jones, C. P. John Barrymore. Cinema Digest 3-5:11
    Ap 7 '33
How I escaped a great lover's doom. Am Mag 115:26
    Ap '33
My son John. Am Mag 115:58 My '33
Danton, C. John the great. Photop 45-3:45 F '34
Rankin, R. Jack the bachelor, John the husband. Photop
    45-6:52 My '34
Danton, C. John Barrymore's kick-back. Photop 49-4:
    62 Ap '36
Three people in Romeo and Juliet. Pict R 37:4 S '36
John Barrymore will air-streamline Shakespeare. News-
    week 9:22 Je 26 '37
People. Lit Digest 124:16 Jl 17 '37
Zeitlin, I. The miracle at the John Barrymores'.
    Photop 52-3:26 Mr '38
Back on Broadway. Life 8:56 F 12 '40
Those dear children. Newsweek 15:39 F 12 '40
Vernon, G. In My dear children. Commonweal 31:367
    F 16 '40
Wyatt, E. V. Moral di-armament. Cath World 150:728
    Mr '40

Gilder, R. Appearance in My dear children. Theatre
Arts 24:234 Ap '40
Zeitlin, I. My life with John. Photop 54-6:26 Je '40
Great profile set in cement. Life 9:63 S 30 '40
McEvoy, J. P. Barrymore, clown prince of Denmark.
Read Digest 38:24 F '41
Barrymores meet. Life 12:35 Mr 9 '42
Benedick forever. Time 39:42 Je 8 '42
Great profile. Newsweek 19:58 Je 8 '42
Obit. Cur Bio '42
Berger, S. M. Clown prince of the American stage.
Sat R 27:5 Ja 8 '44
Fowler's sweet prince. Newsweek 23:68 Ja 10 '44
Wilson, E. Life and times of John Barrymore. New
Yorker 19:58 Ja 22 '44
Young, S. Mr. F's bad boy. New Repub 110:248 F 21
'44
Krutch, J. W. Romantic as actor. Nation 158:255 F 26
'44
Fowler, G. Good nite, sweet prince; abridged. Read
Digest 44:107 Ap '44
Barrymore rides again. Newsweek 36:50 Ag 7 '50
Snyder, L. L. This was Barrymore. Coronet 30:34 S
'51
Berger, S. M. The film career of John Barrymore, inc.
filmog. Films In Review 3-10:481 D '52
Eccentric's eccentric. Time 63:108 Ap 5 '54
With wit and love. Newsweek 43:46 Ap 5 '54
Hecht, B. Last performance. Theatre Arts 38:27 Je '54
Barrymore, D. & Frank, G. My battle with my father.
Excerpt from Too much, too soon. Look 21:76 Mr 19
'57
Damned day the Barrymores buried John. Newsweek 49:
114 Ap 8 '57
Wheeler, D. E. As I remember them. Am Mer 85:112
Ag '57
(See also: BARRYMORE, DIANA; BARRYMORE, ETHEL;
BARRYMORE, JOHN DREW, BARRYMORE, LIONEL;
BARRYMORE FAMILY)

BARRYMORE, JOHN DREW
(Also known as John Blythe Barrymore and John Barry-
more, Jr.)
Thomas, B. Young profile. Colliers 124:27 S 10 '49
Barrymore rides again; John Barrymore and Shakespeare.
Newsweek 36:50 Ag 7 '50
High lonesome. Newsweek 36:92 S 25 '50

Roberts, W.   Zing went the strings of his heart.
  Photop 42-3:44 S '52
What's in a profile?   TV Guide 5-50:22 D 14 '57
(See also: BARRYMORE, DIANA; BARRYMORE, ETHEL;
  BARRYMORE, JOHN; BARRYMORE, LIONEL; BARRY-
  MORE FAMILY)

BARRYMORE, LIONEL
The long lost Lionel.   Photop 12-3:131 Ag '17
Merritt, P.   John and Lionel.   Everybodys 41:31 Ag '19
Lionel Barrymore in Macbeth.   Forum 65:459 Ap '21
Mullett, M. B.   Lionel Barrymore tells how people show
  their age.   Am Mag 93:36 F '22
Present state of the movies.   Ladies Home J 43:25 S '26
Will the movies ever be different?   Ladies Home J 44:
  14 My '27
Pringle, H. F.   Late-blooming Barrymore.   Colliers 90:
  27 O 1 '32
Hamilton, S.   Until death do them part.   Photop 51-4:48
  Ap '37
Taylor, F. J.   Christmas message from America's
  Scrooge; intv.   Bet Hom & Gard 19:15 D '40
Antrim, D. K.   How music has helped in my life.   Etude
  59:805 D '41
Happiest holiday I ever spent.   House B 85:13 Ja '43
Woolf, S. J.   Old Scrooge to the life!, intv.   N. Y. Times
  Mag p18 D 19 '43
Biography.   Cur Bio '43
Bach, Beethoven and Barrymore.   Newsweek 23:82 Mr
  20 '44
Dialogues; orchestral tone poem.   In memoriam.   Musi-
  cian 49:71 Ap '44
Barrymore the composer.   Time 43:54 My 1 '44
Christmas carol by Charles Dickens; radio dramatization.
  Life 17:51 D 25 '44
Lionel Barrymore.   Time 47:45 My 6 '46
Crichton, K.   Barrymore, the lionhearted.   Colliers 123:
  21 Mr 26 '49
Barrymore under a grapefruit tree.   Sat Eve Post 223:
  136 Ag 19 '50
Barrymore, L. ed. by C. Shipp.   We Barrymores!
  Sat Eve Post 223:17 Ag 19; 32 Ag 26; 36 S 2; 34 S 9;
  34 S 16; 34 S 23 '50
Rhodes, R.   Best actor in the family?   Sat R 34:16 My
  12 '51
Obit.   Illus Lond N 225:960 N 27 '54
Closing scene.   Newsweek 44:96 N 29 '54

Obit. Time 64:70 N 29 '54
    Am Ann 1955:71 '55
    Brit Bk Yr 1955:572 '55
    Colliers Yrbk 1955:467 '55
    Cur Bio 16:8 Ja '55
    Screen World 6:223 '55
Downing, R. Lionel Barrymore 1878-1954. Films In
    Review 6-1:8 Ja '55
Clemens, C. Some glimpses of Lionel Barrymore.
    Hobbies 60:106 Jl '55
Shipp, C. Most unforgettable character I've met. Read
    Digest Ag '57
Gray, B. A Lionel Barrymore index. Films In Review
    8-4:220 Ap '62
(See also: BARRYMORE, DIANA; BARRYMORE, ETHEL;
    BARRYMORE, JOHN; BARRYMORE, JOHN DREW;
    BARRYMORE FAMILY)

BARRYMORE FAMILY
Patterson, A. Broadway's royal family. Photop 18-1:30
    Je; 18-2:33 Jl '20
Harriss, J. Apple a debut; first night tradition sacred
    to the Drews and Barrymores. Theatre Arts 53:14
    Ap '31
Hall, L. To the head of the class. Photop 41-3:53 F
    '32
Biery, R. Refereeing the royal family. Photop 42-5:
    28 O '32
Jones, C. P. Barrymores and doubtful taste? Cinema
    Digest 3-8:8 My 8 '33
Rankin, R. The barnstorming Barrymores. Photop 44-
    4:32 S '33
Broun, H. Memoirs of the royal family. New Repub
    93:363 F 2 '38
Royal family. N. Y. Times Mag p18 Ap 12 '42
Barrymores forever. Coronet 27:26 Mr '50
Barrymore, L. We Barrymores; as told to Cameron Shipp.
    Sat Eve Post 223:17 Ag 19; 32 Ag 26; 36 S 2; 34 S 9;
    34 S 16; 34 S 23 '50
(See also: BARRYMORE, DIANA; BARRYMORE, ETHEL;
    BARRYMORE, JOHN; BARRYMORE, JOHN DREW;
    BARRYMORE, LIONEL)

BARTHELMESS, RICHARD
Howe, H. Call Mr. Ponce de Leon. Photop 13-5:39
    Ap '18
Evans, D. A wealthy manufacturer's son. Photop 16-4:

96 S '19

Denton, F.   Dick's new contract.   Photop 18-4:68 S '20

Underhill, H.   What they know about each other.   Photop
27-6: 38 My '25

Walker, H. L.   A plea for privacy.   Photop 34-4:65 S
'28

Steele, J. H.   Intimate portrait of a man with black hair.
Photop 37-4:39 Mr '30

Film pioneers' roll of their living immortals.   Life
40:121 Ja 23 '56

Jacobs, J.   Richard Barthelmess, inc. filmog.   Films
In Review 9-1:12 Ja '58

Obit.   Time 82:47 Ag 23 '63
Illus Lond N 243:283 Ag 24 '63
Newsweek 62:67 Ag 26 '63
Am Ann 1964:735 '64
Brit Bk Yr 1964:621 '64
Screen World 15:219 '64

BARTHOLOMEW, FREDDIE

Hamilton, S.   Copperfield in quest of his youth.   Photop
47-2:68 Ja '35

Shaver.   Am Mag 119:56 Je '35

Hollywood kidnapping.   Time 27:50 Ap 20 '36

Ludewig, M. E.   Freddie himself.   St N 63:18 My '36

Rough-housing for a Fauntleroy.   Lit Digest 122:24 S 26
'36

Hamilton, S.   The Americanization of Freddie Bartholomew.   Photop 50-5:24 N '36

Who's a sissy?   Sr Schol 29:2 Ja 23 '37

Willson, D.   Tears from his heart--and his head.
Photop 51-10:22 O '37

Kutner, N.   Box office babies.   Colliers 103:74 Mr 25
'39

BARTON, JAMES

Kennedy, J. B.   Bouncing Barton.   Colliers 82:19 Ag 11
'28

Biographical sketch.   Time 26:28 S 30 '35

Gehman, R.   James Barton: seasoned showman.   Theatre
Arts 36:28 F '52

Obit.   Newsweek 59:57 Mr 5 '62

BASEHEART, RICHARD

Dern, M.   Well, of course, it isn't exactly Hamlet.
TV Guide 13-25:19 Je 19 '65

BASSERMAN, ALBERT
  Obit. Newsweek 39:70 My 26 '52
    Time 59:86 My 26 '52
    Am Ann 1953:68 '53

BATES, ALAN
  Tomorrow's lead. Plays & Players 7-10:22 Jl '60
  Miller, E. Two ways to skin a cat. Seventeen 22:137
    My '63
  Biography. Cur Bio 30:3 Mr '69

BATES, BARBARA
  Starlet progress. Life 18:107 My 28 '45
  Dennison, T. K. Barbara Bates, inc. filmog. Films In
    Review 20-7:456 Ag/S '69

BATES, FLORENCE
  Obit. Screen World 6:223 '55
  Bodeen, D. Florence Bates, inc. filmog. Films In
    Review 17-10:641 D '66

BAXLEY, BARBARA
  A visit with Barbara Baxley. Theatre 2-11:24 N '60

BAXTER, ANNE
  Beauty with a broken nose. Am Mag 134:97 N '42
  Crichton, K. Lady with a zip. Colliers 110:76 D 12 '42
  All about Anne Baxter. Photop 23-4:55 S '43
  Paul, E. Anne Baxter complex. Photop 25-5:47 O '44
  Parsons, L. O. Surprise ending. Photop 28-2:32 Ja '46
  Rhodes, K. The Hodiaks. Photop 29-4:29 S '46
  Made in Hollywood. Time 59:106 My 5 '52
  Graham, S. As you were, Annie. Photop 43-4:44 Ap
    '53
  Pollock, L. Between heaven and h ... Photop 51-4:46
    Ap '57; 51-5:64 My '57
  Life in a land without television. TV Guide 9-45:15 N 11
    '61

BAXTER, WARNER
  Erskine, L. Sales manager to leading man. Photop 27-
    4:66 Mr '25
  Hastings, T. The Cisco Kid himself. Photop 35-5:34
    Ap 29
  Castle, M. And then there were three. Photop 52-7:
    18 Jl '38
  Davidson, R. Warner Baxter's narrowest escape from

death.   Photop 54-12:68 D '40
Obit.   Newsweek 37:71 My 14 '51
   Time 57:103 My 21 '51
   Am Ann 1952:68 '52
Biography.   NCAB 39:472 '54

BAYNE, BEVERLY
   Craig, J.   La fille au Devant.   Photop 8-5:119 O '15
   Pike, C.   Beverly's baby stare.   Photop 8-6:23 My '18

BEAN, ORSON
   Efron, E.   He talked himself out of a career.   TV Guide
      12-29:15/ Jl 18 '64
   For him this is no joke.   TV Guide 13-19:20 My 8 '65

BEATLES
   New madness; rhythm-and-blues quartet called the Beatles.
      Time 82:64 N 15 '63
   Beatlemania.   Newsweek 62:104 N 18 '63
   Lewis, F.   Britons succumb to Beatlemania.   N. Y.
      Times Mag p124 D 1 '63
   Beatle man: manager for Beatles.   New Yorker 39:23 D
      28 '63
   People are talking about the Beatles, four parody singers,
      now the passion of British young.   Vogue 143:100 Ja
      1 '64
   Green, T.   Here come those Beatles.   Life 56:24 Ja 31
      '64
   Beatles is coming.   Newsweek 63:77 F 3 '64
   Yeah, yeah, yeah: Beatles in New York.   Newsweek 63:
      88 F 17 '64
   Beatlemania hits the U.S.   Sr Schol 84:21 F 21 '64
   Unbarbershop quartet; the Beatles.   Time 83:46 F 21 '64
   Cameron, G.   Yeah-yeah-yeah!   Beatlemania becomes a
      part of US history.   Life 56:34 F 21 '64
   Ridgeway, J.   Feeling of youth: Beatles.   New Repub
      150:6 F 22 '64
   Hiram's report: the Beatles in New York.   New Yorker
      40:21 F 22 '64
   Dempsey, D.   Why the girls scream, weep, flip.   N. Y.
      Times Mag p15 F 23 '64
   George, Paul, Ringo and John: the Beatles in the United
      States.   Newsweek 63:54 F 24 '64
   Riesman, D.   What the Beatles prove about teenagers;
      intv.   U. S. News 56:88 F 24 '64
   British exports booming; Beatles.   Nat R 16:142 F 25 '64
   Beatles' secret.   Reporter 30:16 F 27 '64

Beatles reaction puzzles even psychologists. Sci N L
85:141 F 29 '64

Bean, R. Keeping up with the Beatles. Films & Filming
10-5:9 F '64

Rinzier, A. No soul in Beatlesville. Nation 198:221 Mr
2 '64

Packard, V. Building the Beatle image. Sat Eve Post
237:36 Mr 21 '64

Aronowitz, A. G. Yeah! yeah! yeah! music's gold bugs;
the Beatles. Sat Eve Post 237:30 Mr 21 '64

Miller, E. Bit by the Beatles! Seventeen 23:82 Mr '64

Musel, R. Back to Blighty with the Beatles. TV Guide
12-16:10 Ap 18 '64

York, C. At work--at play. Photop 65-4:6 Ap '64

Osmundsen, J. A. Science looks at Beatlemania. Sci
Digest 55:24 My '64

DeBlasio, E. A date with the Beatles. Photop 65-5:29
My '64

Brandt, S. The girls they hide. Photop 54-6:36 Je '64

Edge, J. Do they believe in God? Photop 66-1:38 Jl '64

Aronowitz, A. G. Return of the Beatles. Sat Eve Post
237:22 Ag 8 '64

Report from Hiram; premiere of Beatles' first picture,
Hard day's night. New Yorker 40:25 Ag 22 '64

Brace yourself, they're back; Beatles. Bsns W p28 Ag
22 '64

Cameron, G. Disaster? Well, not exactly; there stood
the Beatles. Life 57:58A Ag 28 '64

Brien, A. Afterthoughts on the Beatles. Mlle 59:239
Ag '64

Miller, E. What are the Beatles really like? Seventeen
23:236 Ag '64

Ransome, V. Beatles discuss mixed marriages. Photop
66-2:36 Ag '64

Howard, W. The Beatles and Shakespeare. Photo 66-2:
38 Ag '64

Carthew, A. Shaggy Englishman story; British long-hairs
Rolling Stones and the Beatles. N. Y. Times Mag p18
S 6 '64

Hiram and the Animals; comparison with the Beatles.
New Yorker 40:40 S 12 '64

Richards, J. Where they put their hair up. Photop 66-
3:60 S '64

Beatle business; record sales. Time 84:112 O 2 '64

Our American scrapbook. Life 57:105 O 23 '64

What the Beatles have done to hair; teenaged British boys.
Look 28:58 D 29 '64

Magaro, R.   What the police found.   Photop 66-6:37 D
   '64

London, J.   Slow horses and fast women.   Photop 67-1:
   48 Ja '65

Beatlemania: the most or the worst?   Sr Schol 86:10
   F 4 '65

Beware the red Beatles.   Newsweek 65:89A F 15 '65

Buying the Beatles.   Time 85:94 F 19 '65

Beatlemania and the fast buck: Beatle-touched items
   sold at fancy prices.   Christian Cent 82:230 F 24 '65

I wanna hold your stock.   Newsweek 65:70 Mr 1 '65

Thompson, T.   Hear that big sound.   Life My 21 '65

Mopheads, M. B. E.   Newsweek 65:38 Je 28 '65

Levy, A.   What every woman should know about the
   Beatles.   Good H 161:12 Jl '65

Goodman, R.   Day the king of swing met the Beatles.
   Esquire 64:52 Jl '65

Beauty and the Beatles.   McCalls 92:78 Jl '65

Miller, E.   On the scene with the Beatles.   Seventeen
   24:230 Ag '65

Fuller, J. G.   Trade winds; phenomenal success.   Sat
   R 48:14 S 18 '65

Chasins, A.   High-brows vs. no-brows.   McCalls 92:42
   S '65

Blue-chip Beatles.   Newsweek 66:82 O 4 '65

Freed, R.   B is for Beatles and baroque; concerning
   Baroque Beatles book.   Sat R 48:57 D 25 '65

Best of the Beatles.   Time 86:36 D 31 '65

Comden, B.   Letter from Liverpool, almost.   Vogue
   146:120 D '65

Bards of pop.   Newsweek 67:102 Mr 21 '66

Cleave, M.   Old Beatles, a study in paradox.   N. Y.
   Times Mag p10 Jl 3 '66

Schecter, J.   Beatles under wraps in Tokyo.   Life 61:72
   Jl 15 '66

Blues for the Beatles; U.S. tour; reactions to Lennon
   statement.   Newsweek 68:94 Ag 22 '66

Morris, J.   Monarchs of the Beatle empire.   Sat Eve
   Post 239:22 Ag 27 '66

Notes and comment; more popular, or more famous,
   than Jesus.   New Yorker 42:21 Ag 27 '66

Sugg, A.   The Beatles and film art.   Film Heritage 1-4:
   3 Sum '66

Is Beatlemania dead?   North American tour.   Time 88:
   38 S 2 '66

Wescott, J.   From a boy's point of view.   Seventeen
   25:14 S '66

Wikler, E.   Everybody has a Beatle.   Read Digest 89: 72 O '66

Other noises, other notes.   Time 89:63 Mr 3 '67

Corliss, R.   Beatle metaphysics.   Commonweal 86:234 My 12 '67

Mix-master to the Beatles.   Time 89:67 Je 16 '67

Thompson, T.   New far-out Beatles.   Life 62:100 Je 16 '67

Sgt. Pepper; latest album.   New Yorker 43:22 Je 24 '67

Kroll, J.   It's getting better.   Newsweek 69:70 Je 26 '67

Schrag, P.   Facing the music.   Sat R 50:61 Ag 19 '67

Lees, G.   Beatles, op 15; Sgt. Pepper's lonely hearts club band.   Hi Fi 17:94 Ag '67

Messengers.   Time 90:60 S 22 '67

Yurchenco, H.   Those Beatles again.   Am Rec G 34:248 N '67

Jahn, M.   After Sgt. Pepper; Magical mystery tour album.   Sat R 50:55 D 30 '67

Four little Beatles and how they grew.   Read Digest 91: 229 D '67

Christgau, R.   Secular music.   Esquire 68:283 D '67

Kroll, J.   Beatles vs. Stones; Rolling Stones as rivals.   Newsweek 71:62 Ja 1 '68

Fab? chaos; the TV film Magical mystery tour.   Time 91: 60 Ja 5 '68

Coffin, P.   Art beat of the 60's.   Look 32:32 Ja 9 '68

Hazlitt, P.   We learned to live without drugs.   Photop 73-1:37 Ja '68

Buckley, W. F.   Beatles and the guru.   Nat R 20:259 Mr 12 '68

Beatles beating a new path to corporate karma.   Bsns W p40 My 18 '68

Beatles inc.   Newsweek 71:68 My 27 '68

Grunfeld, F. V.   Polyphony and a new vocal quartet.   Horizon 10:56 Spg '68

Hedgepeth, W.   Yellow submarine.   Look 32:37 Jl 23 '68

Framing the Beatles.   Newsweek 72:89 Ag 19 '68

Wilk, M.   Log of the yellow submarine.   McCalls 95:72 Ag '68

Apples for the Beatles; first recordings issued.   Time 92: 59 S 6 '68

Davies, H.   Beatles; excerpt.   Life 65:86 S 13; 60 S 20 '68

Zimmerman, P. D.   Inside Beatles.   Newsweek 72:106 S 30 '68

Goldman, A.   Beatles in oil and water.   Vogue 152:154 O 1 '68

Palmer, R. Danger, Beatles at work. Sat R 51:64 O
   12 '68

Mannerist phase; new album of recordings. Time 92:53
   D 6 '68

Saal, J. Double Beatle. Newsweek 72:109 D 9 '68

Wood, M. Etc; four Beatles, five Stones. Commonweal
   89:439 D 27 '68

Sander, E. Beatles; plain white wrapper. Sat R 51:58
   D 28 '68

Eyes of the Beatles. Vogue 152:198 D '68

Fager, C. E. Be grateful, parents! Christian Cent 86:
   92 Ja 15 '69

(See also: HARRISON, GEORGE; LENNON, JOHN; Mc
   CARTNEY, PAUL; STARR, RINGO)

BEATTY, WARREN

Miller, E. New kind of Hollywood hero. Seventeen 20:
   122 My '61

Rise of Geyger Kroop. Time 78:52 S 1 '61

It's Warren Beatty. Life 51:104 N 3 '61

Cronin, J. Beatty and the two beauties. Photop 60-6:
   54 D '61

Miller, W. On stage. Horizon 4:104 Ja '62

Hoffman, J. Wedding bells for Natalie. Photop 61-2:58
   F '62

Biography. Cur Bio 23:5 My '62
   Same. Cur Bio Yrbk 1962:34 '63

Crowley, W. Their biggest problem is . . . Photop 61-
   6:21 Je '62

Laitin, J. Brash and rumpled star. Sat Eve Post 235:
   26 Jl 14 '62

Somers, A. Are they fighting over Warren? Photop 62-
   1:29 Jl '62

Sherwood, D. Warren, I knew you when. Photop 62-2:32
   Ag '62

Carpozi, G. Good imitation of marriage. Photop 62-6:
   53 D '62

Is the party over? Photop 64-3:64 S '63

Gris, W. What are you, Warren? Photop 64-4:63 O '63

Waterbury, R. What Leslie Caron gives him. Photop
   66-6:53 D '64

Gris, W. It's my duty to marry her. Photop 68-1:50
   Jl '65

Reed, R. Will the real Warren Beatty please stand up.
   Esquire 68:43 Ag '67

Warren Beatty. Vogue 150:94 N 15 '67

Thompson, T. Under the gaze of the charmer. Life 64:

  86 Ap 26 '68
Miron, C. Why Faye Dunaway said no. Photop 73-6:51
  Je '68
Musel, R. Warren Beatty talks. TV Guide 17-12:15 Mr
  22 '69
Webb, M. Her secret dates with Beatty. Photop 75-6:
  56 Je '69

BEAVERS, LOUISE
  Obit. Time 80:84 N 2 '62
  Screen World 14:221 '63

BEBAN, GEORGE
  McGaffey, K. And George did it. Photop 13-3:20 F '18

BECKETT, SCOTTY
  Obit. Screen World 20:232 '69

BEDFORD, BRIAN
  Tomorrow's lead. Plays & Players 6-1:22 O '58
  Emerson, E. Brian Bedford; intv. Film Fan Mo 79:11
  Ja '68

BEECHER, JANET
  Merton, G. The woman with sapphire hair. Photop 46-
  6:38 N '34
  Obit. Screen World 7:221 '56

BEERY, NOAH SR.
  Obit. Time 47:88 Ap 8 '46
  Wood, C. TV personalities biographical sketchbook.
  TV Personalities p139 '57

BEERY, NOAH JR.
  Greggory, D. Never say Noah! Photop 24-3:50 F '44

BEERY, WALLACE
  Biery, R. Wally knows his pachyderms. Photop 43-4:
  57 Mr '33
  They stand out from the crowd. Lit Digest 117:14 Ap 21
  '34
  It's funny about my face. Am Mag 117:50 Je '34
  Packer, E. Wally Beery debunks matrimony. Photop
  46-3:58 Ag '34
  Beery, W. Mrs. Carol, Wally and me. Photop 47-3:
  44 F '35
  Chorus man into star. Cinema Arts 1-1:47 Je '37

Mann, M.   One-man cavalcade.   Photop 20-1:64 D '41
Obit.   Newsweek 33:64 Ap 25 '49
   Time 53:93 Ap 25 '49
Maltin, L.   Wallace Beery, inc. filmog.   Film Fan Mo
   73-74:3 Jl/Ag '67

BEGLEY, ED
Biography.   Cur Bio 17:8 Mr '56
   Same.   Cur Bio Yrbk 1956:43 '57
Millstein, G.   Long-running Ed Begley.   N.Y. Times
   Mag p77 D 9 '56
Changing the stars.   Newsweek 49:106 Je 10 '57
Whitney, D.   He needed no school of acting.   TV Guide
   12-31:18 Ag 1 '64

BEL GEDDES, BARBARA
(See GEDDES, BARBARA BEL)

BELAFONTE, HARRY
Timber's gotta roll.   Time 61:55 Mr 9 '53
Splash with song.   Newsweek 43:84 Mr 29 '54
Whitcomb, J.   Backstage at the birth of a hit.   Cosmop
   136:59 Mr '54
Call me actor.   Theatre Arts 38:14 Jl '54
People are talking about.   Vogue 124:125 D '54
Bravos for Belafonte.   Life 38:132 Ap 25 '55
Belafonte boom.   Look 20:38 Ag 21 '56
Biography.   Cur Bio 17:3 Ja '56
   Same.   Cur Bio Yrbk 1956:45 '57
Van Holmes, J.   Belafonte gives it all he's got.   Sat Eve
   Post 229:28 Ap 20 '57
I wonder why nobody don't like me.   Life 42:85 My 27 '57
Guess again!   Good H 144:70 My '57
Ross, I.   Story of a restless troubadour.   Coronet 42:85
   My '57
Storm over Belafonte.   Look 21:138 Je 25 '57
Wild about Hollywood.   Time 70:66 Jl 1 '57
Lead man holler.   Time 73:40 Mr 2 '59
Hentoff, N.   Faces of Harry Belafonte.   Reporter 21:38
   Ag 20 '59
Morrison, C.   Harry Belafonte: transatlantic troubadour
   Look 23:90 D 8 '59
Coleman, E.   Organization man named Belafonte.   N.Y.
   Times Mag p35 D 13 '59
Harry Belafonte talks to teens.   Seventeen 21:112 Je '62
Gouldthorpe, K.   Big star stomp through old time Harlem.
   Life 60:70 F 4 '66

BELLAMY, MADGE

Smith, A. Peroxide pep. Photop 30-5:31 O '26
Larkin, M. Giving the men a break. Photop 35-4:28
   Mr '29
Albert, K. Bellamy, Bronson, Borden. Photop 40-2:
   70 Jl '31

BELLAMY, RALPH

Fatal marriage. Am Mag 139:64 Ap '45
Ralph Bellamy's new theme song: That's what I like
   about the sleuth! TeleVision Guide p21 N 12 '49
Man against crime. Newsweek 38:50 Ag 20 '51
Frost, B. Ralph Bellamy against crime. TV Guide 4-
   22:16 Je 2 '51
Biography. Cur Bio Yrbk 1951:29 '52
Private eye--with muscles. TV Guide 1-7:16 My 15 '53
Thirty million angels. Theatre Arts 38:74 D '54
Wood, C. TV personalities biographical sketchbook.
   TV Personalities p18 '54
Morehouse, W. Equity's Bellamy. Theatre Arts, 41:20
   N '57
Actor's choice. Time 71:87 My 26 '58
LaCossitt, H. Man who plays F.D.R. Sat Eve Post
   231:41 N 8 '58
Actor and the actress. Cosmop 147:45 N '59
Biography. Am Ann 1959:84 '59
Lewis, R. W. The nice guy who didn't get the girl.
   TV Guide 12-19:15 My 9 '64

BELMONDO, JEAN-PAUL

Schneider, P. E. Punk with charm. N.Y. Times Mag
   p84 My 7 '61
Frizell, B. On screen. Horizon 4:116 N '61
Belmondo and Melville. Film 30:2 Win '61
Breathless man. Time 84:76 Jl 10 '64
Shipman, D. Belmondo. Films & Filming 10-12:7 S '64
Biography. Cur Bio 26:3 D '64
   Same. Cur Bio Yrbk 1965:25 '65
Grenier, R. Son of Bogie. Esquire 65:67 Ja '66
People are talking about . . . Vogue 148:217 O 1 '66
Chelminski, R. Power, spell and free spirit of Belmondo.
   Life 61:111 N 11 '66

BENDIX, WILLIAM

O'Liam, D. Bendix, the magnificent. Colliers 113:16
   Ja 1 '44
Bendix, T. Just my Bill. Photop 25-3:48 Ap '44

Hoary ape. Newsweek 24:82 Jl 3 '44

Shane, T. Hollywood's magnificent mug. Sat Eve Post
217:27 S 2 '44

Explosion. Am Mag 140:64 O '45

Crichton, K. Bendix bats for Ruth. Colliers 122:18 Ag
7 '48

Biography. Cur Bio 9:4 S '48
Same revised. Cur Bio Yrbk 1948:42 '49

Four from Hollywood. TV Guide 6-4:10 Ja 23 '53

Life of Riley: fact or fiction. TV Guide 2-31:10 Jl 31
'54

Day I'd like to live over. Good H 141:253 S '55

Wood, C. TV personalities biographical sketchbook.
TV Personalities p78 '57

He who gets stung. TV Guide 6-10:24 Mr 8 '58

Obit. Time 84:64 D 25 '64
Illus Lond N 245:1023 D 26 '64
Newsweek 64:52 D 28 '64
Cur Bio 26:6 F '65
Cur Bio Yrbk 1965:30 '65
Screen World 16:219 '65

BENNETT, CONSTANCE

Albert, K. How I would manage six famous husbands.
Photop 38-1:68 Je '30

Waterbury, R. Gloria, Connie and the Marquis. Photop
38-3:32 Ag '30

Albert, K. Connie and Lilyan. Photop 39-6:30 My '31

Lang, H. Those amazing Bennett girls and their pappy.
Photop 40-2:67 Jl '31

Biery, R. Why Constance is unpopular in Hollywood.
Photop 41-3:34 F '32

Sylvia tells all about Connie Bennett. Photop 43-3:70
F '33

Taviner, R. Two's a crowd. Photop 43-4:34 Mr '33

Constance Bennett plays decorator in her own beach house.
House & Gard 66:28 Jl '34

Dungaree debut. Life 40:123 My 14 '56

Obit. Time 86:82 Ag 6 '65
Screen World 17:233 '66

Ringgold, G. Constance Bennett, inc. filmog. Films In
Review 16-8:472 O '65

BENNETT, ENID

Copeland, G. Who has a kangaroo? Photop 17-4:44 My
'20

BENNETT, JOAN
Busby, M. It's all over now. Photop 36-3:63 Ag '29
Lang, H. Those amazing Bennett girls and their pappy.
Photop 40-2:67 Jl '31
Taviner, R. Two's a crowd. Photop 43-4:34 Mr '33
Messer, G. Joan marches on--alone! Photop 51-7:16
Jl '37
Hayes, B. Hedy Lamarr vs. Joan Bennett. Photop
53-11:18 O '39
Calling on Joan Bennett; as movie star, mother and wife
of producer, her day is busy. Life 9:124 S 9 '40
Livable informality of my French provincial home.
House & Gard 78 sup23 N '40
Bennett, J. How I licked my bad temper. Photop 21-5:
42 O '42
Biography. NCAB curG:377 '46
Glamorous grandmothers. Coronet 29:122 F '51
Gunplay in Hollywood. Newsweek 38:20 D 24 '51
Triangle in Hollywood. Time 58:59 D 24 '51
Bennett, J. & Freedman, E. Gardens need mystery.
Horticulture 39:622 D '61
Efron, E. No tears for Miss Bennett. TV Guide 15-34:
12 Ag 26 '67
Look of a garden, five floors up. House & Gard 132:
100 Ag '67

BENNY, JACK
Biographical sketch. Time 26:53 O 28 '35
Zeitlin, I. Mr. and Mrs. is the name. Photop 51-11:
22 N '37
Robinson, H. & Patrick, T. Jack Benny. Scrib Mag
103:11 Mr '38
Waukegan wisecracker. Time 33:20 Ap 17 '39
Jell-o's dollface. Time 36:48 D 23 '40
Ten years before the mike. Newsweek 17:60 My 5 '41
Biography. Cur Bio '41
Sprague, D. Valentines from Benny. Photop 20-4:48
Mr '42
Buck Benny's rides. Newsweek 21:94 F '43
Van Ryan, F. This is Jack Benny, who cares? Read
Digest 42:85 Je '43
Baker, G. Joke's on him; intv. Sr Schol 43:17 Ja 24 '44
Benny for Pall Mall. Newsweek 23:83 Mr 6 '44
Beatty, J. Unhappy fiddler. Am Mag 138:28 D '44
Please kick Benny. Newsweek 26:100 D 24'45
Busch, N. F. Jack Benny inc. Life 22:85 F 3 '47
It's Benny two to one. Newsweek 29:66 Mr 31 '47

My current reading. Sat R 31:25 Jl 19 '48
Amory, C. Jack Benny's $400 yaks. Sat Eve Post 221:
  25 N 6 '48
Capital gain on income. Bsns W p20 D 4 '48
Sunday nite scramble. Time 52:63 D 6 '48
Rorty, J. Storm on the air waves. Commonweal 49:
  250 D 17 '48
Benny tries TV. Life 26:50 Ap 4 '49
Buck Benny rides TV. TV Guide 3-43:8 O 28 '50
Same old Benny. Newsweek 36:56 N 6 '50
Ace, G. Big bargain from Waukegan. Sat R 33:31 N 11
  '50
Benny debut on television. Newsweek 36:50 D 4 '50
Benny, J. From vaudeo to video via radio. Colliers
  127:13 Mr 24 '51
Ace, G. Bright new star. Sat R 34:39 D 1 '51
Quiet riot. Newsweek 40:62 N 3 '52
Livingstone, M. I got even with Jack Benny, I married
  him; as told to J. K. Ardmore. Womans H C 80:38
  O '53
Headin' for a new range? TV Guide 2-6:8 F 5 '54
Benny, J. After 39 years, I'm turning 40. Colliers
  133:32 F 19 '54
With champion miser as host $$$ pour like the cham-
  pagne. Life 36:53 Mr 22 '54
Marx, A. No. 1 master of timing. N.Y. Times Mag
  p17 F 13 '55
Farewell to radio. Newsweek 46:71 Ag 29 '55
Saroyan, W. Jack Benny's 39 years. Look 19:51 N 1
  '55
Benny fiddles, and no one burns. TV Guide 3-47:13 N
  19 '55
Benny battles classics. Life 41:63 O 15 '56
Offbeat at Carnegie Hall. Newsweek 48:112 O 15 '56
Carnegie Hall debut. Mus Am 76:22 N 1 '56
Listen to Jack Benny. Colliers 138:6 N 23 '56
Wood, C. TV personalities biographical sketchbook.
  TV Personalities p119 '56
Livingstone, M. ed by H. Markel. Love letter to blue
  eyes. Good H 145:114 O '57
Many happy returns of Benny. Life 44:101 F 24 '58
Benny's autolight dimmed. Sr Schol 72:16 Ap 4 '58
Benny, J. Best advice I ever had. Read Digest 74:75
  Mr '59
Life begins at 39. Newsweek 53:96 Ap 13 '59
Langman, A. W. Television. McCalls 86:6 My '59
Cerf, P. Jack Benny puzzles me. Good H 148:32 Je '59

Jack Benny honored by coin club. Numis 72:1099 S '59
Truman breaks up Benny. Life 47:117 O 12 '59
Who picked up the check. TV Guide 7-45:17 N 7 '59
The best of Benny. TV Guide 8-46:6 N 12 '60
Crashing the automat. Newsweek 56:73 N 21 '60
Nichols, M. Durable wit from Waukegan. Coronet 52:
    16 F '61
Wolters, L. Jack Benny: he's been 39 for 28 years.
    Todays Health 39:24 Mr '61
Second fiddle. Newsweek 57:98 Ap 17 '61
Benny, J. How to tell a joke. Read Digest 79:79 Jl '61
Jack Benny, straight man. Newsweek 58:68 Ag 28 '61
The fiddle squeaks at 10 p. m. TV Guide 9-38:12 S 23 '61
Does Jack look quite up to Paar? Life 52:53 F 9 '62
Him Tarzan? ? ? Life 53:109 D 26 '62
Davidson, B. Buck Benny rides again. Sat Eve Post
    236:27 Mr 2 '63
Uncle Jack. Time 81:60 Mr 8 '63
Benny on Broadway. Newsweek 61:86 Mr 11 '63
Jack Benny and company. TV Guide 11-12:15 Mr 23 '63
Gilman, R. Comics, comics; show at the Ziegfeld.
    Commonweal 78:47 Ap 5 '63
Frank, G. 39. McCalls 90:91 Ap '63
Benny, J. My dad, Jack Benny; as told to A. Hano.
    Good H 157:97 N '63
Biography. Cur Bio 24:5 N '63
    Same. Cur Bio Yrbk 1963:28 '64
Raddatz, L. Jack Benny changes his tune. TV Guide
    12-19:26 My 9 '64
Rubin, B. A sentimental farewell. TV Guide 13-35:15
    Ag 28 '65
Pause. Time 88:84 N 4 '66

BERGEN, CANDICE
    Two models on modeling. Mlle 60:144 N '64
    Candy Bergen; what will she do when she grows up?
        Look 29:39 S 7 '65
    Bergen, C. What I did last summer. Esquire 64:234
        D '65
    Kael, P. Goddess upstages the girls. Life 60:118 Ap 8
        '66
    Bergen, C. Africa: Safari. Vogue 149:146 Ap 1 '67
    Hochstein, R. Candy Bergen, golden girl. Good H 164:
        34 My '67
    Bergen, C. Is Bel Air burning? Esquire 68:138 D '67

BERGEN, EDGAR
  Reynolds, Q. Man who talks to himself. Colliers 99:
    24 Mr 20 '37
  Roe, E. America's eminent dummy: Charlie McCarthy.
    C S Mon Mag p5 Ja 5 '38
  People's choice: comments on Charlie McCarthy.
    Lit Digest 125:16 Ja 8 '38
  Radio revives an ancient art; ventriloquism. Edgar Ber-
    gen and his dummies. Pop Mech 69:402 Mr '38
  Berger, M. Bergen's brazen blockhead. Read Digest
    32:23 Mr '38
  Comeback for Elmer; pal of Charlie McCarthy reborn in
    filmland. Newsweek 12:26 Ag 15 '38
  Baskette, K. He really mows 'em down. Photop 52-12:
    20 D '38
  Man and moppet, Charlie McCarthy. Time 33:28 Mr 20
    '39
  Romance of Betty Lou Riggs and Charlie McCarthy Bergen.
    Newsweek 10:24 S 13 '39
  Woolf, S. J. Charlie McCarthy gives the lowdown in a
    birthday interview. N. Y. Times Mag p9 Ap 14 '40
  Wright, L. Bergen, you're just an old stay-at-home.
    Bet Hom & Gard 18:26 Ag '40
  McEvoy, J. P. McCarthy, $500,000 chunk of wood.
    Read Digest 38:14 Mr '41
  Four-year sensation in wood. Newsweek 17:60 My 19 '41
  Where Edgar Bergen McCarthy-izes. House B 85:86
    Ap '43
  Baker, G. Keeper of the blockhead; intv. Sr Schol 43:
    19 S 20 '43
  Judy for Punch; Effie Klinker. Time 44:42 Ag 20 '44
  Baker, G. Charlie's aunt. Sr Schol 45:32 O 2 '44
  Cultivated groaner; Bergen and mouthpieces. Time 44:
    54 N 20 '44
  Biography. Cur Bio My '45
  It's paunch, prattle, chum. Sr Schol 48:21 Mr 18 '46
  Halferty, G. Television ala Bergen. C S Mon Mag p5
    Mr 22 '47
  Bergen in the big city. Newsweek 30:60 N 17 '47
  Jennings, D. Charlie McCarthy: the double life of Edgar
    Bergen. Colliers 125:13 Ap 29; 22 My 6 '50
  Cornelius, J. Listen, Bergen. Field & Stream 60:82
    Mr '56
  Durable dummy. Newsweek My 14 '56
  Trust Edgar Bergen. TV Guide 4-24:28 Je 16 '56
  Wood, C. TV personalities biographical sketchbook.
    TV Personalities p107 '56

I'm still learning about flying by flying.   Flying 66:46
   Ja '60

BERGEN, POLLY
   Whitcomb, J.   Backstage at the birth of a hit.   Cosmop
      136:58 Mr '54
   Soup expert makes good.   TV Guide 2-40:8 O 2 '54
   Jon Whitcomb backstage at your hit parade.   Cosmop
      137:78 O '54
   Whitcomb, J.   Biographical sketch.   Cosmop 137:78 O
      '54
   Girl near the top.   Look 19:64 Mr 22 '55
   Wood, C.   TV personalities biographical sketchbook.
      TV Personalities p48 '56
   She carried a torch.   TV Guide 5-19:20 My 11 '57
   Torch singers.   Newsweek 49:65 My 20 '57
   Boal, S.   Pretty Polly.   Cosmop 143:53 D '57
   Emmy awards.   Time 71:49 Ap 28 '58
   Zingg, D.   She can't make up her mind.   Look 22:52
      Ap 29 '58
   Paul, D.   Ooh what she said.   Ooh what he answered.
      Photop 54-1:52 Jl '58
   Biography.   Cur Bio 19:14 S '58
      Same.   Cur Bio Yrbk 1958:38 '58
   They hired her to be stupid.   TV Guide 7-6:4 F 7 '59
   Bergen on Broadway.   Look 23:47 My 26 '59
   Pretty Polly in a comedy plunge.   Life 49:57 O 3 '60
   Just Polly and me.   TV Guide 8-41:12 O 8 '60
   All Polly does is purr.   TV Guide 10-2:15 Ja 13 '62
   McClelland, D.   Bancroft and Bergen.   Films In Review
      14-9:573 N '63
   Polly Bergen sets the holiday scene.   Good H 161:38 D
      '65
   Carrying the torch.   Newsweek 67:80 Ja 31 '66
   Beauty and the beast.   Newsweek 72:104 O 7 '68

BERGER, SENTA
   Because I played a marvelous witch.   TV Guide 11-44:
      26 N 2 '63
   Hamilton, S.   Senta of Vienna.   Look 28:87 O 6 '64
   She's Paulette, Hedy and Ava all in one.   Life 59:80 S
      10 '65

BERGERAC, JACQUES
   Ford, E.   Love set.   Photop 43-5:70 My '53
   Johnson, M.   The day Dorothy's secret prayer was an-
      swered.   Photop 56-4:47 O '59

Hollywood's strangest divorce.   Photop 67-2:44 F '65

BERGMAN, INGRID
  Crichton, K.   Big girl.   Colliers 106:13 S 14 '40
  Biography.   Cur Bio '40
  Daugherty, F.   Ingrid Bergman: her heart's in her work.
    C S Mon Mag p4 F 15 '41
  Ingrid Bergman takes a short holiday from Hollywood.
    Life 10:46 F 24 '41
  Baskette, K.   Nordic natural.   Photop 19-5:52 O '41
  Carlile, T. & Speiser, J.   Young Swedish star brings a
    new brand of charm to American screen.   Life 15:98
    Jl 26 '43
  Great new star.   Time 42:55 Ag 2 '43
  Peattie, D. C.   First lady of Hollywood.   Read Digest
    43:39 S '43
  Skolsky, S.   Candid on Ingrid Bergman.   Photop 23-5:
    38 O '43
  Woolf, S. J.   In, but not of Hollywood; intv.   N. Y. Times
    Mag p12 D 26 '43
  Morrison, E.   Thanks for today.   Photop 24-6:38 My '44
  Parsons, L. O.   "Miss Christmas Tree."   Photop 25-5:
    32 O '44
  Harris, E.   Bergman in brief.   Photop 26-2:50 Ja '45
  Steele, J. H.   Portrait of Ingrid Berman.   Photop 27-3:
    36 Ag '45
  Bergman's year.   Life 19:127 N 12 '45
  Nugent, F. S. That phenomenon named Bergman.   N. Y.
    Times Mag p14 D 16 '45
  Following the films; Hollywood's lady of the year.   Sr
    Schol 48:29 F 18 '46
  Peck, G.   Ingrid, spellbinder.   Photop 28-4:32 Mr '46
  Lundberg, H.   Ingrid Bergman.   Am Scand R 34:123 Je
    '46
  Steele, J. H.   The intimate story of Ingrid.   Photop 29-
    1:36 Je; 29-2:42 Jl; 29-3:62 Ag '46
  Ingrid Bergman as Joan of Arc.   N. Y. Times Mag p22
    N 10 '46
  Bergman on Broadway.   Life 21:51 D 2 '46
  Wallace, I.   Smorgasbord circuit.   Colliers 118:11 D 21
    '46
  Brown, J. M.   To the ladies.   Sat R 29:24 D 21 '46
  Woolf, S. J.   Backstage with Miss Bergman.   N. Y.
    Times Mag p16 D 29 '46
  Shipp, C.   Because she's Bergman.   Photop 30-1:41 D
    '46
  Broadway and Bergman.   Newsweek 29:84 Ja 27 '47

Barnett, L.   Ingrid of Lorraine.   Life 22:118 Mr 24 '47
Barnett, L. K.   Writing on life.   Life 22:118 Mr 24 '47
Film as ambassadors; excerpts.   Sr Schol 50:36 Ap 14
  '47
Funke, L.   Broadway stars, 10 years ago and today.
  N.Y. Times Mag Ap 20 '47
Anderson, M.   How Ingrid Bergman became Joan.
  Photop 30-5:36 Ap '47
Maxwell, E.   Triumph for Ingrid.   Photop 31-3:38 Ag '47
Ingrid Bergman.   Life 23:107 D 15 '47
Campbell, K.   Time out for laughter.   Photop 32-1:40
  D '47
Parsons, L. O.   Ingrid--the story of Bergman as a wom-
  an.   Photop 32-3:42 F '48
Fink, H.   I was there.   Photop 33-1:38 Je '48
Martin, P.   Big beautiful Swede.   Sat Eve Post 221:116
  O 30 '48
In Joan of Arc's path.   N.Y. Times Mag p66 N 7 '48
Ingrid as Joan.   Womans H C 75:7 N '48
Maid of Stockholm.   Sr Schol 53:5 D 8 '48
Edwards, C. C.   Children need to play-act.   Parents Mag
  23:30 D '48
Same.   Recreation 42:492 F '49
Steele, J. H.   Swedish homespun.   Photop 34-5:52 Ap '49
Strombolian idyl.   Life 26:48 My 2 '49
Fantasy on the black island.   Time 53:102 My 16 '49
Parsons, L. O.   The Bergman bombshell.   Photop 36-2:
  30 Jl '49
Off the pedestal.   Time 54:78 Ag 15 '49
Weller, G.   Ingrid's Rossellini.   Colliers 124:14 N 12 '49
Memorable make believe.   Coronet 27:18 N '49
Bergman's stromboli.   N.Y. Times Mag p14 D 25 '49
Act of God.   Time 54:51 D 26 '49
Steele, J.   The Bergman love story.   Photop 36-7:36 D
  '49
Basket of ricotta.   Time 55:86 F 13 '50
Ingrid Bergman has a baby.   Life 28:42 F 13 '50
Stromboli bambino.   Newsweek 35:32 F 13 '50
Rossellini and the Rota.   Newsweek 35:72 F 27 '50
Genet.   Letter from Rome.   New Yorker 26:88 Ap 8 '50
Senor and senora.   Time 55:86 Je 5 '50
Reward of patience.   Time 55:40 Je 12 '50
Ingrid's Robertino.   Life 28:39 Je 12 '50
Stockholm to Stromboli.   Coronet 29:117 Ja '51
Swedish mother shows off her Italian son.   Life 30:31 F
  19 '51
Maxwell, E.   The lady in question.   Photop 39-2:34 F '51

New Berman. N. Y. Times Mag p34 Je 29 '52
Ingrid's twins. Life 33:43 Ag 11 '52
Maxwell, E. Do you want Ingrid Bergman back?
    Photop 42-2:39 Ag '52
Ingrid and the hat trick. Theatre Arts 37:17 Mr '53
Ingrid's new role. Colliers 132:30 S 18 '53
She won't go home again. Newsweek 45:50 Mr 14 '55
Joan at the stake. Theatre Arts 39:30 My '55
Ingrid Bergman, the woman America can't forget.
    Coronet 39:53 N '55
Whitcomb, J. Encounter with Ingrid. Cosmop 140:26
    My '56
Ingrid Bergman, or not? Newsweek 48:85 Ag 13 '56
Personality of the month. Films & Filming 2-11:3 Ag
    '56
Bergman's Anastasia. N. Y. Times Mag p25 S 9 '56
Ingrid . . . a fresh start at forty. Look 20:100 S 18 '56
Letter from Paris. New Yorker 32:118 S 29 '56
Bergman, I. with B. Davidson. I am not doing penance
    for anything. Colliers 138:35 O 26 '56
Jones, M. W. Look homeward, Ingrid Bergman. Photop
    50-4:45 O '56
Brilliant return for Ingrid. Life 41:75 N 26 '56
Ingrid's return. Newsweek 49:63 Ja 28 '57
Ingrid and Yul get good news. Life 42:112 Ap 8 '57
Parker, P. Rossellini talks. Photop 52-3:50 S '57
Meltsir, A. The heart has rasons. Photop 52-4:66 O
    '57
Not forever after. Newsweek 50:65 N 18 '57
Happy London get-together. Life 44:49 F 10 '58
Tynan, K. Abundant Miss Bergman. Holiday 24:79 Ag
    '58
Davidson, B. Ingrid Bergman. Look 22:20 S 2; 29 S 16;
    47 O 14 '58
Gardner, M. I'm not afraid of marriage, despite every-
    thing. Photop 54-3:56 S '58
Ingrid Bergman story. McCalls 86:38 N '58
Tynan, K. The abundant Miss Bergman. Films & Film-
    ing 5-3:10 D '58
Biography. Am Ann 1958:85 '58
    Colliers Yrbk 1958:689 '58
Ingrid Bergman to date. Newsweek 53:31 Ja 5 '59
Hoffman, J. The bride cried on her honeymoon. Photop
    55-4:46 Ap '59
Steele, J. H. Ingrid Bergman; an intimate portrait;
    abridged. Good H 149:50 Jl '59
Governess. New Yorker 35:36 O 10 '59

A part for Miss Bergman.   TV Guide 7-42:18 O 17 '59
Gay interlude in a ghost story; rehearsal of Henry James'
    Turn of the screw.   Life 47:175 O 19 '59
She's the greatest.   Newsweek 54:64 O 19 '59
People are talking about.   Vogue 134:126 N 1 '59
Watson, B.   I will always love Roberto.   Photop 57-1:
    22 Ja '60
The children everybody stares at.   Photop 57-4:38 Ap '60
At 43, a star at work.   Newsweek 56:100 D 5 '60
Double bill by Bergman.   Life 50:90 Mr 3 '61
Halsman, P.   Ingrid Bergman.   Look 25:88 Mr 14 '61
Millstein, G.   Praised, blamed, boycotted.   TV Guide
    9-11:5 Mr 18 '61
Ross, L.   Player.   New Yorker 37:100 O 21 '61
Redbook dialogue.   Redbook 118:30 Ja '62
Dawes, A.   Stay away from my children.   Photop 63-2:
    44 F '62
Deardorff, R.   Interview with Ingrid Bergman.   Redbook
    122:52 F '64
Hamilton, J.   Visit.   Look 28:52 Je 16 '64
Hamblin, D.   Hardly anybody knows him--that's the way
    he wants it.   Life 57:133 O 16 '64
Biography.   Cur Bio 26:3 S '65
    Same.   Cur Bio Yrbk 1965:34 '65
Davis, M. S.   New heartbreak in Ingrid Bergman's life.
    Good H 164:54 Ja '67
Musel, R.   Ingrid Bergman was in the studio, lying on
    a prop bed the wrong way around, and. . .   TV Guide
    15-9:19 Mr 4 '67
One thing at a time.   Time 90:53 S 8 '67
Prideaux, T.   Shining return for Ingrid.   Life 63:63 O
    13 '67
Bowers, R. L.   Ingrid Bergman, inc. filmog.   Films In
    Review 19-2:71 F '68
Fallaci, O.   Ingrid Bergman; intv.   Look 32:26 Mr 5 '68
Newsmakers.   Newsweek 73:55 F 24 '69
Davidson, M.   Ingrid Bergman: the new happiness in her
    life.   Good H 168:82 My '69

BERGNER, ELIZABETH
    Dukes, A.   Scene in Europe.   Theatre Arts 18:102 F '34
    Mob stops film starring Jewess.   Newsweek 3:15 Mr 17
        '34
    Manhattan bows to the magic mite.   Lit Digest 119:23
        F 2 '35
    Krutch, J. W.   Elizabeth Bergner.   Nation 140:167 F 6
        '35

Young, S.   Particular and general.   Nat R 82:21 F 13
    '35
Isaacs, E. J. R.   Broadway in review.   Theatre Arts
    19:173 Mr '35
Wyatt, E. V.   Bergner.   Cath World 140:721 Mr '35
Background of an actress.   Theatre Arts 19:227 Mr '35
Crichton, K.   She stops the show.   Colliers 95:11 Ap 20
    '35
Troy, W.   Monologues by Bergner.   Nation 140:668
    Je 5 '35
On the current screen.   Lit Digest 119:26 Je 8 '35
New Rosalind.   Lit Digest 122:24 S 26 '36
Hoellering, F.   Films: sentimental anniversary.   Nation
    149:24 Jl 1 '39
Some film actors who have made themselves known this
    year.   Theatre Arts 26:186 Mr '42
Comeback.   Time 74:70 O 19 '59
What they are doing now.   Show 2-7:108 Jl '62

BERLINGER, WARREN
    Person of promise.   Films & Filming 6-9:32 Je '60

BERNARD, DOROTHY
    Burgess, B.   The girl on the cover.   Photop 10-3:92
        Ag '16
    Obit.   Screen World 7:221 '56

BEVAN, BILLY
    Obit.   Screen World 9:221 '58

BEY, TURHAN
    Bentley, J.   Talking about Turhan Bey.   Photop 24-5:
        58 Ap '44
    Arvad, I.   Ladies' knight.   Photop 26-1:46 D '44
    Parsons, L. O.   Lana talks about Turhan.   Photop 26-5:
        30 Ap '45
    Parsons, L. O.   And so goodbye.   Photop 28-3:32 F '46
    Rosterman, R.   Turhan Bey, inc. filmog.   Films In
        Review 16-4:263 Ap '65

BEYMER, RICHARD
    Tusher, B.   You've made me feel I belong.   Photop 58-
        2:38 Ag '60
    Wall, T.   Have heart--will love.   Photop 60-3:36 S '61
    Miller, E.   Talent bursting at the seams.   Seventeen
        20:92 O '61
    Melstir, A.   Photoplay breaks the big story.   Photop

60-6:38 D '61
Lewis, R. W. Hollywood's new breed of soft young men.
    Sat Eve Post 235:73 D 1 '62

BICKFORD, CHARLES
    Francis R. Big boy Bickford. Photop 37-4:65 Mr '30
    Lang, H. "Red-head" Bickford speaks. Photop 39-1:
        35 D '30
    Whitney, D. Cantankerous Charles Bickford. TV Guide
        15-2:14 Ja 14 '67
    Obit. Newsweek 70:98 N 20 '67
        Time 90:102 N 17 '67
        Brit Bk Yr 1968:587 '68
        Screen World 19:228 '68

BIKEL, THEODORE
    Doubling his talent. Newsweek 51:63 F 24 '58
    Hano, A. Star nobody knows. Coronet 47:156 Ja '60
    Bikel, T. Mirror up to nature. Theatre 2-3:12 Mr '60
    Millstein, G. Theodore Bikel: charisma and chutzpah.
        Esquire 55:110 Ap '61
    New role for Theodore Bikel. U. S. Camera 24:54 Ap '61
    Bikel, T. Pleasures of photography. Pop Phot 50:62
        My '62
    So they say; intv. Mlle 57:234 Ag '63

BILLINGTON, FRANCELIA
    Synon, K. Francelia Billington. Photop 7-1:58 D '14

BINNEY, CONSTANCE
    Johnson, J. Plymouth Rock chicken. Photop 16-4:32 S
        '19
    Heroines made at home. Delin 99:29 O '21

BINNS, EDWARD
    He leads a policeman's life. TV Guide 7-35:8 Ag 29 '59

BISHOP, JULIE
    In the cast. TV Guide 1-5:16 My 1 '53

BISHOP, WILLIAM
    Obit. Screen World 11:215 '60

BISSETT, JACQUELINE
    Ehrlich, H. Sinatra's English import. Look 32:71 Mr
        19 '68

BJORK, ANITA
  Burke, P. E. Fame came too soon to "Miss Julie."
  Films & Filming 3-10:10 Jl '57

BLACKMAN, HONOR
  Carthew, A. All honor Honor. N.Y. Times Mag p73
    Mr 1 '64
  Smith, M. E. Honor's judo defense of honor. Life 60:
    127 My 20 '66

BLACKWELL, CARLYLE
  Willis, R. Magnetic Carlyle Blackwell. Photop 6-1:53
    Je '14
  Hobart, P. A chat with the man on the cover. Feature
    Movie 1-3:7 Ap 15 '15
  Obit. Time 65:76 Je 27 '55
    Screen World 7:222 '56

BLAINE, VIVIAN
  Morse, A. D. Doll in Guys and Dolls. Colliers 127:
    26 Ja 27 '51
  Wood, C. TV personalities biographical sketchbook.
    TV Personalities p36 '56

BLAIR, BETSY
  Kelly, B. It's like this to be Mrs. Gene Kelly. Photop
    25-1:36 Je '44

BLAIR, JANET
  Crichton, K. Hollywood canary. Colliers 110:14 Jl 18
    '42
  Trucker. Am Mag 134:78 Ag '42
  French, W. F. A-to-Z girl. Photop 22-1:43 D '42
  Skolsky, S. Brief on Blair. Photop 23-3:46 Ag '43
  Bush, Janet B. And so we were married. Photop 23-
    5:49 O '43
  Boger, F. My kids, the Kellys. Photop 33-3:54 Ag '48
  Wood, C. TV personalities biographical sketchbook.
    TV Personalities p28 '54
  Caesar's third wife. TV Guide 4-22:5 Je 2 '56
  Fresh pretty faces for fall. Life 41:129 S 24 '56
  Goldberg, H. It's wonderful being a third wife. Cosmop
    141:27 D '56
  Personality of the month. Plays & Players 5-2:3 N '57
  When a woman needs a lift. TV Guide 7-27:17 Jl 18 '59

BLAKE, MADGE
  Blake, G. They couldn't put me on the shelf! as told to

J. N. Bell.   Todays Health 38:19 Mr '60
Bell, J. N.   Grandmother with grease paint.   Todays
Health 38:23 Mr '60

BLANDICK, CLARA
Obit.   Screen World 14:221 '63

BLINN, HOLBROOK
Belasco's teacher's boy.   Photop 10-2:49 Jl '16

BLONDELL, JOAN
Biery, R.   A new picture thief.   Photop 40-4:69 S '31
Reeve, W.   The awakening of Joan Blondell.   Photop 49-
1:45 Ja '36
Mook, S. R.   The Dick Powells' hectic honeymoon.
Photop 51-1:21 Ja '37
Crichton, K.   Double star; story of Dick Powell and Joan
Blondell.   Colliers 99:22 F 20 '37
Pine, D.   Breakup.   Photop 24-5:65 Ap '44
Blondell, J.   Frantic.   Am Mag 146:138 D '48
Forecasts and side glances.   Theatre Arts 36:13 Je '52
deRoos, R.   Joan Blondell: Miss Elevator of 1969.
TV Guide 17-16:35 Ap 19 '69
Maltin, L.   Film Fan Monthly interviews Joan Blondell.
Film Fan Mo 99:3 S '69

BLOOM, CLAIRE
She knew what she wanted.   Time 60:80 N 17 '52
Tynan, K.   Claire Bloom in the limelight.   N.Y. Times
Mag p17 D 14 '52
Kauffmann, S.   Spoken word; recording of Romeo and
Juliet.   Sat R 36:89 N 28 '53
Harvey, E.   TV imports.   Colliers 136:36 O 14 '55
Claire's classic career.   Life 40:86 F 20 '56
Biography.   Cur Bio 17:9 My '56
Same.   Cur Bio Yrbk 1956:59 '57
Gibbs, W.   Theatre; Old Vic company.   New Yorker 32:
71 N 3 '56
Daley, R.   Britain's brainy beauty.   Coronet 43:37 Ap '58
Jennings, C. R.   Bloom in love.   Sat Eve Post 237:70
S 12 '64
Guerin, A.   Beauty and the beast.   Life 59:45 O 29 '65

BLORE, ERIC
Obit.   Illus Lond N 234:445 Mr 14 '59
Newsweek 53:61 Mr 16 '59

Am Ann 1960: 850 '60
Brit Bk Yr 1960:505 '60
Screen World 11:215 '60

BLUE, MONTE
Herzog, D.   Big boy Blue.   Photop 29-6:53 My '26
Francis, R.   The stars pay and pay.   Photop 38-5:69
O '30
Obit.   Illus Lond N 242:313 Mr 2 '63
Newsweek 61:57 Mr 4 '63
Gray, B.   Monte Blue, inc filmog.   Films In Review
14-5:313 My '63
Scott, K. W.   Letter.   Films In Review 14-8:508 O '63
Obit.   Screen World 15:219 '64

BLYTH, ANN
New star is born.   Musician 49:67 Ap '44
Blyth spirit.   Am Mag 148:105 S '49
Blyth, A.   On Easter I remember.   Photop 37-4:34 Ap
'50
Arnold, M.   Angel face.   Photop 39-4:40 Ap '51
Wilson, L.   She's a new woman.   Photop 40-5:40 N '51
Clayton, D.   She's my girl.   Photop 41-5:60 My '52
Hubler, R. G.   Angelic Annie.   Colliers 130:56 S 27 '52
Corwin, J.   She keeps Hollywood guessing.   Photop 42-
3:64 S '52
Waterbury, R.   Ann Blyth's wonderful love story.
Photop 43-4:34 Ap '53
Linet, B.   To love and to cherish.   Photop 44-3:78 S '53
Waterbury, R.   The family Ann married.   Photop 44-5:48
N '53
Noel, T.   Prelude to a lullaby.   Photop 45-3:54 Mr '54
Crain, J.   Portrait of Ann.   Photop 46-3:54 S '54
Senseney, D.   Just what the doctor ordered.   Photop 47-2:
40 F '55
Emmett, R.   Ann Blyth's love bank.   Photop 47-5:69 My
'55
Arnold, M.   Her guardian angel kissed her.   Photop 49-1:
34 Ja '56
Wheatland, C. M. & Sharpe, E.   Young Hollywood at
home.   Ladies Home J 74:64 F '57
Jacobi, E.   Count your blessing.   Photop 51-3:32 Mr '57
Lewis, J.   You don't know Ann Blyth.   Photop 52-6:24
D '57

BLYTHE, BETTY
St. Johns, A. R.   When the Queen of Sheba was a kid.

Boardman, Eleanor

Photop 19-2:50 Ja '21
Patterson, A. When Venus ordered hash. Photop 21-
1:30 D '21

BOARDMAN, ELEANOR
Winship, M. The girl on the cover. Photop 24-4:37 S
'23
Albert, K. Where has this artist been hiding? Photop
39-3:58 F '31

BOGARDE, DIRK
Barker, F. G. Dirk Bogarde is still stage-struck.
Plays & Players 3-3:8 D '55
Bogarde, D. Stop calling me a film star. Films &
Filming 3-4:7 Ja '57
Bogarde, D. In who's who of the critics. Films &
Filming 8-8:13 My '62
Arkadin. Film clips. Sight & Sound 31-4:190 Aut '62
Whitehall, R. Dirk Bogarde. Films & Filming 10-2:13
N '63
Unpublic life. Time 83:66 Ap 3 '64
Biography. Cur Bio 28:7 Jl '67
Same. Cur Bio Yrbk 1967:34 '68

BOGART, HUMPHREY
Albert, K. Meet Humphrey Bogart. Photop 51-7:44 Jl
'37
Rankin, R. Behavior by Bogart. Photop 52-9:22 S '38
Peterson, E. T. Human side of Hollywood he-men. Bet
Hom & Gard 17:22 My '39
Durant, J. Tough on and off; movies' professional
tough guys. Colliers 106:24 Ag 31 '40
Bromfield, L. "Bogie." Photop 18-4:22 Mr '41
Bogart, H. Bogie on the spot. Photop 21-4:64 S '42
Biography. Cur Bio '42
Delehanty, T. Th battling Bogarts. Photop 22-4:30 Mr
'43
Baskette, K. Hollywood's trigger man. Am Mag 135:
43 Je '43
Asher, J. This is Bogart. Photop 24-2:20 Ja '44
Bogart, May M. Bogie--over there. Photop 24-6:28
My '44
Frazier, G. Humphrey Bogart has a hard, unhappy face
and a hard but happy life. Life 16:55 Je 12 '44
Bogart, H. Medal from Hitler. Photop 26-2:28 Ja '45
I stuck my neck out. Sat Eve Post 217:19 F 10 '45
Parsons, L. O. The bewildering Bogarts. Photop 26-3:

28 F '45

Delehanty, T. Bogie and his "slim." Photop 27-2:32
Jl '45

Ashland, J. Bogart and Bacall. Photop 27-5:40 O '45

Bogart, H. In defense of my wife. Photop 29-1:39 Je
'46

Bogart's regret. Newsweek 30:23 D 15 '47

Bogart, H. I'm no communist. Photop 32-4:52 Mr '48

Waterbury, R. It's this way. Photop 33-4:44 S '48

Bogart, H. The most unforgivable character I've met.
Photop 36-2:48 Jl '49

Bogart, H. Listen to me, kid. Photop 36-4:34 S '49

Bogie's Moroccan campaign. Newsweek 34:22 O 10 '49

Night life of the gods. Time 54:27 O 10 '49

Bogart's venture. Newsweek 37:48 Ap 9 '51

Life goes on location in Africa; African queen. Life 31:
172 S 17 '51

Huston, J. African queen; behind-the-scenes story.
Theatre Arts 36:48 F '52

Humphrey Bogart tells the truth about Hepburn. Coronet
31:139 Ap '52

Shipp, C. Adventures of Humphrey Bogart. Sat Eve Post
225:32 Ag 2 '52

Beat the devil. Look 17:128 S 22 '53

Biography. Am Ann 1953:74 '53

Biography. Colliers Yrbk 1953:85 '53

Survivor. Time 63:66 Je 7 '54

Bogart's on television--but not for long. TV Guide 3-22:
7 My 28 '55

Parsons, L. O. Bogie man. Cosmop 139:94 N '55

Bogart on Hollywood. Look 20:97 Ag 21 '56

At Bogart's death, a eulogy for a tough guy. Life 42:44
Ja 28 '57

Obit. Newsweek 49:69 Ja 21 '57
Time 69:80 Ja 21 '57
Illus Lond N 230:141 Ja 26 '57
Life 42:44 Ja 28 '57
Cur Bio 18:3 Mr '57
Cur Bio Yrbk 1957:61 '58
Am Ann 1958:89 '58
Brit Bk Yr 1958:508 '58
Screen World 9:221 '58

Cooke, A. Epitaph for a tough guy. Atlan 199:31 My '57

McCarty, C. Humphrey Bogart, inc. filmog. Films In
Review 8-5:193 My '57

Biography. NCAB 45:558 '62

Bogey worship. Time 83:80 F 7 '64

Bogdanovich, P.   Bogie in excelsis.   Esquire 62:108
   S '64
Bogey boom.   Newsweek 66:94 N 1 '65
Hyanes, J.   Bogie, the biography of Humphrey Bogart;
   excerpt.   Good H 162:54 Ja '66
Weales, G.   Bogart vogue.   Commonweal 83:664 Mr 11
   '66
Zimmermann, G.   Bacall comes back--big.   Look 30:
   95 Mr 22 '66
Laren Bacall talks about Bogart, Sinatra and her new life.
   McCalls 93:24 Jl '66
Frankel, H.   Tough guy and the jet set.   Sat R 49:33
   S 24 '66
Brooks, L.   Humphrey and Bogey.   Sight & Sound 35:18
   Win '66
Berson, D.   Bogie really had cool.   Seventeen 26:16 Ja
   '67
Roseman, E.   In my opinion.   Seventeen 26:268 F '67

BOHM, KARLHEINZ
   Bohm, K.   The world before us.   Films & Filming 6-5:
   11 F '60

BOLAND, MARY
   Kennedy, J. B.   Make them laugh; intv.   Colliers 88:21
   Ag 22 '31
   Hamilton, S.   We want a divorce.   Photop 47-3:46 F '35
   Maddox, B.   Mary Boland's poignant love story.   Photop
   51-2:73 F '37
   Obit.   Time 86:67 Jl 2 '65
   Newsweek 66:61 Jl 5 '65
   Screen World 17:233 '66
   Davis, H. R.   Mary Boland, inc. filmog.   Films In Re-
   view 16-7:453 Ag 5 '65

BOLES, JOHN
   French, J.   Vocal boy makes good.   Photop 36-4:29 S '29
   Lang, H.   John Boles confesses.   Photop 39-2:72 Ja '31
   Rankin, R.   Why women are crazy about John Boles.
   Photop 46-3:45 Ap '34
   Obit.   Time 93:80 Mr 7 '69
   Newsweek 73:93 Mr 10 '69

BOND, WARD
   The man with the trigger-happy tongue.   TV Guide 6-24:
   22 Je 14 '58
   The old wagonmaster gets rolling.   TV Guide 7-15:17 Ap

11'59

Why that old blankety blank! TV Guide 8-47:5 N 19 '60

A farewell to Ward Bond. TV Guide (New York edition)
8-47:A-1 N 19 '60

Mitchell, G. Ward Bond. Films In Review 11-10:635 D
'60

Obit. Newsweek 56:74 N 14 '60
Time 76:104 N 14 '60
Am Ann 1961:840 '61
Brit Bk Yr 1961:511 '61
Screen World 12:219 '61

BONDI, BEULAH
Springer, J. Beulah Bondi, inc. filmog. Films In Review 14-5:282 My '63

BOONE, PAT
Kinney, H. McCalls visits Pat Boone. McCalls 83:4 Je
'56

New pop crop on top. Time 68:43 S 3 '56

Ryan, T. C. Rock 'n' roll battle: Boone vs. Presley.
Colliers 138:109 O 26 '56

Pat Boone. Look 21:83 Ja 22 '57

Farewell to Godfrey. TV Guide 5-10:17 Mr 9 '57

Pat Boone on the trail. Newsweek 49:103 My 13 '57

Ashton, S. The Pat Boone story. Photop 51-6:41 Je '57

Pat Boone--soaring on song. Newsweek 50:52 Ag 19 '57

Why Pat Boone won't go "Hollywood." TV Guide 5-38:8
S 21 '57

Arnold, M. Can an actor stay good? Photop 52-4:79 O
'57

Whitcomb, J. Interview with Pat Boone. Cosmop 143:
66 N '57

Engelsman, N. Young marriage succeeds for Pat Boone.
Parents Mag 32:44 D '57

Nichols, M. Singing actor without overtones. Coronet 43:
8 D '57

Wood, C. TV personalities biographical sketchbook.
TV Personalities p7 '57

Anderson, N. What the home folks think of Pat Boone.
Photop 53-1:26 Ja '58

Boone, P. Mrs. ed. by A. Meltsir. Man I love. Mc
Calls 85:40 F '58

No life or death matter. Newsweek 51:71 Mr 24 '58

Class of '58. TV Guide 6-23:4 Je 7 '58

Clean-cut kid. Time 71:42 Je 9 '58

Hoffman, J. Hollywood's funniest feud is on. Photop

53-6:42 Je '58

All American boy.   Look 22:81 Ag 5 '58

George, M.   I baby-sat for the Boones.   Photop 54-5:48
N '58

Teen commandments.   Time 73:56 Ja 5 '59

Pat Boone boom; with excerpts from Twixt twelve and
twenty.   Life 46:75 F 2 '59

Boone, P.   One day in my life I'm ashamed of.   Photop
55-3:40 Mr '59

The cooga mooga kid is still hot.   TV Guide 7-24:8 Je
13 '59

Biography.   Cur Bio 20:8 Jl '59
Same.   Cur Bio Yrbk 1959:39 '60

Spicer, B. C.   Pat Boone talks to teen agers.   Ladies
Home J 76:52 Ag '59

Divas, G.   I remember when.   Photop 56-5:54 N '59

Christian, F.   Pat Boone surrounded by women.   Cosmop
147:70 D '59

Twas the month before Christmas.   Photop 57-1:24 Ja '60

Silvian, L.   Dear God, could you please speak a little
louder.   Photop 57-5:68 My '60

The things girls do that bug boys most.   Photop 58-4:
44 O '60

Britten, R.   Love thy neighbor.   Photop 59-3:32 Mr '61

Boone, P.   Let's draft every star now.   Photop 60-1:
41 Ja '62

Redbook dialogue.   Redbook 119:15 Je '62

Gideon, N.   His church accuses him.   Photop 62-5:39
N '62

Boone, P.   Why I made that "immoral" movie.   Photop
63-5:52 My '63

Hoffman, J.   He adopts ten boys.   Photop 64-5:49 N '63

Gregory, J.   Why he risks his life.   Photop 67-2:62 F
'65

Whitney, D.   Mr. Clean of song.   TV Guide 15-15:20 Ap
15 '67

BOONE, RICHARD

Healer of the sick.   TV Guide 3-42:4 O 15 '55

A hired gun looks himself over.   TV Guide 5-41:12 O 12
'57

Beefstew, Boone style.   Look 22:65 Je 24 '58

Had stethoscope . . . now have gun.   TV Guide 6-19:8
My 10 '58

Havemann, E.   Return of the strong silent man.   Mc
Calls 86:40 Ja '59

Evolution of an actor.   TV Guide 7-9:17 F 28 '59

Whitcomb, J.   Mr. Paladin of San Francisco.   Cosmop
146:76 My '59

Within sight of never-never land.   TV Guide 8-6:8 F 6
'60

Edson, L.   TV's rebellious cowboy.   Sat Eve Post 233:
23 Ag 6 '60

Gehman, R.   The paradox of Paladin.   TV Guide 9-1:9
Ja 7; 9-2:20 Ja 14; 9-3:25 Ja 21 '61

Schickel, R.   Television's angry gun.   Show 1-2:51 N '61

. . . will travel.   Newsweek 59:51 Ja 22 '62

Whitney, D.   Paladin is off on a new adventure.   TV
Guide 11-35:6 Ag 31 '63

Biography.   Cur Bio 25:7 F '64

Same.   Cur Bio Yrbk 1964:47 '64

BOOTH, KAREN
On her toes.   Am Mag 114:118 Jl '47

BOOTH, SHIRLEY
Long, long ago.   Theatre Arts 34:38 S '50

Brown, J. M.   Shirley Booth to the rescue.   Sat R 34:
23 My 5 '51

Actress.   New Yorker 27:28 My 19 '51

Poling, J.   One touched with genius.   Colliers 127:23
Je 16 '51

Show stopper.   Coronet 31:16 D '51

Gilroy, H.   Hollywood can't change Shirley Booth.   N. Y.
Times Mag p15 Ap 27 '52

Eells, G.   Come home, Shirley Booth.   Theatre Arts 36:
30 O '52

Coughlan, R.   New queen of the drama.   Life 33:128 N1 '52

Kalb, B.   Biographical note.   Sat R 35:27 D 27 '52

Biography.   Cur Bio 14:9 Ap '53

Same.   Cur Bio Yrbk 1953:81 '52

One more for Shirley.   Time 61:110 My 11 '53

Trouper.   Time 62:58 Ag 10 '53

Kaye, J.   Shirley Booth: Broadway's choice.   Coronet
35:48 D '53

Shirley sheds Sheba.   Colliers 133:46 F 19 '54

Bentley, E.   Theatre.   New Repub 130:21 Ap 19 '54

Happy state of Shirley Booth.   Life 36:106 My 17 '54

Biography.   Am Ann 1954:77 '54

Starring Shirley Booth; cape playhouse.   Theatre Arts 39:
70 Ag '55

Eleven fine actors get their dream roles.   Life 44:76 Ap
14 '58

Whitcomb, J.   Shirley Booth.   Cosmop 145:74 S '58

Gelman, M. Shirley Booth. Theatre 2-4:15 Ap '60
Miss Booth as Hazel. Sat Eve Post 234:96 My 27 '61
After chuckles. Newsweek 57:69 My 29 '61
Solving the servant problem. TV Guide 9-40:28 O 7 '61
Congdon, T. At home with Hazel. Sat Eve Post 235:65
 S 22 '62
Musel, R. Miss Booth comes to tea. TV Guide 14-49:
 38 D 3 '66

BORDEN, OLIVE
Mahlon, M. Chicken--Southern style. Photop 29-6:63 My
 '26
Biery, R. It's the easiest job in the movies. Photop
 33-1:42 D '27
Loring, H. Olive in quest of her soul. Photop 37-1:59
 D '29
Albert, K. Bellamy, Bronson, Borden. Photop 40-2:70
 Jl '31
Obit. Time 50:102 O 13 '47

BORG, VEDA ANN
Hall, G. I didn't have any face. Photop 19-4:65 S '41
Ringgold, G. Veda Ann Borg, inc. filmog. Films In
 Review 16-3:188 Mr '65

BORGNINE, ERNEST
Happy switch for a heavy. Life 38:166 Ap 11 '55
Millstein, G. Importance of being Marty. Colliers 136:
 48 Jl 22 '55
Jennings, D. He gets $150,000 a year for being mean.
 Sat Eve Post 228:26 Ag 27 '55
Nice folks the Borgnines. Sat Eve Post 228:96 Ag 27 '55
Promotion on Marty. Time 67:108 Mr 19 '56
Biography. Cur Bio 17:12 Ap '56
 Same. Cur Bio Yrbk 1956:69 '57
Ashton, S. I was letting Marty down. Photop 50-1:58
 Jl '56
Mehling, H. Ernest Borgnine: misfit makes good.
 Coronet 43:31 D '57
Biography. Colliers Yrbk 1957:691 '57
Marty in Hollywood. Time 72:44 S 8 '58
Check all inhibitions at the gate. TV Guide 11-6:10 F 9
 '63
Brossard, C. TV's howling new success. Look 27:32a
 Jl 16 '63

BOSWORTH, HOBART
Corliss, A. & Bartlett, R. They both came back.

Photop 17-5:32 Ap '20
Martin, B. Hobart Bosworth. Cinema Digest 1-10:9 S
19 '32
Obit. Cur Bio F '44

BOW, CLARA
Tully, J. Astonishing life-story of a popular screen star.
Pict R 29:11 N '27
Bow, C. as told to A. R. St. Johns. My life story.
Photop 33-3:30 F; 33-5:56 Ap '28
Shirley, L. Empty hearted. Photop 36-5:29 O '29
Alton, M. Clara's first train ride. Photop 37-2:65 Ja
'30
Hall, L. Seeing Clara Bow. Photop 37-6:38 My '30
Woodward, M. That awful "It!" Photop 38-2:39 Jl '30
Hall, L. What about Clara Bow? Photop 38-5:60 O '30
Jarvis, P. Quit pickin' on me! Photop 39-2:33 Ja '31
Biery, R. Clara's microphone fright. Photop 40-2:31
Jl '31
Lang, H. Roughing it with Clara. Photop 40-4:30 S '31
Vonnell, C. Clara Bow--housewife of Rancho Clarito.
Photop 42-2:28 Jl '32
Melcher, E. S. Clara Bow. Cinema Digest 1-10:9 S 19
'32
Bell, R. Clara is the ideal wife. Photop 44-6:51 N '33
Kirkwood, R. They're Clara's twins. Photop 44-6:51 N
'33
Mrs. Hush. Life 22:120 Mr 31 '47
Behlmer, R. Clara Bow, inc. filmog. Films In Review
14-8:451 O '63
Girl who had it. Time 86:60 O 8 '65
Last act for it girl. Life 59:106B O 8 '65
Obit. Newsweek 66:72 O 11 '65
Screen World 17:234 '66
Taylor, J. R. 20's show people. Sight & Sound 37-4:
199 Aut '68

BOWMAN, LEE
Dudley, F. Lee Bowman, homesteader. Photop 26-6:
52 My '45
Who's who in the cast. TV Guide 5-4:6 Ja 25 '52

BOYD, STEPHEN
Person of promise. Films & Filming 2-8:17 My '56
Nichols, M. Actor to watch. Coronet 47:18 Ja '60
Allen, B. Why a guy wants to stay single. Photop 58-

1:56 Jl '60
Biography.   Cur Bio 22:5 D '61
Same.   Cur Bio Yrbk 1961:66 '62

BOYD, WILLIAM
Spensley, D.   A Boyd in a gilded cage.   Photop 30-6:
91 N '26
Small, C.   Old Hopalong can't miss.   Sat Eve Post 219:
20 Je 14 '47
Life goes on tour with Hopalong Cassidy.   Life 27:150
S 12 '49
Biography.   Cur Bio 11:5 Mr '50
Same.   Cur Bio Yrbk 1950:63 '51
A few kind words in favor of foul play.   TV Guide 3-18:
16 My 6 '50
Tall in the saddle.   Time 55:42 My 22 '50
Jensen, O.   Hopalong hits the jackpot.   Life 28:63 Je 12
'50
Waterbury, R.   Hollywood's greatest love story.   Photop
37-6:46 Je '50
Kiddies in the old corral.   Time 56:18 N 27 '50
Whitney, D.   Inside story of Hopalong Cassidy.   Coronet
29:87 D '50
Hoppy's redeal.   Newsweek 37:52 Ja 8 '51
Tax-ridden Hoppy to unsaddle enterprises.   Bsns W p151
Ja 19 '52
Living legend.   TV Guide 1-17:14 Jl 24 '53

BOYER, CHARLES
Reeve, W.   The man of the hour.   Photop 48-1:32 Je '35
Hamilton, S.   Boyer breaks his bonds.   Photop 51-9:38
S '37
Steele, J. H.   Portrait with a French accent.   Photop
52-7:63 Jl '38
Dunne, I.   Charles.   Photop 53-10:25 O '39
Morse, W. Jr.   I watched Charles Boyer go away to war.
Photop 53-12:23 D '39
Sharpe, H.   Man of many moments.   Photop 54-7:26 Jl;
54-8:24 Ag; 54-9:72 S '40
Wanger, W.   Film phenomena.   Sat R 26:22 Mr 13 '43
Biography.   Cur Bio '43
Schallert, E.   Heritage on a hilltop.   Photop 25-4:52 S '44
Porter, A.   M'sieu Bwa-yea.   Colliers 119:20 My 17 '47
Maxwell, E.   Deep are his roots.   Photop 33-2:52 Jl '48
Boyer on Broadway.   Life 26:49 Ja 3 '49
Four Hollywood veterans go to hell on Broadway.   Life
31:46 N5 '51

Four-star chat. New Yorker 28:26 Ap 19 '52
Martin, Boyer and Kind sir: a powerful box office team.
    Newsweek 42:56 N 9 '53
Gentleman ladykiller. Newsweek 50:61 D 30 '57
As they see themselves. Newsweek 56:90 Jl 11 '60
He left the basbah 25 years ago. TV Guide 10-44:10 N
    3 '62
Charles Boyer. Plays & Players 11-1:9 O '63
Bedroom pirate. Time 84:66 S 11 '64

BRACKEN, EDDIE
    Greggory, D. The unbreakable Bracken. Photop 24-4:
        59 Mr '44
    Biography. Cur Bio O '44
    Chapman, J. It's fun to be Bracken. Photop 27-1:38
        Je '45
    Darbyshire, M. B. As a family man, he's a natural.
        Am Home 42:29 O '49
    Wood, C. TV personalities biographical sketchbook.
        TV Personalities p87 '57

BRADNA, OLYMPE
    Sobo, L. Here is Bradna. Photop 52-8:14 Ag '38

BRADY, ALICE
    Youth and the stage. Womans H C 41:22 N '14
    Sayford, I. S. Alice Brady vs. William A. Photop 10-4:
        47 S '16
    Hilliker, K. Pretty soft! Photop 14-2:25 Jl '18
    Boone, A. Keeping up with Alice. Photop 18-6:64 N '20
    Patterson, A. Alice-sit-by-the-fire. Photop 24-5:56 O
        '23
    It's not what you wear; it's how you wear it. Womans
        H C 57-73 Mr '30
    Spensley, D. The unbreakable Brady. Photop 52-6:30
        Je '38
    Biography. DAB sup2:58 '58
    Bodeen, D. Alice Brady, inc. filmog. Films In Review
        17-9:555 N '66

BRADY, SCOTT
    Arnold, M. Hollywood bachelor. Photop 38-3:42 S '50
    MacGregor, R. Two brothers. Photop 41-4:46 Ap '52
    Hall, G. What really goes on with Scott Brady and
        Dorothy Malone? Photop 42-2:54 Ag '52
    Waterbury, R. Afraid to fall in love. Photop 45-1:34
        Ja '54

Ott, B. He's your man, if . . . Photop 46-1:58 Jl '54
Nichols, M. Horseback detective. Coronet 49:21 Ap '61

BRAND, NEVILLE
Wallace Beery, Humphrey Bogart and me. TV Guide 14-26:20 Je 25 '66

BRANDO, JOCELYN
The Brandos. Life 24:53 Mr 22 '48
A Brando named Jocelyn. TV Guide 7-36:20 S 5 '59

BRANDO, MARLON
The Brandos. Life 24:53 Mr 22 '48
Semple, L. Jr. Young man from everywhere. Theatre Arts 32:26 O '48
Preparing for paraplegia; actor trains for movie about crippled veteran. Life 28:129 Je 12 '50
Biographical note. Time 56:80 Jl 24 '50
Strauss, T. Brilliant brat. Life 29:49 Jl 31 '50
Maxwell, E. That mad man Marlon. Photop 38-6:40 D '50
Biography. Cur Bio 13:11 Ap '52
Same. Cur Bio Yrbk 1952:62 '53
Johnson, G. Marlon Brando: actor on impulse. Coronet 32:75 Jl '52
Hopper, H. Hollywood's new sex boat. Photop 42-1:58 Jl '52
Here's Brando. Colliers 130:24 N 1 '52
Julius Caesar, Brando and a top cast. Life 34:135 Ap 20 '53
Martin, P. Star who sneers at Hollywood. Sat Eve Post 225:32 Je 6 '53
Lardner, J. While Egypt burns. Newsweek 43:54 Mr 1 '54
Bolstad, H. The wild one. Photop 45-6:66 Je '54
Love and gore on the docks. Life 37:45 Jl 19 '54
Ager, C. Brando in search of himself. N.Y. Times Mag p24 Jl 25 '54
Malden, K. My friend Brando. Photop 46-3:61 S '54
Tiger in the reeds. Time 64:58 O 11 '54
Harvey, E. Napoleon Brando. Colliers 134:108 O 29 '54
People. Time 64:57 D 6 '54
Corwin, J. The devil is a gentleman. Photop 47-1:24 Ja '55
Lerman, L. Charm boys. Mlle 40:161 F '55
Pursuit of happiness. Photop 47-3:39 Mr '55
Marlon and Grace. Life 38:117 Ap 11 '55

Itria, H. Marlon Brando story: I am myself. Look 19:
34 My 17 '55
Gehman, R. Marlon Brando story. Cosmop 138:43 My
'55
Jacobi, E. A character--but still Brando.   Photop
47-6:62 Je '55
Artful dodger. Newsweek 46:44 Ag 22 '55
The visible invisible Brando. Photop 48-3:54 S '55
Ardmore, J. K. Brando--why dolls love the guy.
Womans H C 82:22 N '55
Knefler, C. Luck is a lady for Brando. Photop 49-2:
41 F '56
Who's an Okinawan now? Life 40:138 Ap 23 '56
Amour and the man. Sat R 39:29 O 13 '56
Lane, L. Why the rebel craze is here to stay. Photop
50-5:56 N '56
Weales, G. Movies: the crazy, mixed-up kids take over.
Reporter 15:40 D 13 '56
Ryan, T. C. Banzai Brando. Colliers 138:58 D 21 '56
Biography. Am Ann 1956:87 '56
Brit Bk Yr 1956:115 '56
Colliers Yrbk 1956:514 '56
Gray, N. Search for faith. Photop 51-6:60 Je '57
Marlon Brando at work. Newsweek 50:92 Ag 12 '57
Capote, T. Duke in his domain. New Yorker 33:53 N 9
'57
Ericson, O. The heart never betrays. Photop 53-2:
42 F '58
Rush, B. Brando, the young lion. Films & Filming 4-
6:10 Mr '58
Down beatnik. Time 72:53 O 13 '58
Scott, J. A. How to be a success in show business .
Cosmop 145:66 N '58
Brando directing. Newsweek 53:86 Ja 12 '59
Hawley, E. Six days before love died. Photop 55-1:59
Ja '59
Gehman, R. Mrs. Marlon Brando; who she really is.
McCalls 86:36 Jl '59
Malden, K. The two faces of Brando. Films & Filming
5-11:7 Ag '59
Nichols, M. Many moods of Marlon Brando. Coronet
46:30 O '59
Why he always turns his back on love. Photop 57-2:38
F '60
Brando's break into a new field. Life 48:105 Ap 4 '60
$6,000,000 method. Time 77:72 Mr 24 '61
Nugent, J. P. Talk with the star. Newsweek 57:90

Ap 3 '61

York, C. Brando's secret marriage to Movita. Photop
60-1:69 Jl '61

MacDonald, D. Three years, six million, one film. Esquire 56:24 O '61

York, C. The slap that said I love you. Photop 61-3:
16 Mr '62

Anderson, N. Anna tells all about Marlon. Photop 61-5:
53 My '62

Davidson, B. Mutiny of Marlon Brando. Sat Eve Post
235:18 Je 16 '62

Talk with a star. Newsweek 60:118 N 19 '62

McVay, D. The Brando mutiny. Films & Filming 9-3:
24 D '62

Ambassador Brando. Life 54:45 My 10 '63

Hoffman, J. Brando's $5,000,000 punch. Photop 63-5:37
My '63

Brando fathered my baby. Photop 64-4:27 O '63

Brando fights for civil rights. Ebony 18:60 O '63

Eyles, A. The other Brando. Films & Filming 11-4:7
Ja '65

We're having lunch today with Marlon Brando, folks; intv.
Esquire 65:98 F '66

Kael, P. Marlon Brando, an American hero. Atlan
217:72 Mr '66

Hamilton, J. Charlie and his countess. Look 30:96 Ap
19 '66

Steele, R. Meet Marlon Brando. Film Heritage 2-1:2
Fall '66

BRASSELLE, KEEFE
Harbert, R. Where there's a will. Good H 137:16 O '53
Waters, H. F. Worms' eye view. Newsweek 72:59 S 23
'68

BRAZZI, ROSSANO
Brazzi as a heavy lover. Life 39:59 Jl 25 '55
Meyerson, E. Continental charmer. Photop 48-4:65 O
'55
Lerman, L. Male attraction. Mlle 42:152 F '56
Russo, M. He leaves his heart in Rome. Photop 50-2:
52 Ag '56
deRoulf, P. How to have a love affair. Photop 51-2:52
F '57
Nichols, M. Brassy Brazzi: he's sure of his mettle.
Coronet 42:8 S '57
McCalls visits. McCalls 85:14 Ap '58

Johnson, R.   Rossano's revenge.   Sat Eve Post 231:31
   Ja 31 '59
Biography.   Cur Bio 22:7 My '61
   same.   Cur Bio Yrbk 1961:70 '62

BREAMER, SYLVIA
   Johnson, J.   The daughter of "The Powerful."   Photop
      15-1:74 D '18
   Johaneson, B.   The girl with hypnotic eyes.   Photop 25-
      3:54 F '24

BRENNAN, WALTER
   Old pro.   Newsweek 51:65 F 3 '58
   This is the real McCoy.   TV Guide 6-31:20 Ag 2 '58
   What'll we do with grandpa?   Todays Health 36:24 O '58
   A man in his right mind.   TV Guide 7-10:17 Mr 7 '59
   A mutual admiration society.   TV Guide 8-4:5 Ja 23 '60
   Couple of agile codgers.   Life 49:61 O 17 '60
   Bell, J. N.   My kids don't owe me a thing.   Todays
      Health 40:20 D '62
   Dern, M.   Foxy grampa in a business suit.   TV Guide
      13-15:24 Ap 10 '65
   See, C.   An old actor stands fast in the changing world.
      TV Guide 16-13:10 Mr 30 '68

BRENT, EVELYN
   Biery, R.   Suicide never pays.   Photop 33-6:32 My '28
   Albert, K.   She eats and tells.   Photop 39-2:40 Ja '31

BRENT, GEORGE
   Biery, R.   We present two splendid new screen personali-
      ties.   Photop 42-1:67 Je '32
   Lane, J.   He's jinx-proof now.   Photop 46-6:58 N '34
   Proctor, K.   Nobody ever heard of her.   Photop 51-8:
      22 Ag '37
   Fletcher, A. W.   Reborn!   Photop 53-4:18 Ap '39
   Sharpe, H.   Beginning--bright victory.   Photop 53-6:22
      Je '39; 53-7:66 Jl '39
   Sheridan, A.   George.   Photop 54-9:18 S '40
   Cheatham, M.   George Brent tells: Why Ann Sheridan
      and I won't marry.   Photop 19-4:30 S '41
   Jefferson, S.   Why Ann Sheridan and George Brent have
      separated.   Photop 22-1:66 D '42
   Why George Brent came out of retirement.   TV Guide
      5-11:17 Mr 16 '57

BRIAN, DAVID
 Waterbury, R. Look ma, he's famous. Photop 38-1:50
   Jl '50
 Mr. D. A. Takes the stand. TV Guide 2-26:20 Je 25 '54
 The party's over. TV Guide 4-12:13 Mr 24 '56
 Wood, C. TV personalities biographical sketchbook.
   TV Personalities p23 '57

BRICE, ROSETTA
 Rosetta Brice. Feature Movie 1-4:52 My 5 '15

BRIDGES, LLOYD
 The explosive Mr. Bridges. TV Guide 6-15:17 Ap 12 '58
 Off the deep end. Time 71:61 Je 9 '58
 Aqualung actor. TV Guide 6-39:20 S 27 '58
 The happiest water boy since Gunga Din. TV Guide 7-
   26:17 Je 27 '59
 Nichols, M. Making a big splash. Coronet 48:18 Je '60
 The gentle muscleman. TV Guide 11-9:6 Mr 2 '63
 Goodwin, F. How they put a skin diver on a horse.
   TV Guide 13-47:8 N 20 '64

BRITT, MAY
 Sumptuous Swedish smorgasbord. Life 43:11 Ag 12 '57
 May Britt, sultry with a quiet way. Life 47:68 Ag 17 '59
 Wedding day for Sammy and May. Life 47:117 N 28 '60
 Britt, M. Why I married Sammy Davis Jr. Ebony 16:
   97 Ja '61
 Corbin, J. My baby belongs to the world. Photop 60-4:
   40 O '61
 Somers, A. No one can take them from me. Photop 61-
   3:39 Mr '62
 Robbins, F. Why we're adopting a baby. Photop 62-2:56
   Ag '62
 Somers, A. We'll have a dozen babies. Photop 62-4:27
   O '62
 Robbins, F. Children of a mixed marriage. Photop 63-3:
   29 Mr '63
 Carpozi, G. Jr. How Sammy changed me. Photop 63-5:
   39 My '63
 Camber, G. How May changed me. Photop 64-1:68 Jl '63
 Lyle, J. Their friendship with Sammy and May. Photop
   66-4:43 O '64
 Newsmakers. Newsweek 70:52 D 4 '67
 Camber, G. What he did to May. Photop 73-2:39 F '68
 Kerr, D. May to wed white man. Photop 73-4:42 Ap '68

BRITTON, BARBARA
   Barbara Britton: private eyeful. TV Guide 2-13:15 Mr
   26 '54

BRITTON, PAMELA
   They laughed when she played it straight. TV Guide 12-
   41:26 O 10 '64

BROCKWELL, GLADYS
   Kingsley, G. Rich girl, poor girl. Photop 11-5:127 Ap
   '17
   Porter, V. H. Miss goody two-shoes. Photop 14-2:39
   Jl '18

BRODERICK, HELEN
   Obit. Newsweek 54:59 O 5 '59

BROMBERG, EDWARD J.
   Obit. Newsweek 38:70 D 17 '51
      Time 58:98 D 17 '51

BROMFIELD, JOHN
   Wood, C. TV personalities biographical sketchbook.
   TV Personalities p35 '57
   The sheriff was promoted. TV Guide 7-26:8 Je 27 '59

BRONCHO BILLY
   See: ANDERSON, G. M. "BRONCHO BILLY"

BRONSON, BETTY
   Albert, K. Bellamy, Bronson, Borden. Photop 40-2:70
   Jl '31

BROOK, CLIVE
   Woodward, M. Mr. Brook hates tea. Photop 39-2:77 Ja
   '31

BROOKS, LOUISE
   Card, J. The intense isolation of Louise Brooks. Sight
   & Sound 27-5:240 Sum '58
   Brooks, L. Gish & Garbo, the executive war on stars.
   Sight & Sound 28-1:13 Win '58/9
   Brooks, L. Pabst and Lulu. Sight & Sound 34-3:123
   Sum '65
   Brooks, L. Charlie Chaplin remembered. Film Culture
   40:5 Spg '66
   Brooks, L. Humphrey and Bogey. Sight & Sound 36-1:

Brophy, Edward

18 Win '66/7

BROPHY, EDWARD
Obit. Screen World 12:219 '61

BROWN, JAMES
Winters, L. Streamlined Texan. Photop 23-3:44 Ag '43
Harris, E. Bringing up Jim Brown. Photop 25-4:59 S
'44

BROWN, JIM
Syracuse gets off the ground. Life 41:147 O 8 '56
Brown of the Browns. Time 72:66 N 10 '58
Brown's run of records. Life 45:125 N 17 '58
Gross, M. All-around Jimmy Brown. Sat Eve Post 231:
31 N 22 '58
Masin, H. J Jim-dandy! Sr Schol 75:21 N 11 '59
Cleveland's Jim Brown; the big breakaway. Look 23:108
N 24 '59
Meet Mr. Fullback. Sr Schol 81:22 O 31 '62
Knack for running. Time 82:66 O 4 '63
Maule, T. Plan that worked; Cleveland Brows vs. N.Y.
Giants. Sports Illus 19:16 O 21 '63
Flynn, J. He's the greatest since Jim Thorpe. Life 55:
47 O 25 '63
Jimmy the Giant killer. Time 82:84 O 25 '63
Two men named Brown. Newsweek 62:88 O 28 '63
People are talking about Jim Brown of the Cleveland
Browns. Vogue 142:122 D '63
Poinsett, A. Pro football's mightiest player. Ebony 19:
32 Ja '64
From pigskins to redskins. Life 57:67 S 18 '64
Biography. Cur Bio 25:12 S '64
Same. Cur Bio Yrbk 1964:56 '64
Brown, J. My case against Paul Brown; excerpt from
Off my chest. Look 28:62 O 6 '64
Brown, J. Football bruisers I've bumped into; excerpt
from Off my chest. Look 28:104 O 20 '64
Brown on Brown. Newsweek 64:62 N 16 '64
Poinsett, A. Controversial Jim Brown. Ebony 20:65 D
'64
Explosive Mr. Brown. Ebony 20:57 Mr '65
Look at me, man! Time 86:80 N 26 '65
Game of the brave. Newsweek 67:97 My 23 '66
New day for Black Rock. Time 88:48 Jl 22 '66
Maule, T. Curtain falls on a long run. Sports Illus 25:
30 Jl 25 '66

Sanders, C. L.   Why I quit football.   Ebony 22:119 D '66
Warga, W.   Footage instead of yardage for Jim Brown.
   Life 62:103 My 19 '67
Brown power.   Newsweek 71:75 Ja 15 '68
Masin, H. L.   Mr. Fullback and Mr. Halfback.   Sr Schol
   93:40 S 27 '68
Sanders, C. L.   Film star Jim Brown.   Ebony 24:192
   D '68
Woodley, R.   He likes to keep you psyched.   Life 66:69
   My 23 '69

BROWN, JOE E.
Hamilton, S. Whooie! Here comes Joe E.   Photop 42-6:
   32 N '32
Lucky papa!   Am Mag 121:50 My '36
Elmer.   Time 36:44 Ag 5 '40
Funnyman's report.   Time 41:56 My 10 '43
Hendrick, K.   Laugh-maker with a serious outlook.
   C S Mon Mag p5 Ag 14 '43
On the go Joe.   Newsweek 23:76 F 28 '44
Burned up.   Am Mag 137:60 Ap '44
Killers without hate.   Am Mag 138:17 S '44
Biography.   Cur Bio F '45
Goofy gooneys.   Read Digest 46:75 Ap '45
Johnston, A.   Comedy.   New Yorker 21:26 Jl 7 '45
First break.   Theatre Arts 32:42 O '48
Monroe, K.   That battling buffoon named Brown.   Sat
   Eve Post 224:22 D 8; 30 D 15 '51
Holiday, K.   Lessons of sorrow.   Bet Hom & Gard 30:
   109 N '52

BROWN, JOHN MACK
Albert, K.   Ask Dad--he knows.   Photop 34-6:59 N '28
What they are doing now.   Show 2-8:106 Ag '62

BROWN, VANESSA
Porter, A.   Four Cinderellas.   Colliers 119:18 F 1 '47
Brain.   Am Mag 143:129 Mr '47
Sweet Vanessa Brown.   Life 33:148 D 8 '52
Goldberg, H.   Her brains didn't get in her way.
   Cosmop 134:24 Mr '53
Love of four mediums.   Theatre Arts 37:11 My '53
Wood, C.   TV personalities biographical sketchbook.
   TV Personalities p76 '56

BROWN, WINNIE
St. Johns, A. R.   Stunting into stardom.   Photop 23-1:39 D'22

BROWNE, CORAL
   Glamour from the bush.   Plays & Players 2-5:9 F '55

BRUCE, DAVID
   Erwin, L.   Scotch and sober.   Photop 28-1:47 D '45

BRUCE, NIGEL
   Daugherty, F.   Baker Street regulars; Rathbone and
      Bruce make pictures based on Doyle stories and fill in
      the times between with a radio program.   C S Mon
      Mag p7 Ag 19 '44
   Obit.   Illus Lond N 223:612 O 17 '53
      Newsweek 42:77 O 19 '53
      Time 62:104 O 19 '53
      Am Ann 1954:89 '54
      Brit Bk Yr 1954:526 '54
      Screen World 5:208 '54

BRUCE, VIRGINIA
   Maxwell, V.   "I hate to leave John Gilbert."   Photop 45-
      5:34 Ap '34
   Hall, G.   Why Virginia Bruce won't marry for five years.
      Photop 48-6:30 N '35
   Hunt, J. L.   Show a sleeping beauty awoke to glamour.
      Photop 50-4:22 O '36
   Small, F.   Three cornered love.   Photop 51-3:34 Mr '37
   Baskette, K.   Second chance at love.   Photop 52-2:24
      F '38
   My heart is set on colonial.   House & Gard 77:44 F '40

BRYAN, JANE
   Hamilton, S.   Janey-Paney.   Photop 53-11:32 N '39

BRYNNER, YUL
   Brynner rex.   New Yorker 27:24 Ap 21 '51
   Brynner, Y.   King and I.   Good H 141:52 Jl '55
   King, his camera and a film triumph.   Life 40:109 My 28
      '56
   Sayre, J.   Yul Brynner: who do women find him irre-
      sistible?   Colliers 138:32 Jl 6 '56
   Biography.   Cur Bio 17:19 S '56
      Same.   Cur Bio Yrbk 1956:80 '57
   Archerd, A.   Who needs hair?   Photop 51-2:64 F '57
   Head of hair for a head of skin.   Life 42:140 Mr 18 '57
   Ingrid and Yul get good news.   Life 42:112 Ap 8 '57
   Whitcomb, J.   Bald box office king.   Cosmop 142:35
      My '57

Hubler, R. G. Yul Brynner, jack of all mimes. Coronet
    42:131 Jl '57
Mineo, S. The king and me. Photop 52-4:54 O '57
Yul Brynner--golden egghead. Newsweek 51:100 My 19
    '58
Wag at the wig-fitting session. Life 45:61 N 10 '58
Martin, P. I call on Yul Brynner. Sat Eve Post 231:24
    N 22 '58
Biography. Am Ann 1958:107 '58
Refugee aid. U. N. Rev 6:2 O '59
Gardner, M. Why do they label him fraud? Photop 57-
    3:40 Mr '60
Brynner's bride. Life 48:102 Ap 25 '60
Where real drama is. Newsweek 56:88 D 12 '60
Miller, E. Tony Curtis and Yul Brynner among the cos-
    sacks. Seventeen 21:92 O '62

BUCHANAN, EDGAR
    It's easier than pulling teeth. TV Guide 13-44:24 O 30
        '65

BUCHANAN, JACK
    Triple trouble. Colliers 132:44 Jl 25 '53
    Obit. Newsweek 50:72 O 28 '57
        Time 70:96 O 28 '57
        Screen World 9:221 '58

BUCHHOLZ, HORST
    Advance notice. Vogue 134:143 S 15 '59
    Biography. Cur Bio 21:12 Mr '60
        Same. Cur Bio Yrbk 1960:57 '61
    The girl in the picture. Films & Filming 6-7:31 Ap '60
    Henry Bookholt. Time 78:52 Ag 4 '61
    Miller, E. Pretty brunette and a German boat. Seven-
        teen 20:113 N '61
    Britten, R. Crack-up! Photop 60-6:40 D '61
    Friedman, F. What a lover! Photop 61-2:38 F '62
    People are talking about . . . Vogue 139:82 Ap 15 '62
    Buchholz, H. The ego and I. Films & Filming 8-7:9
        Ap '62

BULL, PETER
    Bull, P. Waiting for God knows what. Plays & Players
        3-8:7 My '56

BUNNY, JOHN
    Pemberton, R. B. Man seen daily by millions. Am Mag

78:60 Ag '14
Lanier, H. W.   Coquelin of the movies.   World's Work
    29:566 Mr '15
Collins, F. L.   Motion picture roll of honor.   Good H
    95:62 Ag '32

BUONO, VICTOR
Luft, H. G.   Victor Buono.   Films In Review 14-3:190
    Mr '63

BURKE, BILLIE
My simple rules for beauty.   Delin 77:510 Je '11
Dale, A.   Bonnie Billie Burke.   Cosmop 52:412 F '12
Charming Billie.   Cosmop 55:263 Jl '13
Underhill, H.   All feminine except the "Billie."   Photop
    13-1:55 D '17
On acting and babies.   Am Mag 86:58 Ag '18
Johnson, J.   Lending enchantment to distance.   Photop
    15-6:43 My '19
Cole, C. C.   Topknots and souls.   Delin 97:30 S '20
Billie Burke remembers by herself.   Delin 104:10 My;
    12 Je '24
Cantor, E. & Freedman, D.   Ziefeld and his follies.
    Colliers 93:24 Ja 27 '34
Calhoun, D.   A romance that is stronger than death.
    Photop 48-4:70 S '35
Darbyshire, M. B.   Families can live happily side by
    side.   Am Home 38:22 Ag '47
Burke, B.   With a feather on my nose, with Cameron
    Shipp; excerpts.   Colliers 122:18 S 25; 19 O 2; 28 O
    9 '48
Busy life.   Time 52:38 O 4 '48
Collinge, P.   Vive le white plumage.   Sat R 32:17 Je 25
    '49
Burke, B.   With a feather on my nose, with Cameron
    Shipp; excerpts.   Good H 149:94 O '59
Ziegfeld, P.   Ziegfeld's girl; excerpts. Ladies Home J
    81:62 Jl; 104 Ag '64

BURKE, JAMES
Obit.   Screen World 20:232 '69

BURNETTE, SMILEY
Hobbyist of the month.   Pop Mech 87:148 Ap '47
Obit.   Screen World 19:229 '68

BURNS, GEORGE
 Burns, G. Gracie Allen as I know her. Ind Woman 19:
  198 Jl '40
 Straightman. Time 42:58 D 13 '48
 Biography. Cur Bio 12:13 Mr '51
  Same. Cur Bio Yrbk 1951:75 '52
 Playing it straight. TV Guide 1-39:5 D 25 '53
 Burns, G. I love her, that's why; excerpt from autobiog-
  raphy. Coronet 39:82 Ap '56
 George Burns, an old cowhand himself, spoofs the west-
  erns. TV Guide 5-39:18 S 28 '57
 Burns without Allen. Time 71:46 Mr 3 '58
 Eells, G. Improbable tycoon. Look 22:34 Mr 18 '58
 Riding alone. TV Guide 6-43:17 O 25 '58
 No longer stylish. TV Guide 7-23:17 Je 6 '59
 (See also: BURNS AND ALLEN)

BURNS AND ALLEN
 Hamilton, S. By the Grace of Georgie. Photop 52-4:27 Ap '38
 Darbyshire, M. B. Radio stars build a home; Hollywood
  home of George Burns and Gracie Allen. Arts & Dec
  48:25 Ag '38
 Baker, G. Backstage with Burns & Allen; intv. Sr Schol
  42:20 Ap 19 '43
 Kaye, J. George burns while Gracie fiddles. Pageant
  p104 Je '50
 Hands tell the (funny) story. TV Guide 2-44:5 N 6 '54
 Wood, C. TV personalities biographical sketchbook.
  TV Personalities p14 '54
 Burns, Allen and Burns. TV Guide 4-34:24 Ag 25 '56
 Burns and Allen. Newsweek 49:94 Je 24 '57
 Gracie ends act with George. Life 45:87 S 22 '58
 (See also: ALLEN, GRACIE; BURNS, GEORGE)

BURR, RAYMOND
 Nichols, M. Murder makes the grade. Coronet 44:16
  Ag '58
 Raymond Burr, Perry Mason's prisoner. Look 22:54 S
  2 '58
 TV's legal eagle. TV Guide 6-36:17 S 6 '58
 The incredible case of Raymond Burr. TV Guide 7-8:20
  F 21 '59
 Johnson, R. TV's make-believe lawyer. Sat Eve Post
  232:26 O 3 '59
 These guns for hire. Time 74:52 O 26 '59
 Gehman, R. The case of the oversize actor. TV Guide
  9-9:8 Mr 4; 9-10:17 Mr 11; 9-11:24 Mr 18 '61

Biography.   Cur Bio 22:15 S '61
   Same.   Cur Bio Yrbk 1961:88 '62
TV's Perry Mason.   Look 25:54 O 10 '61
Whitney, D.   Pleading his own case.   TV Guide 13-30:
   15 Jl 24 '65
Jennings, C. R.   Burr for the prosecution.   TV Guide
   15-37:24 S 16 '67
The day I died.   Photop 73-1:24 Ja '68
What she made him shed.   Photop 74-6:32 D '68
Efron, E.   He puts the iron in Ironside.   TV Guide 17-
   7:26 F 15 '69

BURTON, CHARLOTTE
Shannon, B.   A good little sport.   Photop 11-1:135 D '16

BURTON, RICHARD
Hubler, R. G.   Angriest star in Hollywood.   Sat Eve
   Post 226:30 O 3 '53
Wild Welshman.   Look 17:75 S 8 '53
Barker, R.   Hollywood to Hamlet.   Plays & Players 1-
   4:4 Ja '54
Burton, S.   I wouldn't want him tamed.   Photop 45-3:64
   Mr '54
Booth bows again.   Life 38:55 Ja 24 '55
Buckley, M.   Burton, the Welsh rarebit.   Photop 47-5:
   67 My '55
Virile Welshman.   Coronet 39:10 Ja '56
Longing for a cigarette.   Plays & Players 3-5:7 F '56
Talks with the star.   Newsweek 59:94 D 12 '60
Biography.   Cur Bio 21:4 D '60
   Same.   Cur Bio Yrbk 1960:68 '61
Hamilton, L.   Churchill's ghost voice.   Sr Schol 78:9
   Mr 15 '61
Brossard, C.   Hottest actor around.   Look 25:54a My 23
   '61
Gelb, A. and Gelb, B.   Actor with two lives.   Sat Eve
   Post 235:64 Ja 27 '62
York, C.   Who is this man they link with Liz?   Photop
   61-5:8 My '62
York, C.   The night they destroyed Eddie.   Photop 61-6:
   4 Je '62
Skolsky, S.   Their strange marriage deal.   Photop 62-1:
   45 Jl '62
Richards, J.   The shameless lovers.   Photop 62-4:38 O
   '62
Richard Burton.   Films & Filming 9-1:7 O '62
Hoffman, J.   Wedding bells toll their doom.   Photop

62-5:44 N '62

Davis, D.   Liz loses Burton.   Photop 62-6:46 D '62

Edwards, D.   Her love deal with the Burtons.   Photop
63-2:48 F '63

DeBlasio, E.   How he got that way.   Photop 63-2:51 F
'63

Man on the billboard.   Time 81:70 Ap 26 '63

Carpozi, G. Jr.   Mob beats up Burton.   Photop 63-4:14
Ap '63

Taylor, E.   Elizabeth Taylor talks about Cleopatra to J.
Hamilton.   Look 27:41 My 7 '63

Millionairess.   Time 81:50 Je 7 '63

Mr. Cleopatra.   New Statesm 66:106 Jl 19 '63

Anatomy of an actor.   Read Digest 83:104 Jl '63

Joya, M.   Sybil's plan to ruin Liz.   Photop 64-2:29 Ag
'63

DeBlasio, E.   What Burton does to Liz.   Photop 64-3:33
S '63

Brewer, D.   What Eddie could tell him.   Photop 64-4:50
O '63

Hopper, H.   Passion and waste.   Photop 64-5:41 N '63

Perils of Mexican divorce.   Time 82:34 D 27 '63

Brewer, D.   Burton two-timing Liz.   Photop 64-6:47 D
'63

Funny thing happened on the way to decorum.   Time 83:
56 Ja 3 '64

Burton and the girls.   Look 28:40 Ja 28 '64

Roddy, J.   Visit with Richard Burton.   Look 28:47 Ja 28
'64

Wayne, D.   Report from Mexico.   Photop 65-1:30 Ja '64

Dickenliz in Toronto.   Newsweek 63:78 F 10 '64

Burton, R.   Candid look at Beckett and myself.   Life 56:
85 Mr 13 '64

Hammon, J.   Liz gets Burton, abuse and all.   Photop
65-3:40 Mr '64

Prince of thought.   Time 83:65 Ap 17 '64

Lyle, J.   Can Burton hold Liz, and his liquor?   Photop
65-4:52 Ap '64

Wills, G.   Theater: N.Y. performance of Hamlet.   Nat
R 16:458 Je 2 '64

Hall, J.   Moment-by-moment wedding scoop.   Photop
65-6:46 Je '64

Something to write home about.   Time 84:62 Jl 3 '64

Victor, T.   Drama the cameras missed.   Sat Eve Post
237:24 Jl 11 '64

Prideaux, T.   Liz and Dick put iambics in the big time.
Life 57:12 Jl 24 '64

York, C. The night they shared a room with Eddie.
   Photop 66-1:20 Jl '64
Rogoff, G. Hamlet of brain and passion. Hi Fi 14:51
   Jl '64
McLaughlin, J. Burton's Hamlet. Cath World 199:308
   Ag '64
Carpozi, G. Burton's incurable disease. Photop 66-3:
   46 S '64
Beginning writer. Time 84:82 O 30 '64
Lyle, J. Their friendship with Sammy and May. Photop
   66-4:43 O '64
Meehan, T. Success et cetera. Show 4-9:32 O '64
Somers, A. How she makes him prove his love. Photop
   66-5:62 N '64
Valentine, L. How they're making you forget. Photop
   66-5:41 N '64
We will dance. Newsweek 64:73 D 21 '64
Hershey, L. Other Burton. McCalls 92:86 Ja '65
Somers, A. He offers her another man. Photop 67-1:23
   Ja '65
Hoffman, J. Burton crawls for Liz. Photop 67-2:41 F
   '65
Burton writes of Taylor. Vogue 145:128 Mr 1 '65
Hamilton, J. King and queen. Look 29:26 Mr 9 '65
Hoffman, J. Her nights with Richard. Photop 67-4:41
   Ap '65
Hyams, J. Mind and heart of Richard Burton. Good H
   160:84 Je '65
Hoffman, J. Burton's ruining me with liquor. Photop
   68-1:59 Jl '65
Valentine, L. The only girl who said no. Photop 68-2:
   33 Ag '65
Joy. McCalls 93:25 D '65
Roddy, J. Elizabeth Taylor and Richard Burton: the
   night of the brawl. Look 30:42 F 8 '66
Smith, M. Burtons play Faustus at Oxford as a favor to
   Richard's old tutor. Life 60:79 Mr 4 '66
Smith, M. Liz launches 1,000 ships: Faustus at Oxford.
   Life 60:78 Mr 4 '66
Bawd of Avon. Time 87:58 Je 3 '66
Davis, S. Jr. Richard Burton. McCalls 94:99 O '66
Braddon, R. Richard Burton to Liz: I love thee not.
   Sat Eve Post 239:88 D 3 '66
Sage, T. Who's afraid of Dr. Faustus? Nat R 18:1319 D 27 '66
Redfield, W. Night Elizabeth Taylor said so what? and
   Richard Burton kicked the television set in; excerpt
   from Letters from an actor. Esquire 67:108 Ja '67

His Liz: a scheming charmer. Life 62:78 F 24 '67

Rosponi, L. Burtons in Dahomey. Vogue 149:92 Ap 15 '67

Garrison, L. On location with Richard and Elizabeth (and 145 friends). N. Y. Times Mag p30 My 7 '67

On location with Richard and Liz: why they're never dull. Look 31:64 Je 27 '67

Brossard, C. It's a mad, mad world, 'ol boy; intv. Look 31:69 Je 27 '67

Happy anniversary Elizabeth and Richard; tributes from seven friends. McCalls 94:68 Je '67

Peter Glenville talks about the Burtons. Vogue 150:282 S 1 '67

Valentine, L. What he gets from liquor. Photop 72-6: 46 D '67

Pepper, C. G. Voyage with the Burtons. McCalls 95: 56 Ja '68

Reluctant Hamlet reviews the tale of how it got to be or not to be. Life 64:8 F 9 '68

Musel, R. The Burtons turn to TV for fun and profit. TV Guide 16-22:16 Je 1 '68

Perry, A. How his drinking saved his life. Photop 73-6:54 Je '68

Sheed, W. Burton and Taylor must go. Esquire 70:173 O '68

Thompson, T. While Burton romances Rex, Liz weighs her power and her future. Life 66-65 Ja 17 '69

Birstein, A. Liz Taylor and Richard Burton; what it's like to be walking investments. Vogue 153:100 F 15 '69

O'Brien, F. I won't be a puppet. Photop 75-3:40 Mr '69

Conner, P. A search for world without pain. Photop 76-1:64 Jl '69

Musel, R. Elizabeth wouldn't like this at all. TV Guide 17-42:20 O 18 '69

BUSCH, MAE

St. Johns, A. R. She's a nut--but I like her. Photop 21-4:26 Mr '22

Summers, M. P. Mae Busch. Films In Review 7-3: 141 Mr '56

BUSH, PAULINE

Posner, G. A. Pretty, petite Pauline Bush. Photop 5-2:29 Ja '14

Thein, M. A biography. Feature Movie 2-8:25 Jl 25 '15

BUSHMAN, FRANCIS X.
Synon, K. Francis X. Bushman, romanticist. Photop
6-2:55 Jl '14
Neiss, L. J. Fifteen minutes with the man on the cover.
Feature Movie 1-1:4 Mr 15 '15
Biery, R. Who killed Francis X. Bushman? Photop
33-2:34 Ja '28
Kent, T. Ex-millionaire. Photop 39-2:35 Ja '31
Martin, P. First king of swoon; intv. Sat Eve Post 217:
14 Ap 28 '45
Profile unimpaired. Time 50:92 S 22 '47
Speaking of pictures. Life 24:10 F 2 '48
Johnson, G. Hollywood's greatest lover. Coronet 32:28
S '52
Amour and the man. Sat R 39:29 O 13 '56
. . . and then I met this blonde. TV Guide 4-50:24 D
15 '56
With Francis X. Newsweek 59:97 My 8 '61
What they are doing now. Show 2-8:106 Ag '62
Obit. Time 88:77 S 2 '66
Illus Lond N 249:11 S 3 '66
Brit Bk Yr 1967:590 '67
Screen World 18:232 '67
First movie star. Newsweek 68:22 S 5 '66

BUTTERWORTH, CHARLES
Collins, F. L. He made a fortune by looking dumb!
Photop 47-6:30 My '35
Obit. Newsweek 27:56 Je 24 '46
Time 47:78 Je 24 '46

BUTTONS, RED
Next week, a Cadillac? Time 60:54 O 27 '52
New face. Newsweek 40:68 N 10 '52
Red Buttons lampoons Hollywood muscle men. Look 17:
32 Ja 27 '53
Millstein, G. Four Red Buttons and how they grew.
N. Y. Times Mag p14 F 22 '53
Ho ho song. Newsweek 41:86 Ap 6 '53
Strange things are happening to Red Buttons. TV Guide
1-8:17 My 22 '53
Red Buttons: Minsky's was just like Harvard. News-
week 42:60 S 28 '53
Millstein, G. Red Buttons. Colliers 132:23 O 16 '53
Humility pays for Red Buttons. TV Guide 2-7:5 F 12 '54
Too much for one man. Life 36:163 Je 7 '54
Buttons at bat again. TV Guide 2-42:13 O 16 '54

Wood, C.   TV personalities biographical sketchbook.
    TV Personalities p22 '54
Frosting on the cake.   Newsweek 47:104 Ap 9 '56
McCalls visits.   McCalls 85:20 D '57
Biography.   Cur Bio 19:21 S '58
    Same.   Cur Bio Yrbk 1958:70 '58
Maas, P.   Return of Red Buttons.   Coronet 45:48 F '59
Elf said grrrrrrf.   Newsweek 56:76 Ag 15 '60
Hobson, D.   Is this man an imposter?   TV Guide 14-22:
    22 My 28 '66

BYINGTON, SPRING
Attention, mothers-in-law.   TV Guide 2-49:13 D 4 '54
Wood, C.   TV personalities biographical sketchbook.
    TV Personalities p148 '54
TV's happiest outlaws.   Look 19:178 D 13 '55
Flying grandmother.   TV Guide 4-10:13 Mr 10 '56
Biography.   Cur Bio 17:25 S '56
    Same.   Cur Bio Yrbk 1956:94 '57
Who's who cooks.   Good H 144:10 My '57
For the older woman.   TV Guide 7-11:12 Mr 14 '59

BYRNES, EDWARD
Byrnes, E.   Why doesn't a fellow ever get over his first
    love?   Photop 55-4:66 Ap '59
Accent on youth.   TV Guide 7-19:17 My 9 '59
Jukebox.   Time 73:72 My 11 '59
Kookie wows the kids.   Look 23:73 Jl 7 '59
Borie, M.   Someone to watch over me.   Photop 56-2:46
    Ag '59
Nichols, M.   Edd B: confident Kookie.   Coronet 46:16
    Ag '59
Borie, M.   Is she really going Kookie?   Photop 56-3:34
    S '59
Are you Kookie too?   Photop 56-5:46 N '59
Where's Kookie going?   Photop 57-4:29 Ap '60
The fine art of building a star.   TV Guide 8-35:17 Ag 27
    '60
Williams, J.   Kookie, we're gonna mash your face.
    Photop 58-4:52 O '60

CABOT, BRUCE

Stevens, G. Divorce taught them how truly they were married. Photop 48-7:50 D '35

CABOT, SEBASTIAN

He uses his beard and bulk shamelessly. TV Guide 9-17:7 Ap 29 '61

Whitney, D. The great faffler. TV Guide 15-16:16 Ap 22 '67

Gould, E. Britain's largest export. TV Guide 15-50:20 D 16 '67

CAGNEY, JAMES

Lang, H. Jimmy from the "Jungle." Photop 40-2:49 Jl '31

Pringle, H. F. Tough, by request. Colliers 90:22 S 3 '32

York, C. Red-headed rebel. Photop 43-1:45 D '32

Banton, R. He can't even find a friend. Photop 44-3:70 Ag '33

Rankin, R. If one Cagney's good, two should be better. Photop 44-5:75 O '33

Maddox, B. The "tough" from the chorus. Photop 45-3:69 F '34

On the current screen. Lit Digest 117:43 Ap 7 '34

Johnston, A. They toughened him up. Womans H C 61:18 N '34

Baldwin, L. Why Jimmy Cagney took a walk. Photop 50-5:21 N '36

Ferguson, O. Great guy. New Repub 92:271 O 13 '37

Hamilton, S. Like Ferdinand--he loves to smell flowers. Photop 53-2:28 F '39

Durant, J. Tough on and off. Colliers 106:24 Ag 31 '40

Tully, J. Big-time small guy. Photop 54-8:10 Ag '40

Haynes, H. Should love wait? Photop 18-4:34 Mr '41

Biography. Cur Bio '42

Steele, J. H. Portrait of a shy guy. Photop 23-5:53 O '43

Paul, E. Man without an axe. Photop 27-4:52 S '45

Brown, J. M. Cagney rides again. Sat R 32:28 O 1 '49

Gimp is back, still rough on Ruth. Life 38:67 Je 20 '55

Parsons, L. O. Cagney's year. Cosmop 138:24 Je '55

Meyerson, E. Live and learn. Photop 48-2:70 Ag '55

Berquist, L. New craze for Cagney. Look 19:98 S 20 '55

Shipp, C. Cagney. Colliers 136:30 O 28 '55

Benz, H. Gentle tough of Martha's Vineyard. Coronet 39:134 N '55

Cagney, J. How I got this way; as told to P. Martin. Sat Eve Post 228:17 Ja 7; 32 Ja 14; 30 Ja 21 '56

Who's who cooks. Good H 143:10 O '56

Cagney plays Lon Chaney. Look 21:126 Je 11 '57

Cagney's Lon Chaney. Newsweek 50:88 Ag 19 '57

Chaney chills 'em again. Life 43:105 S 2 '57

Miller, D. James Cagney, inc. filmog. Films In Review 9-7:361 Ag/S '58

James Cagney interviewed. Sight & Sound 28-1:25 Win '58/9

James Cagney talking. Films & Filming 5-6:12 Mr '59

Personality of the month. Films & Filming 8-6:7 Mr '62

Roman, R. C. Yankee Doodle Cagney. Dance Mag 41:58 Jl '67

Where are they now? Newsweek 71:16 Ap 22 '68

CAGNEY, JEANNE

Smith, H. A. Cantankerous Cagneys. Sat Eve Post 216:9 O 2 '43

Long, J. Time of her life. Am Mag 146:42 S '48

CAIN, ROBERT

Obit. Screen World 6:223 '55

CAINE, MICHAEL

People are talking about. Vogue 146:154 N 1 '65

Gouldthrope, K. Success of a sometime spy. Life 61:105 O 21 '66

Steinem, G. M. What's 'e got? N. Y. Times Mag p66 D 4 '66

Lawrenson, H. Caine file. Esquire 66:260 D '66

Miller, E. Cool character called Caine. Seventeen 25:116 D '66

Young man shows his medals. Time 89:66 F 17 '67

Lear, M. W. Caine mutiny. McCalls 94:87 Mr '67

McCarry, C. Hot actor for a cool time. Sat Eve Post 240:94 My 20 '67

Fallaci, O. Michael Caine talks. Look 31:85 My 30 '67

Birmingham, S. Sudden fame of Michael Caine. Holiday 41:81 Je '67

Hamill, P. New roughneck breed of ladies' men. Good H 165:94 O '67

Biography. Cur Bio 29:5 My '68

Same.   Cur Bio Yrbk 1968:72 '69

CALLAN, MICHAEL
   Gautschy, D.   The story of a marriage.   Photop 60-3:
    46 S '61
   Lewis, R. W.   Hollywood's new breed of soft young men.
    Sat Eve Post 235:77 D 1 '62
   Fessier, M. Jr.   He plays a hot second base for the
    daisies.   TV Guide 14-51:15 D 17 '66

CALHERN, LOUIS
   Hartwell, D.   Man who startled Hollywood.   Sat Eve Post
    223:40 My 26 '51
   Biography.   Cur Bio 12:13 Jl '51
    Same.   Cur Bio Yrbk 1951:87 '52
   Obit.   Illus Lond N 228:565 My 19 '56
    Newsweek 47:76 My 21 '56
    Time 67:95 My 21 '56
    Cur Bio 17:19 Jl '56
    Cur Bio Yrbk 1956:98 '57
    Am Ann   1957:118 '57
    Screen World 8:221 '57
   Biography.   NCAB 45:517 '62

CALHOUN, RORY
   Walker, H. L.   Smokey.   Photop 31-3:66 Ag '47
   Walker, H. L.   The life of Rory.   Photop 32-3:64 F '48
   Walker, H. L.   Weekend wedding.   Photop 33-6:24 N '48
   Scott, D.   Rory's gone Hollywood.   Photop 42-4:68 O '52
   Ford, E.   Terrific trio.   Photop 43-4:32 Ap '53
   Leon, R.   Domesticated dreamboat.   Photop 43-6:54 Je
    '53
   Arnold, M.   Keeping a date with love.   Photop 44-3:56
    S '53
   Senseney, D.   So glad they met.   Photop 46-5:58 N '54
   Oppenheimer, P.   The crackerjack-of-all-trades.   Photop
    47-2:42 F '55
   He-man Calhoun.   Photop 47-3:88 Mr '55
   Ott, B.   Love has charms.   Photop 47-4:45 Ap '55
   Balling, F. D.   Love in the shadow of fear.   Photop
    48-4:46 O '55
   Connolly, M.   Impertinent interview.   Photop 48-6:36 D
    '55
   Arnold, M.   The day that decided Rory Calhoun's life.
    Photop 49-3:41 Mr '56
   Calhoun, R.   Look kid how stupid can you be?   Photop
    51-2:48 F '57

Calhoun, R. Cindy, oh Cindy. Photop 52-1:46 Jl '57
Musicianly boxer. Mus Am 78:9 Ja 1 '58
Smile when you say that pardner. TV Guide 7-5:24 Ja
     31 '59
He rides the range with both feet on the ground. TV
     Guide 8-7:12 F 13 '60

CALVET, CORINNE
    Corinne Calvet. Life 22:87 My 26 '47
    Replacement for Rita? Life 26:77 My 2 '49
    Colby, A. French dressing. Photop 36-7:56 D '49
    Martin, P. Hollywood's French threat. Sat Eve Post
        223:31 D 2 '50

CALVERT, CATHERINE
    Valentine, S. The careers of Catherine Calvert. Photop
        19-6:62 My '21

CALVERT, PHYLLIS
    Books into films. Pub W 151:438 Ja 25 '47
    Phyllis Calvert. Life 24:129 Je 14 '48

CAMBRIDGE, GODFREY
    Higgins, R. Godfrey Cambridge lives 53 blocks from
        Harlem. TV Guide 16-19:18 My 11 '68
    Biography. Cur Bio 30:11 Mr '69

CAMERON, DONALD
    Obit. Screen World 7:222 '56

CAMERON, ROD
    Shipp, C. Frontier guy. Photop 29-2:60 Jl '46
    The scholarly cop. TV Guide 6-25:22 Je 21 '58

CAMPBELL, WILLIAM
    Johnson, H. Sassy, but successful. Photop 48-1:11 Jl
        '55
    Harris, R. The Bill's overdue. Photop 49-1:40 Ja '56

CANOVA, JUDY
    Crichton, K. Hillbilly Judy. Colliers 109:17 My 16 '42
    Judy comes down the hill. Newsweek 26:102 D 17 '45

CANTINFLAS
    Creel, G. Mexico's Charlie Chaplin. Colliers 109:62
        My 30 '42
    Millan, V. C. Turbulent harlequin. Inter Am 1:29 Je

'42
King of Mexican clowns. Sr Schol 42:9 Mr 29 '43
Hinojosa, M. Latin Americans chortle with Cantinflas.
   Rotarian 64:15 Ap '44
Cantinflas trouble. Newsweek 27:54 Mr 25 '46
Oliver, M. R. Cantinflas. Hollywood Q 2-3:252 Ap '47
Ross, B. Mexico's Chaplin. Sight & Sound 17-66:87
   Sum '48
Villada, R. F. He makes Mexico laugh. Americas 5:6
   Mr '53
Eighty days with Cantinflas. Look 20:144 D 11 '56
Hellyer, D. Cantinflas, the Mexican mirthquake. Coro-
   net 42:147 Je '57
Gerald, Y. The comedy of Cantinflas. Films In Re-
   view 9-1:6 Ja '58
Mexican jumping bean. Newsweek 55:94 Mr 7 '60
Condon, R. Cantinflas. Holiday 28:161 D '60
Keating, B. Journey to the heartland. Holiday 32:146
   O '62
Playing it straight. Time 81:19 F 1 '63
Day, B. Mexico's little nobody who made good. Read
   Digest 89:221 O '66
Traveler, consider my Mexico; ed by R. Joseph.
   Esquire 66:144 N '66

CANTOR, EDDIE
   Mullet, M. B. We all like the medicine ex-Doctor Eddie
      Cantor gives. Am Mag 98:34 Jl '24
   Cantor, E. Why I like Hollywood better than the Bronx.
      Photop 30-6 N '26
   Now you tell one. Colliers 80:13 D 24 '27
   Freedman, D. My life in your hands. Sat Eve Post
      201:3 O 6; 28 O 13; 26 O 20; 20 O 27; 39 N 3 '28
   Aches have it. Colliers 83:32 Ap 20 '29
   One and one. Colliers 84:17 Jl 13 '29
   Freedman, D. Yoo-hoo! prosperity! Sat Eve Post 204:
      3 Ap 15 '31
   Freedman, D. I'm glad my five are girls. Am Mag 113:
      42 Ja '32
   Freedman, D. Who's hooey in Hollywood. Sat Eve Post
      204:6 Ap 16; 28 My 21; 205 Jl 2 '32
   Eddie Cantor gives a party. Ladies Home J 49:9 Jl '32
   Hamilton, E. Eddie goes Spanish. Photop 43-1:50 D '32
   Ziegfeld and his Follies. Colliers 93:7 Ja 13; 22 Ja 20;
      24 Ja 27; 18 F 3; 18 F 10; 22 F 17 '34
   What price acting? Sat Eve Post 206:8 Je 23 '34
   You oughta be in pictures. Sat Eve Post 207:29 O 20 '34

First time I died. Am Mag 121:47 Ja '36

Pic-ups. Pict R 37:34 Ja '36

Dear Ida; wedding anniversary letter. Am Mag 123:43
  Ja '36

For whose benefit? Sat Eve Post 208:14 Ap 25 '36

Cantor, M. Dad has his day. Good H 104:34 Ap '37

Five that never fail me. Read Digest 37:39 N '40

West, S. What is behind the popular song. Etude 58:
  804 D '40

It's a state of mind. Read Digest 38:76 Ap '41

Baker, G. Here's my favorite; intv. Sr Schol 39:17 S
  29 '41

Biography. Cur Bio '41

Burnham, D. Benjo eyes. Commonweal 35:295 Ja 9 '42

What's in a name? Womans H C 75:117 F '48

Bowes, V. His brother's keeper. Colliers 122:50 D 4
  '48

Banjo eyes bounces home. TV Guide 3-36:16 S 9 '50

Rotating comics. Time 56:83 S 25 '50

Eddie Cantor: good citizen. TV Guide 4-16:8 Ap 21 '51

Cantor, E. How I beg for money; as told to C. Shipp.
  Sat Eve Post 224:32 O 27 '51

Lords of laughter. Coronet 30:72 O '51

Hospitals can be fun. Read Digest 59:13 O '51

God help me. Ladies Home J 68:63 D '51

Cantor, E. Me and my heart attack. Look 17:4 Ja 13
  '53

Eddie Cantor's Rx for living. TV Guide 1-14:4 Jl 3 '53

Greater than the h-bomb. Read Digest 63:7 S '53

Biography. Cur Bio 15:28 My '54
  Same. Cur Bio Yrbk 1954:152 '54

Wood, C. TV personalities biographical sketchbook.
  TV Personalities p102 '54

If you knew Eddie. Newsweek 45:38 F 7 '55

Debus, A. G. Current collectors' recordings. Hobbies
  59:28 F '55

Cantor, E. My greatest discovery. Coronet 38:147 Je
  '55.

Cantor, E. Day I was fired. Read Digest 67:119 O '55

Cantor, E. Grandma was a matchmaker; excerpt from
  autobiography. Take my life. McCalls 84:34 Je '57

Cantor, E. If it hand't been for grandma; excerpt from
  autobiography Take my life. Read Digest 71:186 Jl '57

Mr. San Francisco. Coronet 45:140 F '59

That four-letter word, love; excerpt from The way I see
  it. Look 24:76 F 16 '60

Most unforgettable character I've met. Read Digest 76:

179 Mr '60
State of mind. Read Digest 80:182B Je '62
Obit. Time 84:112 O 16 '64
    Illus Lond N 245:613 O 17 '64
    Cur Bio 26:7 Ja '65
    Cur Bio Yrbk 1965:69 '65
    Screen World 16:220 '65

CAPRICE, JUNE
    Stevens, S. It didn't happen! Photop 17-2:101 Ja '20

CAPUCINE
    Beauty under wraps. Look 24:86 Mr 15 '60
    Harritz, R. Unknown star from France. Cosmop 148:
        10 Ap '60
    Hottest icicle. Time 86:89 D 10 '65

CARDINALE, CLAUDIA
    Next love goddess; dialogue. Esquire 55:108 My '61
    Show business. Time 78:45 Jl 18 '61
    People on the way up. Sat Eve Post 235:26 F 3 '62
    People are talking about. Vogue 139:88 Mr 15 '62
    Clamour over Claudia. Look 26:109 Je 19 '62
    Mitgang, H. On screen: Claudia Cardinale. Horizon
        5:38 Ja '63
    Lane, J. F. C. C. Films & Filming 9-4:19 Ja '63
    Hamil, P. Square world of Claudia Cardinale. Sat Eve
        Post 237:62 F 29 '64
    She'd rather lose money than be a cliche. Life 61:52
        Jl 8 '66
    New seven deadly sins. Esquire 66:190 D '66

CAREW, ORA
    Obit. Screen World 7:222 '56

CAREY, HARRY Sr.
    Jordan, J. From city streets to a rancho. Photop 21-4:
        32 Mr '22
    Harry Carey. New Yorker 17:16 O 18 '41
    Obit. Newsweek 30:52 S 29 '47
        Time 50:94 S 29 '47
    Riggan, B. Damn the crocodiles, keep the cameras roll-
        ing! Am Heritage 19:38 Je '68

CAREY, MACDONALD
    Arnold, M. Leave it to Macdonald Carey. Photop 33-5:
        60 O '48

Waterbury, R.   Star in your home.   Photop 34-6:66 My
   '49
Wheeler, L.   Where living's fun.   Photop 41-2:60 F '52
Wood, C.   TV personalities biographical sketchbook.
   TV Personalities p87 '56
Raddatz, L.   The dean of medicine (Hollywood division).
   TV Guide 17-47:26 N 22 '69

CAREY, PHIL
Wood, C.   TV personalities biographical sketchbook.
   TV Personalities p18 '57
These Gunns for hire.   Time 74:52 O 26 '59

CARLISLE, MARY
Hayes, J.   Little girl, don't cry!   Photop 45-4:37 Mr '34

CARLSON, RICHARD
Carlson is an actor and author.   Life 26:38 Ja 31 '49
Stars born in Chicago.   Life 26:37 Ja 31 '49
Biographical note.   Colliers 126:22 Jl 8 '50
Diary of a Hollywood safari.   Colliers 126:22 Jl 8; 32
   Jl 15; 20 Jl 22 '50
Same abridged with title Hollywood safari.   Read Digest
   57:45 O '50
Actor, writer, traveler: now he's a TV hero who fights
   Communism.   TV Guide 1-36:5 D 4 '53
Wood, C.   TV personalities biographical sketchbook.
   TV Personalities p52 '57

CARMICHAEL, HOAGY
Martin, D.   New films with notable music.   Etude 59:13
   Ja '41
Biography.   Cur Bio '41
Stars dust Hoagy.   Newsweek 25:97 Je 4 '45
Mathews, S.   This is the house that Stardust built.
   House B 88:96 Mr '46
Restrained off-blue.   Time 48:85 N 25 '45
People who read and write.   N. Y. Times Bk R p8 D 8
   '46
Martin, P.   Star-dust troubadour. Sat Eve Post 220:22
   N 8 '47
Indiana melody; Brown county in autumn.   Time 54:33
   D 26 '49
Hubler, R. G.   Hoagy Carmichael: mealncholy minstrel.
   Coronet 37:116 N '54
They're playing our song.   Time 66:77 O 24 '55
Marek, G.   Silver anniversary of Stardust.   Good H 141:

17 S '55
Freeman, B. & Kolodin, I.   Hoagy.   Sat R 52:43 Je 28
    '69

CARNOVSKY, MORRIS
Yours for a better life.   Theatre Arts 32:46 Je '48
Funke, L. & Booth, J. E.   Actor's method: his life.
    N. Y. Times Mag p47 O 1 '61
Everyman's disasters; Connecticut's triumph.   Time 82:
    44 Ag 16 '63

CAROL, MARTINE
France's favorite blonde.   Look 20:93 F 21 '56
Boost for French films.   Bsns W p103 Je 30 '56
France's Monroe.   New Yorker 32:14 Jl 7 '56
Obit.   Illus Lond N 250:13 F 11 '67
    Time 89:64 F 17 '67
    Newsweek 69:73 F 20 '67
    Screen World 19:229 '68

CAROL SUE
Earle, E.   Three fur coats.   Photop 37-1:36 D '29
Ladd, S.   I married a "killer."   Photop 22-1:45 D '42
St. Johns, A. R.   What you don't know about Alan Ladd's
    marriage.   Photop 23-2:28 Jl '43
Ladd, A.   The woman I love.   Photop 33-4:52 S '48

CARON, LESLIE
Hormel, G.   The most discussed girl in Hollywood.
    Photop 41-6:37 Je '52
Shipp, C.   Mademoiselle in blue jeans.   Womans H C
    79:32 D '52
    Same abridged.   Read Digest 62:137 F '53
Two looks at Leslie Caron.   Life 34:77 Mr 16 '53
Caron, L.   You don't have to be popular.   Photop 43-6:
    40 Je '53
Charmer on tiptoe.   Newsweek 43:75 F 1 '54
On the international scene.   Dance Mag 28:31 F '54
Caron carries on.   Colliers 133:32 My 28 '54
Biography.   Cur Bio 15:20 S '54
    Same.   Cur Bio Yrbk 1954:157 '54
Steele, J. H.   Pixie from Paris.   Photop 47-5:64 My '55
Biddle, M. T.   Companion in Paris.   Womans H C 83:4
    O '55
Britton, B.   Duckling into swan.   Photop 48-4:50 O '55
Balling, F. D.   Have luck, will travel.   Photop 49-6:46
    Je '56

Karhanek-Pal, F. Leslie Caron draws a reply. Dance
 Mag 32:38 F '58
McCalls visits. McCalls 85:10 My '58
Whitcomb, J. Leslie Caron as Gigi. Cosmop 144:76
 My '58
Whitcomb, J. Lunch with Leslie Caron. Cosmop 144:
 77 My '58
O'Donnell, M. Why--it's Leslie Caron. Photop 55-1:
 24 Ja '59
Lemon, R. Glamour girls off-duty. Newsweek 55:60 Ja
 4 '60
Whitcomb, J. Subterranean Miss Caron. Cosmop 148:
 18 Ja '60
Chic Caron. Look 24:91 Je 7 '60
Personalities of the month. Plays & Players 8-4:3 Ja
 '61
Leslie on a lark. Coronet 49:129 Ap '61
Caron, L. Making the mighty three-in-one into Logan's
 Fanny. Films & Filming 7-10:7 Jl '61
Kean, A. Reaction to the Berlin crisis. Photop 61-1:50
 Ja '62
Jennings, C. R. Waif becomes a woman. Sat Eve Post
 236:22 S 14 '63
Joel, L. Ballet is an adolescent passion. Dance Mag
 37:26 O '63
Accused of adultery! Photop 66-3:52 S '64
Waterbury, R. What Leslie Caron gives him. Photop
 66-6:53 D '64
Gris, H. It's my duty to marry her. Photop 68-1:50
 Jl '65
Unisexing with Caron and Cavett. TV Guide 17-41:37
 O 11 '69

CARPENTER, CARLETON
 Whitcomb, J. Backstage at the birth of a hit. Cosmop
  136:59 Mr '54

CARRADINE, DAVID
 Deloos, R. David Carradine rides the new wave--in a
  saddle. TV Guide 14-51:24 D 17 '66

CARRADINE, JOHN
 Crichton, K. Ghost of Shakespeare. Colliers 111:40 My
  29 '43
 Second front: Carradine's Hamlet. Time 42:32 N 8 '43
 Martin, P. Hamlet isn't hunry anymore. Sat Eve Post
  216:11 Ap 22 '44

Mank, G. W.   John Carradine, inc. filmog.   Films In
  Review 19-4:255 Ap '68

CARRILLO, LEO
Taylor, F. J.   Leo the caballero.   Sat Eve Post 219:26
  Jl '46
Obit.   Time 78:99 S 22 '61
  Am Ann 1962:848 '62
  Screen World 13:219 '62

CARROLL, DIAHANN
Tables for two.   New Yorker 33:75 Ag 10 '57
Diahann can act too.   Life 47:57 D 7 '59
Bottom of the top.   Time 79:48 D 7 '59
Hands at the heart of a song.   Life 47:57 D 7 '59
Paris bound with Diahann.   Life 51:67 N 3 '61
Talk with a star.   Newsweek 59:85 Mr 26 '62
Fancy wrappings and sweet music for Diahann.   Life 52:
  11 Ap 27 '62
Kelly, V.   Diahann Carroll: show stopper.   Look 26:
  110 My 22 '62
Broadway's newest star.   Ebony 17:40 Jl '62
Biography.   Cur Bio 23:15 S '62
  Same.   Cur Bio Yrbk 1962:74 '63
Gallic-American spectacular.   Ebony 22:36 Ap '67
Efron, E.   Success is not her problem.   TV Guide 15-
  21:12 My 27 '67
Shayon, R. L.   Julia: a political relevance?   Sat R 51:
  37 Jl 20 '68
Wolff, A.   Diahann Carroll: a new kind of glamour on
  TV.   Look 32:66 O 29 '68
Diahann's dash is designer's dish.   Life 65:88 N 8 '68
Entertaining Diahann Carroll.   Harper Baz 102:236 N '68
Julia.   Ebony 24:56 N '68
Smith, M.   A doll known to cry.   Photop 74-5:60 N '68
Wonderful world of color.   Time 92:70 D 13 '68
Chance, W.   Locked in her room.   Photop 76-2:35 Ag '69
Goode, B.   Love for Don Marshall threatened.   Photop
  76-5:60 N '69

CARROLL, JOHN
Asher, J.   Velvet volcano.   Photop 54-12:18 D '40

CARROLL, LEO G.
Gresham, W. L.   Mama and papa; intv.   Theatre Arts
  29:221 Ap '45
Wood, C.   TV personalities biographical sketchbook.

.TV Personalities p143 '54
U. N. C. L. E.'s uncle.   TV Guide 13-31:12 Jl 31 '65

CARROLL, MADELEINE
Foster, I.   Here is England's favorite charmer.   Photop
46-2:32 Jl '34
Crichton, K.   Camera shy.   Colliers 98:9 N 14 '36
Hartley, K.   Play truth or consequences with Madeleine
Carroll.   Photop 53-12:24 D '39
Burton, J.   Love in exile.   Photop 21-6:65 N '42
Madeleine's greatest role wins the French people.
Newsweek 26:78 O 1 '45
Biography.   Cur Bio 10:17 Ap '49
Same.   Cur Bio Yrbk 1949:94 '50
Hughes, C.   Strange career of Madeleine Carroll.
Coronet 28:150 My '50

CARROLL, NANCY
Corbin, E.   The littlest rebel in Hollywood.   Photop 36-
6:63 N '29
Baldwyn, F.   Her name in lights.   Photop 38-5:65 O '30
Springer, J.   Nancy Carroll.   Films In Review 7-4:155
Ap '56
Classic kitten.   Show 2-9:108 S '62
Springer, J.   Nancy Carroll filmography.   Films In Re-
view 15-5:287 My '64
Obit.   Time 86:72 Ag 13 '65
Newsweek 66:59 Ag 16 '65
Screen World 17:234 '66
Springer, J.   Nancy Carroll.   Films In Review 16-8:521
O '65

CARSON, JACK
Wilkinson, L.   Shy show off.   Photop 24-2:46 Ja '44
Novak, M.   Big guy.   Photop 28-2:48 Ja '46
Morgan, D.   My handicap--Jack Carson.   Photop 30-5:
54 Ap '47
Obit.   Time 81:74 Ja 11 '63
Newsweek 61:49 Ja 14 '63
Brit Bk Yr 1964:622 '64
Screen World 15:219 '64
Doerfler, B.   Jack Carson, inc. filmog.   Films In Re-
view 14-6:380 Je/Jl '63

CARSON, JEANNIE
Harvey, E.   TV imports.   Colliers 136:34 O 14 '55
Restless redhead.   Look 19:75 O 18 '55

Taking a fling in TV.   TV Guide 4-52:17 D 29 '56
Second tomato.   TV Guide 6-4:28 Ja 25 '58

CARSON, SUNSET
Lackey, W.   Sunset Carson, inc. filmog.   Film Fan Mo
92:20 F '69

CARTER, HELENA
Phi beta beauty.   Am Mag 147:102 Ja '49

CARTER, JANIS
Liebshen's lady.   TV Guide 3-6:20 F 5 '55

CARVER, LOUISE
Obit.   Screen World 8:221 '57

CARVER, LYNNE
Obit.   Screen World 7:222 '56

CASARES, MARIA
People of talent.   Sight & Sound 24-4:201 Spg '55

CASS, PEGGY
Efron, E.   She can act--but not on TV.   TV Guide 12-33:
15 Ag 15 '64

CASSAVETES, JOHN
Broadway love story.   Look 21:62 Je 11 '57
No torn shirts for him.   TV Guide 5-40:18 O 5 '57
The chip's off his shoulder.   TV Guide 7-48:28 N 28 '59
$40,000 method.   Time 77:72 Mr 24 '61
People on the way up.   Sat Eve Post 235:26 Ap 7 '62
Faces of the husbands.   New Yorker 45:32 Mr 15 '69
Biography.   Cur Bio 30:10 Jl '69

CATLETT, WALTER
Obit.   Brit Bk Yr 1961:512 '61
Screen World 12:219 '61

CAULFIELD, JOAN
Franchey, J.   Caulfield system.   Colliers 118:15 S 7 '46
Star from nowhere.   Am Mag 142:151 N '46
Harris, E.   Call for Joan Caulfield.   Photop 30-2:46
Ja '47
Caulfield, J.   I like it here.   Photop 31-2:48 Jl '47
Caulfield, J.   Tinsel 'round my finger.   Photop 32-1:
68 D '47

Caulfield, J.   Mistakes Hollywood girls make with men.
   Photop 32-6:72 My '48
McElory, J.   Breakfast in Hollywood.   Photop 36-2:60
   Je '49
Petty girl.   Life 28:75 F 6 '50
Gould, J.   TV's top comediennes.   N.Y. Times Mag p17
   D 27 '53
Scott, M.   Joan Caulfield.   Cosmop 136:27 Ja '54
Biography.   Cur Bio 15:33 My '54
   Same.   Cur Bio Yrbk 1954:164 '54
Wood, C.   TV personalities biographical sketchbook.
   TV Personalities p52 '54
Thomas, B.   Can a baby save my marriage?   Photop
   57-5:74 My '60

CHADWICK, HELENE
   Evans, D.   A nice girl from Main St.   Photop 22-3:36
      Ag '22
   Obit.   Cur Bio '40

CHAKIRIS, GEORGE
   Stanford, J.   The boy who makes you forget.   Photop
      61-4:46 Ap '62
   Tusher, B.   Hate! Photop 62-4:34 O '62
   Lewis, R. W.   Hollywood's new breed of soft young men.
      Sat Eve Post 235:76 D 1 '62
   Gable, B.   Hear your heroes.   Seventeen 22:62 Ja '63
   Miller, E.   In search of George Chakiris.   Seventeen
      23:136 Mr '64
   Philmus, L. C.   What bugs me about women.   Photop
      65-6:62 Je '64

CHAMBERLAIN, RICHARD
   My son, the doctor.   TV Guide 9-50:15 D 16 '61
   Wall, T.   Which doctor would you call?   Photop 61-3:
      30 Mr '62
   Wall, T.   Yoweee! Photop 61-5:36 My '62
   We accuse you . . .   Photop 62-1:56 Jl '62
   Davidson, M.   Television's very personal physicians,
      Kildare and Casey.   McCalls 89:66 Ag '62
   Miller, E.   Richard Chamberlain plays TV's Doctor Kil-
      dare.   Seventeen 21:116 S '62
   TV's Dr. Kildare.   Look 26:137 N 20 '62
   Ray, C.   He's like a rash with me.   Photop 63-2:43
      F '63
   Efron, E.   He inspires women.   TV Guide 11-11:8 Mr
      16 '63

Durslag, M. Dr. Kildare is a doll. Sat Eve Post 236:
   14 Mr 30 '63
Who's your dream doctor? Photop 63-3:37 Mr '63
Baskette, K. Dick Chamberlain's life story. Photop
   63-6:39 Je; 64-1:52 Jl '63
Biography. Cur Bio 24:9 Jl '63
   Same. Cur Bio Yrbk 1963:64 '64
Old Doc Kildare. TV Guide 11-38:15 S 21 '63
I want to make love. Photop 64-6:56 D '63
Richard Chamberlain as he sees himself. TV Guide 12-
   10:15 Mr 7 '64
Ellis, F. Is he dating a married woman? Photop 65-4:
   36 Ap '64
Borie, M. If you lived with him. Photop 66-1:58 Jl '64
Ardmore, J. I can't wait to get to work. Photop 66-4:
   40 O '64
Balling, F. D. Misery can be a friend. Photop 67-2:
   56 F '65
Joya, M. The night he ran for his life. Photop 68-2:
   64 Ag '65
Pep pills for Dr. Kildare. TV Guide 13-50:10 D 11 '65
Bowers, J. From TV to Tiffany's in one wild leap.
   Sat Eve Post 239:97 N 19 '66
Musel, R. You have to look after yourself. TV Guide
   16-43:38 O 26 '68
Buckley, P. Qui est vous, Richard Chamberlain? After
   Dark 11-3:20 Jl '69

CHAMPION, GOWER
   Hazards in four mediums. Theatre Arts 36:74 D '52
   Biography. Cur Bio 14:39 S '53
      Same. Cur Bio Yrbk 1953:110 '53
   Wood, C. TV personalities biographical sketchbook.
      TV Personalities p148 '57
   Tap-happy hot director. Life 50:90 My 5 '61
   Gower Champion. Dance Mag 38:33 Mr '64
   Gates, G. B. Broadway's Champion. Holiday 37:87 F
      '65
   (See also: CHAMPIONS)

CHAMPION, MARGE
   Biography. Cur Bio 14:39 S '53
      Same. Cur Bio Yrbk 1953:110 '53
   Wood, C. TV personalities biographical sketchbook.
      TV Personalities p148 '57
   (See also: CHAMPIONS)

CHAMPIONS (Marge and Gower)
    Madeira, E. A.   Dancers' way with fashion.   Womans
        H C 77:112 Jl '50
    Their dance steps are the cats'.   Am Mag 153:48 Ja '52
    Dudley, F.   Mr. and Mrs. Darling.   Photop 41-3:46 Mr
        '52
    Champions of Hollywood; dancers in a great tradition.
        Newsweek 39:56 Je 23 '52
    Cahn, R.   Dance is born.   Colliers 130:42 Jl 12 '52
    Arnold, M.   Just right for each other.   Photop 43-4:36
        Ap '53
    Harris, E.   Marge and Gower Champion.   Cosmop 135:
        10 Jl '53
    Barr, M.   The Champions.   Dance Mag 28:13 S '54
    French, M. G.   Husbands of four beautiful women tell us
        why she looks good to me.   McCalls 82:104 Ag '55
    Champions prepare to entertain royal visitors.   Dance
        Mag 31:50 D '57
    Duncan, D.   Ballet helps ballroom?   Dance 32:65 Jl '58;
        Reply 32:66 O '58
    Hochstein, R.   Booster shots for the midway marriage.
        Good H 155:34 O '62

CHANDLER, GEORGE
    The face is familiar.   TV Guide 6-21:22 My 24 '58

CHANDLER, JEFF
    Arnold, M.   Jeff.   Photop 39-2:56 F '51
    Chandler, J.   They're in love with love.   Photop 41-6:
        42 Je '52
    Arnold, M.   His lady carries a torch.   Photop 44-2:48
        Ag '53
    Scott, D.   When love is just a memory.   Photop 44-5:11
        N '53
    Corwin, J.   Jeff's other love.   Photop 45-1:50 Ja '54
    Linet, B.   Giant heart.   Photop 46-4:62 O '54
    Roberts, W.   Sentimental rebel.   Photop 47-4:40 Ap '55
    Scott, D.   They kissed and made up.   Photop 47-6:8 Je
        '55
    Obit.   Illus Lond N 238:1079 Je 24 '61
        Newsweek 57:65 Je 26 '61
        Screen World 13:219 '62
    Jordan, D.   Jeff Chandler, inc. filmog.   Films In Re-
        view 12-7:446 Ag /S '61
    Waterbury, R.   Daddy, we'll always love you.   Photop
        60-3:52 S '61

CHANEY, LON Sr.
  Kennedy, J. B.   His faces are his fortune; intv.
    Colliers 77:21 My 8 '26
  Waterbury, R.   The true story of Lon Chaney.   Photop
    33-1:32 D '27; 33-2:36 Ja; 33-3:56 F '28
  Lang, H.   Chaney talks.   Photop 37-6:75 My '30
  Lights out for Lon Chaney.   Lit Digest 106:37 S 13 '30
  Locan, C. A.   The Lon Chaney I knew.   Photop 38-6:
    58 N '30
  Collins, F. L.   Motion picture roll of honor.   Good H
    95:62 Ag '32
  Mitchell, G.   Lon Chaney 1886-1930, inc. filmog.   Films
    In Review 6-10:497 D '53
  Haley, A.   Man with a thousand faces.   Coronet 39:175
    D '55
  Knight, A.   So well remembered.   Sat R 40:25 Ag 17 '57
  Cagney's Lon Chaney.   Newsweek 50:88 Ag 19 '57
  Chaney chills 'em again.   Life 43:105 S 2 '57

CHANNING, CAROL
  Gentlemen prefer blondes.   Life 27:68 D 26 '49
  New star.   New Yorker 25:14 D 24 '49
  Brown, J. M.   Modern Lorelei.   Sat R 32:28 D 31 '49
  Keating, J.   Return of Lorelei Lee.   Colliers 125:30 Ja
    7 '50
  Wonderful leveling off.   Time 55:50 Ja 9 '50
  Hine, A.   Three smart blondes.   Holiday 10:6 S '51
  Audience in the act.   Theatre Arts 38:69 O '54
  Kaleidoscopic Channing.   Life 39:154 N 28 '55
  Broadway brings back the vamp.   Look 19:108 N 29 '55
  Double whammy.   Am Mag 161:53 Mr '56
  Watt, D.   Tables for two.   New Yorker 33:114 Ja 25 '58
  Couple of well skates.   Life 45:193 D 22 '58
  At home with the Lunts.   Theatre Arts 45:23 Ap '61
  Millstein, G.   Goodbye, Lorelei; hello, Dolly!   Sat Eve
    Post 237:78 F 22 '64
  Dolly.   New Yorker 40:23 F 29 '64
  Ehrlich, H.   New Carol Channing.   Look 28:58 My 19 '64
  Kerr, W.   Love letters of a tough critic.   Life 56:114 Je
    19 '64
  Pace-setters; intv.   Mlle 59:283 Ag '64
  Biography.   Cur Bio 25:17 S '64
    Same.   Cur Bio Yrbk 1964:76 '64
  Channing's dream.   Esquire 63:58 Ja '65
  Ace, G.   Jonathan Winters of our discontent.   Sat R
    48:14 Ap 24 '65
  New doll in town.   Newsweek 66:74 Ag 16 '65

At home with Carol Channing. House & Gard 128:211
  S '65
Operation Big Daddy. Time 89:19 Ja 27 '67
Sidney, H. Full evening of brotherliness. Life 62:30D
  Ja 27 '67

CHAPLIN, CHARLES
  Charlie Chaplin. Photop 7-3:35 F '15
  Some expressions! McClure 45:27 Jl '15
  Carr, H. C. Charlie Chaplin's story. Photop 8-2:27
    Jl; 8-3:43 Ag; 8-4:107 S; 8-5:97 O '15
  Adams, F. P. Plutarch lights of history. Harper 62:
    300 Mr 25 '16
  Smith, E. H. Charlie Chaplin's million-dollar walk.
    McClure 47:26 Jl '16
  O'Higgins, H. Charlie Chaplin's art. New Repub 10:16
    F 3 '17
  Ramsey, T. Chaplin--and how he does it. Photop 12-4:
    19 S '17
  Wagner, R. Mr. Charles Spencer Chaplin, the man you
    don't know. Ladies Home J 35:82 Ag '18
  Johnson, J. Charles, not Charlie. Photop 14-4:81 S '18
  What people laugh at. Am Mag 86:34 N '18
  Peltret, E. Chaplin's new contract. Photop 15-3:72 F
    '19
  Biby, E. A. How pictures discovered Charlie Chaplin.
    Photop 15-5:70 Ap '19
  Charlie Chaplin says laughs are produced by rules. Lit
    Digest 61:80 My 3 '19
  Charlie Chaplin is too tragic to play Hamlet. Cur
    Opinion 70:187 F '21
  Ervine, St. J. Mr. Charles Chaplin. Liv Age 309:107
    Ap 9 '21
  Jordan, J. Mother o' mine. Photop 20-2:45 Jl '21
  Charlie Chaplin's art dissected. Lit Digest 71:26 O 8 '21
  Burke, T. Tragic comedian. Outlook 130:100 Ja 18 '22
    Same abridged. Lit Digest 72:48 Ja 28 '22
  Science and Charlie Chaplin. Lit Digest 72:68 Ja 28 '22
  Chaplin, C. Charlies abroad. Photop 21-1:64 D '21; 21-
    2:20 Ja '22
  Wright, W. H. Charlie's great secret. Photop 21-3:40
    F '22
  Charlie Chaplin as a comedian contemplates suicide.
    Cur Opinion 72:209 F '22
  How Charlie Chaplin does it. World's Work 43:425 F '22
  Young, S. Dear Mr. Chaplin. New Repub 31:358 Ag
    23 '22

We have come to stay. Ladies Home J 39:12 O '22
In defense of myself. Colliers 70:8 N 11 '22
St. Johns, A. R. The loves of Charlie Chaplin. Photop
    23-3:28 F '23
Charlie Chaplin. Sunset 51:29 Jl'23
Does the public know what it wants? Ladies Home J 40:
    40 O '23
How much of Chaplin does Charlie own? Lit Digest 80:
    44 F 2 '24
Can art be popular? Ladies Home J 41:34 O '24
York, C. Charlie's unromantic wedding. Photop 27-3:
    35 F '25
Bercovici, K. Charlie Chaplin. Colliers 76:5 Ag 15 '25
Wilson, E. New Chaplin comedy. New Repub 44:45 S
    2 '25
Reniers, P. Chaplin moves his stake to Alaska. Ind
    115:368 S 26 '25
Ervine, St. J. & King, H. Two English views of Chaplin.
    Liv Age 327:370 N 14 '25
Woollcott, A. Sandman's magic. Colliers 77:13 Ja 30
    '26
St. Johns, I. Everything's rosy at Charlie's. Photop
    29-3:35 F '26
Young, S. Charlot in Rome. New Repub 48:217 O 13 '26
Tully, J. Charlie Chaplin, his real life story. Pict R
    28:8 Ja; 19 F; 22 Mr; 22 Ap '27
deBeauplan, R. From Charlot to Chaplin. Liv Age 333:
    311 Ag 15 '27
Young, S. Charlie Chaplin. New Repub 53:313 F 8 '28
Bakshy, A. Charlie Chaplin. Nation 126:247 F 29 '28
Bonnie Prince Charlie of the custard pies. Lit Digest
    93:36 Mr 24 '28
Chaplin as Puck. Bookm 67:177 Ap '28
Hollriegel, A. Charles Chaplin at home. Liv Age 334:
    1068 Jl '28
Bercovici, K. Day with Charlie Chaplin. Harper 158:
    42 D '28
Frank, W. Charles Chaplin. Scrib Mag 86:237 S '29
Kisch, E. E. I work with Charlie Chaplin. Liv Age
    337:230 O 15 '29
Lang, H. No talkies for Charlie. Photop 37-6:47 My '30
Rose, D. Silence is requested. No. Am 230:127 Jl '30
Charlie Chaplin and talking pictures. Theatre Arts 14:
    908 N '30
Bercovici, K. My friend Charlie Chaplin. Delin 117:
    12 D '30
Peet, C. Chaplin's sanctification. Outlook 157:271

F 18 '31

Seldes, G. Chaplin's masterpieces; City lights. New
   Repub 66:46 F 25 '31

Charlie Chaplin defies the talkies. Lit Digest 108:28
   F 28 '31

Bakshy, A. Charlie Chaplin falters. Nation 132:250 Mr
   4 '31

Skinner, R. D. City lights. Commonweal 13:553 Mr 18
   '31

Sir Charlie? Commonweal 13:537 Mr 18 '31

Good word for the talkies. Lit Digest 108:17 Mr 21 '31

Woollcott, A. Charlie, as ever was. Colliers 87:18 Mr
   28 '31

Arnett, K. Still kicking around. Photop 39-4:39 Mr '31

Wettach, A. My colleague Charlie Chaplin. Liv Age
   340:43 Mr '31

Fergusson, F. City lights. Bookm 73:184 Ap '31

John Bull hit by a Chaplin pie. Lit Digest 109:10 My 23
   '31

In the driftway. Nation 132:583 My 27 '31

If Charlie plagiarized, what then? Lit Digest 110:17 S
   12 '31

Bartlett, A. C. Charlie Chaplin's no-man; intv. Am Mag
   112:78 O '31

Charlie Chaplin and talkies. R of Rs 86:49 Ag '32

Bercovici, K. Little stories of big men. Good H 98:
   148 Ja '34

Comedian sees the world; autobiography. Womans H C
   60: 7 S; 15 O; 15 N; 21 D '33; 61 Ja '34

Rozas, L. T. Charlie Chaplin's decline. Liv Age 346:
   319 Je '34

Darnton, C. The woman who found Charlie Chaplin.
   Photop 46-3:27 Ag '34

Churchill, W. Everybody's language; can silent movies
   come back. Colliers 96:24 O 26 '35

Taviner, R. What love has done for Chaplin. Photop
   48-5:28 O '35

Chaplin: machine age Don Quixote. Lit Digest 120:26 N
   2 '35

Bewildered little fellow bucking modern times. Newsweek
   7:18 F 8 '36

Mullen, S. M. Chaplin, master of pantomime, laughter
   and tears. Sr Schol 28:24 F 15 '36

Van Doren, M. Charlie Chaplin. Nation 142:232 F 19
   '36

No. 1 player. Sr Schol 29:25 N 21 '36

Waley, H. D. Is this Charlie. Sight & Sound 7-25:10

Spr '38

Charlie's lost again. C S Mon Mag p13 Je 1 '38

Childhood recollections. Read Digest 33:69 D '38

Scripteaser; Great dictator's provisional script. Time
   34:24 Ag 7 '39

Cooke, A. Charlie Chaplin. Atlan 164:176 Ag '39
   Same abridged. Read Digest 35:34 S '39

Chaplin's new film. Cur Hist 51:52 S '39

Crichton, K. Ride 'em Charlie! Colliers 105:20 Mr 16
   '40

Comedy has its limits. Christian Cent 57:816 Je 26 '40

Pringle, H. F. Story of two mustaches. Ladies Home J
   57:18 Jl '40

Charlie Chaplin's dictator. Life 9:53 S 2 '40

Daughtery, F. Two millions' worth of laughter. C S
   Mon Mag p 7 S 7 '40

Van Gelder, R. Chaplin draws a keen weapon. N. Y.
   Times Mag p8 S 8 '40

Great dictator. Sr Schol 37:32 S 16 '40

Willson, D. Chaplin talks. Photop 54-12:20 D '40

Biography. Cur Bio '40

Wilson, R. The new mystery of Mr. and Mrs. Chaplin.
   Photop 18-2:56 Ja '41

Frye, N. Great Charlie. Canad Forum 21:148 Ag '41

Farber, M. Little fellow. New Repub 106:606 My 4 '42

Hirschfeld, A. Man with both feet in clouds. N. Y.
   Times Mag p12 Jl 26 '42

Hitler and Chaplin at 54. N. Y. Times Mag p17 Ap 18 '43

Chaplin and Joan. Newsweek 21:49 Je 21 '43

St. Johns, A. R. Case against Chaplin. Photop 23-4:
   35 S '43

Chaplin as villain. Newsweek 23:46 F 21 '44

Man and woman. Time 43:24 Ap 3 '44

Charlie and Wayne. Newsweek 23:29 Ap 10 '44

Fleming, J. Modern times in Moscow. Newsweek 23:42
   My 15 '44

Just a Peter Pan. Time 45:15 Ja 1 '45

Case of Carol Ann. Life 18:30 Ja 8 '45

Father for Carol Ann. Newsweek 25:41 Ap 30 '45

Eiseinstein, S. M. tr. by Herbert Marshall. Charlie the
   grown-up. Sight & Sound 15:53 Sum '46

Laugh's on us. Nation 175:440 N 15 '52

Genet. Letter from Paris. New Yorker 28:175 N 15 '52

Unrehearsed Chaplin comedy. Life 33:51 N 17 '52

Bentley, E. Chaplin's mea culpa. New Repub 127:30 N
   17 '52

Barrett, W. Charlie as Charles. Am Mer 75:90 N '52

Huie, W. B.   Mr. Chaplin and the 5th freedom.   Am Mer
    75:123 N '52
Miller, E.   Limelight: a great comedian sums up his life.
    Theatre Arts 36:76 N '52
Kerr, W.   Lineage of Limelight.   Theatre Arts 36:72 N
    '52
New light on Limelight.   Reporter 8:1 Ja 6 '53
Mr. Ferrer and Mr. Chaplin: threat by American Legion.
    Nation 176:90 Ja 31 '53
Process of dissolution.   Commonweal 57:441 F 6 '53
Tallenay, J. L.   Tragic vision of Charles Chaplin.
    Commonweal 57:451 F 6 '53
Murray, W.   Limelight, Chaplin and his censors.
    Nation 176:247 Mr 21 '53
Glick, N.   Chaplin's film romance.   Commentary 15:295
    Mr '53
Cane and bowler.   Newsweek 41:37 Ap 27 '53
Biography.   Colliers Yrbk 1953:128 '53
Micha, R.   Chaplin as Don Juan.   Sight & Sound 23-3:
    132 Ja/Mr '54
People of the week.   U.S. News 36:14 F 19 '54
Little man and a plot.   Newsweek 43:48 Je 14 '54
Anderson, L.   In search of Charlie.   Sight & Sound 24-
    1:4 Je/S '54
Double play.   Sat Eve Post 227:10 S 4 '54
Ferguson, O.   Hallelujah, bum again.   New Repub 131:44
    N 22 '54
Unfunny fellow.   Newsweek 46:31 N 21 '55
Film pioneers' roll of their living immortals.   Life 40:
    123 Ja 23 '56
Callenbach, E.   Great Chaplin chase.   Nation 183:96 Ag
    4 '56
Halle, L. J.   Foreign relations and domestic behavior.
    Sat R 39:11 O 13 '56
Baker, P.   Clown with a frown.   Films & Filming 3-11:
    7 Ag '57
Lane, J. F.   My life as Chaplin's leading lady; intv. with
    Dawn Addams.   Films & Filming 3-11:12 Ag '57
Hinxman, M.   An interview with Chaplin.   Sight & Sound
    27-2:76 Aut '57
Unfunny Charlie Chaplin.   Newsweek 50:108 S 9 '57
Chaplin and the little guy.   New Statesm 54:308 S 14 '57
Unfunny comic.   Time 70:48 S 23 '57
Kaufman, W.   Saturday Review goes to the movies.   Sat
    R 40:26 S 28 '57
Lee, P.   Whither Chaplin?   America 98:12 O 5 '57
Fulford, R.   Chaplin; a king in decline.   New Repub

137:22 O 7 '57

Felheim, M.   Monarch in exile.   Reporter 17:43 O 17 '57

O'Donnell, J. P.   Charlie Chaplin's stormy exile.   Sat
Eve Post 230:19 Mr 8; 44 Mr 15; 36 Mr 22 '58

Why Chaplin paid up.   Newsweek 53:39 Ja 12 '59

Mayer, A. L.   The origins of United Artists.   Films In
Review 10-7:390 Ag/S '59

Baggy little man now.   Newsweek 54:120 N 9 '59

Giesler, J.   Chaplin case; as told to P. Martin.   Sat
Eve Post 232:38 N 21 '59

Ross, W.   Charlie Chaplin; clown without a country.
Coronet 48:121 Je '60

Crowther, B.   Modern, mellower times of Mr. Chaplin.
N. Y. Times Mag p52 N 6 '60

Biography.   Cur Bio 22:13 Mr '61

Rosen, C.   The saddest story of all.   Photop 59-5:50 My
'61

Spears, J.   Chaplin's collaborators.   Films In Review
13-1:18 Ja '62

Charlie Chaplin.   Time 79:59 My 4 '62

Charlie Chaplin.   America 107:561 Ag 4 '62

Clurman, H.   Oona, Oxford, America and the book;
intv.   Esquire 58:86 N '62

Biography.   Cur Bio Yrbk 1961:100 '62

Charles the great.   Newsweek 64:78 Jl 27 '64

Brownlow, K.   The early days of Charles Chaplin.   Film
40:12 Sum '64

Lemay, H.   Tantalizing look behind Chaplin's mask; his
autobiography.   Life 57:24 O 2 '64

Little tramp as told to himself.   Time 84:132 O 2 '64

Kauffman, S.   Man named Chaffin.   New Repub 151:19
O 3 '64

Tramp.   Newsweek 64:112 O 5 '64

Knight, A.   Travels with Charlie and friends.   Sat R
47:45 O 10 '64

Houseman, J.   Charlie's Chaplin.   Nation 199:222 O 12
'64

Junker, H.   Real life of the tramp.   Commonweal 81:104
O 16 '64

Hatch, R.   Dapper wayfarer.   Harper 229:129 O '64

Wyndham, F.   Charles Chaplin at ease.   Vogue 144:112
N 15 '64

McVay, D.   Chaplin revisited.   Films & Filming 11-2:
10 N '64

Russell, F.   Only the little tramp matters.   Nat R 16:
1066 D 1 '64

Gill, B.   Books.   New Yorker 40:236 D 12 '64

Cotes, P.   The little fellow's self portrait.   Films &
   Filming 11-3:11 D '64
Correction to Only the little tramp matters.   Nat R 17:
   77 Ja 26 '65
Muggeridge, M.   Books.   Esquire 63:54 F '65
Macdonald, D.   On Chaplin, Verdoux and Agee.   Esquire
   63:18 Ap '65
Frank, G.   Charles Chaplin and his children.   Ladies
   Home J 82:70 My '65
Chaplin takes a walk.   Sight & Sound 35-1:20 Win '65
Robinson, D.   Chaplin meets the press.   Sight & Sound
   34:20 Win '65
Chaplin, G. ed. by E. Miller.   Entrancing new actress.
   Seventeen 24:95 D '65
Hamblin, D. J.   Passionate clown comes back.   Life 60:
   80A Ap 1 '66
Hamilton, J.   Charlie and his countess.   Look 30:96 Ap
   19 '66
Custard pie of creation.   Newsweek 67:90 Je 6 '66
Brooks, L.   Charles Chaplin remembered.   Film Culture
   40:5 Spg '66
Bentley, E.   Charlie Chaplin and Peggy Hopkins Joyce.
   Moviegoer 3:10 Sum '66
Gilliatt, P.   Genius of Chaplin.   Vogue 148:94 Jl '66
Chaplin in the limelight.   Illus Lond N 249:20 D 31 '66
Meryman, R.   Ageless master's anatomy of comedy.
   Life 62:80 Mr 10 '67
Kenner, H.   Anatomy of tepidity.   Nat R 15:599 My 30
   '67
Madeen, D.   Harlequin's stick, Charlie's cane.   Film Q
   22-1:10 Fall '68

CHAPLIN, GERALDINE
New Chaplin in limelight.   Life 56:75 Ja 31 '64
Charlie Chaplin's daughter.   Vogue 143:146 F 1 '64
Deardorff, R.   Charlie Chaplin's daughter.   Redbook
   124:58 Mr '65
A female Chaplin makes the movies.   Look 29:57 Ap 20
   '65
Miller, E.   Entrancing new actress.   Seventeen 24:92
   D '65
Martin, H. H.   Two loves of Dr. Zhivago.   Sat Eve Post
   239:26 Ja 15 '66
Geraldine Chaplin.   Vogue 147:136 F 1 '66
Brash Paris styles on tanbark.   Life 60:88 Mr 11 '66
Beauty life.   Mlle 62:138 Mr '66

CHAPLIN, SYDNEY (1926-   )
Another Chaplin rises.   Life 42:74 F 11 '57

CHAPLIN, SYDNEY (1885-1965)
Obit.   Screen World 17:234 '66

CHAPMAN, MARGUERITE
Slugger.   Am Mag 136:126 O '43

CHARISSE, CYD
Speaking of pictures.   Life 22:24 Ap 7 '47
Dreier, H.   Hobby house.   Photop 37-4:58 Ap '50
Arnold, M.   Prairie flower.   Photop 40-4:62 O '51
Finklea and Austerlitz, alias Charisse and Astaire.
    Newsweek 42:48 Jl 6 '53
Harvey, E.   Legs and a legend.   Colliers 133:24 Mr 5
    '54
Bell, P.   Dance for your figure.   McCalls 81:54 Mr '54
Biography.   Cur Bio 15:16 Ja '54
    Same.   Cur Bio Yrbk 1954:171 '54
Every girl should have a chance to dance.   Good H 140:
    20 Ja '55
Wilson, E.   The sexiest girl in town.   Photop 50-1:56
    Jl '56
Whatland, C. M. & Sharpe, E.   Young Hollywood at
    home.   Ladies Home J 74:70 Je '57
Whitcomb, J.   Miss Exquisite Legs.   Cosmop 142:70 Je
    '57
Knight, A.   Dance in the movies.   Dance Mag 31:10 Jl
    '57
Meet Cyd Charisse.   N. Y. Times Mag p102 N 22 '59
Clark, R.   Meet Cyd Charisse.   Dance Mag 33:78 D '59
On-the-spot report on an American beauty.   Good H 150:
    101 Je '60

CHARLESON, MARY
Reel chats and news.   Feature Movie 1-1:41 Mr 15 '15
Obit.   Screen World 13:219 '62

CHASE, CHARLEY
Obit.   Cur Bio '40
Maltin, L.   Charley Chase.   Film Fan Mo 97-8:5 Jl/Ag
    '69
Doran, A.   Working with Charley Chase.   Film Fan Mo
    97-8:29 Jl/Ag '69
Gilbert, B.   Charley Chase.   Film Fan Mo 97-8:31 Jl/
    Ag '69

Geltzer, G. The films of Charley Chase. Film Fan Mo
97-8:32 Jl/Ag '69

CHASE, ILKA
Pringle, H. F. Hangarian for Helen. Colliers 106:12
O 26 '40
Ilka and her ilk. Newsweek 19:62 Mr 30 '42
Biography. Cur Bio '42
My country 'tis of thee. Womans H C 70:21 My '43
Gordon, J. Silky Ilka. Am Mag 137:26 Ap '44
"The Chase" is on TV. TeleVision Guide 2-32:8 Ag 6
'49
Culinary guide for imbeciles who like to eat. Vogue
125:80 Je '55
Must your husband look that way? Womans H C 83:48
Ap '56
Happy heart. Vogue 128:113 D '56

CHATTERTON, RUTH
Albert, K. That old devil, camera. Photop 35-6:65 My
'19
Hall, L. The destiny fighter. Photop 38-2:43 Jl '30
Waite, E. Sometimes it pays to jump overboard. Am
Mag 111:72 Je '31
Condon, F. Laughing lady. Sat Eve Post 204:34 N 28
'31
Biery, R. $750,000 and danger. Photop 41-5:42 Ap '32
Quirk, M. A. From lady to Judy O'Grady. Photop 43-
4:57 Mr '33
Vernon, G. Leave her to heaven. Commonweal 31:455
Mr 15 '40
Breit, H. Talk with Miss Ruth Chatterton. N. Y. Times
Bk R p14 Ag 27 '50
Obit. Time 78:92 D 1 '61
Illus Lond N 239:979 D 2 '61
Newsweek 58:61 D 4 '61
Pub W 180:40 D 18 '61
Am Ann 1962:849 '62
Screen World 13:219 '62
Carr, C. L. Ruth Chatterton, inc. filmog. Films In
Review 13-1:7 Ja '62

CHEKHOV, MICHAEL
Character studies. Theatre Arts 19:250 Ap '35
Chekhov theatre studio. Theatre Arts 22:733 O '38
Chekhov theatre studio moves to America. Theatre Arts
23:84 F '39

Chekhov theatre branching out on a new method of train-
ing young acting groups.   Theatre Arts 24:692 O '40
Actor must have three selves.   Theatre Arts 36:30 D '52
Obit.   Time 66:114 O 10 '55
Screen World 7:222 '56

CHERRILL, VIRGINIA
York, C.   Girl wanted--no experience required.   Photop
35-2:34 Ja '29

CHEVALIER, MAURICE
Gavroche in Hollywood.   Lit Digest 101:25 My 18 '29
Spensley, D.   Songs across the sea.   Photop 36-4:41 S
'29
Zeitlin, I.   Chevalier of France!   Photop 38-2:37 Jl;
38-3:72 Ag; 38-4:68 S '30
Luckiest man in the world.   Lit Digest 107:22 O 18 '30
How I got that way.   Sat Eve Post 204:8 Ag 8 '31
Zeitlin, I.   Ginsburg!   Photop 41-1:65 D '31
Skinner, R. D.   Play and screen.   Commonweal 15:470
F 24 '32
Grant, J.   Why Chevalier sits alone.   Photop 42-6:29 N
'32
Behind the scenes with Chevalier.   Lit Digest 114:14 D
10 '32
Shawell, J.   What Chevalier thinks of women.   Pict R
35:16 N '33
Hunt, J. L.   The unhappy Mr. Chevalier.   Photop 47-1:
69 D '34
Chevalier as ever.   Newsweek 29:84 Mr 24 '47
Shop talk.   Pub W 151:1939 Ap 5 '47
Biography.   Cur Bio 9:12 Ja '48
Same, revised.   Cur Bio Yrbk 1948:99 '49
Lader, L.   Maurice Chevalier: Prince Charming at
sixty.   Coronet 25:75 N '48
Rhodes, R.   Place Pigalle, boul' Mich' Chevalier.
Sat R 32:27 O 22 '49
Ageless troubadour.   Coronet 27:6 D '49
Old hands across the sea.   Life 37:121 D 6 '54
Daubeny, P.   The French straw hat.   Plays & Players
2-3:6 D '54
Daubeny, P.   The man she loved.   Plays & Players 2-4:
8 Ja '55
Daubeny, P.   Young as ever.   Plays & Players 2-5:11
F '55
People are talking about . . .   Vogue 126:110 S 15 '55
Giniger, H.   Bonjour again, Maurice.   N. Y. Times Mag

p19 S 18 '55
Gibbs, W. Theatre. New Yorker 31:97 O 8 '55
Memory, sweet memory. Newsweek 46:75 O 10 '55
Old favorite in Manhattan. Time 66:53 O 10 '55
Harvey, E. TV imports. Colliers 136:35 O 14 '55
Lewis, T. Theatre. America 94:81 O 15 '55
Hayes, R. Stage. Commonweal 63:62 O 21 '55
Wyatt, E. V. Maurice Chevalier. Cath World 182:143
    N '55
Tables for two. New Yorker 31:215 D 3 '55
Maurice Chevalier. Theatre Arts 39:20 D '55
Farewell to romance. Newsweek 50:106 O 7 '57
Wood, C. TV personalities biographical sketchbook.
    TV Personalities p98 '57
Same Chevalier. Life 44:113 Ap 28 '58
People are talking about . . . Vogue 131:90 Je '58
Thank heaven for little girls. Look 22:42 Ag 19 '58
Martin, P. I call on Maurice Chevalier. Sat Eve Post
    231:26 Ag 30 '58
Mackay, M. Charmer. Newsweek 53:51 Mr 2 '59
Chevalier, M. Best advice I ever had. Read Digest
    74:97 My '59
Wolters, L. Life begins at 70, says Maurice Chevalier.
    Todays Health 37:19 Ag '59
Chevalier, M. With love; abridged. McCalls 87:94 My;
    76 Je '60
As they see themselves. Newsweek 59:90 Jl 11 '60
Romp for two ageless troubadours. Life 50:77 Mr 10 '61
Chevalier, M. My life is a song. Music J 19:9 Ap '61
Chevalier, M. I've been lucky. Seventeen 21:98 Jl '62
Solo. New Yorker 38:25 F 16 '63
Schneider, P. E. Seventy-five and still a one-man show.
    N.Y. Times Mag p34 S 8 '63
Love affair. Newsweek 65:100 Ap 12 '65
Hewes, H. Maurice Chevalier at 77. Sat R 48:44 Ap
    17 '65
Lewis, T. Maurice Chevalier at 77. America 112:590
    Ap 17 '65
Sheed, W. Chevalier at 77. Commonweal 82:155 Ap 23
    '65
Kupferberg, H. Le veritable Maurice. Atlan 219:111
    Ja '67
Newsmakers. Newsweek 71:52 F 26 '68
Ehrlich, H. Chevalier at 80. Look 32:30 My 28 '68
Biography. Cur Bio 30:13 Mr '69

CHILDERS, NAOMI
Craig, G. The girl on the cover. Photop 11-2:55 Ja '17
Obit. Screen World 16:220 '65

CHRISTIAN, LINDA
Fink, H. I was there. Photop 33-3:46 Ag '48
Parsons, L. O. I'm going to marry Ty Power. Photop
    33-4:36 S '48
And circuses. Time 53:18 F 7 '49
Tyrone and Linda get married. Life 26:32 F 7 '49
Viva Ty! viva Linda! Newsweek 33:34 F 7 '49
Non-Catholic marriage is no marriage. Christian Cent
    66:165 F 9 '49
Christian, L. How lucky can you be? Photop 36-6:36 N '49
Gentlemen jokesters. Time 71:37 Ap 7 '58
Latins and Linda. Newsweek 51:46 Ap 7 '58
Baby's ungallant farewell to Linda's arms. Life 44:40
    Ap 7 '58
Goldberg, H. & O'Conner, B. Linda Christian. Cosmop
    147:69 Jl '59
Have nymphhet, will travel. Time 89:49 My 12 '67

CHRISTIE, JULIE
Star is weaned. Time 82:57 S 6 '63
Hamilton, J. Julie Christie: a star in eleven minutes.
    Look 28:40 Ag 25 '64
Voom! voom! It's Julie Christie. Newsweek 66:88 D
    20 '65
Martin, H. H. Two loves of Dr. Zhivago. Sat Eve
    Post 239:26 Ja 15 '66
People are talking about . . . Vogue 147:138 F 1 '66
Hamilton, J. Julie Christie: a new international darling.
    Look 30:93 Mr 8 '66
Beauty life. Mlle 62:138 Mr '66
Personalities of the week. Illus Lond N 248:15 Ap 2;
    10 Ap 30 '66
Liber, N. ed. Style and verve of an antigoddess; intv.
    Life 60:61 Ap 29 '66
Mortimer, P. Julie Christie talks about mates and
    morals; intv. Ladies Home J 83:88 Je '66
Miller, E. Success can feel like a razor's edge.
    Seventeen 25:104 Jl '66
Ronal, M. Lively arts. Sr Schol 89:30 S 30 '66
Glanville, B. Julie Christie: a face made for film.
    Holiday 40:95 S '66
Biography. Cur Bio 27:7 S '66
    Same. Cur Bio Yrbk 1966:47 '67

Flink, S. Lusty new role for Julie Christie. Look 31:
59 Mr 21 '67
Fallaci, O. Strange, empty success of Julie Christie.
Look 31:66 Mr 21 '67

CHRISTOPHER, JORDAN
Bergquist, L. Wild scene at Arthur. Look 29:40 N 30
'65
Lerman, L. Four most likely to succeed. Mlle 65:158
S '67

CHRISTIANS, MADY
Hamilton, S. The smile that hides a tear. Photop 46-
4:70 S '34

CHRISTY, ANN
Denton, F. More luck o' the Irish. Photop 33-5:63 Ap
'28

CIANELLI, EDUARDO
Eduardo Cianelli tribute. Film Fan Mo 101:18 N '69

CILENTO, DIANE
Diane Cilento talks to Robert Rietly. Plays & Players
10-8:14 My '63

CLAIRE, INA
Dainty Quaker girl. Cosmop 55:837 N '13
Sumner, K. Ina Claire describes people who are easy
to imitate. Am Mag 89:36 F '20
Little studies in ill-temper. Overland 82:171 Ap '24
Make faces, please. Ladies Home J 43:25 Jl '26
Roberts, K. Dress for Cinderella. Colliers 84:23 Jl
27 '29
Roberts, K. Pajama parties. Colliers 85:16 Ja 18 '30
Roberts, K. Not a single failure, yet. Pict R 31:6 Ja
'30
Hall, L. Ina Claire laughs last, and loudest. Photop
39-4:42 Mr '31
James, F. I couldn't stay. Photop 43-6:51 My '33
Brown, J. M. Peg Woffington to Ina Claire. Theatre
Arts 17:955 D '33
Parrott, U. Ina Claire; intv. Sat Eve Post 207:35 Ja
12 '35
Eustis, M. Actor attacks his part. Theatre Arts 21:
126 F '37
Brown, J. M. To the ladies. Sat R 29:23 D 21 '46

Ina Claire. Life 22:51 F 10 '47
Busch, N. F. Ina Claire; her great career does credit
   to taste of U. S. audiences. Life 22:56 F 10 '47
Morehouse, W. Ina Claire on Nob Hill. Theatre Arts
   35:26 Ag '51
Claire confidential. Theatre Arts 38:14 My '54

CLARK, DANE
Deere, D. The Dane takes over. Photop 27-1:45 Je '45
Walker, D. Romantic lug. Photop 27-6:50 N '45
Dudley, F. Galahad in gloves. Photop 28-3:40 F '46
Parsons, L. O. Hell or hero? Photop 28-5:32 Ap '46
Who's who in the cast. TV Guide 4-17:24 Ap 28 '51
Nichols, M. Battling bantam. Coronet 47:17 D '59
Wood, C. TV personalities biographical sketchbook.
   TV Personalities p80 '57

CLARK, FRED
Obit. Time 92:82 D 13 '68
   Screen World 20:232 '69

CLARK, MARGUERITE
Dale, A. Petite Marguerite. Cosmop 53:547 S '12
Bacon, G. V. Little Miss Practicality. Photop 9-4:34
   Mr '16
Two most popular women in America. Everybodys 34:
   782 Je '16
The Peter Pan of the movies. Photop 11-1:75 D '16
From comic opera to moving pictures. Am Mag 84:42
   D '17
O'Reilly, E. S. She says to me, says she . . .
   Photop 13-2:49 Ja '18
Evans, D. Grand crossing impressions. Photop 14-2:
   58 Jl '18
True fairy-story. Everybodys 39:23 S '18
Washburn, B. Marguerite Clark today. Photop 28-5:
   28 Ap '25
Obit. Cur Bio '40
Bordeen, D. Marguerite Clark, inc. filmog. Films In
   Review 15-10:611 D '64

CLARK, PETULA
Pretty pet. Newsweek 65:82 F 8 '65
Everyone's pet. Time 85:52 Ap 23 '65
Harman, C. Pappy, listen to Petula. Life 59:23 D 10
   '65
Rollin, B. Petula Clark: Little lady with a big beat.

Look 30:M7 Ag 23 '66
Whitney, D.   The 'downtown' girl goes way uptown.
  TV Guide 15-3:12 Ja 21 '67
Stolley, R. B.   Petula.   Life 62:79 Je 9 '67
Gould, G.   Search for Petula Clark.   Hi Fi 17:67 N '67
Gardiner, H.   Pet's pets.   Photop 73-5:100 My '68
Levy, A.   Is Petula Clark another Julie Andrews?
  Good H 168:88 Mr '69

CLARKE, MAE
Lang, H.   I'll have vanilla.   Photop 41-2:72 Ja '32
Taviner, R.   The gamest girl in Hollywood.   Photop 43-
  5:49 Ap '33

CLAYTON, ETHEL
Vance, E.   Ethel Clayton at home.   Photop 7-2:124 Ja
  '15
Clayton, E.   What my pictures tell me a wife should be.
  Photop 8-2:52 Jl '15
St. Johns, A. R.   A cross in the garden.   Photop 15-6:
  48 My '19
Valentine, S.   Home wanted.   Photop 19-2:69 Ja '21
Obit.   Screen World 18:233 '67

CLAYTON, MARGUERITE
Scott, D.   Friends everywhere.   Photop 14-5:27 O '18

CLEVELAND, GEORGE
Wood, C.   TV personalities biographical sketchbook.
  TV Personalities p16 '54

CLIFT, MONTGOMERY
Montgomery Clift.   Life 25:73 Ag 16 '48
Crichton, K.   Week's preview.   Colliers 122:64 O 9 '48
Roberts, W.   The Montgomery Clift story.   Photop 34-5:
  36 Ap '49
Hodges, R. B.   What would $100,000 do to you?   Am
  Mag 147:42 Je '49
Hurst, T.   What it's like to date Montgomery Clift.
  Photop 36-2:42 Jl '49
Frank, S.   Hollywood's new dreamboat.   Sat Eve Post
  222:30 Ag 27 '49
Maxwell, E.   Tall, dark and different.   Photop 36-4:38
  S '49
Hollywood personality.   Good H 129:10 O '49
Leiser, E.   No time for company.   Photop 37-1:42 Ja
  '50

Steele, J. Restless rebel. Photop 38-1:48 Jl '50
Maxwell, E. The new Montgomery Clift cut. Photop
    40-6:56 D '51
Arnold, M. Nobody asked him. Photop 44-6:52 D '53
Corwin, J. Montgomery Clift's tragic love story.
    Photop 45-5:40 My '54
Biography. Cur Bio 15:25 Jl '54
    Same. Cur Bio Yrbk 1954:183 '54
Kingsley, G. Forget the mystery, meet the man.
    Photop 46-6:44 D '54
Cole, C. Eyes that say more than words. Films &
    Filming 2-12:13 S '56
Harris, E. Montgomery Clift . . . strange young man.
    McCalls 84:32 Ja '57
Gehman, R. Flight from fear. Photop 51-3:35 Mr '57
Gehman, R. Monty's brush with death. Photop 51-4:
    58 Ap '57
Talk with a star. Newsweek 51:98 Ap 7 '58
Shipp, C. Hollywood's shocking rumor. Photop 54-2:
    74 Ag '58
Whitcomb, J. Moody Montgomery Clift. Cosmop 147:
    28 N '59
Twinkle-think. Newsweek 60:63 D 24 '62
Zinnemann, F. Montgomery Clift. Sight & Sound 35-4:
    204 Aut '66
Obit. Brit Bk Yr 1967:591 '67
    Cur Bio 27:46 S '66
    Cur Bio Yrbk 1966:464 '67
    Illus Lond N 249:8 Jl 30 '66
    Newsweek 68:54 Ag 1 '66
    Time 88:68 Jl 29 '66
    Screen World 18:233 '67
Long, B. Winner who lost. Vogue 148:70 N 15 '66
Roman, R. C. Montgomery Clift, inc. filmog. Films
    In Review 17-9:541 N '66
Thom, R. Montgomery Clift; a small place in the sun.
    Esquire 67:105 Mr '67

CLYDE, ANDY
    An actor who can live with himself. TV Guide 8-47:28
        N 19 '60
    Obit. Screen World 19:229 '68

COBB, LEE J.
    Higher call. New Yorker 25:21 Mr 26 '49
    Cobb, L. J. Take my advice. Films & Filming 5-2:
        7 N '58

He wears well. Newsweek 53:98 Ja 26 '59
Victory by ridicule. Time 74:66 N 23 '59
Biography. Cur Bio 21:13 F '60
    Same. Cur Bio Yrbk 1960:90 '61
Nichols, M. Lee J. Cobb: man of the ages. Coronet
    49:16 N '60
Raddatz, L. Rebirth of an actor. TV Guide 11-43:18
    O 26 '63
As flies to wanton boys. Time 92:92 N 15 '68

COBURN, CHARLES
Biography. Cur Bio Je '44
Berch, B. Charles Coburn, the monocled cupid. Photop
    26-2:52 Ja '45
Coburn swings out at 72. Life 28:97 Mr 27 '50
Manning, G. Monocle from Georgia. Colliers 126:28
    Ag 19 '50
Gay old blade. TV Guide 4-24:17 Je 16 '56
Dance: what it means to me. Dance Mag 31:18 Je '57
Obit. Time 78:76 S 8 '61
    Illus Lond N 239:426 S 9 '61
    Newsweek 58:69 S 11 '61
    Am Ann 1962:849 '62
    Cur Bio 22:7 N '61
    Cur Bio Yrbk 1961:108 '62
    Screen World 13:219 '62
Osborne, B. Charles Coburn, inc. filmog. Films In
    Review 12-8:499 O '61

COBURN, JAMES
People are talking about . . . Vogue 148:114 O 15 '66
Weisenreder, E. B. Letter. Films In Review 17-9:
    600 N '66
Beyond the ego. Time 89:76 My 26 '67
Redbook dialogue. Redbook 129:64 O '67
James Coburn: star of a new American stripe. Vogue
    151:119 F 1 '68

COCHRAN, STEVE
Parsons, L. O. Big guy! Big future! Big romance?
    Photop 40-1:42 Jl '51
Downing, H. Lonely Lochinvar. Photop 44-1:46 Jl '53
Obit. Time 86:84 Jl 9 '65
    Newsweek 66:64 Jl 12 '65
    Screen World 17:235 '66

CODY, IRON EYES
Raddatz, L. Him Hollywood Indian. TV Guide 12-29:
10 Jl 18 '64

CODY, LEW
St. Johns, A. R. Confessions of a male vampire.
Photop 15-4:28 Mr '19
Cody, L. A reformed villain. Photop 22-2:50 Jl '22
St. Johns, A. R. The butterfly man and the little clown.
Photop 36-2:38 Jl '29
North, J. They saved his life with laughter. Photop
40-1:66 Je '31

COLBERT, CLAUDETTE
Kennedy, J. B. Woman from Paris. Colliers 85:21 F
15 '30
Parsons, H. She wants to paint. Photop 37-5:37 Ap '30
Condon, F. Upward progress of a Chauchoin. Sat Eve
Post 204:30 D 26 '31
Hall, L. Claudette battles on. Photop 42-1:31 Je '32
Henderson, J. Claudette Colbert. Cinema Digest 1-10:
9 S 19 '32
Patrick, C. Claudette's "Eve Dive." Cinema Digest
4-3:15 My 29 '33
Beatty, J. She was such a nice girl. Am Mag 120:58 S '35
LaCava, G. "The fretting frog"--the story of Claudette
Colbert's leap to the top. Photop 48-6:26 N '35
Stevens, M. This time it's no modern marriage.
Photop 49-2:22 F '36
Taylor, A. Claudette Colbert's climb to stardom.
Photop 50-5:14 N; 50-6:50 D '36; 51-1:72 Ja '37
Sharpe, H. The romance of Claudette Colbert's second
honeymoon. Photop 52-2:20 F '38
Crichton, K. Career girl. Colliers 103:11 Ja 28 '39
Hartley, K.   Play truth or consequences with Claudette
Colbert. Photop 53-3:24 Mr '39
Colbert, C. as told to Jack Smalley. Why I like Holly-
wood. Photop 54-2:67 F '40
Fletcher, A. W. How Claudette Colbert lives. Photop
54-12:24 D '40
Fletcher, A. W. She chooses enchantment. Photop 18-
2:51 Ja '41
Colbert, C. I was self-conscious. Photop 22-4:51 Mr
'43
Biography. Cur Bio Ja '45
Dudley, F. Eternally Claudette. Photop 31-5:46 O '47
Colbert, C. I remember grandma. Sat Eve Post 222:

31 Mr 25 '50
Wheeler, L.   English with a French accent.   Photop 41-3:
    62 Mr '52
The lady says no!   TV Guide 3-16:13 Ap 16 '55
Woman.   TV Guide 7-20:8 My 16 '59
Fraser, P. L.   Claudette Colbert puzzles me.   Good H
    149:32 Jl '59
Nominations for the late, late.   N. Y. Times Mag p24
    F 28 '60
Tornabene, L.   Lunch date with Claudette Colbert.
    Cosmop 149:14 Jl '60
Claudette Colbert--dressed to the life.   Vogue 136:215
    S 1 '60
Richards, S.   A visit with Claudette Colbert.   Theatre
    3-2:20 F '61
Claudette Colbert's other home in the sun.   House B
    106:98 Ja '64
Biography.   Cur Bio 25:14 My '64
    Same.   Cur Bio Yrbk 1964:83 '64

COLBY, ANITA
Cover girl.   Time 45:39 Ja 8 '45
Holiday look on the ski slope.   Holiday 11:79 Ja '52
Holiday look on a cruise.   Holiday 11:91 Mr '52
Holiday look at the beach.   Holiday 11:145 My '52
Holiday look.   Holiday 12:105 S '52
Great American bath.   Look 18:44 S 7 '54
In defense of the single woman.   Look 19:36 N 29 '55
Where are they now?   Newsweek 72:14 S 30 '68

COLEMAN, NANCY
Crichton, K.   You don't need glamor.   Colliers 110:12
    Ag 15 '42
Bentley, J.   She's solid!   Photop 23-2:59 Jl '43
Star going up.   Am Mag 138:138 N '44

COLLEANO, BONAR
Obit.   Screen World 10:221 '59

COLLIER, CONSTANCE
Rankin, R.   A middle-aged woman ran away with the
    show.   Photop 47-6:28 My '35
Playwrights at their own first nights.   Theatre Arts 25:
    888 D '41
Lambs like grease paint.   Atlan 173:105 Mr '44
Biography.   Cur Bio 15:27 Jl '54
    Same.   Cur Bio Yrbk 1954:193 '54

Obit. Cur Bio 16:16 Je '55
Illus Lond N 226:837 My 7 '55
Newsweek 45:69 My 9 '55
Time 65:102 My 9 '55
Am Ann 1956:154 '56
Brit Bk Yr 1956:509 '56
Cur Bio Yrbk 1955:132 '56
Screen World 7:223 '56

COLLINS, JOAN
Presenting Joan Collins. Look 19:39 S 6 '55
Downing, H. Cool, crazy and jolly exciting. Photop 48-5:56 N '55
Bolstad, H. The lady is dangerous. Photop 49-1:43 Ja '56
Wilson, E. Shock trouper. Photop 50-3:56 S '56
Whitcomb, J. On location with The opposite sex. Cosmop 141:68 O '56
Collins, Mrs. E. My daughter Joan. Photop 51-1:26 Ja '57
Clement, C. She learned to say no. Photop 51-5:48 My '57
Maynard, J. What's wrong with me. Photop 52-5:71 N '57
Lemon, R. Glamour girls off-duty. Newsweek 55:60 Ja 4 '60
Christy, G. Nothing matters when you're in love. Photop 57-4:58 Ap '60

COLLINS, RAY
Obit. Screen World 17:235 '66

COLMAN, RONALD
Spensley, D. The rival Nordic lovers. Photop 28-5:28 O '25
Waterbury, R. Ronald talks at last. Photop 29-2:29 Ja '26
Albert, K. Exposing Ronald! Photop 37-3:63 F '30
Colman, R. The way I see it. Photop 40-4:65 S '31
Bahn, C. B. Ronald Colman. Cinema Digest 1-13:15 O 31 '32
Torring, R. Ronald's painted mustache. Photop 44-3: 51 Ag '33
Zeitlin, I. Rough sketch of a gentleman. Photop 51-12: 28 D '37
Castle, M. And then there were three. Photop 52-7: 18 Jl '38

Hall, G.   Romantic recluse.   Photop 53-1:12 Ja '39;
    53-2:66 F '39
Hartley, K.   Play truth or consequences with Ronald
    Colman.   Photop 54-3:16 Mr '40
Steele, J. H.   Portrait of a casual sophisticate.   Photop
    ` 22-2:30 Ja '43
Biography.   Cur Bio '43
Biographical note.   Time 51:99 F 23 '48
Waterbury, R.   His double life.   Photop 33-1:46 Je '48
Kilocycle prexy.   Time 56:83 N 6 '50
Wood, C.   TV personalities biographical sketchbook.
    TV Personalities p49 '54
Film pioneers' roll of their living immortals.   Life 40:
    121 Ja 23 '56
Jacobs, J.   Ronald Colman, inc. filmog.   Films In Re-
    view 9-4:175 Ap '58
Letters.   Films In Review 9-5:280 My '58
Departure of a debonair star.   Life 44:74 Je 2 '58
Matinee idol.   Time 71:84 Je 2 '58
Obit.   Am Ann 1959:160 '59
    Brit Bk Yr 1959:508 '59
    Cur Bio 19:28 S '58
    Cur Bio Yrbk 1958:99 '58
    Illus Lond N 232:925 My 31 '58
    Life 44:74 Je 2 '58
    Time 71:100 My 26; 84 Je 2 '58
    Screen World 10:221 '59
Biography.   NCAB 43:476 '61

COMER, ANJANETTE
    When a woman makes up her mind.   TV Guide 12-29:26
        Jl 18 '64

COMPSON, BETTY
    Yost, R. M. Jr.   Rescued from the river.   Photop 17-1:
        74 D '19
    St. Johns, A. R.   Betty and Jobyna.   Photop 24-6:52
        N '23
    Tully, J.   Betty Compson.   Pict R 29:6 Ja '28
    Foster, D.   Too many guests.   Photop 38-3:39 Ag '30
    Woodward, M.   Unbeatable Betty.   Photop 39-4:69 Mr '31
    Keen, J. H.   Betty Compson.   Cinema Digest 1-8:6 Ag
        22 '32
    Bodeen, D.   Betty Compson, inc. filmog.   Films In
        Review 17-7:396 Ag/S '66

COMPTON, JOYCE
Maltin, L. Joyce Compton.   Film Fan Mo 102:19 D '69

CONKLIN, CHESTER
Sayford, I. S.   Chester Conklin and fame's ladder.
Photop 10-1:84 Je '16
Leamy, H.   Back of Chester's whiskers.   Colliers 82:
16 S 29 '28
Where are they now?   Newsweek 67:16 Je 6 '66

CONNERY, SEAN
Devil of a fellow, this Bond.   Life 54:100B My 24 '63
Canny Scot.   Time 83:78 Ja 10 '64
T-shirted beer-lover as the suave spy.   Life 56:55 Ap 3
'64
Hamill, P.   Bottled in Bond: Sean Connery.   Sat Eve
Post 237:32 Je 6 '64
Sean Connery; the reluctant James Bond.   Look 28:83 S
8 '64
Random, E.   Licensed ladykiller.   Photop 66-3:54 S '64
Mosley, L.   Mr. Kisskiss Bangbang.   N.Y. Times Mag
p38 N 22 '64
Tornebene, L.   Tomorrow's stars.   Good H 160:20 Mr
'65
Bondomania.   Time 85:59 Je 11 '65
Zimmermann, G.   James Bond conquers all in Thunder-
ball.   Look 29:45 Jl 13 '65
Zinsser, W. K.   Big Bond bonanza.   Sat Eve Post 238:
76 Jl 17 '65
Stewart-Gordon, F.   007-the spy with the golden touch.
Read Digest 87:113 O '65
Allen, B.   Sean Connery takes over Rock Point.   Mlle
62:127 D '65
Biography.   Cur Bio 27:8 Ja '66
Same.   Cur Bio Yrbk 1966:54 '67
dePaul, J.   What goes on in my bedroom.   Photop 69-5:
33 My '66

CONNOLLY, WALTER
Charm begins at forty.   Lit Digest 119:19 Mr 23 '35
Obit.   Newsweek 15:6 Je 10 '40
Time 35:88 Je 10 '40
Cur Bio '40

CONNORS, BUCK
He was never "fired" from a job.   Photop 4-2:133 Jl '14

CONNORS, CHUCK
  Herbert, R. Once a ballplayer. Good H 137:16 Jl '53
    '53
  He finally made the big leagues. TV Guide 7-6:24 F 7
    '59
  Nichols, M. Brooklyn Dodge of bullets. Coronet 45:12
    F '59
  The rifleman was a ham. TV Guide 7-34:8 Ag 22 '59
  He deals in sentiment, not slaying. TV Guide 8-11:20 Mr
    12 '60
  Eells, G. Chuck Connors, man of dimension. Look 24:
    56J Je 21 '60
  Boys have a ball at dad's work. Life 49:117 O 3 '60
  Now he's back on target. TV Guide 10-3:15 Ja 20 '62
  Kessner, J. Any man can be a husband. Photop 66-4:
    67 O '64
  Back to civvies--the hard way. TV Guide 13-3:6 Ja 23
    '65
  Durslag, M. Nuts to everything but golf. TV Guide 13-
    43:19 O 23 '65
  Hobson, D. This cowboy hobnobs with governors, sena-
    tors, Modac and Sloopy--not to mention a pair of
    Garys. TV Guide 16-4:22 Ja 27 '68

CONNORS, MIKE
  And he never loses his balance. TV Guide 8-11:12 Mr
    12 '60
  Prelutsky, B. How old is Mike Connors? Don't ask.
    TV Guide 67-39:12 S 30 '67
  Wood, A. A private eye's private life. Photop 74-6:
    37 D '68

CONRIED, HANS
  The accent's on versatility. TV Guide 8-17:28 Ap 23 '60
  He plays Conried to the hilt. TV Guide 11-35:15 Ag 31
    '63

CONSTANTINE, EDDIE
  American in Paris. Time 66:74 N 14 '55
  Frenchman from Los Angeles. Newsweek 48:83 O 1 '56
  People are talking about . . . Vogue 128:237 S 1 '56
  The star who didn't come home. Show 2-5:100 My '62
  Constantine the great. Newsweek 66:70B S 6 '65
  Nolan, J. E. Eddie Constantine, inc. filmog. Films In
    Review 19-7:431 Ag/S '68
  Lindsay, M. Interview. Cinema 4-4:17 D '68

CONTE, RICHARD
    Wheeler, L.   Ideas for rent.   Photop 38-5:60 N '50

CONWAY, TOM
    Richards, J. M.   Tom Conway, inc. filmog.   Films In
        Review 18-9:592 N '67
    Obit.   Screen World 19:230 '68
    Pitts, M. R.   Tom Conway, inc. filmog.   Film Fan Mo
        99:16 S '69

COOGAN, JACKIE
    Jordan, J.   Tipperary and the kid.   Photop 20-1:58 Je '21
    Coogan, J.   Jackie turns author.   Photop 22-1:40 Je '22
    St. Johns, A. R.   The kid who earned a million.   Photop
        23-3:45 F '23
    Biggers, E. D.   Open letter to Jackie Coogan.   Colliers
        71:11 Mr 31 '23
    Sangster, M.   How they raise Jackie Coogan.   Photop
        23-6:36 My '23
    Wilson, T.   Wonder child who is just a natural boy.
        Am Mag 96:36 Ag '23
    Howe, H.   What's going to happen to Jackie Coogan?
        Photop 25-1:38 D '23
    Jackie in English and French eyes.   Lit Digest 83:30 N15 '24
    Jackie's European diary.   Photop 27-1:39 D '24; 27-2:78
        Ja; 27-3:53 F; 27-4:63 Mr '25
    Eichel, L. P.   When Jackie Coogan was a little boy.
        Colliers 75:42 F 7 '25
    Wood, J.   Jackie Coogan in London.   Forum 76:392 S '26
    Jackie Coogan has the right idea about drawing.   School
        Arts 26:72 O '26
    Bernsteins' arithmetic faces court test in Jackie's suit for
        $4,000,000.   Newsweek 11:28 Ap 25 '38
    Kid.   Time 31:41 My 2 '38
    Rhea, M.   The kid makes good.   Photop 25-2:62 Jl '44
    Kid comes back.   Life 20:62 F 4 '46
    Kid's kid.   Theatre Arts 37:17 Mr '53
    Nichols, M.   Child stars who came back.   Coronet 48:
        80 Mr '58
    The kid comes back.   TV Guide 5-28:10 Jl 20 '59
    York, C.   His tomorrows have only yesterday.   Photop
        59-6:56 Je '61
    Hane, A.   The kid is dead . . . not Coogan.   TV Guide
        13-39:22 Jl 24 '65

COOK, DONALD
    Biography.   Cur Bio 15:34 Jl '54

Same.   Cur Bio Yrbk 1954:202 '54
Perils of leisure.   New Repub 140:17 Ja 19 '59
Obit.   Newsweek 58:76 O 16 '61
    Cur Bio 22:6 D '61
    Cur Bio Yrbk 1961:113 '62
    Am Ann 1962:849 '62
    Screen World 13:219 '62

COOPER, BEN
Craig, R.   Cooper's 21 and terrific.   Photop 48-2:40
    Ag '55
Cooper, Mr. & Mrs. B.   Ben--pardon our pride.
    Photop 49-4:50 Ap '56
Ben Cooper, U. S. A.   Photop 51-4:82 Ap '57

COOPER, GARY
Spensley, D.   The big boy tells his story.   Photop 35-5:
    64 Ap; 35-6:70 My '29
Busby, M.   The new two-gun man.   Photop 37-5:50 Ap
    '30
Leslie, M.   I'm through being bossed.   Photop 42-5:34
    O '32
Jamison, J.   Cary vs. Gary.   Photop 43-2:33 Ja '33
Maxwell, V.   Can a man love two women at the same
    time?   Photop 45-3:32 F '34
Beatty, J.   Keep your shoes shined; intv.   Womans H C
    63:85 O '35
When I was a boy.   St N 63:21 N '35
Douglas, F.   The Gary Coopers plan a house at Beverly
    Hills.   Arts & Dec 43:15 N '35
Hunt, J. L.   Why Gary's gone rural.   Photop 50-2:30 Ag
    '36
Connell, R.   Mr. Cooper goes to town.   Pict R 38:12 O
    '36
St. Johns, A. R.   Gary, the great.   Photop 52-4:18 Ap
    '38
McCrea, J.   My friend Coop!   Photop 53-10:20 O '39
Coop.   Time 37:78 Mr 3 '41
Rhea, M.   The law of averages.   Photop 18-4:32 Mr '41
Hunting at Sun Valley with the Gary Coopers and Ernest
    Hemingways.   Life 11:116 N 24 '41
Biography.   Cur Bio '41
Nugent, F. S.   All-American man.   N. Y. Times Mag p18
    Jl 5 '42
French, W. F.   What Hollywood thinks of Gary Cooper.
    Photop 21-3:39 Ag '42
Beatty, J.   Super-duper Cooper.   Am Mag 134-34 N '42

St. Johns, A. R.   Gary wraps it up.   Photop 23-6:32
N '43

Hartung, P. T.   Gary and Cary.   Commonweal 40:547
S 22 '44

Maxwell, E.   American natural.   Photop 26-1:38 D '44

Daugherty, F.   He's the type.   C S Mon Mag p9 Je 30
'45

Johnson, N.   Along came Cooper.   Photop 27-3:38 Ag '45

Arvad, I.   Call for Coop.   Photop 28-1:54 D '45

Cooper, G.   Philadelphia story.   Newsweek 30:21 Ag 18
'47

Howe, H.   Life in the dog house.   Photop 32-6:66 My '48

Life visits Gary Cooper.   Life 26:128 Mr 7 '49

Martin, P.   That man Cooper.   Sat Eve Post 222:22 Ja
14 '50

Parsons, L. O.   Restless hearts.   Photop 39-3:50 Mr '51

25th anniversary for Gary Cooper.   Life 33:22 Ag 25 '52

Gary Cooper spears a kahala in Samoa.   Colliers 130:37
D 20 '52

Gary Cooper, an American tourist.   Colliers 132:46 S 4
'53

Maugham, W. S.   Gary Cooper.   Plays & Players 1-3:4
D '53

Harvey, E.   Coop gets girl, Burt gets bullet.   Colliers
134:72 Ag 6 '54

Biography.   Am Ann 1954:172 '54

Gary Cooper, strong and silent for thirty years.   Look
19:35 F 8 '55

Hubler, R. C.   Gary Cooper: Mr. American.   Coronet
38:21 Je '55

Cooper, G.   Well, it was this way; as told to G. Scullin.
Sat Eve Post 228:17 F 18; 28 F 25; 32 Mr 3; 40 Mr
10; 46 Mr 17; 36 Mr 24; 36 Mr 31; 36 Ap 7 '56
Same abridged.   Read Digest 69:69 Jl; 144 Ag '56

Cooper does a Crosby.   Look 20:100 Ag 7 '56

McCalls visits.   McCalls 84:22 Je '57

Gary, Cary remain frisky past fifty.   Life 43:79 Ag 12
'57

Hatful of heroes by Gary.   Life 45:8 S 1 '58

Kauffmann, S.   Little respect, there!   New Repub 141:
22 N 30 '59

Clarens, C.   Gary Cooper, inc. filmog.   Films In Review 10-10:577 D '59

Urge stays on.   Newsweek 56:100 D 12 '60

Cooper, G.   I took a good look at myself and this is what
I saw; as told to L. Slater.   McCalls 88:62 Ja '61

Strong but not silent.   TV Guide 9-12:8 Mr 25 '61

Sad news of Cooper.   Life 50:74A Ap 28 '61
O'Neil, P.   Hollywood mourns a good man.   Life My 26
    '61
Morgan, T. B.   American hero grows older.   Esquire
    55:63 My '61
Obit.   Cur Bio 22:13 Jl '61
    Illus Lond N 238:851 My 20 '61
    Newsweek 57:25 My 22 '61
    Time 77:54 My 19 '61
    Am Ann 1962:189 '62
    Cur Bio Yrbk 1961:113 '62
    Screen World 13:221 '62
Gordon, S.   Gary Cooper's last trip home.   Look 25:53
    Jl 18 '61
Dinter, C.   Tribute to a great guy--Coop.   Photop 60-1:
    46 Jl '61
Miron, C.   Gary Cooper's daughter to enter convent.
    Photop 60-2:52 Ag '61
Anthony, P.   A lesson for every woman.   Photop 60-4:
    58 O '61
Hyatt, D. B.   Gary Cooper.   McCalls 90:97 Mr '63
Gary Cooper and the real west.   Pop Phot 52:36 Ap '63
Cooper, Mrs. G.   How I faced tomorrow; as told to
    George Christy.   Good H 157:81 S '63
Biography.   NCAB 48:53 '65

COOPER, GLADYS
    Miss Gladys Cooper.   Vogue 127:96 Ap 1 '56
    Morley, R.   Gladys Cooper.   McCalls 94:106 O '66

COOPER, JACKIE
    Mook, S. R.   Man about town.   Photop 41-2:54 Ja '32
    Beatty, J.   Little boy with a big pay check.   Am Mag
        113:22 Mr '32
    Lang, H.   Jackie is head man.   Photop 44-1:37 Je '33
    Clarkson, E. P.   Boy and his room; intv.   Parents Mag
        13:48 Ap '38
    Proctor, K.   No runaway marriage for these two.
        Photop 20-2:28 Ja '42
    Fletcher, A. W.   Jackie had a friend named Mabel.
        Photop 20-4:62 Mr '42
    Goldberg, H.   Nobody wanted me to grow up.   Cosmop
        139:64 N '55
    Haunted by his past.   TV Guide 4-30:17 Ag 4 '56
    Wood, C.   TV personalities biographical sketchbook.
        TV Personalities p41 '56
    Nichols, M.   Child stars who came back.   Coronet 43:

86 Mr '58
Can "Skippy" do it again?   TV Guide 6-35:17 Ag 30 '58
Birth of a show.   TV Guide 7-39:8 S 26 '59
Hano, A.   How Skippy finally grew up.   Coronet 49:67
   Ja '61
Cooper, J.   Unfortunately I was rich; as told to R. Kahn.
   Sat Eve Post 234:28 Mr 25 '61
DeRoos, R.   When the wise guys were wrong.   TV Guide
   13-45:6 N 6; 13-46:15 N 13 '65

COOTE, ROBERT
He can't resist the open road.   TV Guide 13-15:15 Ap
   10 '65

CORBIN, GLADYS
Hartford, A.   Gladys Corbin, inc. filmog.   Film Fan
   Mo 94:21 Ap '69

CORD, ALEX
Yockenee-poo!   Newsweek 66:79 Ag 30 '65

COREY, WENDELL
Kingsley, K.   Their marriage is a laugh.   Photop 43-3:
   92 Mr '53
Obit.   Newsweek 72:137 N 18 '68
   Time 92:58 N 22 '68
   Screen World 20:233 '69

CORTEZ, RICARDO
Spensley, D.   Ricardo--the first.   Photop 28-4:63 S '25
Quirk, J. R.   Hollywood's greatest true love story.
   Photop 37-5:38 Ap '30
Lieber, E.   Ricardo is a riddle.   Photop 42-6:45 N '32
Star finally gets a chance to live through a movie.
   Newsweek 4:24 Ag 4 '34

COSTELLO, DOLORES
St. Johns, I.   That exquisite Dolores.   Photop 29-5:36
   Ap '26
Freund, E. R.   Dolores Costello--gallant lady.   Photop
   49-2:34 F '36

COSTELLO, HELENE
Obit.   Screen World 9:221 '58

COSTELLO, LOU
Biography.   Cur Bio '41

Costello's courage.   Newsweek 22:98 N 15 '43
Costello, L.   God made me well.   Photop 24-1:40 D '43
Mother's day; Costellos celebrate.   Womans H C 76:162
    My '49
Lou Costello plays it straight.   TV Guide 6-44:28 N 1 '58
Obit.   Am Ann 1960:851 '60
    Brit Bk Yr 1960:506 '60
    Cur Bio 20:14 My '59
    Cur Bio Yrbk 1959:80 '60
    Illus Lond N 234:445 Mr 14 '59
    Newsweek 53:61 Mr 16 '59
    Time 73:86 Mr 16 '59
    Screen World 11:216 '60
(See also: ABBOTT AND COSTELLO)

COSTELLO, MAURICE
    The idol of yesteryear.   Photop 41-6:60 My '32
    Obit.   Newsweek 36:67 N 6 '50
        Time 56:71 N 6 '50

COTTEN, JOSEPH
    Crichton, K.   King Cotten.   Colliers 110:60 O 10 '42
    Heyn, E. V.   A guy called Joe.   Photop 22-6:44 My '43
    Steele, J. H   Portrait in C.   Photop 26-3:58 F '45
    Cotten, J.   Confessions of a lazy guy.   Photop 27-1:36
        Je; 27-2:58 Jl '45
    Smith, A. M.   Circus clowns are actor's hobby.   Hobbies
        50:21 F '46
    Maxwell, E.   100% Cotten.   Photop 32-1:42 D '47
    Regular Joe.   Theatre Arts 38:12 Ap '54
    Wood, C.   TV personalities biographical sketchbook.
        TV Personalities p66 '56
    Red carpet treatment.   TV Guide 5-10:28 Mr 9 '57
    Liston, J.   At home with Joseph Cotten.   Am Home 64:
        6 N '61
    The elegant ex-potato-salad salesman.   TV Guide 12-11:
        24 Mr 14 '64

COULORIS, GEORGE
    Gilder, R.   Actors in their stride.   Theatre Arts 27:
        268 My '43

COURTENAY, TOM
    Blue-eyed boy.   Time 80:55 S 14 '62
    Courtenay, T.   The loneliness of the long distance runner.
        Films & Filming 8-12:10 S '62
    Biography.   Cur Bio 25:17 My '64

Same Cur Bio Yrbk 1964:88 '64

COURTLAND, JEROME
   Ames, M.   Introducing Cojo.   Photop 28-5:60 Ap '46

COURTOT, MARGUERITE
   Gaddis, P.   Marguerite Courtot, a "reel" girl.   Photop
      6-2:84 Jl '14
   Courtot: Well, who is she?   Photop 8-1:120 Je '15
   Howard, L.   How I teach my gowns to act.   Photop 9-
      3:89 F '16
   Smith, A.   She hates Broadway.   Photop 17-3:118 F '20

COY, JOHNNY
   Delehanty, T.   Johnny jump-up.   Photop 28-2:52 Ja '46
   Harris, E.   He thinks on his feet.   Photop 28-6:51 My
      '46

CRABBE, BUSTER
   Kaleidoscope interviews Buster Crabbe, inc. filmog.
      Kaleidoscope 2-2:entire issue. n. d.
   Crabbe, B.   Seven-day wonder diet.   TV Guide 4-17:16
      Ap 28 '51
   The Four Buster Crabbes.   TV Guide 5-11:35 Mr 14 '52
   Tarzan and son join the Legion.   TV Guide 3-28:20 Jl 9
      '55
   Wood, C.   TV personalities biographical sketchbook.
      TV Personalities p92 '57

CRAIG, HELEN
   Crichton, K.   Stage-struck.   Colliers 107:18 Ap 5 '41

CRAIG, JAMES
   French, J. R.   Craig's life.   Photop 23-4:66 S '43
   Bentley, J.   Big Jim Craig.   Photop 25-2:50 Jl '44

CRAIN, JEANNE
   Overnight rise to movie stardom.   Life 17:73 S 4 '44
   Graham, S.   C. for Circe.   Photop 26-1:36 D '44
   Perkins, L.   Photolife of Jeanne Crain.   Photop 26-6:48
      My '45
   Parsons, L. O.   Fair and fancy free.   Photop 28-1:44
      D '45
   Deere, D.   Scenic wonder.   Photop 28-3:60 F '46
   Waterbury, R.   Runaway bride.   Photop 28-5:30 Ap;
      28-6:36 My '46
   St. Johns, E.   One dream for two.   Photop 29-3:34 Ag '46

Science puts oomph into Jeanne Crain's bubble bath.
   Life 21:12 S 30 '46
Brinkman, P.   This is my wife.   Photop 30-3:60 F '47
St. Johns, E.   First year.   Photop 30-5:43 Ap '47
Waterbury, R.   Our baby is here.   Photop 31-2:31 Jl '47
St. Johns, E.   Dear baby.   Photop 31-5:40 O '47
Dailey, D.   Lover girl.   Photop 32-1:42 Je '48
Maxwell, E.   Smartest girl in town.   Photop 33-5:54 O
   '48
Crain, J.   How to keep marriage romantic.   Photop
   34-3:42 F '49
Brinkman, P.   On a pink cloud with Jeanne Crain.
   Photop 37-5:58 My '50
Wheeler, L.   Plot for a home.   Photop 40-1:60 Jl '51
Biography.   Cur Bio 12:17 N '51
   Same.   Cur Bio Yrbk 1951:142 '52
Dudley, F.   Seventh heaven.   Photop 42-6:48 D '52
Crain, J.   Portrait of Ann.   Photop 46-3:54 S '54
Service, F.   No stranger to paradise.   Photop 46-5:48
   N '54
Meltsir, A.   From California to London in bedlam.
   Photop 48-1:43 Jl '55
Parmeter, A.   What Jeanne dreams, she gets!   Photop
   49-1:47 Ja '56
Albert, D.   Stamped by scandal!   Photop 50-1:62 Jl '56
Hegedorn, R.   Jeanne Crain, inc. filmog.   Films In Re-
   view 17-5:327 My '66
McClelland, D.   Jeanne Crain, inc. filmog.   Films In
   Review 20-6:357 Je/Jl '69

CRANE, RICHARD
   Hamilton, S.   Cashing in on Richard Crane.   Photop 25-
      4:58 S '44
   Dudley, F.   Time out for love.   Photop 26-5:40 Ap '45
   Raker, A.   Letter, inc. filmog.   Films In Review 20-6:
      386 Je/Jl '69

CRAVEN, FRANK
   Sumner, K.   He didn't want to be poor all of his life.
      Am Mag 92:34 Ag '21

CRAWFORD, BRODERICK
   Biography.   Cur Bio 11:12 Ap '50
      Same.   Cur Bio Yrbk 1950:105 '51
   Wheeler, L.   And all through the house.   Photop 38-6:
      56 D '50
   Parsons, L. O.   What happens to Academy Award win-

ners?   Cosmop 136:18 Mr '54
Kramer, S.   Into surgery for Not as a stranger.
   Colliers 135:78 F 4 '55
Just call him softy.   TV Guide 5-17:17 Ap 27 '57
Wood, C.   TV personalities biographical sketchbook.
   TV Personalities p22 '57
Amery, C.   Celebrity register.   McCalls 91:88 O '63

CRAWFORD, JOAN
   Biery, R.   The story of a dancing girl.   Photop 34-4:34
      S; 34-5:68 O; 34-6:42 N '28
   Hughes, F.   Filmland's royal family (second edition).
      Photop 36-6:37 N '29
   Ogden, E.   Hey, Doug!   Just look what's going on here!
      Photop 39-4:40 Mr '31
   Albert, K.   Why they said Joan was "high hat."   Photop
      40-3:65 Ag '31
   Pringle, H. F.   Joan and Doug.   Colliers 89:19 Ja 16 '32
   Horton, H.   The girl with the haunted face.   Photop
      42-2:42 Jl '32
   Shawell, J.   Evolution of Joan Crawford.   Pict R 34:14
      Ja '33
   Bahn, C. B.   Joan Crawford.   Cinema Digest 4-5:10 Je
      12 '33
   Job of keeping at the top.   Sat Eve Post 205:14 Je 17
      '33
   Arnold, F.   Joan's heart still beats for Doug.   Photop
      44-4:60 S '33
   Jamison, J.   I'd rather know Joan than anyone else, says
      Franchot Tone.   Photop 44-6:38 N '33
   Hunt, F.   I meet Miss Crawford.   Photop 45-3:36 F '34
   Baskette, K.   The new ambitions of Joan Crawford.
      Photop 47-3:76 F '35
   Manners, D.   The girl without a past.   Photop 48-5:32
      O '35
   Manners, D.   Second marriage.   Photop 49-5:24 My '36
   Zeitlin, I.   Why Joan Crawford remains great.   Photop
      50-4:45 O '36
   St. Johns, A. R.   Joan Crawford, the dramatic rise of
      a self-made star.   Photop 51-10:26 O; 51-11:64 N;
      51-12:70 D '37
   Crawford, J.   How to be friends with your ex-husbands.
      Photop 53-8:12 Ag '39
   Crawford, J.   What's wrong with dancing?   Photop 53-11:
      20 N '39
   Waterbury, R.   Love is laughter.   Photop 21-5:66 O '42
   I couldn't ask for more.   Ladies Home J 59:13 D '42

Crawford, J. I've been lonely. Photop 22-5:56 Ap '43
Crawford, J. These lives are at stake! Photop 23-2:
  48 Jl '43
Crichton, K. Lady in waiting. Colliers 114:13 O 28 '44
Biography. Cur Bio 7:13 Ja '46
  Same, revised. Cur Bio Yrbk 1946:132 '47
Waterbury, R. Stormy passage for Joan and Phil.
  Photop 28-4:29 Mr '46
Joan Crawford at home in New York. Am Home 35:42
  Mr '46
Divorced. Newsweek 27:54 My 6 '46
Parsons, L. O. You're welcome, Joan. Photop 29-1:
  34 Je '46
Fourth Joan Crawford. Newsweek 26:102 O 15 '46
Crawford, J. I have learned. Photop 29-5:40 O '46
Fletcher, A. W. Return of romance? Photop 29-6:36
  N '46
Maxwell, E. Mademoiselle la Chandelier. Photop 30-3:
  56 F '47
Marshman, D. Second rise of Joan Crawford. Life 22:45
  Je 23 '47
Wald, J. I took one look at her. Photop 31-1:46 Je '47
Waterbury, R. Un-possessed. Photop 31-3:34 Ag '47
Crawford, J. I'm an adopted mother. Photop 32-3:40
  F '48
Fink, H. I was there. Photop 33-2:66 Jl '48
Graham, S. The house that Joan built. Photop 33-4:50
  S '48
Frazier, G. Handsome Joan from San Antone. Colliers
  123:15 Mr 12 '49
Fink, H. I was there. Photop 34-5:56 Ap '49
Morgan, M. Joan Crawford is my "manager." TV
  Guide 3-26:16 Jl 1 '50
They made me a myth--Joan Crawford, daughter of the
  American Revolution. Sight & Sound 21-4:162 Ap/Je
  '52
Hine, A. You mustn't miss Joan. Holiday 12:26 N '52
Jon Whitcomb's page. Cosmop 134:94 Ja '53
Harvey, E. Crawford dances again. Colliers 132:13
  Jl 4 '53
Young lady of ten. Sat Eve Post 226:104 Ag 22 '53
Joan goes back to old ways. Life 35:110 N 9 '53
Ardmore, J. K. Story I've never told. Womans H C
  82:44 Ja; 40 F '55
Knight, A. Hardy perennials. Sat R 38:21 O 29 '55
Meltsir, A. Two women and a dream. Photop 48-5:60
  N '55

Goldsmith, B. L.   Joan Crawford introduces her daughter
  to show business.   Womans H C 83:13 Ag '56
Quirk, L. J.   Joan Crawford, inc. filmog.   Films In
  Review 7-10:481 D '56
Wood, C.   TV personalities biographical sketchbook.
  TV Personalities p53 '56
Crawford, J.   God's greatest gift to me.   Photop 52-6:
  50 D '57
Living it up with Pepsi.   Time 71:92 My 19 '58
If it's alive, it's dead.   Newsweek 53:64 Ja 5 '59
Kay, S.   Who put the fingerprints on Joan Crawford's
  wall?   Photop 55-4:56 Ap '59
Crawford, J.   Its' such a fascinating busines . . . as
  told to J. Ardmore.   Ptr Ink 268:48 Jl 10 '59
Blake, E.   No one to come home to.   Photop 56-1:72 Jl
  '59
Gehman, R.   Joan Crawford.   McCalls 86:41 S '59
Durable charms of Joan the queen.   Life 47:136 O 5 '59
Dinter, C.   Joan.   Photop 57-1:46 Ja '60
Crawford, J.   This is my story; excerpt from autobiog-
  raphy Portrait of Joan.   Good H 155:58 Jl '62
Shall we dance? thud!   Joan Crawford learning judo.
  Life 53:57 S 28 '62
It's not all glitter.   Seventeen 21:104 D '62
Corbin, J.   Why she had to learn judo.   Photop 63-4:66
  Ap '63
Other life of Joan Crawford.   Bsns W p91 S 21 '63
Amory, C.   Celebrity register.   McCalls 91:118 O '63
Oulahan, R.   Well-planned Crawford.   Life 56:11 F 21
  '64
Braun, E.   Forty years a queen.   Films & Filming 11-
  8:7 My '65
Lyon, N.   Second fame; good fame.   Vogue 146:212 N 1
  '65
Bowers, R. L.   Joan Crawford's latest decade.   Films
  In Review 17-6:366 Je/Jl '66
Biography.   Cur Bio 27:12 S '66
  Same.   Cur Bio Yrbk 1966:59 '67
Lady in the dark.   TV Guide 17-13:8 Ag 16 '69

CRAWFORD, MICHAEL
  Prideaux, T.   I'd fall thirty floors for a laugh.   Life 62:
    70 Mr 10 '67
  Pleasure bumps.   Time 89:41 Je 2 '67

CREHAN, JOSEPH
  Obit.   Screen World 18:233 '67

CRENNA, RICHARD
   The man with the squeak.   TV Guide 9-20:12 My 20 '61
   Slattery's saga.   Newsweek 65:82 My 31 '65
   Whitney, D.   Beaten at the polls.   TV Guide 13-46:12
      N 13 '65

CREWS, LAURA HOPE
   Eaton, W. P.   Carrying on the torch.   Am Mag 76:46 O
      '13
   Lang, H.   Glory by proxy.   Photop 38-1:71 Je '30
   Hopkins, U. N.   American tradition in the Beverly Hills
      home of Laura Hope Crews.   Arts & Dec 49:10 O '38
   Obit.   Newsweek 20:8 N 23 '42
      Time 40:74 N 23 '42
      Cur Bio '43

CRISP, DONALD
   Mitchell, G.   Letter.   Films In Review 12-3:189 Mr '61

CRISTAL, LINDA
   Hamilton, J.   Girl who travels alone.   Look 24:107 Jl 19
      '60
   Warning: it can mean only one thing.   Photop 58-5:
      48 N '60
   Galanoy, T.   She doesn't need a script.   TV Guide 16-24:
      24 Je 15 '68
   Terry, P.   Linda's love for Sidney Poitier.   Photop 74-
      6:38 D '68

CRONYN, HUME
   Notes on film acting.   Theatre Arts 33:45 Je '49
   Diesel, L.   Round-the-clock with the Cronyns.   Theatre
      Arts 36:44 F '52
   Biography.   Cur Bio 17:17 Mr '56
      Same.   Cur Bio Yrbk 1946:132 '57
   Tynan, K.   A for effort, O for obstinacy.   New Yorker
      35:82 Ap 25 '59
   Hayes, R.   Three by two.   Commonweal 70:206 My 22 '59
   Dear Diary.   Theatre Arts 45:12 Jl '61
   Ross, L.   Player.   New Yorker 37:103 O 21 '61

CROSBY, BING
   Reynolds, Q.   Kid from Spokane.   Colliers 95:20 Ap 27
      '35
   Taviner, R.   Time out for twins.   Photop 48-2:65 Jl '35
   Ryan, D.   The secret of Bing Crosby's greatness. Photop
      48:72 O '35

Harris, S. Bing Crosby Inc. unlimited. Photop 50-3:21
  S '36
Epler, S. E. Bing Crosby honored with degree of doctor
  of philosophy in music by Gonzaga university. Sch &
  Soc 46:760 D 11 '37
Lawrence, C. Newest of the Bing Crosby homes in San
  Fernando valley. Arts & Dec 49:3 D '38
Binyon, C. Close-up of the groaner. Photop 53-2:22 F
  '39
O'Hara, J. Bing Crosby's phonograph recording of Ballad
  for Americans. Newsweek 16:62 S 16 '40
Groaner. Time 37:92 Ap 7 '41
Biography. Cur Bio '41
Smith, H. A. Bing, king of groaners. Sat Eve Post
  215:9 O 31; 26 N 7 '42
Boone, A. R. Crosby research foundation. Nations Bus
  31:22 F '43
Martin, M. I sing for Bing. Am Mag 135:44 Ap '43
  Same. Read Digest 42:34 Je '43
Proctor, K. Play truth or consequences with Bing Crosby.
  Photop 23-1:48 Je '43
Rhythm boys. Time 42:70 Jl 19 '43
Smith, H. A. Bing, king of the groaners; abridged.
  Read Digest 43:74 Jl '43
Bing's secret weapons. Am Mag 136:128 D '43
Keen, H. Race track production line. Flying 34:67 My
  '44
Delehanty, T. Going Bing's way. Photop 25-3:47 Ag '44
Parsons, L. O. Bing-as I know him. Photop 26-1:32
  D '44
Crosby, B. Christmas 1944. Photop 26-2:21 Ja '45
Nugent, F. S. At home with the Crosby team. N.Y.
  Times Mag p16 Mr 4 '45
Follen, V. With a song in his heart. Photop 26-6:30
  My '45
Barnett, L. Bing, Inc. Life 18:86 Je 18 '45
I got plenty of mousetraps. Am Mag 140:32 Jl '45
Barnett, L. Bing, Inc. abridged. Read Digest 47:30
  S '45
Crosby meets court. Newsweek 27:78 Ja 14 '46
Crosby's contract. Bsns W p87 Ja 26 '46
Going his way is a nation's habit after twenty years of
  Crosby's song. Newsweek 27:66 Ja 28 '46
Sponsor vs. star. Adv & Sell 39:104 F '46
Maxwell, E. King Bing. Photop 28-4:48 Mr '46
Arnold, M. Cowboy Crosby. Photop 28-4:50 Mr '46
Canned Crosby. Newsweek 28:56 Ag 26 '46

Philco signs Bing. Bsns W p40 Ag 31 '46
Cohen, M. Inking in Bing Crosby. Photop 29-4:62 S '46
Crosby dead or alive. Newsweek 28:96 N 25 '46
Biography. NCAB cur G:163 '46
Great |throat. Fortune 35:128 Ja '47
World-wide groaner. Time 45:88 Mr 26 '47
Arnold, M. Man at the top. Photop 30-4:32 Mr '47
On wax. New Yorker 23:20 Je 14 '47
Bing's still king. Newsweek 30:94 N 24 '47
Arnold, M. Christmas gift. Photop 32-1:36 D '47
Bing's party. Time 51:52 Ja 19 '48
Brack, A. I was there. Photop 32-4:60 Mr '48
Edwards, R. Play truth or consequences with Bing
    Crosby. Photop 32-5:46 Ap '48
Sammes, F. R. Million-dollar minstrel. Photop 32-6:
    55 My '48
Parsons, L. O. "My Bing:" Dixie Crosby talks.
    Photop 32-6:56 My '48
Hope, B. I and Hope. Photop 32-6:58 My '48
Morrow, B. Checked shirt and tails. Photop 32-6:59
    My '48
Crosby, H. L. Sr. He's my boy. Photop 32-6:60 My '48
Wood, T. Bing Crosby, mousetrap builder. N. Y.
    Times Mag p17 Je 6 '48
Shane, T. Road to the 19th hole. Colliers 122:29 Ag
    14 '48
Maxwell, E. Bing's my dish. Photop 33-3:44 Ag '48
Crosby, B. How I got my goat. Sat Eve Post 221:20
    O 16 '48
Minute maid's man. Time 52:91 O 18 '48
Sher, J. Bing and his priates. Photop 33-5:38 O '48
New stars for CBS. Newsweek 33:49 Ja 31 '49
Westmore, W. Make mine Crosby style. Photop 34-3:
    44 F '49
Mr. Harper. After hours. Harper 199:99 Ag '49
Bing Crosby lives here. House B 91:46 Ag '49
Duncan, G. Bing Crosby and his four sons. Coronet
    27:43 N '49
Thomas, B. The Crosby myth. Photop 37-6:52 Je '50
Shearer, E. Gary Crosby and friend. Colliers 127:12
    Ja 6 '51
Good citizen pays his taxes. Sr Schol 57:5 Ja 10 '51
Bing and his boys. Newsweek 37:42 Je 25 '51
Pryor, T. M. Dr. Crosby's remedy. N. Y. Times Mag
    p18 My 4 '52
Hoffman, I. Bing's big break. Coronet 31:133 Ap '52
All night stand. Time 59:45 Je 30 '52

Mr. Harper. One of Bing's things. Harper 204:94 Je
'52

Hopper, H. Dixie. Photop 43-2:44 F '53

Crosby, B. Call me lucky, as told to Pete Martin; a-
bridged. Sat Eve Post 225:17 F 14; 22 F 21; 30 F 28;
36 Mr 7; 40 Mr 14; 36 Mr 21; 38 Mr 28; 30 Ap 4 '53

Bing Crosby's biggest gamble. TV Guide 1-6:6 My 8 '53

Balliett, W. Mr. Boop-doop-a-doop. Sat R 36:17 Je
27 '53

Lucky Bing. Newsweek 41:92 Je 29 '53

Biography. Cur Bio 14:19 Je '53
  Same. Cur Bio Yrbk 1953:130 '53

Bathroom baritone. Time 62:98 Jl 13 '53

Rita, Marlene and the farmer's daughter. Life 35:65
Ag 3 '53

The reluctant dragon. TV Guide 2-1:5 Ja 1 '54

With $15,000,000 Bing wants to slowly bow out. News-
week 43:38 Ja 4 '54

Bing-come-lately; Bing Crosby show. Life 36:57 Ja 11
'54

Hunt, J. Bing walks alone. Photop 45-2:48 F '54

Bing sing. Newsweek 44:68 S 13 '54

Two misters play sisters. Colliers 134:74 O 15 '54

Crosby, B. My four sons--and me. McCalls 82:37 O
'54

I never had to scream. Look 18:75 N 2 '54

Country girl. N. Y. Times Mag p39 N 14 '54

Bing on binge. Life 37:106 D 6 '54

Bing Crosby and Grace Kelly try for Academy Award.
Look 18:163 D 14 '54

New millionaires. Time 64:64 D 27 '54

Arnold, M. Bing-goes that Crosby myth. Photop 47-6:
57 Je '55

My competition has a crew cut. Coronet 38:24 S '55

Hobson, W. Crosby and Christmas and such. Sat R
38:62 N 26 '55

First time I sant Silent night. Good H 141:42 D '55

Austin, J. Mr. Bing, God bless him! Am Home 55:43
F '56

Weinman, M. High jinks in High society. Colliers 137:
32 Je 8 '56

Little, S. Decorating ideas from Bing Crosby's house.
House B 98:114 S '56

Kurnitz, H. Crosby moves in High society. Holiday
20:69 S '56

Crosby family album. McCalls 84:50 D '56

Martin, P. I call on Bing Crosby. Sat Eve Post 229:

38 My 11 '57

Talk with the star. Newsweek 50:89 Jl 8 '57

Shanley, J. P. Television; special program on behalf of
the Edsel car. America 98:118 O 26 '57

Lardner, J. Air. New Yorker 33:114 N 2 '57

Martin, P. I call on Kathy Grant Crosby. Sat Eve
Post 230:28 Ap 5 '58

Kamm, H. Bing talks. Look 22:46 My 13 '58

Crosby, Bob. I hated being Bing's brother; as told to
M. Abramson. Look 22:57 Jl 22 '58

Bing's boys on their own. Life 45:85 S 15 '58

Posner, C. Why Bing and Kathy need this baby so much.
Photop 51-3:51 S '58

Davidson, M. Kitchen for Bing and Kathy. Ladies
Home J 75:70 S '58

Old master. Time 72:53 O 13 '58

Gordon, S. Meet Mrs. Crosby and little Bing. Look 23:
25 Ja 20 '59

Keeping his hand in. TV Guide 7-9:14 F 28 '59

Slater, L. Crisis for the Crosbys: what's bothering
Bing's boys. McCalls 86:58 My '59

Davidson, B. Crosbys of Hollywood. Look 24:34 Je 7
'60

Crosby, B. How I want to bring up my daughter; ed by
B. Willett. Ladies Home J 77:80 O '60

Romp for two ageless troubadours. Life 50:77 Mr 10 '61

Defresne, F. Bing would rather go fishing. Field &
Stream 66:48 D '61

Who's the new champ? She's Bing's girl. Life 52:43
Mr 2 '62

Bing's second family. Look 26:16 Jl 17 '62

Hope, B. Bob tells on Bing. Music J 20:27 S '62

Hume, R. Hollywood's Bing. Films & Filming 9-1:64
O '62

Bing tags a marlin. Field & Stream 67:31 D '62

Crosby, K. G. Bing and I. Good H 156:86 Mr '63

Hamburger, P. Notes for a gazetteer; Crosbyana room
of Crosby library at Gonzaga university. New Yorker
39:198 O 26 '63

Bing's back. Newsweek 67:78 Ja 24 '66

Davidson, B. Old Dad has a long way to slide. Sat Eve
Post 239:28 Ap 9 '66

Davidson, M. & Rale, B. Bing Crosby and his new
movie: Stagecoach. Sat Eve Post 239:30 Ap 9 '66

Conrad, B. Good new life of Bing Crosby. Good H 162:
88 My '66

Crosby, B. My second family. Ladies Home J 83:81

My '66
Durslag, M. The sweet life. TV Guide 15-3:24 Ja 21 '67
Williams, M. Columbia, Epic and Crosby. Sat R 51:56
    Je 29 '68
Marill, A. H. Bing Crosby, inc. filmog. Films In Re-
    view 19-6:321 Je/Jl '68
A Crosby fishing-and-tall story expedition. TV Guide 17-
    35:25 Ag 30 '69

CROSBY, GARY
    Home on the range? Time 56-45 Ag 7 '50
    Biographical note. Sr Schol 57:3 O 4 '50
    Shearer, L. Gary Crosby and friend. Colliers 127:12
        Ja 6 '51
    Gary Crosby turns into a second groaner. Life 31:37 Jl
        30 '51
    Bingle Jr. Time 63:55 Je 21 '54
    That's my boy. Newsweek 43:55 Je 21 '54
    Bing Crosby's boy Gary. Look 18:40 Ag 10 '54
    Crosby, B. My competition has a crew cut. Coronet
        38:24 S '55
    Wood, C. TV personalities biographical sketchbook.
        TV Personalities p49 '56
    Bing's son says it. Newsweek 52:90 D 1 '58
    Davidson, M. Gary Crosby, a man's victory over alco-
        holism. Good H 165:93 S '67

CROWLEY, PAT
    Parsons, L. O. Ambitious Cinderella. Cosmop 135:6
        Jl '53
    Harbert, R. Cinderella succeeds. Good H 137:16 Ag '53
    Tootsie role. Colliers 132:60 O 2 '53
    Pacific paradise. Look 18:14 Ja 12 '54
    Life visits a Hollywood homebody. Life 36:128 Mr 29 '54
    Meyerson, E. Date with a dream. Photop 45-4:68 Ap
        '54
    The girl from Olyphant. TV Guide 8-5:24 Ja 30 '60
    DeRoos, R. Daisies grow better with pepper. TV Guide
        14-5:16 Ja 29 '66

CULP, ROBERT
    Hobson, D. He bears witness to his beliefs. TV Guide
        14-3:10 Ja 15 '66
    Color him funny. Newsweek 67:76 Ja 31 '66
    Fleming, A. I hate a woman who clings. Photop 72-6:
        24 D '67

CUMMINGS, CONSTANCE
  Keating, R.   When Connie was down and out.   Photop
    45-1:71 D '33

CUMMINGS, ROBERT
  Steele, J. H.   Hollywood at home.   Photop 18-2:48 Ja '41
  Rhea, M.   Another eagle takes the air.   Photop 20-6:
    46 My '42
  Canfield, A.   Wedding in the rain.   Photop 27-1:64 Je
    '45
  One more for TV.   Newsweek 40:69 N 17 '52
  Up-and-coming Cummings.   TV Guide 3-15:13 Ap 9 '55
  Biography.   Cur Bio 17:15 Ja '56
    Same.   Cur Bio Yrbk 1956:134 '57
  1,000-watt bulb.   Time 67:109 Ap 9 '56
  Wood, C.   TV personalities biographical sketchbook.
    TV Personalities p143 '56
  Eells, G.   Life and times of a perennial juvenile.   Look
    22:110 O 14 '58
  Nichols, M.   Pill-powered juvenile.   Coronet 45:12 Je
    '59
  Health is no game.   TV Guide 8-12:12 Mr 19 '60
  Greenwood, J. R.   Meet Bob Cummings, pilot, actor,
    businessman.   Flying 66:45 Mr '60

CUMMINS, PEGGY
  Peggy Cummins; 19-year-old Irish girl may play gaudy
    heroine of Forever Amber.   Life 19:133 N 19 '45
  Reid, A.   Peggy in Amberland.   Colliers 117:19 My 25
    '46
  Deere, D.   Bit of Ireland.   Photop 31-3:42 Ag '47
  Her Irish heart was breaking.   Am Mag 144:121 O '47

CUNARD, GRACE
  The biography of Grace Cunard.   Feature Movie 2-6:44
    Je 25 '15
  Obit.   Screen World 19:230 '68

CURRIE, FINLAY
  Obit.   Screen World 20:233 '69

CURRIER, FRANK
  St. Johns, I.   The daddy of them all.   Photop 30-3:33 Ag
    '26

CURTIS, ALAN
  Hayes, B.   When Sonja Henie met Alan Curtis.   Photop

54-4:26 Ap '40
Obit. Time 61:94 F 9 '53
Screen World 5:208 '54

CURTIS, TONY
Curtis, T. Across a crowded room. Photop 39-2:38 F
'51
Steele, J. H. He's a natural. Photop 39-5:50 My '51
Janet's and Tony's home sweet home. Photop 40-5:54 N
'51
Waterbury, R. Their rules for romance. Photop 40-6:
39 D '51
Martin, P. Perils of being a young movie star. Sat
Eve Post 224:22 F 9 '52
Waterbury, R. The love you give. Photop 41-5:48 My
'52
Curtis, T. Our first year. Photop 41-6:56 Je '52
Lewis, J. I'm in love with my best friend's wife.
Photop 42-2:58 Ag '52
Brown, F. The threat to the Tony Curtis-Janet Leigh
marriage. Photop 43-2:48 '53
Waterbury, R. Happiness quiz. Photop 43-5:48 My '53
Parsons, L. O. It's tough to stay married in Hollywood.
Cosmop 135:9 Ag '53
Swanson, P. No sad songs. Photop 44-4:54 O '53
King and queen of hearts. Look 18:50 F 23 '54
Leigh, J. Spoil the brute! Photop 45-2:50 F '54
Corwin, J. Love those in-laws. Photop 45-4:66 Ap '54
Bolstad, H. Tony's days of decision. Photop 46-2:34 Ag
'54
Arnold, M. When love is enough. Photop 46-4:58 O '54
Curtis, T. Get with it kids. Photop 47-2:51 F '55
Steele, J. H What's the difference. Photop 47-3:49
Mr '55
Downing, H. Man alive. Photop 47-5:40 My '55
Hopper, H. Young men of Hollywood. Coronet 38:54 Jl
'55
Curtis, T. Be a doll for a guy. Photop 48-2:52 Ag '55
Waterbury, R. Boy did I goof. Photop 48-3:63 S '55
Parisian picnic. Look 19:90 N 29 '55
Jones, M. W. Having wonderful time. Photop 48-6:58
D '55
Debut: Janet Leigh's first baby. Look 20:20 N 13 '56
Meltsir, A. Once upon a time. Photop 50-6:60 D '56
Jessup, S. Rebel in a button-down collar. Photop 51-5:
51 My '57
Curtis, T. Running scared. Photop 52-1:54 Jl '57

Tony gets the brush.   Photop 52-5:66 N '57

Nichols, M.   Idle dreamer to self-made idol.   Coronet
43:10 Ja '58

Talk with a star.   Newsweek Je 30 '58

Divas, G.   I've never had a birthday party.   Photop 54-
5:56 N '58

Day, D.   I won't break these resolutions.   Photop 55-2:
48 F '59

Michaels, E.   If only my dad could have lived to see you.
Photop 55-5:52 My '59

Biography.   Cur Bio 20:14 My '59
Cur Bio Yrbk 1959:82 '60

Mommy, Daddy says God does like ice cream.   Photop
56-1:40 Jl '59

Johnson, R.   Wonderful world of Tony Curtis.   Sat Eve
Post 232:26 Jl 25 '59

Hano, A.   Angry idol from Third Ave.   Coronet 46:102
S '59

Downs R.   There will be no divorce.   Photop 57-1:50
Ja '60

Ardmore, J.   Would he marry you all over again.
Photop 58-2:46 Ag '60

A quiet afternoon with Janet and Tony.   Photop 58-4:54
O '60

Dinter, C.   Mommy, what church does Santa Claus go to?
Photop 59-1:32 Ja '61

How to become a star today.   Newsweek 57:92 F 27 '61

Knight, A.   Film actor prepares.   Sat R 44:36 Mr 4 '61

Day, D.   Janet, don't let your castles crumble.   Photop
60-2:48 Ag '61

It's time you opened your eyes.   Photop 60-4:36 O '61

Alexander, S.   Bee-yoody-ful life of a movie caliph.
Life 51:161 N 17 '61

Tony Curtis photographs Sergeants 3.   Ebony 17:43 Ap '62

Janet tells: why I left Tony.   Photop 61-6:18 Je '62

Bacon, J.   I can't help crying inside.   Photop 61-6:28 Je
'62

How hypnotism saved me!   Photop 62-3:38 S '62

Miller, E.   Tony Curtis and Yul Brynner among the Cos-
sacks.   Seventeen 21:92 O '62

Meet Mrs. Tony Curtis II.   Photop 62-4:29 O '62

Gideon, N.   Second wife but not second best.   Photop 62-
6:25 D '62

Look who's marrying Tony.   Life 54:35 F 22 '63

Gideon, N.   What do lovers do all day?   Photop 63-3:39
Mr '63

Mr. and Mrs. Tony Curtis.   Photop 63-5:49 My '63

Lewis, R. W.   Tony Curtis: it's a brand new ballgame.
Sat Eve Post 241:39 Mr 23 '68

CUSHING, PETER
Nolan, J. E.   Five TV heavies.   Film Fan Mo 92:15 F
'69

CYBULSKI, ZBIGNIEW
Person of promise.   Films & Filming 5-12:17 S '59
Personality of the month.   Films & Filming 8-2:7 N '61
Zbigniew Cybulski.   Film 31:25 Spg '62
Man in the green lenses.   Time 84:71 D 18 '64
Obit.   Screen World 19:230 '68

DAHL, ARLENE

Design for stardom. Am Mag 147:95 Mr '49
Colby, A. Oh what a beautiful Dahl. Photop 36-5:60 '49
Wilson, L. Designing woman. Photop 40-2:58 Ag '51
Ford, E. Too busy for love? Photop 43-2:68 F '53
Swanson, P. From Lana to Arlene. Photop 43-5:34 My '53
Kingsley, K. Two's company. Photop 44-1:48 Jl '53
Dahl, A. How to handle men. Photop 44-5:58 N '53
Wood, C. TV personalities biographical sketchbook. TV Personalities p109 '56
People are talking about. Vogue 129:136 Ap 1 '57
Finlay, J. F. Film and TV. Cath World 185:221 Je '57
Flirt with a fluttery fan. Life 52:61 My 4 '62

DAILEY, DAN

Asher, J. Dangerous Dan. Photop 32-2:64 Ja '48
Deere, D. He's looking over a four-leaf clover. Photop 32-6:46 My '48
Dailey, D. Lover girl. Photop 33-1:42 Je '48
Arnold, M. Rhythm man. Photop 34-6:60 My '49
Parsons, L. O. Second chance. Photop 36-5:34 O '49
Weiner, W. L. Unfancy Dan. Colliers 125:28 Ap 1 '50
Parsons, L. O. Lost--their blue heaven. Photop 38-6:52 D '50
Parsons, L. O. The life he saved. Photop 40-2:40 Ag '51
Raddatz, L. Dailey for governor. TV Guide 17-46:26 N 15 '69

DALE, ESTHER

Obit. Screen World 13:219 '62

DALEY, CASS

Ugly duckling. Time 47:62 Ja 28 '46
Campbell, K. They preferred gaiety to grandeur. Am Home 36:24 N '46

DALL, JOHN

Fletcher, A. W. All about John Dall. Photop 27-5:44 O '45

DALTON, AUDREY

Scott, D. Those Irish eyes are smiling. Photop 45-1:52 Ja '54

Waterbury, R.   Undivided heart.   Photop 46-3:68 S '54

DALTON, DOROTHY
Blackwood, J. H.   Dorothy Dalton's "I will."   Photop
14-3:92 Ag '18
Mantle, B.   The voice in the dark.   Photop 17-6:35 My
'20

DAMITA, LILI
Kennedy, J. B.   Lily vs. ballet.   Colliers 85:17 Ap 26
'30
Biery, R.   Lili's coming back.   Photop 40-5:56 O '31

DAMON, MARK
Christy, G.   Guess things happen that way.   Photop 55-
1:54 Ja '59

DANA, VIOLA
Interpreter of youth.   Cosmop 55:124 Je '13
Bartlett, R.   A melody for the viola.   Photop 12-5:69
O '17
St. Johns, I.   It's no laughing matter.   Photop 28-2:58
Jl '25

D'ANDREA, TOM
Actor cooks; with recipes.   Am Home 39:133 My '48

DANDRIDGE, DOROTHY
Shy no more.   Life 31:65 N 5 '51
Eye and ear specialist.   Time 59:50 F 4 '52
Forecasts and side glances.   Theatre Arts 36:13 Mr '52
Bright road for Dandridge.   Theatre Arts 37:12 My '53
New beauty for Bizet.   Life 37:87 N 1 '54
Parsons, L. O.   Dorothy Dandridge stars in a great new
movie.   Cosmop 137:4 D '54
Two for the show.   Time 65:42 My 2 '55
Robinson, L.   Private world of Dorothy Dandridge.
Ebony 17:116 Je '62
Obit.   Newsweek 66:66 S 20 '65
Time 86:124 S 17 '65
Screen World 17:235 '66
Robinson, L.   Dorothy Dandridge: Hollywood's tragic
enigma.   Ebony 21:70 Mr '66

DANIELL, HENRY
Gray, B.   Henry Daniell, inc. filmog. Films In Review

D '63
Obit.   Screen World 15:220 '64

DANIELS, BEBE
Fair, J.   Some Bebe!   Photop 14-6:57 N '18
Jordan, J.   A belle of Bogota.   Photop 19-2:46 Ja '21
St. Johns, A. R.   The most popular girl in Hollywood.
    Photop 22-6:33 N '22
Dix, R.   Why I have never married Bebe Daniels.
    Photop 25-2:30 Ja '24
Spensley, D.   The evolution of Bebe.   Photop 28-6:34
    N '25
Hyland, D.   Pictures or football?   Photop 34-4:38 S '28
Lang, H.   Bebe and Ben.   Photop 38-2:73 Jl '30
Whitney, P. D.   Then and now.   N. Y. Times Mag p22
    F 24 '54
The story behind "This is your life, Bebe Daniels"   TV
    Guide 2-47:2 N 20 '54
Where are they now?   Newsweek 49:26 My 6 '57
What are they doing now?   Show 2-8:106 Ag '62
Bodeen, D.   Bebe Daniels, inc. filmog.   Films In Review
    15-7:413 Ag/S '64
Bodeen, D.   Bebe Daniels.   Films In Review 15-10:639
    D '64

DANTINE, HELMUT
Hamilton, S.   Important import.   Photop 23-5:59 O '43
Asher, J.   American from Vienna.   Photop 27-6:44 N '45

DARIN, BOBBY
Splish becomes splash.   Newsweek 54:84 O 19 '59
Bobby's back in town.   TV Guide 7-52:20 D 26 '59
Alexander, S.   I want to be a legend by 25.   Life 48:49
    Ja 11 '60
Baskette, K.   Wise guy.   Photop 57-4:48 Ap '60
Dinter, C.   Do we have the right to marry?   Photop 58-
    2:68 Ag '60
Siegel, M.   He's all wrong for me.   Photop 58-6:66 D
    '60
Gehman, R.   The astoundingly brash character of Darin.
    TV Guide 9-4:9 Ja 28 '61
Johnson, M.   Uncensored!   Sandra Dee elopes with Bobby
    Darin.   Photop 59-2:58 F '61
2-1/2 months to go.   Time 77:82 Mr 10 '61
Siegel, M.   Runaway honeymoon.   Photop 59-3:26 Mr '61
Linn, E.   Little singer with a big ego.   Sat Eve Post

234:27 My 6 '61

Borie, M.   At last--Sandra breaks the silence.   Photop
   59-5:34 My '61

I'll see my wife anytime I want.   Photop 60-1:54 Jl '61

Miller, E.   Bobby Darin: man on the move.   Seventeen
   20:80 Jl '61

Corbin, J.   Waiting for baby.   Photop 60-2:34 Ag '61

Waterbury, R.   The dangers facing their baby.   Photop
   60-3:34 S '61

Davidson, B.   Bobby Darin and Paul Anka: boy wonders,
   but why?   McCalls 89:110 O '61

Wilder, G.   A '62 Dodd for the Darins.   Photop 61-3:6
   Mr '62

Look at me.   Newsweek 59:109 Ap 9 '62

Why I played a film bigot.   Ebony 18:45 N '62

Biography.   Cur Bio 24:9 Mr '63
   Same.   Cur Bio Yrbk 1963:98 '64

York, C.   Why she walked out on Bobby.   Photop 63-6:
   16 Je '63

Six quitters.   Esquire 62:103 S '64

Dee, S.   Peter Pan is out!   Seventeen 25:158 Mr '66

Artell, T.   A chip off the old block.   Photop 69-5:64 My
   '66

DARMOND, GRACE
   Lincoln, W.   Filmland's youngest star.   Feature Movie
      5-1:13 Ja '16
   Obit.   Screen World 15:220 '64

DARNELL, LINDA
   Hall, G.   The boy Linda Darnell loves.   Photop 18-5:53
      Ap '41
   Fletcher, A. W.   How Linda Darnell lives.   Photop 19-
      6:46 N '41
   Surmelian, L.   This is how it happened.   Photop 23-2:
      32 Jl '43
   Darnell, L.   I'm glad I married an older man.   Photop
      24-3:52 F '44
   Linda Darnell.   Life 17:49 Jl 3 '44
   Scott, D.   Siren in slacks.   Photop 28-4:58 Mr '46
   Porter, A.   Forever Linda.   Colliers 118:16 N 2 '46
   Parsons, L. O.   Linda, woman of the year.   Photop 29-
      6:38 N '46
   Graham, S.   Can't say goodbye.   Photop 30-6:68 My '47
   Darnell, L.   Don't rush into divorce.   Photop 32-4:73
      Mr '48
   Maxwell, E.   In search of Linda Darnell.   Photop 36-2:

40 Je '49

Darnell, L.   Should girls marry older men?   Photop 40-
3:35 S '51

Obit.   Time 85:100 Ap 16 '65
Screen World 17:235 '66

Haranis, C.   She walked in beauty.   Photop 68-1:8 Jl '65

Baskette, K.   Needless tragedy of Linda Darnell.   Good
H 161:42 S '65

Roman, R. C.   Linda Darnell, inc. filmog.   Films In
Review 17-8:473 O '66

DARREN, JAMES
Albright, D.   Can a teenager be ready for marriage?
Photop 53-5:32 My '58

Christy, G.   Why is it so tough to make a girl understand how/ you feel?   Photop 55-6:64 Je '59

Person of promise.   Films & Filming 6-3:17 D '59

Christy, G.   James Darren marries Evy Norlund.   Photop
57-5:44 My '60

Christy, G.   Honeymoon--it couldn't last forever.   Photop
58-2:48 Ag '60

Henderson, B.   What's going on here?   Photop 60-4:50
O '61

Dinter, C.   Evy, have I lost a son?   Photop 61-4:65 Ap
'62

Can they live together.   Photop 64-5:52 N '63

Harmetz, A.   It has to be a boy.   Photop 65-4:68 Ap '64

A teenage idol passes 30.   TV Guide 15-25:14 Je 24 '67

DARRIEUX, DANIELLE
Roberts, K.   Mademoiselle from gay Paree.   Colliers
100:14 D 18 '37

Steele, J. H.   Portrait in Bordeaux red.   Photop 52-9:
32 S '38

Whitehall, R.   Danielle Darrieux.   Films & Filming 8-
3:12 D '61

DARWELL, JANE
Biography.   Cur Bio '41

Obit.   Cur Bio 28:43 O '67
Cur Bio Yrbk 1967:474 '68
Newsweek 70:73 Ag 28 '67
Time 90:65 Ag 25 '67
Screen World 19:230 '68

DAUPHIN, CLAUDE
Wood, C.   TV personalities biographical sketchbook.

TV Personalities p38 '56
For peanuts and the art of Ayme.   Theatre Arts 42:25
Je '58

DAVALOS, RICHARD
Service, F. Determined Davalos.   Photop 48-1:141 Jl
'55

DAVENPORT, HARRY
Obit. Newsweek 34:53 Ag 22 '49
Time 54:77 Ag 22 '49
Jones, K. D. Harry Davenport, inc. filmog.   Films In
Review 17-6:390 Je/Jl '66

DAVIDSON, JOHN
Higgins, R. Soloist who's eager to harmonize.   TV Guide
14-31:12 Jl 30 '66
Buckley, P. John Davidson: the square that never was.
After Dark 11-4:30 Ag '69

DAVIES, MARION
Evans, D. Galatea on Riverside Drive.   Photop 16-5:62
O '19
Broderick, H. Pretty soft to be a star, eh? Photop 20-
4:43 S '21
St. Johns, A. R. An impression of Marion Davies.
Photop 27-2:59 Ja '25
Howe, H. The local favorite.   Photop 29-6:58 My '26
York, C. You can never be an actor.   Photop 34-2:78
Jl '28
Biery, R. Marion's philosophy.   Photop 41-3:68 F '32
Moffit, J. C. Choice of Marion Davies brings squawk.
Cinema Digest 1-6:7 Jl 25 '32
Lang, H. She even laughs off landslides.   Photop 44-1:
42 Je '33
Gaines, W. P. Marion Davies' secrets of success.
Photop 47-3:53 F '35
Swanson, P. Sunday night at Marion Davies'.   Cinema
Arts 1-1:34 Je '37
Hail and farewell.   Time 58:50 Ag 27 '51
Hearst's bombshell.   Time 58:57 S 3 '51
Hedda cuts a queen.   Newsweek 38:46 S 3 '51
Hearst empire.   Bsns W p110 S 22 '51
Marion Davies: consultant.   Time 58:90 N 5 '51
Marion gets married.   Life 31:44 N 12 '51
Back page wedding.   Newsweek 38:61 N 12 '51
Fate and Uncle Horace.   Time 58:24 N 12 '51

Life goes to a big Marion Davies party.   Life 33:133 O
   20 '52
Hearst vs. Brown.   Time 60:65 N 24 '52
Tycoon Davies.   Time 66:56 Ag 1 '55
Obit.   Am Ann 1962:850 '62
   Illus Lond N 239:547 S 30 '61
   Newsweek 58:36 O 2 '61
   Time 78:69 S 29 '61
   Screen World 13:221 '62
Taylor, J. R.   20's show people.   Sight & Sound 37-4:
   200 Aut '68

DAVIS, BETTE
   Lieber, E.   She was afraid to wed.   Photop 43-1:55
      D '32
   Crichton, K.   Bad, but very good.   Colliers 94:18 N 17
      '34
   Baskette, K.   The girl they tried to forget.   Photop 47-
      6:26 My '35
   Rankin, R.   I think women are awful, says Bette Davis.
      Photop 48-4:48 S '35
   Smalley, J.   One year with Oscar.   Photop 51-8:55 Ag
      '37
   Popeye the magnificent.   Time 31:33 Mr 28 '38
   Mainwaring, D.   Hollywood melodies.   Good H 106:40 Ap
      '38
   Randin, R.   The "golden goose" reaches thirty.   Photop
      52-8:10 Ag '38
   Rankin, R.   What really happened to Bette Davis' mar-
      riage?   Photop 52-12:24 D '38
   Wags; Tailwagger foundation.   Am Mag 127:91 Mr '39
   Fletcher, A. W.   Reborn!   Photop 53-4:18 Ap '39
   Henderson, M.   Gallant lady.   Good H 108:38 Je '39
   Erskine, J.   The queen's office hours.   Photop 53-12:
      17 D '39
   Davis, B.   Code for American girls.   Photop 54-9:17 S
      '40
   Davis, B.   Don't be a draft bride.   Photop 18-2:26 Ja '41
   Jefferson, S.   Scoop!   The man Bette Davis married.
      Photop 18-4:57 Mr '41
   Birthday party at Littleton, New Hampshire.   Life 10:
      126 Ap 28 '41
   Davis, B.   Is a girl's past ever her own?   Photop 19-5:
      34 O '41
   Walker, H. L.   Save those tears!   The philosophy of
      Bette Davis.   Photop 25-1:47 Je '44
   Steele, J. H.   Portrait of the dynamic Davis.   Photop 26-

1:56 D '44

Swanson, P.   The lady and the corporal.   Photop 26-2:
24 Ja '45

Paul, E.   Yankee with verve.   Photop 27-3:46 Ag '45

Ashland, J.   Invitation to the wedding of Bette and William Grant Sherry.   Photop 28-3:27 F '46

Becker, M. L.   Leaders are readers.   Sr Schol 48:16
Ap 1 '46

Crocker, H.   Assignment in Hollywood.   Good H 122:12
My '46

Parsons, L. O.   My baby will be a Yankee.   Photop 30-
2:32 Ja '47

Gilmore, H.   Visit to Sugar Hill.   Photop 30-4:51 Mr '47

Romero, R.   Great roles reborn.   Theatre Arts 31:56
Mr '47

Davis, B.   My new life.   Photop 32-2:52 Ja '48

Maury, M.   Alias Bette Davis.   Photop 34-4:48 Mr '49

Davis, B.   Things my mother taught me.   Am Mag 148:
50 N '49

Parsons, L. O.   Bitter choice.   Photop 38-1:34 Jl '50

Wilson, L.   That old magic.   Photop 39-3:38 Mr '51

Lambert, G.   Portrait of an actress.   Sight & Sound 21-
1:12 Ag/S '51

Millstein, G.   Bette Davis turns from buskin to bumps.
N. Y. Times Mag p 22 O 19 '52

Zeitlin, I.   The present is perfect.   Photop 42-4:58 O
'52

Bette goes to Broadway.   Colliers 130:20 N 29 '52

Great lady whoops it up.   Life 33:24 D 29 '52

Holiday geegaws: a dancing Davis.   Theatre Arts 36:15
D '52

Nathan, G. J.   Davis and the sour apple tree.   Theatre
Arts 37:68 Mr '53

Biography.   Cur Bio 14:19 Mr '53
Same.   Cur Bio Yrbk 1953:144 '53

Bette as Bess.   N. Y. Times Mag p31 Jl 3 '55

Davis, B.   All about me; with B. Davidson.   Colliers
136:27 N 25; 36 D 9 '55

Quirk, L. J.   Bette Davis, inc. filmog.   Films In Review 6-10:481 D '55

Cole, C.   I was not found on a soda fountain stool; intv.
Films & Filming 2-8:6 My '56

Baker, P.   All about Bette.   Films & Filming 2-8:7
My '56

Gray, M.   This is a storm in a Russian teacup.   Films
& Filming 2-8:10 My '56

Bette Davis, her films and the men who made them; intv.

Films & Filming 2-8:12 My '56

Bette Davis serves notice. TV Guide 6-22:17 My 31 '58

Davis, B. I think . . . Films & Filming 5-8:33 My '59

Bette can can-can. TV Guide 7-41:12 O 10 '59

Two by two across the USA. Life 47:61 D 21 '59

Hayes, R. Galesburg and Arcadia. Commonweal 73:72
    O 14 '60

Bette Davis plays Apple Annie. Look 25:62d N 7 '61

Davis, B. Lonely life, abridged. Ladies H J 79:40 Je;
    69 Jl; 36 S '62

Hamilton, J. B. D. Merrill, Bette Davis' daughter.
    Look 26:83 D 18 '62

Awaiting her day in court. TV Guide 11-4:15 Ja 26 '63

Bette for Burr; Perry Mason show. Newsweek 61:80 Ja
    28 '63

Shipman, D. Whatever happened to Bette Davis? Films
    & Filming 9-7:8 Ap '63

Dyer, P. J. Meeting Baby Jane. Sight & Sound 32-3:
    118 Sum '63

Baskette, K. Bette Davis' biggest victory. Good H 157:
    30 Ag '63

Anderson, N. What I'm telling my daughter. Photop
    64-3:62 S '63

Brown, L. Bette Davis. Film Careers 1-3:4 My '64

Hanson, J. All about Eve. Film Careers 1-3:26 My '64

Brock, R. Bette's Oscars. Film Careers 1-3:30 My '64

Shaw, B. P. Bette Davis film index. Film Careers 1-
    3:34 My '64

Merchant, W. Lesson in survival; intv. Holiday 36:83
    Ag '64

Moshier, W. F. A Bette Davis retrospective. Films In
    Review 15-7:449 Ag/S '64

Ringgold, G. Bette Davis. Films In Review 15-8:509 O
    '64

Mothner, I. Pro. Look 29:20 Mr 9 '65

Davis, B. What is a star? Films & Filming 11-12:5
    S '65

Bette Davis goes west . . . with a wallop. TV Guide
    14-31:3 Jl 30 '66

When I was sixteen. Good H 167:99 O '68

Ringgold, G. Bette Davis, inc. filmog. Screen Facts
    9:1 n. d.

DAVIS, JIM

    Tregaskis, R. Jim Davis comes home. Sat Eve Post
        218:17 F 9 '46

DAVIS, JOAN
     Crichton, K.   Action!   Colliers 102:11 O 22 '38
     Hamilton, S.   Lady clown.   Photop 53-4:25 My '39
     Biography.   Cur Bio Je '45
     Radio comedienne.   Life 19:93 O 1 '45
     Co-op Joan.   Newsweek 30:58 O 20 '47
     Lucy's TV sister.   Newsweek 40:63 N 3 '52
     Joan Davis.   TV Guide 6-2:6 Ja 9 '53
     Gould, J.   TV's top comediennes.   N. Y. Times Mag
        p17 D 27 '53
     Crazy mixed-up kid.   TV Guide 2-27:15 Jl 2 '54
     Ardmore, J. K.   I'll never quit now.   Woman H C 81:
        14 N '54
     Wood, C.   TV personalities biographical sketchbook.
        TV Personalities p150 '54
     Jordan, D.   Joan Davis, inc. filmog.   Films In Review
        12-9:574 N '61
     Obit.   Illus Lond N 238:941 Je 3 '61
        Newsweek 57:64 Je 5 '61
        Time 77:86 Je 2 '61
        Am Ann 1962:850 '62
        Cur Bio 22:23 S '61
        Cur Bio Yrbk 1961:128 '62
        Screen World 13:221 '62

DAVIS, NANCY
     Silver-spooned starlet.   Am Mag 150:58 Ag '50
     California's stylish first lady, size 6.   Life 62:55 My 19
        '67
     Harney, S.   Are you ready to be seen?   Ladies Home J.
        84:34 Ag '67
     Gordon, S.   California's leading lady.   Look 31:37 O 31
        '67
     Harris, E.   What is Nancy Reagan really, really like?
        Look 31:40 O 31 '67
     Didion, J.   Pretty Nancy.   Sat Eve Post 241:20 Je 1 '68

DAVIS, OSSIE
     Mr. and Mrs. Broadway.   Ebony 16:111 F '61
     Suddenly Ossie and Ruby are everywhere.   Life 55:110
        D 6 '63
     English language is my enemy!   Negro Hist Bul 30:18 Ap
        '67

DAVIS, SAMMY JR.
     Nice fellow.   Time 65:65 Ap 18 '55
     Seeman, B.   Starring Sammy Davis Jr.   Coronet 39:87

D '55

Biography. Cur Bio 17:38 S '56
   Same. Cur Bio Yrbk 1956:144 '57

Wolfe, M. F. Mr. Wonderful with a 35. Pop Phot 41:
   89 Ag '57

Duncan, D. Name dropper. Dance Mag 33:21 Ag '59

Jewish Negro. Time 75:38 F 1 '60

Martin, P. I call on Sammy Davis Jr. Sat Eve Post
   232:44 My 21 '60

Wedding day for Sammy and May. Life 49:117 N 28 '60

Britt, M. Why I married Sammy Davis Jr. Ebony 16:
   97 Ja '61

Corbin, J. My baby belongs to the world. Photop 60-
   4:40 O '61

For the queen and commoners. Ebony 17:30 Ja '62

Somers, A. No one can take them from me. Photop 61-
   3:39 Mr '62

Corbin, J. Command performance. Photop 61-6:46 Je
   '62

Robbins, F. Why we're adopting a baby. Photop 62-2:
   56 Ag '62

Dark side of the masque. Time 80:56 Ag 24 '62

Somers, A. We'll have a dozen babies. Photop 62-4:27
   O '62

Robbins, F. Children of a mixed marriage. Photop 63-
   3:29 Mr '63

Carpozi, G. Jr. How Sammy changed me. Photop 63-5:
   39 My '63

Camber, G. How May changed me. Photop 64-1:68 Jl
   '63

Hoffman, J. Two negroes fight for integration. Photop
   64-4:58 O '63

What Sammy Davis can tell them. Photop 65-3:37 Mr '64

Smith, J. A. Why is mommy white? Photop 4:33
   Ap '64

Lyle, J. Their friendship with Sammy and May. Photop
   66-4:43 O '64

Thompson, T. Five month ordeal with a whole career at
   stake. Life 57:92 N 13 '64

Davis, S. I'm glad my son's so happy. Photop 66-5:44
   N '64

Home life of May Britt and Golden Boy. Ebony 20:137 D
   '64

Armbrister, T. Don't call him junior anymore. Sat Eve
   Post 238:89 F 13 '65

Goode, B. How I was led back to God. Photop 68-1:
   33 Jl '65

I gotta get bigger. Newsweek 66:80 Ag 9 '65
Davis, S. Jr. Yes I can, excerpt. Harper 231:87 Ag '65
Davis, S. Jr. Yes I can, excerpt. Ladies H J 82: 77
   Ag '65
Man of many selves. Time 86:92 N 5 '65
Thompson, T. Sammy could and did. Life 59:21 N 5 '65
Davis, S. Jr. Yes I can, excerpt. Ebony 21:151 D '65
Make Sammy shuffle? Sat R 49:22 F 5 '66
Sammy Davis Jr., busiest man in show business. Ebony
   21:165 Ap '66
Shayon, R. L. Yes he can. Sat R 49:38 My 21 '66
Ebert, A. What do you hear, baby? TV Guide 14-28:4
   Jl 9; 14-29:22 Jl 16 '66
Is my mixed marriage mixing up my kids? Ebony 21:124
   O '66
Newsmakers. Newsweek 70:52 D 4 '67
Camber, G. What he did to May. Photop 73-2:39 F '68
Does my son have cancer? Photop 73-3:52 Mr '68
Kerr, D. May to wed white man. Photop 73-4:42 Ap '68
O'Brien, F. New color-blind couple. Photop 76-2:56 Ag
   '69

DAW, MARJORIE
   Peltret, E. She's in the "waities." Photop 14-2:45 Jl
      '18
   Merritt, P. Creed of the ingenue. Everybodys 42:53 Je
      '20

DAWN, HAZEL
   Roseate Dawn. Cosmop 55:694 O '13
   Mason, E. W. Mrs. The Dawn on the cover. Photop
      10-5:84 O '16
   Dawn of a bright era. Theatre Arts 43:29 S '59
   Setting the record straight. Theatre Arts 43:94 O '59
   What are they doing now? Show 2-3:96 Mr '62

DAWN, MARPESSA
   America's Dawn comes up in France. Life 48:57 Mr 14
      '60
   Girl on the go in Paris. Ebony 20:100 My '65

DAY, DENNIS
   Day out, Day in. Newsweek 27:62 Mr 25 '46
   Gilrain, E. Join the Dennis Days for a barbecue. Bet
      Hom & Gard 32:89 S '54
   Wood, C. TV personalities biographical sketchbook.
      TV Personalities p97 '54

Liston, J.   Dennis Days do a kid-proof remodeling.
Am Home 65:12 O '62

DAY, DORIS
Doris crashes through.   Am Mag 147:113 My '49
Swanson, P.   Oh, what a lovely Day.   Photop 36-2:46
Jl '49
Barnett, H. & Barnett, A.   She's a real warm Day.
Colliers 125:16 Ja 7 '50
Howe, H.   Happy Day.   Photop 37-6:60 Je '50
Day, A.   For sentimental reasons.   Photop 40-2:36 Jl '51
Zeitlin, I.   No blue notes.   Photop 41-2:42 F '52
Waterbury, R.   Life is for living.   Photop 41-3:42 Mr
'52
Wheeler, L.   Sunny side up.   Photop 41-4:54 Ap '52
All eyes on Doris Day.   Colliers 130:10 Ag 9 '52
Swanson, P.   It's a big wide wonderful world.   Photop
42-3:48 S '52
Goodwin, M.   And along came Dodo.   Photop 43-2:42 F
'53
Day, D.   Be happy, you're lucky.   Photop 44-2:34 Ag '53
Parsons, L. O.   It's a great Day.   Cosmop 136:6 Ja '54
Help Doris Day get well.   Photop 45-2:34 F '54
Biography.   Cur Bio 15:24 Ap '54
Same.   Cur Bio Yrbk 1954:225 '54
Day, D.   I'm well again.   Photop 45-5:46 My '54
Lucky me.   Photop 46-1:56 Jl '54
Maynard, J.   Wake up and live!   Photop 46-3:44 S '54
Steele, J. H.   All the things she is.   Photop 46-6:64 D
'54
Jacobi, E.   If you like what you love you're in luck.
Photop 47-2:49 F '55
Hall, G.   Some wives have secrets.   Photop 47-5:46 My
'55
Roberts, W.   Atom blonde.   Photop 47-6:39 Je '55
Oppenheimer, P.   Having a memorable time.   Photop 48-
2:69 Ag '55
Connolly, M.   Impertinent interview.   Photop 48-4:4 O '55
Shipp, C.   Hollywood's girl next door.   Cosmop 140:58
Ap '56
Ott, B.   Whistle bait.   Photop 49-5:48 My '56
Alpert, H.   Enough.   Enough.   Sat R 39:29 N 17 '56
Scullin, G.   Escape to happiness.   Photop 51-4:68 Ap;
51-5:58 My; 51-6:68 Je '57
Whitcomb, J.   Man with a big voice.   Cosmop 143:16 S
'57
Don't believe everything they're saying about me.   Photop

54-4:38 O '58

This is the co-star. Newsweek 55:121 Ap 11 '60

Newman, E. If I were 17 again. Photop 57-5:66 My '60

Mrs. Preston, I am going to kill you. Life 49:136A O
10 '60

Davidson, B. Doris Day. Look 25:36 Je 20 '61

Day, D. What I want most for Christmas. Photop 59-1:
30 Ja '61

Frank, L. A preview of spring. Photop 61-5:42 My '62

Capp, A. The Day dream. Show 2-12:72 D '62

Doris Day's divorce. Photop 63-1:4 Ja '63

Kahn, R. Is there a Doris Day? Ladies Home J 80:62
Jl '63

Tomato on top is Doris. Life 55:105 S 27 '63

Melcher, T. Doris Day I know. Good H 157:88 O '63

In the Garden of Eden with Doris Day. Look 27:138 D
17 '63

Johnson, M. Is she giving up her religion? Photop 65-
5:48 My '64

Sanders, A. Her life with Granny Clampett. Photop 66-
1:42 Jl '64

Doris Day cuts up. Good H 161:72 O '65

Bell, J. N. Hollywood interview; canonizing the super-
ficial. Sat R 49:115 O 8 '66

How to stay young. Ladies Home J 84:72 My '67

Ardmore, J. She rides by day, hides by night. Photop
73-1:53 Ja '68

Ardmore, J. If my son's a hippie, so am I. Photop 73-
6:36 Je '68

Bascombe, L. Last words to her husband. Photop 74-1:
47 Jl '68

Rollin, B. Doris Day: Miss Apple Pie hits TV. Look
32:54 N 26 '68

Whitney, D. All sugar, no spice. TV Guide 16-52:18
D 28 '68

Fleming, A. I want wolf whistles. Photop 75-1:27 Ja
'69

The three times she loved. Photop 76-2:62 Ag '69

Julie, E. Her midnight tears. Photop 76-5:50 N '69

Wasserman, J. L. I don't even like apple pie. TV
Guide 17-49:30 D 6 '69

DAY, LARAINE

Starlet Laraine Day clicks in her first important film role.
Life 8:54 Mr 25 '40

Amateur. Am Mag 131:82 Ap '41

Crichton, K. Great Day. Colliers 107:14 Je 7 '41

Day, L.   Don't be ashamed to pray.   Photop 23-3:32 Ag
'43

Harris, E.   If you were Laraine Day's house guest.
Photop 24-6:50 My '44

Case of Leo and Laraine.   Life 22:37 F 3 '47

Don't you want me to be happy.   Time 49:22 F 3 '47

Parsons, L. O.   I'd marry him all over again.   Photop
31-3:32 Ag '47

Day, L.   The care and feeding of a baseball manager.
TV Guide 3-25:16 Je 24 '50

Durocher, L.   Safe at home.   TV Guide 3-35:8 S 2 '50

Day, L.   How to enjoy baseball.   TV Guide 4-22:28 Je
2 '51

Small, C.   Laraine taught Leo nice guys finish first.
Colliers 129:22 Mr 8 '52

Reynolds, Q.   He won it the hard way.   Read Digest 60:
37 Ap '52

Hutchens, J. K.   On an author.   N. Y. Trib Bk R p2
My 4 '52

Biography.   Cur Bio 14:49 S '53
Same.   Cur Bio Yrbk 1953:150 '53

Laraine Day: the umpire Leo married.   Look 19:55 Ag
9 '55

DEACON, RICHARD
This face is worth a fortune.   TV Guide 17-6:15 F 8 '69

DEAN, JAMES
Ringgold, G.   James Dean, inc. filmog.   Screen Facts
8:1 n. d.

I predict these will be the bright new stars of 1955.
Look 19:17 Ja 11 '55

Next successes.   Vogue 125:170 F 1 '55

Moody new star.   Life 38:125 Mr 7 '55

Parsons, L. O.   James Dean--new face with future.
Cosmop 138:44 Mr '55

Skolsky, S.   Demon Dean.   Photop 48-1:38 Jl '55

Hopper, H.   Young men of Hollywood.   Coronet 38:56 Jl
'55

Obit.   Am Ann 1956:201 '56
Colliers Yrbk 1957:693 '57
Newsweek 46:76 O 10 '55
Time 66:114 O 10 '55
Screen World 7:223 '56

Roth, S. H.   Late James Dean.   Colliers 136:62 N 25 '55

Wood, N.   You haven't heard the half about Jimmy.
Photop 48-5:55 N '55

Hunt, E. H.   To James Dean.   Photop 49-1:50 Ja '56

Dean, E. W.   James Dean--the boy I loved.   Photop
49-3:57 Mr '56

Star that won't dim.   Newsweek 47:122 Je 18 '56

Dean of the one-shotters.   Time 68:54 S 3 '56

Goodman, E.   Delirium over dead star.   Life 41:75 S
24 '56

Bast, W.   There was a boy.   Photop 50-3:39 S; 50-4:48
O; 50-5:52 N '56

Alpert, H.   It's Dean, Dean, Dean.   Sat R 39:28 O 13
'56

Scullin, G.   James Dean; the legend and the facts.
Look 20:121 O 16 '56

Honor, E.   Hollywood tragedies.   Cosmop 141:38 O '56

Dean cult.   Time 68:63 N 26 '56

Mitgang, H.   Strange James Dean death cult.   Coronet
41:111 N '56

Weales, G.   Movies: the crazy, mixed-up kids take
over.   Reporter 15:40 D 13 '56

Cole, C.   The Dean myth.   Films & Filming 3-4:17 Ja
'57

Astrachan, S.   New lost generation.   New Repub 136:22
F 18 '57

Knight, A.   Celluloid monument.   Sat R 40:20 Ag 3 '57

Sheridan, E.   In memory of Jimmy.   Photop 52-4:70 O
'57

Wood, C.   TV personalities biographical sketchbook.
TV Personalities p133 '57

Tanner, L.   Best years of their lives.   Coronet 47:92
Mr '60

Roth, S. H.   Assignment I'll never forget: James Dean.
Pop Phot 51:71 Jl '62

Winters, S.   Loneliest years of my life.   Seventeen 21:
148 S '62

Meltsir, A.   Life after death.   Photop 64-3:40 S '63

Bean, R.   Dean--ten years after.   Films & Filming 12-
1:12 O '65

DEAN, JULIE
Woodward, H. B.   Those famous girls.   Mlle 42:60 Ja '56

DEAN, PRISCILLA
St. Johns, A. R.   Priscilla pins her hair back.   Photop
16-5:32 O '19

Winship, M.   Oh, why did they name you Priscilla?
Photop 25-4:71 Mr '24

DE CAMP, ROSEMARY

Zeitlin, I.   The girl with a hundred faces.   Photop 20-4:
38 Mr '42

Wood, C.   TV personalities biographical sketchbook.
TV Personalities p145 '56

Hobson, D.   She worked with Orson Wells when he was
thin.   TV Guide 17-27:32 Jl 5 '69

DE CARLO, YVONNE

Sheridan, M.   Salome on rye.   Colliers 115:56 My 5 '45

Deere, D.   Yvonne, where she danced.   Photop 28-4:46
Mr '46

Fisher, G.   Yippee Yvonne.   Photop 29-1:62 Je '46

Eaton, H.   Blue jeans and mink.   Photop 30-2:35 Ja '47

St. Johns, E.   Dusky dreamer.   Photop 33-4:62 S '48

One man's mambo.   Colliers 131:68 Je 13 '53

Eisenberg, H.   Life can be beautiful.   Photop 51-5:52
My '57

Durslag, M.   The prince of Iran was wild about her.
TV Guide 13-1:22 Ja 2 '65

DE CORDOBA, PEDRO

Lavery, E.   Pedro De Cordoba.   Cath World 172:111 N
'50

Wyatt, E. V.   Theatre.   Cath World 172:147 N '50

DeCORDOVA, ARTURO

Eaton, H.   The man with two countries.   Photop 27-3:55
Ag '45

Wilkinson, L.   Man from Mexico.   Photop 28-6:66 My '46

DEE, FRANCES

Biery, R.   She talked too much.   Photop 41-4:57 Mr '32

Wilkinson, L. A.   What makes love tick?   Photop 52-12:
28 D '38

Dudley, F.   McCrea Inc.   Photop 25-2:52 Jl '44

We and our boys live country style; ed. by J. Morris.
Parents Mag 25:40 Ap '50

DEE, RUBY

Mr. and Mrs. Broadway.   Ebony 16:111 F '61

Suddenly Ossie and Ruby are everywhere.   Life 55:110
D 6 '63

Coleman, E.   Gags and good intentions can't tame a
shrew.   Life 59:13 Jl 23 '65

DEE, SANDRA

Dee, S. Fear: it can be lonely. Photop 53-5:54 My '58
Borie, M. My first real date. Photop 54-3:31 S '58
Borie, M. Why Johnny doesn't go for Sandra. Photop
    54-5:59 N '58
Dee, S. I've got the mumps. Photop 55-4:42 Ap '59
Bringing up mother. Coronet 45:89 My '59
I giggle. Newsweek 53:104 Je 8 '59
Nobody ever carries my books to school. Photop 55-6:
    60 Je '59
Borie, M. Is she really going Kookie? Photop 56-3:34
    S '59
Borie, M. You'll never guess. Photop 56-4:50 O '59
Rosenka, A. Why don't you tell the truth about your
    father. Photop 56-6:38 D '59
Anderson, N. Strictly personal. Photop 57-4:32 Ap '60
Johnson, M. I told a real whopper. Photop 58-1:38 Jl '60
If I were Lana Turner . . . Photop 58-6:24 D '60
Johnson, M. Uncensored! Sandra Dee elopes with Bobby
    Darin. Photop 59-2:58 F '61
Siegel, M. Runaway honeymoon. Photop 59-3:26 Mr '61
Hamilton, S. Her mother's side of the story. Photop
    59-4:29 Ap '61
Borie, M. At last--Sandra breaks the silence. Photop
    59-5:34 My '61
Corbin, J. Waiting for baby. Photop 60-2:34 Ag '61
Waterbury, R. The dangers awaiting their baby. Photop
    60-3:34 S '61
Rand, F. What if it's a girl? Photop 60-4:33 O '61
Wilder, G. A '62 Dodd for the Darins. Photop 61-3:6
    Mr '62
Robbins, F. I'm afraid to show my baby. Photop 63-2:
    67 F '63
Jennings, C. R. Odd Odyssey of Sandra Dee. Sat Eve
    Post 236:22 Je 22 '63
York, C. Why she walked out on Bobby. Photop 63-6:
    16 Je '63
Ardmore, J. I'm in a state of shock. Photop 64-2:46
    Ag '63
Can they live together? Photop 64-5:52 N '63
Artell, T. A chip off the old block. Photop 69-5:64
    My '66

DE FORE, DON

Bowers, L. Dapper Don. Photop 29-5:70 O '46
Waterbury, R. Star in your home. Photop 34-5:54 Ap
    '49

Wood, C. TV personalities biographical sketchbook.
TV Personalities p100 '56
Roughest job in television. TV Guide 10-40:15 O 6 '62

DE GRASSE, SAM
Obit. Screen World 5:208 '54

DeHAVEN, GLORIA
Waterbury, R. Glorious DeHaven. Photop 25-6:54 N '44
Waterbury, R. The difference is you. Photop 26-4:32
Mr '45
Perkins, L. Photolife of Gloria DeHaven. Photop 27-4:
54 S '45
Sharpe, H. Triangle. Photop 28-5:58 Ap '46
Higgins, R. Growing up the hard way. TV Guide 14-26:
Je 25 '66
Oderman, S. Gloria DeHaven. Film Fan Mo 92:3 F '69
Maltin, L. Film Fan Monthly interviews Gloria DeHaven,
inc. filmog. Film Fan Mo 92:7 F '69

DE HAVILLAND, OLIVIA
Reeve, W. She's one in a million. Photop 49-2:51 F
'36
Armstrong, G. School's out. Colliers 99:24 F 6 '37
Beatty, J. Dreams do come true. Am Mag 124:34 S '37
Spensley, D. Victorian . . . with variations. Photop
52-9:26 S '38
Hartley, K. Play truth or consequences with Olivia De
Havilland. Photop 53-9:24 S '39
Zeitlin, I. How Olivia sees her sister's romance.
Photop 53-11:27 N '39
Morse, W. Jr. We have a wonderful time together.
Photop 54-4:64 Ap '40
Haynes, H. Should love wait? Photop 18-4:34 Mr '41
Fletcher, A. W. Sister act. Photop 19-4:42 S '41
Zarat, I. I feel like a heel. Photop 20-2:26 Ja '42
Jensen, O. O. Sister act. Life 12:88 My 4 '42
Hamilton, S. Olivia DeHavilland on the spot. Photop
22-3:40 F '43
Burton, J. New love for Livvie. Photop 23-2:34 Jl '43
Skolsky, S. Loose-leaf on Livvie DeHavilland. Photop
23-4:50 S '43
Harris, E. If you were Olivia DeHavilland's house guest.
Photop 24-4:56 Mr '44
Biography. Cur Bio '44
Waterbury, R. Olivia DeHavilland hit her stride.
Photop 29-4:52 S '46

Ormiston, R. Yankee bride. Photop 29-6:74 N '46
Shearer, L. Recipe for a movie star. N. Y. Times Mag
  p17 Mr 30 '47
Parsons, L. O. Enter Marcus. Photop 30-4:36 Mr '47
Howe, H. How dreamy can you get. Photop 30-6:62
  My '47
We made our closet to fit. Womans H C 75:74 N '48
Shocker. Time 52:44 D 20 '48
Maxwell, E. Lady of distinction. Photop 34-6:52 My '49
Two-time winner. Life 28:33 Ap 3 '50
Poling, J. Olivia's world is the stage. Colliers 127:14
  Ja 13 '51
Nathan, G. J. Wherefore art thou Candida? Theatre
  Arts 36:18 Je '52
Brown, H. Breakup! Photop 42-2:35 Ag '52
Connolly, M. New lease on love. Photop 43-4:68 Ap '53
Kramer, S. Into surgery for: Not as a stranger.
  Colliers 135:78 F 4 '55
New Olivia DeHavilland says what she thinks. Newsweek
  50:112 N 4 '57
Hubler, R. G. Olivia--the bellicose belle. Coronet 44:
  95 Jl '58
DeHavilland, O. Best advice I ever had. Read Digest
  76:122 Mr '60
Biography. NCAB curI:351 '60
DeHavilland, O. Where am I? I'm in France, that's
  where! McCalls 88:54 Ag '61
Ardmore, J. Gone with the wind--fate broke its promises.
  Photop 60-2:29 Ag '61
Doyle, N. Olivia DeHavilland, inc. filmog. Films In
  Review 13-2:71 F '62
Look who wrote a book. Life 52:55 Je 1 '62
DeHavilland, O. Come out fighting. Films & Filming
  12-6:19 Mr '66
Biography. Cur Bio 27:12 N '66
  Same. Cur Bio Yrbk 1966:74 '67
Where are they now? Newsweek 69:20 Ap 10 '67
Dream that never died. Look 31:113 D 12 '67

DEKKER, ALBERT
  Obit. Newsweek 71:73 My 20 '68
    Time 91:86 My 17 '68
    Screen World 20:233 '69

deLACY, PHILIPPE
  Don, V. J. The war orphan. Photop 34-2:40 Jl '28

de la MOTTE, MARGUERITE
  Winship, M. Out of Arabian nights. Photop 21-5:40 Ap
    '22
  Obit. Time 55:91 Mr 20 '50

DELON, ALAIN
  Person of promise. Films & Filming 5-8:12 My '59
  Alain Delon. Life 56:75 F 24 '64
  Biography. Cur Bio 25:9 Ap '64
    Cur Bio Yrbk 1964:106 '64
  Bean, R. Reaching for the world. Films & Filming 11-
    5:9 F '65
  Tornabene, L. Tomorrow's stars. Good H 160:26 Mr
    '65

DEL RIO, DOLORES
  Albert, K. Dolores vs. the jinx. Photop 40-3:69 Ag '31
  Lieber, E. What price stardom? Photop 42-4:57 S '32
  Biery, R. How many lives has Dolores Del Rio? Photop
    44-5:60 O '33
  Franklin, K. Dolores extols passive love. Photop 45-
    5:39 Ap '34
  Hunt, J. L. The beauty who sits alone. Photop 47-1:
    34 D '34
  Return of Dolores. Newsweek 51:53 Ap 28 '58
  Bodeen, D. Dolores Del Rio, inc. filmog. Films In
    Review 18-5:266 My '67
  Gomez-Sicre, J. Dolores Del Rio; excerpts. Americas
    19:8 N '67

DEMAREST, WILLIAM
  Muir, F. Sourpuss Bill. Sat Eve Post 218:17 F 23 '46
  Raddatz, L. Little Willie Demarest--65 years later.
    TV Guide 14-29:16 Jl 16 '66

DEMONGEOT, MYLENE
  Person of promise. Films & Filming 4-1:31 O '57
  Whitcomb, J. Bonjour tristesse on location. Cosmop
    144:76 Mr '58

DEMPSTER, CAROL
  Robbins, E. M. The two strange women. Photop 14-3:
    86 Ag '19
  Evans, D. Griffith's newest heroine. Photop 21-3:31 F
    '22
  Herzog, D. The mystery girl of pictures. Photop 28-2:
    54 Jl '25

Biery, R. I don't care if I never make another picture.
  Photop 34-3:55 Ag '28

DENEUVE, CATHERINE
  Harris, G. T. Sister stars of France. Look 29:90 Je
    1 '65
  Catherine of France. Esquire 65:143 Ap '66
  Catherine Deneuve. Life 66:32 Ja 24 '69
  Belle de jour. Time 91:106 Ap 26 '68
  Ehrlich, H. Catherine Deneuve. Look 32:62 Ap 30 '68
  Deneuve: making it in America. Newsweek 72:42 Ag 26
    '68

DENNING, RICHARD
  Wood, C. TV personalities biographical sketchbook.
    TV Personalities p106 '54
  Too good to be true. TV Guide 9-16:24 Ap 22 '61
  Raddatz, L. A beachcomber goes to work. TV Guide
    17-20:24 My 17 '69

DENNIS, SANDY
  Two in the center. Time 83:64 Mr 6 '64
  Any Wednesday's Sandy. Look 28:101 Je 16 '64
  Kerr, W. Love letters of a tough critic. Life 56:113
    Je 19 '64
  Hoban, R. New ingenue. Holiday 37:131 Mr '65
  Miller, E. Anyone you know? Seventeen 26:118 Je '67
  Talent without tinsel. Time 90:54 S 1 '67
  Hurwitz, H. L. High school principal looks Up the down
    staircase. Sr Schol 91:sup 16 O 5 '67
  Warga, W. Girl with a good grip on chaos. Life 64:65
    F 9 '68
  Biography. Cur Bio 30:3 Ja '69

DENNY, REGINALD
  Spensley, D. The fall guy. Photop 30-1:35 Je '26
  Ogden, E. Discovered--Reginald Denny! Photop 38-1:43
    Je '30
  Reggie's robot. Am Mag 147:96 F '49
  Ex-super. New Yorker 34:20 Je 28 '58
  Obit. Time 89:69 Je 30 '67
    Brit Bk Yr 1968:588 '68
    Screen World 19:231 '68

DEREK, JOHN
  Bogart, H. Listen to me, kid. Photop 36-4:34 S '49
  Waterbury, R. The kid who never cried. Photop 36-7:

40 D '49

Zeitlin, I.   Now it can be told.   Photop 38-4:32 O '50

Perkins, L.   Photolife of John Derek.   Photop 40-1:50
Jl '51

Derek, P.   The quiet one.   Photop 42-2:48 Ag '52

Armstrong, G.   Is Hollywood destroying John Derek?
Photop 43-4:48 Ap '53

Derek, J.   I have a terrible time.   Photop 44-2:56 Ag
'53

Tusher, B.   Everything's jake for Johnny.   Photop 44-6:
50 D '53

Waterbury, R.   The triumphant years.   Photop 45-5:64
My '54

Downing, H.   Miracle at the crossroads.   Photop 46-4:
68 O '54

Arnold, M.   The big gamble.   Photop 47-4:65 Ap '55

Phillips, D.   You need love in your life.   Photop 41-2:
46 Ag '55

Scott, D.   The truth behind John Derek's bust-up.
Photop 48-6:45 D '55

Downing, H.   When does a husband think divorce is justi-
fied?   Photop 50-4:72 O '56

Hamilton, J.   Ursula Andress of Dr. No: beauty finds
its way.   Look 26:72 D 31 '62

Ursula major.   Newsweek 64:79B Jl 20 '64

DE RITA, JOE
(See: THREE STOOGES)

DE ROCHE, CHARLES
St. Johns, A. R.   Mister Charles De Roche.   Photop
24-6:51 N '23

DESMOND, WILLIAM
St. Johns, A. R.   Here comes the groom!   Photop 16-4:
36 S '19

St. Johns, A. R.   An interview with a baby.   Photop 18-
4:31 S '20

DEVINE, ANDY
Rankin, R.   200 pounds of Irishman.   Photop 43-5:43
Ap '33

Wild Bill Hickok's pardner.   TV Guide 1-22:A12 Ag 28
'53

Hi ya, Bill!   TV Guide 5-18:17 My 4 '57

Wood, C.   TV personalities biographical sketchbook.
TV Personalities p59 '56

deWILDE, BRANDON
  Tot in buskin. New Yorker 25:20 Ja 28 '50
  Funke, L. Acting is child's play. N. Y. Times Mag p24
    Mr 2 '52
  Berger, M. Double life of Brandon deWilde. N. Y.
    Times Mag p19 My 24 '53
  Long, J. Have you a little whiz-kid in your home?
    Am Mag 157:22 Ja '54
  Jamie on TV. TV Guide 2-6:17 F 5 '54
  Struggle with a boy. Sat Eve Post 226:192 My 22 '54
  Zolotow, M. Star who'd rather play marbles. Sat Eve
    Post 226:44 My 22 '54
  Nice kids in tale of trouble. Life 47:69 Ag 24 '59
  Christy, G. First love is . . . Photop 56-4:34 O '59
  Johnson, A. What girls don't understand about boys and
    vice versa. Photop 56-6:44 D '59
  Miller, E. Say hello to Brandon deWilde. Seventeen
    21:148 My '62

DE WOLFE, BILLY
  Whitcomb, J. Backstage at the birth of a hit. Cosmop
    136:58 Mr '54

DEXTER, ANTHONY
  Waterbury, R. Double life. Photop 40-3:56 S '51
  Campbell, K. Look out Tony Dexter. Photop 41-2:44
    F '52

DICKINSON, ANGIE
  Season for an actress. TV Guide 4-26:5 Je 30 '56
  Movie discoverer's latest find. Life 45:163 N 17 '58
  Person of promise. Films & Filming 6-2:17 N '59

DICKSON, GLORIA
  Girl of the month. Good H 105:38 Ag '37

DIETRICH, MARLENE
  Albert, K. She threatens Garbo's throne. Photop 39-1:
    60 D '30
  Hall, L. Garbo vs. Dietrich. Photop 39-3:50 F '31
  Condon, F. Greta and Marlene. Sat Eve Post 203:29
    My 30 '31
  Hall, L. The perils of Marlene. Photop 39-6:37 My '31
  Lowe, C. Marlene Dietrich in person. Pict R 32:4 Ag
    '31
  Biery, R. She's not a parrot. Photop 40-5:67 O '31
  Evans, K. Will Marlene break the spell? Photop 41-3:

76 F '32

Potter, M.   Marlene Dietrich.   Cinema Digest 1-13:14
    O 31 '32

Biery, R.   Is Dietrich through?   Photop 43-2:28 Ja '33

Biery, R.   Marlene is free at last.   Photop 44-2:31 Jl
    '33

Shawell, J.   Garbo or Dietrich?   Pict R 34:16 Jl '33

Baker, K.   War clouds in the West?   Photop 45-1:47 D
    '33

Lang, J.   The revolt against Dietrich.   Photop 46-4:28
    S '34

Reeve, W.   What is Dietrich's destiny?   Photop 48-2:29
    Jl '35

Green, C.   For the first and last time Dietrich talks.
    Photop 48-7:42 D '35

Biographical sketch.   Time 28:40 N 30 '36

Marlene Dietrich breaks ankle saving Baby X in studio
    fall.   Life 11:38 S 8 '41

French, W. F.   What Hollywood thinks about Marlene
    Dietrich.   Photop 20-5:48 Ap '42

Gilded Dietrich.   Life 15:119 N 29 '43

Dietrich returns.   N. Y. Times Mag p36 S 22 '46

Blue angel returns.   N. Y. Times Mag p30 Je 13 '48

Steals the show.   Life 25:59 Ag 9 '48

Knuath, P.   Grandmother, Dietrich.   Life 25:64 Ag 9 '48

Glamorous grandmothers.   Coronet 29:122 F '51

Robinson, S.   I couldn't compete with my mother.
    Ladies Home J 68:54 O '51

Still champion.   Time 59:40 Ja 21 '52

George, M.   Marlene Dietrich's beginning.   Films In
    Review 3-2:77 F '52

Weinberg, H. G.   Weinberg on Dietrich.   Films In Re-
    view 3-3:141 Mr '52

Marvelous Marlene.   Coronet 32:101 My '52

Weltschmerz.   Time 60:64 Ag 4 '52

Hemingway, E.   Tribute to mamma from papa.   Life 33:
    92 Ag 18 '52

Sargeant, W.   Dietrich and her magic myth.   Life 33:
    86 Ag 18 '52

Marlene's joint; recording of Cafe Istanbul.   New Yorker
    28:33 N 29 '52

Sargeant, W.   Durable Dietrich.   Read Digest 61:65 D
    '52

Biography.   Cur Bio 14:24 Ja '53
    Same.   Cur Bio Yrbk 1953:158 '53

Marlene Dietrich as the ringmaster.   Vogue 121:44 My
    15 '53

Weinberg, H. G.   Has Von Sternberg discovered a Japanese Dietrich?   Theatre Arts 37:26 Ag '53

Schiller, R.   Miraculous Marlene.   Womans H C 80:36 Jl; 40 Ag '53

Lyons, S. R.   Her mother's daughter.   Good H 137:57 O '53

Fusses over ladies and a ladies' man.   Life 36:24 Ja 11 '54

How to be loved.   Ladies Home J 71:36 Ja '54

O'Hara, J.   Appointment with O'Hara.   Colliers 133:6 Mr 19 '54

Dietrich--the body and the soul.   Colliers 133:25 My 14 '54

How to be loved; abridged.   Read Digest 65:28 Jl '54

Knight, A.   Marlene Dietrich; notes on a living legend.   Films In Review 5-10:497 D '54

Magic lingers.   Time 65:46 Ap 4 '55

Mr. Harper.   After hours; the kraut woman.   Harper 210: 82 My '55

People.   Time 66:37 Jl 18 '55

James, T. F.   Picture album of beautiful women in America.   Cosmop 140:29 Je '56

Lane, J. F.   Give her dirt--and hard work.   Films & Filming 3-3:13 D '56

Danger of being beautiful.   McCalls 84:52 Mr '57

My favorite Christmas present.   McCalls 85:8 D '57

What Dietrich will do.   Newsweek 52:52 S 1 '58

Kaplan, R.   Marlene; the bewitching grandmother.   Coronet 47:99 D '59

Davidson, B.   Dietrich legend.   McCalls 87:70 Mr '60

Blue angel's return.   Newsweek 55:86 My 2 '60

Suitcase in Berlin.   Newsweek 55:80 My 16 '60

Germans welcome Marlene home.   Life 48:103 My 23 '60

Are you keeping your man happy?   Photop 58-5:44 N '60

Marlene Dietrich: a picture history.   Look 25:56 O 24 '61

Marlene Dietrich's ABCs; condensation.   Look 25:42 O 24 '61

Whitehall, R.   The blue angel.   Films & Filming 9-1:18 O '62

Two old pros.   Time 83:44 My 29 '64

Marlene Dietrich.   Plays & Players 12-3:7 D '64

Higham, C.   Dietrich in Sydney.   Sight & Sound 34:23 Win '65

Higham, C.   Marlene today.   Films In Review 16-10:652 D '65

Old gal in town.   Time 90:84 O 20 '67

Kroll, J.   The kraut.   Newsweek 70:113 O 23 '67.
Biography.   Cur Bio 29:10 F '68
Lady doth protest.   Newsweek 72:58 S 16 '68
Davis, J. K.   Marlene: the magic of a precise pro.
   Life 65:6 N 8 '68
Biography.   Cur Bio Yrbk 1968:112 '69

DILLER, PHYLLIS
   Going muu muu; or, trapeze trauma.   N. Y. Times Mag
      p14 Je 22 '58
   Killer Diller.   Time 77:56 Mr 24 '61
   Haley, A.   Phyllis Diller; the unlikeliest star.   Sat Eve
      Post 235:26 Mr 31 '62
   Rubber-faced comic.   Life 54:57 My 17 '63
   Crail, I.   Mr. America; you don't have a chance.   TV
      Guide 13-23:10 Je 5 '65
   Swisher, V. H.   Funny Phyllis Diller is serious about
      ballet.   Dance Mag 40:28 Ja '66
   Reddy, J.   TV's killer Diller.   Read Digest 89:90 N '66
   Allen, W.   Serious side of Diller; intv.   Hobbies 71:124
      D '66
   Lewis, R. W.   Doris Day and Abraham Lincoln share a
      connecting bath.   TV Guide 15-8:19 F 25 '67
   Redbook dialogue.   Redbook 129:58 My '67
   Biography.   Cur Bio 28:12 Jl '67
   Same.   Cur Bio Yrbk 1967:98 '68
   Erwin, R.   Phyllis Diller begins her own comic strip.
      Ed & Pub 101:37 Ja 6 '68
   Smith, M.   How to trim a Christmas tree.   Photop 73-
      1:58 Ja '68
   What she made him shed.   Photop 74-6:32 D '68
   Resnick, S.   They drove me from church.   Photop 75-2:
      43 F '69
   Wasserman, J.   A two-time loser plans her next assault
      on TV.   TV Guide 17-13:14 Mr 29 '69

DILLMAN, BRADFORD
   Knowles, J.   Hell's kitchen to Broadway in 3 acts.
      Holiday 21:91 F '57
   Person of promise.   Films & Filming 5-3:17 D '58
   Talk with a new star.   Newsweek 53:118 Ap 13 '59
   Biography.   Cur Bio 21:14 Ja '60
   Same.   Cur Bio Yrbk 1960:114 '61

DINGLE, CHARLES
   Obit.   Newsweek 47:69 Ja 30 '56
      Time 67:88 Ja 30 '56

DIX, RICHARD
    Dix, R. Why I have never married Bebe Daniels.
        Photop 25-2:30 Ja '24
    Johaneson, B. That saving sense of humor. Photop 25-
        6:67 My '24
    Dix, R. How it feels to become a star. Photop 27-2:
        51 Ja '25
    Colling, B. Tire of "single cussedness." Photop 28-3:
        63 Ag '25
    Herzog, D. Mr. Columbus Dix. Photop 30-2:69 Jl '26
    York, C. Still the most eligible young man. Photop 30-
        4:74 S '26
    Colman, J. He was not afraid to die. Photop 34-2:31
        Jl '28
    Reilly, R. S. When Ernest sniffed grease paint the world
        lost a doctor. Am Mag 108:78 S '29
    Obit. Illus Lond N 215:503 O 1 '49
        Newsweek 34:60 O 3 '49
        Time 54:65 O 3 '49
    Biography. NCAB 37:450 '51
    Bodeen, D. Richard Dix, inc. filmog. Films In Review
        17-8:487 O '66

DODD, CLAIRE
    Schwartz, W. Claire Dodd. Films In Review 18-5:319
        My '67

DOMERGUE, FAITH
    Hollywood's new generation. Life 24:93 My 24 '48
    Faith Domergue: she follows Harlow and Russell. Life
        29:79 Jl 17 '50
    She couldn't say yes. Am Mag 150:62 S '50
    Hughes' Miss Domergue. Newsweek 37:74 Ja 8 '51
    Arnold, M. Faith--and five million dollars. Photop 39-
        3:60 Mr '51

DONAHUE, TROY
    Borie, M. Sixteen minutes after the picture was taken.
        Photop 57-2:42 F '60
    Person of promise. Films & Filming 6-7:17 Ap '60
    Barrett, R. Just building castles in the sand. Photop
        57-6:64 Je '60
    Dinter, C. Trapped. Photop 58-6:60 D '60
    Gautschy, D. Announcing his engagement. Photop 59-5:
        54 My '61
    He is so in 'Surfside 6'. TV Guide 9-33:17 Ag 19 '61
    Newcomb, E. We want Troy. Photop 60-3:54 S '61

Corbin, J. Nobody can take Troy from me. Photop 60-3:58 S '61

Miller, E. How does it look when I kiss her? Seventeen 20:150 S '61

Troy beats up Lili Kardell! Photop 60-5:58 N '61

Baskette, K. Here's my heart. Photop 60-6:30 D '61; 61-1:30 Ja '62

deRoos, R. The answer to a million dreams. TV Guide 10-8:6 F 24 '62

Lint, J. A man shouldn't wear the pants. Photop 62-2:50 Ag '62

Efron, E. The perfect couple--on screen. TV Guide 10-35:15 S 1 '62

Krantz, J. Night they invented Troy Donahue. McCalls 89:130 S '62

Woods, M. Who's imitating Rock. Photop 62-3:29 S '62

Lewis, R. W. Hollywood's new breed of soft young men. Sat Eve Post 235:74 D 1 '62

Somers, A. Love is a violent agreement. Photop 63-2:71 F '63

Somers, A. The big rumor--they're married. Photop 63-3:62 Mr '63

Ormandy, E. When we're getting married. Photop 64-4:45 O '63

Suzanne finally said "yes." Photop 65-2:38 F '64

Gregory, J. With this kiss. Photop 65-3:6 Mr '64

Miller, E. Straight from the shoulder. Seventeen 23:140 My '64

How marriage changed us. Photop 65-6:33 Je '64

Honeymoon killed by love. Photop 66-4:54 O '64

DONAT, ROBERT

Conlon, P. The world is yours, Mr. Donat. Photop 47-1:40 D '34

Boehnel, W. Don't argue with Donat. Photop 49-2:21 F '36

Pringle, H. F. No more swords. Colliers 98:16 O 17 '36

LeJeune, C. Dollars to Donat. Photop 53-8:61 Ag '39

It is by dying . . . Newsweek 52:60 Jl 21 '58

Obit. Am Ann 1959:221 '59

   Illus Lond N 232:1019 Je 14 '58

   Newsweek 51:80 Je 16 '58

   Time 71:78 Je 23 '58

   Brit Bk Yr 1959:509 '59

   Screen World 10:222 '59

DONATH, LUDWIG
  Acting in opera.   Opera N 30:6 Ap 16 '66
  Obit.   Time 90:104 O 13 '67
    Screen World 19:231 '68

DONLEVY, BRIAN
  Franchey, J. R.   Don't hitch your wagon.   Photop 20-2:
    36 Ja '42
  Harris, E.   Tell me a love story.   Photop 23-2:47 Jl
    '43
  Introduction.   Am Mag 136:52 Ag '43
  Donlevy, B.   I'm like this.   Photop 26-2:44 Ja '45
  Waterbury, R.   Star in your home.   Photop 36-1:62 Je
    '49

DONNELL, JEFF
  Deere, D.   Jeff Donnell in a jiffy.   Photop 24-5:47 Ap
    '44
  Alice is a girl named Jeff.   TV Guide 3-24:20 Je 11 '55

DORAN, ANN
  Her owls are worth more than a hoot.   TV Guide 8-48:12
    N 26 '60

DORLEAC, FRANÇOISE
  Françoise Dorleac, gamine fatale.   Vogue 144:144 O 1 '64
  Young actress tries them all on.   Life 58:54 Mr 5 '65
  Harris, T. G.   Sister stars of France.   Look 29:90 Je
    1 '65
  Miller, E.   Actress alone.   Seventeen 25:164 N '66
  Obit.   Screen World 19:231 '68

DORN, PHILIP
  Surmelian, L.   The indomitable Dutch.   Photop 22-6:51
    My '43

DORO, MARIE
  Winsome Marie Doro.   Cosmop 54:844 My '13
  Bartlett, R.   My lady o' dreams.   Photop 14-1:23 Je '18
  Blum, D.   Ten beauties of the American stage.   Theatre
    Arts 36:68 S '52
  Obit.   Screen World 8:222 '57

DORS, DIANA
  Visible export.   Time 66:116 O 10 '55
  Plimsoll line, sailors beware.   Life 39:70 D 5 '55
  DeRoulf, P.   Watch out for Dors.   Photop 51-1:34 Ja '57

Sex's scientific side.   Theatre Arts 41:14 S '57
Whitehall, R.   D. D.   Films & Filming 9-4:21 Ja '63

D'ORSAY, FIFI
 Albert, K.   She wants beeg family.   Photop 37-5:63 Ap
  '30
 What are they doing now?   Show 2-8:106 Ag '62

DOUGLAS, DONNA
 Ardmore, J.   I love my baby, but . . . Photop 65-2:50
  F '64
 Gregory, J.   I had to make up my own religion.   Photop
  66-1:56 Jl '64

DOUGLAS, KIRK
 Callahan, M.   Meet the champ.   Photop 36-3:52 Ag '49
 Swanson, P.   There was a boy.   Photop 37-5:68 My '50
 Hill, G.   Hollywood's heavy heartthrob.   Colliers 128:20
  Jl 21 '51
 Biography.   Cur Bio 13:15 Mr '52
  Same.   Cur Bio Yrbk 1952:155 '53
 Swanson, P.   For men only.   Photop 42-4:44 O '52
 Katleman, I.   Life is a B script.   Coronet 33:138 F '53
 Armstrong, G.   Is it really love.   Photop 43-3:68 Mr '53
 Gould, H.   Ready for love.   Photop 44-4:44 O '53
 Ball, E.   Kirk's island of safety.   Photop 47-2:52 F '55
 Balling, F. D.   When a star finds heaven.   Photop 47-6:
  65 Je '55
 Block, M.   For sale: one pair of traveling boots.
  Photop 48-5:59 N '55
 Roberts, W.   Inherited--a world of love.   Photop 49-4:
  54 Ap '56
 Drivin' Douglas.   Coronet 40:6 Ag '56
 Kirk Douglas as Van Gogh.   Life 41:62 O 1 '56
 Maynard, J.   What can money buy?   Photop 50-5:72 N
  '56
 Douglas, K.   Actor in me; as told to P. Martin.   Sat
  Eve Post 229:20 Je 22; 30 Jl 29 '57
 Massing the Vikings.   Newsweek 50:96 Ag 26 '57
 Whitcomb, J.   Kirk Douglas makes a violent movie.
  Cosmop 144:16 Je '58
 Dream coming true.   Newsweek 53:110 Mr 9 '59
 Dean, B.   The day he booked a seat on flight 375.
  Photop 59-1:38 Ja '61
 Douglas, K.   Using my two heads.   Films & Filming 7-
  9:10 Je '61
 Talk with a star.   Newsweek 59:87 Je 18 '62

Douglas, Mrs. K.   My awful wedded husband.   Sat Eve
   Post 235:62 N 24 '62
Fox, J. Kirk Douglas.   Can Art 20:58 Ja '63
Redbook readers talk with Kirk Douglas; intv.   Redbook
   126:72 Ap '66

DOUGLAS, MELVYN
   Sharpe, H.   Melvyn of the movies.   Photop 53-2:16 F;
      53-3:67 Mr; 53-4:67 Ap '39
   From the bill of fare.   Nation 150:625 My 18 '40
   Binyon, C.   Memo on Melvyn.   Photop 54-5:24 My '40
   Reid, S.   Is Melvyn Douglas a communist?   Photop 54-
      9:23 S '40
   Mulvey, K.   Keeping up with Hollywood.   Womans H C
      69:6 F '42
   Biography.   Cur Bio '42
   Number one movie fan.   New Repub. 114:541 Ap 15 '46
   Leonard, H.   Present and accounted for.   Sight & Sound
      15-59:86 Aut '46
   Douglas, H. G.   World I want for children.   Parents
      Mag 24:24 Mr '49
   Discovering Darrow.   New Repub 136:14 My 27 '57
   Millstein, G.   Melvyn Douglas.   Theatre Arts 44:30 Ja
      '60
   Richards, S.   A visit with Melvyn Douglas.   Theatre 2-
      6:22 Je '60
   Biography.   Am Ann 1961:223 '61

DOUGLAS, PAUL
   Phillips, W.   Week's preview.   Colliers 123:40 Ja 22 '49
   Ruark, B.   Lover with a ball bat.   Colliers 124:20 O 1
      '49
   Love that brute!   Life 27:117 O 10 '49
   Waterbury, R.   That new man!   Photop 36-5:50 O '49
   That man Douglas.   N.Y. Times Mag p40 N 6 '49
   Paul Douglas: demon to daddy.   Life 30:118 Mr 12 '51
   Douglas, P.   Take my wife.   Photop 41-2:58 F '52
   The conscientious ham.   TV Guide 6-45:28 N 8 '58
   Obit.   Am Ann 1960:852 '60
      Brit Bk Yr 1960:507 '60
      Newsweek 54:92 S 21 '59
      Time 74:100 S 21 '59
      Screen World 11:216 '60

DOVE, BILLIE
   What are they doing now?   Show 2-8:106 Ag '62
   Schwartz, W.   Filmography.   Films In Review 19-1:64 Ja '68

DOW, PEGGY
  Medicine to movies. Am Mag 149:107 Mr '50
  Her face is her fortune. Life 29:67 Ag 7 '50
  Arnold, M. Divided heart. Photop 41-2:52 F '52
  Hagen, R. Peggy Dow, inc. filmog. Films In Review
    15-8:517 O '64

DOWNS, CATHY
  Girl in a glass skirt. Life 22:142 Ap 7 '47

DRAKE, BETSY
  Roberts, W. Cinderella is a girl named Betsy Drake.
    Photop 33-6:42 N '48
  Bets on Betsy. Am Mag 146:118 N '48
  Parsons, L. O. They've got marriage on their minds.
    Photop 37-1:30 Ja '50

DRAKE, DONNA
  Crichton, K. Personality kid. Colliers 109:20 Ap 25 '42

DRAKE, TOM
  Arnold, M. Moody vagabond. Photop 26-4:58 Mr '45
  Walker, H. L. He married his first love. Photop 26-
    6:43 My '45
  Drake, T. Double talk. Photop 27-3:40 Ag '45
  Steele, J. H. Portrait of a realist. Photop 27-6:48 N
    '45
  Hamilton, S. Parting without tears. Photop 29-2:31 Jl
    '46
  Sharpe, H. Taking Tom Drake apart. Photop 29-3:48
    Ag '46
  Harris, E. Operation Drake. Photop 31-1:48 Je '47

DRESSER, LOUISE
  Tully, J. On the banks of the Wabash. Photop 27-6:43
    My '25
  Tully, J. Louise Dresser. Pict R 29:2 F '28
  Albert, K. Two true troupers. Photop 37-4:34 Mr '30
  Obit. Time 85:106 Ap 30 '65
    Screen World 17:236 '66

DRESSLER, MARIE
  Albert, K. Two true troupers. Photop 37-4:34 Mr '30
  Busby, M. Three's a crowd. Photop 38-1:77 Je '30
  Kennedy, J. B. Working girl; intv. Colliers 86:16 N 1
    '30
  Kiesling, B. C. When Hollywood cried real tears.

Photop 39-3:43 F '31

North, J.   Don't expect too much.   Photop 40-4:45 S '31

Jarvis, J.   Queen Marie of Hollywood.   Photop 41-2:32
Ja '32

Williams, M. B.   Down and up again.   Sat Eve Post 205:
28 S 10 '32

Dressler, M. as told by A. R. St. Johns.   Marie Dressler's own story.   Photop 42-4:28 S; 42-5:57 O; 42-6:
48 N '32

They stand out in a crowd.   Lit Digest 116:11 O 7 '33

Shawell, J.   Marie Dressler turns down a fortune.
Pict R 35:11 Jl '34

Great film star passes.   Lit Digest 118:8 Ag 4 '34

Marie Dressler dies, ending a brilliant comeback.
Newsweek 4:24 Ag 4 '34

For Hollywood to ponder.   Commonweal 20:358 Ag 10 '34

Packer, E.   She was the noblest lady of them all.
Photop 46-5:28 O '34

DREW, ELLEN

Sobol, L.   Mama is in the movies now.   Photop 53-1:16
Ja '39

Crichton, K.   Second chance.   Colliers 103:15 Je 17 '39

Cinderella.   Am Mag 130:83 D '40

Service, F.   Sticking pins in Cinderella.   Photop 18-5:
70 Ap '41

DRIVAS, ROBERT

Zachary, R.   I don't want to be the boy next door.
After Dark 11-4:18 Ag '69

DRU, JOANNE

Swanson, P.   Hey there, Haymes!   Photop 26-3:36 F '45

Madison, A.   Horseshoe Haymes.   Photop 27-6:60 N '45

Haymes, D.   Us.   Photop 31-1:54 Je '47

Chandler, D.   Mama has glamor.   Colliers 124:32 D 17
'49

Colby, A.   Mother is a glamour girl.   Photop 37-2:52
F '50

Waterbury, R.   Joannie and Johnnie are sweethearts.
Photop 38-5:42 N '50

But, darling, do I look pretty?   TV Guide 9-22:14 Je 3
'61

DRURY, JAMES

Whitney, D.   The Garbo of the sagebrush.   TV Guide 11-
18:18 My 4 '63

York, C. His wedding! A Photoplay exclusive. Photop
74-1:7 Jl '68
Discriminating against dames. Photop 76-6:48 D '69

DUFF, HOWARD
Sher, J. From Hut 67 to Hollywood. Photop 33-4:48
S '48
Meshikow, M. Mr. Soft Touch. Photop 36-6:50 N '49
Duff, H. That's sex, girls. Photop 37-4:50 Ap '50
Wood, C. TV personalities biographical sketchbook.
TV Personalities p 16 '57
Mr. Duff and Ida. TV Guide 5-22:17 Je 1 '57
Raddatz, L. The Howard Duff syndrome. TV Guide 15-
22:19 Je 3 '67

DUGGAN, ANDREW
Raddatz, L. The Dugan with the double 'G'. TV Guide
17-31:21 Ag 2 '69

DUKE, PATTY
Old pro at ten. Time 74:83 O 12 '59
Patty Duke . . . a small miracle. Look 23:53 N 24 '59
Balch, J. Miracle named Patty. Theatre Arts 44:28
Ja '60
Nichols, M. Star at thirteen. Coronet 48:131 Jl '60
People on the way up. Sat Eve Post 234:31 O 7 '61
We could have talked all night. Seventeen 21:44 Ja '62
Hollywood scene. Seventeen 21:10 Ja '62
Gallant lady meets herself when young. Life 52:89 Mr
23 '62
Prideaux, T. Patty and the gift of love. Life 52:93 Mr
30 '62
Star bright. Sr Schol 80:24 Ap 11 '62
Biography. Cur Bio 24:32 S '63
Same. Cur Bio Yrbk 1963:117 '64
Miss Patty Duke. TV Guide 11-52:6 D 28 '63
I believe. Seventeen 23:102 Ja '64
Gillespie, A. Double life of Patty Duke. Good H 158:
52 Ap '64
Corbin, J. Pin-up #17. Photop 65-4:56 Ap '64
Gregory, J. The man behind her wedding. Photop 66-
3:45 S '64
Applegate, E. I want my husband to marry Patty.
Photop 66-5:72 N '64
Aaaaaaaah-wow! Newsweek 66:106 O 18 '65
Rollins, B. Dames in the Valley of the dolls. Look 31:
56 S 5 '67

Reynolds, L.   In psychiatric hospital.   Photop 75-5:50
  My '69
Scott, B.   Adam West could love her.   Photop 76-1:60
  Jl '69

DULLEA, KEIR
  Haunting new face.   Life 56:115 Je 12 '64
  Miller, E.   Romantic at large.   Seventeen 24:145 N '65
  Dullea, K.   Way to the top.   Films & Filming 12-3:5
    D '65
  Bean, R.   Portrait of a young actor on his way to the
    top.   Films & Filming 12-3:5 D '65

DUMONT, MARGARET
  Crichton, K.   Don't call me a stooge.   Colliers 99:18
    My 15 '37
  Obit.   Newsweek 65:64 Mr 22 '65
    Time 85:92 Mr 19 '65
    Screen World 17:236 '66

DUNAWAY, FAYE
  Hamilton, J.   Fay Dunaway; the farmer's granddaughter.
    Look 30:108 D 13 '66
  Day or night Faye's a girl with go.   Life 64:74 Ja 12 '68
  Maas, P.   New fashion star is born.   Ladies H J 85:75
    F '68
  Fay Dunaway; star, symbol, style.   Newsweek 71:42 Mr
    4 '68
  Beauty register.   Vogue 151:220 My '68
  Miron, C.   Why Fay Dunaway said no.   Photop 73-6:51
    Je '68
  Langguth, A. J.   Do you still love me?   asked Faye
    Dunaway.   Sat Eve Post 241:30 S 7 '68
  Hamilton, J.   Faye and the Italian.   Look 33:44 Ja 21 '69
  Brandt, S.   In love with Mastroianni.   Photop 75-1:39
    Ja '69

DUNCAN, MARY
  Howe, H.   Hollywood's new slayer.   Photop 36-3:43 Ag
    '29
  Busby, M.   Crystal-gazing with Mary.   Photop 38-6:72
    N '30

DUNCAN, WILLIAM
  Obit.   Screen World 13:221 '62

DUNN, JAMES
   North, J. Jimmie hates sandwiches. Photop 40-6:35 N'31
   Dunn, J. I got my second chance.   Photop 27-4:58 S '45
   Wood, C. TV personalities biographical sketchbook.
     TV Personalities p85 '56
   What are they doing now? Show 2-7:108 Jl '62
   Obit. Newsweek 70:89 S 18 '67
     Screen World 19:231 '68

DUNN, MICHAEL
   Small talk. Newsweek 62:72 N 18 '63
   Dwarf's full-size success. Life 56:43 F 14 '64
   Lurie, D. I'm no cutie-midget needing a mother; intv.
     Life 56:50 F 14 '64
   Elf's progress. Time 86:54 Jl 30 '65
   Higgins, R. He casts a long shadow. TV Guide 15-27:
     22 Jl 8 '67

DUNNE, IRENE
   Biery, R. Irene's secret marriage.   Photop 39-5:35 Ap
     '31
   Condon, F. She made a hole in one. Sat Eve Post 204:
     91 Je 11 '32
   Maxwell, V. Don't live with your mother-in-law.
     Photop 44-4:74 S '33
   Shuler, M. Working and waiting. C S Mon Mag p3 F
     12 '36
   Hamilton, S. This is really Irene Dunne. Photop 49-4:
     26 Ap '36
   Fletcher, A. W. The true and tender story of Irene
     Dunne's daughter. Photop 52-6:20 Je '38
   St. Johns, A. R. How Irene Dunne succeeded without
     glamour. Photop 53-5:24 My '39
   Boyer, C. Irene. Photop 53-10:24 O '39
   Proctor, K. Play truth or consequences with Irene Dunne.
     Photop 21-2:41 Jl '42
   Dignified. Am Mag 134:84 Ag '42
   Ormiston, R. To make you happier. Photop 24-5:56 Ap
     '44
   St. Johns, A. R. Thank you Irene Dunne. Photop 25-4:
     34 S '44
   Beatty, J. Lady Irene. Am Mag 138:28 N '44
   Biography. Cur Bio Ag '45
   Maxwell, E. A very special woman. Photop 32-2:44 Ja
     '48
   Young, L. I remember Irene Dunne. Photop 33-3:36 Ag
     '48

American queen; extra chins help Irene Dunne portray
  Victoria. Life 29:81 S 11 '50
Lieber, E.   Just a nice person, eh?   Photop 42-3:45
  Ag '52
Report on economic conditions in non-self-governing ter-
  ritories. U.S. Dept. State Bul 37:895 D 2 '57
Cerf, P. Irene Dunne's first job. Good H 146:116 F
  '58
Freedom is responsibility; address Ja 9, 1959.   Vital
  Speeches 25:283 F 15 '59
Birmingham, S. What have they done to Irene Dunne.
  McCalls 91:100 Ag '64

DUNNOCK, MILDRED
  Biography. Cur Bio 16:54 S '55
  Same. Cur Bio Yrbk 1955:175 '56

DUPREZ, JUNE
  Roberts, B. June Duprez, inc. filmog.   Films In Re-
    view 19-2:128 F '68

DURANTE, JIMMY
  Seldes, G. Jimmy is exhubilant.   New Repub 57:247 Ja
    16 '29
  Hamilton, S. Hollywood's new lover.   Photop 41-6:30
    My '32
  Stewart, D. O. The love life of Jimmy Durante. Photop
    42-3:58 Ag '32
  Hamilton, S. A farewell to charms.   Photop 43-5:29 Ap
    '33
  Kennedy, J. B. Tough dollar. Colliers 92:19 Jl 22 '33
  Hamilton, S. A tornado? No! Lupe and Jimmy.
    Photop 45-1:30 D '33
  Poet sues Durante. Newsweek 3:34 Mr 31 '34
  When I was a boy. St N 63:21 N '35
  Laughter. Am Mag 123:61 My '37
  Ferguson, O. Great Durante. New Repub 98:102 Mr 1
    '39
  Parker, D. Hollywood rediscovers Schnozzle.   Colliers
    113:24 Ja 8 '44
  Jimmy, that well-dressed man.   Time 43:71 Ja 24 '44
    Same, abridged with title Jimmy Durante comes back.
    Read Digest 44:43 Ap '44
  Hutchins, J. K. Durante's away but not for long.   N.Y.
    Times Mag p20 Je 4 '44
  Teamwork. Am Mag 139:64 F '45
  Million gags, one Durante. Newsweek 27:92 Je 17 '46

Biography. Cur Bio 7:22 S '46
  Same revised. Cur Bio Yrbk 1946:166 '47
Nichols, L. Lament for the age of clowns. N.Y.
  Times Mag p12 F 1 '48
Zolotow, M. No people like show people; abridged.
  Sat Eve Post 223:22 Jl 15 '50
Hobson, W. Hits and misses. Sat R 33:68 S 30 '50
Jimmy Durante Claus. TV Guide 3-51:12 O 23 '50
Great Schnozzola. Newsweek 36:58 N 13 '50
One-man show. Time 56:52 D 11 '50
Big screen. Life 30:93 My 21 '51
McEvoy, J. P. Stupendious Jimmy Durante. Read
  Digest 58:21 Je '51
Fowler, G. Schnozzola; the story of Jimmy Durante.
  Colliers 127:13 Je 30; 128 Jl 7; 24 Jl 14; 24 Jl 21;
  26 Jl 28; 26 Ag 4 '51
On the pedasill. Time 58:118 S 24 '51
New stories about Jimmy Durante. TV Guide 4-40:8 O
  5 '51
Lords of laughter. Coronet 30:71 O '51
Hotchner, A. E. Dizzy day of Jimmy Durante. Read
  Digest 60:41 Mr '52
The mystery of Mrs. Calabash. TV Guide 5-16:4 Ap 16
  '52
Perelman, S. J. Great nosepiece. Holiday 11:87 Je '52
Durante, J. The only kid I ever hated. TV Guide 6-10:
  4 Mr 6 '53
Uncle Jimmy. TV Guide 1-33:15 N 13 '53
Wood, C. TV personalities biographical sketchbook.
  TV Personalities p100 '54
Those Copa girls. Coronet 38:75 My '55
Day I'd like to live over. Good H 141:215 N '55
The Durante men's club. TV Guide 4-7:13 F 18 '56
Mehling, H. Living legends. Todays Health 36:10 D '58
Dinter, C. Goodbye Mrs. Calabash . . . forgive me.
  Photop 58-1:52 Jl '60
Backbreaker. Newsweek 58:80 Jl 17 '61
McCarthy, J. Jimmy the well-dressed man. Holiday
  31:113 Ja '62
Reynolds, Q. The indestructible enigma: an affectionate
  biography. Show 2-2:60 F '62
Reddy, J. Wild world of Jimmy Durante. Read Digest
  83:202 N '63
Moore, S. And another who never went away. Life 58:
  12 Ap 9 '65
Whitney, D. Da Schnozz. TV Guide 17-52:22 D 27 '69

DURBIN, DEANNA

Proctor, K. It's lonely being a child prodigy. Photop
   51-6:26 Je '37
Henderson, J. The private life of Deanna Durbin.
   Photop 51-12:22 D '37
Tully, J. Fifteen and famous. Sr Schol 31:12 Ja 15 '38
Bell, L. P. Girl of the month. Good H 106:35 Ja '38
Crichton, J. Nice and young. Colliers 101:19 My 21 '38
Wright, J. How Deanna Durbin hurdles the awkward age.
   Photop 52-11:14 N '38
Queen in her own house. C S Mon Mag p13 Je 3 '39
Deanna Durbin; how Deanna got into the movies and what
   she found there. Fortune 20:66 O '39
Lemmon, B. Musical debutante. Etude 58:76 F '40
Fletcher, A. W. How Deanna Durbin lives. Photop 54-
   8:20 Ag '40
MacKaye, M. Mighty atoms of Hollywood. Ladies Home
   J 57:19 S '40
Deanna Durbin, grown to young womanhood makes her
   eighth straight hit. Life 9:85 O 21 '40
Herendeen, A. Inside story of a successful young movie
   star. Parents Mag 15:29 N '40
Lovely Lana and sweet Deanna are belles of birthday ball.
   Life 10:30 F 10 '41
Martin, D. Musical films and their makers. Etude 59:
   84 F '41
Dearest Deanna. Time 37:29 Je 16 '41
St. Johns, A. R. Hollywood's greatest love story.
   Photop 19-1:28 Je; 19-2:42 Jl '41
Crichton, K. Pygmalion the kid. Colliers 108:14 S 27
   '41
Hammon, M. Just married. Good H 113:4 S '41
Biography. Cur Bio '41
New home of Deanna Durbin Paul, most famous bride of
   the year. House B 84:48 S '42
Arvey, V. Music gave me a career. Etude 61:429 Jl
   '43
Durbin, D. Happiness. Photop 23-6:47 N '43
Parsons, L. Divorce for Deanna. Photop 24-2:18 Ja '44
Deanna Durbin becomes a mature dramatic star. Life
   17:52 Jl 3 '44
Bentley, J. Deanna's in love. Photop 25-4:29 S '44
Skolsky, S. Deanna--with variations. Photop 27-6:58
   N '45
Schroeder, C. Finale. Photop 32-5:74 Ap '48
Parsons, L. O. No help wanted. Photop 33-5:42 O '48
Three little girls grow up. Good H 129:168 S '49

Certain restlessness. Time 54:94 N 7 '49
Where are they now? Newsweek 51:18 Ja 27 '58
Ringgold, G. Deanna Durbin, inc. filmog. Screen
   Facts 5:1 n. d.

DURFEE, MINTA
   Bartlett, R. Somebody loves a fat man. Photop 10-3:
      105 Ag '16

DURYEA, DAN
   Frightful father. Am Mag 141:134 Ja '46
   Martin, P. Screen's No. 1 heel. Sat Eve Post 220:28
      Mr 13 '48
   Canfield, A. That's the way the money goes. Photop
      39-4:110 Ap '51
   Look who's a hero! TV Guide 3-23:16 Je 4 '55
   Labelle, P. Filmography. Films In Review 18-6:384
      Je/Jl '67
   Obit. Newsweek 71:88 Je 17 '68
      Time 91:88 Je 14 '68
      Screen World 20:233 '69

DVORAK, ANN
   Biery, R. We present two splendid new screen person-
      alities. Photop 42-1:66 Je '32
   Cinema clippings. Cinema Digest 1-6:27 Jl 25 '32
   Lloyd, B. An extra girl's diary. Photop 42-2:74 Jl '32
   Ramsey, W. In sickness and in health. Photop 49-2:76
      F '36
   Darbyshire, M. B. Ann Dvorak lives simply. Bet Hom
      & Gard 25:174 Ap '47
   McClelland, D. Ann Dvorak, underground goddess, inc.
      filmog. Film Fan Mo 95:3 My '69

EARLE, EDWARD
    deRonalf, J. Edward Earle--indifferent idol. Photop 8-
      1:36 Je '15
    Dolber, J. Our Mary's first leading man. Photop 13-
      4:65 Mr '18

EASTWOOD, CLINT
    This cowboy feels he's got it made. TV Guide 9-5:8 F
      4 '61
    Dynamite on horseback. TV Guide 10-48:24 D 1 '62
    New formula for violence. Life 62:95 Ap 14 '67

EATON, SHIRLEY
    Person of promise. Films & Filming 2-11:9 Ag '56

EBSON, BUDDY
    Prince of the wild frontier. TV Guide 3-32:4 Ag 6 '55
    Essoe, G. The star who became a puppet who became
      a star. TV Guide 17-41:40 O 11 '69

EBURNE, MAUDE
    Obit. Screen World 12:219 '61

EDDY, HELEN JEROME
    McGaffey, K. Helpful Helen. Photop 14-1:65 Je '18
    Boone, A. We'd hate to eat her biscuits. Photop 19-5:
      62 Ap '21

EDDY, NELSON
    They stand out from the crowd. Lit Digest 119:25 Mr 30
      '35
    Collins, F. L. The ladies say he's got what it takes.
      Photop 48-2:34 Jl '35
    Crichton, K. Singing for a living. Colliers 98:21 Ag 15
      '36
    Sharpe, H. Private life of Nelson Eddy. Photop 50-2:
      24 Ag; 50-3:56 S; 50-4:72 O '36
    Steele, J. H. Portrait of a man walking alone. Photop
      52-12:32 D '38
    Hamilton, S. I'll tell you about my marriage. Photop
      53-4:32 Ap '39
    Laine, J. Success in voice study. Etude 57:695 N '39
    MacDonald, J. Nelson. Photop 54-6:23 Je '40
    Daugherty, F. J. American baritone. C S Mon Mag p7
      D 13 '41

MacDonald, J. What I don't like about Nelson Eddy.
Photop 21-3:55 Ag '42
Antrim, D. K. Who should have a singing career?
Etude 61:77 F '43
Biography. Cur Bio '43
Brick top. Time 44:58 O 30 '44
Biographical note. Mus Am 70:270 F '50
Sabin, R. Nelson Eddy, story-teller in song. Mus Am
71:5 Ja 15 '51
Mammy's little Nelson. Time 61:56 Je 22 '53
Obit. Time 89:100 Mr 17 '67
Newsweek 69:78 Mr 20 '67
Opera News 31:30 Ap 15 '67
Cur Bio 28:45 My '67
Cur Bio Yrbk 1967:475 '68
Brit Bk Yr 1968:589 '68
Screen World 19:231 '67

EDWARDS, ALAN
Obit. Screen World 6:223 '55

EDWARDS, CLIFF
Cliff "Ukulele Ike" Edwards. TV Guide 2-30:8 Je 23 '49

EDWARDS, VINCE
deRoos, R. Yes, there is a doctor in the house. TV
Guide 10-1:6 Ja 6 '62
Wall, T. Which doctor would you call? Photop 61-3:
30 Mr '62
Wallace, R. Surly surgeon on the upsurge. Life 52:94
Ap 20 '62
Kelly, V. Ben Casey; TV's dour doctor. Look 26:38
My 8 '62
Davidson, B. TV's surly medico. Sat Eve Post 235:62
My 12 '62
Lee, J. Are you the girl to make him smile? Photop
61-5:60 My '62
The real Vince Edwards. Photop 61-6:58 Je '62
Zoine, B. His twin brother's exclusive story. Photop
62-1:66 Jl '62
Davidson, B. Television's very personal physicians;
Kildare and Casey. McCalls 89:66 Ag '62
Wall, T. How to cure a broken heart. Photop 62-3:51
S '62
Vince Edwards stands accused! Photop 62-4:54 O '62
Biography. Cur Bio 23:3 O '62
Same. Cur Bio Yrbk 1962:117 '63

Baskette, K.   Book-length life story.   Photop 62-5:30 N;
   62-6:51 D '62
Paul, C.   The man he can't stop punishing.   Photop 63-
   2:46 F '63
How Ben Casey operated in Las Vegas.   TV Guide 11-21:
   6 My 25 '63
Who's your dream doctor?   Photop 63-3:37 Mr '63
Haranis, C.   Is he breaking his mother's heart?   Photop
   63-4:58 Ap '63
Little pretty pocketbook.   PTA Mag 57:17 Ap '63
Carpozi, G. Jr.   The girl who waits for him.   Photop
   64-1:41 Jl '63
Hughes, E.   His recipes for lovers.   Photop 64-5:49 N
   '63
Edwards, V.   My battle with Ben Casey.   Seventeen 23:
   130 F '64
Anybody know what kind of mood Vince-baby is in today?
   TV Guide 12-14:6 Ap 4 '64
Terry, P.   The girl who took him from Sherry.   Photop
   65-4:38 Ap '64
Fessier, M.   Teen marriages are ridiculous.   Photop
   65-5:56 My '64
DeBlasio, E.   The girl he can never forget.   Photop 66-
   4:56 O '64
Gehman, R.   Physician, heal thyself.   TV Guide 13-14:
   19 Ap 3 '65
Whitney, D.   Vince baby plays it cool.   TV Guide 15-7:6
   F 18 '67

EGAN, RICHARD
   Waterbury, R.   He lost his shirt and became a star.
      Photop 47-5:63 My '55
   Hopper, H.   Young man of Hollywood.   Coronet 38:55 Jl
      '55
   Phillips, D.   The masculine most.   Photop 49-1:38 Ja '56
   Egan, R.   Is college really necessary?   Photop 50-1:68
      Jl '56
   Hardy, P.   Will you marry me?   Photop 53-6:62 Je '58
   "Where are we, Mommy?" asked Boom-boom.   TV
      Guide 11-15:15 Ap 13 '63

EGGAR, SAMANTHA
   Mothner, I.   Girl named Sam.   Look 28:90 O 20 '64
   Samantha Eggar: red hair, freckles, talent to burn.
      Vogue 149:134 Mr 15 '67
   Ellis, E.   Mama Sam.   Photop 74-1:60 Jl '68

EILERS, SALLY
  Lathem, M. Sally's not a "bad girl." Photop 41-1:78
    D '31

EKBERG, ANITA
  Beautiful maid from Malmo. Life 31:133 O 8 '51
  Fleming, T. J. Multimillion Monroe doctrine. Cosmop
    139:60 Jl '55
  Women who fascinate men. Look 20:57 Mr 6 '56
  Jones, M. W. Swedish dish. Photop 49-3:36 Mr '56
  Malmo maid makes good. Life 40:90 Je 16 '56
  Lerman, L. Prettiest girl in town. Mlle 43:78 Je '56
  People are talking about . . . Vogue 128:132 Ag 1 '56
  Locke, C. Red hot iceberg. Photop 51-2:58 F '57
  Etter, B. Danger signals in love. Photop 53-6:39 Je '58
  Swings and arrows of outraged Ekberg. Life 49:28 O 31
    '60
  Morin, L. Anita Ekberg, inc. filmog. Films In Review
    14-10:636 D '63

ELAM, JACK
  The picture of a classic villain. TV Guide 11-22:15 Je
    1 '63

ELDRIDGE, FLORENCE
  Kahn, J. M. Wandering with the Marches. Photop 41-1:
    52 D '31
  Funke, L. Broadway husband and wife teams. N. Y.
    Times Mag p19 Ja 12 '47
  March story. Newsweek 35:49 Ja 2 '50

ELG, TAINA
  Fleming, T. J. Multimillion Monroe doctrine. Cosmop
    139:60 Jl '55
  Three movie beauties star in California clothes. Look
    21:75 Je 11 '57
  In the news. Dance Mag 32:32 Ja '58

ELLIOTT, "WILD BILL"
  Obit. Screen World 17:236 '66
  McCleary, C. Letter, inc. filmog. Films In Review 20-
    6:390 Je/Jl '69

ELY, RON
  Lewis, R. W. It shouldn't happen to an ape man. TV
    Guide 14-48:22 N 26 '66

EMERSON, FAYE
Deere, D.   The girl with two lives.   Photop 27-3:54
   Ag '45
Faye Emerson: Town crier in a mink stole!   TV Guide
   3-3:12 Ja 21 '50
Faye sheds a husband, sees a fight.   Life 28:39 Ja 23 '50
Hamburger, P.   Television.   New Yorker 26:101 Ap 8 '50
Faye's decollete makes TV melee.   Life 28:87 Ap 10 '50
Emerson, F.   The low down on low-neck gowns.   TV
   Guide 3-15:20 Ap 15 '50
Not too heavy.   Time 55:57 Ap 24 '50
If Faye Emerson were president.   TV Guide 3-22:8 Je 3
   '50
Emerson, F.   You make my program!   TV Guide 3-46:8
   N 18 '50
Emerson, F.   TV hostess.   TV Guide 4-4:20 Ja 27 '51
Martin, P.   Blonde bombshell of TV.   Sat Eve Post 223:
   24 Je 30 '51
Shayon, R. L.   Two bravos and one raspberry.   Sat R
   34:32 Ag 11 '51
Biography.   Cur Bio S '51
Fayzie's flabbergasted.   TV Guide 3-8:13 F 19 '55
Gibbs, W.   Theatre.   New Yorker 32:60 Ja 12 '57
Wood, C.   TV personalities biographical sketchbook.
   TV Personalities p75 '57
Where are they now?   Newsweek 68:20 N 28 '66

EMERSON, HOPE
Obit.   Screen World 12:221 '61

EMERY, GILBERT
Squads right.   Everybodys 38:31 My '18
Shellhase, G.   Gilbert Emery, inc. filmog.   Films In
   Review 18-10:661 D '67

EMERY, JOHN
Obit.   Screen World 16:220 '65

ERDMAN, RICHARD
He can't get over Errol Flynn.   TV Guide 9-22:24 Je 3
   '61

ERICKSON, LEIF
On the record.   Time 48:16 Jl 29 '46
Time for honesty.   Am Mer 80:109 Je '55
Terry, P.   Married after two children.   Photop 73-6:68
   Je '68

Whitney, D.   Trail to the High Chapparal.   TV Guide
    17-34:16 Ag 23 '69

ERROL, LEON
    Mullett, M. B.   Leon Errol tells what it is to be a
        comic actor.   Am Mag 93:18 Ja '22
    Kennedy, J. B.   Drunk who never drinks; intv.   Colliers
        79:11 Je 18 '27
    Obit.   Newsweek 38:71 O 22 '51
        Time 58:13 O 22 '51

ERWIN, STUART
    Ellis, T.   He's not so dumb.   Photop 40-5:33 O '31
    Hamilton, S.   It's the way he says it.   Photop 42-5:60 O
        '32
    My kids won't let me.   Am Mag 153:18 Je '52
    Wood, C.   TV personalities biographical sketchbook.
        TV Personalities p62 '56
    Obit.   Newsweek 71:41 Ja 1 '68
        Screen World 19:232 '68

EVANS, DALE
    Dusek, J.   I was there.   Photop 32-2:54 Ja '48
    Evans, D.   I lived a lie.   Photop 32-5:62 Ap '48
    Kingsley, K.   With open hearts.   Photop 43-2:82 F '53
    Wood, C.   TV personalities biographical sketchbook.
        TV Personalities p138 '54
    Man and wife.   Time 65:55 Mr 7 '55
    Gill, T. A.   Evangelists three.   Christian Cent 72:370
        Mr 23 '55
    Davis, E. M.   Answer is God: the inspiring personal
        story of Dale Evans and Roy Rogers and the miracle
        that changed their lives.   Sat R 38:19 D 10 '55
    Biography.   Cur Bio 17:56 S '56
        Same.   Cur Bio Yrbk 1956:525 '57
    Raftery, G.   Life with a bestseller; Angel unaware.
        Lib J 84:232 Ja 15 '59
    Davidson, M.   Are they going to be headed off at the
        pass?   TV Guide 10-49:10 D 8 '62

EVANS, EDITH
    Griffith, H.   English stage album.   Theatre Arts 15:765
        S '31
    Prima donna's tantrums; role of Irela in Evensong.   Lit
        Digest 115:16 F 18 '33
    Brown, J. M.   Doctor and the Dame.   Sat R 33:30 O 14
        '50

Golden legend. Plays & Players 1-7:4 Ap '54
Biography. Cur Bio 17:16 Je '56
  Same. Cur Bio Yrbk 1956:166 '57
Dame Edith. New Yorker 36:31 Ja 21 '61
Hobson, H. Edith Evans--a profile. Plays & Players
  11-3:14 D '63
Goodwin, I. Grand Dame. Newsweek 71:88 Ap 1 '68

EVANS, JOAN
  Eunson, D. We let our daughter go to Hollywood. Am
    Mag 146:32 N '48
  Evans, J. I'm Hollywood's Cinderella. Photop 34-2:30
    Ja '49
  Evans, J. This is the bitter truth. Photop 36-7:50 D
    '49
  Evans, J. Me and boys. Photop 37-6:44 Je '50
  Evans, J. Farley--so right, so wrong. Photop 38-5:
    48 N '50
  Wheeler, B. Teenage heaven. Photop 39-4:60 Ap '51
  Hopper, H. Act your age, Joan Evans. Photop 40-4:
    48 O '51

EVANS, MADGE
  Biery, R. How Madge Evans grew to stardom. Photop
    41-1:40 D '31
  Lieber, E. Her tongue in her cheek. Photop 43-2:69
    Ja '33
  Stevens, G. Why Madge Evans has never married.
    Photop 50-1:36 Jl '36

EVANS, MAURICE
  Reed, E. Some actors, season of 1935-36. Theatre
    Arts 20:440 Je '36
  Richard II: emancipated bookkeeper star of best stage
    performance in 30 years. Lit Digest 123:23 F 20 '37
  Sherburne, E. C. Stage classics as best sellers; Richard
    II with Maurice Evans starred. C S Mon Mag p4 Ap
    7 '37
  Happy birthday, Mr. Shakespeare! Maurice Evans makes
    Richard II a smash hit. Sr Schol 30:5 Ap 24 '37
  Eaton, W. P. Shakespeare with a difference. Atlan
    159:474 Ap '37
  Roberts, K. He answers his fan mail. Colliers 100:55
    O 23 '37
  Uncut Hamlet. Sat R 19:8 N 26 '38
  Nathan, G. J. True Jack Falstaff. Newsweek 13:30 F
    13 '39

Gilder, R.   Maurice Evan's full-length Hamlet.   Theatre
    Arts 24:86 F '40
Old play in Manhattan.   Time 35:53 Ap 22 '40
Biography.   Cur Bio 1940
Strauss, T.   Maurice Evans: Shakespeare's man.
    Theatre Arts 26:161 Mr '42
Ammerman, G.   Shakespeare as the GI's do it.   N. Y.
    Times Mag p22 Ja 28 '45
Reynolds, Q.   G. I. Hamlet.   Colliers 115:14 Mr 24 '45
G. I. Hamlet; Maurice Evans made Shakespeare a soldier
    hit.   Life 20:57 Ja 7 '46
Gilder, R.   Broadway in review; Maurice Evans' produc-
    tion of Hamlet.   Theatre Arts 30:75 F '46
Doyle, L. F.   Mr. Evans and Shakespeare.   America
    74:616 Mr 16 '46
Evans, Shaw, Shakespeare.   Newsweek 31:88 My 17 '48
Brown, J. M.   Brush off your Shakespeare.   Sat R 32:
    26 N 5 '49
Whiteside, T.   Old Vic for New York.   N. Y. Times Mag
    p10 Ja 1 '50
Phelan, K.   New York City theatre company.   Common-
    weal 51:414 Ja 20 '50
Long, long ago.   Theatre Arts 34:38 S '50
Biography.   NCAB.   cur H:155 '52
Video rushes in where angels fear . . .   Life 36:53 F 8
    '54
Show business is all business.   Theatre Arts 38:12 Ap '54
Merrill, J. F.   TV's Mr. Shakespeare.   Sr Schol 65:6
    N 17 '54
Zolotow, M.   Foxy dreamer of Broadway.   Sat Eve Post
    228:36 O 22 '55
Bentley, B.   No time for playwrights.   Theatre Arts 39:
    30 D '55
Some reminiscences of Shaw.   Theatre Arts 43:17 N '59
Bringing Evans back to the bard.   N. Y. Times Mag p65
    N 6 '60
Richards, S.   At home with Maurice Evans.   Theatre 2-
    12:20 D '60
Biography.   Cur Bio 22:22 Je '61
    Same Cur Bio Yrbk 1961:146 '62
Million dollars worth of make-up obliterates some famous
    faces; making up of Planet of the apes.   Life 63:82
    Ag 18 '67
Guestward ho.   Time 90:82 D 8 '67

EVANS, ROBERT
New movie star.   McCalls 84:17 Ag '57

New pictures. Time 70:59 S 2 '57
Return to the matinee idol. Photop 52-5:49 N '57
Person to person. Films & Filming 4-4:17 Ja '58
Hamilton, S. The week Bob Evans almost died. Photop
    54-2:6 Ag '58
Sands, G. The boy who couldn't cry. Photop 54-6:48 D
    '58
Breisky, B. How I stumbled into the movies. Sat Eve
    Post 232:26 Ag 15 '59
Evans, R. If only she were here. Photop 57-1:46 Ja
    '60
Wall, T. From Miss to Mrs. to mystery. Photop 61-2:
    46 F '62
Why Eddie stole his girl. Photop 64-4:47 O '63
Three to get ready. Time 91:104 Ap 12 '68
Mills, J. Why should he have it? Life 66:62 Mr 7 '69

EVELYN, JUDITH
    Davis, L. & Cleveland, J. Perils of Judy. Colliers
        109:14 Ap 11 '42
    Obit. Screen World 19:232 '68

EVEREST, BARBARA
    Obit. Screen World 20:234 '69

EWELL, TOM
    Comic actor. New Yorker 28:30 D 13 '52
    Wilson, J. S. Tom Ewell's twenty year itch. Theatre
        Arts 37:18 My '53
    Zolotow, M. Mysterious audience. Theatre Arts 38:78
        Je '54
    Mitgang, H. Tom Ewell's twenty year itch. N. Y. Times
        Mag p32 S 19 '54
    At home with Tom Ewell. Theatre 2-5:18 My '60
    A study in misery. TV Guide 8-49:8 D 3 '60
    Biography. Cur Bio 22:17 My '61
        Same. Cur Bio Yrbk 1961:149 '62

EYTHE, WILLIAM
    Walker, H. L. Eyeful of Eythe. Photop 26-2:30 Ja '45
    Kilgallen, D. Man from Mars. Photop 27-5:42 O '45
    Eythe, W. Royal command performance. Photop 30-3:
        62 F '47
    Eythe, W. I met the menace. Photop 31-4:48 S '47
    Obit. Time 69:88 F 4 '57
        Screen World 9:223 '58

FABIAN

Fabian. Man! This was a perfect date. Photop
56-2: 42 Ag '59

Simon, T. Can you resist his eyes? Photop 56-3:
47 S '59

Hoffman, J. I've got to say goodbye. Photop 57-3:
30 Mr '60

Brother, a good thing nobody can read daydreams.
Photop 58-6:26 D '60

Randall, L. What's it like to be Fabian? Photop
59-4:54 Ap '61

Jaffe, G. This is how it all began. Photop 60-2:
56 Ag '61

Anthony, P. The revenge of Fabian Forte. Photop
61-1:52 Ja '62

Henderson, B. A man too soon. Photop 61-5:47
My '62

Tusher, W. My love for Fabian. Photop 65-3:44
Mr '64

FABRAY, NANETTE

Zolotow, M. Danger: Broadway beauty at work.
Colliers 125:26 F 11 '50

Triple trouble. Colliers 132:44 Jl 25 '53

Caesar's TV wife. Look 19:89 Mr 8 '55

Zolotow, M. I'm home at last. Cosmop 138:31
My '55

Biography. Cur Bio 17:29 Ja '56

Same. Cur Bio Yrbk 1956:168 '57

Shipp, C. Girl in high gear. Sat Eve Post 228:30
Ja 28 '56

Wood, C. TV personalities biographical sketchbook.
TV Personalities p114 '56

Hochstein, R., ed. One battle I had to win.
Good H 156:88 My '63

FAIRBANKS, DOUGLAS SR.

Owen, K. Old Doc Cheerful. Photop 10-2:95
Jl '16

Crul, G. Close-up of Douglas Fairbanks. Every-
  bodys 35:729 D '16
Combining play with work. Am Mag 84:33 Jl '17
Lane, R. W. How I became a great actress; ten
  minutes in a bar-room with Douglas Fairbanks
  the optimist. Sunset 40:35 Ap '18
If I were bringing up your children. Womans H C
  46:24 Jul '19
Woollcott, A. Strenuous honeymoon. Everybodys
  43:36 N '20
One reel of autobiography. Colliers 67:10
  Je 18 '21
Fairbanks makes d'Artagnan into a French cowboy.
  Lit Digest 70:28 S 17 '21
Larkin, M. How Doug keeps fit. Outing 80:206
  Ag '22
How I keep running on 'high. Am Mag 94:36 Ag '22
Let me say this for films. Ladies Home J 39:13
  S '22
Why big pictures. Ladies Home J 41:7 Mr '24
Films for the fifty million. Ladies Home J 41:27
  Ap '24
Taylor, C. K. Most popular man in the world.
  Outlook 138:683 D 24 '24
Swashbuckling with Doug on a painted ocean. Lit
  Digest 89:34 Ap 10 '26
Taylor, C. K. Doug gets away with it; The black
  pirate. Outlook 142:560 Ap 14 '26
Lindsay, V. Great Douglas Fairbanks. Ladies Home
  J 43:12 Ag '26
When Doug, the gaucho, hurls his trusty bolas.
  Lit Digest 95:26 D 31 '27
Bakshy, A. Douglas Fairbanks. Nation 126:104
  Ja 25 '28
Vivian, C. H. What kind of boy was Doug?
  Sunset 61:38 O '28
Collins, F. L. Douglas Fairbank's successors.
  Womans H C 56:25 F '29
Hall, L. How about Mary and Doug? Photop 38-3:
  42 Ag '30
Paddock, C. If you think you can. Colliers 88:24
  N 28 '31
Foster, A. So comes the end of the rainbow trail.
  Photop 44-4:28 S '33

Mercer, J.   The Fairbanks' social war is on.
   Photop 50-2:22   Ag '36
Last leap.   Time 34:30   D 25 '39
Obit.   Newsweek 14:25   D 25 '39
   Cur Bio '40
Fairbanks story.   Newsweek 41:108   My 11 '53
Pickford, M.   My whole life.   McCalls 81:44
   My: 43   Je '54
Fishwick, M.   Aesop in Hollywood.   Sat R 37:7
   Jl 10 '54
Biography.   DAB sup2:172 '58
Mayer, A. L.   The origins of United Artists.
   Films In Review   10-7:390   Ag/S '59

FAIRBANKS, DOUGLAS JR.
   Bradley, E.   Not like Dad.   Photop 35-3:50   F '29
   Hughes, F.   Filmland's royal family (second
      edition).   Photop 36-6:37   N '29
   Pringle, H. F.   Joan and Doug.   Colliers 89:19
      Ja 16 '32
   Jr; autobiography.   Sat Eve Post 204:11   My 14 '32
   Arnold, F.   Joan's heart still beats for Doug.
      Photop 44-4:60   S '33
   Hayden, K.   These are my plans.   Photop 44-6:30
      N '33
   Steele, J. H.   Portrait of a young man looking at
      life.   Photop 52-10:22   O '38
   Hollywood ambassador.   Sr Schol 39:8   Ap 28 '41
   Fairbanks strews good will through South America.
      Life   10:24   Je 2 '41
   Fairbanks, D. Jr.   If I were editor.   Photop 19-6:
      39   N '41
   Biography.   Cur Bio '41
   Morse, W. Jr.   In the face of death.   Photop
      21-1:26   Je '42
   Leonard, H.   Present and accounted for.   Sight &
      Sound 15-59:87   Aut '46
   Heads American relief for Korea.   U.S.   Dept State
      Bul 24:413   Mr 12 '51
   Four from Hollywood.   TV Guide 6-4:11   Ja 23 '53
   By a little finger.   Time 61:33   Ja 26 '53
   Sir Douglas Fairbanks.   Newsweek 46:37   Jl 18'55
   Biography.   Cur Bio 17:16   F '56
      Same Cur Bio Yrbk 1956:172   '57

Eying three new TV careers.   TV Guide 5-6:14
   F 9 '57
Travel techniques.   Vogue 129:78 Ap 15 '57
People of the week.   U.S. News 42:20 Je 28
   '57
McCalls visits Douglas Fairbanks Jr.--host to the
   Queen.   McCalls 85:12 My '58
Who killed chivalry?   McCalls 92:117 N '64
Efron, E. Back on stage . . . momentarily.
   TV Guide 13-19:22 My 8'65
Men in vogue; intv.   Vogue 148:53   Ag 15 '66

FALCONETTI, MARIE (Known as Falconetti)
   Winge, J. H. Dryer and Falconetti. Sight & Sound
   18-72:18 n.d.

FALK, PETER
   Miron, C.   Visiting day at the Peter Falks!
      Photop 59-5:68 My '61
   Close but no cigar.   Newsweek 59:60 My 28 '62
   The evolution of an efficiency expert.   TV Guide
      10-26:8   Je 30 '62
   Adams, C. A Cary Grant I ain't.   Photop 62-4:
      36 O '62
   Gehman, R.   O'Brien's behind the 8-ball. TV
      Guide 14-2:12 Ja 8 '66
   Heinz, W. C. They kill you with silence.   Sat
      Eve Post 239:91 F 26 '66
   Kaleidoscope interviews Peter Falk. Kaleidoscope
      2-3: 19 n.d.

FARENTINO, JAMES
   We did it.   Photop 76-6:44 D '69

FARLEY, DOT
   Willis, R.   Comedienne, tragedienne, and photo-
      playwright.   Photop 6-6:139 N '14

FARMER, FRANCES
   Baskette, K.   Miss sex appeal of '37.   Photop 51-2:45
      F '37
   Crichton, K.   I dress as I like.   Colliers 99:21 My 8
      '37
   Frank, G.   Return of an actress.   Coronet 43:44 F '58

FARNUM, DUSTIN
   Owen, K.   Dustin Farnum; intv.   Photop 8-2:128 Jl '15
   Handy, T. B.   The Corsican brothers.   Photop 16-6:28
      N '19

FARNUM, WILLIAM
   Eyck, J. T.   Bill Farnum.   Photop 8-5:110 O '15
   Eyck, J. T.   The crimson corpuscle of the celluloid.
      Photop 12-6:17 N '17
   Handy, T. B.   The Corsican brothers.   Photop 16-6:28
      N '19
   Schader, F. H.   The man who fought alone.   Photop 33-
      2:30 Ja '28
   Obit.   Time 61:99 Je 15 '53
      Newsweek 41:70 Je 15 '53
      Am Ann 1954:232 '54
      Brit Bk Yr 1954:527 '54
      Screen World 5:208 '54

FARR, FELICIA
   Three miffed misses frame frustration.   Life 40:22 Ap
      23 '56
   Baby sitter supreme.   TV Guide 5-38:29 S 21 '57
   Farr, F.   My husband, Jack Lemmon; ed by M. David-
      son.   Good H 160:58 Ap '65

FARRELL, CHARLES
   Hall, L.   Charlie has to fight!   Photop 40-2:30 Jl '31
   Taviner, R.   Charlie goes on his own.   Photop 43-3:
      45 F '33
   Baskette, K.   The new Charles Farrell.   Photop 45-1:
      33 D '33
   Who's who in the cast.   TV Guide 5-34:37 Ag 22 '52
   Gehman, R.   Storm behind My little Margie.   Cosmop
      135:8 D '53
   The man from Seventh heaven.   TV Guide 2-11:13 Mr 12
      '54
   Wood, C.   TV personalities biographical sketchbook.
      TV Personalities p67 '54
   What are they doing now?   Show 2-8:106 Ag '62

Wright, A. Charlie's seventh heaven. Sports Illus 18:
  36 Ap 15 '63

FARRELL, GLENDA
  Palmer, G. They discovered friendship through heartbreak. Photop 51-6:48 Je '37

FARROW, MIA
  Dern, M. The third of the seven little Farrows. TV
    Guide 12-40:15 O 3 '64
  Gordon, S. Mia Farrow; an actress in search of a char-
    acter. Look 28:72 D 1 '64
  Mia. Newsweek 65:31 Ja 4 '65
  York, C. Sinatra to marry Mia Farrow. Photop 67-2:
    14 F '65
  Thompson, T. Seagoing soap opera of Captain Sinatra.
    Life 59:34B Ag 20 '65
  Voyage of the Southern Breeze. Time 86:64 Ag 20 '65
  Extraordinary girl; ed by E. Miller. Seventeen 24:136
    O '65
  Vogue's eye view: who's a breakaway? Vogue 147:71
    Ap 15 '66
  Somers, A. He's gotta marry her now. Photop 69-5:37
    My '66
  Fun couples. Newsweek 68:58 Jl 25 '66
  Mia to Mrs. in four minutes. Life 61:46A Jl 29 '66
  Thompson, T. Mia. Look 62:75 My 5 '67
  Knickerbocker, S. ed. Mia; intv. McCalls 94:70 My '67
  Scott, V. Mia Farrow's swinging life with Frank Sinatra.
    Ladies Home J 84:84 My '67
  Hamilton, J. Working Sinatras. Look 31:86 O 31 '67
  Newsmakers. Newsweek 70:52 D 4 '67
  Wood, A. Why I'm seeing Maharishi. Photop 73-1:39
    Ja '68
  York, C. Why he was glad to let Mia go. Photop 73-2:
    50 F '68
  O'Brien, F. How she begged Sinatra. Photop 73-4:50 Ap
    '68
  An almost unprintable talk. Photop 73-5:64 My '68
  Hamilton, J. Rosemary's baby. Look 32:91 Je 25 '68
  Tabori, L. Mia Farrow talks; intv. Ladies Home J 85:
    59 Ag '68
  Her divorce--with love. Photop 74-5:36 N '68
  Cocks, J. Moonchild and the fifth Beatle. Time 93:50
    F 7 '69
  Riley, N. Their shocking love scenes. Photop 75-2:39
    F '69

Kerr, M. A.   Why she sobs to strangers.   Photop 75-3:
   52 Mr '69
Ellis, E.   And the married musician.   Photop 75-5:69
   My '69
Dee, S.   Her hush-hush house call.   Photop 75-6:42 Je
   '69

FAWCETT, GEORGE
   Schmid, P. J.   George Fawcett talks on motion pictures.
      Feature Movie 5-1:28 Ja '16
   Biography.   NCAB 35:325 '49

FAYE, ALICE
   Roberts, K.   Singing star.   Colliers 101:18 My 14 '38
   Hayes, B.   Give it another chance.   Photop 52-11:28 N
      '38
   Hartley, K.   Play truth or consequences with Alice Faye.
      Photop 53-4:20 Ap '39
   St. Johns, A. R.   Tenth avenue girl.   Photop 53-10:17
      O; 53-11:24 N; 53-12:68 D '39
   Waterbury, R.   Don, Alice and Ty.   Photop 54-4:14 Ap
      '40
   Fletcher, A. W.   How Alice Fay lives.   Photop 18-6:43
      My '41
   Hamilton, S.   My bride, Alice Faye.   Photop 19-3:26 Ag
      '41
   West, R.   They named the baby Junior.   Photop 21-3:32
      Ag '42
   St. Johns, A. R.   Listen to me, Alice Faye!   Photop
      23-3:26 Ag '43
   Parsons, L. O.   You wouldn't know Alice Faye.   Photop
      25-4:30 S '44
   Schallert, E.   Reconversion of Alice Faye.   Photop 28-1:
      50 D '45
   Moshier, W. F.   Alice Faye, inc. filmog.   Films In
      Review 12-8:474 O '61
   Barrett, M.   Alice Faye, I love you.   Show 2-7:8 Jl '62

FAYE, JULIA
   Obit.   Screen World 18:234 '67

FAYLEN, FRANK
   Formerly Frank Faylen.   TV Guide 11-3:26 Ja 19 '63

FAZENDA, LOUISE
   She quit at the altar.   Photop 12-3:26 Ag '17
   Corliss, A.   Fazenda--comic Venus.   Photop 13-5:67

Ap '18

Squier, E. L. They said she couldn't cook. Photop 16-6:
64 N '19

Busby, M. You don't have to be beautiful. Photop 37-
2:47 Ja '30

Lang, H. She wants to thrill us to tears! Photop 40-
1:67 Je '31

Meredith, E. The miracle of Louise Fazenda's baby.
Photop 44-3:33 Ag '33

Roberts, K. Lady can take it. Colliers 101:19 Je 11 '38

Lee, R. Louise Fazenda. Films In Review 13-7:444
Ag/S '62

Obit. Time 79:86 Ap 27 '62
Brit Bk Yr 1963:869 '63
Screen World 14:222 '63

FEALY, MAUDE
Synon, K. The apple of Paris--and Maude Fealy.
Photop 6-3:98 Ag '14

FELLOWES, ROCKCLIFFE
St. Johns, I. Coming into his own. Photop 27-3:58 F
'25

FENTON, LESLIE
Howe, H. He threw away a million. Photop 36-6:41
N '29

Albert, K. Why Leslie Fenton came back. Photop 39-3:
45 F '31

Ramsey, W. In sickness and in health. Photop 49-2:76
F '36

FERGUSON, ELSIE
Craig, R. H. Unguessed riddle. Cosmop 54:269 Ja '13

Underhill, H. The rise of Elsie Ferguson. Photop 8-5:
41 Ap '18

Raftery, H. Elsie or Alla? Photop 14-2:22 Jl '18

Ferguson, E. Clothes and good taste. Photop 17-4:57
My '20

Ferguson, E. My husband. Photop 21-2:38 Ja '22

Beauty and the plain woman. Ladies Home J 44:32 Je '27

Outrageous confusion. Newsweek 22:96 N 15 '43

Biography. Cur Bio F '44

Blum, D. Ten beauties of the American stage. Theatre
Arts 36:70 S '52

Obit. Cur Bio 23:11 Ja '62
Cur Bio Yrbk 1962:127 '63

Screen World 13:222 '62
Bodeen, D. Elsie Ferguson, inc. filmog. Films In Review 15-9:551 N '64

FERGUSON, HELEN
Winship, M. From dishes to drama. Photop 21-1:37 D '21

FERNANDEL
Silent interview. Life 25:88 D 27 '48
Gallery of Americans. Look 17:40 O 6 '53
Biography. Cur Bio 16:5 O '55
   Same. Cur Bio Yrbk 1955:203 '56
Gerald, Y. Fernandel's comic style. Films In Review 11-3:141 Mr '60

FERRER, JOSE
Underwood, M. Joe and Uta. Colliers 113:20 My 20 '44
Biography. Cur Bio My '44
Old play in Manhattan. Time 48:78 O 21 '46
Frank, S. Broadway's new matinee idol. Sat Eve Post 219:28 Mr 8 '47
Funke, L. Broadway stars--ten years ago and today. N.Y. Times Mag p25 Ap 20 '47
Best actor. Life 25:51 D 20 '48
Television no terror. Theatre Arts 33:46 Ap '49
Advice to the players. C S Mon Mag p15 Ag 19 '50
Hine, A. People and prospects. Holiday 9:22 F '51
Mr. Harper. After hours. Harper 202:102 F '51
Bardolatry. Time 57:82 Mr 19 '51
Millstein, G. All the stage is his world. N.Y. Times Mag p20 Mr 25 '51
Oscars for Jose and Judy. Life 30:38 Ap 9 '51
Alig, W. B. Starring Jose Ferrer. Americas 3:9 S '51
Brown, J. M. Amazing Mr. Ferrer. Sat R 35:22 F 9 '52
Phenomenon called Ferrer. Life 39:99 F 11 '52
Forecasts and side glances. Theatre Arts 36:13 Ap '52
Theatre Arts spotlights. Theatre Arts 36:52 My '52
Shrinking of Jose Ferrer. Life 33:51 S 29 '52
Mr. Ferrer and Mr. Chaplin; threat by American Legion. Nation 176:90 Ja 31 '53
Gibbs, W. Theatre. New Yorker 29:76 D 19 '53
Millstein, G. Fabulous Jose Ferrer. Colliers 132:34 D 25 '53
Haves, H. Happy hunchback. Sat R 36:27 D 26 '53
Biography. Am Ann 1953:241 '53

Hayes, R.   Portrait of the artist as Mr. Ferrer.
Commonweal 59:378 Ja 15 '54
Four parts in eight weeks.   Theatre Arts 38:32 Ja '54
Peet, C.   All around star.   Sr Schol 64:6 Mr 3 '54
Frazier, G.   Jose Ferrer; stage-master.   Coronet 36:
83 Je '54
Clooney, R.   On being Mrs. Jose Ferrer; as told to M.
L. Runbeck.   Good H 142:66 My '56
McCalls visits.   McCalls 84:6 Jl '57
Jose sings out.   Newsweek 56:98 Jl 25 '60
Kolodin, I.   Name is Ferrer, not Farrar; acting in Gian-
ni Schicchi.   Sat R 43:33 O 8 '60
Gelman, M.   Jose Ferrer.   Theatre 3-1:21 Ja '61
Condon, R.   Ole Jose.   Holiday 29:123 Mr '61
Meltsir, A.   Highly improbable, uproariously happy mar-
riage of Rosemary Clooney and Jose Ferrer.   Coronet
50:145 Ag '61
Funke, L. & Booth, J. E.   Actor's method: his life.
N. Y.   Times Mag p35 O 1 '61
Corbin, J.   Break-up.   Photop 61-1:6 Ja '62
Ferrer, J.   In who's who of the critics.   Films & Film-
ing 8-8:14 My '62
Ferrer, J.   Cyrano and others; intv.   Films & Filming
8-10:13 Jl '62

FERRER, MEL
Making of a movie matador.   Life 29:55 Jl 10 '50
Hill, G.   Jet propulsion, Hollywood type.   Colliers 126:
28 Jl 29 '50
Hine, A.   People and prospects.   Holiday 9:22 F '51
Life in the afternoon.   Newsweek 37:54 Ap 23 '51
La Jolla players.   Theatre Arts 35:4 Ag '51
Idyl for Audrey.   Life 39:44 Jl 18 '55
Jones, M. W.   My husband doesn't ruin me.   Photop 49-
4:52 Ap '56
Tolstoy, Ferrer, Hepburn, $6 million.   Newsweek 48:53
Jl 30 '56
Scandal in rehearsal.   Life 42:56 F 4 '57
Celebrities on a stylish spree.   Life 47:103 S 7 '59

FETCHIT, STEPIN
Howe, H.   Stepin's high colored past.   Photop 36-1:31
Je '29
Where are they now?   Newsweek 70:22 N 20 '67

FIELD, BETTY
Franchey, J. R.   Casual cyclone.   Photop 19-4:53 S '41

Crichton, K.   Understudy to success.   Colliers 109:21 Mr
   28 '42
Valentine, E. R.   Three's a family and a stage team.
   N. Y. Times Mag p14 S 12 '43
Nichols, L.   Gallery of leading ladies.   N. Y. Times Mag
   p20 Mr 3 '46
Crichton, K.   Papa's dreamgirl.   Colliers 118:14 Ag 31
   '46
Funke, L.   Broadway husband and wife teams.   N. Y.
   Times Mag p18 Ja 12 '47
Biography.   Cur Bio 20:16 S '59
   Same.   Cur Bio Yrbk 1959:116 '60
Out islands are in.   Vogue 141:132 F 15 '63

FIELD, SHIRLEY ANN
   Cockney makes good.   Look 26:63 Ap 24 '62
   Gutwillig, R.   On screen.   Horizon 5:36 Mr '63

FIELDS, GRACIE
   Caruso's successor.   Time 31:22 F 28 '38
   Davis, L. & Cleveland, J.   Sing, Gracie, sing!   Colliers
      108:15 Ag 9 '41
   Biography.   Cur Bio '41
   Davis, L. & Cleveland, J.   Sing, Gracie, sing! excerpts.
      Read Digest 41:13 Jl '42
   Lanchashire lass.   Newsweek 20:80 O 19 '42
   Grycie.   Time 40:59 N 9 '42
   English comedienne mugs and sings.   Life 13:124 D 21
      '42
   Heylbut, R.   Secret of public reaction; intv.   Etude 61:
      100 F '43
   Dolson, H.   Our Gracie.   Read Digest 42:22 Ap '43
   Morgan, A. L.   Return to radio.   Etude 61:782 D '43
   Our Gracie.   Time 50:52 S 1 '47
   Star can act, too.   Newsweek Mr 31 '58
   Personalities of the week.   Illus Lond N 247:15 Jl 10 '65

FIELDS, W. C.
   Waterbury, R.   The old Army game.   Photop 28-5:68 O
      '25
   Cary, H.   Loneliest man in the movies.   Colliers 76:26
      N 28 '25
   Mallett, M. B.   Bill Fields disliked his label so he
      laughed it off; intv.   Am Mag 101:18 Ja '26
   How the films fought shy of Bill Fields.   Lit Digest 88:
      52 F 20 '26
   Brown, H.   W. C. Fields and the cosmos.   Nation 132:

24 Ja 7 '31

Anything for a laugh.   Am Mag 118:73 S '34

Hamilton, S.   A red-nosed Romeo.   Photop 47-1:32 D '34

Ferguson, O.   Great McGonigle.   New Repub 84:48 Ag
21 '35

Comedian in new screen role after winning back his health.
Lit Digest 121:19 Je 20 '36

Hamilton, S.   Dangerous days of Bill Fields.   Photop 50-
1:30 Jl '36

Hamilton, S.   Who knows what is funny?   Sat Eve Post
211:10 Ag 6 '38

Hamilton, S.   That man's here again.   Photop 51-8:16
Ag '37

Carnegie, D.   Funny-man Fields.   Sr Schol 31:7 O 9 '37

Ferguson, O.   Old fashioned way.   New Repub 103:900 D
30 '40

Funnyman W. C. Fields has his own way of keeping fit.
Life 10:104 My 12 '41

Ferguson, O.   Happy endings.   New Repub 105:622 N 10
'41

Cerf, B.   Trade winds.   Sat R 27:20 Je 3 '44

Pompous bluff, the genial fraud.   Nation 164:3 Ja 4 '47

Priestley, J. B.   W. C. Fields.   New Statesm 33:8 Ja
4 '47

Gentle grifter.   Time 49:54 Ja 6 '47

Red-nosed, raspy-voiced funnyman dies on Christmas day.
Newsweek 29:19 Ja 6 '47

W. C. Fields.   Life 22:63 Ja 6 '47

Local man.   New Yorker 22:78 Ja 25 '47

Priestley, J. B.   W. C. Fields.   Atlan 179:43 Mr '47

Taylor, R. L.   W. C. Fields: rowdy king of comedy.
Sat Eve Post 221:19 My 21; 24 My 28; 26 Je 4; 37 Je
11; 30 Je 18; 30 Je 25; 222:34 Jl 2; 30 Jl 9 '49

Self-made curmudgeon.   Time 54:108 O 17 '49

Taylor, R. L.   W. C. Fields; rowdy king of comedy; excerpts.   Read Digest 55:143 D '49

Starr, C.   Film forum.   Sat R 33:28 Ag 26 '50

Tynan, K.   Toby Jug and bottle.   Sight & Sound 19-10:
395 F '51

Ghosts of W. C. Fields: whom did he marry?   and when?
Newsweek 38:28 S 10 '51

Eccentric's eccentric.   Time 63:108 Ap 5 '54

With wit and love.   Newsweek 43:96 Ap 5 '54

Durgnat, R.   Subversion in the Fields.   Films & Filming 12-3:42 D '65

Flatley, G.   Who was he?   N. Y. Times Mag p114 Ap
24 '66

Markfield, W.   Dark geography of W. C. Fields.   N. Y.
    Times Mag p32 Ap 24 '66
Zimmerman, P. D.   Great debunker.   Newsweek 69:88
    Ap 3 '67
Robinson, D.   Dukinfield meets McGargle, creation of a
    character.   Sight & Sound 36:125 Sum '67
Ford, C.   One and only W. C. Fields.   Harper 235:65
    O '67
Ford, C.   W. C. Fields, the one and only.   Read Digest
    91:158 N '67
Jacobs, J.   Days of wine and legends.   Reporter 38:49
    Ja 25 '68
Handlin, O.   Fear and laughter.   Atlan 221:116 Ja '68

FINCH, PETER
    Personality of the month.   Films & Filming 6-12:5 S '60
    Finch, P.   Peter, Peter pumpkin eater.   Films & Film-
        ing 10-9:7 Je '64

FINE, LARRY
    (See: THREE STOOGES)

FINNEY, ALBERT
    Tomorrow's lead.   Plays & Players 5-10:24 Jl '58
    First Finney.   Time 77:64 F 24 '61
    Waggoner, W.   Next Olivier.   N. Y. Times Mag p43 Mr
        26 '61
    Albert Finney and Mary Ure talk about acting.   Sight &
        Sound 30-2:56 Spg '61
    Albert the First.   New Statesm 62:116 Jl 28 '61
    Brien, A.   European portfolio.   Theatre Arts 46:61 F '62
    Miller, E.   Enthusiastic actors dig a classic!   Seventeen
        22:14 F '63
    LaBadie, D. W.   Albert Finney and "Tom Jones."   Show
        3-6:64 Je '63
    Prideaux, T.   Thirst for greatness.   Life 55:125 O 11
        '63
    Actor Finney: he needs the Everests.   Newsweek 62:56
        O 28 '63
    Williamson, A.   Albert Finney.   Theatre Arts 47:30 O '63
    Biography.   Cur Bio 24:8 O '63
        Same.   Cur Bio Yrbk 1963:132 '64
    Finney, the flesh and the devil.   Look 27:76 N 19 '63
    Tornabene, L.   Tomorrow's stars.   Good H 160:20 Mr
        '65
    Burnett, H. ed.   Face to face, excerpts.   Harper 230:
        61 Ap '65

FITZGERALD, BARRY
Crichton, K. Actor who doesn't care. Colliers 114:12
S 16 '44
Stanley, F. Fitzgerald meets fame and he frowns. N.Y.
Times Mag p14 Ja 14 '45
Nugent, F. S. Barry Fitzgerald--the shanghaied Irish-
man. Photop 26-2:53 Ja '45
Biography. Cur Bio F '45
Homeward bound. New Yorker 21:16 Jl 28 '45
Fitzgerald, B. Once was enough for me. Photop 27-4:
59 S '45
I'm a clerk. Am Mag 140:64 N '45
Reynolds, H. Barry Fitzgerald, visitor. Commonweal
45:399 Ja 31 '47
Wallace, I. Barry go bragh! Colliers 122:22 Jl 10 '48
Obit. Time 77:78 Ja 13 '61
Newsweek 57:57 Ja 16 '61
Cur Bio 22:24 F '61
Cur Bio Yrbk 1961:160 '62
Illus Lond N 238:69 Ja 14 '61
Am Ann 1962:851 '62
Screen World 13:222 '62

FITZGERALD, GERALDINE
Crichton, K. She'd rather be Irish. Colliers 105:11 Ap
20 '40
Morse, W. Jr. Time out for a lullaby. Photop 54-5:
74 My '40
Franchey, J. R. "Pixie." Photop 19-3:54 Ag '41
Victim's explanation. Time 46:94 Ag 27 '45
Role I liked best. Sat Eve Post 219:98 Ag 24 '46
Meet our cover girl. Am Home 55:6 My '56

FLEMING, RHONDA
Sunday school teacher. Am Mag 141:137 Mr '46
Rhonda Fleming. Life 26:103 Mr 14 '49
Colby, A. Have a beautiful time. Photop 38-1:64 Jl '50

FLIPPEN, JAY C.
Look who's in the Navy. TV Guide 10-50:6 D 15 '62

FLYNN, ERROL
Reeve, W. The astounding story of Errol Flynn.
Photop 49-4:28 Ap '36
Crichton, K. From reef to reef. Colliers 98:40 O 10
'36
Hall, L. The madcap love of the Errol Flynns. Photop

51-2:32 F '37
Night in town.   Colliers 99:22 Ap 24 '37
Flynn, E.   What really happened to me in Spain.   Photop
51-7:12 Jl '37
Flynn, E.   Young man about Hollywood.   Photop 51-8:24
Ag '37
Flynn, E.   Hollywood women, heaven preserve them.
Photop 51-9:29 S '37
Flynn, E.   Hollywood morals, if any!   Photop 51-10:31
O '37
Flynn, E.   Hollywood's not so ancient mariners.   Photop
52-1:17 Ja '38
Not that I'm ungrateful.   Womans H C 65:64 Ja '38
Flynn, E.   Ensenada--the land of tamales and tequila.
Photop 52-2:26 F '38
Flynn, E.   The seamy side of Hollywood.   Photop 52-4:
28 Ap '38
Picaresque story.   Time 31:57 My 16 '38
Flynn, E.   Let's hunt for treasure.   Photop 53-4:22 Ap
'39
Steele, J. H.   Portrait of a man who goes places.
Photop 53-8:38 Ag '39
Erskine, J.   The queen's office hours.   Photop 53-12:
17 D '39
Ulman, W. A. Jr.   The man who found a country.
Photop 54-12:27 D '40
Mulvey, K.   Biographical sketch.   Womans H C 68:19
Ja '41
Zarat, I.   I feel like a heel about Errol.   Photop 20-2:
26 Ja '42
What's happened to Errol Flynn?   Photop 21-5:26 O '42
Trial and Errol.   Newsweek 21:39 F 15 '43
St. Johns, A. R.   What I think about the Errol Flynn
case.   Photop 22-3:26 F '43
St. Johns, A. R.   Errol Flynn begins again.   Photop 23-
5:30 O '43
Hamilton, S.   The girl in Errol Flynn's life.   Photop
25-1:28 Je '44
Steele, J. H.   Portrait of a restless soul.   Photop 25-5:
62 O '44
Parsons, L. O.   Nora Eddington talks about her mar-
riage.   Photop 27-2:30 Jl '45
First fling.   Time 47:94 F 25 '46
Cooper, M.   Flynn vs. Flynn.   Photop 29-1:56 Je '46
Lait, G.   Mr. and Mrs. Mariner.   Photop 29-5:45 O '46
Hamilton, S.   The Mickey Flynn.   Photop 33-3:48 Ag '48
Parsons, L. O.   Tangled lives.   Photop 36-1:34 Je '49

Parsons, L. O.   Errol Flynn and the princess.   Photop
   37-2:33 F '50
Graham, S.   She can handle him.   Photop 42-3:68 S '52
Obit.   Illus Lond N 235:509 O 24 '59
   Life 47:133 O 26 '59
   Newsweek 54:45 O 26 '59
   Time 74:104 O 26 '59
   Am Ann 1960:852 '60
   Brit Bk Yr 1960:508 '60
   Screen World 11:219 '60
That handsome rake.   Newsweek 55:61 Ja 4 '60
14,001 nights.   Time 75:44 Ja 4 '60
Hamilton, S.   Exit laughing.   Photop 57-1:36 Ja '60
Thomas, A.   Errol Flynn.   Films In Review 11-1:7 Ja
   '60
Roman, R. C.   Filmography.   Films in Review 11-1:15
   Ja '60
Winchell, Putnam dispute My wicked, wicked ways.
   Pub W 177:22 Ap 11 '60

FLYNN, SEAN
Swatch off the old swashbuckler.   Life 51:83 S 8 '61

FOCH, NINA
Thruelson, R.   Young actress.   Sat Eve Post 220:32 S
   6 '47
Who's interested in money?   TV Guide 5-24:24 Je 15 '57

FONDA, HENRY
Smalley, J.   Henry Fonda's new love story.   Photop 50-6:
   45 D '36
Morse, W. Jr.   A boy from Omaha.   Photop 54-11:26
   N; 54-12:66 D '40
Peacock, H. F. & Schoentgen, J. F.   Out of Henry
   Fonda's attic.   Photop 19-2:62 Jl '41
Woolf, S. J.   Henry Fonda gives a recipe for a hit.
   N.Y. Times Mag p20 Ap 25 '48
Coons, R.   Country slicker.   Photop 33-1:52 Je '48
My current reading.   Sat R 31:29 Jl 31 '48
Shearer, M. P.   Why the Fondas' house functions smooth-
   ly.   House B 90:50 Jl '48
Everything about our house can take a beating.   House B
   90:46 Jl '48
Fondas' formula for successful living.   House B 90:40
   Jl '48
Meet farmer Fonda.   House B 90:74 Jl '48
Fonda, H.   Dad and me.   Am Mag 146:94 Ag '48

Biography.   Cur Bio Yrbk 1948:216 '49

Poling, J.   Mr Roberts is a banker now.   Colliers 128:
30 D 15 '51

Benchley, N.   Offstage.   Theatre Arts 35:44 D '51

Edwards, J.   Unusual case of Henry Fonda.   Coronet
33:40 Mr '53

Fonda-Nolan duel.   Vogue 123:100 Mr 15 '54

Clown swaps frown; dramatization of Emmett Kelly's Autobiography.   Life 38:113 Mr 7 '55

Kinney, H.   McCalls visits Henry Fonda.   McCalls 83:
4 S '56

Personality of the month.   Films & Filming 3-11:5 Ag '57

Brownstone remade.   Vogue 131:109 Ja 15 '58

Morton, F.   Unspectacular hero.   Holiday 24:117 N '58

Whitcomb, J.   Father's daughter.   Cosmop 149:11 Jl '59

Singing in the rain.   Newsweek 54:83 Ag 10 '59

The marshal's on the level.   TV Guide 8-4:12 Ja 23 '60

Prideaux, T.   Flowering of a new Fonda.   Life 48:71 F
22 '60

Henry Fonda and his daughter Jane.   Vogue 135:135 Mr 1
'60

Markel, H.   Henry Fonda's daughter goes into orbit.
Good H 150:32 Mr '60

Henry Fonda.   Theatre 2-11:21 N '60

Springer, J.   Henry Fonda, inc. filmog.   Films In Review 11-9:519 N '60

Ross, L.   Profile.   New Yorker 37:61 O 28 '61

Springtime for Henry.   Time 79:43 F 16 '62

Cowie, P.   Fonda.   Films & Filming 8-7:22 Ap '62

Fonda on Fonda.   Films & Filming 9-5:7 F '63

Davidson, B.   Oldest Fonda.   McCalls 90:89 My '63

Hagen, R.   Fonda: without a method.   Films & Filming
12-9:40 Je '66

Springer, J.   Henry Fonda's last six years.   Films In
Review 17-7:393 Ag/S '66

FONDA, JANE

Kinney, H.   McCalls visits Henry Fonda.   McCalls 83:
4 S '56

Inevitable discovery of Jane Fonda.   Look 23:123 N 10
'59

Prideaux, T.   Flowering of a new Fonda.   Life 48:71 F
22 '60

Henry Fonda and his daughter Jane.   Vogue 135:135 Mr
1 '60

Markel, H.   Henry Fonda's daughter goes into orbit. Good
H 150:32 Mr '60

Whitcomb, J. Father's daughter. Cosmop 149:11 Jl '60
Person of promise. Films & Filming 6-10:17 Jl '60
Barclay, C. Look what's happened to my plain Jane.
   Photop 58-2:52 Ag '60
Spotlight. Life 51:118 O 27 '61
People on the way up. Sat Eve Post 234:22 D 16 '61
Springtime for Henry. Time 79:43 F 16 '62
Kauffman, S. Rise of Jane Fonda. New Repub 147:26 N
   24 '62
Who'll be the next goddess? Newsweek 60:96 D 10 '62
Aronowitz, A. Lady Jane. Sat Eve Post 236:22 Mr 23
   '63
U. S. Jane conquers Paris. Life 56:75 Ja 10 '64
Biography. Cur Bio 25:19 Jl '64
   Same. Cur Bio Yrbk 1964:128 '64
Diffused Jane Fonda. U. S. Camera 29:60 Jl '66
Blonde black panther. Time 88:76 S 9 '66
Thompson, T. Up and away with Jane Fonda. Life 64:
   66 Mr 29 '68
Ellis, E. The naked truth about her. Photop 74-2:57
   Ag '68
Ehrlich, H. Jane Fonda; shining in two new roles.
   Look 33:70 My 13 '69

FONDA, PETER
   Springtime for Henry. Time 79:43 F 16 '62
   Miller, E. Peter Fonda on his own. Seventeen 22:208
      Ag '63
   Tornabene, L. Tomorrow's stars. Good H 160:20 Mr
      '65
   Reed, R. Holden Caulfield at 27. Esquire 69:70 F '68
   Thoughts and attitudes about Easy rider. Film 56:24 Aut
      '69

FONTAINE, JOAN
   Zeitlin, I. How Olivia sees her sister's romance.
      Photop 53-11:27 N '39
   Fletcher, A. W. Hollywood at home. Photop 54-7:18
      Jl '40
   Fletcher, A. W. Sister act. Photop 19-4:42 S '41
   Daugherty, F. Not so little sister. C S Mon Mag p6
      Mr 21 '42
   Baskette, K. Olivia's little sister. Am Mag 133:20 Ap
      '42
   Surmelian, L. These above all. Photop 20-5:32 Ap '42
   Waterbury, R. Personal conquest. Photop 21-1:34 Je;
      21-2:52 Jl '42

Jensen, O. O. Sister act; Joan Fontaine and Olivia De
    Havilland spurred on by rivalry to separate success.
    Life 12:88 My 4 '42
Interesting people at home.   House & Gard 85:36 Ag '42
Surmelian, L. I won't deny the rumors.   Photop 21-6:
    30 N '42
Sharpe, H. Categorically speaking.   Photop 23-6:50 N
    '43
Skolsky, S. Jottings on Joan.   Photop 24-4:40 Mr '44
Bentley, J. And now goodbye.   Photop 25-1| Je '44
Fletcher, A. W. Fontaine's fling.   Photop 26-1:34 D '44
Biography. Cur Bio My '44
Fontaine, J. Come into the kitchen darling.   Photop 28-
    6:64 My '46
Harris, E. Gay elopement.   Photop 29-3:24 Ag '46
Fontaine, J. Missy Dozier's bank account.   Photop 34-
    5:62 Ap '49
Parsons, L. O. The story of a divorce.   Photop 39-2:46
    F '51
Theatre arts gallery.   Theatre Arts 39:64 Ja '55
Anderson, J. ed. Cooking is my second love.   Ladies
    Home J 76:86 O '59
Anthony, P. The whole truth.   Photop 61-3:40 Mr '62
Carlyle, J. Joan Fontaine, inc. filmog.   Films In Re-
    view 14-3:146 Mr '63
Armory, C. Celebrity register.   McCalls 90:158 Ag '63
Where are they now?   Newsweek 69:20 Ap 10 '67

FOOTE, COURTENAY
    Brooke, F. A modern wit and a distinguished actor.
        Photop 6-6:75 N '14

FORBES, RALPH
    Obit.   Newsweek 37:57 Ap 9 '51
        Time 57:93 Ap 9 '51
        Am Ann 1952:255 '52

FORD, CONSTANCE
    Model behavior.   Theatre Arts 36:17 D '52
    Wood, C. TV personalities biographical sketchbook.
        TV Personalities p139 '56
    This Ford just stands still.   TV Guide 5-51:16 D 21 '57

FORD, FRANCIS
    Obit.   Screen World 5:208 '54

FORD, GLENN
    Hamman, M. Odyssey of an ugly duckling. Good H 112:
      11 My '41
    Franchey, J. R. No sex appeal? Photop 19-5:38 O '41
    Ford, G. My pals Brenda and Bill. Photop 21-1:52 Je
      '42
    Cummings, M. To Ellie with love. Photop 22-2:26 Ja '43
    Cummings, M. Order of the wedding day. Photop 24-
      2:24 Ja '44
    Asher, J. Watch Glenn Ford go by. Photop 29-2:46 Jl
      '46
    Perkins, L. Photolife of Glenn Ford. Photop 29-5:50 O
      '46
    Asher, J. We have a home. Photop 31-4:42 S '47
    Ford, G. Difficult--that's me. Photop 34-2:40 Ja '49
    Coons, R. '49 Fords. Photop 36-4:62 S '49
    Ford, G. They are men's women. Photop 41-4:48 Ap
      '52
    Wilder, J. Secrets behind Hollywood heartbreaks.
      Photop 42-5:48 N '52
    Ford, E. P. For the love of Pete. Photop 46-4:64 O '54
    Parsons, L. O. Interrupted melody. Cosmop 138:18 Ap
      '55
    Ardmore, J. K. At home with the Glenn Fords. Parents
      Mag 30:50 N '55
    Maynard, J. This I believe. Photop 48-6:60 D '55
    Arnold, M. It's fun to fight. Photop 49-4:40 Ap '56
    Ford, G. The whole world over. Photop 51-1:32 Ja '57
    Nest egg of talent is hatched. Coronet 41:12a Ja '57
    Ford, G. I can always escape; as told to J. K. Ardmore.
      Sat Eve Post 230:18 Ja 4 '58
    King of the box office. Newsweek 53:120 My 11 '59
    Biography. Cur Bio 20:10 Je '59
      Same. Cur Bio Yrbk 1959:125 '60
    Downing, H. Last interview. Photop 56-2:56 Ag '59
    What Glenn Ford's hiding from Debbie. Photop 58-1:42
      Jl '60
    Ardmore, J. Glenn, will you marry Debbie? Photop
      58-5:26 N '60
    Rowland, T. When's the marriage? Photop 59-5:56 My
      '61
    Connie and Glenn run to Paris. Photop 61-4:60 Ap '62
    Corbin, J. Connie and Glen to marry, if . . . Photop
      61-5:26 My '62
    Corbin, J. Did he betray his bride-to-be? Photop 63-
      6:46 Je '63
    Finnigan, J. The man who came to the movies--to stay.

TV Guide 16-51:16 D 21 '68
Allen, J. Why she couldn't love him. Photop 75-6:62
Je '69

FORD, HARRISON
Valentine, S. But he doesn't have a chance. Photop 17-
2:49 Ja '20
Obit. Screen World 9:223 '58

FORD, PAUL
Wood, C. TV personalities biographical sketchbook.
TV Personalities p131 '56
This eagle's a sitting duck. TV Guide 5-12:22 Mr 23 '57
Mr. Weaver. New Yorker 36:34 Ap 16 '60

FORD, WALLACE
Tully, J. He started life on a doorstep. Photop 44-5:
40 O '33
Obit. Newsweek 67:67 Je 20 '66
Screen World 18:235 '67

FORMAN, TOM
Carr, A. Tom Forman. Feature Movie 2-7:50 Jl 10 '15
Boone, A. Rich men, poor men and actors. Photop
16-5:36 O '19

FORREST, ALLAN
Obit. Cur Bio '41

FORREST, ANN
Jordan, J. A daughter of the vikings. Photop 20-3:41
Ag '21

FORREST, SALLY
Chandler, D. It pays to get fired. Colliers 125:34 Ja
21 '50
Mulvey, K. The Forrest party plan. Photop 39-1:52
Ja '51
Asher, J. Love walked right in. Photop 39-2:52 F '51

FORSYTHE, JOHN
A matter of delicate balance. TV Guide 7-48:12 N 28 '59
Nichols, M. Cuties and a cliche. Coronet 50:14 Je '61
Hano, A. No doubt being a star is fun, fun, fun. TV
Guide 13-52 D 25 '65

FORTESCUE, KENNETH
  Person of promise. Films & Filming 6-6:17 Mr '60

FOSTER, DIANNE
  Don't turn your back on Dianne. TV Guide 9-20:28 My
    20 '61

FOSTER, PRESTON
  Cap'n John of the Cheryl Ann. TV Guide 3-21:5 My 21 '55
  Wood, C. TV personalities biographical sketchbook.
    TV Personalities p63 '57

FOSTER, SUSANNA
  Foster, S. What d'you mean, sweet sixteen? Photop
    18-6:33 My '41
  Franchey, J. A. Wonderful gamin. Colliers 107:16 Je
    14 '41
  Wilkinson, L. Oh Susanna! Photop 24-3:51 F '44
  Foster, S. Cadets on call. Photop 26-1:62 D '44
  Susie socks. Am Mag 139:130 My '45

FOULGER, BYRON
  McClure, A. The unsung heroes: Byron Foulger. Film
    Fan Mo 95:17 My '69

FOXE, EARLE
  Tierney, A. They loved a bandit. Photop 6-1:94 D '16

FRANCIOSA, ANTHONY
  Names to remember. Vogue 127:117 My 1 '56
  Anthony Franciosa: hothead newcomer. Look 21:92 Ag
    20 '57
  Bast, B. Watch this man! Photop 52-2:50 Ag '57
  Sheppard, D. The truth about my son. Photop 52-4:53
    O '57
  Nichols, M. Anthony Franciosa; at war with himself.
    Coronet 43:8 N '57
  To thine own self be true. Photop 53-4:68 Ap '58
  Michaels, E. Why a guy looks at other women. Photop
    56-5:52 N '59
  Biography. Cur Bio 22:15 Jl '61
    Same. Cur Bio Yrbk 1961:165 '62
  Hano, A. Mr. Franciosa changes his spots. TV Guide
    12-46:8 N 14 '64

FRANCIS, ANNE
  Wise, E. Hard luck Annie. Photop 48-4:48 O '55

Miss Francis and Mr. Smidgeon.   TV Guide 6-45:24 N 8
   '58
Lewis, R. W.   Honey West's earrings explode; so does
   Anne Francis.   TV Guide 13-41:19 O 9 '65

FRANCIS, CONNIE
Francis, C.   I love you . . . I never want to see you
   again.   Photop 55-6:56 Je '59
Christy, G.   Can I ever get him back again?   Photop 56-
   5:51 N '59
Marziglian, I.   Let's all go over to Connie Francis' pajama party.   Photop 56-6:50 D '59
Perlberg, R.   Gee, will I ever get married?   Photop
   58-4:42 O '60
Francis, C.   Will I mess up everything again?   Photop
   58-6:30 D '60
Perlberg, R.   No one guessed her secret.   Photop 59-6:
   54 Je '61
Stanford, J.   We hear you're getting married.   Photop
   60-3:44 S '61

FRANCIS, KAY
Hall, L.   Vamping with sound.   Photop 36-5:51 O '29
Hall, L.   Just three years.   Photop 42-5:48 O '32
Maxwell, V.   Just life and love.   Photop 44-1:76 Je '33
Roberts, K.   Acting in a business way; intv.   Colliers
   95:14 Mr 16 '35
Hamilton, S.   Okay Francis!   Photop 49-3:30 Mr '36
Don't try your luck out here!   Pict R 38:16 Ja '37
Maxwell, E.   It's romance again for Kay Francis.
   Photop 52-5:24 My '38
Mook, S. R.   I can't wait to be forgotten.   Photop 53-3:
   32 Mr '39
Kay Francis lives here.   House & Gard 76:52 O '39
Pyle, E.   Four good soldiers.   Sr Schol 42:2 Mr 29 '43
Paris, J. R. Jr. & Ringgold, G.   Kay Francis, inc.
   filmog.   Films In Review 15-2:65 F '64
Obit.   Newsweek 72:103 S 9 '68
   Time 92:68 S 6 '68
   Screen World 20:234 '69

FRANCIS, ROBERT
Obit.   Time 66:73 Ag 15 '55
   Screen World 7:223 '56

FRANCISCUS, JAMES
Goodwin, F.   It's back to school for a yule grad.

TV Guide 11-46:19 N 16 '63
Corbin, J. Pinup #16. Photop 65-1:54 Ja '64
Wood, A. Teacher with a bedside manner. Photop 65-
5:46 My '64
Artell, T. Daddy is a lover. Photop 66-1:45 Jl '64
Miller, E. Mr. Novak cuts class. Seventeen 23:141 S
'64
Bascombe, L. He looks so nice--but is he? Photop 67-
1:29 Ja '65
Tornabene, L. Tomorrow's stars. Good H 160:24 Mr
'65
Arrested by the police. Photop 68-2:8 Ag '65

FRANZ, EDUARD
Nothing of the actor except the ability. TV Guide 12-26:
6 Jl 4 '64

FRAWLEY, WILLIAM
Conlon, S. The "rediscovery" of Bill Frawley. Photop
47-2:58 Ja '35
Lucy's neighbors. TV Guide 6-12:4 Mr 20 '53
They love Lucy. Am Mag 155:55 Je '53
The Mertzes, and how they got that way. TV Guide 2-
52:5 D 25 '54
Wood, C. TV personalities biographical sketchbook.
TV Personalities p141 '57
He calls 'em as he sees 'em. TV Guide 9-31:4 Ag 5 '61
Obit. Newsweek 67:93 Mr 14 '66
Time 87:69 Mr 11 '66
Screen World 18:235 '67
Gray, B. William Frawley, inc. filmog. Films In Re-
view 17-5:324 My '66

FREDERICK, PAULINE
Biblical heroine. Cosmop 54:846 My '13
Pauline Frederick. Photop 7-3:56 F '15
Johnson, J. "Polly" Frederick; intv. Photop 8-5:62 O
'15
Frederick, P. Directors I have known. Photop 15-6:28
My '19
Patterson, A. The tragedies of Pauline Frederick.
Photop 23-5:28 Ap '23
St. Johns, A. R. What has happened to Pauline Fred-
erick? Photop 30-4:63 S '26
Bodeen, D. Pauline Frederick, inc. filmog. Films In
Review 16-2:69 F '65

FREEMAN, HOWARD
   Obit.   Screen World 19:232 '68

FREEMAN, MONA
   Babes.   Am Mag 145:117 Je '48
   McElroy, J.   Breakfast in Hollywood.   Photop 34-6:70
      My '49
   Hine, H.   Teen tot Mona Freeman discovers that a star's
      New York vacation closely resembles work.   Holiday
      7:24 Je '50
   Howe, H.   Mrs. Pat.   Photop 38-1:58 Jl '50
   Wheeler, L.   Halfway house.   Photop 38-3:58 S '50
   Corwin, J.   Unpredictable Mona.   Photop 43-5:38 My '53
   Gravin, R.   Filmography.   Films In Review 19-1:63 Ja
      '68

FROBE, GERT
   Man you love to hate.   Time 86:94 N 12 '65

FULLER, MARY
   Baker, C.   The girl on the cover; intv.   Photop 8-1:99
      Je '15
   Somewhere in France.   Photop 10-6:41 N '16
   Smith, F. J.   Photoplay finds Mary Fuller.   Photop 26-3:
      58 Ag '24

FUNICELLO, ANNETTE
   Fair weather ahead.   TV Guide 6-21:28 My 24 '58
   So long, Mickey.   TV Guide 7-8:17 F 21 '59
   Coy, K.   Why did I ever let him talk me into going
      steady?   Photop 55-5:62 My '59
   Anderson, N.   What is an Annette?   Photop 56-3:56 S '59
   Funicello, M.   Anka's okay, but Annette, she's in love.
      Photop 57-1:26 Ja '60
   Nichols, M.   Stardom bound.   Coronet 47:72 Ja '60
   Barclay, C.   What I learned about men since last Mon-
      day.   Photop 57-5:42 My '60
   Hamilton, S.   What happened to those wedding bells?
      Photop 57-6:61 Je '60
   Baskette, K.   When Paul took Annette home to his mother.
      Photop 58-2:62 Ag '60
   I'm just myself.   Seventeen 21:66 Ja '62
   She's the idol of little boys, and big ones too.   TV Guide
      11-41:12 O 12 '63
   Ardmore, J.   I'm going to have twins.   Photop 68-1:46
      Jl '65
   Resnick, S.   I'm afraid for my baby.   Photop 69-5:38 My '66

GABLE, CLARK

Lang, H.   What a man!   Photop 40-5:34 O '31
Quirk, J. R.   About Clark Gable.   Photop 40-6:67 N '31
Biery, R.   "I'm not so sure" says Clark Gable.   Photop 41-2:69 Ja '32
Biery, R.   Will Clark Gable last?   Photop 42-3:67 Ag '32
Biery, R.   Why Clark Gable says "I am paid not to think."   Photop 43-1:28 D '32
Lieber, E.   "I'd do it again" says Clark.   Photop 43-6: 30 My '33
French, W. F.   Clark Gable cuts the apron strings.   Photop 45-5:38 Ap '34
Pringle, H. F.   It's a living.   Colliers 94:17 D 8 '34
Biographical sketch.   Lit Digest 120:26 Ag 24 '35
When I was a boy.   St N 63:21 N '35
Greene, C.   Why Gable has stayed on top.   Photop 48-6: 24 N '35
St. Johns, A. R.   Love, fame and the Clark Gables.   Photop 49-2:14 F '36
Slap 'em for luck; autobiography.   Am Mag 122:35 S '36
Hastings, D.   Clark Gable's romantic plight.   Photop 50-3:12 S '36
Small, F.   Gable answers the call of the wild.   Photop 51-6:36 Je '37
Tully, J.   Clark Gable without women.   Cinema Arts 1-3:28 S '37
Doherty, E.   Can the Gable-Lombard love story have a happy ending?   Photop 52-5:18 My '38
Hamilton, S.   At last! Mrs. Clark Gable talks.   Photop 52-12:18 D '38
St. Johns, A. R.   Tyrone learns from Clark.   Photop 53-9:18 S '39
I was afraid of Rhett Butler.   Womans H C 67:17 F '40
Gable, C. as told to Ruth Waterbury.   Vivien Leigh, Rhett Butler and I.   Photop 54-2:12 F '40
McEvoy, J. P.   Joe Lucky.   Sat Eve Post 212:22 My 4 '40
Pringle, H. F.   Mr. and Mrs. Clark Gable.   Ladies Home J 57:20 My '40
Fletcher, A. W.   How Clark Gable and Carole Lombard live.   Photop 54-10:30 O '40
Why Janet Gaynor walked home.   Am Mag 131:42 Ap '41
Hamilton, S.   Gable--on the spot.   Photop 18-5:36 Ap '41

Waterbury, R.   What the loss of Carole Lombard means
   to Clark Gable.   Photop 20-5:28 Ap '42
Waterbury, R.   How Clark Gable is conquering loneliness.
   Photop 21-3:34 Ag '42
Your individual degree of discipline has national world
   value.   Educ Vict 1:12 N 16 '42
Glory's price.   Time 42:15 N 8 '43
Ruggles, W.   Investigation.   Am Mag 137:60 Mr '44
St. Johns, A. R.   A personal story on Clark Gable.
   Photop 24-4:32 Mr; 24-5:30 Ap '44
Schallert, E.   The girl in Clark Gable's wife.   Photop
   25-1:29 Je '44
Biography.   Cur Bio My '45
Canfield, A.   This week: Clark Gable.   Colliers 117:56
   Ja 19 '46
Public details of Clark Gable's private life.   Time 47:
   94 F 11 '46
Peters, S.   My Hollywood friends.   Photop 28-3:48 F '46
Fletcher, A. W.   Return of a romance?   Photop 29-6:36
   N '46
Parsons, L. O.   Mister "King."   Photop 31-6:40 N '47
LeRoy, M.   I saw a star.   Photop 33-3:38 Ag '48
Man behind the Gable fable.   Colliers 123:24 F 12 '49
Maxwell, E.   Gable fable.   Photop 36-1:52 Je '49
Waterbury, R.   The king takes a lady.   Photop 37-3:48
   Mr '50
Canfield, A.   What keeps Gable clicking?   Coronet 28:
   55 Ag '50
Maxwell, E.   Gable's in love again.   Photop 42-4:46 O
   '52
New bather, same Gable.   Life 34:80 Ja 26 '53
Glamour in Africa; filming Mogambo.   Look 17:41 Je 2
   '53
Siedel, F.   Boy called Billy.   Coronet 34:148 Jl '53
Parsons, L. O.   King Clark returns.   Cosmop 135:10 O
   '53
Who, Gable?   Colliers 133:26 Ja 8 '54
Shipp, C.   Gable saga.   Cosmop 139:19 Je '54
Clark Gable: the lonely man.   Look 18:60 S 7 '54
Garceau, J.   Reply to Gable: the lonely man.   Look 18:
   22 S 21 '54
Knight, A.   Hardy perennials.   Sat R 38:21 O 29 '55
McCarthy, J.   Clark Gable; his life story.   Look 19:63
   O 4; 103 O 18; 96 N 1 '55
Mrs. Gable keeps her eye on the king while he makes a
   movie with four queens.   Look 20:61 S 4 '56
Amour and the man.   Sat R 39:29 O 13 '56

King: he was leery of playing Rhett Butler. Newsweek
    48:70 D 24 '56
Kish, F. She calls him "papa" but she calls him
    "darling." Photop 51-2:68 F '57
Martin, P. I call on Clark Gable. Sat Eve Post 230:24
    O 5 '57
Indestructible Gable. Life 44:59 Ap 7 '58
Downs, R. How does it feel to die. Photop 57-2:58 F
    '60
Mathison, R. Who's a misfit? filming of The Misfits.
    Newsweek 56:102 S 12 '60
Nichols, M. Legend grows mellow. Coronet 48:14 S '60
Davidson, B. Clark Gable in his 60th year. McCalls
    88:66 N '60
Just before heart attack. Life 49:95 N 21 '60
Clark Gable is dead; a last intimate look. Life 49:92 N
    28 '60
Gable: the king is dead. Newsweek 56:27 N 28 '60
Hero's exit. Time 76:61 N 28 '60
Obit. Illus Lond N 237:961 N 26 '60
    Life 49:35N 28 '60
    Am Ann 1961:292 '61
    Brit Bk Yr 1961:514 '61
    Cur Bio 22:24 Ja '61
    Screen World 12:221 '61
Goode, J. Revealing talk of an old pro. Life 50:54B
    Ja 13 '61
Famous pair, and a finale. Life 50:53 Ja 13 '61
Gordon, S. Gable: last look at a king. Look 25:63 Ja
    31 '61
Allen, P. Without me, Clark Gable would never be a
    father. Photop 59-1:50 Ja '61
Gable's last movie. Look 25:57 Ja 31 '61
Weatherby, W. J. Misfits: epic or requiem? Sat R
    44:26 F 4 '61
For us the king will never die. Photop 59-2:70 F '61
Handsome heir to the fabled Gable. Life 50:99 Ap 14 '61
Hoffman, J. The secret Clark Gable and Kay never
    shared. Photop 59-4:36 Ap '61
Hamilton, S. Gable's son. Photop 60-1:32 Jl '61
Gable, K. Clark Gable; a personal portrait, abridged.
    Look 25:68 Ag 29 '61
Garceau, J. Dear Mr. G, abridged. Ladies Home J
    78:24 Jl; 42 Ag; 66 S '61
Scott, V. Life without Clark. Coronet 50:106 O '61
Samuels, C. King: the story of Clark Gable, abridged.
    Good H 153:72 O; 68 N '61

Rochlen, K.   The plot to steal my baby.   Photop 61-1:44
   Ja '62
Gordon, S.   Story of John Clark Gable; baby in the spot-
   light.   Look 26:22 Jl 3 '62

GABIN, JEAN
   Morse, W. Jr.   Escape from the Nazis.   Photop 19-2:36
      Jl '41
   Biography.   Cur Bio '41
   Mulvey, K.   I escaped the invader.   Womans H C 69:6
      Ja '42
   It happened overnight; how I became a platinum blond.
      Am Mag 134:124 Jl '42
   Surmelian, L.   The love dilemma of Jean Gabin.   Photop
      21-2:66 Jl '42
   And Gabin goes gaily on.   Newsweek 44:86 Jl 19 '54
   Nolan, J. E.   Jean Gabin, inc. filmog.   Films in Review
      14-4:193 Ap '63
   Cowie, P.   Jean Gabin.   Films & Filming 10-5:12 F '64
   Playing to the crowd.   Newsweek 63:38 My 11 '64

GABOR, EVA
   Gabbing with the Gabors.   Colliers 130:28 S 6 '52
   Whitcomb, J.   Lunch with Eva Gabor.   Cosmop 144:78
      My '58
   It is written in the goulash.   TV Guide 8-15:24 Ap 9 '60
   Whitney, D.   When a 'cheec Hongarian' found herself in a
      barnyard.   TV Guide 14-36:15 S 3 '66
   DeRoos, R.   Eva.   TV Guide 15-35:16 S 2 '67
   Biography.   Cur Bio 29:19 Jl '68
      Same.   Cur Bio Yrbk 1968:136 '69
   Taylor, T.   I hate to sleep alone.   Photop 75-5:36 My
      '69

GABOR, ZSA ZSA
   Another Gabor.   Life 31:103 O 15 '51
   Gabbing with the Gabors.   Colliers 130:28 S 6 '52
   Bride seemed sad.   Newsweek 43:22 Ja 11 '54
   Fusses over ladies and a ladies' man.   Life 36:24 Ja 11
      '54
   Gabor, Z. Z.   Men in my life.   Coronet 37:131 Ja '55
   New TV executive.   Fortune 56:77 O '57
   Real nice party group.   Life 44:153 My 26 '58
   Martin, P.   I call on Zsa Zsa Gabor.   Sat Eve Post
      231:44 S 13 '58
   How to write a book.   Time 73:37 Mr 9 '59
   Zsa Zsa Gabor woman.   TV Guide 7-21:24 My 23 '59

Celebrities on a stylish spree. Life 47:103 S 7 '59
Serious non-writer. New Yorker 36:16 Jl 30 '60
Nichols, M. Busy business of being Zsa Zsa. Coronet
    48:50 Ag '60
Douglas, A. Zsa Zsa Gabor portrays great literary
    heroines. Cosmop 149:42 Ag '60
Gabor, Z. Z. Zsa Zsa Gabor; my story, abridged. Mc
    Calls 87:66 Ag; 120 S; 106 O '60
Gabor, Z. Z. To love is weakness. Photop 62-5:42 N
    '62
Efron, E. Zsa Zsa talks about Zsa Zsa. TV Guide 16-
    12:14 Mr 23 '68

GALLAGHER, SKEETS
    Obit. Time 65:103 Je '55
    Screen World 7:223 '56

GAM, RITA
    TV leading ladies. Life 32:144 My 5 '52
    Silent siren. Life 33:103 S 15 '52
    Look, ma, I'm talkin'! Look 17:41 My 19 '53
    Gam, R. That Kelly girl and me. Photop 47-4:48 Ap '55
    Mrs. Thomas Guinzburg. Vogue 137:112 F 15 '61

GARAT, HENRI
    Obit. Screen World 11:216 '60

GARBO, GRETA
    West, M. That Stockholm Venus. Photop 29-6:36 My '26
    Biery, R. The story of Greta Garbo. Photop 33-5:30
        Ap; 33-6:36 My; 34-1:64 Je '28
    Wayne, P. Woman of Scandinavia. Pict R 31:6 O '29
    Hall, L. Garbo-maniacs. Photop 37-2:60 Ja '30
    Skinner, R. D. Greta Garbo in Anna Christies. Com-
        monweal 11:590 Mr 26 '30
    Sundborg, A. That Gustafsson girl. Photop 37-5:40 Ap;
        37-6:40 My '30
    Palmborg, R. P. The private life of Greta Garbo.
        Photop 38-4:38 S; 38-5:36 O '30
    Hall, L. Garbo vs. Dietrich. Photop 39-3:50 F '31
    Albert, K. Did Brown and Garbo fight? Photop 39-4:33
        Mr '31
    Albert, K. Exploding the Garbo myth. Photop 39-5:70
        Ap '31
    Condon, F. Greta and Marlene. Sat Eve Post 203:29
        My 30 '31
    Clive, F. Greta Garbo, the woman nobody knows.

Liv Age 340:369 Je '31

Hall, L.   See Garbo first.   Photop 40-2:61 Jl '31

Marshall, M.   With benefit of Garbo.   Nation 133:526 N 11 '31

Biery, R.   Hollywood's cruelty to Greta Garbo.   Photop 41-2:28 Ja '32

Wheelright, R.   When Nordic met Latin.   Photop 41-3: 45 F '32

Condon, F.   Lady who lives behind a wall.   Sat Eve Post 204:31 Mr 26 '32

Albert, K.   How Garbo's fear of people started.   Photop 41-4:28 Mr '32

York, C.   One more Garbo fan.   Photop 41-6:67 My '32

Garbo at sea.   Cinema Digest 1-8:30 Ag 22 '32

Hall, L.   Garbo, she can go home.   Photop 42-3:33 Ag '32

Young, S.   Film note: Greta Garbo.   New Repub 72:176 S 28 '32

Ingwerson, A.   No Chaplin honors for Garbo.   Photop 42-6:30 N '32

Ingwerson, A.   Did Garbo marry Stiller?   Photop 43-2: 47 Ja '33

Martin, H.   Greta Garbo.   Cinema Digest 3-4:11 Ap 10 '33

Cummings, A.   Is the Garbo rage over?   Photop 43-5:36 Ap '33

Hall, H.   Garbo greater?   Cinema Digest 3-8:3 My 8 '33

Shawell, J.   Garbo or Dietrich.   Pict R 34:16 Jl '33

Hodgekins, A.   Garbo's gamble.   Photop 44-2:37 Jl '33

Stevers, M.   Now I can help you.   Photop 44-5:74 O '33

Dale, H.   Two queens were born in Sweden.   Photop 44-5:29 O '33

On the screen.   Lit Digest 117:34 Ja 13 '34

Troy, W.   Garbo and screen acting.   Nation 138:112 Ja 24 '34

Maxwell, V.   The amazing story behind Garbo's choice of Gilbert.   Photop 45-2:32 Ja '34

Clairmont, L.   Greta Garbo wanted to be a tight rope walker.   Photop 45-6:28 My '34

Baskette, K.   Guessing time for Garbo.   Photop 46-4:55 S '34

Wiles, O.   What it's like to work with Garbo.   Photop 46-6:43 N '34

Troy, W.   New Garbo?   Nation 139:721 D 19 '34

Rinehart, M. R.   Women of the year.   Pict R 36:7 Ja '35

Aydelotte, W.   A heroine to her tailor.   Photop 47-6:44 My '35

On the current screen. Lit Digest 120:21 S 21 '35
Adrian answers 20 questions on Garbo. Photop 48-4:36
   S '35
Taylor, W. E. I had tea with Garbo! C S Mon Mag
   p16 Mr 25 '36
Mason, J. Garbo talks at last! Photop 50-1:48 Jl '36
Madame Sylvia. Garbo's glamour--mystery or misery.
   Photop 50-6:56 D '36
Canfield, M. C. Letter to Garbo. Theatre Arts 21:951
   D '37
Simmons, J. I won't marry Stokowski says Greta Garbo.
   Photop 52-1:16 Ja '38
Idyl. Time 31:50 Mr 14 '38
Marianne. Great lady. Photop 53-7:15 Jl '39
Churchill, D. W. Legend laughs. N. Y. Times Mag p4
   Ja 14 '40
   Same abridged. Read Digest 36:113 Ap '40
Garbo shedding clothes and mystery, swims, skis and
   dances. Life 11:86 S 29 '41
Phelps, W. L. I wish I'd met. Good H 114:39 Ja '42
Palmborg, R. P. Garbo finds herself. Photop 20-4:54
   Mr '42
Here comes Garbo. Time 52:72 Ag 30 '48
Return of the duchess. Time 53:94 Je 6 '49
Worden, H. Greta Garbo, sphinx without a secret.
   Coronet 26:134 Jl '49
Swedish-American becomes citizen of the U. S. Life 30:
   30 F 19 '51
Behind the mask. Coronet 30:109 Jl '51
New style of Garbo. Life 31:53 O 8 '51
Huff, T. The career of Greta Garbo, inc. filmog.
   Films In Review 2-10:1 D '51
Benchley, N. This is Garbo. Colliers 129:13 Mr 1 '52
Benchley, N. Beautiful myth. Read Digest 61:17 Jl '52
Birch, L. Incognita. New Statesm 44:714 D 13 '52
Tynan, K. Garbo. Sight & Sound 23-4:187 Ap/Je '54
Bainbridge, J. Great Garbo, excerpts from Garbo.
   Life 38:84 Ja 10; 76 Ja 17; 112 Ja 24 '55
Biography. Cur Bio 16:20 Ap '55
Garbo at Capri. Look 19:84 S 6 '55
Greatest stars. Cosmop 141:28 O '56
Fleet, S. Garbo: the lost star. Films & Filming 3-3:
   14 D '56
Biography. Cur Bio Yrbk 1955:221 '56
Garbo visits Liz. Photop 54-2:54 Ag '58
Brooks, L. Gish and Garbo, the executive war on stars.

Sight & Sound 28-1:13 Win '58/9

Peck, S.   Still a mystery.   N.Y. Times Mag p62 S 18 '60

Garbo chill.   Newsweek 57:79 Ja 16 '61

Britten, R.   Caught off-guard.   Photop 59-6:62 Je '61

La dolce Greta.   Newsweek 61:89 Mr 11 '63

Good grief! Garbo?   Life 54:55 Ap 5 '63

Levy, A.   Garbo walks! Show 3-6:60 Je '63

Quigly, I.   Garbo, Garbo, Garbo.   Spectator (Lond) 211: 290 S 6 '63

Whitehall, R.   Garbo--how good was she?   Films & Filming 9-12:42 S '63

Timeless beauty and greatest of film stars: Greta Garbo. Illus Lond N 243:917 N 30 '63

Cruise, E. J.   Great Garbo.   Seventeen 23:28 Ja '64

Alpert, H.   Saga of G. Lovisa Gustafsoon.   N.Y. Times Mag p26 S 5 '65

Barthes, R.   Garbo's face.   Moviegoer 3:8 Sum '66

Kroll, J.   Garbo.   Newsweek 72:76 Jl 22 '68

GARDNER, AVA

Hollywood's new generation.   Life 24:99 My 24 '48

Martin, P.   Tarheel tornado.   Sat Eve Post 220:32 Je 5 '48

Swanson, P.   Don't be unhappy.   Photop 37-3:60 Mr '50

Home-town girl.   Good H 130:325 Ap '50

Carlile, T.   The truth about Ava.   Photop 39-1:26 Ja '51

Maxwell, E.   The Gardner-Sinatra jigsaw.   Photop 40-1: 48 Jl '51

Farmer's daughter.   Time 58:68 S 3 '51

How Ava Gardner fooled Hollywood.   Photop 40-4:52 O '51

Well, said Frankie, we finally made it.   Life 31:49 N 19 '51

Fink, H.   I was there.   Photop 40-6:66 D '51

Waterbury, R.   The life and loves of Ava Gardner. Photop 41-2:37 F '52

Clarke, S.   Why they are the battling Sinatras.   Photop 41-6:38 Je '52

Ava and her times.   Newsweek 40:93 N 24 '52

Why is a movie star?   Look 17:54 F 10 '53

Attwood, W.   London memo from William Attwood. Subject: Ava.   Look 17:56 F 10 '53

Glamour in Africa; filming Mogambo.   Look 17:41 Je 2 '53

Man who wouldn't look at Ava.   Look 17:32 O 6 '53

Corwin, J.   Cease fire.   Photop 44-6:33 D '53

Ava Gardner--beauty.   Vogue 123:147 F 1 '54

Arnold, M.   Lonesome on top of the world.   Photop 45-
   2:58 F '54
New light on Ava.   Life 36:139 Ap 12 '54
End of the affair.   Time 63:102 Je 21 '54
Ava Gardner plays the gypsy.   Colliers 134:28 Jl 23 '54
Speaking of pictures.   Life 37:16 O 18 '54
Lardner, J.   Public love.   Newsweek 44:88 D 13 '54
LaBarre, H.   Ava in Pakistan.   Cosmop 140:70 Mr '56
Hyams, J.   Private hell of Ava Gardner.   Look 20:143
   N '27; 103 D 11 '56
Nichols, M.   Barefoot girl with dressing.   Coronet 41:8
   Ap '57
Waterbury, R.   Ava Gardner's dry tears.   Photop 51-4:
   60 Ap '57
Joyce, A.   The woman behind the headlines.   Photop 52-
   4:49 O '57
Graves, R.   Toast to Ava Gardner.   New Yorker 34:34
   Ap 26 '58
Whitcomb, J.   Goya's artistic violence makes an exciting
   movie.   Cosmop 146:68 Ja '59
Watson, B.   Haunted.   Photop 56-5:79 N '59
Jaffe, R.   Private demons of Ava Gardner.   Good H
   152:68 Mr '61
Miron, C.   Ava at 38.   Photop 59-6:24 Je '61
Todd, R.   Did Ava strike out with Roger?   Photop 61-1:
   46 Ja '62
Biography.   Cur Bio 26:23 Mr '65
   Same.   Cur Bio Yrbk 1963:153 '65
Vincent, M.   Ava Gardner, inc. filmog.   Films In Re-
   view 16-6:343 Je/Jl '65
Reed, R.   Ava; life in the afternoon.   Esquire 67:102 My
   '67

GARDINER, REGINALD
DeRoos, R.   I'm the longest-haired gent who ever lived.
   TV Guide 15-26:12 Jl 1 '67

GARDNER, HELEN
Darnell, J.   A day spent with Helen Gardner.   Photop
   5-2:72 Ja '14
Two Helens.   New Yorker 35:17 Ja 9 '60
Obit.   Screen World 20:234 '69

GARFIELD, JOHN
No. 1 male cinema discovery of 1938.   Time 33:50 Ja 30
   '39
Zeitlin, I.   It pays to be tough.   Photop 53-1:17 Ja '39

Crichton, K.   No part too tough.   Colliers 103:11 Ap 13
    '39
Show business as usual.   Theatre Arts 27:117 Mr '43
Garfield, J.   Speaking of Garfield.   Photop 22-6:52 My
    '43
Paul, E.   Citizen Garfield.   Photop 28-1:38 D '45
Our part in Body and soul.   Opportunity 26:20 Ja '48
Garfield, Mrs. J.   John's other life.   Photop 32-4:70 Mr
    '48
Biography.   Cur Bio 9:16 Ap '48
    Same.   Cur Bio Yrbk 1948:236 '49
Door of mystery.   Coronet 29:24 Ap '51
Death of a Golden boy.   Newsweek 39:24 Je 2 '52
Tough guy.   Time 59:92 Je 2 '52
Obit.   Life 32:36 Je 2 '52
    Cur Bio 13:22 Jl '52
    Am Ann 1953:271 '53
    Cur Bio Yrbk 1952:204 '53
John Garfield.   Sight & Sound 22-1:3 Jl/S '52
Roman, R. C.   John Garfield, inc. filmog.   Films In
    Review 11-6:325 Je/Jl '60

GARGAN, WILLIAM
    Bosworth, C.   A good pal is worth three dollars.   Photop
        46-2:34 Jl '34
    Bill Gargan as "Martin Kane."   TV Guide 2-38:8 S 17 '49
    Kane quartet of Martin Kane, private eye.   Newsweek 35:
        52 Mr 27 '50
    Wall, C. B.   William Gargan's finest role.   Read Digest
        42:49 S '63
    Bill Gargan's greatest role.   Life 59:63 D 3 '65
    Biography.   Cur Bio 30:6 Ja '69
    Gargan, W.   Why me? an autobiography; abridged.
        Good H 168:92 Mr '69

GARLAND, BEVERLY
    Won't somebody remember me?   TV Guide 6-41:24 O 11
        '58
    McClelland, D.   Ill-used actresses, inc. filmog.   Films
        In Review 14-10:638 D '63
    She's finally getting a chance to laugh out loud.   TV
        Guide 13-6:23 F 6 '65

GARLAND, JUDY
    Jot.   Am Mag 125:114 My '38
    MacKaye, M.   Might atoms of Hollywood.   Ladies Home
        J 57:19 S '40

Willson, D. A Garland for Judy. Photop 54-9:32 S '40

Waterbury, R. Boys--and Judy Garland. Photop 54-12:
14 D '40

York, C. The marriage dilemma of Judy Garland.
Photop 18-6:27 My '41

Biography. Cur Bio '41

Reid, S. The private life of Judy Garland Rose. Photop
21-6:38 N '42

Palms, J. & Dawson, C. Pocketful o' songs. Photop
22-1:54 D '42; 22-2:48 Ja; 22-3:50 F '43

Judy's symphonic jive. Newsweek 22:80 Jl 12 '43

Skolsky, S. Judy Garland--victory model. Photop 23-2:
30 Jl '43

Garland, J. Lonely girl. Photop 23-6:30 N '43

Baby Nora Bayes. Time 42:90 D 27 '43

Parsons, L. O. The mystery of Judy Garland. Photop
25-2:28 Jl '44

Nathan, R. To Judy Garland. Photop 25-5:36 O '44

St. Johns, A. R. Love song for Judy Garland. Photop
26-5:28 Ap; 26-6:40 My '45

Ormiston, R. Halfway to heaven. Photop 27-5:34 O '45

St. Johns, A. R. Judy. Photop 27-6:30 N '45

St. Johns, E. Million dollar lullaby. Photop 29-6:60 N
'46

Maxwell, E. Liza, Liza, smile at me. Photop 30-6:40
My '47

St. Johns, E. The truth about Judy Garland's health.
Photop 31-6:46 N '47

Arnold, M. The punch in Judy Garland. Photop 33-4:
40 S '48

Parsons, L. O. Spotlight on Liza. Photop 34-5:44 Ap
'49

Payne, V. Report on Judy Garland. Photop 36-3:33
Ag '49

Three little girls grow up. Good H 129:168 S '49

Working girl. Time 54:101 N 14 '49

Alsop, C. Judy's singing again. Photop 36-6:34 N '49

Judy couldn't relax. Newsweek 36:14 Jl 3 '50

Parsons, L. O. The only hope. Photop 38-3:33 S '50

Judy goes boom. Life 30:49 Ap 23 '51

Star turns Judy Garland. Sight & Sound 20-2:53 Je '51

Pepper, B. No sad songs for Judy Garland. Photop
40-2:35 Ag '51

Judy comes back. Life 31:105 O 29 '51

Clurman, H. Punch and Judy. New Repub 125:21 N 26
'51

Kass, R. Films and TV. Cath World 174:223 D '51
Linet, B. I was there. Photop 41-1:29 Ja '52
Warren, J. New name for happiness. Photop 41-2:95
     F '52
Benchley, N. Offstage. Theatre Arts 36:18 F '52
Judy's triumph. Newsweek 39:90 Mr 10 '52
Fadiman, C. Judy and Juan; two high moments. Holiday
     11:6 Mr '52
Maxwell, E. Let's stop coddling Judy Garland. Photop
     41-4:42 Ap '52
Hotchner, A. E. Judy Garland's rainbow. Read Digest
     61:73 Ag '52
Biography. Cur Bio 13:7 D '52
     Same. Cur Bio Yrbk 1952:204 '53
Graham, S. What's wrong with Judy Garland and her
     mother? Photop 42-6:64 D '52
Corwin, J. Mother's day. Photop 43-2:76 F '53
Little girl, big voice. N. Y. Times Mag p50 Ja 24 '54
Harvey, E. Star is reborn. Colliers 133:32 Ap 30 '54
Star is reborn. Look 18:63 My 18 '54
New day for Judy. Life 37:163 S 13 '54
Hopper, H. No more tears for Judy. Womans H C 81:
     27 S '54
Triumph for Hollywood. Newsweek 44:86 N 1 '54
Goode, B. Judy's painting the clouds with sunshine.
     Photop 46-5:70 N '54
How not to love a woman. Coronet 37:41 F '55
Shipp, C. Star who thinks nobody loves her. Sat Eve
     Post 227:28 Ap 2 '55
How not to love a woman, abridged. Read Digest 66:
     115 My '55
Lorna goes on unrehearsed at rehearsal. Life 39:87 O
     10 '55
Clurman, H. Theatre. Nation 183:314 O 13 '56
Judy at the Palace. Dance Mag 30:29 N '56
Hyams, J. Crack-up. Photop 51-1:38 Ja '57
Garland, J. Real me; as told to J. Hyams. McCalls
     84:78 Ap '57
Lyle, J. The day a marriage died. Photop 53-6:49 Je
     '58
Judy Garland at the Met. Newsweek 53:112 My 11 '59
Tynan. K. Theatre; engagement at the Metropolitan opera
     house. New Yorker 35:79 My 23 '59
Over and over the rainbow. Time 77:52 My 5 '61
Alexander, S. Judy's new rainbow. Life 50:108 Je 2 '61
Lipsitt, R. Judy at Carnegie. Theatre 3-6:11 Je '61
McVay, D. Judy Garland. Films & Filming 8-1:10 O '61

Redbook dialogue.   Redbook 118:60 N '61
Four for posterity.   Look 26:84 Ja 16 '62
Barber, R.   Eternal magic for Judy Garland.   Good H
    154:53 Ja '62
Davidson, B.   Judy, another look at the rainbow.   Mc
    Calls 89:95 Ja '62
Hamilton, J.   Judy.   Look 26:101 Ap 10 '62
deToledano, R.   Cult of Judy.   Nat R 13:154 Ap 28 '62
Rosterman, R.   Judy Garland, inc. filmog.   Films In
    Review 13-4:206 Ap '62
New new Garland.   Time 80:57 N 16 '62
Cantan, S.   Liza Minnelli: Judy's daughter bows in.
    Look 27:51 My 21 '63
Judy and Mickey reunited.   Life 55:47 Jl 19 '63
Poirier, N.   Momma's girl; Judy Garland's daughter.
    Sat Eve Post 236:30 O 5 '63
Whitney, D.   The great Garland gamble.   TV Guide 11-
    42:20 O 19 '63
Question mark.   Newsweek 62:70 N 4 '63
Lewis, R. W.   TV troubles of Judy Garland.   Sat Eve
    Post 236:93 D 7 '63
Second generation--Garland style.   Sr Schol 84:14 Ja 31
    '64
Garland, J.   There'll always be an encore.   McCalls 91:
    54 Ja; 64 F '64
Dickens, H.   Judy Garland.   Film Careers 1-2:3 Mr '64
Ringgold, G.   Judy on TV.   Film Careers 1-2:20 Mr '64
Connor, E.   The Wizard of Oz.   Film Careers 1-2:23
    Mr '64
Barbour, A. G.   The Garland hit parade.   Film Careers
    1-2:28 Mr '64
McCarty, C.   Judy's film index and song notes.   Film
    Careers 1-2:36 Mr '64
Martin, W.   A fan is born.   Film Careers 1-2:60 Mr '64
Scott, V.   Judy's story of the show that failed.   TV Guide
    12-18:10 My 2 '64
Two old pros.   Time 83:44 My 29 '64
Triumph of Judy's Liza.   Life 58:82 My 28 '65
Albie, E.   Judy Garland.   McCalls 94:103 O '66
Seance at the Palace.   Time 90:40 Ag 18 '67
Lewis, T.   Judy Garland at home at the Palace.   Amer-
    ica 117:208 Ag 26 '67
Plot against Judy Garland.   Ladies Home J 84:64 Ag '67
Korall, B.   Garland phenomenon.   Sat R 50:66 S 30 '67
Davidson, M.   My mom and I; intv. with Liza Minelli.
    Good H 167:72 Jl '68
Goldman, W.   Judy floats.   Esquire 71:78 Ja '69

Green, T. I had her pills under lock. Photop 76-2:44
 Ag '69
Kearley, J. Judy. Film 55:19 Sum '69

GARNER, JAMES
 Can he outdraw the champs? TV Guide 5-45:17 N 9 '57
 Free wheeling slick. Time 70:37 D 30 '57
 Asher, J. Maverick. Photop 53-3:48 Mr '58
 Person of promise. Films & Filming 4-8:12 My '58
 TV's midas touch. Look 22:70 S 16 '58
 Martin, P. I call on Bret Maverick. Sat Eve Post 231:
  20 O 11 '58
 Funniest brother act since the Marxes. TV Guide 7-3:17
  Ja 17 '59
 Hoffman, J. Nobody ever seemed to want to love me.
  Photop 56-4:38 O '59
 The cowboys' lament. TV Guide 7-47:17 N 21 '59
 Still a maverick. TV Guide 9-12:14 Mr 25 '61
 Corbin, J. Pinup #15. Photop 64-3:45 S '63
 Kessner, J. I've never made a mistake. Photop 64-5:
  63 N '63
 Miller, E. James Garner makes the scene. Seventeen
  23:122 O '64
 Norbye, J. P. James Garner drives at Monte Carlo.
  Pop Sci 189:78 Ag '66
 Scott, D. James Garner really races in Grand prix.
  Pop Sci 189:78 Ag '66
 Biography. Cur Bio 27:20 N '66
  Same. Cur Bio Yrbk 1966:117 '67
 See, C. Garner is a grump. TV Guide 16-45:14 N 9 '68

GARNER, PEGGY ANN
 Three little movie girls. Life 18:76 F 26 '45
 Junior miss. Life 19:51 Jl 23 '45
 Roberts, W. Peg of our hearts. Photop 27-2:50 Jl '45

GARON, PAULINE
 Winship, M. Enter the DeMille Blonde. Photop 23-2:
  33 Ja '23

GARRETT, BETTY
 Garrett, B. I'm just wild about Larry Parks. Photop
  33-5:48 O '48
 Betty has the voice. Am Mag 148:110 Ag '49
 Colby, A. Keep it secret. Photop 37-6:64 Je '50
 Chapman, P. Dig this crazy rhythm girl. Photop 49-1:
  39 Ja '56

McClelland, D.   Waste.   Films In Review 13-2:126 F '62

GARSON, GREER
  Crichton, K.   Bright beauty.   Colliers 105:11 My 18 '40
  Baskette, K.   The battling duchess of Garson.   Photop
      54-10:27 O '40
  Waterbury, R.   Redheaded rebel.   Photop 18-3:54 F; 18-
      4:54 Mr '41
  Greer Garson's poodles are sent to school for manners.
      Life 10:80 Je 23 '41
  Griswold, J. B.   Redheaded buzz saw.   Am Mag 133:42
      F '42
  Daughtery, F.   Good-bye, Mrs. Chips!   C S Mon Mag
      p 16 My 9 '42
  Strauss, T.   I wasn't born with a bustle.   N. Y. Times
      Mag p14 Jl 19 '42
  Emerson, B.   Secret romance.   Photop 21-3:26 Ag '42
  Mrs. Miniver steps out.   N. Y. Times Mag p33 S 27 '42
  Steele, J. H.   Portrait of a lady with red hair.   Photop
      22-1:40 D '42
  Biography.   Cur Bio '42
  Jefferson, S.   Why Hollywood told Greer Garson: don't
      marry.   Photop 22-3:28 F '43
  Life calls on Greer Garson in Hollywood.   Life 14:90
      Ap 12 '43
  Jefferson, S.   Navy lady.   Photop 23-5:29 O '43
  Ideal woman.   Time 42:54 D 20 '43
  Skolsky, S.   Grace-note on Greer Garson.   Photop 24-3:
      34 F '44
  Parsons, L. O.   A story from the heart of Greer Garson.
      Photop 25-3:28 Ag '44
  Gardner, M.   Glorified Mrs; off-stage close-up.   Ladies
      Home J 61:20 S '44
  Maxwell, E.   Gold medal lady.   Photop 26-6:26 My '45
  Howe, H.   Redheaded woman.   Photop 27-6:47 N '45
  Sammis, F. R.   First lady--second time.   Photop 28-4:
      37 Mr '46
  Waterbury, R.   Second chance.   Photop 29-5:39 O '46
  Martin, P.   Hollywood's fabulous female.   Sat Eve Post
      219:22 D 28 '46
  Parsons, L. O.   Search for happiness.   Photop 32-1:34
      D '47
  Speaking of pictures.   Life 24:21 Je 7 '48
  Garson, G.   That prize Pidgeon.   Photop 34-4:62 Mr '49
  Bell, P.   Greer Garson says: beauty is a state of mind.
      McCalls 81:110 Je '54
  Why Greer Garson wants to chew scenery on TV.   TV

Guide 3-14:15 Ap 2 '55
Unexpected Eleanor. Life 49:84 S 12 '60
Greer Garson plays Mrs. F. D. R. Theatre 2-9:24 S '60
Luft, H. G. Greer Garson, inc. filmog. Films In Review 12-3:152 Mr '61
Garson, G. I love to dramatize food; as told to J. Anderson. Ladies Home J 78:71 Je '61

GASSMAN, VITTORIO
Winters, S. The man I married. Photop 43-5:58 My '53
Rogers, M. Together again. Photop 44-2:24 Ag '53
Italy's man of a thousand faces. Films & Filming 5-7:29 Ap '59
Mankin, P. Good omens from Italy. New Repub 143:19 Jl 18 '60
Lane, J. F. Rise of the matador. Plays & Players 10-9:18 Je '63
Biography. Cur Bio 25:8 O '64
    Same. Cur Bio Yrbk 1964:141 '64
Davis, M. S. Hamlet who wants to play clowns. N. Y. Times Mag p46 S 19 '65

GATES, NANCY
Career or family. TV Guide 7-47:28 N 21 '59

GAUNTIER, GENE
Condon, M. Hot chocolate and reminiscences at nine of the morning. Photop 7-2:69 Ja '15
Blazing the trail. Womans H C 55:7 O; 25 N; 15 D '28; 56:13 Ja; 20 F; 18 Mr '29

GAVIN, JOHN
Non-neurotic newcomer. Look 22:65 Jl 22 '58
Slater, L. McCalls visits. McCalls 85:6 Ag '58
Ardmore, J. Rebel with a cause. Photop 61-6:48 Je '62
Biography. Cur Bio 23:26 S '62
    Same. Cur Bio Yrbk 1962:147 '63
Lewis, J. D. But you can't ride a horse in striped pants. TV Guide 12-21:15 My 23 '64

GAYNOR, JANET
Tully, J. Janet Gaynor. Pict R 29:4 Mr '28
Spensley, D. My life--so far. Photop 35-1:34 D '28; 35-2:50 Ja '29
Parsons, H. Janet goes to war. Photop 38-3:38 Ag '30
Albert, K. On the job! Photop 38-6:33 N '30
Fidler, J. M. Marian and Janet. Photop 42-2:73 Jl '32

Fidler, J. M.   Now what next, Janet?   Photop 43-4:37
 Mr '33
Maxwell, V.   Janet chooses her man.   Photop 43-5:35
 Ap '33
Hamilton, S.   The imp they call Janet.   Photop 44-6:71
 N '33
Holdom, C.   Janet of the films.   C S Mon Mag p3 Jl 24
 '35
Hamman, M.   Their lucky break.   Pict R 38:64 D '36
Bailey, K.   A star is born again.   Photop 51-7:36 Jl '37
Hayes, B.   How Tyrone Power won the lonely heart of
 Janet Gaynor.   Photop 52-1:14 Ja '38
Waterbury, R.   Happiness for Janet--designed by Adrian.
 Photop 53-11:26 N '39
Adrian's Africa.   House & Gard 96:180 O '49
Carr, C. L.   Janet Gaynor, inc. filmog.   Films In Re-
 view 10-8:470 O '59
Where are they now?   Newsweek 61:20 Ap 15 '63

GAYNOR, MITZI
Gaynor, M.   With all my love.   Photop 40-5:44 N '51
Goodman, E.   Mitzi's a merry madcap.   Colliers 129:15
 F 16 '52
Wilson, L.   They call her sparkle plenty.   Photop 41-4:
 62 Ap '52
Roberts, W.   Her happiness is showing.   Photop 42-1:58
 Jl '52
Arnold, M.   The strange romance of Mitzi Gaynor.
 Photop 42-4:48 O '52
Corwin, J.   Change of heart.   Photop 43-1:68 Ja '53
Swanson, P.   Mitzi made up her mind.   Photop 44-6:60
 D '53
Emmett, R.   Pandemonium reigned in paradise.   Photop
 47-6:61 Je '55
Phillips, D.   What she goes for she gets.   Photop 48-4:
 68 O '55
Maddox, T.   The bride vanished.   Photop 49-5:44 My '56
Bundle of ginger.   Coronet 40:10 My '56
Bean, J.   My princess yum yum.   Photop 50-2:50 Ag '56
McCalls visits.   McCalls 85:14 Ap '58
Johnson, R.   She made it the second time.   Sat Eve Post
 231:32 Ag 23 '58
Bester, A.   Mitzi the gypsy.   Holiday 27:131 Je '60
Mitzi fractures Las Vegas.   Life 51:48 Ag 4 '61
Como, W.   On the gypsy circuit.   Dance Mag 41:20 F
 '67
Prelutsky, B.   Mitzi keeps it light.   TV Guide 16-41:

12 O 12 '68

GAZZARA, BEN
Serious Sicilian. New Yorker 31:25 Ap 23 '55
Durslag, M. The egghead flatfoot. TV Guide 11-41:8
O 12 '63
All about that nude love scene. Photop 66-5:50 N '64
Condon, M. They remember Ben . . . TV Guide 15-1:
18 Ja 7 '67
Biography. Cur Bio 28:19 N '67
Same. Cur Bio Yrbk 1967:134 '68
Efron, E. When are you going to die? TV Guide 16-5:
15 F 3 '68

GEDDES, BARBARA BEL
Houghton, N. Tomorrow arrives today. Theatre Arts
30:82 F '46
Nichols, L. Gallery of leading ladies. N. Y. Times Mag
p21 Mr 3 '46
Sink or swim. Am Mag 144:113 Ag '47
New star! Barbara Bel Geddes. Life 24:65 Ap 12 '48
Biography. Cur Bio 9:15 Jl '48
Same. Cur Bio Yrbk 1948:238 '49
Swanson, P. The Bel Geddes plan. Photop 33-5:44 O
'48
Geddes, B. B. Our life with Susan; ed by J. Alvin.
Parents Mag 25:32 S '50
Miss Bel Geddes. New Yorker 27:28 Ap 7 '51
Rising star. Time 57:78 Ap 9 '51
Gelman, M. Barbara Bel Geddes. Theatre 3-2:17 F '61
Can witty women win in love? Life 50:70 Ap 14 '61

GENDRON, PIERRE
Obit. Screen World 8:222 '57

GENN, LEO
Actor and lawyer. New Yorker 22:25 F 15 '47

GEORGE, GLADYS
They stand out from the crowd. Lit Digest 119:10 Ja 19
'35
Crichton, K. Life on the strand. Colliers 95:19 Mr 9
'35
Rinehart, M. R. Valiant picture for a valiant star.
Womans H C 63:57 O '36
Obit. Newsweek 44:59 D 20 '54
Time 64:64 D 20 '54

Am |Ann 1955:290 '55
Brit Bk Yr 1955:576 '55
Screen World 6:223 '55

GERAGHTY, CARMELITA
Geraghty, T. J.   Fathering a film star.   Photop 34-4:71
S '28
Obit.   Screen World 18:235 '67

GERRARD, CHARLES
Copeland, G.   Taking advantage of a villain.   Photop 17-
4:52 My '20

GHOSTLEY, ALICE
New faces.   Theatre Arts 36:19 Ag '52
Higgins, B.   Alice in blunderland.   TV Guide 12-21:8 My
23 '64

GIBSON, HOOT
Baskette, K.   Cruising cowboy.   Photop 45-6:45 My '34
Ager, C.   Then and now.   N. Y. Times Mag p62 S 20 '59
Hard-riding Hoot.   Newsweek 60:19 S 3 '62
Obit.   Time 80:64 Ag 31 '62
Am Ann 1963:759 '63
Brit Bk Yr 1963:869 '63
Screen World 14:222 '63

GIBSON, WYNNE
Biery, R.   Down to two cents.   Photop 41-6:40 My '32

GIELGUD, JOHN
Shackleton, E.   English stage album.   Theatre Arts 15:
770 S '31
Dukes, A.   English scene: John Gielgud's Hamlet.
Theatre Arts 19:84 F '35
John Gielgud shows New York a memorable Hamlet.
Newsweek 8:27 O 17 '36
Actor to Elsinore.   Time 28:44 O 19 '36
Morley, C.   Mr. Gielgud's Hamlet.   Sat R 14:13 O 24
'36
Season's first guests.   Theatre Arts 20:819 O '36
Isaacs, E. J. R.   West End on Broadway, John Geilgud's
Hamlet.   Theatre Arts 20:841 N '36
Pringle, H. F.   Hamlet in high.   Colliers 99:17 Ja 30 '37
Actor prepares.   Theatre Arts 21:30 Ja '37
Eaton, W. P.   Shakespeare with a difference.   Atlan 159:
474 Ap '37

Artist's apprenticeship; chapters from an autobiography.
   Theatre Arts 21:357 My 453 Je '37
In the margin. Theatre Arts 21:798 O '37
Dukes, A. English scene: Gielgud's Richard II. Theatre
   Arts 21:845 N '37
Actor's dilemma. Theatre Arts 23:274 Ap '39
John Gielgud's life. Newsweek 14:25 Jl 17 '39
Anderson, J. To the manner born. Sat R 20:13 Ag 5 '39
Gilder, R. Three actors. Theatre Arts 23:761 O '39
Before Macbeth. Theatre Arts 26:112 F '42
Dukes, A. Gielgud Macbeth. Theatre Arts 26:615 O '42
Christmas party in Gibraltar. Theatre Arts 27:277 My
   '43
Staging Love for love. Theatre Arts 27:662 N '43
Haymarket and the New. Theatre Arts 29:166 Mr '45
Reynolds, J. Gielgud as Raskolnikoff. Theatre Arts 30:
   640 N '46
Dent, A. John Gielgud; actor. Theatre Arts 31:25 F '47
Gilder, R. Wit and the prat-fall. Theatre Arts 31:16 Ap
   '47
Biography. Cur Bio 8:13 Ap '47
   Same. Cur Bio Yrbk 1947:240 '48
Granville-Barker's Shakespeare. Theatre Arts 31:48 O
   '47
Stevens, V. Gielgud rehearses Medea. Theatre Arts
   31:31 N '47
Speak the speech, I pray you. Theatre Arts 35:49 Ap '51
Barker, R. Actor of steel. Plays & Player 1-1:4 O '53
Golden voice. Plays & Players 2-11:8 Ag '55
Personality of the month. Plays & Players 3-8:3 My '56
Staying a star. Plays & Players 4-3:7 D '56
To the glory of Gielgud. Newsweek 49:70 Je 17 '57
Hewes, H. Great Gielgud. Sat R 41:20 D 27 '58
Clurman, H. Theatre. Nation 188:39 Ja 10 '59
Tynan, K. Theatre. New Yorker 34:68 Ja 10 '59
New recital on Broadway. Time 73:66 Ja 12 '59
Shakespearean sorcerer. Newsweek 53:56 Ja 12 '59
Talk with a star. Newsweek 53:56 Ja 12 '59
Hewes, H. One man in his Shakespeare. Sat R 42:74
   Ja 17 '59
A Shakespearean speaks his mind. Theatre Arts 43:69
   Ja '59
Driver, T. F. Gielgud's Broadway triumph. New Repub
   140:20 F 2 '59
Hayes, R. Stage; Ages of man. Commonweal 69:521 F
   13 '59
Wyatt, E. V. R. Shakespeare's Ages of man. Cath

World 188:505 Mr '59
Shakespeare's Ages of man.   Theatre Arts 43:10 Mr '59
Brustein, R. S.   Sir John at a standstill.   New Repub
     141:21 O 5 '59
Vidal, G.   Sir John, by a nose.   Reporter 21:38 O 15 '59
Dickinson, H.   Readers or rhapsodies?   Q. J. Speech Ed
     45:258 O '59
Urge to act, an incurable fever.   N. Y. Times Mag p42
     F 14 '60
Funke, L. & Booth, J. E.   Actor's method; his life.
     N. Y. Times Mag p34 D 1 '61
Ross, L.   Player.   New Yorker 37:110 N 4 '61
Personality of the month.   Plays & Players 9-3:3 D '61
Hobson, H.   On tape: an intv.   Show 2-1:58 Ja '62
Roberts, P.   Scandal at the Haymarket.   Plays & Players
     9-7:9 Ap '62
Shakespeare's Babbitt?   Harper 225:6 Ag '62
Pumphrey, A.   Tale of two knights.   Theatre Arts 47:18
     Ja '63
Gielgud, J.   Talks about acting.   Plays & Players 10-
     9:14 Je '63
Gielgud, J.   Directing the classics.   Plays & Players 11-
     2:16 N '63
Stewart, R. S.   John Gielgud and Edward Albee talk about
     the theatre.   Atlan 215:61 Ap '65
In a strange land.   Opera News 30:8 F 12 '66
Redfield, W.   Night Elizabeth Taylor said so what? and
     Richard Burton kicked the television set in.   Esquire
     67:108 Ja '67
Hewes, H.   Theatre.   Sat R 50:51 F 11 '67
Burton, R.   Reluctant Hamlet reviews the tale of how it
     got to be or not to be.   Life 64:8 F 9 '68
Arkadin.   Film clips.   Sight & Sound 37-4:210 Aut '68

GIFFORD, FRANCES
     Pin-up politico.   Am Mag 143:127 My '47

GILBERT, BILLY
     Maltin, L.   The films of Billy Gilbert, inc. filmog.
          Film Fan Mo 63:3 Ja '67
     Ware, H.   Billy Gilbert, inc. filmog.   Films In Review
          19-4:252 Ap '68

GILBERT, JOHN
     St. Johns, I.   I told you so.   Photop 27-4:43 Mr '25
     Spensley, D.   The rival Nordic lovers.   Photop 28-5:28
          O '25

St. Johns, I. Can Jack Gilbert get away with it?
     Photop 29-4:66 Mr '26
Gilbert, J. Jack Gilbert writes his own story. Photop
     34-1:32 Je '28; 34-2:36 Jl '28; 34-3:68 Ag '28; 34-4:
     41 S '28
Waterbury, R. The girl Jack Gilbert married. Photop
     36-2:30 Jl '29
St. Johns, A. R. Why Jack Gilbert got married. Photop
     36-3:36 Ag '29
Albert, K. Is Jack Gilbert through? Photop 37-3:29 F
     '30
Foster, D. Gilbert's voice is all right. Photop 38-1:37
     Je '30
Moffit, J. C. John Gilbert. Cinema Digest 1-9:12 S 5
     '32
Jones, C. P. John Gilbert. Cinema Digest 1-11:10 O 3
     '32
Stevers, M. Now I can help you. Photop 44-5:74 O '33
Rankin, R. Reunion in the palace. Photop 44-6:31 N '33
Maxwell, V. The amazing story behind Garbo's choice of
     Gilbert. Photop 45-2:32 Ja '34
Maxwell, V. I hate to leave John Gilbert--Virginia Bruce.
     Photop 45-5:34 Ap '34
St. Johns, A. R. What defeated Jack Gilbert? Photop
     48-1:26 Je '35
Obit. Time 27:59 Ja 20 '36
St. Johns, A. R. The tragic truth about John Gilbert's
     death. Photop 49-3:34 Mr '36
Quirk, L. J. John Gilbert. Films In Review 7-3:101
     Mr '56
Amour and the man. Sat R 39:29 O 13 '56
Biography. DAB sup2:232 '58
Davis, H. R. John Gilbert filmography. Films In Re-
     view 13-8:477 O '62

GILLMORE, MARGALO
     Four flights up; excerpt. McCalls 91:84 Mr '64

GILMORE, VIRGINIA
     Crichton, K. Gilmore the gamin. Colliers 108:14 N 15
     '41

GINGOLD, HERMIONE
     Stokes, S. English spotlight. Theatre Arts 30:673 N '46
     Pure Gingold. Theatre Arts 33:14 D '49
     Bundle from Britain. Theatre Arts 37:14 D '53
     No tea. New Yorker 29:20 Ja 16 '54

Whitcomb, J.   Backstage at the birth of a hit.   Cosmop
136:56 Mr '54
Gingold, H.   Thoughts in the sun.   Plays & Players 2-
12:9 S '55
Half Tallulah--half Groucho.   TV Guide 6-13:20 Mr 29 '58
Biography.   Cur Bio 19:15 O '58
  Same.   Cur Bio Yrbk 1958:165 '58
Eimeri, S.   Can women be funny?   Mlle 56:150 N '62
Trewin, J. C.   Hermione Gingold.   Plays & Players 13-
2:7 N '65

GISH, DOROTHY
Willis, R.   I go a-calling on the Gish girls.   Photop 7-1:
36 D '14
Evans, D.   Grand crossings impressions.   Photop 14-4:
72 S '18
St. Johns, A. R.   Black sheep Gish.   Photop 15-2:36 Ja
'19
Evans, D.   Seriously speaking.   Photop 18-6:30 N '20
Patterson, A.   The Gish girls talk about each other.
Photop 20-1:29 Je '21
Gish, D.   Largely a matter of love.   Photop 21-4:37 Mr
'22
And so I'm a comedienne.   Ladies Home J.   42:7 Jl '25
They stand out from the crowd.   Lit Digest 117:11 Mr 17
'34
Biography.   Cur Bio Ag '44
Nichols, L.   Gallery of leading ladies.   N. Y. Times Mag
p20 Mr 3 '46
Williams, R. L.   Gallant Gish girls.   Life 31:115 Ag 20
'51
Kuhn, I. C.   Sixty years in show business.   Nat R 14:
504 Je 18 '63
Obit.   Newsweek 71:88 Je 17 '68
  Time 91:88 Je 14 '68
  Cur Bio 29:41 S '68
  Cur Bio Yrbk 1968:455 '69
  Screen World 20:234 '69
Bodeen, D.   Dorothy Gish, inc. filmog.   Films In Re-
view 19-7:393 Ag/S '68

GISH, LILLIAN
Willis, R.   I go a-calling on the Gish girls.   Photop 7-1:
36 D '14
Johnson, J.   The real Lillian Gish.   Photop 14-3:24 Ag
'18
Patterson, A.   The Gish girls talk about each other.

Photop 20-1:29 Je '21

Evans, D.   The girl on the cover.   Photop 21-1:38 D '21

Hergesheimer, J.   Lillian Gish.   Am Mer 1:397 Ap '24

Beginning young.   Ladies Home J 42:19 S '25

Quirk, J. R.   The enigma of the screen.   Photop 29-4:
    63 Mr '26

Hall, L.   Lillian fights alone.   Photop 35-5:63 Ap '29

Krutch, J. W.   Lillian Gish keeps a secret.   Nation 130:
    554 My 7 '30

Lillian Gish revives town.   Cinema Digest 1-7:28 Ag 8 '32

Young, S.   Dames aux camelias.   New Repub. 73:214
    Ja 4 '33

Lillian Gish, a real actress in 9 Pine Street.   Newsweek
    1:28 My 6 '33

Biography.   Cur Bio Ag '44

I made war propaganda.   Scrib Com 11:7 N '41

Letter from Lillian.   Theatre Arts 33:4 S '49

Williams, R. L.   Gallant Gish girls.   Life 31:115 Ag 20
    '51

Film pioneers' roll of their living immortals.   Life 40:
    122 Ja 23 '56

Gish, L.   Silence was our virtue.   Films & Filming 4-3:
    9 D '57

Conversations with Lillian Gish.   Sight & Sound 27-3:128
    Win '57/58

Brooks, L.   Gish and Garbo, the executive war on stars.
    Sight & Sound 28-1:13 Win '58/59

Peck, S.   Then and now: Lillian Gish.   N. Y. Times Mag
    p70 Ap 17 '60

Tozzi, R.   Lillian Gish, inc. filmog.   Films In Review
    13-10:577 D '62

Lillian Gish.   Film Culture Spg/Sum '65

Stern, H.   The age of innocence returns.   After Dark 11-
    2:16 Je '69

GLASS, GASTON
    Obit.   Screen World 17:236 '66

GLAUM, LOUISE
    Howe, H.   Vampire or ingenue?   Photop 14-3:33 Ag '18

GLEASON, JAMES
    Mullett, M. B.   Why Jimmie Gleason wants to raise
        mules; the history of Is zat so?   Intv.   Am Mag 100:
        34 N '25
    Obit.   Illus Lond N 234:715 Ap 25 '59
        Time 73:80 Ap 27 '59

Wilson Lib Bul 33:714 Je '59
Am Ann 1960:853 '60
Brit Bk Yr 1960:508 '60
Screen World 11:219 '60

GODDARD, PAULETTE
Crichton, K.   Perils of Paulette.   Colliers 104:11 S 2 '39
Campbell, M.   The perils of Paulette.   Photop 53-9:32 S '39
Bryan, K.   If you want to get there.   Photop 54-11:16 N '40
Budget house for a box office beauty.   Am Home 27:14 My '42
St. Johns, A. R.   Paulette Goddard--woman of daring. Photop 21-4:28 S '42
Addison, R.   Paulette's in love.   Photop 22-3:66 F '43
French, W. F.   What Hollywood thinks of Paulette Goddard.   Photop 22-6:43 My '43
Skolsky, S.   Paulette on Paulette Goddard.   Photop 24-1:36 D '43
Harris, E.   If you were Paulette Goddard's house guest. Photop 25-1:50 Je '44
Goddard, P.   I went to the end of the line.   Photop 25-3:32 Ag '44
Waterbury, R.   Exclusive on Paulette Goddard and Burgess Meredith.   Photop 25-3:62 Ag '44
Mystery of Paulette Goddard.   Life 19:124 D 17 '45
Meredith, B.   This is my wife.   Photop 29-5:62 O '46
Biography.   Cur Bio 7:13 N '46
Miss Goddard as a Wildean wit.   N.Y. Times Mag p20 D 21 '47
Howe, H.   Golden dish.   Photop 33-6:50 N '48
Benson, E.   The films of Paulette Goddard.   Film Fan Mo 72:3 Je '67

GODOWSKY, DAGMAR
Godowsky, D.   She wants to be the wickedest woman on the screen.   Photop 25-6:86 My '24
Laughs with father.   Am Mer 56:319 Mr '43
Shadows from a lunarium.   Time 71:102 F 24 '58

GOODWIN, BILL
Announcer's exit.   Time 45:52 Ja 8 '45
Wood, C.   TV personalities biographical sketchbook. TV Personalities p140 '57
Obit.   Newsweek 51:73 My 19 '58

GORCEY, LEO
    Obit. Newsweek 73:7 Je 16 '69
       Time 93:90 Je 13 '69

GORDON, C. HENRY
    Rankin, R. Ladies love villains.   Photop 45-1:72 D '33
    Obit. Cur Bio '41

GORDON, HUNTLEY
    Obit. Screen World 8:222 '57

GORDON, MARY
    Baskette, K. A present for mother.   Photop 48-6:44 N
       '35

GORDON, RUTH
    Money wasn't everything; autobiography.   Forum 101:99
       F '39
       Same, abridged.   Read Digest 34:82 Mr '39
    Look in your glass; autobiography.   Atlant 164:145 Ag '39;
       302 S; 474 O '39
       Excerpts.   Sr Schol 35:21E D 11 '39
    Three-star classic.   Time 40:45 D 21 '42
    Biography.   Cur Bio '43
    Crichton, K. Gifted Gordon.   Colliers 113:75 My 27 '44
    Houghton, N. Kanins on Broadway.   Theatre Arts 30:
       731 D '46
    Ruth went on to big stage career.   Life 22:60 Ja 6 '47
    Funke, L. Broadway husband and wife teams.   N.Y.
       Times Mag p19 Ja 12 '47
    Teenagers go on the air.   Wilson Lib Bul 23:181 O '48
    Leading lady; drama, with biographical sketch.   Theatre
       Arts 34:58 F '50
    Legitimate Laughton.   Theatre Arts 34:30 N '50
    Alpert, H. In the beginning.   Sat R 36:43 O 3 '53
    Enchantress from never-never land.   Sat R 39:18 Ap 28
       '56

GORING, MARIUS
    Hatch, R. Movies.   New Repub 120:30 Ja 31 '49
    Marius Goring.   Plays & Players 11-6:7 Mr '64

GOUDAL, JETTA
    Howe, H. A Parisian Chinese lily.   Photop 24-3:50 Ag
       '23
    Busby, M. Sunday night at Jetta's.   Photop 37-6:60 My
       '30

GRABLE, BETTY

Crichton, K. Out on two limbs. Colliers 107:66 My 17
'41

Grable, B. How I keep my figure. Photop 18-6:36 My
'41

Sharpe, H. What makes Betty run? Photop 20-6:40 My;
21-1:48 Je '42

St. Johns, A. R. What you don't know about the Betty
Grable-George Raft romance. Photop 22-5:26 Ap '43

Skolsky, S. The champ Betty Grable. Photop 23-1:30 Je
'43

Fletcher, A. W. What about Betty Grable and Harry
James? Photop 23-3:25 Ag '43

Harris, E. The enchanted couple. Photop 26-4:34 Mr
'45

Kutner, N. Betty Grable's secret date. Photop 27-5:47
O '45

Deere, D. If you were the ranch guest of Betty Grable.
Photop 28-6:46 My '46

Dudley, F. It's a joke, son. Photop 29-3:52 Ag '46

Grable, B. It's like this with Harry and me. Photop
29-6:54 N '46

Howe, H. It's the darndest thing. Photop 30-5:53 Ap '47

Waterbury, R. They'll remember mama. Photop 32-2:
38 Ja '48

Grable, B. Rules for wives. Photop 32-5:50 Ap '48

Living the daydream. Time 52:40 Ag 23 '48

Blue, A. Her divided heart. Photop 34-2:48 Ja '49

Howe, H. Beautiful blonde from Calabasas Ranch.
Photop 34-5:58 Ap '49

Scott, D. Blonde bonanza. Photop 36-6:42 S '49

Martin, P. World's most popular blonde. Sat Eve Post
222:26 Ap 15 '50

Arnold, M. Betty takes a bow. Photop 42-1:56 Jl '52

Rogers, M. Betty's other life. Photop 43-2:54 F '53

Corwin, J. Nice going, Mrs. James! Photop 44-1:54
Jl '53

Meltsir, A. Two women and a dream. Photop 48-5:60
N '55

Wood, C. TV personalities biographical sketchbook.
TV Personalities p33 '57

Ham and legs. Time 73:68 Ap 13 '59

Ringgold, G. Betty Grable, inc. filmog. Screen Facts
4:1 n. d.

GRAHAME, GLORIA

Budding star. Life 21:77 O 21 '46

Hollywood's new generation.   Life 24:94 My 24 '48
Hagen, R.   Gloria Grahame, inc. filmog.   Screen Facts
   1-6:39 n. d.

GRANDIN, ETHEL
   Condon, M.   Rain, and the radiant Ethel Grandin.
   Photop 6-1:91 Je '14

GRANGER, DOROTHY
   Maltin, L.   Dorothy Granger, inc. filmog.   Film Fan Mo
   100:3 O '69

GRANGER, FARLEY
   Granger, F.   I go to war.   Photop 25-2:30 Jl '44
   Shea, S.   Finding out about Farley Granger.   Photop 25-
   5:38 O '44
   Arnold, M.   Subject to change.   Photop 34-4:56 Mr '49
   Harris, E.   Impetuous bachelor.   Photop 37-3:44 Mr '50
   Zeitlin, I.   All his life.   Photop 38-1:36 Jl '50
   Fletcher, A. W.   Talk about Farley Granger.   Photop 38-
   5:44 N '50
   Maxwell, E.   His very own.   Photop 38-5:46 N '50
   Evans, J.   Farley--so right, so wrong.   Photop 38-5:48
   N '50
   Winters, S.   You can't help loving that man.   Photop
   38-5:50 N '50
   Granger, F.   What ails me.   Photop 39-3:44 Mr '51
   Zeitlin, I.   Their love is like this.   Photop 40-2:52 Ag
   '51
   Gwynn, E.   Long engagements are fun.   Photop 40-6:62
   D '51
   Granger, F.   Girls ruin romance.   Photop 41-6:40 Je '52
   Linet, B.   Look what's happening to Farley.   Photop 44-
   1:50 Jl '53

GRANGER, STEWART
   Carlson, R.   Diary of a Hollywood safari.   Colliers 126:
   22 Jl 8; 32 Jl 15 '50
   Same abridged with title Hollywood safari.   Read Digest
   57:45 O '50
   Waterbury, R.   A toast to love.   Photop 39-4:42 Ap '51
   Martin, P.   Movies' beautiful brute.   Sat Eve Post 224:
   24 D 22 '51
   Gallant Granger.   Life 32:71 My 26 '52
   Zeitlin, I.   Trouble in paradise?   Photop 42-6:38 D '52
   Granger, S.   Love story.   Photop 43-2:50 F '53
   Murray, M.   Why the Stewart Granger marriage won't

fail.   Photop 43-5:56 My '53

Armstrong, G.   This is Stewart Granger.   Photop 44-5:
50 N '53

Steele, J.   Granger.   Photop 45-2:54 F '54

Howe, H.   He kissed her--if only he hadn't.   Photop 45-
5:59 My '54

Maynard, J.   Look who's smiling.   Photop 47-5:48 My '55

Phillips, D.   A doll's life with a guy.   Photop 48-3:59
S '55

Waterbury, R.   Confession of a husband in love.   Photop
49-2:67 F '56

Manning, D.   They're expecting a living doll.   Photop
50-1:44 Jl '56

Reich, I.   Nothing in common.   Photop 55-2:50 F '59

End of a dream.   Photop 58-5:62 O '60

GRANT, CARY

Melcher, E. S.   Cary Grant.   Cinema Digest 1-13:14 O
31 '32

Jamison, J.   Cary vs. Gary.   Photop 43-2:33 Ja '33

Hunt, J. L.   We will never understand Cary Grant in
Hollywood.   Photop 48-3:46 Ag '35

Reeve, W.   The reluctant bachelor.   Photop 49-6:48 Je
'36

Lane, V. T.   How Grant took Hollywood.   Photop 52-5:22
My '38

Waterbury, R.   The gay romance of Cary Grant.   Photop
53-4:26 Ap '39

Roberts, A.   Cash and Cary.   Photop 54-2:22 F '40

Biographical note.   Time 35:86 My 20 '40

Steele, J. H.   How Cary Grant lives.   Photop 54-9:20
S '40

Stein, H.   Cary Grant's million dollar romance.   Photop
54-11:14 N '40

Biography.   Cur Bio '41

Jefferson, S.   Matrimony deferred.   Photop 21-5:65 O '42

Steele, J. H.   Portrait of "U. S." Grant.   Photop 22-4:52
Mr '43

Parsons, L. O.   The married life of the Cary Grants.
Photop 24-3:30 F '44

Hartung, P. T.   Gary and Cary.   Commonweal 40:547 S
22 '44

Maxwell, E.   Heartbreak story.   Photop 25-5:30 O '44

Parsons, L. O.   What next for Cary Grant?   Photop 27-
3:32 Ag '45

Waterbury, R.   Notorious gentleman.   Photop 30-2:38 Ja
'47

Arnold, M.   Portrait in quicksilver.   Photop 31-6:70 N
'47
Maxwell, E.   That angel Cary.   Photop 32-5:44 Ap '48
Grant, C.   She's my dream wife.   Photop 33-3:50 Ag '48
Martin, P.   How Grant took Hollywood.   Sat Eve Post
221:22 F 19 '49
Parsons, L. O.   They've got marriage on their minds.
Photop 37-1:30 Ja '50
Lerman, L.   Charm Boys.   Mlle 40:160 F '55
Cary Grant . . . of enduring charm.   Look 19:95 Ag 23
'55
Parsons, L. O.   Cary Grant stars in a Cosmopolitan
story.   Cosmop 139:86 O '55
Amour and the man.   Sat R 39:29 O 13 '56
Desmond, C.   He'll never win an oscar.   Photop 51-3:
52 Mr '57
Rakish Hollywood star who simply won't grow old.
Newsweek 49:108 Jl 24 '57
Gary, Cary remain frisky past fifty.   Life 43:79 Ag 12
'57
Hubler, R. G.   Cary Grant--Hollywood's indestructible
pro.   Coronet 42:35 Ag '57
Zittell, E.   What's Cary up to?   Photop 52-6:42 D '57
Happy London get-together.   Life 44:49 F 10 '58
Harris, E.   Riddle of Cary Grant.   McCalls 85:51 S '58
Laraine, N.   We love each other but . . .   Photop 55-1:56
Ja '59
Berquist, L.   Curious story behind the new Cary Grant.
Look 23:50 S 1 '59
Women like them.   Vogue 134:110 N 15 '59
Hamilton, S.   Confidential file.   Photop 57-4:52 Ap '60
Gehman, R.   Ageless Cary Grant.   Good H 151:64 S '60
Grant, C.   What it means to be a star.   Films & Film-
ing 7-10:12 Jl '61
Roman, R. C.   Cary Grant, inc. filmog.   Films In Re-
view 12-10:577 D '61
Thyssen, G.   Dinner on his bed.   Photop 61-3:66 Mr '62
Old Cary Grant fine.   Time 80:40 Jl 27 '62
Davidson, M.   Cary Grant; as his best friends (and ex-
friends) know him.   Good H 155:80 N '62
Grant, C.   Archie Leach.   Ladies Home J 80:50 Ja; 23
Mr; 86 Ap '63
How many titles of these Cary Grant movies can you
name?   Ladies Home J 80:46 Mr '63
Lyle, J.   To the sexiest sixty-year-old.   Photop 65-2:
43 F '64
Unlikely role for hairy Cary.   Life 57:99 D 18 '64

New look for Cary Grant. Good H 160:44 Ja '65
Rivers, N. He can't wait to be a father. Photop 67-2:
    29 F '65
Biography. Cur Bio 26:21 N '65
    Same. Cur Bio Yrbk 1965:170 '65
Jamieson, R. Why I waited to be a father. Photop 69-
    5:57 My '66
Gordon, S. Cary Grant: the perennial dreamboat in a
    new role. Look 30:70 Jl 26 '66
Graham, D. What LSD is doing to him. Photop 72-2:38
    Ag '67
Ace, G. Until wealth do us part. Sat R 50:10 S 23 '67
Battelle, P. Mrs. Cary Grant talks about marrying and
    divorcing Cary Grant. Ladies Home J 85:107 Ap '68
O'Brien, F. His shocking divorce. Photop 73-6:14 Je
    '68
Levy, R. To catch a star. Duns R 92:90 S '68
How a star fits a director's chair. Bsns W p92 D 21 '68
Owen, J. The widow he wants for a wife. Photop 76-6:
    60 D '69

GRANT, KATHRYN
    Ashton, S. Love is never a mistake. Photop 52-1:60
        Jl '57
    Martin, P. I call on Kathryn Grant Crosby. Sat Eve
        Post 230:28 Ap 5 '58
    Bing talks. Look 22:46 My 13 '58
    Posner, C. Why Bing and Kathryn need this baby so
        much. Photop 54-3:51 S '58
    Gordon, S. Meet Mrs. Crosby and little Bing. Look 23:
        25 Ja 20 '59
    Mrs. Bing Crosby, student nurse. Look 27:98 Mr 12 '63
    Crosby, K. G. Bing and I. Good H 156:86 Mr '63

GRANT, LEE
    Considine, S. Lee Grant, Hollywood starlet! After
        Dark 11-8:24 D '69

GRANVILLE, BONITA
    Proctor, K. No runaway marriage for these two. Photop
        20-2:28 Ja '42
    Granville, B. My wartime morals. Photop 23-4:36 S '43
    Granville, B. Volunteer for cheer. Photop 26-3:48 F '45

GRAPEWIN, CHARLES
    Obit. Time 67:88 F 13 '56
        Screen World 8:222 '57

GRAVES, PETER
  Raddatz, L. He didn't catch the train. TV Guide 14-27:
    12 Jl 2 '66
  Waterbury, R. Big brother is not watching. Photop 74-
    5:56 N '68
  deRoos, R. Let's have a little awe for Peter Graves.
    TV Guide 17-6:21 F 8 '69

GRAVES, RALPH
  Boone, A. Griffith's first blonde hero. Photop 16-5:54
    O '19

GRAY, ALEXANDER
  Busby, M. Born to sing. Photop 38-2:67 Jl '30

GRAY, COLEEN
  Farmer's daughter. Am Mag 145:111 Mr '48
  Wood, C. TV personalities biographical sketchbook.
    TV Personalities p89 '56
  A stripped gear of the star system. TV Guide 7-16:21
    Ap 18 '59
  Raddatz, L. Right soap opera . . . wrong Coleen.
    TV Guide 15-41:21 O 14 '67

GRAY, DOLORES
  Stump, A. Movie star who acts like one. Am Mag 161:
    28 F '56
  Whitcomb, J. On location with The opposite sex.
    Cosmop 141:68 O '56
  Whitcomb, J. Party in Copenhagen. Cosmop 146:70 Ap
    '59

GRAY, GILDA
  Smith, A. This girl danced and made the piper pay.
    Photop 28-5:38 O '25
  Golden girl. Time 75:43 Ja 4 '60
  She shook the nation. Newsweek 55:14 Ja 4 '60

GRAYSON, KATHRYN
  Cades, H. R. Keep your eyes on her. Womans H C 68:
    90 Je '41
  Anders, J. The man Kathryn Grayson married. Photop
    19-5:68 O '41
  Waterbury, R. Kathryn Grayson's fight for happiness.
    Photop 22-1:65 D '42
  Grayson, K. Are American women good wartime wives?
    Photop 24-4:28 Mr '44

Parsons, L. O.   The miracle of Kathryn Grayson and
  Johnny Shelton.   Photop 27-6:28 N '45
Arnold, M.   K-K-K-Katie!   Photop 29-2:48 Jl '46
Graham, S.   Katie and Johnnie are sweethearts.   Photop
  30-2:60 Ja '47
Deere, D.   This time for keeps.   Photop 31-5:36 O '47
Grayson, K.   That's my Johnnie.   Photop 32-1:58 Je '48
Hopper, H.   The truth about the Kathryn Grayson-Mario
  Lanza feud.   Photop 41-4:40 Ap '52
Asklund, G.   Singing in the movies.   Etude 70:16 N '52
MacRae, G.   Listen, Kate.   Photop 43-4:76 Ap '53
TV and a handful of beads.   TV Guide 5-20:20 My 18 '57

GREEN, HARRY
  Obit.   Screen World 10:222 '59

GREEN, MITZI
  Ogden, E.   Mitzi has boy-trouble.   Photop 37-3:41 F '30
  Denton, F.   Mitzi on the job.   Photop 40-3:28 Ag '31
  Albert, R.   Come on back, Mitzi.   Photop 42-2:41 Jl '32
  Pringle, H. F.   Big girl now.   Colliers 100:17 Jl 24 '37
  Bye-bye babies.   Newsweek 26:89 Jl 16 '45
  Obit.   Newsweek 73:123 Je 9 '69
    Time 93:98 Je 6 '69

GREENE, LORNE
  Patriarch of the Ponderosa.   TV Guide 9-19:20 My 13 '61
  He likes to cook.   Bet Hom & Gard 43:80 Jl '65
  Dunne, J. G.   And now to the Nugget.   TV Guide 13-36:
    18 S 4 '65
  Lewis, R. W.   Bonanza.   Sat Eve Post 238:84 D 4 '65

GREENE, RICHARD
  Steele, J. H.   Portrait in Scotch plaid with shamrocks.
    Photop 53-12:32 D '39
  The British Hopalong.   TV Guide 4-27:8 Jl 7 '56
  Wood, C.   TV personalities biographical sketchbook.
    TV Personalities p132 '56

GREENSTREET, SYDNEY
  Kutner, N.   If you were housekeeper for Sydney Green-
    street.   Good H 116:33 Ap '43
  Biography.   Cur Bio '43
  Movie murderer.   Life 18:49 Ap 2 '45
  Greenstreet plays the great huckster.   Life 22:51 Mr 31
    '47
  Dickens, H.   Sydney Greenstreet, inc. filmog.   Screen

Facts 8:40 n.d.
Obit. Newsweek 43:47 F 1 '54
        Time 63:70 F 1 '54
        Illus Lond N 224:163 Ja 30 '54
        Am Ann 1955:311 '55
        Brit Bk Yr 1955:576 '55
        Cur Bio 15:27 Mr '54
        Cur Bio Yrbk 1954:309 '54
        Screen World 6:223 '55

GREENWOOD, CHARLOTTE
    Mullett, M. B.   Tall, thin, awkward girl becomes a
        Broadway star.   Am Mag 96:34 D '23
    Long-legged Letty makes money striding across country's
        stages.   Newsweek 10:24 O 18 '37
    Crichton, K.   Lady Longlegs.   Colliers 101:15 Ja 15 '38

GREENWOOD, JOAN
    Tune-up time for rising stars.   Life 36:66 Ja 25 '54
    Four young stars, will they be great?   Vogue 123:110
        Ap 1 '54
    Biography.   Cur Bio 15:43 My '54
        Same.   Cur Bio Yrbk 1954:309 '54
    Kitten on the quai.   Plays & Players 2-6:5 Mr '55
    People of talent.   Sight & Sound 25-4:191 Spg '56

GREER, JANE
    Jane Greer.   Life 22:91 Je 2 '47
    Marshall, J.   Jaunt with Janie.   Colliers 121:78 My 22
        '48

GREGORY, JAMES
    TV's hidden light.   House & Gard 109:231 My '56
    Recreating the career of a tough cop.   TV Guide 7-33:8
        Ag 15 '59

GRENFELL, JOYCE
    Overheards.   Vogue 126:136 O 1 '55
    Gibbs, W.   Theatre.   New Yorker 31:90 O 22 '55
    Joyce Grenfell requests the pleasure.   Newsweek 46:54 O
        24 '55
    Joyce Grenfell requests the pleasure.   Time 66:86 O 24
        '55
    Hewes, H.   Broadway postscript.   Sat R 38:20 O 29 '55
    Theatre; Joyce Grenfell requests the pleasure.   America
        94:138 O 29 '55
    Hayes, R.   Belle of St. Trinian's.   Commonweal 63:166

N 18 '55
Walker and talker.   New Yorker 31:41 N 19 '55
Wyatt, E. V. R.   Joyce Grenfell requests.   Cath World
   182:224 D '55
Joyce Grenfell requests the pleasure.   Theatre Arts 39:
   20 D '55
Personality of the month.   Plays & Players 5-1:3 O '57
Biography.   Cur Bio 19:15 Mr '58
   Same.   Cur Bio Yrbk 1958:175 '58
Tiger and the lady.   Time 71:76 Ap 21 '58
Driver, T. F.   Cleverness vs. artistry.   Christian Cent
   75:533 Ap 30 '58
How to play the game of talk.   Vogue 132:115 D '58

GREY, LITA
   St. Johns, I.   Chaplin's new find.   Photop 26-4:68 S '24

GRIFFIES, ETHEL
   McClelland, D.   Ethel Griffies: in a class by herself.
      Film Fan Mo 73/74:33 Jl/Ag '67
   Biography.   Cur Bio 29:19 Ja '68
      Same.   Cur Bio Yrbk 1968:169 '69

GRIFFITH, ANDY
   Hillbilly's a hit.   Newsweek 46:55 O 31 '55
   Lerman, L.   Male attraction.   Mlle 42:151 F '56
   Guitar-thumping demagogue.   Life 42:68 My 27 '57
   Millstein, G.   Strange chronicle of Andy Griffith.   N. Y.
      Times Mag p17 Je 2 '57
   Elliot, L.   Andy Griffith; yokel boy makes good.
      Coronet 42:105 O '57
   Biography.   Cur Bio 21:12 My '60
      Same.   Cur Bio Yrbk 1960:169 '61
   Doin' what comes natural.   TV Guide 8-40:28 O 1 '60
   Edson, L.   Cornball with the steel-trap mind.   TV Guide
      9-4:17 Ja 28; 9-5:17 F 4 '61
   Morrison, C.   Andy Griffith; sheriff of Mayberry.   Look
      27:80a Ap 9 '63
   Freeman, D.   I think I'm gaining on myself.   Sat Eve
      Post 237:69 Ja 25 '64
   Dern, M.   A southern sheriff faces some problems.
      TV Guide 13-17:5 Ap 24 '65
   Condon, M.   He never left home.   TV Guide 14-23:15
      Je 4 '66
   Lewis, R. W.   The wonderous Andy Griffith TV machine.
      TV Guide 16-28:16 Jl 13; 16-29:28 Jl 20 '68

GRIFFITH, CORINNE
  Craig, M. Trapped in Flatbush. Photop 15-2:80 Ja '19
  Evans, D. The girl on the cover. Photop 21-2:38 Ja '22
  St. Johns, A. R. Why men go crazy about Corinne Grif-
    fith. Photop 25-1:36 D '23
  Busby, M. Exit--Corinne Griffith. Photop 37-6:33 My
    '30
  Watkins, F. Corinne Griffith. Films In Review 10-9:
    566 N '59
  Robinson, E. Letter Films In Review 10-10:631 D '59
  Teichart, R. E. Corinne Griffith. Films In Review 11-
    1:58 Ja '60
  What are they doing now? Show 2-3:96 Mr '62

GRIFFITH, HUGH
  Squire Hugh. Time 82:38 D 27 '63
  Hugh Griffith. Plays & Players 11-9:7 Je '64

GRIFFITH, RAYMOND
  Obit. Screen World 9:223 '58

GRIMES, TAMMY
  Grimy Tams. Time 72:36 D 29 '58
  Kooky girl's success. Life 46:42 Ja 5 '59
  People are talking about. Vogue 133:95 Ap 1 '59
  Stang, J. Clown as a lady. N. Y. Times Mag p101 Mr
    20 '60
  Off beat honey-blonde. Newsweek 55:105 My 23 '60
  Tammy Grimes. Vogue 136:180 S 15 '60
  Talk with a star. Newsweek 56:61 N 14 '60
  Keating, J. Tammy Grimes. Theatre Arts 46:20 N '60
  Tammy, the unsinkable Miss Grimes. Life 49:141 D 5
    '60
  Portrait painter and an actress. Life 50:89 My 19 '61
  Bester, A. Unsinkable Tammy Grimes. Holiday 31:99
    F '62
  Biography. Cur Bio 23:23 Jl '62
    Same. Cur Bio Yrbk 1962:170 '63
  Lapham, L. H. Illusive, elusive Miss Tammy Grimes.
    Sat Eve Post 237:60 Ap 4 '64

GUILD, NANCY
  In the cast. TV Guide 1-3:12 Ap 17 '53

GUILFOYLE, PAUL
  Obit. Newsweek 58:47 Jl 10 '61

GUINNESS, ALEC

Alec's way. Time 49:55 My 12 '47
Biographical note. Theatre Arts 33:48 Mr '49
Eliot and Guinness. New Yorker 25:25 F 4 '50
Kind hearts and coronets. Life 28:79 Je 19 '50
Brown, J. M. My goodness! my Guinness! Sat R 33:
    30 Jl 15 '50
Biography. Cur Bio 11:18 O '50
    Same. Cur Bio Yrbk 1950:206 '51
Messrs. Guinness. N. Y. Times Mag p54 O 14 '51
Watts, S. Guinness is what Guinness acts. N. Y. Times
    Mag p18 Ap 6 '52
Newman, J. Guinness--man of many faces. Colliers
    130:26 Jl 26 '52
Alpert, H. Mr. Guinness does it again. Sat R 35:31
    O 11 '52
Birnbaum, A. Onward and upward with Guinness. N. Y.
    Times Mag p31 O 26 '52
Alec the great. Life 33:131 N 24 '52
Artist views the critic. Atlan 191:51 Mr '53
Guinness steps out. N. Y. Times Mag p36 Ap 30 '53
One man's mambo. Colliers 131:68 Je 13 '53
Knight, A. Man in the ironic mask. Sat R 36:34 S 26
    '53
Bent, F. Alec Guinness: man of many parts. Coronet
    34:87 O '53
Biography. Colliers Yrbk 1953:320 '53
Theatrical chameleon. Plays & Players 1-8:4 My '54
Father Brown. N. Y. Times Mag p40 O 24 '54
Guinness as a cardinal. Newsweek 46:118 D 12 '55
Guinness is good for three more. Life 40:81 Mr 26 '56
Alec Guinness of Britain; the comedian who captured
    America. Newsweek 47:65 Ap 16 '56
Personality of the month. Films & Filming 2-7:3 Ap '56
The man in the rubber mask. Plays & Players 3-9:5 Je
    '56
Ruse, J. He always steals the show. Sat Eve Post 230:
    19 Ja 25 '58
Least likely to succeed. Time 71:52 Ap 21 '58
Whitcomb, J. Alec Guinness. Cosmop 145:80 O '58
People are talking about. Vogue 133:93 Ja 1 '59
Biography. Am Ann 1959:316 '59
Biography. Colliers Yrbk 1959:697 '59
Personality of the month. Plays & Players 7-8:3 My '60
Guinness, A. In who's who of the critics. Films &
    Filming 8-8:14 My '62
Guinness, A. SAG. Esquire 57:123 My '62

Robin, A.   Living legends.   Todays Health 40:75 Je '62
Trewin, J. C.   Alec Guinness: a profile.   Plays &
    Players 11-2:9 N '63
Peck, S.   Gamut of Guinness.   N. Y. Times Mag p18 F
    '64
Strolling player.   New Yorker 39:30 F 8 '64
Catching up with the evasive Sir Alec.   Life 56:61 Je 5
    '64
Kerr, W.   Love letters of a tough critic.   Life 56:114
    Je 19 '64
Alec Guinness as Dylan.   Am Rec G 30:1143 Ag '64
Meehan, T.   Between actors.   Show 4-11:28 D '64
Guinness, A.   Life with a pinch of salt.   Films & Film-
    ing 12-2:5 N '65
People are talking about . . .   Vogue 151:65 Ja 15 '68

GWENN, EDMUND
Charm begins at forty.   Lit Digest 119:19 Mr 23 '35
Biography.   Cur Bio '43
Obit.   Illus Lond N 235:241 S 12 '59
    Time 74:100 S 21 '59
    Am Ann 1960:853 '60
    Cur Bio 20:3 N '59
    Cur Bio Yrbk 1959:165 '60
    Screen World 11:220 '60

GWYNNE, ANNE
Gwyne, A. & Sheridan, A.   Uniform date-iquette.
    Photop 23-3:36 Ag '43

HAAS, HUGO
Biographical note. Time 58:102 Ag 27 '51
Obit. Screen World 19:233 '68

HACKATHORNE, GEORGE
Winship, M. A real "Merton of the movies." Photop
26-2:76 Jl '24

HACKETT, BUDDY
Take artist. Time 68:86 O 8 '56
Born to be funny. TV Guide 4-46:9 N 17 '56
Wood, C. TV personalities biographical sketchbook.
TV Personalities p37 '57
Eliot, A. Buddy and the Bruegel. Vogue 145:132 F 1 '65
Biography. Cur Bio 26:23 My '65
Same. Cur Bio Yrbk 1965:182 '65

HACKETT, FLORENCE
Ambush. New Repub 29:42 D 7 '21
On his majesty's service. New Repub 29:203 Ja 18 '22
Obit. Screen World 6:224 '55

HACKETT, JOAN
People on the way up. Sat Eve Post 235:26 Mr 10 '62
15 gypsies lived upstairs. TV Guide 11-5:12 F 2 '63
On the brink. Time 81:80 Ap 12 '63

HACKETT, RAYMOND
Obit. Screen World 10:222 '59

HAGEN, JEAN
Good girl gone right. TV Guide 2-25:12 Je 18 '54
Wood, C. TV personalities biographical sketchbook.
TV Personalities p22 '54
She's sick of goodies. TV Guide 3-30:20 Jl 23 '55
Hagen, R. Jean Hagen, inc. filmog. Film Fan Mo 90:
7 D '68

HAINES, WILLIAM
Howe, H. Bullied into pictures. Photop 26-5:45 O '24
Spensley, D. The kidding kid. Photop 30-5:81 O '26
Busby, M. The wisecracker reveals himself. Photop 36-
4:68 S; 36-5:56 O '29

HALE, ALAN SR.
   Obit. Newsweek 35:51 Ja 30 '50
     Time 55:74 Ja 30 '50

HALE, BARBARA
   Barbara Hale. Life 20:111 Ap 22 '46
   Walker, H. L. Hale to Williams. Photop 29-5:58 O '46
   Porter, A. Four Cinderellas. Colliers 119:18 F 1 '47
   Double feature. Am Mag 146:118 Jl '48
   Williams, B. No one else could take her place. Photop
     37-1:40 Ja '50
   Pardon her blushes. TV Guide 6-27:20 Jl 5 '58
   Gehman, R. The case of the silent secretary. TV Guide
     10-9:22 Mr 3 '62

HALE, CREIGHTON
   Obit. Screen World 16:237 '66

HALE, GEORGIA
   Tully, J. The girl with the broken ankle. Photop 28-3:
     58 Ag '25

HALE, JONATHAN
   Obit. Screen World 18:236 '67

HALE, LOUISE CLOSSER
   Inside life of the stage. Bookm 24:557 F; 25:55 Mr '07
   Actress, a romance of the theatre. Ladies Home J 25:
     7 S; 13 O; 21 N; 26:21 D '08; 19 Ja; 19 F '09
   Arrested pursuit. Harper 53:22 Ja 2 '09
   Seven stages of the stage. Delin 73:772 Je '09
   Ophelia and the center of the stage. Colliers 45:15 My
     21 '10
   Theatre: a school for discipline. Delin 75:487 Je '10
   Unconventional life. Delin 87:9 N '15
   What the day's work means to me. Bookm 42:454 D '15
   Filming the snoopers. McClure 47:20 Jl '16
   Merely actresses. Ladies Home J 35:113 O '18
   Our family album. Ladies Home J 42:34 S '25
   New stage fright: talking pictures. Harper 161:417 S
     '30
   Tragedy and comedy in the talkies. Womans H C 15:18
     O '30
   Benet, W. R. Obit. Sat R 10:33 Ag 5 '33

HALL, GRAYSON
   Hall, G. & Wright, G. The road to off-Broadway.

Theatre 2-11:22 N '60

HALL, JUANITA
    After 21 years. Time 53:74 Je 6 '49
    Anderson, D. Show stopper. Theatre Arts 36:26 O '52
    Obit. Newsweek 71:86 Mr 11 '68
        Time 91:92 Mr 8 '68

HALL, PORTER
    Obit. Newsweek 42:77 O 19 '53
        Screen World 5:208 '54

HALL, THURSTON
    Obit. Screen World 9:222 '58

HALSEY, BRETT
    Corbin, J. Our marriage was a sin. Photop 61-4:58
        Ap '62
    He follows the sun. TV Guide 10-27:15 Jl 7 '62

HALTON, CHARLES
    McClure, A. The unsung heroes: Charles Halton.
        Film Fan Mo 79:15 Ja '68

HAMILTON, GEORGE
    Hamilton, J. George Hamilton: rich boy makes good.
        Look 24:54a Mr 29 '60
    Borie, M. Can you keep my secret? Photop 57-5:56
        My '60
    Corbin, J. Is there a happy ending for Susan? Photop
        59-6:30 Je '61
    Wall, T. The night George danced with Lolita. Photop
        62-4:57 O '62
    Lewis, R. W. Hollywood's new breed of soft young men.
        Sat Eve Post 235:75 D 1 '62
    Denis, P. You don't need money--just name. Photop
        65-3:42 Mr '64
    Jennings, C. R. It's all George. Show 4-5:74 My '64
    Brossard, C. George Hamilton: elegant young rebel.
        Look 30:76 Mr 22 '66
    New girl in town. Time 87:21 Mr 22 '66
    Hollywood house party. Newsweek 67:36 Mr 28 '66
    That Hamilton man. Newsweek 67:27 Ap 4 '66
    First family suitors: their military status. U. S. News
        60:22 Ap 25 '66
    Byers, M. What kind of guy is George? Lynda Bird's
        dashing Hollywood beau. Life 60:51 My 13 '66

That wonderful, terrible life of the President's daughters.
  Newsweek 67:36 My 23 '66
Graham, S.   Close-up: George Hamilton; intv.   McCalls
  93:42 S '66
Charley, my boy?   Time 88:37 O 7 '66
As draft pressures mount.   U. S. News 61:8 N 7 '66
Number one; draft deferment.   Newsweek 68:38 N 7 '66

HAMILTON, HALE
  Craig, M.   A cave-man of culture.   Photop 15-4:49 Mr
    '19
  Obit.   Cur Bio '42

HAMILTON, MAHLON
  Obit.   Screen World 12:221 '61

HAMMERSTEIN, ELAINE
  Obit.   Newsweek 32:54 Ag 23 '48

HAMPDEN, WALTER
  Romance comes to our stage: production of Cyrano de
    Bergerac.   Lit Digest 79:28 N 24 '23
  Macgowan, K.   Month of Duse and the red letter day of
    Hampden as actor-director.   Theatre Arts 8:2 Ja '24
  Hamilton, C.   Walter Hampden, actor, manager.
    World's Work 47:410 F '24
  Young, S.   Mr. Walter Hampden.   New Repub 45:272 Ja
    27 '26
  Pretense.   Am Mag 119:11 Ap '35
  Walter Hampden defends Cyrano's nose for the last time.
    Newsweek 7:44 My 9 '36
  Vernon, G.   Adieu a Cyrano.   Commonweal 24:76 My 15
    '36
  Vernon, G.   Walter Hampden to end his career as a
    theatrical producer.   Commonweal 25:639 Ap 2 '37
  Biography.   Cur Bio 14:33 My '53
    Same.   Cur Bio Yrbk 1953:244 '53
  Obit.   Newsweek 45:64 Je 20 '55
    Time 65:90 Je 20 '55
    Hobbies 60:108 S '55
    Cur Bio 16:57 S '55
    Cur Bio Yrbk 1955:256 '56
    Am Ann 1956:321 '56
    Brit Bk Yr 1956:513 '56
    Screen World 7:223 '56
  Downing, R.   Walter Hampden, June 30, 1879 - June 11,
    1955.   Films In Review 6-7:310 Ag/S '55

Biography. NCAB 44:34 '62
Rachow, L. A. Walter Hampden memorial library.
   Wilson Lib Bul 38:656 Ap '64

HAMPTON, HOPE
   Evans, D. A Broadway farmerette. Photop 20-6:42 N
      '22
   Johaneson, B. Who and what is Hope Hampton?
      Photop 24-6:56 N '23

HANDWORTH, OCTAVIA
   Carr, A. Octavia Handworth. Feature Movie 2-7:50 Jl
      10 '15

HANSEN, JUANITA
   Obit. Screen World 13:222 '62

HANSON, LARS
   Obit. Screen World 17:237 '66

HARAREET, HAYA
   Nichols, M. Stardom bound. Coronet 47:71 Ja '60
   People are talking about. Vogue 135:85 Ap 15 '60
   Person of promise. Films & Filming 6-8:17 My '60

HARDIN, TY
   'Cheyenne' tries a new star. TV Guide 6-36:24 S 6 '58
   Day, D. Darling, I think I'm going to be a father.
      Photop 56-6:66 D '59
   Help wanted party. Photop 57-2:50 F '60
   Ty stands for Typhoon. TV Guide 8-29:12 Jl 16 '60
   Hoffman, J. How a dream of love turns into a night-
      mare. Photop 58-3:62 S '60

HARDING, ANN
   Your crowning glory. Ladies Home J 44:19 Mr '27
   Busby, M. That sex appeal voice. Photop 36-5:40 O '29
   Hamilton, S. Annie, the moom-pitcher star. Photop
      41-6:45 My '32
   Henderson, J. Tear up contract? Cinema Digest 1-6:
      7 Jl 25 '32
   North, J. The strange case of Ann Harding. Photop
      42-3:32 Ag '32
   Nash, E. G. My sister, Ann Harding. Photop 43-4:
      40 Mr; 43-5:32 Ap; 43-6:53 My '33
   Melcher, E. Ann Harding and George Arliss. Cinema
      Digest 3-7:11 My 1 '33

HARDWICKE, CEDRIC
  I look at the audience. Theatre Arts 15:758 S '31
  Schackleton, E. English stage album. Theatre Arts 15:
    768 S '31
  Cooke, A. Crux in English acting. Theatre Arts 16:705
    S '32
  Season's first guests. Theatre Arts 20:825 O '36
  Jamison, J. Dead men tell tales. Photop 51-9:80 S '37
  Moribund craft of acting. Theatre Arts 23:106 F '39
  Devil's advocate. New Yorker 22:22 Ap 6 '46
  Biography. Cur Bio O '49
  Four Hollywood veterans go to hell on Broadway. Life
    31:46 N 5 '51
  Four-star chat. New Yorker 28:26 Ap 19 '52
  Hewes, H. Sir Cedric in Shawland. Sat R 35:26 My 17
    '52
  American home for Shakespeare. Theatre Arts 38:66 Ja
    '54
  Our theatre in the fifties. Theatre Arts 38:30 F '54
  Lawyer who dared. Coronet 35:91 Ap '54
  Actor stakes his claim. Theatre Arts 42:66 F '58
  Talk with a star. Newsweek 53:82 Mr 2 '59
  Actor as author. Newsweek 57:106 Mr 20 '61
  Mrs. G's professor conducts a class off campus. TV
    Guide 10-10:15 Mr 10 '62
  Roman, R. C. Cedric Hardwicke, inc. filmog. Films
    In Review 16-1:8 Ja '65
  Obit. Screen World 16:220 '65

HARDY, OLIVER
  Where are they now? Newsweek 50:18 Jl 15 '57
  Obit. Illus Lond N 231:275 Ag 17 '57
    Newsweek 50:61 Ag 19 '57
    Time 70:76 Ag 19 '57
    Am Ann 1958:336 '58
    Brit Bk Yr 1958:512 '58
    Screen World 9:223 '58
  (See also: LAUREL AND HARDY)

HARLAN, KENNETH
  Obit. Screen World 19:233 '68

HARLAN, OTIS
  Obit. Newsweek 15:2 Ja 29 '40
    Cur Bio '40

HARLOW, JEAN
  Hall, L. Hell's angel. Photop 39-2:69 Ja '31
  Condon, F. Kansas City platinum. Sat Eve Post 204:35
    S 19 '31
  Burton, C. The big Harlow holdup. Photop 44-6:45 N '33
  Rankin, R. Jean battles a sea of rumors. Photop 45-5:
    32 Ap '34
  Biographical sketch. Time 26:26 Ag 19 '35
  Obit. Newsweek 9:26 Je 12 '37
    Time 29:30 Je 14 '37
  Film funeral. Time 29:46 Je 21 '37
  St. Johns, A. R. The Jean Harlow story Hollywood sup-
    pressed. Photop 51-8:19 Ag '37
  Baldwin, F. The love story Jean Harlow asked me to
    write. Photop 51-10:20 O '37
  Honor, E. Hollywood tragedies. Cosmop 141:38 O '56
  Biography. DAB sup2:285 '58
  St. Johns, A. R. The Jean Harlow story Hollywood sup-
    pressed. Photop 59-2:40 F '61
  Hopper, H. That dirty Harlow book. Photop 67-2:36 F
    '65

HARRIS, BARBARA
  Invitation to a future. Wilson Lib Bul 32:30 Ja '58
  Girl-child. Time 79:48 My 11 '62
  Barbara Harris is funny. Esquire 58:100 N '62
  On a clear day a battalion of Barbaras. Newsweek 66:
    84 N 1 '65
  In lights it spells Harris. Time 86:71 D 3 '65
  Rollin, B. Barbara Harris: Broadway's new all-female
    funnygirl. Look 29:139 D 14 '65
  Up soars her pink balloon. Life 59:79 D 17 '65
  Birmingham, S. Other Barbara, the other Harris.
    Holiday 39:91 Je '66
  Nichols, M. Mike Nichols talks about Barbara Harris.
    Life 61:106 D 16 '66
  People are talking about . . . Vogue 148:214 D '66
  Biography. Cur Bio 29:14 Ap '68
    Same. Cur Bio Yrbk 1968:173 '69

HARRIS, JULIE
  Sun shines for Julie Harris. Life 28:63 Ja 23 '50
  Half her age. Coronet 29:124 D '50
  Brown, J. M. Star bright. Sat R 34:26 D 22 '51
  Bad little good girl. Life 31:51 D 24 '51
  Wallace, R. Julie Harris. Life 32:154 Ap 7 '52
  Anderson, D. Show stopper. Theatre Arts 36:67 Jl '52

On the road with Julie Harris.   Colliers 131:42 Ja 17 '53
Harbert, R.   Assignment in Hollywood.   Good H 136:18 Ap
'53
Julie on the primrose path.   Life 36:59 F 15 '54
Four young stars, will they be great?   Vogue 123:109 Ap
1 '54
Millstein, G.   Unexceptionable Julie Harris.   N. Y. Times
Mag p14 N 6 '55
Fiery particle.   Time 66:76 N 28 '55
Julie Harris: best actress?   Newsweek 46:110 N 28 '55
Hewes, H.   Saint Joan.   Sat R 38:38 D 3 '55
Biography.   Cur Bio 17:20 F '56
Same.   Cur Bio Yrbk 1956:250 '57
Merrill, J. F.   Quicksilver and genius.   Sr Schol 68:6
Mr 15 '56
Harris, J. as told to B. Friedan.   I was afraid to have
a baby.   McCalls 84:68 D '56
Same abridged.   Read Digest 70:42 Ap '57
Biography.   Am Ann 1957:344 '57
Eleven fine actors get their dream roles.   Life 44:76 Ap
14 '58
Julie Harris in one for the road.   Life 46:57 Ja 19 '59
Forever trying to climb the wall.   TV Guide 7-46:14 N
14 '59
Talk with a star.   Newsweek 58:73 O 30 '61
Millstein, G.   Star's struggle on Broadway.   N. Y. Times
Mag p28 N 5 '61
Julie jumps from cutie pie to queen.   Life 51:59 D 1 '61
Keating, J.   Theatre Arts gallery.   Theatre Arts 46:20
Ja '62
Julie Harris.   Vogue 139:113 F 1 '62
Julie Harris.   Film 35:21 Spg '63
Promise! Oh what a lovely word.   Seventeen 22:138 O
'63
Brower, B.   A saint is a saint, you know.   Sat Eve Post
237:22 D 5 '64
Higgins, R.   She lights the stage with a bright flame.
TV Guide 13-14:14 Ap 3 '65
In lights it spells Harris.   Time 86:71 D 3 '65

HARRIS, PHIL
Hayes, B.   Give it another chance.   Photop 52-11:28 N
'38
Hamilton, S.   "My bride" Alice Faye.   Photop 19-3:26
Ag '41
West, R.   They named the baby junior.   Photop 21-3:32
Ag '42

HARRIS, RICHARD
   Biography. Cur Bio 25:25 My '64
     Same. Cur Bio Yrbk 1964:183 '64
   Harris, R. My two faces. Films & Filming 11-7:5 Ap
     '65
   Borgzinner, J. Limerick lad in Arthur's court. Life
     63:70 S 22 '67

HARRIS, ROSEMARY
   Medley of grievous things. Mlle 60:171 Ap '65
   Hallowell, J. Broadway finds a new first lady. Life 60:
     57 My 6 '66
   Chameleon on a tarton. Time 88:74 D 9 '66
   Biography. Cur Bio 28:18 S '67
     Same. Cur Bio Yrbk 1967:162 '68
   Ehrlich, H. Actors' favorite actress. Look 32:M15 O
     15 '68

HARRISON, GEORGE
   Biography. Cur Bio 27:23 N '66
     Same. Cur Bio Yrbk 1966:157 '67
   Reid, C. Ravi Shankar and George Beatles. N. Y.
     Times Mag p28 My 7 '67
   Thomas, M. George Harrison tells it like it is; intv.
     Holiday 43:111 F '68
   Carre, G. He and wife face pot charge. Photop 75-6:14
     Je '69
   (See also: BEATLES)

HARRISON, REX
   Howe, H. Rex Harrison. Photop 29-6:58 N '46
   Biography. Cur Bio 8:26 Ja '47
     Same. Cur Bio Yrbk 1947:275 '48
   Maxwell, E. Rex and his queen. Photop 32-3:60 F '48
   Martin, P. Hollywood's vaguest star. Sat Eve Post 220:
     25 My 15 '48
   New team. New Yorker 26:14 D 30 '50
   Farewell and hail. Newsweek 38:79 Ag 13 '51
   Hewes, H. Rex perplexed. Sat R 35:26 My 10 '52
   Barker, R. A player king. Plays & Players 2-2:19 N
     '54
   Charmer. Time 68:42 Jl 23 '56
   Shaw and the actor. Theatre Arts 41:29 Mr '57
   Another Harrison on the horizon. Life 43:47 S 30 '57
   Britain is smitten by Fair lady. Life 44:20 My 12 '58
   Dinter, C. Till death do us part. Photop 56-6:46 D '59
   Stars at rehearsal. Newsweek 55:78 F 1 '60

Personality of the month.   Plays & Players 8-1:3 O '60
Hamilton, J.   Rex Harrison and his own fair lady.
Look 27:72 Je 18 '63
Gordon, S.   My fair lady's dream come true.   Look 28:
60 F 25 '64
Seidenbaum, A.   Rex Harrison.   McCalls 92:98 O '64
Hamilton, J.   Rich, restless life of Rex Harrison.
Look 29:62 N 2 '65
Behlmer, R.   Rex Harrison, inc. filmog.   Films In Re-
view 16-10:593 D '65
Debonair Rex now a celebrated doctor.   Life 61:122 S
30 '66
Men in Vogue.   Vogue S 30 '66
Russ, L.   Why Rex Harrison is Dr. Dolittle.   Pub W
192:22 D 11 '67
King Rex.   Newsweek 71:84 Ja 29 '68

HARRON, ROBERT
Peltret, E.   Griffith's boy--Bobby.   Photop 13-5:20 Ap
'18
Dunham, H.   Bobby Harron, inc. filmog.   Films In Review 14-10:607 D '63
Braff, R.   Robert Harron, inc. filmog.   Films In Review
19-4:253 Ap '68

HART, DOLORES
Hart, D.   Girl-boy miracle.   Photop 53-6:45 Je '58
Hart, D.   Private note to Elvis.   Photop 54-2:56 Ag '58
LeBarre, H.   Pub crawling from sundown to dawn.
Cosmop 146:46 Ap '59
Hamilton, J.   Pleasure of his company.   Look 23:58 Jl
7 '59
The girl with 65,000 greeting cards.   TV Guide 8-45:12
N 5 '60
Hart, D.   How I got into the movies.   Ladies Home J
78:64 My '61
Persons of promise.   Films & Filming 7-10:13 Jl '61
Dolores Hart: alive as an actress.   Look 25:51 D 19 '61
Block, M.   How much money is a husband worth?   Photop
60-6:36 D '61
Denis, P.   Introducing the Jerry Lewis look.   Photop 62-
1:31 Jl '62
Hart, D.   I was grabbed by the police.   Photop 62-6:58
D '62
Joya, M.   Why I want to be a nun.   Photop 64-3:56 S '63
Camber, G.   Her life as a nun.   Photop 65-3:38 Mr '64
Denis, P.   The day she became Sister Judith.   Photop

66-4:52 O '64

HART, WILLIAM S.
Vosges, H. What Bill Hart told in the maid's room.
  Photop 12-4:81 S '17
Hart, W. S. My pinto and me. Photop 17-3:58 F '20
Crowell, M. Famous two-gun star of the movies. Am
  Mag 92:18 Jl '21
Flagg, J. M. Bill Hart. Photop 21-6:23 My '22
Patterson, A. The screen's saddest hero. Photop 28-4:
  48 S '25
Frisbie, R. D. Williamu cowboy. Photop 33-5:64 Ap
  '28
Shaffer, R. After four years. Photop 36-5:36 O '29
Daugherty, F. Ol' Bill Hart is coming back! Photop
  39-1:50 D '30
Van Gelder, R. Two-gun man at 70; William S. Hart
  talks about the good old days. N. Y. Times Mag p13
  D 8 '40
Obit. Newsweek 28:48 Jl 1 '46
  Time 48:70 Jl 1 '46
  Cur Bio 7:20 Jl '46
  Cur Bio Yrbk 1946:246 '47
Mitchell, G. William S. Hart. Films In Review 6-4:
  145 Ap '55
Dewar, J. William S. Hart ranch. L. Angeles Mus Q
  14:16 Sum '58

HARTMAN, ELIZABETH
Schmidt, L. A. Me, Biff. Look 30:M14 My 31 '66
Ex-waif pops up as sexpot. Life 62:43 Mr 24 '67
Miller, E. Daydreamer talks; intv. Seventeen 27:130 N
  '68

HARTMAN, GRETCHEN
Evans, D. The lady of the names. Photop 15-1:46 D
  '18

HARVEY, LAURENCE
Lerman, L. Male attraction. Mlle 42:151 F '56
Spiv no more. Newsweek 53:91 Je 29 '59
Martin, P. I call on Laurence Harvey. Sat Eve Post
  232:32 Je 11 '60
Biography. Cur Bio 22:21 My '61
  Same. Cur Bio Yrbk 1961:195 '62
Harvey, L. Following my actor's instinct. Films &
  Filming 8-1:22 O '61

Boy prince.   Time 82:84 D 6 '63

Stanbrook, A.   Laurence Harvey.   Films & Filming 10-
8:42 My '64

Shorter, E.   Laurence Harvey: a profile.   Plays &
Players 11-12:8 S '64

Lawrencson, H.   1/5 of Laurence Harvey.   Esquire 70:
93 Ag '68

HARVEY, LILLIAN

Donaldson, G.   Lilian Harvey, inc. filmog.   Films In Review 18-9:587 N '67

Obit.   Screen World 20:235 '69

HASSO, SIGNE

Swedish hunch.   Am Mag 138:130 S '44

McClelland, D.   Signe Hasso, inc. filmog.   Films In
Review 18-9:589 N '67

Manzi, I.   Filmography.   Films In Review 19-2:123 F '68

HATFIELD, HURD

Harris, E.   Bohemian buccaneer.   Photop 27-6:40 N '45

Fletcher, A. W.   The heritage of Hurd.   Photop 29-1:64
Je '46

HATTON, RAYMOND

Corliss, A.   That mean guy Hatton.   Photop 10-6:57 N
'16

Corliss, A.   The all-around king.   Photop 13-2:105 Ja
'18

Hatton, F.   Over the bumps with Raymond.   Photop 28-2:
82 Jl '25

HAVER, JUNE

Movie star.   Life 17:71 D 4 '44

Marshall, J.   Fightin' Irish.   Colliers 115:20 Ja 20 '45

Graham, S.   When it's June Haver.   Photop 26-5:45 Ap
'45

Janis, E.   Hustle-along Haver.   Photop 28-3:44 F '46

Parsons, L. O.   Smoke screen.   Photop 28-4:30 Mr '46

This prodigy made good.   Am Mag 141:143 Je '46

Haver, J.   Date bait.   Photop 29-5:43 O '46

Cashin, B.   If you're smart.   Photop 30-5:51 Ap '47

Downing, H.   This side of heaven.   Photop 31-3:48 Ag
'47

Parsons, L. O.   The biggest mistake of my life.
Photop 32-2:36 Ja '48

Howe, H.   She says it with music.   Photop 33-3:42 Ag '48

Roberts, W. Found: the silver lining. Photop 36-5:36
  O '49
Waterbury, R. End of a love story. Photop 37-1:29 Ja
  '50
Zeitlin, I. How June Haver overcame heartache. Photop
  37-6:42 Je '50
Scott, D. Twenty minutes past five. Photop 40-3:44 S
  '51
Zeitlin, I. June Haver--and the familiar stranger.
  Photop 40-6:58 D '51
Nun next door. Time 61:66 F 16 '53
Haver, J. Don't be my valentine. Photop 43-2:70 F '53
Wilkie, J. Farewell, Haver. Photop 43-5:44 My '53
Film star leaves convent. Life 35:60 O 12 '53
Senseney, D. The day fate smiled. Photop 46-1:44 Jl
  '54

HAVER, PHYLLIS
St. Johns, A. R. Goodbye, bathing girl! Photop 20-4:
  32 S '21
Leamy, H. She came up spluttering. Colliers 82:20 O
  20 '28
Obit. Screen World 12:221 '61

HAVOC, JUNE
Crichton, K. Havoc in Hollywood. Colliers 110:20 Ag 8
  '42
Dreier, H. Seaside paradise. Photop 38-2:68 Ag '50
Millstein, G. Summer theatre versus Broadway. N. Y.
  Times Mag p20 Ag 3 '52
She wouldn't give up. Look 17:113 My 5 '53
Havoc's here. TV Guide 2-44:16 O 30 '54
Wood, C. TV personalities biographical sketchbook.
  TV Personalities p123 '54
The moth and the flame. TV Guide 5-27:4 Jl 6 '57
June talks back. TV Guide 5-48:24 N 30 '57
Saga of dainty June. Time 73:54 Je 1 '59
Fuller, J. Trade winds. Sat R 42:6 Je 13 '59

HAWKINS, JACK
People are talking about. Vogue 127:119 My 1 '56
Biography. Cur Bio 20:5 N '59
  Same. Cur Bio Yrbk 1959:174 '60
Newsmakers. Newsweek 69:60 Mr 20 '67

HAWLEY, ORMI
Miss Hawley loses admirer. Feature Movie 1-1:41 Mr

15 '15
Thein, M.   A chat with Ormi Hawley.   Feature Movie
2-8:22 Jl 25 '15

HAWLEY, WANDA
Courtland, V.   Victuals and voice.   Photop 17-2:44 Ja '20

HAWN, GOLDIE
Raddatz, L.   Recognition comes to Goldie Hawn.   TV
Guide 16-26:12 Je 29 '68
Girls from Laugh In.   Newsweek 73:62 Ja 27 '69
People are talking about.   Vogue 153:192 My '69

HAWORTH, JILL
Hamilton, J.   Little girl from Exodus.   Look 25:112 Mr
28 '61
Cook, G.   Three days to grow up.   Photop 60-1:48 Jl '61
My romance with a Beatle.   Photop 65-5:72 My '64
Miller, E.   I've lost my English accent.   Seventeen 24:
68 Ja '65

HAYAKAWA, SESSUE
Kinglsey, G.   That splash of saffron.   Photop 9-4:139
Mr '16
Hayakawa, Japanese screen star.   Lit Digest 55:70 N 3
'17
Is the higher art of the movies to come from Japan?
Sessue Hayakawa on the screen.   Cur Opinion 64:30
Ja '18
Enter the villain.   Newsweek 51:62 Mr 17 '58
Risen sun.   New Yorker 35:16 Ag 1 '59
Hubler, R.   Honorable bad guy.   Coronet 50:146 My '61
Biography.   Cur Bio 23:36 S '62
Same.   Cur Bio Yrbk 1962:194 '63
Watkins, F.   Sessue Hayakawa.   Films In Review 17-6:
391 Je/Jl '66

HAYDEN, STERLING
Biographical sketch.   Time 37:93 F 17 '41
Ormiston, R.   Could you tame Sterling Hayden?   Photop
19-6:34 N '41
Gilmore, H.   Exclusive!   The real reason Sterling Hay-
den quit Hollywood.   Photop 20-1:30 D '41
Burton, J.   Love in exile.   Photop 21-6:65 N '42
Adventurer.   Time 57:104 Ap 23 '51
To break out.   Time 73:62 F 9 '59
Hayden's wanderer idyl.   Life 47:55 D 14 '59

HAYES, GEORGE "GABBY"

Hayes, G.   Granddaddy "Wild Fred" Hayes and Buffalo
   Bill.   TV Guide 3-40:28 O 7 '50
Gabby Hayes: real oldtimer.   TV Guide 4-41:16 O 12 '51
Hayes, G.   Advice to campers.   TV Guide 5-25:51 Je 20
   '52
Hayes, G.   Uncle Wrong-Way Hayes and the subway.   TV
   Guide 5-43:41 O 24 '52
Hayes, G.   When cousin bigwind got out of control.   TV
   Guide 1-8:A6 My 22 '53
Wood, C.   TV personalities biographical sketchbook.
   TV Personalities p37 '56
Obit.   Time 93:67 F 21 '69
   Newsweek 73:101 F 24 '69

HAYES, HELEN

Merritt, P.   Girl who is April.   Everybodys 40:39 Ap '19
Sumner, K.   Star at nineteen.   Am Mag 91:34 Mr '21
Adams, M.   Young ladies of the stage.   Woman Cit 8:10
   Ap 19 '24
Concerning Helen Hayes.   Drama 19:136 F '29
Kennedy, J. B.   Lucky lady; intv.   Colliers 83:33 Mr 30
   '29
Roberts, K.   Front-page family.   Colliers 87:30 Je 13 '31
Skinner, R. D.   Helen Hayes' screen debut.   Commonweal
   15:77 N 18 '31
Skinner, R. D.   Good fairy.   Commonweal 15:187 D 16 '31
Lieber, E.   No headlines for Helen.   Photop 42-5:70 O
   '32
Breuer, E.   Helen Hayes, first lady of the screen.   Pict
   R 34:14 Ap '33
Biery, R.   Why I'll return to the stage.   Photop 43-6:69
   My '33
Cole, C. C.   Candles of the Lord.   Delin 123:21 D '33
Dressing a personality.   Good H 98:62 Mr '34
Ray, M. B.   Preserve the cook; intv.   Colliers 93:34
   Ap 14 '34
Hunt, F.   Helen Hayes.   Photop 46-3:53 Ap '34
Helen Hayes ends her screen career; intv.   Lit Digest
   120:21 Jl 20 '35
Helen millennial.   Time 26:22 D 30 '35
Just living; autobiography.   Ladies Home J 53:8 Ap '36
   Same, abridged.   Lit Digest 121:22 My 9 '36
Pinchot, A.   Not in the picture; sidelights on celebrities.
   Delin 128:19 My '36
Discipline.   Am Mag 122:11 Ag '36
Victoria Regina; the high noon of English 19th Century

taste in the house of Helen Hayes.   House & Gard 70:
20 Ag '36

Eustis, M.   Actor attacks his part.   Theatre Arts 20:798
O '36

Arell, R.   Flaws that made fortunes.   Delin 130:46 Mr
'37

Helen Hayes reigns in a garden.   House & Gard 72:52 Ag
'37

Helen Hayes' new play.   Newsweek 14:31 Jl 17 '39

Harriman, M. C.   Helen Hayes and Mr. MacArthur.
Ladies Home J 56:28 O '39

Brown, C. H.   Mary, this is your mother.   Sat Eve Post
212:5 N 4; 16 N 11; 16 N 18; 16 N 25; 20 D 9; 26 D 16;
16 D 23; 26 D 30 '39

Valentine, E. R.   To Helen Hayes it's a puzzle; what wins
hearts as well as popular acclaim for an actress.
N. Y. Times Mag p8 D 1 '40

Hughes, C.   Leading and vibrant ladies.   N. Y. Times
Mag p10 Ja 4 '42

McEvoy, J. P.   MacArthurs.   Read Digest 40:15 Mr '42

Biography.   Cur Bio '42

Happiest holiday I ever spent.   House B 85:13 Ja '43

When ladies meet.   Ind Woman 22:65 Mr '43

Harriman, M. C.   Life with Helen Hayes.   N. Y. Times
Mag p16 My 16 '43

Enter, a great lady.   Read Digest 44:70 Mr '44

Baker, G.   Her world's a stage.   Sr Schol 44:17 Ap 24
'44

Political drama.   N. Y. Times Mag p16 Ag 27 '44

Summer theatre.   Life 21:84 Ag 5 '46

My life with music.   Etude 64:425 Ag '46

Biographical note.   Etude 64:425 Ag '46

Helen Hayes dances.   N. Y. Times Mag p30 O 27 '46

Helen herself.   Newsweek 28:92 N 11 '46

Happy birthday.   Life 21:79 N 18 '46

Brown, J. M.   To the ladies.   Sat R 29:23 D 21 '46

Funke, L.   Broadway husband and wife teams.   N. Y.
Times Mag p19 Ja 12 '47

Funke, L.   Broadway stars--ten years ago and today.
N. Y. Times Mag p24 Ap 20 '47

Most unforgettable character I've met.   Read Digest 51:
16 S '47

ANTA.   Theatre Arts 31:33 O '47

My current reading.   Sat R 31:27 Ag 28 '48

Helen Hayes on the air.   Newsweek 33:46 F 14 '49

Where are the new stars?   Theatre Arts 33:49 O '49

Funke, L.   Helen Hayes album.   N. Y. Times Mag p30

O 8 '50

Helen Hayes: new career, new aim in life.   C S Mon
   Mag p14 N 11 '50

Memo on intention to call a National theatre assembly.
   Theatre Arts 35:46 Ja '51

Ten most memorable stage performances.   Colliers 128:
   20 S 22 '51

Great ladies of the U. S. stage.   Life 31:120 N 19 '51

In my darkest hour, hope.   Read Digest 60:1 Mr '52

Theatre for the world.   Theatre Arts 36:30 Mr '52

Hinem, A.   Helen on Hollywood.   Holiday 11:16 Ap '52

Martin, P.   Helen Hayes tries Hollywood again.   Sat Eve
   Post 225:20 Ag 30 '52

Taking the curse off the classics.   Theatre Arts 37:65
   S '53

Play is worth a thousand speeches.   Nat Parent Teach 48:
   26 My '54

First lady's festival.   Theatre Arts 38:24 Jl '54

Helen Hayes and son.   Life 37:76 Ag 2 '54

Meegan, J.   When Arthur Godfrey met Helen Hayes.
   Coronet 37:25 D '54

Old hit.   Newsweek 45:43 Ja 3 '55

Funke, L.   Helen Hayes theatre.   N. Y. Times Mag p28
   N 20 '55

MacArthur, J. & Dowling R.   Happy anniversary, dear
   Helen.   Theatre Arts 39:14 D '55

Grand night for Helen.   Life 40:101 Ja 16 '56

Start a little theater.   Rotarian 88:6 Ja '56

Helen Hayes anniversary album.   Theatre Arts 40:32 F
   '56

MacArthur, J. as told to S. Fields.   Meet my Helen
   Hayes.   McCalls 83:40 F '56

Spelvin, G.   To London with love, or, A haymaker by
   Helen.   Theatre Arts 40:62 D '56

Biography.   Colliers Yrbk 1956:524 '56

Biography.   Cur Bio 17:33 O '56

   Same.   Cur Bio Yrbk 1956:258 '57

Hayes, H. as told to N. Kutner.   Of all my stages.
   Good H 144:69 F; 80 Mr '57

Talk with two stars.   Newsweek 50:84 N 25 '57

Biography.   Time 70:91 N 25 '57

Hayes, H.   Best advice I ever had.   Read Digest 73:88
   S '58

Ten best for a repertory theatre.   N. Y. Times Mag p19
   N 9 '58

Hayes, H.   Helen Hayes relives her roles.   N. Y. Times
   Mag p40 D 7 '58

Landmark in a long career. Theatre Arts 42:74 D '58
She can't resist. Newsweek 53:104 Ap 27 '59
Schulberg, L. Touch of magic. Commonweal 70:305 Je
    19 '59
Franklin, R. First lady's fond memories. Theatre Arts
    43:17 S '59
Biography. Am Ann 1959:320 '59
Hayes, H. You just can't depend on God. Show 1-1:88
    O '61
MacArthur, J. My mother, Helen Hayes; as told to A.
    Whitman. Good H 154:68 F '62
In memory of Mary. Newsweek 62:104 O 21 '63
Hunt, G. P. She has been in Life 54 times. Life 55:3 N
    1 '63
I bid adieu to things. Life 55:99 N 1 '63
Hayes, H. Gift of job; excerpts. McCalls 92:73 S '65
Hayes, H. Charlie; excerpt from A Gift of joy. Read
    Digest 87:126 N '65
Successful autographing tours by three personalities.
    Pub W 188:53 D 13 '65
Hayes, H. My faith in prayer; excerpt from A gift of
    joy. Read Digest 87:55 D '65
Hayes, H. Queen and I; excerpt from A gift of joy.
    Read Digest 88:103 Ap '66
Weales, G. One for the road. Reporter 34:54 My 19 '66
Childhood in New York. McCalls 95:97 D '67
Helen Hayes own story: my loves remembered; excerpt
    from On Reflection. Good H 167:88 N '68

HAYMES, DICK
    Swanson, P. Hey there, Haymes! Photop 26-3:36 F '45
    Madison, A. Horseshoe Haymes. Photop 27-6:60 N '45
    Howe, H. Vagabond on a gold stallion. Photop 28-5:46
        Ap '46
    Dudley, F. It's a joke son. Photop 29-3:52 Ag '46
    Dick Haymes, camera hobbyist. Am Home 36:64 N '46
    Haymes, D. Us. Photop 31-1:54 Je '47
    Parsons, L. O. Tangled lives. Photop 34-1:34 Je '49
    Nevada wedding. Life 35:35 O 5 '53
    Unfrumptious wedding. Time 62:45 O 5 '53
    Muir, F. She's the marrying kind. Photop 44-4:48 O
        '53

HAYWARD, LOUIS
    Reed, E. New faces: 1935. Theatre Arts 19:275 Ap
        '35
    Small, F. It was hate at first sight. Photop 50-4:66

O '36

How Mr. and Mrs. Hayward live.   Photop 20-1:48 D '41

Wood, C.   TV personalities biographical sketchbook.
TV Personalities p53 '57

HAYWARD, SUSAN

Wilkinson, L. A.   Sweet Susan Hayward.   Photop 25-2:
51 Jl '44

Franchey, J.   Susan the nonesuch.   Colliers 114:24 D
2 '44

Ashland, J.   Sweet pepper.   Photop 31-4:44 S '47

Arnold, M.   Brooklyn goes to bat.   Photop 37-3:52 Mr
'50

Waterbury, R.   This is Susan Hayward.   Photop 39-5:52
My '51

Wood, T.   Unlazy Susan.   Colliers 128:20 Ag 18 '51

Froman, J.   She lived my life.   Photop 42-1:46 Jl '52

Zeitlin, I.   Three loves has Susan Hayward.   Photop 42-
5:41 N '52

Biography.   Cur Bio 14:37 My '53

Roberts, G.   With a song in their hearts.   Photop 43-6:
56 Je '53

If you knew Susan.   Look 17:64 Jl 14 '53

Privilege of the podium; Mrs. Margaret Harpstrite and
the Barkers.   Time 62:26 N 30 '53

Corwin, J.   Smashup.   Photop 44-5:36 N '53

Corwin, J.   Jeff's other love.   Photop 45-1:50 Ja '54

Block, M.   Mom's no quitter.   Photop 46-2:60 Ag '54

Manning, D.   Brooklyn's child is full of faith.   Photop
48-1:59 Jl '55

Lane, M.   I know Susan's secret!   Photop 48-5:86 N '55

Susan Hayward bids for an Academy award.   Look 19:
104 D 13 '55

Alpert, H.   Tragedy, happy ending style.   Sat R 39:56 Ja
7 '56

Emmitt, R.   Susan Hayward: trouble bait.   Photop 49-
2:50 F '56

Whitcomb, J.   Songbird Susan.   Cosmop 140:61 F '56

Brooklyn, bombshell.   Coronet 39:6 Ap '56

Johnson, H.   God has not forgotten me.   Photop 55-3:66
Mr '59

Jennings, D.   Hollywood's late-blooming redhead.   Sat
Eve Post 232:14 Jl 11 '59

Graves, J.   Look at me, love me, anyone!   Photop 56-
2:58 Ag '59

Biography.   Am Ann 1960:332 '60

McClelland, D.   Susan Hayward, inc. filmog.   Films In

Review 13-5 My '62
McClelland, D.   The Brooklyn Bernhardt.   Films &
Filming 11-6:11 Mr '65
I can't live in Hollywood.   Photop 74-1:56 Jl '68

HAYWORTH, RITA
Best-dressed.   Am Mag 131:74 F '41
Hover, H.   You could do it too.   Photop 18-3:22 F '41
Crichton, K.   Rita the rage.   Colliers 107:18 My 3 '41
California Carmen.   Time 38:90 N 10 '41
Steele, J. H.   Portrait of a shy glamour girl.   Photop
20-3:40 F '42
Parker, S.   Love and Rita Hayworth.   Photop 21-2:26
Jl '42
Waterbury, R.   The romance Hollywood doesn't like.
Photop 21-6:28 N '42
Beatty, J.   Sweetheart of the A. E. F.   Am Mag 134:42
D '42
Cover girl; Rita learns new role.   Life 14:74 Ja 18 '43
Addison, R.   When Rita Hayworth said goodby to Vic Ma-
ture.   Photop 22-4:47 Mr '43
Addison, R.   Breakup--the truth about Rita Hayworth
and Victor Mature.   Photop 23-3:28 Ag '43
GI Oscar winner.   Life 18:30 Jl 16 '45
Parsons, L. O.   Intermission for romance.   Photop 28-6:
30 My '46
Vidor, C.   Exciting woman.   Photop 29-3:42 Ag '46
Deere, D.   Feet that danced.   Photop 29-6:47 N '46
Parsons, L. O.   It's like this.   Photop 31-2:36 Jl '47
Sargeant, W.   Cult of the love goddess in America.
Life 23:80 N 10 '47
Deere, D.   Rita Hayworth lives here.   Photop 31-6:72
N '47
Fink, H.   I was there.   Photop 32-1:52 D '47
Parsons, L. O.   Ask the boss.   Photop 32-4:50 Mr '48
Carmen Hayworth.   Newsweek 32:78 Ag 23 '48
Lait, J.   Sho' is all woman.   Photop 33-6:46 N '48
Maxwell, E.   Love affair.   Photop 34-3:34 F '49
Maxwell, E.   Transatlantic call to Rita and Aly.   Photop
34-5:34 Ap '49
Coughlan, R.   The Aga, the Aly and the Rita.   Life 26:
125 My 16 '49
Oui, oui.   Time 53:27 Je 6 '49
Prominent couple married.   Life 26:57 Je 6 '49
Liebling, A. J.   Right up Louella's Ali.   New Yorker
25:86 Je 11 '49
Coughlan, R.   The Aga, the Aly and the Rita, abridged.

Read Digest 55:136 Ag '49

Parsons, L. O.   I saw Rita Hayworth marry Aly Khan.
  Photop 36-3:34 Ag '49

Maxwell, E.   The fabulous life.   Photop 36-5:40 O '49

Yasmin.   Time 55:84 Ja 9 '50

Rita's baby has world premiere.   Life 28:34 Ja 16 '50

Maxwell, E.   Title to happiness.   Photop 38-1:40 Jl '50

Onward and upward.   Time 57:98 My 7 '51

Landry, B.   I remember Rita.   Colliers 128:18 Jl 28 '51

Maxwell, E.   The princess abdicates.   Photop 40-2:50
  Ag '51

Wilson, L.   Should Rita Hayworth change?   Photop 40-6:
  46 D '51

Johnson, G.   Does Rita want career or love?   Coronet
  31:62 Ja '52

Maxwell, E.   The girl who came back.   Photop 41-6:60
  Je '52

Corwin, J.   The not-so-private life of Rita Hayworth.
  Photop 42-4:50 O '52

Return of a love goddess.   Cosmop 134:66 Ap '53

Harvey, E.   Here's Rita as Sadie.   Colliers 132:14 Jl
  11 '53

Nevada wedding.   Life 35:35 O 5 '53

Unfrumptious wedding.   Time 62:45 O 5 '53

Muir, F.   She's the marrying kind.   Photop 44-4:48 O
  '53

Rita, Rebecca and Yasmin.   Newsweek 43:54 My 3 '54

Prince on a mission.   Newsweek 44:45 Ag 9 '54

People.   Time 66:46 S 26 '55

Courts and contracts.   Newsweek 47:40 Ja 9 '56

Whitcomb, J.   2,243 miles from Broadway.   Cosmop 142:
  18 Ja '57

Rita rips into Zip.   Life 43:97 O 14 '57

Out of bondage.   Look 22:50 Ja 21 '58

Mills, J. R.   The love goddess.   Photop 53-2:40 F '58

Rita without glamour.   Life 47:125 O 26 '59

Hunter, A.   Surrendered.   Photop 56-5:75 N '59

Biography.   Cur Bio 21:14 My '60
  Cur Bio Yrbk 1960:184 '61

Reynolds, L.   I'll run away ... I'll elope.   Photop 60-4:
  48 O '61

Connell, E. S. Jr.   Brief essay on the subject of celebrity
  with numerous digressions and particular attention to
  the actress Rita Hayworth.   Esquire 63:114 Mr '65

Ringgold, G.   Rita Hayworth, inc. filmog.   Screen Facts
  1-2:1 n. d.

HEATHERTON, JOEY
  Rising star learns to shine; intv. Seventeen 20:66 Ja'61
  This is Joey. TV Guide 11-35:25 Ag 31 '63
  Astor, G. Joey Heatherton: heavenly body entering orbit.
    Look 30:95 Ja 8 '66

HECKART, EILEEN
  Anderson, D. Eileen Heckart. Theatre Arts 42:70 F '58
  Biography. Cur Bio 19:18 Je '58
  Same. Cur Bio Yrbk 1958:188 '58

HEDISON, DAVID
  Torpedoed by success? TV Guide 14-29:10 Jl 16 '66
  His littlest Armenian. Photop 76-6:56 D '69

HEDREN, TIPPI
  Hamilton, J. Hitchcock's new Grace Kelly. Look 26:53
    D 4 '62
  Hedren, T. I cried at my wedding. Photop 67-1:54 Ja
    '65

HEFLIN, VAN
  Some film actors who have made themselves known this
    year. Theatre Arts 26:184 Mr '42
  Zarat, I. A guy a girl could love. Photop 22-1:56 D
    '42
  Biography. Cur Bio '43
  Scott, D. Voyager. Photop 30-2:58 Ja '47
  Actor goes to school. Theatre Arts 34:36 O '50
  Actor's long voyage home. Theatre Arts 37:15 Ja '53
  Raddatz, L. And then his symmetricals began to slip.
    TV Guide 11-52:15 D 28 '63

HELTON, PEGGY
  Weisenreder, E. B. Letter. Films In Review 19-9:592
    N '68

HEMMINGS, DAVID
  People are talking about . . . Vogue 149:94 F 15 '67
  Lerman, L. International movie report. Mlle 64:118 F
    '67
  Miller, E. It doesn't come easy. Seventeen 26:153 My
    '67
  Ehrlich, H. Light brigade charges again. Look 32:58
    F 6 '68
  Redbook dialogue. Redbook 131:70 Jl '68
  Reeves, A. Love becomes legal. Photop 75-2:54 F '69

HENDRIX, WANDA
   Murphy, A. Why I'm not afraid to marry Wanda Hendrix.
      Photop 34-2:26 Ja '47
   Hero and actress. Life 23:106 N 17 '47
   Proctor, K. Love is young. Photop 32-5:52 Ap '48
   Hollywood's new generation. Life 24:94 My 24 '48
   She's a big girl now. Am Mag 146:111 D '48
   Mulvey, K. Searching party. Photop 36-4:56 S '49
   Hendrix, W. Hero's wife. Photop 36-7:30 D '49
   Colby, A. Make trouble pay dividends in beauty. Photop
      37-3:62 Mr '50

HENIE, SONJA
   Skating. Newsweek 3:24 Mr 17 '34
   Astaire on ice. Time 27:57 Mr 30 '36
   Top. Am Mag 123:98 Ap '37
   Hayes, B. Shadows across the ice. Photop 51-8:42 Ag
      '37
   Beatty, J. $1,000,000 on ice. Am Mag 124:32 N '37
   Sharpe, H. Skating through life. Photop 51-11:14 N;
      51-12:30 D '37; 52-1:62 Ja '38
   Portmann, D. Why Sonja Henie won't marry. Photop
      52-4:24 Ap '38
   Lester, B. B. One in a million. C S Mon Mag p4 O 19
      '38
   Rhea, M. Sonja Henie's new prince charming. Photop
      53-3:28 Mr '39
   Gee-whizzer. Time 34:51 Jl 17 '39
   Fabulous Sonja Henie. Newsweek 15:38 Ja 29 '40
   Hayes, B. When Sonja Henie met Alan Curtis. Photop
      54-4:26 Ap '40
   Biography. Cur Bio '40
   McEvoy, J. P. She happens on ice. Read Digest 39:41
      N '41
   Henie, S. Way of a winner. Photop 23-5:72 O '43
   Graham, S. People will say they're in love. Photop 29-
      1:32 Je '46
   Porter, A. Frozen assets; Sonja Henie and her Holly-
      wood ice revue. Colliers 119:76 Ja 25 '47
   Ice queen. Time 51:50 F 2 '48
   Hot stuff on ice. Newsweek 32:86 O 25 '48
   Biography. Cur Bio 13:18 Ja '52
      Same. Cur Bio Yrbk 1952:258 '53
   Hot feud for icy gold. Life 32:46 F 4 '52
   Marriage go-round. Time 77:44 Ja 6 '61
   What are they doing now? Show 2-3:97 Mr '62
   Where are they now? Newsweek 63:14 F 10 '64

HENREID, PAUL
   Rhea, M. Strangers in arms. Photop 20-4:44 Mr '42
   Sharpe, H. Enter Paul Henreid. Photop 22-2:37 Ja '43
   Henreid, P. How to have a happy marriage. Photop
      24-3:38 F '44
   Deere, D. Hearthside pirate. Photop 29-1:50 Je '46
   Henreid, P. The actor as director. Films In Review
      3-6:270 Je/Jl '52
   Nolan, J. E. Films on TV. Films In Review 20-5:305
      My '69

HEPBURN, AUDREY
   Gigi. New Yorker 27:32 D 8 '51
   Audrey is a hit. Life 31:103 D 10 '51
   Miller, G. Search for Gigi. Theatre Arts 36:48 Jl '52
   Hewes, H. Stars who danced. Sat R 35:28 N 15 '52
   Princess apparent. Time 62:60 S 7 '53
   Hartung, P. T. Star is born. Commonweal 58:586 S 18
      '53
   Parsons, L. O. Audrey Hepburn--greatest since Garbo?
      Cosmop 135:10 S '53
   Audrey Hepburn, many-sided charmer. Life 35:127 D 7
      '53
   Connolly, M. Who needs beauty. Photop 45-1:48 Ja '54
   Mlle merit awards. Mlle 38:82 Ja '54
   On stardom's way. Coronet 35:46 Ja '54
   Herrmann, H. M. Half nymph, half wunderkind. N. Y.
      Times Mag p15 F 14 '54
   Whitcomb, J. Dear valentine. Cosmop 136:91 F '54
   Clurman, H. Letter to Audrey Hepburn. Nation 178:206
      Mr 6 '54
   Another triumph for Audrey. Life 36:60 Mr 8 '54
   Biography. Cur Bio 15:27 Mr '54
      Same. Cur Bio Yrbk 1954:331 '54
   Four young stars, will they be great? Vogue 123:108
      Ap 1 '54
   Winner; New York portion of Hollywood's Academy awards.
      New Yorker 30:22 Ap 3 '54
   Audrey waits for Academy decision. Life 36:137 Ap 5 '54
   Audrey scores twice. Sr Schol 64:19 Ap 7 '54
   Swanson, P. Knee-deep in stardust. Photop 45-4:58
      Ap '54
   Fields, S. Audrey Hepburn. McCalls 81:61 Jl '54
   Beaton, C. Audrey Hepburn. Vogue 124:129 N 1 '54
   Harris, R. Audrey Hepburn--the girl, the gamin and the
      star. Photop 47-3:61 Mr '55
   Idyl for Audrey. Life 39:44 Jl 18 '55

Abramson, M. Audrey Hepburn. Cosmop 139:26 O '55

Biography. Am Ann 1955:322 '55

Biography. Colliers Yrbk 1955:476 '55

Jones, M. W. My husband doesn't ruin me. Photop 49-4:52 Ap '56

Tolstoy, Ferrer, Hepburn, $6 million. Newsweek 48:53 Jl 30 '56

War and peace; Audrey Hepburn plays a classic heroine. Womans H C 83:40 S '56

Maynard, J. Audrey Hepburn's harvest of the heart. Photop 50-3:42 S '56

Hawkins, W. Interview with Audrey Hepburn. Dance Mag 30:17 O '56

Nichols, M. Audrey Hepburn goes back to the bar. Coronet 41:44 N '56

Scandal in rehearsal; Mayerling. Life 42:56 F 4 '57

Cook, P. Photographer and his model make a pretty movie. Cosmop 142:50 F '57

Jones, M. W. The small private world of Audrey Hepburn. Photop 51-2:66 F '57

Ed Feingersh shoots a star in motion. Pop Phot 40:76 Ap '57

Chi-chi Cinderella. Look 21:116 My 14 '57

Knight, A. Choreography for camera; Funny face. Dance Mag 31:16 My '57

Clement, C. Look where you're going Audrey. Photop 51-6:46 Je '57

McCalls visits. McCalls 84:22 Je '57

Allen, A. Please, God, help me to walk again. Photop 55-5:58 My '59

Lovely Audrey in religious role. Life 46:141 Je 8 '59

Waldman, J. Audrey's fantastic figure. Cosmop 146:63 Je '59

Harris, E. Audrey Hepburn. Good H 149:60 Ag '59

Celebrities on a stylish spree. Life 47:103 S 7 '59

Hamilton, J. Audrey Hepburn and her strong son. Look 24:89 N 8 '60

Britten, R. Audrey's happiest moment. Photop 59-4:50 Ap '61

Barbar, R. Delightful riddle of Audrey Hepburn. Good H 155:61 Ag '62

Looks in fashion. Vogue 141:83 Ja 1 '63

Cary Grant, Audrey Hepburn. Look 27:87 D 17 '63

Gordon, S. My fair lady's dream come true. Look 28:60 F 25 '64

Brett, S. Audrey Hepburn. Films & Filming 10-6:8 Mr '64

Who says it's a dog's life?   Good H 158:82 Mr '64

Seidenbaum, G.   Audrey Hepburn; making of My fair lady.
   McCalls 92:96 O '64

Leduc, V.   Steal-scening with Hepburn and O'Toole.
   Vogue 147:172 Ap 1 '66

Look at Audrey Hepburn score!   Ladies Home J 84:60 Ja
   '68

Dowty, L.   Audrey Hepburn makes the scene.   Good H
   165:84 Ag '67

Waterbury, R.   Her marriage breakup.   Photop 72-6:34
   D '67

Audrey and Andrea.   Vogue 153:109 Mr 15 '69

Tyron, M. & Collins, P.   Brides at 39--mothers at 40?
   Photop 76-5:56 N '69

HEPBURN, KATHARINE

Temple, M.   She stole his best scenes.   Photop 43-2:82
   Ja '33

Melcher, E.   Screen sensations of the year.   Cinema
   Digest 3-5:9 Ap 7 '33

Cohen, H. W.   Katharine Hepburn.   Cinema Digest 3-7:
   12 My 1 '33

Hamilton, S.   Well! well! so this is Hollywood.   Photop
   44-3:71 Ag '33

On the screen.   Lit Digest 116:16 S 2 '33

Pringle, H. F.   Mind of her own.   Colliers 92:21 O 28
   '33

Croy, H.   Women capture screen honors for 1933. Lit
   Digest 116:42 N 4 '33

Tazelaar, M.   Katharine Hepburn's rise to fame.   Lit
   Digest 116:29 D 30 '33

Young, S.   Miss Katharine Hepburn.   New Repub 77:281
   Ja 17 '34

Maxwell, V.   Katharine Hepburn's inferiority complex.
   Photop 45-2:52 Ja '34

Reed, E.   Roster of new faces.   Theatre Arts 18:54 Ja
   '34

Morse, W. Jr.   The power behind the Hollywood throne.
   Photop 45-3:31 F '34

Shawell, J.   Hollywood's strange girl.   Pict R 35:11 Ap
   '34

Dressing a personality.   Good H 98:60 My '34

Johnston, A.   Hepburn legend.   Womans H C 61:12 Je
   '34

Baker, K.   What's ahead for Hepburn?   Photop 46-2:69
   Jl '34

Ferguson, O.   Two show figures.   New Repub 84:104

S 4 '35

Baskette, K. Is Hepburn killing her own career? Photop
    48-4:38 S '35

Jackson, A. Hepburn from A to B. Cinema Arts 1-2:
    20 Jl '37

Brilliant playing in Holiday turns tables on critics.
    Newsweek 11:21 Je 13 '38

Kaufmann, A. What! Another Scarlett O'Hara? Photop
    52-8:64 Ag '38

Jensen, O. O. Hepburns; seven members of a fabulous
    Hartford family express themselves at any cost. Life
    8:46 Ja 22 '40

    Same, abridged. Read Digest 36:102 Mr '40

Baskette, K. What happened to Hepburn? Photop 54-12:
    19 D '40

Philadelphia story. Life 10:31 Ja 6 '41

Wilkinson, L. A. & Bryan, J. 3rd. Hepburn story.
    Sat Eve Post 214:9 N 29; 26 D 6; 24 D 13; 16 D 27 '41;
    20 Ja 3 '42

Hepburn in Hartford. Life 12:78 My 11 '42

Biography. Cur Bio '42

Woolf, S. J. She's a different Miss Hepburn; intv.
    N. Y. Times Mag p18 N 28 '43

Crichton, K. Kate the great. Colliers 112:24 D 4 '43

Cukor, G. Forever Kate. Photop 32-3:68 F '48

MacGregor, A. Katie's hep. Photop 37-4:62 Ap '50

Life goes on location in Africa; African queen. Life 31:
    172 S 17 '51

Huston, J. African queen; behind the scenes story.
    Theatre Arts 36:48 F '52

Bogart, H. Humphrey Bogart tells the truth about Hep-
    burn. Coronet 31:139 Ap '52

Watts, S. Katharine Hepburn vs. George Bernard Shaw.
    N. Y. Times Mag p17 Jl 13 '52

Hepburn story. Time 60:60 S 1 '52

    Same abridged. Read Digest 61:87 N '52

Marshall, M. Drama. Nation 175:413 N 1 '52

Brown, J. M. Katharine without Petruchio: Millionairess.
    Sat R 35:25 N 1 '52

Bentley, E. Unbuoyant billions. New Repub 127:22 N 3
    '52

Monthly critical review: Kid Hepburn vs. Rocky Shaw.
    Theatre Arts 36:18 N '52

Spelvin, G. Tomahawks out, men! here comes Hepburn
    with a London hit! Theatre Arts 36:22 D '52

Hepburn in Venice. N. Y. Times Mag p66 S 19 '54

Hepburn takes a plunge. Look 18:60 N 2 '54

Summertime, U.S.A.   Cosmop 138:126 My '55
Kalb, B.   Star.   Sat R 38:34 Je 18 '55
Mason, G.   Katharine the great.   Films & Filming 2-
    11:7 Ag '56
Katie's latest capers.   Look 20:161 D 11 '56
When co-stars get together.   Newsweek 49:118 My 27 '57
Tozzi, R. V.   Katharine Hepburn, inc. filmog.   Films In
    Review 8-10:481 D '57
Life congratulates Hepburn and her gams.   Life 28:47 F
    20 '60
Talk with a star.   Newsweek 55:97 Je 13 '60
Williams, T.   Five fiery ladies.   Life 50:88 F 3 '61
Talk with a star.   Newsweek 60:109 O 15 '62
To Lawrence Langer.   Theatre Arts 47:11 My '63
Cowie, P.   Katharine Hepburn.   Films & Filming 9-9:21
    Je '63
Hamilton, J.   Last visit with two undimmed stars.   Look
    31:26 Jl 11 '67
Newquist, R.   Special kind of magic; abridged.   McCalls
    94:64 Jl '67
Israel, L.   Last of the honest-to-God ladies.   Esquire
    68:14 N '67
Newsmakers.   Newsweek 71:36 Ja 1 '68
Frook, L.   Aunt Kate.   Life 64:61 Ja 5 '68
Ardmore, J.   Woman without a husband.   Photop 73-2:56
    F '68
Miller, K.   Kath and her Aunt Kate.   Seventeen 27:134
    F '68
Feibleman, P. S.   Unsinkable Kate.   Look 32:63 Ag 6 '68
Tildesley, A.   Kate the great!   Photop 74-2:28 Ag '68
Graham, S.   Spencer Tracy and Katharine Hepburn.
    Ladies Home J 85:94 D '68
Tynan, K.   Great Kate.   Vogue 153:87 Ap 15 '69

HERBERT, HEYES
    Obit.   Screen World 10:222 '59

HERBERT, HOLMES
    Obit.   Screen World 8:222 '57

HERBERT, HUGH
    Hartley, K.   Hugh Herbert isn't all he wise-cracks to be.
        Photop 50-5:36 N '36
    Hamilton, S.   Woo, woo--and I do mean woo.   Photop
        52-8:63 Ag '38
    Peterson, E. T.   Cinema's culinary cut-up.   Bet Hom &
        Gard 16:16 Ag '38

Hexagonal Hugh Herbert.   Newsweek 15:46 Je 3 '40
Obit.   Newsweek 39:79 Mr 24 '52
   Time 59:98 Mr 24 '52
   Am Ann 1953:305 '53

HERNANDEZ, JUANO
Zegri, A.   Spanish Americans invade Broadway.
   Americas 10:30 N '58

HERSHOLT, JEAN
Crichton, K.   He's the doctor; playing doctor to the Dione
   quintuplets.   Colliers 97:17 Ap 4 '36
Five little stars.   Womans H C 66:20 Je '39
Bianco, M.   Jean Hersholt's Andersen.   Horn Bk 20:164
   My '44
Biography.   Cur Bio D '44
The two never met.   Sat R 29:18 D 21 '46
My current reading.   Sat R 31:14 F 14 '48
Presented the University of California at Los Angeles
   library with 180 Danish plays.   Lib J 73:552 Ap 1 '48
Obit.   Newsweek 47:78 Je 11 '56
   Time 67:87 Je 11 '56
   Am Ann 1957:347 '57
   Brit Bk Yr 1957:575 '57
   Cur Bio 17:43 S '56
   Cur Bio Yrbk 1956:262 '57
   Screen World 8:222 '57
   Biography.   NCAB 42:652 '58

HESTON, CHARLTON
Who's who in the cast.   TV Guide 4-3:28 Ja 20 '51
Linet, B.   I was there.   Photop 41-6:50 Je '52
Waterbury, R.   Charlton loves Lydia.   Photop 43-6:60 Je
   '53
Ott, B.   Their marriage is a lifetime honeymoon.
   Photop 45-4:62 Ap '54
Waterbury, R.   There'll be some changes made.   Photop
   46-6:50 D '54
Limke, H.   Bringing up baby.   Photop 48-4:53 O '55
Engelsman, N.   Top billing for the youngest Heston.
   Parents Mag 31:40 Ag '56
Nichols, M.   Moses from Michigan.   Coronet 40:8 O '56
Baby who plays Moses.   McCalls 84:20 N '56
Downing, H.   For if ye believe.   Photop 50-6:46 D '56
Goldsmith, B. L.   Midwestern Moses.   Womans H C 84:
   13 Ja '57
DeRoulf, P.   Charlton Heston sounds off on men and

matrimony. Photop 51-5:50 My '57
Biography. Cur Bio 18:26 My '57
   Same. Cur Bio Yrbk 1957:253 '58
Steele, J. H. Unmasking Charlton Heston. Photop 53-
   1:51 Ja '58
Davidson, B. House that Ben-Hur built. Look 24:56J
   My 24 '60
Martin, P. I call on Ben-Hur. Sat Eve Post 233:20 Ag
   20 '60
Gale, B. Charlton Heston's race to stardom. Coronet
   49:156 N '60
Roud, R. The French line. Sight & Sound 29-4:171
   Aut '60
Biography. Am Ann 1961:328 '61
Heston, C. Mammoth movies I have known. Films &
   Filming 8-7:16 Ap '62
Hoffman, J. The Heston affair. Photop 61-5:70 My '62
Liston, J. At home with Charlton Heston. Am Home
   65:14 My '62
Maddox, T. I found my father in a phone book. Photop
   66-4:46 O '64
Agony and the ecstasy of Michelangelo. Look 29:41 Mr
   9 '65
Hamill, P. Heston; larger than life. Sat Eve Post 238:
   87 Jl 3 '65
Seiberling, D. Trying to be a genius. Life 59:75 N 12
   '65
Redbook dialogue. Redbook 126:68 D '65
Graven image. Time 88:43 Ag 12 '66
Higham, C. Charlton Heston. Sight & Sound 35-4:169
   Aut '66
Finnigan, J. Fighting on another front. TV Guide 15-24:
   12 Je 17 '67
1968: a new year in better shape. Vogue 151:67 Ja 1
   '68
Webb, M. Nude scene that went too far. Photop 75-3:
   54 Mr '69
Hoffman, J. Gives his all for Shakespeare. Photop 76-
   6:63 D '69

HEYDT, LOUIS JEAN
   Obit. Newsweek 55:42 F 8 '60

HICKMAN, DWAYNE
   Most envied man on the campus. TV Guide 4-49:20 D 8
      '56
   The many loves and lives of Dobie Gillis. TV Guide 7-

41:17 O 10 '59
Hickman, D. I win Tuesday's loving looks.   Photop 56-
  5:56 N '59
Nichols, M.   Career policy pays off.   Coronet 48:10 Jl
  '60
Formula for TV success.   Look 25:50a My 9 '61
Now he can relax.   TV Guide 9-35:17 S 2 '61
Miller, E.   I was a teenager for 10 years.   Seventeen
  24:94 Je '65

HICKS, RUSSELL
  Obit.   Screen World 9:223 '58

HINDS, SAMUEL S.
  The face is familiar.   Cinema Arts 1-1:38 Je '37
  Sterling, E.   Face is familiar; once-wealthy lawyer, now
    is lawyer before camera.   Am Mag 126:61 D '38
  Obit.   Time 52:88 O 25 '48
  Doctor, lawyer, merchant, judge-casting always called
    Sam Hinds.   Life 25:56 N 29 '48
  Jones, K.   Letter, inc. filmog.   Films In Review 17-7:
    462 Ag/S '66

HINES, JOHNNY
  Pike, C.   Everybody calls him 'Johnny.'   Photop 15-5:43
    Ap '19
  Boyle, M.   Johnny on the jump.   Photop 28-3:76 Ag '25

HINGLE, PAT
  Harity, R.   Patience of Job.   Cosmop 147:8 Ag '59
  Biography.   Cur Bio 26:20 Ap '65
    Same.   Cur Bio Yrbk 1965:198 '65

HILL, ARTHUR
  Biography.   Am Ann 1964:660 '64

HILL, STEVEN
  Raddatz, L.   He didn't come out of a cookie cutter.
    TV Guide 15-6:20 F 11 '67

HILLER, WENDY
  Reed, E.   Some actors, season of 1935-36.   Theatre
    Arts 20:442 Je '36
  Hobson, H.   Wendy Hiller strides to fame.   C S Mon Mag
    p4 My 11 '40
  Chute, M.   Girl with the "immoral" hair.   Photop 19-1:
    68 Je '41

Biography.   Cur Bio '41
Breit, H.   Shavian darling.   N. Y. Times Mag p61 S 28
    '47
Heiress.   Time 50:70 O 13 '47
My current reading.   Sat R 30:8 D 27 '47

HILLIARD, HARRIET
(See NELSON, HARRIET)

HITCHCOCK, RAYMOND
    Parmer, C.   I'm looking for a place to die!   Colliers
        78:25 O 2 '26

HOBBES, HALLIWELL
    Obit.   Screen World 14:222 '63

HODGES, EDDIE
    Hot tots.   Newsweek 51:58 Ja 13 '58
    Anderson, D.   Show stopper.   Theatre Arts 42:62 Je '58
    Harlib, M. E.   Everybody loves Eddie.   Coronet 44:97
        Ag '58

HODIAK, JOHN
    Proctor, K.   Hi, Hody!   Photop 25-1:56 Je '44
    Maury, M.   Strictly USA.   Photop 26-5:36 Ap '45
    Parsons, L. O.   Surprise ending.   Photop 28-2:32 Ja '46
    Howe, H.   Family bachelor.   Photop 28-6:54 My '46
    Rhodes, K.   The Hodiaks.   Photop 29-4:29 S '46
    Obit.   Newsweek 46:61 O 31 '55
        Time 66:92 O 31 '55
        Am Ann 1956:328 '56
        Brit Bk Yr 1956:513 '56
        Screen World 7:225 '56

HOFFMAN, DUSTIN
    Zeitlin, D.   Homely non-hero, Dustin Hoffman gets an un-
        likely role in Mike Nichols' The graduate.   Life 63:111
        N 24 '67
    I plummeted to stardom.   Newsweek 71:86 Ja 22 '68
    Reynolds, L.   His mother's story.   Photop 73-6:45 Je '68
    Kerr, D.   His own story.   Photop 73-6:45 Je '68
    We talk with Dustin Hoffman; intv.   Mlle 67:368 Ag '68
    Chapman, D.   Graduate turns bum.   Look 32:66 S 17 '68
    Gussow, M.   Dustin.   McCalls 95:66 S '68
    Lear, M. W.   Dustin Hoffman; the man behind the smile.
        Redbook 131:66 S '68
    Cocks, J.   Moonchild and the fifth Beatle. Time 93:50 F 7 '69

HOLBROOK, HAL

Malcolm, D. F.   Off Broadway.   New Yorker 35:80 Ap 18 '59

Millstein, G.   One as Twain.   N. Y. Times Mag p24 Ap 19 '59

Mark Twain tonight!   Time 73:71 Ap 20 '59

Lewis, T.   Mark Twain tonight!   America 101:351 My 16 '59

Fuller, J. G.   Trade Winds.   Sat R 42:6 My 30 '59

Broadway's Mark Twain.   Newsweek 53:58 Je 1 '59

Wyatt, E. V. R.   Mark Twain tonight!   Cath World 189: 241 Je '59

Twain comes to town; Holbrook monologues.   Theatre Arts 43:6 Je '59

Clurman, H.   Hal Holbrook's Mark Twain tonight! Nation 189:79 Ag 15 '59

Prideaux, T.   Twain's amazing twin.   Life 47:81 O 19 '59

Twain to the life.   Theatre Arts 43:71 O '59

Biography.   Cur Bio 22:23 My '61

Same.   Cur Bio Yrbk 1961:206 '62

Funniest lies: Mark Twain tonight!   Time 87:63 Ap 1 '66

Lewis, T.   Mark Twain tonight!   America 114:605 Ap 23 '66

Mark Twain tonight, Hal Holbrook this morning.   New Yorker 42:44 Ap 23 '66

Prideaux, T.   Mark Twain on Holbrook.   Life 60:16 My 13 '66

Schickel, R.   Hal Holbrook tonight!   Holiday 40:103 Ag '66

HOLDEN, FAY

Cosby, V.   Ma Hardy advises.   Photop 18-3:20 F '41

HOLDEN, WILLIAM

Franchey, J. R.   That's Holden for you.   Photop 54-7:10 Jl '40

Ford, G.   My pals Brenda and Bill.   Photop 21-1:52 Je '42

Asher, J.   Happiness is a thing called Bill.   Photop 31-5: 48 O '47

Howe, H.   Dear husband.   Photop 38-4:36 O '50

Nugent, F. S.   Golden Holden.   Colliers 127:30 Je 2 '51

Swanson, P.   Mr. Dynamite.   Photop 41-1:40 Ja '52

Biographical note.   Newsweek 43:93 My 3 '54

Stronger sex makes strong box office.   Life 36:93 My 31 '54

Biography.   Cur Bio 15:47 Je '54

Same. Cur Bio Yrbk 1954:338 '54
Martin, P. Hollywood's most improbable star. Sat Eve
    Post 227:33 Ag 28; 30 S 4 '54
Senseney, D. The guy with the grin. Photop 46-3:47
    S '54
Phillips, D. Average score: terrific. Photop 47-4:37
    Ap '55
Bocca, G. William Holden, Hollywood's golden boy.
    Cosmop 139:28 S '55
Conquest of Smiling Jim. Time 67:62 F 27 '56
Moller, E. My boss, Bill. Photop 49-4:56 Ap '56
Hubler, R. G. Bill Holden: I.Q. at box office.
    Coronet 40:108 Jl '56
Busy star at work. Newsweek 50:104 O 28 '57
Plimmer, C. & Plimmer, D. Extraordinary ordinary guy.
    N. Y. Times Mag p57 Ja 19 '58
Kinney, H. McCalls visits. McCalls 85:8 Ag '58
Ross, L. Player. New Yorker 37:111 O 21 '61
Miller, E. Modern movie star. Seventeen 21:106 F '62
Talk with a star. Newsweek 59:96 Ap 23 '62
Still the golden boy. McCalls 89:48 Jl '62
Waterbury, R. The truth about his helath. Photop 62-4:
    60 O '62
Coughlan, R. Two birds bet a million on a club in the
    bush. Sports Illus 18:84 My 20 '63
Corbin, J. The wrong kind of love. Photop 65-5:54 My
    '64
Film rites in Kenya. Time 92:96 S 13 '68
Whitney, D. To Africa, with love. TV Guide 17-12:23
    Mr 22 '69

HOLLIDAY, JUDY
Born yesterday. Life 20:81 F 25 '46
Rainy afternoon. New Yorker 22:18 Mr 2 '46
Nichols, L. Gallery of leading ladies. N. Y. Times Mag
    p21 Mr 3 '46
Davis, L. It's a living. Colliers 117:15 Je 15 '46
Dumb blonde in Hollywood. Life 28:77 F 13 '50
Biographical note. Newsweek 37:57 Ja 1 '51
Herrmann, H. M. Hey-hey-day of a dumb blonde. N. Y.
    Times Mag p16 Mr 4 '51
Sargeant, W. Judy Holliday. Life 30:107 Ap 2 '51
Oscars for Jose and Judy. Life 30:38 Ap 9 '51
Biography. Cur Bio 12:29 Ap '51
    Same. Cur Bio Yrbk 1951:279 '52
Swanson, P. Happy Holliday. Photop 39-5:58 My '51
Hine, A. Three smart blondes. Holiday 10:6 S '51

Harvey, E. Judy Holliday takes her own glamor picture.
  Colliers 129:42 Ja 26 '52
Off on a Holliday. Newsweek 40:38 C 6 '52
Happy Holliday. TV Guide 3-9:17 F 26 '55
Judy Holliday tells her story of Greenwich village.
  Coronet 37:83 Mr '55
Bird, V. Holliday's blond surprise. Sat Eve Post 228:
  26 D 31 '55
Hobson, L. Z. Trade winds. Sat R 39:6 Ag 4 '56
Judy Holliday in Bells are ringing. Vogue 128:110 D '56
Judy at the switchboard. Life 42:69 F 11 '57
Langner, L. Whole weeks of Hollidays. Theatre Arts
  41:27 Mr '57
Judy Holliday takes a singing lesson. McCalls 85:26 O
  '57
Eleven fine actors get their dream roles. Life 44:76 Ap
  14 '58
Whitcomb, J. Judy and the Bells. Cosmop 148:29 F '60
Talk with a star. Newsweek 55:92 Je 27 '60
Prideaux, T. They're still ringing the bells. Life 49:
  45 Jl 25 '60
People are talking about. Vogue 136:152 O 1 '60
Gelman, M. Judy Holliday. Theatre 2-10:26 O '60
Obit. Time 85:50 Je 18 '65
  Cur Bio 26:15 Jl '65
  Cur Bio Yrbk 1965:203 '65
  Screen World 17:237 '66
Bright girl. Newsweek 65:87 Je 21 '65
Ace, G. Curtain slowly descends. Sat R 48:12 Jl 17 '65

HOLLIMAN, EARL
  Nichols, M. Broken-nosed buckaroo. Coronet 47:12
    Ja '60
  Even his friends told him. TV Guide 8-27:24 Jl 2 '60
  Inside hysteria. TV Guide 11-7:10 F 16 '63
  Swisher, V. H. Earl Holliman rediscovered: serious
    actor or wild west star. After Dark 11-1:16 My '69

HOLLISTER, ALICE
  Gaddis, P. Taking tea with Alice Hollister. Photop 7-
    3:87 F '15

HOLLOWAY, STERLING
  Hey rookie! in North Africa. Theatre Arts 28:247 Ap '44

HOLM, CELESTE
  Biography. Cur Bio Ap '44

Armstrong, G. Gorgeous Okie. Colliers 113:16 Je 10
  '44
Mann, A. They got a song. Colliers 114:12 D 9 '44
Have you met Celeste Holm? Good H 129:10 S '49
Merson, B. Holm was never like this. Colliers 127:28
  Ap 28 '51
Laughing stars. Theatre Arts 35:29 Ap '51
Massage for Celeste. Life 31:29 Jl 2 '51
Who's who in the cast. TV Guide 5-33:32 Ag 15 '52
King and Celeste. Theatre Arts 36:15 Ag '52
Clothes co-star in comedy. Look 18:116 F 23 '54
Stage reclaims its own. Theatre Arts 38:28 Mr '54
Can Celeste be real? Newsweek 44:62 O 25 '54
Wood, C. TV personalities biographical sketchbook.
  TV Personalities p42 '54
A visit with Celeste Holm. Theatre 2-12:24 D '60
UN international school. Parents Mag 39:66 F '64
Friends. New Yorker 42:24 F 4 '67
To Oklahoma! Look 32:50 Ap 2 '68

HOLMES, HELEN
  The girl on the cover; intv. Photop 7-4:53 Mr '15
  Thomas, J. A biography. Feature Movie 2-8:24 Jl 25
    '15
  Burden, A. The girl who keeps a railroad; intv.
    Photop 8-2:89 Jl '15
  Craig, G. When Helen rented a baby. Photop 11-4:82
    Mr '17
  Obit. Sch & Soc 48:719 D 3 '38

HOLMES, PHILLIPS
  Foster, D. The battle of Phil Holmes vs. the world.
    Photop 39-1:76 D '30
  Obit. Cur Bio '42

HOLMES, TAYLOR
  Business of beauty. Sat Eve Post 204:14 Ag 22 '31
  Obit. Newsweek 54:90 O 12 '59
    Brit Bk Yr 1960:509 '60
    Screen World 11:220 '60

HOLT, GEORGE
  Richards, W. Unmasking a villain. Photop 6-4:59 S '14

HOLT, JACK
  Jordan, J. Wanted: a chance to ride. Photop 20-3:34
    Ag '21

Evans, D.   The man uncomfortable.   Photop 22-6:30 N
    '22
Taggart, H.   Jack Holt, regular he-man.   Photop 26-2:
    58 Jl '24
Howe, H.   His last fifty cents.   Photop 30-2:91 Jl '26
Hamilton, S.   He's no romeo, but . . .   Photop 42-4:76
    S '32
Vandour, C.   Holt and sons.   Photop 21-6:47 N '42
Obit.   Newsweek 37:64 Ja 29 '51
    Time 57:86 Ja 29 '51
    Pub W 159:800 F 3 '51

HOLT, TIM
    Vandour, C.   Holt and sons.   Photop 21-6:47 N '42

HOMOLKA, OSCAR
    Homolka.   New Yorker 20:24 D 2 '44
    Nolan, J. E.   Five TV heavies.   Film Fan Mo 92:15 F
        '69

HOPE, BOB
    Steele, J. H.   Portrait of the man with the chin.   Photop
        54-4:19 Ap '40
    Hamilton, S.   Thanks for the memories.   Photop 54-10:
        22 O; 54-11:70 N '40
    Biographical sketch.   Time 38:64 Jl 7 '41
    Johnston, A.   Bob Hope; star U. S. comic has made his
        public laugh ever since a tree fell on him.   Life 11:
        102 O 27 '41
    Proctor, K.   Play truth or consequences with Bob Hope.
        Photop 20-1:46 D '41
    Biography.   Cur Bio '41
    Radio year full of Hope; gagster dethrones Jack Benny as
        No. 1 dial entertainer.   Newsweek 19:48 Ja 5 '42
    Griswold, J. B.   That dope Hope.   Am Mag 133:40 Ja
        '42
    What's in a name?   Am Mag 134:56 N '42
    Hope, B.   Alaska here I come.   Photop 22-2:18 Ja '43
    Ad-libbing comedian co-stars with Dorothy Lamour in
        Goldwyn's They got me covered.   Life 14:43 F 15 '43
    Hope for humanity.   Time 42:43 S 20 '43
    Hope, B.   My favorite sarong.   Photop 23-5:46 O '43
    Where there's Hope there's life.   Read Digest 43:56 N '43
    Bob Hope's challenge.   Theatre Arts 27:634 N '43
    Kids mob Bob Hope; opening of Y. M. C. A. camp for war
        workers' sons.   Life 15:36 D 20 '43
    Sullivan, E.   Bob Hope, hero without uniform.   Photop

24-1:28 D '43

Sure-fire gags for the foxhole.   N. Y. Times Mag p16 My
    28 '44

Hope, D.   My life with a gagster.   Womans H C 71:10
    My '44

I never left home; excerpts.   Life 17:41 Ag 7 '44

Thank God the G. I. can laugh.   Read Digest 45:41 Ag '44

Cerf, B.   Trade winds; I never left home;   Sat R 27:16
    S 9 '44

Bob Hope's seven faces.   N. Y. Times Mag p24 S 10 '44

Miller, M.   G. I. gag man.   Sr Schol 45:13 S 11 '44

Kilgallen, D.   Nicest guy in the world.   Photop 26-1:40
    D '44

I never left home campaign.   Pub W 147:1114 Mr 10 '45

Hope springs financial.   Newsweek 27:61 My 6 '46

Brown, J. M.   While there's Hope.   Sat R 29:22 O 5 '46

So this is peace; excerpts.   Life 21:119 O 21 '46

Hope, inc.   Time 48:94 N 18 '46

Deere, D.   If you were Bob Hope's house guest.   Photop
    31-1:66 Je '47

Howe, H.   Where there's Hope.   Photop 32-2:50 Ja '48

Speaking of pictures.   Life 24:24 Ap 19 '48

Hope, B.   I and Crosby.   Photop 32-6:58 My '48

Shane, T.   Road to the 19th hole.   Colliers 122:20 Ag
    14 '48

Tomorrow is a new day.   Am Mag 147:21 Mr '49

Hope, D.   He's a good man to have around.   Photop
    34-4:38 Mr '49

Hope, B.   Meet my family.   Parents Mag 24:32 D '49

Hope, Mrs. A.   My nephew Bob Hope.   Photop 37-1:38
    Ja '50

$1,500-a-minute program; Bob Hope makes long-awaited
    debut.   Life 28:83 Ap 24 '50

Unaccustomed view.   Newsweek 35:52 Je 5 '50

New Hope.   Newsweek 35:55 Je 19 '50

Great comedian says: people are great.   Coronet 28:25
    Je '50

Lords of laughter.   Coronet 30:83 O '51

Hope for housewives.   Newsweek 40:60 D 15 '52

Rosten, L.   Gags and riches.   Look 17:102 F 24 '53

Harris, E.   Bob Hope for the housewife.   McCalls 80:
    38 Ap '53

Quick change artist.   TV Guide 1-9:18 My 29 '53

Biography.   Cur Bio 14:31 O '53
    Same.   Cur Bio Yrbk 1953:274 '53

Hope, D. ed. by J. K. Ardmore.   My life is full of Hope.
    Womans H C 80:42 N '53

Bob (round the world) Hope.   TV Guide 1-38:8 D 18 '53
Busy Mr. Hope.   Sat Eve Post 226:120 F 13 '54
Behind the scenes.   Sat Eve Post 226:156 Mr 27 '54
Hope, B. ed. by P. Martin.   This is on me.   Sat Eve
    Post 226:17 F 13; 22 F 20; 20 F 27; 22 Mr 6; 24 Mr
    13; 20 Mr 20; 38 Mr 27; 30 Ap 3; 30 Ap 10 '54
Abroad with Bob Hope.   Newsweek 44:92 N 22 '54
Old hands across the sea.   Life 37:121 D 6 '54
Thanks for the many thanks.   Good H 140:16 My '55
Knight, A.   Whence this pleasing Hope?   Sat R 38:23 Jl
    9 '55
My rules for golf.   Coronet 38:67 Jl '55
Hope, B.   My favorite mother-in-law; as told to E. Har-
    ris.   McCalls 83:29 O '55
Tumble for tumbling Hope.   Life 40:36 Ja 9 '56
Ex-partners.   Time 68:108 O 15 '56
Have talent, will travel.   TV Guide 5-4:8 Ja 26 '57
High, S.   His miracle is youngsters.   Read Digest 70:
    178 Mr '57
Comic and commissars.   Newsweek 51:62 Mr 31 '58
Robert returns to 'Roberta.'   TV Guide 6-31:8 Ag 2 '58
Martin, P.   I call on Bob Hope.   Sat Eve Post 230:32
    Ap 26 '58
Hope, B.   I found the Russians can laugh too.   Look 22:
    22 Je 10 '58
Hope revives his Roberta role.   Theatre Arts 42:20 S '58
The future still Hopeful.   TV Guide 7-21:17 My 23 '59
Hoffman, J.   There are still so many more things I'd
    like to see.   Photop 55-6:58 Je '59
Wolters, L.   Why Bob Hope put on the brakes.   Todays
    Health 37:24 Jl '59
Hope, B.   Women in my life; as told to E. Harris.
    McCalls 87:76 O '59
Reddy, J.   My exclusive interview with Bob Hope.   Read
    Digest 75:55 D '59
Long live Hope.   Newsweek 55:66 Mr 7 '60
Open season on politicians.   TV Guide 8-43:14 O 22 '60
Sexy eyes over Hope's shoulder.   Life 50:107 Mr 17 '61
Backbreaker.   Newsweek 58:80 Jl 17 '61
Hilarious heyday of eternal Hope.   Life 52:92 My 11 '62
Crosby, B.   Bing tells on Bob.   Mus J 20:26 S '62
Durslag, M.   40 years and $10,000,000 later . . .
    TV Guide 10-46:4 N 17 '62
NAB votes top award to Bob Hope.   Broadcasting 64:32
    Ja 21 '63
Olsen, J.   Hope: all kinds of a nut about sports.
    Sports Illus 18:65 Je 3 '63

Reddy, J.   Around the world with Bob Hope.   Read
    Digest 82:140 Je '63
Fish don't applaud.   Time 82:67 O 25 '63
Linn, E.   Bob Hope in the road to golf.   Sat Eve Post
    236:28 N 9 '63
Hope, B.   Mr. Hope at the nab.   Sponsor 17:44 Ap 8
    '64
Dick--please be good, so I can bow.   TV Guide 12-15:
    26 Ap 11 '64
Bob Hope wins tenth annual Travel award.   Travel 121:
    36 Je '64
Holiday Hope.   Time 85:51 Ja 8 '65
Bob Hope on Vietnam; intv.   Nations Bus 54:44 F '66
Armbrister, T.   G. I.'s best friend.   Sat Eve Post 239:
    93 Mr 12 '66
Gordon, M.   They remember Bob when his name was
    Les.   TV Guide 14-16:10 Ap 16 '66
Things aren't that simple.   Seventeen 25:130 D '66
Well, that's what it says in my crystal ball.   Ladies
    Home J 84:14 Ja '67
Waterbury, R.   Private life of a public man.   Photop 71-
    6:68 Je '67
Comedian as hero.   Time 90:58 D 22 '67
Christmas in Vietnam: Bob Hope style.   U. S. News 64:
    8 Ja 1 '68
Raddatz, L.   Hope's greatest "road show."   TV Guide
    16-2:21 Ja 13 '68
Rollin, B.   Bob Hope hits the road he never left.   Look
    32:44 Ja 23 '68
Wright, A.   Golf is a game of Hope.   Sports Illus 28:44
    F 12 '68
Bob, everybody's Hope.   Read Digest 91:124 Mr '68
Robinson, D.   Eight famous Americans tell of The day I
    was proudest of my wife; intvs.   Good H 167:75 Ag
    '68
Champlin, C.   Have you heard this one, Mr. President?
    McCalls 96:113 N '68
Where there's golf, there's Hope.   Holiday 44:50 N '68
Album of Christmas jokes.   Ladies Home J 85:86 D '68
Bacon, J.   Bob Hope and his $150,000,000 bankroll.
    TV Guide 17-2:20 Ja 11 '69

HOPE, GLORIA
Henderson, F.   A ripe olive.   Photop 16-6:38 N '19

HOPKINS, MIRIAM
Hughes, A.   "Li'l Gawgia" gets glamour!   Photop 41-4:

66 Mr '32
Make mine a speakeasy. Colliers 90:31 Ag 27 '32
They stand out from the crowd. Lit Digest 119:38 Je 22
'35
Cummings, M. A day with Miriam Hopkins. Photop 49-
4:56 Ap '36
Sharpe, H. Is it love at last for Miriam Hopkins?
Photop 51-5:24 My '37
Miriam acts up. Newsweek 26:52 D 31 '45
Malton, L. The films of Miriam Hopkins, inc. filmog.
Film Fan Mo 71:3 My '67

HOPPER, DENNIS
Southern, T. Loved house of the Dennis Hoppers.
Vogue 146:138 Ag 1 '65

HORNE, GEOFFREY
Person of promise. Films & Filming 4-5:16 F '58

HORNE, LENA
Chocolate cream chanteuse. Time 41:62 Ja 4 '43
Song seller. Newsweek 21:65 Ja 4 '43
Young Negro with haunting voice charms New York with
old songs. Life 14:20 Ja 4 '43
Crichton, K. Horne solo. Colliers 111:12 Je 26 '43
Biography. Cur Bio Je '44
Paul, E. Naturally Lena Horne. Photop 25-4:38 S '44
Lena in Paris. Time 50:67 D 8 '47
Lena Horne. Life 25:101 O 18 '48
Watt, D. Tables for two. New Yorker 32:95 F 2 '57
Lena lights up Jamaica. Life 43:112 N 18 '57
Feinstein, H. Lena Horne speaks freely. Ebony 18:61
My '63
Horne, L. I just want to be myself. Show 3-9:62 Ag
'63
Horne, L. My life with Lennie; excerpt from Lena.
Ebony 21:176 N '65
Successful autographing tours by three personalities.
Pub W 188:53 D 13 '65
Noble, J. L. Three-horned dilemma facing Negro women.
Ebony 21:118 Ag '66
Backstage. Ebony 23:26 Jl '68
Pierce, P. Lena at 51. Ebony 23:125 Jl '68

HORTON, CLARA MARIE
Brandon, F. M. Little Clara Marie Horton. Photop
6-5:35 O '13

Condon, M.   The littlest leading lady.   Photop 6-6:89
  S '14
Handy, T. B.   Sweet sixteen--plus!   Photop 16-4:67 S '19

HORTON, EDWARD EVERETT
  Crichton, K.   Comedy, six days a week.   Colliers 98:22
    Jl 18 '36
  Tour.   Time 36:62 Jl 22 '40
  Biography.   Cur Bio 7:25 D '46
    Same revised.   Cur Bio Yrbk 1946:270 '47
  Edward and Henry; the summer theater.   Time 50:54 Jl
    7 '47
  Veteran.   New Yorker 24:13 Ag 7 '48
  Roaring Chicken is one active bird.   TV Guide 13-42:12
    O 16 '65

HORTON, ROBERT
  Ford, E.   Elopement.   Photop 44-5:80 N '53
  Westward ho, Robert Horton.   TV Guide 6-33:8 Ag 16 '58
  Horton, R.   Everybody at home was picking on me.
    Photop 55-2:68 F '59
  Swisher, V.   Three little words.   Photop 59-4:64 Ap '61
  All his fights weren't with the Indians.   TV Guide 9-25:
    17 Je 24 '61
  Johnson, R.   Big ego, big talent.   Sat Eve Post 234:98
    D 23 '61
  Whitney, D.   Ride 'em, Sigmund Freud.   TV Guide 14-10:
    14 Mr 5 '66

HOTELEY, MAE
  Gaddis, P.   Mae Hoteley: philosopher and optimist.
    Photop 6-3:120 Ag '14

HOWARD, CURLY
  (See: THREE STOOGES)

HOWARD, JOHN
  To John Howard.   House & Gard 77:15 Mr '40
  Wood, C.   TV personalities biographical sketchbook.
    TV Personalities p72 '57

HOWARD, LESLIE
  Where the actor ends.   Sat Eve Post 202:39 Je 28 '30
  Woodward, M.   A nervous wreck.   Photop 40-5:66 O '31
  Personalities prominent in the press.   Cinema Digest 1-
    3:7 Je 13 '32
  Albert, A.   Not a sock in a hundred reels.   Photop 42-

3:35 Ag '32

Maxwell, V. Leslie Howard's lucky coin. Photop 45-4:
69 Mr '34

Shawell, J. Leslie Howard pays a debt. Pict R 35:7
Je '34

Bosworth, C. A good pal is worth three dollars.
Photop 46-2:34 Jl '34

Isaacs, E. J. R. Broadway in review. Theatre Arts 19:
169 Mr '35

Crichton, K. Very quiet actor. Colliers 95:24 My 4 '35

Romeo at home. Liv Age 350:512 Ag '36

Krutch, J. W. Leslie Howard's Hamlet. Nation 143:612
N 21 '36

Isaacs, E. J. R. Large men, large steeds; Leslie
Howard's production of Hamlet. Theatre Arts 21:7
Ja '37

My movie lot is not a happy one. Read Digest 31:41 S
'37

Men of free France. Liv Age 359:164 O '40

Hobson, H. Leslie Howard, Anglo-American interpreter.
C S Mon Mag p7 O 18 '41

Leslie Howard. Newsweek 21:92 Je 14 '43

Obit. Cur Bio '43

Dickins, H. Leslie Howard, inc. filmog. Films In Review 10-4:198 Ap '59

Biography. DNB 1941-1950:414 '59

HOWARD, MOE
(See: THREE STOOGES)

HOWARD, SHEMP
Obit. Screen World 7:225 '56

HOWARD, TREVOR
Personality of the month. Plays & Players 1-3:3 D '53
Every woman's man. Plays & Players 1-10:4 Jl '54
Elephants' friend on his hearth. Life 45:109 O 27 '58
Sandenbergh, B. Trevor Howard. Films In Review 15-
3:190 Mr '64
Biography. Cur Bio 25:30 Jl '64
Same. Cur Bio Yrbk 1964:203 '64

HOWES, SALLY ANN
Stang, J. My (new) fair lady. N. Y. Times Mag p18 Ja
5 '58
Fiery fair lady takes over. Life 44:51 Mr 3 '58

HUDSON, ROCHELLE
   Taviner, R. On the set with Will Rogers. Photop 48-3:
      36 Ag '35
   Wood, C. TV personalities biographical sketchbook.
      TV Personalities p130 '54

HUDSON, ROCK
   Hubler, R. G. How to create a movie star. Sat Eve
      Post 225:26 S 27 '52
   Preble, B. Bachelor's bedlam. Photop 42-3:52 S '52
   Hudson, R. I was the shyest guy in town. Photop 43-1:
      38 Ja '53
   Arnold, M. Hudson never looked better. Photop 43-3:
      50 Mr '53
   Hudson, R. Has anybody seen my gal? Photop 43-6:
      48 Je '53
   Walsh, R. Not bad for a country kid. Photop 44-3:40
      S '53
   Arnold, M. Rock's mystery girl. Photop 44-5:38 N '53
   Noel, T. Rock's a good man to have around. Photop
      45-4:48 Ap '54
   Hudson, R. Don't call that boy a square. Photop 46-
      1:46 Jl '54
   Two careers take a turn. Life 37:51 S 6 '54
   Edwards, R. Rock's magnificent obsession. Photop 46-
      3:38 S '54
   Fitzsimons, C. Sure, Ireland must be heaven. Photop
      46-5:8 N '54
   Hudson, R. The giving is easy. Photop 46-6:60 D '54
   Manning, R. Rock Hudson's love affair with the U.S.A.
      Photop 47-1:40 Ja '55
   Olsen, Mrs. K. My son, your years become you.
      Photop 47-3:42 Mr '55
   Townsend, P. Bachelor daze. Photop 47-5:53 My '55
   Allen, D. Hudson's hideaway. Photop 48-1:44 Jl '55
   Limke, H. Never a dull moment. Photop 48-3:45 S '55
   Simple life of a busy bachelor. Life 39:129 O 3 '55
   Ott, B. The Hudson got hep. Photop 49-1:28 Ja '56
   Balling, F. D. Planning a heavenly love nest. Photop
      50-3:44 S '56
   Ott, B. The man who almost got away. Photop 50-6:
      36 D '56
   Hyams, J. Why women are in love with Rock Hudson.
      McCalls 84:52 F '57
   Hyams, J. The Rock Hudson story. Photop 51-2:43 F;
      51-3:48 Mr '57
   Downing, H. Give a man room to grow. Photop 51-5:

70 My '57

Nichols, M.   Rock known as Hudson.   Coronet 42:14 Je
'57

Ott, B.   A long way from home.   Photop 52-2:46 Ag '57

Can Rock's marriage be saved?   Photop 53-2:55 F '58

Harris, E.   Rock Hudson: why he is no. 1.   Look 22:
47 Mr 18 '58

Shayon, R. L.   Easy as ABC.   Sat R 41:23 My 10 '58

Allen, D.   Search for happiness.   Photop 53-5:38 My '58

Lyle, J.   Is there a second chance for Rock's heart?
Photop 54-4:32 O '58

Rock Hudson's personal letter to you.   Photop 54-6:21
D '58

Lardner, J.   Air; big party.   New Yorker 35:22 N 21 '59

I'm Rock's best gal but he treats me like a dog.   Photop
57-2:48 F '60

Martin, P.   I call on Rock Hudson.   Sat Eve Post 233:
16 Jl 23 '60

Warning: it can mean only one thing.   Photop 58-5:48
N '60

Divas, G.   I was scheduled to die.   Photop 59-1:52 Ja
'61

Biography.   Cur Bio 22:25 O '61
Same.   Cur Bio Yrbk 1961:211 '62

Rowland, T.   Me big star--Rock Hudson.   Photop 60-6:
50 D '61

Waterbury, R.   Why they keep it a secret.   Photop 61-1:
60 Ja '62

Kiss that breaks up Rock.   Life 52:65 F 16 '62

Lyle, J.   I love you darling.   Photop 63-2:57 F '62

Corbin, J.   Your guide to the modern wolf.   Photop 63-
2:32 F '62

Baskette, K.   Is he the next Cary Grant?   Good H 156:
81 Ap '63

Somers, A.   I slept in Rock Hudson's bed.   Photop 65-1:
30 Ja '64

Dawes, A.   King of the movie mattress.   Photop 67-1:35
Ja '65

Webb, M.   He talks about himself.   Photop 75-5:43 My '69

HUFF, LOUISE
Shirk, A. H.   Do you believe in fairies?   Photop 14-2:
63 Jl '18
Shannon, B.   Dante was wrong.   Photop 18-3:30 Ag '20

HUGHES, GARETH
Oursler, F.   Star in the desert.   Read Digest 60:99 Mr '52

Obit.   Screen World 17:237 '66

HUGHES, LLOYD
  Mahlon, M.   Just an American youth.   Photop 29-5:38
    Ap '26
  Obit.   Screen World 10:222 '59

HULETTE, GLADYS
  Beatty, J.   Don't call it 'beauty and the beast.'   Photop
    10-6:75 N '61
  Bartlett, R.   The personality test.   Photop 14-5:59 O '18
  Hulette, G.   More tears, please!   Photop 35-4:60 Mr '29

HULL, HENRY
  Crichton, K.   Ace in the role.   Colliers 93:26 My 19 '34

HULL, JOSEPHINE
  Gresham, W. L.   Comedienne from Radcliffe; intv.
    Theatre Arts 29:346 Je '45
  Biography.   Cur Bio 14:35 O '53
    Same.   Cur Bio Yrbk 1953:283 '53
  Josephine the great.   Life 35:65 N 23 '53
  Josephine Bedlam Hull.   New Yorker 29:40 N 28 '53
  Obit.   Newsweek 49:76 Mr 25 '57
    Time 69:104 Mr 25 '57
    Am Ann 1958:351 '58
    Cur Bio 18:28 My '57
    Cur Bio Yrbk 1957:271 '58
    Screen World 9:223 '58

HUME, BENITA
  Wood, C.   TV personalities biographical sketchbook.
    TV Personalities p48 '54
  Obit.   Newsweek 70:67 N 13 '67
    Screen World 19:233 '68

HUNT, JIMMY
  Harbert, R.   Assignment in Hollywood.   Good H 137:16
    D '53

HUNT, MARSHA
  Crichton, K.   Booted off the lot.   Colliers 108:14 O 4 '41
  Dudley, F.   The okay kid.   Photop 22-2:50 Ja '43
  They come from Chicago.   Theatre Arts 35:44 Jl '51
  Briggs, C.   Marsha Hunt, inc. filmog.   Films In Re-
    view 14-8:511 O '63
  Natural.   Vogue 153:134 Ja 1 '69

HUNT, MARTITA
  Personality of the month.   Plays & Players 1-4:3 D '53
  Obit.   Time 93:72 Je 20 '69

HUNTER, GLENN
  Mullett, M. B.   Gleen Hunter made his debut in an apple
    orchard; intv.   Am Mag 101:34 My '26
  Obit.   Cur Bio 7:31 Mr '46
    Cur Bio Yrbk 1946:275 '47

HUNTER, IAN
  Chute, M.   Ian Hunter--and the high seas.   Photop 52-2:
    32 F '38

HUNTER, JEFF
  Rogers, M.   The dangerous years.   Photop 42-6:44 D '52
  Dudley, F.   Darling, wish you were here.   Photop 43-5:
    50 My '53
  Leon, R.   Hunter's paradise.   Photop 44-5:60 N '53
  Hunter, J.   So nice to come home to.   Photop 45-3:46 Mr
    '54
  Johnson, H.   Barbara's shining hour.   Photop 46-3:51 S
    '54
  Arnold, M.   He got out from behind the 8 ball.   Photop
    50-1:64 Jl '56
  Hunter, J.   Actor's choice.   Films & Filming 8-7:17 Ap
    '62
  Ten push-ups and I simmer down.   TV Guide 12-2:26 Ja
    11 '64
  His sudden death.   Photop 76-2:22 Ag '69

HUNTER, KIM
  Marine takes a wife.   Life 16:89 Mr 13 '44
  England's Miss America.   Am Mag 143:135 Ap '47
  Katcher, D. L.   Talented Hunter.   Colliers 129:44 Mr 8
    '52
  Biography.   Cur Bio 13:23 My '52
    Same.   Cur Bio Yrbk 1952:281 '53
  Kim for success.   Vogue 125:108 Ap 1 '55

HUNTER, ROSS
  Alpert, H.   Happy producers make happy movies.   Sat R
    Ap 15 '67
  Biography.   Cur Bio 28:16 D '67
    Same.   Cur Bio Yrbk 1967:191 '68
  Gittelson, N.   Give a good movie: Airport.   Harper Baz
    102:32 D '68

HUNTER, TAB

Asher, J. He couldn't fail. Photop 43-1:66 Ja '53
Linet, B. Bachelor on his own. Photop 44-2:46 Ag '53
Hunter, T. Why Debbie's my ideal. Photop 45-2:40 F '54
Hunter, T. Let him go. Photop 45-5:42 My '54
Clayton, D. Tab--and they call him dreamboat. Photop 46-2:48 Ag '54
Hunter, T. Build your date line. Photop 46-4:56 O '54
Hunter, T. Don't rush me. Photop 46-6:52 D '54
Hunter, T. My Hawaiian diary. Photop 47-3:53 Mr '55
Hunter, T. I'm in love with a wonderful mom. Photop 47-5:45 My '55
Hopper, H. Young men of Hollywood. Coronet 38:52 Jl '55
Lint, J. E. That's sex, girls. Photop 48-2:56 Ag '55
Block, M. Don't be too big to believe. Photop 49-2:60 F '56
Downing, H. Tab Hunter: caught in that tender trap? Photop 50-1:48 Jl '56
Maynard, J. Why Tab Hunter has become Hollywood's biggest headache. Photop 51-1:36 Ja '57
Hunter, T. Blackout. Photop 54-1:37 Jl '58
Koch, L. I'll wear Tab Hunter's bracelet forever. Photop 55-4:70 Ap '59
Blond bachelor of Malibu Beach. TV Guide 8-44:18 O 29 '60
Alexander, S. Could this man beat his dog. Life 49:51 N 21 '60
Nichols, M. Hunter's gamble is paying off. Coronet 49:14 D '60
Ardmore, J. Too late. Photop 59-3:24 Mr '61
Hunter, F. Let's put an end to the tale. Photop 59-4:46 Ap '61
Asher, J. You be the judge. Photop 61-3:44 Mr '62

HURLOCK, MADELINE

St. Johns, I. Who says vampires are through? Photop 27-2:64 Ja '25

HURST, PAUL

Ware, H. Paul Hurst, inc. filmog. Films In Review 18-10:659 D '67

HUSSEY, OLIVIA

People are talking about . . . Vogue 150:88 Ag 1 '67
Simons, M. New Romeo and Juliet. Look 31:52 O 17

'67

Miller, E.   Love is the sweetest thing.   Seventeen 27:83
   Ja '68

HUSSEY, RUTH

Crichton, K.   Sleeping beauty.   Colliers 106:12 D 21 '40
Walker, H. L.   Act of providence.   Photop 18-3:29 F '41
Hot potato.   Am Mag 132:82 Jl '41
Hussey, R.   Why I read movie magazines.   Photop 20-
   6:44 My '42
Albert, D.   Destination--happiness!   Photop 21-6:68 N '42
Nichols, L.   Gallery of leading ladies.   N. Y. Times Mag
   p21 Mr 3 '46

HUSTON, WALTER

Huston's poetic Lincoln.   Lit Digest 106:15 S 20 '30
Parsons, H.   The peerless Huston!   Photop 39-1:68 D '30
Kennedy, J. B.   Shrinking star.   Colliers 87:19 My 2 '31
Hamilton, S.   He won't argue.   Photop 41-4:68 Mr '32
Shackleton, W. D   Walter Huston shuns pictures.   Photop
   46-3:72 Ag '34
Walter Huston's Othello.   Newsweek 9:31 Ja 16 '37
Biography.   Cur Bio 10:32 F '49
   Same.   Cur Bio Yrbk 1949:289 '50
Obit.   Newsweek 35:68 Ap 17 '50
   Time 55:96 Ap 17 '50
   Illus Lond N 216:616 Ap 22 '50
   Cur Bio 11:25 My '50
   Cur Bio Yrbk 1950:269 '51

HUTTON, BETTY

Jittery.   Am Mag 131:94 Mr '41
Crichton, K.   Blond blitz.   Colliers 110:14 O 31 '42
Jitterbug girl sings and acts in Happy go lucky.   Life 14:
   64 Mr 22 '43
Lowrance, D.   Star-spangled blonde.   Photop 22-5:42 Ap
   '43
Frenchey, J. R.   Sunday punch girl.   Photop 24-1:47 D
   '43
That man.   Am Mag 136:50 D '43
Othman, F. C   Huttontot.   Sat Eve Post 216:27 Je 10 '44
Harris, E.   If you were Betty Hutton's house guest.
   Photop 26-5:48 Ap '45
St. Johns, A. R.   Life of a dynamo.   Photop 28-2:30 Ja
   '46
Howe, H.   Champagne and pretzels.   Photop 29-1:42 Je
   '46

Scott, D. Betty Hutton and Buttercup. Photop 30-4:60 Mr
    '47
Tomboys of the screen. Newsweek 30:92 Jl 7 '47
Hutton, B. I'm a new woman. Photop 31-6:48 N '47
Edwards, R. Play truth or consequences with Betty
    Hutton. Photop 33-1:60 Je '48
Hutton, B. I'd rather be a mother. Photop 34-3:60 F
    '49
Hutton, B. I call him the Katzenjammer Kid. Photop
    36-6:42 N '49
This side of happiness. Time 55:66 Ap 24 '50
Biography. Cur Bio 11:30 Je '50
    Same. Cur Bio Yrbk 1950:269 '51
Parsons, L. O. I can't believe it. Photop 38-4:34 O '50
Zeitlin, I. All in her lifetime. Photop 39-3:46 Mr '51
Wheeler, L. Pint-sized paradise. Photop 40-4:60 O '51
Zeitlin, I. She dared him to marry her. Photop 42-1:38
    Jl '52
Betty Hutton's album. Coronet 34:85 Ag '53
Hutton hits Manhattan. Look 17:69 D 15 '53
Easy does it. Theatre Arts 37:15 D '53
Betty Hutton's biggest one-night stand. TV Guide 2-37:5
    S 11 '54
Why Betty Hutton flopped on TV. TV Guide 2-42:3 O 16
    '54
Hutton, B. This is my story. Photop 50-6:44 D '56
She rules the roost. TV Guide 7-47:8 N 21 '59

HUTTON, JIM
    Miller, E. Growing pains in Hollywood. Seventeen 21:
        126 Mr '62
    Meltsir, A. His kooky, private world. Photop 62-2:62
        Ag '62
    Lint, J. Hollywood killed our marriage. Photop 64-5:57
        N '63

HUTTON, ROBERT
    Harris, E. Hutton heart-to-heart. Photop 26-1:58 D '44
    Deere, D. He's Hutton. Photop 27-2:36 Jl '45
    Hutton, R. My romantic mistakes. Photop 30-2:54 Ja
        '47

HYER, MARTHA
    Ott, B. The girl who refused to get lost. Photop 50-4:
        66 O '56

HYLAND, PEGGY
    Bartlett, R.   Peggy and America discover each other.
        Photop 10-2:69 Jl '16

INCE, JOHN
  Briscoe, J.   Why film favorites forsook the footlights.
    Photop 6-2:95 Jl '14

INESCORT, FRIEDA
  Tyranny of they.   Harper 154:791 My '27
  Louis Bromfield of Mansfield.   Sat R 10:629 Ap 14 '34

IRELAND, JOHN
  Waterbury, R.   Joannie and Johnnie are sweethearts.
    Photop 38-5:42 N '50

IRWIN, MAY
  Business of the stage as career.   Cosmop 28:655 Ap '00
  Reamer, L.   Irwin in Belle of Bridgeport.   Harper 44:
    1094 N 17 '00
  Williams, W.   Past laughter.   Sat Eve Post 203:42 Ap
    25 '31
  Biography.   DAB sup2:335 '58
  Walsh, J.   Six comediennes.   Hobbies 68:35 Je; 32 Jl '63

IVAN, ROSILAND
  McClelland, D.   The unsung heroes: Rosiland Ivan.
    Film Fan Mo 80:17 F '68

IVES, BURL
  Army troubadour.   Time 40:62 Jl 27 '42
  Kantor, M.   Troubadour.   Colliers 113:21 Ap 15 '44
  Singin' for a livin'.   Newsweek 24:103 O 2 '44
  Ross, H.   Just a guy who sings.   Sat Eve Post 217:12
    Ap 14 '45
  Houseboat party.   Life 19:82 Jl 2 '45
  Blue-tail fly.   Time 46:71 S 24 '45
  Anthony, T.   Wayfaring minstrel.   Etude 63:688 D '45
  Biography.   Cur Bio 7:24 Ja '46
    Same.   Cur Bio Yrbk 1946:278 '47
  Antrim, D. K.   15,000 songs you wrote.   Bet Hom &
    Gard 25:56 O '46
  Long, J.   Aunt Kate's big boy.   Am Mag 143:36 Ap '47
  Reynolds, H.   America's top folksong singer.   C S Mon
    Mag p8 D 4 '48
  Berger, M.   Wandering minstrel, Ives.   Sat R 32:20 Ja
    8 '49

Kolodin, I. Ferrier, Ives, Danco and Arie. Sat R 32:
  56 Ag 27 '49
Morse, A. D. Notes from my song bag. Parents Mag
  25:40 O '50
American folk songs. Mus Am 71:20 F '51
Rediscovery of our own folk songs. House & Gard 101:
  79 F '52
Breit, H. Ambassador. N. Y. Times Bk R p8 N 23 '53
Breit, H. Ride 'em! N. Y. Times Bk R p8 N 14 '54
Holmes, C. 20th century troubadour. Holiday 19:14 F
  '56
Home for the wayfaring stranger. Theatre Arts 40:70 My
  '56
Ives, B. How I met my wife. McCalls 85:54 Ja '58
Man who sang the blue-tail fly. Newsweek 52:94 S 8 '58
Abramson, M. Big Daddy's own ballad. Coronet 47:158
  Mr '60
Biography. Cur Bio 21:19 My '60
  Same. Cur Bio Yrbk 1960:202 '61
Burl Ives, Manhattan troubadour. Look 25:48a Mr 14 '61
He likes to cook. Bet Hom & Gard 40:48 N '62
Dear wafarers. Seventeen 24:264 Ag '65
Sloane, G. Ives sings a song of the sea; intv. Motor B
  117:42 Mr '66
Joseph, R. Traveler, consider my Bahamas; intv.
  Esquire 67:120 Mr '67

JACKSON, ANNE

At home with Eli Wallach and Anne Jackson. Theatre
3-1:16 Ja '61
Talk with the stars. Newsweek 61:56 F 18 '63
What's with the Wallachs? at home or onstage its Luv.
Life 58:79 Ja 8 '65
Robinson, D. Eight famous Americans tell of the day I
was proudest of my wife; intv. Good H 167:77 Ag '68

JAECKEL, RICHARD

Deere, D. Everything's Jaeckel. Photop 25-2:36 Jl '44
Dudley, F. The tired admiral. Photop 25-6:62 N '44

JAFFE, SAM

Whitney, D. The courtship of Sam Jaffe. TV Guide 11-
1:18 Ja 5 '63

JAGGER, DEAN

Raddatz, L. The principal was a dropout. TV Guide
12-16:15 Ap 18 '64

JANIS, CONRAD

Time out for Conrad. Theatre Arts 37:17 Mr '53
Millstein, G. Jazz temple on Times Square; Child's
Paramount Restaurant. N.Y. Times Mag p25 N 29 '53

JANNINGS, EMIL

Howe, J. Four kings from Brooklyn. Photop 23:31 Ja
'23
Reniers, P. Shadow stage. Ind 114:327 Mr 21 '25
Johnson, J. A visit with Emil Jannings. Photop 29-3:
46 F '26
Jannings on America. Liv Age 332:81 Ja 1 '27
Jannings now an American film star. Lit Digest 94:22
Jl 23 '27
Reniers, P. Shadow stage. Ind 119:114 Jl 30 '27
Wilson, E. Jannings' first American film. New Repub
51:283 Ag 3 '27
Smith, H. H. Big boy of Hollywood. Outlook 150:806
S 19 '28
Why I left the films. Liv Age 338:554 Jl 1 '30
Jannings' first talkie. Liv Age 338:622 Jl 15 '30
Blue Angel, first sound film of Emil Jannings. Common-
weal 13:242 D 31 '30

Bahn, C. B.   Jannings--Laughton duel?   Cinema Digest
   3-5:9 Ap 7 '33
Obit.   Time 55:71 Ja 9 '50
   France Illus 6:4 Ja 14 '50
   Illus Lond N 216:59 Ja 14 '50
   Newsweek 35:54 Ja 16 '50

JANSSEN, DAVID
Wood, C.   TV personalities biographical sketchbook.
   TV Personalities p91 '57
The 25th man.   TV Guide 6-16:17 Ap 19 '58
These guns for hire.   Time 74:50 O 26 '59
Whitney, D.   He never did much running.   TV Guide 11-
   44:6 N 2 '63
Dawes, A.   Pin up #19.   Photop 66-2:56 Ag '64
Johnson, N.   A guy has to be a heel.   Photop 66-5:68 N
   '64
Hano, A.   David's drooping.   TV Guide 13-10:14 Mr 6
   '65
The fuge.   Newsweek 65:94 Ap 26 '65
Gordon, S.   TV's longest chase.   Look 29:M10 My 18 '65
Artist Ronald Searle captures the fugitive with his trusty
   3b.   TV Guide 14-4:11 Ja 22 '66
Biography.   Cur Bio 28:13 Mr '67
   Same.   Cur Bio Yrbk 1967:196 '68
Ardmore, J.   The truth about everything.   Photop 72-2:
   33 Ag '67
Green, J.   Torn between two women.   Photop 74-6:64 D
   '68
His nights with girlfriend.   Photop 75-3:46 Mr '69
Terry, P.   Love trap--girl who fell in.   Photop 76-2:70
   Ag '69

JARMAN, CLAUDE JR.
Claude Jarman went to Hollywood because of his long yel-
   low hair.   Life 22:68 F 17 '47
Waterbury, R.   Howdy Jody.   Photop 31-1:44 Je '47
Jarman, C. Sr.   My boy and I; ed. by T. Morris & J.
   Morris.   Parents Mag 24:38 N '49

JASON, RICK
The not-so-secret life of Rick Jason.   TV Guide 12-19:
   6 My 9 '64

JEAN, GLORIA
Jones, S. A.   Girl with a voice.   Colliers 104:22 O 14
   '39

Willson, D.   Baby skylark.   Photop 54-7:62 Jl '40
Lemmon, B.   Star enters her 'teens.   Etude 59:76 F '41
Where are they now?   Newsweek 51:18 Ja 27 '58

JEANMARIE, RENEE
Watt, D.   Musical events.   New Yorker 26:135 N 11 '50
Friedrichsen, F.   New Goldwyn girl.   Colliers 129:22
    My 3 '52
Biography.   Cur Bio 13:29 N '52
    Same.   Cur Bio Yrbk 1952:289 '53
Tune-up time for rising stars.   Life 36:68 Ja 25 '54
Hewes, H.   Girl who likes to try everything.   Sat R 37:
    30 F 20 '54
News on toes: an American hit from Paris.   Newsweek
    43:68 Mr 1 '54
French firecracker.   Look 18:81 Mr 9 '54
Girl in pink tights.   Newsweek 43:63 Mr 15 '54
Clurman, H.   Theatre.   Nation 178:246 Mr 20 '54
Ballerina sings.   N.Y. Times Mag p37 Mr 28 '54
Jeanmarie shouts for love.   Life 36:67 Mr 29 '54
People are talking about . . .   Vogue 123:95 Ap 15 '54
Making of a movie; Anything Goes.   Coronet 38:41 Ag '55
Dancer sings.   N.Y. Times Mag p51 Mr 10 '57
Return of Jeanmarie.   Newsweek 51:75 Mr 3 '58
Vaughan, D.   Shop talk with Roland Petit and Zizi.
    Dance Mag 32:42 My '58
Hering, D.   Les Ballets de Paris at Broadway Theatre.
    Dance Mag 32:35 Je '58
Fun to be me.   Newsweek 64:93 N 30 '64

JEFFREYS, ANNE
Marshall, J.   Honey from the B's.   Colliers 119:22 My
    3 '47
TV's loveliest ghost.   TV Guide 2-23:10 Je 4 '54

JENKINS, ALLEN
Maddox, B.   The "toughs" from the chorus.   Photop 45-
    3:69 F '34
Wood, C.   TV personalities biographical sketchbook.
    TV Personalities p136 '57

JENKINS, BUTCH
Hamilton, S.   Butch, the baby menace.   Photop 23-3:
    52 Ag '43

JENKS, FRANK
He follows in Flack's tracks.   TV Guide 2-29:12 Jl 17 '54

Obit.   Screen World 14:222 '63

JENS, SALOME
    Stock, D.   Salome Jens; the queen of off-Broadway.
        Esquire 55:106 F '61
    Jennings, C. R. On stage.   Horizon 4:102 Ja '62

JERGENS, ADELE
    Marshall, J.   SRO on a coral isle.   Colliers 116:30 N
        24 '45

JERGENS, DIANE
    Phillips, D.   Hey, we're engaged.   Photop 54-3:36 S '58
    Borie, M. & Marshutz, R.   Shh!   Don't tell anyone, we
        eloped.   Photop 54-6:43 D '58
    Borie, M.   We couldn't tell if our love was real.
        Photop 55-1:48 Jl '59

JOHNS, GLYNIS
    Forecasts and side glances.   Theatre Arts 36:13 F '52
    Thackery, T. Jr.   The offspring of Tinker Bell and a
        computer.   TV Guide 11-50:12 D 14 '63

JOHNSON, CELIA
    Two and two make Celia.   Time 50:85 D 15 '47
    No thrill in fame.   Plays & Players 1-10:4 Jl '54
    Personality of the month.   Plays & Players 8-2:3 N '60

JOHNSON, EDITH
    Pretty Edith Johnson.   Feature Movie 5-2:22 Mr '16

JOHNSON, KATIE
    Obit.   Screen World 9:223 '58

JOHNSON, KAY
    Burton, S.   She's dynamite.   Photop 37-1:37 D '29

JOHNSON, RITA
    Obit.   Screen World 17:237 '66

JOHNSON, VAN
    Greggory, D.   Guy with a grin.   Photop 23-4:44 S '43
    Johnson, V.   I was just thinking.   Photop 25-1:45 Je '44
    New matinee idol.   Life 17:47 N 13 '44
    Janis, E.   Visit from Van Johnson.   Photop 25-6:38 N
        '44
    Biographical sketch.   Time 44:93 D 4 '44

Johnson, V.   My life.   Photop 26-3:30 F '45; 26-4:47
  Mr '45
Martin, P.   Bobby-sox blitzer.   Sat Eve Post 217:16 Je
  30 '45
Biography.   Cur Bio Jl '45
St Johns, A. R.   The truth about Van Johnson's health.
  Photop 27-2:28 Jl '45
Allyson, J.   The Van Johnson I know.   Photop 27-4:36
  S '45
Butterfield, R.   Van Johnson.   Life 19:114 N 5 '45
Peters, S.   My Hollywood friends.   Photop 28-1:30 D '45
St. Johns, A. R.   Heart of a Yankee.   Photop 28-3:30 F;
  28-4:34 Mr; 28-5:42 Ap '46
Graham, S.   People will say they're in love.   Photop
  29-1:32 Je '46
Mamlok, M.   Van hands down.   Photop 29-4:44 S '46
Parsons, L. O.   Untold love story.   Photop 30-1:38 D '46
Jefferson, S. & Pritchett, F.   The Van Johnson-Evie and
  Keenan Wynn triangle.   Photop 30-4:34 Mr '47
Graham, S.   The verdict on Van.   Photop 32-3:48 F '48
Johnson, V.   My new life.   Photop 33-4:38 S '48
Parsons, L. O.   They've had to take it.   Photop 34-4:46
  Mr '49
McElroy, J.   Breakfast in Hollywood.   Photop 36-1:54 Je
  '49
Johnson, V. Hey, Sugar.   Photop 38-3:46 S '50
Steele, J. H.   Rhode Island redhead.   Photop 40-4:50 O
  '51
Phillips, D. Van Johnson learned no man walks alone.
  Photop 47-3:47 Mr '55
Johnson, Mrs. V.   Portrait of the man I love.   Photop
  49-6:52 Je '56
Davidson, M. & Davidson, B.   Van Johnson: back from
  the edge.   McCalls 90:87 Ag '63
Haranis, C.   Thoughts on an old wedding ring.   Photop
  65-6:72 Je '64

JOLSON, AL
  If I don't get laughs and don't get applause--the mirror
    will show me who is to blame.   Am Mag 87:18 Ap '19
  Kaufman, S.   Other side of Al Jolson.   Everybodys 44:
    16 Ap '21
  Here's one you'll like.   Illus World 38:665 Ja '23
  Fleming, J.   King of cork.   Illus World 38:663 Ja '23
  Seldes, G.   Demoniac in the American theatre.   Dial
    75:303 S '23
  Skinner, R. D.   Al Jolson again.   Commonweal 11:715

Ap 23 '30

Hutchens, J. Al Jolson and others. Theatre Arts 15: 366 My '31

French, W. A. Only Al Jolson wanted to play. Photop 45-4:31 Mr '34

Harris, R. And now there is Al Jolson Jr. Photop 48-2: 24 Jl '35

Green, C. Yours truly rural, Al Jolson. Photop 49-5:28 My '36

Jolson comes back in new musical. Life 9:60 Jl 29 '40

Krutch, J. W. Al Jolson and his mammy. Nation 151: 281 S 28 '40

Biography. Cur Bio '40

Woolf, S. J. Army minstrel. N. Y. Times Mag p19 S 27 '42

Happy ending. Time 49:52 My 26 '47

Switcheroo. Time 50:78 O 6 '47

Zolotow, M. Ageless Al. Read Digest 54:73 Ja '49

Jolson sings again. Life 27:93 S 12 '49

Obit. Newsweek 36:28 O 30 '50
    Time 56:89 O 30 '50
    Scholastic 57:16 N 1 '50

Death of a Jazz Singer. Life 29:115 N 6 '50

Lardner, J. Minstrel memories. Newsweek 36:87 N 6 '50

Obit. Cur Bio 11:25 D '50
    Cur Bio Yrbk 1950:281 '51

Debus, A. G. Records of Al Jolson. Hobbies 60:25 Ap; 27 My; 27 Je; 27 Jl; 27 Ag '56

JONES, ALLAN

Baskette, K. Choir-boy in Hollywood. Photop 50-4:31 O '36

My worst flop. Am Mag 136:50 Jl '43

JONES, "BUCK" CHARLES

Jordan, J. A rodeo Romeo. Photop 20-5:42 O '21

Tully, J. A top rider. Photop 29-2:78 Ja '26

Crichton, K. Horse-opera star. Colliers 97:55 My 9 '36

Griswold, J. B. King of the giddyaps. Am Mag 125:43 Ja '38

Obit. Cur Bio '43

Gordon, A. Buck Jones, inc. filmog. Films In Review 11-3:187 Mr '60

JONES, CAROLYN

One of the Jones girls. TV Guide 5-21:24 My 25 '57

Jones, C. & Adams, N. Don't be difficult. Photop 54-
1:65 Jl '58

Spelling, A. My wife, Carolyn Jones. Photop 54-3:59
S '58

Noveau success. Newsweek 53:96 Mr 23 '59

Carolyn . . . an extraordinary Jones. Look 23:110 Ap
28 '59

Prankish girl's gags in plaster. Life 47:9 Jl 20 '59

Biography. Cur Bio 28:15 Mr '67
Same. Cur Bio Yrbk 1967:208 '68

JONES, CHRISTOPHER
Fessier, M. Jr. Even his haircuts make waves. TV
Guide 14-14:19 Ap 2 '66

Reynolds, L. I didn't know I was married. Photop 74-
5:45 N '68

JONES, DEAN
Jones refuses to keep up with the Joneses. TV Guide 11-
5:22 F 2 '63

JONES, JENNIFER
Crichton, K. Name is Jennifer. Colliers 111:78 Ap 24
'43

Miracle girl. Am Mag 135:28 My 43

Meet two rising stars. Ladies Home J 61:85 Ja '44

Saint from Tulsa. Newsweek 23:75 F 7 '44

Bentley, J. Jennifer Jones--please read. Photop 24-4:
38 Mr '44

Biography. Cur Bio My '44

St. Johns, A. R. Who is Bernadette? Photop 25-1:34 Je
'44

Beatty, J. Keeping up with the Jones girl. Am Mag
138:28 O '44

Parsons, L. O. Bob Walker talks about Jennifer Jones.
Photop 25-6:30 N '44

Carey, R. Jennifer Jones speaks for herself. Photop
27-4:29 S '45

Arnold, M. The amazing Miss Jones. Photop 28-2:36
Ja '46

Maxwell, E. Jennifer Jones, my paradoxical friend.
Photop 28-5:34 Ap '46

Colby, A. That dream girl Jennifer Jones. Photop 29-4:
46 S '46

Arnold, M. Jennifer--the fabulous life of a girl named
Jones. Photop 31-4:64 S '47

Pritchett, F. Portrait of Jenny. Photop 32-3:62 F '48

Jennifer Jones. Life 25:119 D 13 '48
Parsons, L. O. I predict a honeymoon. Photop 34-3:32
    F '49
Peck, G. Jenny and Miss Jones. Photop 36-1:44 Je '49
Maxwell, E. New horizons. Photop 36-6:32 N '49
Hume, R. She saw the vision--and became a star; inc.
    filmog. Films & Filming 2-9:15 Je '56
Posner, C. The mystery of Jennifer Jones. Photop 53-
    4:53 Ap '58
Doyle, N. Jennifer Jones, inc. filmog. Films In Review
    13-7:390 Ag/S '61
Carpozzi, G. I tried to die. Photop 73-2:8 F '68

JONES, SHIRLEY
    People are talking about . . . Vogue 125:121 My 1 '55
    Shirley Jones, the girl from Oklahoma. Look 19:86 Ap
        5 '55
    Whitcomb, J. Miss Jones of Oklahoma. Cosmop 138:40
        Je '55
    Jacobi, E. Everything's going her way. Photop 48-5:41
        N '55
    Carousel is a movie clambake too. Life 40:90 F 6 '56
    Cinderella on a carousel. Coronet 39:8 Mr '56
    Phillips, D. Sugar puss. Photop 49-3:42 Mr '56
    Cinderella comes home. Am Mag 161:50 Je '56
    Good life of a Hollywood bad girl. Look 25:146 N 21 '61
    Biography. Cur Bio 22:28 O '61
        Same. Cur Bio Yrbk 1961:225 '62
    Martin, P. Backstage with Shirley Jones. Sat Eve Post
        235:42 Ja 13 '62
    Balling, F. The greatest miracle of all. Photop 61-5:
        45 My '62
    Meltsir, A. Daredevil with the apple pie face. Photop
        63-2:74 F '63
    Gardiner, H. Babies, just babies. Photop 64-3:42 S '63
    Sanders, A. The stranger in my bed. Photop 66-5:37
        N '64

JORDAN, DOROTHY
    Hamilton, S. Would you believe it? Photop 42-3:40 Ag
        '32

JORY, VICTOR
    Wood, C. TV personalities biographical sketchbook.
        TV Personalities p80 '56
    A good actor and he knows it. TV Guide 8-36:12 S 3 '60

JOURDAN, LOUIS
    English lesson. Life 21:91 S 30 '46
    Downing, H. That new man. Photop 32-6:68 My '48
    Wood, C. TV personalities biographical sketchbook.
        TV Personalities p39 '56
    Lardner, R. Jourdan, the glamorous Gaul. Coronet
        48:88 My '60
    Biography. Cur Bio 28:18 Ja '67
    Same. Cur Bio Yrbk 1967:211 '68

JOY, LEATRICE
    Winship, M. Gloria's successor. Photop 22-3:31 Ag '22

JOY, NICHOLAS
    Obit. Time 83:74 Mr 27 '64
        Screen World 16:223 '65

JOYCE, ALICE
    Venus of the movies. Cosmop 55:839 N '13
    Martin, M. Alice Joyce advises. Photop 6-2:71 Jl '14
    Gaddis, P. Alice Joyce, honeymoon truant. Photop 7-
        6:27 My '15
    Smith, F. J. Alice for short. Photop 12-5:77 O '17
    Patterson, A. The lady of vast silences. Photop 17-4:
        85 My '20
    Darling, E. V. Alice, where have you been? Photop
        25-6:72 My '24
    Obit. Time 66:110 O 17 '55
        Screen World 7:225 '56
        Brit Bk Yr 1956:514 '56

JOYCE, BRENDA
    Crichton, K. Unsophisticated lady. Colliers 105:12 My
        4 '40
    Jefferson, S. Brenda defies the rule. Photop 18-5:30
        Ap '41

JOYCE, PEGGY HOPKINS
    St. Johns, I. What is that lure of Peggy Joyce? Photop
        28-6:28 N '25
    Joyce, P. H. Why women love diamonds. Photop 34-5:
        29 O '28

JUDGE, ARLINE
    Taylor, A. Happiness comes again to Arline Judge.
        Photop 51-5:50 My '37

JURGENS, CURT
Talk with Herr Jurgens.   Newsweek 51:91 Ap 28 '58

KANE, GAIL
 Woen, K. Gail Kane, a Juno of the desert. Photop 9-
   6:54 My '16
 Quirk, J. R. Who-zat lady? Photop 13-6:77 My '18
 Obit. Screen World 18:237 '67

KARLOFF, BORIS
 Gordon, A. Boris Karloff. Cinema 5-1:3 n. d.
 Everson, W. K. Frankenstein, Dracula, Karloff and
   Lugosi. Screen Facts 7:38 n. d.
 Rankin, R. Meet the monster. Photop 43-2:60 Ja '33
 Peterson, E. T. Human side of Hollywood he-men. Bet
   Hom & Gard 17-22 My '39
 Cinnamon and old toast. New Yorker 16:10 F 1 '41
 Pringle, H. F. Gentle monster. Colliers 108:60 S 20
   '41
 Biography. Cur Bio '41
 Baker, G. Here's my favorite; intv. Sr Schol 40:22 Ap
   20 '42
 Thriller diller. Newsweek 34:55 O 3 '49
 Grafton, S. All he needed was one good scare. Good H
   141:66 Ag '55
 Wicked wolf's tail: preparing for Little Red Riding Hood.
   Life 41:115 D 17 '56
 Karloff, B. My life as a monster. Films & Filming 4-
   2:11 N '57
 Love that monster. TV Guide 6-2:14 Ja 11 '58
 Being a monster is really a game. TV Guide 8-42:17 O
   15 '60
 How they sweated out the chills. TV Guide 9-18:17 My
   6 '61
 Karloff, B. Memoirs of a monster; as told to A. & H.
   Eisenberg. Sat Eve Post 235:77 N 3 '62
 Roman, R. C. Boris Karloff, inc. filmog. Films In
   Review 15-7:389 Ag /S '64
 Rosenberg, S. Horrible truth about Frankenstein. Life
   64:74C Mr 15 '68
 Obit. Time 93:81 F 14 '69
 Gentle monster. Newsweek 73:100 F 17 '69
 Obit. Cur Bio 30:44 Mr '69
 Nolan, J. D. Karloff on TV. Film Fan Mo 102:3 D '69

KARNS, ROSCOE
 Roscoe Karns has outlasted all other TV detectives.

TV Guide 1-18:20 Jl 31 '53
Now where do you want this here acting done? TV Guide
9-10:28 Mr 11 '61

KASHFI, ANNA
Nichols, M.   Foreign accent in starlets.   Coronet 40:50
Ag '56
Gehman, R.   Mrs. Marlon Brando: who she really is.
McCalls 86:36 Jl '59
York, C.   The slap that said I love you.   Photop 61-3:
16 Mr '62
Anderson, N.   Anna tells all about Marlon.   Photop 61-5:
53 My '62

KASZNAR, KURT
Whitney, D.   He acted his way out of a paper bag.
TV Guide 17-43:19 O 25 '69

KAUFMANN, CHRISTINE
Person of promise.   Films & Filming 7-9:19 Je '61
Meet Mrs. Tony Curtis II.   Photop 62-4:29 O '62
Gideon, N.   Second wife but not second best.   Photop
62-6:25 D '62
Mr. and Mrs. Tony Curtis.   Photop 63-5:49 My '63

KAYE, DANNY
Davis, L. & Cleveland, J.   Funny man.   Colliers 107:
18 Ap 12 '41
Strauss, T.   Melody in Kaye.   N.Y. Times Mag p10 N
16 '41
Biography.   Cur Bio '41
Dautman, I.   Blitz from Brooklyn.   Photop 24-6:58 My
'44
Danny Kaye satirizes the familiar nightclub pest.   Life
17:10 O 16 '44
Kaye, S. F.   It's like this to be Mrs. Danny Kaye.
Photop 25-5:58 O '44
Kaye-o.   Newsweek 25:82 Ja 15 '45
Mile-a-minute mugger.   Time 45:48 Ja 15 '45
Albert, D.   Head on Danny's shoulders.   Am Mag 139:
40 F '45
Brown, J. M.   Royal line.   Sat R 28:22 Jl 14 '45
Janis, E.   Chrysanthemum top.   Photop 27-5:54 O '45
Git gat gittle.   Time 47:63 Mr 11 '46
Cerf, B.   Trade winds.   Sat R 29:38 Mr 23 '46
Howe, H.   Svengali of scat.   Photop 29-5:56 O '46
Kaye, D.   Once I was a toomler; ed by K. Crichton.

Colliers 123:30 My 14 '49
Traveling salesman in London. Time 53:76 Je 13 '49
Danny conquers England. Life 26:47 Je 13 '49
Gibbs, E. Ambassador from Brooklyn. Life 26:50 Je
    13 '49
Over the magazine editor's desk. C S Mon Mag p15 D 10
    '49
American comedy at Palladium. Holiday 6:162 D '49
Brown, J. M. Incomparable Danny. Sat R 33:30 Ja 21
    '50
Morris, J. A. World's highest paid buffoon. Sat Eve
    Post 222:30 Je 10 '50
Kerr, W. Undoing of Danny Kaye. Theatre Arts 35:41
    Ag '51
Ugly duckling: Danny Kaye retells the story. Coronet
    33:111 N '52
Biography. Cur Bio 13:31 N '52
    Same. Cur Bio Yrbk 1952:298 '53
Millstein, G. Rise and rise of Danny Kaye. N. Y. Times
    Mag p19 Ja 18 '53
King Kaye in the palace. Colliers 131:18 Ja 24 '53
White, S. Mr. Kaye reappears. Look 11:4 Ja 27 '53
Brown, J. M. Okaye. Sat R 36:26 Mr 21 '53
Kass, R. Film & TV; Danny Kaye at the Palace theatre.
    Cath World 176:462 Mr '53
Fun can be work; ballet in Knock on wood. Dance Mag
    27:21 D '53
Acrobatics for Danny Kaye. Life 36:133 Mr 22 '54
Knight, A. Color, comedy and Kaye. Sat R 37:36 Ap
    10 '54
People are talking about . . . Vogue 123:94 Ap 15 '54
Bentley, E. Theatre. New Repub 130:21 Ap 19 '54
Danny Kaye begins tour as UNICEF ambassador-at-large.
    U. N. Bul 16:401 My 15 '54
U. N. presents: Danny Kaye. N. Y. Times Mag p25 Jl
    4 '54
Ardmore, J. K. Danny Kaye's favorite role. Parents
    Mag 29:46 Jl '54
Two misters play sisters. Colliers 134:74 O 15 '54
All for the world's children. Look 18:96 N 16 '54
Lerman, L. Charm boys. Mlle 40:162 F '55
Kaye, S. F. Memo to my husband. Photop 47-3:57 Mr
    '55
Not born a fool. New Statesm 49:810 Je 11 '55
Comic knighthood for Kaye. Life 40:93 Ja 30 '56
Johnson, G. Touch of Pagliacci. Coronet 39:128 F '56
Goldsmith, B. Danny Kaye's story: the sorrow behind

the jester. Womans H C 83:12 Ap '56

Kaye, D. Ambassador-at-large. Colliers 138:32 N 9 '56

All for the children. Newsweek 48:109 D 10 '56

Good seed. Time 68:47 D 10 '56

Danny Kaye and friends on UNICEF; intv. Rotarian 90:
18 F '57

Danny Kaye leaps the language barrier. CTA J 53:39 F
'57

Baton for a comedian. Newsweek 49:64 Ap 15 '57

Annual Mr. Travel award presented to Danny Kaye.
Travel 107:16 Ap '57

Danny Kaye clown prince. Sr Schol 71:10 D 6 '57

Children: the future of the world. Nat Educ Assn J 46:
567 D '57

Biography. Colliers Yrbk 1957:701 '57

Danny Kaye picture book. McCalls 85:12 Ja '58

Peck, S. Danny Kaye in the circus. N.Y. Times Mag
p30 Mr 9 '58

Kolodin, I. & Chasins, A. Not-so-secret musical life of
Danny Kaye. Sat R 41:37 Mr 29 '58

Martin, P. I call on Danny Kaye. Sat Eve Post 231:18
Ag 9 '58

Mehling, H. Living legends. Todays Health 36:7 O '58

Flesh of the stars. Newsweek 52:98 D 8 '58

Kaye, Mrs. D. Men I married. Coronet 46:30 Jl '59

Bester, A. Danny Kaye. Holiday 26:77 Ag '59

Kaye, D. How does TV affect our children. TV Guide
8-13:7 Mr 26 '60

Exit Jerry, enter Danny. Newsweek 56:69 S 5 '60

Making Kaye O.K. N.Y. Times Mag p88 O 23 '60

A great clown finally comes to TV. TV Guide 8-44:12 O
29 '60

Liston, J. At home with Danny Kaye. Am Home 68:4
N '60

Tornabene, L. Lunch date with Danny Kaye. Cosmop
149:22 N '60

Soliloquy. Newsweek 58:62 N 6 '61

Conductor in disarray is Maestro Danny Kaye. Look 26:
62a Ap 24 '62

Happiest man. Read Digest 82:94 Mr '63

Innocent delight. Time 81:68 Ap 19 '63

McCarten, J. Theatre; entertainment at the Ziegfeld.
New Yorker Ap 20 '63

A-okaye. Newsweek 61:90 Ap 22 '63

Zinsser, W. K. Day there was no money; publicity stunt
in Winsted, Conn. Reporter 29:46 S 12 '63

Wednesday question: want to watch Danny Kaye?

Newsweek 62:43 D 23 '63

DeRoos, R. He's satisfied with perfection. TV Guide
12-5:27 F 1 '64

Casey, G. & Nagle, T. Danny Kaye. Flying 74:46 Mr
'64

Fun on TV. Dance Mag 38:31 N '64

Whitney, D. The seven faces of Danny Kaye. TV Guide
13-2:15 Ja 9 '65

Danny Kaye's own story: if I can learn to fly, you can
learn to fly. Pop Sci 190:76 Ja '67

KAYE, STUBBY

Anderson, D. Stubby Kaye, showstopper. Theatre Arts
36:39 F '52

How I learned a lesson in parenthood. Read Digest 75:
79 S '59

Fuller, J. G. Trade winds. Sat R 43:8 S 24 '60

KEANE, RAYMOND

Spensley, D. One in 10,000. Photop 29-6:78 My '26

KEATON, BUSTER

Keaton, B. Before and after taking. Photop 20-4:31 S
'21

St. Johns, A. R. Interviewing Joseph Talmadge Keaton.
Photop 22-5:51 O '22

Why I never smile. Ladies Home J 43:20 Je '26

Moffit, J. C. Page one publicity with premieres.
Cinema Digest 1-7:9 Ag 8 '32

Reid, A. Strictly for laughs. Colliers 113:66 Je 10 '44

Agee, J. Great stone face. Life 27:82 S 5 '49

Gloomy Buster is back again; Keaton is up to his old
tricks on TV. Life 28:145 Mr 13 '50

Shulman, M. Then and now. N.Y. Times Mag p19 My
9 '54

Buster at bay. Life 39:132 D 12 '55

Film pioneers' roll of their living immortals. Life 40:
119 Ja 23 '56

Old comic and pupil. Life 42:91 My 6 '57

Bishop, C. Great stone face. Film Q 12:10 Fall '58

Bishop, C. Interview with Buster Keaton. Film Q 12:
15 Fall '58

Baxter, B. Buster Keaton. Film 18:8 '58

DeRoos, R. Biggest laugh in movie history. Coronet
46:98 Ag '59

Celebrities on a stylish spree. Life 47:103 S 7 '59

Robinson, D. Buster. Sight & Sound 29:41 Win '59

Great stone face talks.   Newsweek 55:90 Ja 25 '60
Still playing it deadpan.   Life 49:132 O 10 '60
Happy pro.   New Yorker 39:36 Ap 27 '63
Beckett; production of his first screenplay for Evergreen
    theatre.   New Yorker 40:22 Ag 8 '64
Watch out, Buster, you're being watched.   Life 57:85
    Ag 14 '64
Brownlow, K.   Buster Keaton; intv.   Film 42:6 Win '64
Gillett, J. & Blue, J.   Keaton at Venice.   Sight & Sound
    34:26 Win '65
Lorca, F. G.   Buster Keaton takes a walk.   Sight &
    Sound 35-1:24 Win '65
Scold and the Sphinx.   Time 87:52 F 11 '66
Agee, J.   Buster Keaton; excerpt from Agee on film.
    Life 60:63 F 11 '66
Obit.   Time 87:82 F 11 '66
    Nat R 18:167 F 22 '66
    Brit Bk Yr 1967:595 '67
    Screen World 18:237 '67
Morgenstern, J.   What a Buster!   Newsweek 67:30 F 14
    '66
Houston, P.   Buster.   Sight & Sound 35-2:72 Spg '66
Friedman, A. B.   Interview.   Film Q 19-4:2 Sum '66
Rhode, E.   Buster Keaton.   Encounter 29:35 D '67
Houston, P.   The great blank page.   Sight & Sound 37-
    2:63 Spg '68

KEDROVA, LILA
    Zorba's woman.   Films & Filming 11-8:51 My '65

KEEL, HOWARD
    Arnold, M.   Even Keel.   Photop 38-4:58 O '50
    Zeitlin, I.   Many brave hearts.   Photop 40-4:40 O '51
    Armstrong, G.   Howard Keel's untold story.   Photop
        42-5:36 N '52
    Bailey, C.   Keel's kingdom.   Photop 46-2:8 Ag '54
    Shipp, C.   Howard's booming baritone.   Sat Eve Post
        228:22 O 15 '55

KEELER, RUBY
    St. Johns, A. R.   Give this little girl a hand.   Photop
        47-5:26 Ap '35
    Harris, R.   And now there is Al Jolson Jr.   Photop 48-
        2:24 Jl '35
    Where are they now?   Newsweek 49:26 My 6 '57

KEENAN, FRANK
  Role as Hon. John Grigsby. Harper 46:310 Mr 8 '02

KEENE, TOM
  Edwards, J. Tom Keene, inc. filmog. Films In Review
    14-8:502 O '63
  Obit. Screen World 15:220 '64

KEITH, BRIAN
  Wood, C. TV personalities biographical sketchbook.
    TV Personalities p111 '56
  Hano, A. Keith and kin. TV Guide 14-40:15 O 1 '66
  Waterbury, R. Love is playing family. Photop 73-2:59
    F '68
  Ardmore, J. Little ego trouble. Photop 74-5:52 N '68
  Allen, J. He couldn't save his marriage. Photop 76-1:
    34 Jl '69
  Riley, N. Mother talks about boyhood. Photop 76-2:68
    Ag '69
  Brian Keith in love. Photop 76-5:66 N '69

KEITH, IAN
  Obit. Newsweek 55:68 Ap 4 '60
    Screen World 12:222 '61

KELLEY, DeFOREST
  Where is the welcome mat? TV Guide 16-34:20 Ag 24 '68

KELLY, CLAIRE
  Person of promise. Films & Filming 5-4:17 Ja '59

KELLY, DOROTHY
  Bartlett, R. Dorothy Kelly. Photop 9-2:45 Ja '16
  Bartlett, R. The girl on the cover. Photop 10-6:88 N '16

KELLY, GENE
  Proctor, K. Hey, Irish! Photop 22-6:36 My '43
  Harris, E. If you were Gene Kelly's house guest.
    Photop 24-3:54 F '44
  Kelly, B. It's like this to be Mrs. Gene Kelly. Photop
    Photop 25-1:36 Je '44
  Arnold, M. Keeping up with Gene Kelly. Photop 26-2:
    38 Ja '45
  Crichton, K. Dancing master. Colliers 115:20 My 19
    '45
  Enton, H. Where's Gene Kelly? Photop 27-6:56 N '45
  Biography. Cur Bio D '45

Frazier, G. Starboard bound. Photop 28-2:47 Ja '46
Isaacs, H. R. Portrait of a dancing actor. Theatre
    Arts 30:149 Mr '46
Boger, F. My kids, the Kellys. Photop 33-3:54 Ag '48
Biographical note. Newsweek 35:84 Mr 27 '50
Martin, P. Fastest moving star in pictures. Sat Eve
    Post 223:24 Jl 8 '50
Chandler, D. Strictly from hunger. Photop 41-2:56 F
    '52
Sakol, J. Traveling man. Photop 42-2:50 Ag '52
Gene Kelly's invitation to the dance. Look 17:88 Mr 24
    '53
Gene Kelly: man in motion. Coronet 35:105 N '53
Harvey, E. Legs and a legend. Colliers 133:24 Mr 5
    '54
Knight, A. Invitation to the dance. Dance Mag 30:14 Je
    '56
Wood, C. TV personalities biographical sketchbook.
    TV Personalities p13 '57
Musical comedy is serious business. Theatre Arts 42:
    18 D '58
Alpert, H. Old friends in new jobs; producing Flower
    drum song. Dance Mag 32:52 D '58
Brazel, A. Dancing is a man's game. Dance Mag 33:
    30 F '59
Dance Magazine's 1958 award winner. Dance Mag 33:
    31 Mr '59
Dance Magazine's annual awards. Dance Mag 33:31 Ap
    '59
Shayon, R. L. Shall we dance? Sat R 42:61 My 16 '59
Kelly's Pontiac show. Dance Mag 33:36 Je '59
An evening with Fred Astaire and Gene Kelly. TV Guide
    7-44:8 O 31 '59
Making ballet jump. Newsweek 56:83 Jl 18 '60
Gene Kelly's French frolic. Life 49:55 Ag 29 '60
September calendar; Museum of modern art presents a
    Gene Kelly dance film festival. Dance Mag 36:36 S
    '62
Behlmer, R. Gene Kelly, inc. filmog. Films In Review
    15-1:6 Ja '64
Amory, C. Celebrity register. McCalls 91:66 Mr '64
Cutts, J. Kelly. Films & Filming 10-11:38 Ag '64;
    10-12:34 S '64
Some notes for young dancers. Dance Mag 39:49 S '65
Dancing in the dark. Dance Mag 39:103 D '65
Sextuple threat. Time 90:56 Ag 4 '67

KELLY, GRACE

> Who's who in the cast--Grace Kelly. TV Guide 3-32:16
>   Ag 12 '50
> TV leading ladies. Life 32:142 My 5 '52
> New films: Mogambo. Newsweek 42:100 O 12 '53
> Hollywood's hottest property. Life 36:117 Ap 26 '54
> Kelly's cool film beauty. Newsweek 43:96 My 17 '54
> Biographical note. Time 63:102 My 24 '54
> Grace Kelly, most wanted woman. Look 18:60 Je 15 '54
> Martin, P. Luckiest girl in Hollywood. Sat Eve Post
>   227:28 O 30 '54
> Bolstad, H. How do you do, Miss Kelly. Photop 46-6:
>   46 D '54
> I predict Grace Kelly will be most popular woman star
>   of year. Look 19:18 Ja 11 '55
> Girl in white gloves. Time 65:46 Ja 31 '55
> Taves, I. Seven Graces. McCalls 82:30 Ja '55
> Cohen, M. The lady is a go-getter. Photop 47-2:45 F
>   '55
> People are talking about . . . Vogue 125:130 Mr 1 '55
> Biography. Cur Bio 16:31 Mr '55
> Marlon and Grace. Life 38:117 Ap 11 '55
> Madeira, E. & Callahan, R. Grace Kelly tells how to
>   travel light. Womans H C 82:46 Ap '55
> McCarthy, J. Genteel Miss Kelly. Cosmop 138:26 Ap
>   '55
> Gam, R. That girl Kelly and me. Photop 47-4:48 Ap '55
> Grace's Riviera romance. Life 38:14 My 30 '55
> Harvey, E. Key to Kelly. Colliers 135:37 Je 24 '55
> Lerman, L. I'll take vanilla! Mlle 41:80 Je '55
> Grace Kelly in the ads. America 93:506 Ag 27 '55
> Charade, P. All actors are a little nutty, says Grace
>   Kelly. Photop 48-4:48 O '55
> Schwartz, D. Films. New Repub 133:21 N 28 '55
> Kelly, Mrs. J. B. My daughter Grace. Good H 141:78
>   N '55
> Philadelphia princess. Time 67:21 Ja 16 '56
> Romance that's got everything. Life 40:17 Ja 16 '56
> Gisele, Oleg and Jean-Pierre were forgotten. Life 40:
>   22 Ja 16 '56
> Bricklayer's daughter. Newsweek 47:20 Ja 16 '56
> Prince and the papers. Time 67:69 Ja 23 '56
> Weinmann, M. Hollywood's queen becomes a princess.
>   Colliers 137:22 Mr 2 '56
> Keeping it dignified. Time 67:63 Mr 26 '56
> Kurnitz, H. Antic arts. Holiday 19:77 Mr '56
> Parton, M. What Make Grace Kelly different. Ladies

Home J 73:68 Mr '56

Women who fascinate men.   Look 20:93 Ap 3 '56

Erwin, R.   Antics of 250 newsmen scare Grace Kelly at
   ship interview.   Ed & Pub 89:13 Ap 7 '56

And now here comes the bride.   Life 40:45 Ap 9 '56

Come to the wedding.   TV Guide 4-15:5 Ap 14 '56

Love for three dimples.   Time 67:23 Ap 16 '56

Mob and princess-to-be.   Newsweek 47:70 Ap 16 '56

Members of the wedding.   Commonweal 64:65 Ap 20 '56

Grace Kelly and U. S. hoopla.   America 95:74 Ap 21 '56

Madness in Monaco.   Newsweek 47:90 Ap 23 '56

What is Grace up to?   Life 40:197 Ap 23 '56

Cousins, N.   Statement and apology.   Sat R 39:20 Ap 28
   '56

Moon over Monte Carlo.   Time 67:33 Ap 30 '56

Movies' pretty princess assumes a real life title.   Life
   40:36 Ap 30 '56

Waterbury, R.   A prince catches a star.   Photop 49-4:
   44 Ap '56

Bolstad, H.   The story of how it all happened.   Photop
   49-4:46 Ap '56

Kahn, E. J.   Cute and not so cute.   New Yorker 40:158
   My 5 '56

Noble pair in the palace.   Life 40:66 My 14 '56

Canfield, A.   The rocky road to paradise.   Photop 50-1:
   20 Jl '56

Kleiman, R.   Where Grace Kelly is princess and there
   are almost no taxes.   U. S. News 41:54 S 7 '56

Schary, D.   Who made Miss Kelly?   Sat R 39:16 O 20 '56

Biography.   Am Ann 1956:405 '56
   Brit Bk Yr 1956:387 '56
   Colliers Yrbk 1956:526 '56
   Cur Bio Yrbk 1955:324 '56

Moskin, J. R.   Princess Grace, prepares for her baby.
   Colliers 139:57 Ja 4 '57

Arthur, W. B.   Grace Kelly's life as a princess.   Look
   21:27 F 5 '57

Sutton, H.   Show at the palace.   Sat R 40:31 My 11 '57

Honor, E.   Princess Grace's royal obligations.   Cosmop
   143:53 Jl '57

Mann, J.   Is Grace getting bored?   Photop 52-5:54 N '57

Arthur, W. B.   Prince Rainier of Monaco.   Look 21:24
   D 24 '57

Biography.   Colliers Yrbk 1957:701 '57

Not to have a home.   America 98:392 Ja 4 '58

Taub, P.   The nursery tale of the little prince.   Photop
   54-2:49 Ag '58

Arthur, W. B.   Princess and the palace.   Look 23:54 Ag
   18 '59
Hoffman, J.   If only I could tell my husband.   Photop
   56-3:62 S '59
Princess on a conquest of Paris.   Life 47:175 O 26 '59
Martin, P.   I call on Princess Grace.   Sat Eve Post
   232:13 Ja 23; 26 Ja 30; 31 F 6 '60
Franklin, G.   Monaco's years of Grace.   Coronet 47:151
   Ap '60
Britten, R.   Please God don't let my father see me cry.
   Photop 58-3:56 S '60
Hoffman, J.   The whispers about Princess Grace and her
   husband.   Photop 58-6:21 D '60
Galante, P.   How it all began.   Look 25:48 Ap 11 '61
Arthur, W. B.   Princess Grace after five years.   Look
   25:42 Ap 11 '61
Anybody seen Kelly?   Newsweek 57:44 Je 19 '61
Ireland takes a Kelly to its heart.   Life 50:38 Je 23 '61
Buchwald, A.   How I lost $50,000 in my spare time.
   Sat R 44:50 O 14 '61
Fisher, G. & Fisher, H.   Prince and I.   Ladies Home J
   78:56 O '61
Loutzenhiser, J. K.   Grace Kelly, inc. filmog.   Films
   In Review 13-4:245 Ap '62
Reigning beauties.   Time 79:30 Je 8 '62
Carpozi, G.   Who's forcing her comeback?   Photop 62-1:
   35 Jl '62
Samuels, C.   Troubled heart of Grace Kelly.   Good H
   155:82 O '62
Princess Grace takes a TV tour of her principality.
   Life 54:55 Ja 25 '63
Hamilton, J.   Princess Grace; a new role.   Look 27:64
   F 12 '63
Grace of Graustark.   Time 81:42 F 22 '63
Anthony, P.   What she can't show on TV.   Photop 63-3:
   54 Mr '63
Rainier III, Prince of Monaco.   Memoirs of Monaco; as
   told to Serge Fliegers.   McCalls 90:81 Ap '63
Massie, R.   Grace of Kelly.   Sat Eve Post 236:18 Je 8
   '63
Is Grace jealous of Jackie?   Photop 63-6:54 Je '63
Obolensky, H.   How Princess Grace chooses children's
   clothes.   Redbook 121:61 Ag '63
Davidson, M.   What Princess Grace likes and doesn't
   like about the life she leads.   Good H 160:59 Ja '65
King, M.   Princess Grace: how she lovingly raises her
   children; as told to S. Fliegers.   Good H 162:74 F '66

Walters, B. How now, Princess Grace? Ladies Home J
  83:65 N '66
Hawkins, P. Prince Rainier tells of "our life together."
  Good H 164:100 Mr '67
Ehrlich, H. Jamaica holiday for Princess Grace. Look
  31:38 Ap 4 '67

KELLY, NANCY
  Condon, F. Has anybody here seen Kelly? Colliers 103:
    17 Ja 21 '38
  Three stars brighter than ever. Vogue 125:89 Ap 15 '55
  From her to maturity. Theatre Arts 39:28 Ap '55
  Biography. Cur Bio 16:41 Je '55
    Same. Cur Bio Yrbk 1955:325 '56

KELLY, PATSY
  Crichton, K. Haphazard Patsy. Colliers 97:32 Ap 18 '36

KELLY, PAUL
  Art and criticism: a Marxian interpretation. Canad
    Forum 13:294 My '33
  Obit. Newsweek 48:89 N 19 '56
    Time 68:94 N 19 '56
    Screen World 8:223 '57
  Biography. NCAB 44:78 '62

KELLY, TOMMY
  Zeitlin, I. Adventures of Tommy Kelly. Photop 52-4:
    26 Ap '38

KENDALL, KAY
  Harvey, E. TV imports. Colliers 136:39 O 14 '55
  People are talking about . . . Vogue 130:110 Ag 15 '57
  Millstein, G. How to be funny though beautiful. N. Y.
    Times Mag p34 S 15 '57
  Another Harrison on the horizon. Life 43:47 S 30 '57
  Barratt, M. E. & M. Movies: flashing star. Good H
    145:38 N '57
  Obit. Illus Lond N 235:241 S 12 '59
    Newsweek 54:84 S 14 '59
    Time 74:96 S 14 '59
  Demarest, M. Blithe spirit is gone. Life 47:111 S 21
    '59
  Dinter, C. Till death do us part. Photop 56-6:46 D '59
  Robbins, J. & Robbins, J. Kay Kendall. Good H 150:
    161 Mr '60
    Same abridged with title: All that love could do.

Read Digest 76:79 Je '60
Obit.   Screen World 11:220 '60
Kurnitz, H.   Kay Kendall.   McCalls 94:100 O '66

KENNEDY, ARTHUR
Peck, S.   Growth and growing pains of an actor.
N. Y. Times Mag p20 F 15 '53
Biography.   Cur Bio 22:8 N '61
Same.   Cur Bio Yrbk 1961:239 '62

KENNEDY, EDGAR
Obit.   Newsweek 32:63 N 22 '48
Time 52:98 N 22 '48
Passing of a slow burn.   Life 25:55 N 29 '48
Maltin, L.   Edgar Kennedy, inc. filmog.   Film Fan Mo
78:3 D '67

KENNEDY, GEORGE
Kerr, M. A.   Cool hand George.   Photop 74-1:20 Jl '68

KENNEDY, MADGE
Evans, D.   Grand crossings impressions.   Photop 14-5:
58 O '18
Allison, D.   Nee Madge Kennedy.   Photop 15-2:62 Ja '19
Broun, H.   Madge Kennedy's return to the stage in
Cornered.   Colliers 67:15 Ja 8 '21
Gray, A.   Madge Kennedy is lucky, but she doesn't trust
luck; intv.   Am Mag 99:34 F '25

KENYON, DORIS
Burgess, B.   Result: Doris Kenyon, star.   Photop 10-5:
104 O '16
Perry, M.   The little girl in the parsonage.   Photop 18-
5:34 O '20

KERR, DEBORAH
Meyer, J.   Deborah Kerr, inc. filmog.   Screen Facts
19:1 n. d.
Pratt, W. J.   Letter.   Screen Facts 20:63 n. d.
Star is born.   Time 49:95 F 10 '47
Hollywood nabs Deborah Kerr.   Life 22:59 Ap 7 '47
Biography.   Cur Bio 8:31 S '47
Same Cur Bio Yrbk 1947:350 '48
Crichton, K.   Huckster's lady.   Colliers 120:50 O 4 '47
Graham, S.   Deborah Kerr.   Photop 31-6:68 N '47
Carlson, R.   Diary of a Hollywood safari.   Colliers 126:
22 Jl 8 '50

Same abridged with title Hollywood safari. Read
Digest 57:45 O '50
Perils of Deborah in savage Africa. Life 29:149 N 13 '50
I love being a mother; ed by J. Morris. Parents Mag
26:34 N '51
Granger, S. Love story. Photop 43-2:50 F '53
Breit, H. Deborah Kerr, minus the icicles. N. Y.
Times Mag p14 O 11 '53
Tea and sympathy. Life 35:121 O 19 '53
Whitcomb, J. Dear valentine. Cosmop 136:91 F '54
Stage reclaims its own. Theatre Arts 38:30 Mr '54
What makes a woman desirable; intv. ed by A. Scheinfeld.
Cosmop 136:18 Ap '54
Kerr, D. What Hollywood did to me; as told to P. Mar-
tin. Sat Eve Post 226:17 Je 5 '54
What I know of love; ed by B. L. Goldsmith. Womans
H C 83:18 Jl '56
Harris, R. The lady dared. Photop 50-2:62 Ag '56
Marks, R. W. Woman all women want to be: Deborah
Kerr. Colliers 138:32 D 7 '56
Eisenberg, H. What every woman needs. Photop 52-3:
42 S '57
My favorite Christmas present. McCalls 85:12 D '57
McCalls visits Deborah Kerr. McCalls 85:11 Ja '58
Hubler, R. G. Hollywood's elegant redhead. Coronet
43:142 Ja '58
Bonjour Riviera. Vogue 131:108 F 15 '58
Meltsir, A. Happiness: this is my life. Photop 53-5:
48 My '58
Lewis, J. What does a woman do when, to keep her
children, she must lose her husband? Photop 54-3:
45 S '58
Culver, M. After a year of silence. Photop 56-4:30 O
'59
Kerr, D. Days and nights of the iguana. Esquire 61:128
My '64
Wilkie, J. Deborah Kerr: the lady is a scamp. Good
H 160:87 F '65
Redbook dialogue. Redbook 125:50 My '65

KERR, JOHN
Tryout theatre. Theatre Arts 29:56 Ja '45
Anderson, D. First time on Broadway. Theatre Arts 37:
75 F '53
John Kerr of Tea and sympathy. Vogue 122:90 N 15 '53
Art for money's sake. Newsweek 47:126 My 14 '56
Emmett, R. Detour to destiny. Photop 49-5:56 My '56

Woman doctor goes to sea.   Ind Woman 35:7 Ag '56
Goldsmith, B. L. Fall films and a new star.   Womans
    H C 83:22 O '56
DeRoulf, P. The searching years.   Photop 50-6:54 D '56
Kelly, Q. Actor without dungarees.   Films & Filming
    3-9:9 Je '57
A sensitive young man.   TV Guide 5-27:12 Jl 6 '57

KERRIGAN, J. WARREN
    Thien, M. A chat with the man on the cover. .Feature
        Movie 2-6:7 Je 25 '15
    Henry, W. M. The great god Kerrigan.   Photop 9-3:32
        F '16
    Shaffer, R. Hollywood's only contented man.   Photop
        39-2:48 Ja '31
    Obit. Time 49:77 Je 23 '47

KERRY, MARGARET
    Chierichetti, D. Margaret Kerry.   Film Fan Mo 96:7
        Je '69

KERRY, NORMAN
    Obit. Newsweek 47:71 Ja 23 '56
        Time 67:91 Ja 23 '56
        Screen World 8:223 '57

KEY, KATHLEEN
    Obit. Screen World 6:224 '55

KEYES, EVELYN
    Holliday, K. Atlanta belle.   Colliers 109:22 Ja 3 '42
    Skolsky, S. My romance with Evelyn Keyes.   Photop
        31-2:50 Jl '47
    What's my type?   Am Mag 144:109 N '47
    Howe, H. Beauty in bedlam.   Photop 33-2:60 Jl '48

KIBBEE, GUY
    Crichton, K. Out of character.   Colliers 95:30 Mr 23
        '35
    Obit. Newsweek 47:67 Je 4 '56
        Time 67:104 Je 4 '56
        Screen World 8:223 '57
        Brit Bk Yr 1957:576 '57

KILBRIDE, PERCY
    Wilson, L. & McClure, D. Ma and Pa Kettle--Holly-
        wood gold mine.   Colliers 128:22 D 8 '51

Wilson, N. Y.   The Kettles.   Films In Review 5-10:524
    D '54
Obit.   Time 84:81 D 18 '64
    Newsweek 64:57 D 21 '56
    Screen World 16:223 '65

KILBURN, TERRY
    Poetic justice.   Theatre Arts 38:15 Ja '54

KING, ANDREA
    Navy wife.   Am Mag 140:122 Ag '45

KING, ANITA
    Kingsley, G.   All-around Anita.   Photop 10-3:143 Ag '16
    Obit.   Screen World 15:220 '64

KING, BRADLEY
    Winship, M.   No, Bradley King is not "Mr."   Photop 26-
    2:63 Jl '24

KING, MOLLIE
    Eyck, J. T.   Mollie of Manhattan.   Photop 12-5 O '17

KINGSTON, WINIFRED
    Davis, L.   The girl on the cover talks.   Photop 7-2:35
    Ja '15
    Corliss, A.   Dustin's sweetheart.   Photop 10-1:40 Je '16
    Obit.   Screen World 19:235 '68

KIRK, LISA
    Lisa Kirk, TV guest star.   TV Guide 3-15:8 Ap 15 '50
    Her name could be nostalgia.   TV Guide 8-16:8 Ap 16 '60

KIRK, PHYLLIS
    Who wouldn't help Phyllis?   Am Mag 151:61 Ja '51
    Studious starlet.   Life 30:67 My 7 '51
    Flapper of the '50's.   TV Guide 5-16:21 Ap 20 '57
    The return of 'The thin man.'   TV Guide 5-43 O 26 '57
    Phyllis gets the last word--natch.   TV Guide 6-22:8 My
    31 '58
    McClelland, D.   Letter inc. filmog.   Films In Review
    15-1:62 Ja '64

KLEMPERER, WERNER
    Whitney, D.   His podium is a prison camp.   TV Guide
    14-4:22 Ja 22 '66
    Mays, C.   I've had three religions.   Photop 73-5:75 My '68

KLUGMAN, JACK
  Dunne, J. G. The complete schnook. TV Guide 12-52:
    15 D 26 '64

KNIGHT, SHIRLEY
  A Knight to remember. TV Guide 8-9:24 F 27 '60

KNOTTS, DON
  Gehman, R. A mouse of a different color. TV Guide
    10-19:18 My 12 '62
  Hobson, D. The wages of fear. TV Guide 15-42:14 O
    21 '67
  Davidson, M. The ultimate square makes the scene.
    TV Guide 17-47:18 N 22 '69

KNOX, ALEXANDER
  Hilton, J. A rather remarkable man. Photop 26-3:42
    F '45
  Knox, A. Acting and behaving. Hollywood Q 1-3:260
    Ap '46
  Knox, A. Performance under pressure. Hollywood Q
    3-2:159 Win '47
  Closing door; drama; with note. Theatre Arts 34:62 My
    '50

KNUDSON, PEGGY
  Beautiful baritone. TV Guide 3-21:12 My 21 '55

KOHNER, SUSAN
  She pays papa 10 percent. TV Guide 5-39:16 S 28 '57
  Borie, M. Can you keep my secret? Photop 57-5:56
    My '60
  Susan Kohner lives here. Seventeen 20:112 My '61
  Corbin, J. Is there a happy ending for Susan? Photop
    59-6:30 Je '61
  Kohner, S. In who's who of the critics. Films & Film-
    ing 8-8:15 My '62
  Wall, T. The night George danced with Lolita. Photop
    62-4:57 O '62
  Krantz, J. High cost of making the scene. Ladies Home
    J 84:106 S '67

KOLB, CLARENCE
  Obit. Screen World 16:223 '65

KORVIN, CHARLES
  Dennison, F. Czech double check. Photop 28-3:50 F '46

KOSLECK, MARTIN
Hollywood /misogynist.   Time 26:23 Jl 15 '35
His fans hate him.   Am Mag 135:120 Ap '43
Greenberg, J.   Martin Kosleck, inc. filmog.   Films In
   Review 18-9:586 N '67

KOVACS, ERNIE
Uncle Ernie Kovacs.   Newsweek 41:70 Ja 12 '53
The man with the hole in his head.   TV Guide 1-8:20
   My 22 '53
At the ballet.   Dance Mag 29:22 Ap '55
Krazy Kovacs.   Look 20:20 D 11 '56
Wood, C.   TV personalities biographical sketchbook.
   TV Personalities p153 '56
Utility expert.   Time 69:66 Ja 28 '57
Electronic comic and his TV tricks.   Life 42:167 Ap 15
   '57
This is no gag.   Newsweek 49:56 Je 3 '57
Martin, P.   I call on Edie Adams and Ernie Kovacs.
   Sat Eve Post 230:16 D 28 '57
Biography.   Cur Bio 19:22 F '58
   Same.   Cur Bio Yrbk 1958:234 '58
Morton, F.   Ernie Kovacs: the last spontaneous man.
   Holiday 24:87 O '58
10-5/8 years ahead of his time.   TV Guide 9-35:8 S 2
   '61
King Leer.   Newsweek 58:64 S 18 '61
Schickel, R.   The real Ernie Kovacs is standing up.
   Show 1-3:80 D '61
Obit.   Time 79:82 Ja 19 '62
   Illus Lond N 240:110 Ja 20 '62
   Newsweek 59:60 Ja 22 '62
   Pub W 181:197 Ja 22 '62
   Cur Bio 23:22 Mr '62
   Cur Bio Yrbk 1962:244 '63
   Am Ann 1963:761 '63
   Brit Bk Yr 1963:872 '63
   Screen World 14:222 '63
Lardner, R.   Ernie Kovacs.   Sat R 45:6 F 10 '62
Cocchi, J.   Ernie Kovacs, inc. filmog.   Films In Re-
   view 13-2:120 F '62
Camber, G.   Ernie, farewell.   Photop 61-4:50 Ap '62
Ernie Kovacs.   Film 32:6 Sum '62
Torre, M.   How I survived.   Redbook 119:46 S '62
Lewis, R. W.   Year in the life of Edie Adams.   Sat
   Eve Post 236:24 Ap 13 '63

KRAUSS, WERNER
    Obit. Screen World 11:220 '60

KREUGER, KURT
    Walker, H. L. Sensational Swiss. Photop 28-4:40 Mr
    '46

KRUGER, OTTO
    Campbell, K. When the enterprising burglar's not a-
    burgling. Am Home 35:18 Ja '46
    Ten things that make my heart beat faster. Good H
    143:150 S '56
    Wood, C. TV personalities biographical sketchbook.
    TV Personalities p138 '57

KWAN, NANCY
    Take tea and see. Time 75:78 Ap 11 '60
    Whitcomb, J. New Suzie Wong. Cosmop 148:10 Je '60
    Enter Suzie Wong. Life 49:55 O 24 '60
    Bad girls, good heroines. Look 24:84 D 6 '60
    Divas, G. The other world of Suzie Wong. Photop 59-
    4:60 Ap '61
    Joel, L. Three points of view. Dance Mag 35:40 N '61
    Martin, P. Backstage with Nancy Kwan. Sat Eve Post
    235:40 F 10 '62
    Davidson, B. Chinese doll. McCalls 89:86 F '62

KYO, MACHIKO
    Trumbull, R. Rising star of Japan. N. Y. Times Mag
    p25 Ap 24 '55
    Beauty from Osaka. Newsweek 46:116 O 10 '55
    People are talking about. Vogue 126:115 D '55
    Lerman, L. Prettiest girl in town. Mlle 43:76 Je '56
    Eastern star looks west. Life 41:143 D 3 '56
    Rothwell, J. Rashomon girl tries western comedy.
    Films & Filming 3-6:6 Mr '57

LA BADIE, FLORENCE
    Condon, M.   The girl on the cover.   Photop 6-3:53 Ag
        '14
    Bacon, G. V.   An impromptu interview.   Photop 11-1:
        124 D '16

LADD, ALAN
    Franchey, J. R.   This Ladd for hire.   Photop 21-4:36 S
        '42
    Ladd, S.   I married a "killer."   Photop 22-1:45 D '42
    St. Johns, A. R.   What you don't know about Alan Ladd's
        marriage.   Photop 23-2:28 Jl '43
    Ladd, A.   A soldier's code for women.   Photop 23-5:34
        O '43
    Biography.   Cur Bio '43
    Muir, F.   Alan Ladd comes home.   Photop 24-3:26 F '44
    Proctor, K.   Play truth or consequences with Alan Ladd.
        Photop 25-3:36 Ag '44
    Harris, E.   If you were Alan Ladd's house guest.   Photop
        25-6:50 N '44
    Quinn, M.   About face--Alan Ladd.   Photop 26-3:47 F '45
    Watch out for the wounded.   Am Mag 139:60 Je '45
    Perkins, L.   Photolife of Alan Ladd.   Photop 27-2:52 Jl
        '45
    Janis, E.   The song and gun man.   Photop 28-2:38 Ja '46
    Cary, R.   The mad Ladds.   Photop 28-5:37 Ap '46
    Sharpe, H.   Ladd adds up.   Photop 29-4:41 S '46
    Deere, D.   High dive.   Photop 30-3:46 F '47
    Roberts, W.   The littlest Ladd.   Photop 31-3:50 Ag '47
    Edwards, R.   Play truth or consequences with Alan Ladd.
        Photop 32-4:58 Mr '48
    Waterbury, R.   Boss man.   Photop 33-2:62 Jl '48
    Ladd, A.   The woman I love.   Photop 33-4:52 S '48
    Hutton, B.   I call him the Katzenjammer Kid.   Photop
        36-6:42 N '49
    Swanson, P.   These precious things.   Photop 37-4:54 Ap
        '50
    Dreier, H.   Their place in the sun.   Photop 38-1:60 Jl
        '50
    Swanson, P.   Last laugh.   Photop 38-3:50 S '50
    Zeitlin, I.   Nine years with love.   Photop 40-1:56 Jl '51
    DeRoos, R.   Hollywood's favorite Ladd.   Colliers 130:28
        S 20 '52
    Hubler, R. G.   Hollywood's unlikely hero.   Sat Eve Post

229:24 F 9 '57

Arnold, M.   The reluctant traveler.   Photop 51-6:56 Je
'57

Ardmore, J. K.   Two Ladds and a dog.   Parents Mag
33:52 Ag '58

Ladd, A.   The things I really wanted to tell my son.
Photop 56-6:54 D '59

Liston, J.   At home with Alan Ladd.   Am Home 63:12
O '60

Obit.   Illus Lond N 244:207 F 8 '64
Time 83:98 F 7 '64
Newsweek 63:57 F 10 '64
Cur Bio 25:23 Mr '64
Cur Bio Yrbk 1964:241 '64

Alan Ladd: a remembrance.   Photop 65-4:28 Ap '64

Roman, R. C.   Alan Ladd, inc. filmog.   Films In Review 15-4:199 Ap '64

LADD, DAVID
Roberts, W.   The littlest Ladd.   Photop 31-3:50 Ag '47
Grayson, J.   Our little ham.   Photop 54-1:68 Jl '58
Ardmore, J. K.   Two Ladds and a dog.   Parents Mag
33:52 Ag '58

LAHR, BERT
Kennedy, J. B.   Eyes left.   Colliers 86:13 D 27 '30
Farewell to the clowns.   Life 22:75 My 19 '47
First break.   Theatre Arts 32:42 O '48
Windsor knot.   Colliers 123:38 My 5 '49
$6.60 comedian.   Time 58:46 O 1 '51
Biography.   Cur Bio 13:23 Ja '52
Same.   Cur Bio Yrbk 1952:324 '53
Zolotow, M.   Broadway's saddest clown.   Sat Eve Post
224:34 My 31 '52
Hamburger, P.   Television.   New Yorker 29:80 Ja 9 '54
Lahr in the middle riddle.   Life 40:155 My 7 '56
Bert Lahr, what every candidate should know.   Colliers
138:24 Ag 31 '56
Millstein, G.   Comic discourses on comedy.   N. Y.
Times Mag p27 Mr 31 '57
People are talking about . . .   Vogue 129:84 Ap 15 '57
Bert Lahr and the wit business.   Newsweek 49:69 Ap 22
'57
Bedroom bedlam with Bert Lahr.   Life 42:122 My 13 '57
Up, up from the gung, gung.   Life 42:127 My 13 '57
Morton, F.   Bert Lahr: clown.   Holiday 23:123 Mr '58
Eleven fine actors get their dream roles.   Life 44:76

Ap 14 '58

Talk with a star. Newsweek 54:108 N 16 '59

Whose voice? Lestoil vs. Bert Lahr. Newsweek 59:88
Je 11 '62

Funny man. New Yorker 38:25 Ja 26 '63

Perelman, S. J. LAHRge world. Theatre Arts 47:20
F '63

Ungaluk, mukaluk. Newsweet 63:56 Mr 2 '64

Kerr, W. Love letters of a tough critic. Life 56:113
Je 19 '64

Anderson, J. Bert Lahr and the beauties. Dance Mag
38:24 S '64

Pisthetairosin Ypsi. Newsweek 68:85 Jl 11 '68

Ciardi, J. Manner of speaking; on purifying the antiqui-
ties in Ypsilanti. Sat R 49:22 Ag 13 '66

Notes and comments. New Yorker 43:37 D 16 '67

Obit. Time 90:104 D 15 '67
Newsweek 70:70 D 18 '67
Brit Bk Yr 1968:593 '68
Cur Bio 29:46 F '68
Cur Bio Yrbk 1968:457 '69
Screen World 19:235 '68

LAKE, ALICE
Peltret, E. It's a hard life! Photop 15-1:39 D '18
Obit. Screen World 19:235 '68

LAKE, ARTHUR
Wood, C. TV personalities biographical sketchbook.
TV Personalities p29 '57

LAKE, VERONICA
Paramount's bid for year's best glamor starlet. Life 10:
82 Mr 3 '41
Cadet flyers show their wings to defense film star.
Life 10:53 Ap 14 '41
Lake, V. I almost gave up. Photop 19-3:46 Ag '41
Ormiston, R. Little Miss Dynamite. Photop 21-3:36
Ag; 21-4:52 S '42
Lake, V. Are you a woman without a man? Photop 22-
2:40 Ja '43
Busch, N. I, Veronica Lake. Life 14:76 My 17 '43
Skolsky, S. Short for Ronni. Photop 22-6:40 My '43
Hopper, H. Veronica Lake's marriage breakup. Photop
23-4:40 S '43
Waterbury, R. What's wrong with Veronica Lake?
Photop 25-5:34 O '44

Lake, V.   You wouldn't know me.   Photop 27-5:56 O '45
Veronica Lake.   Life 22:99 Ap 7 '47
deToth, A.   Marriage is such fun.   Photop 33-3:58 Ap '48
Harmon, B.   Letter, inc. film listing.   Films In Review
    20-7:453 Ag/S '69

LA MARR, BARBARA
St. Johns, A. R.   The girl who was too beautiful.
    Photop 22-1:20 Je '22
LaMarr, B.   Why I adopted a baby.   Photop 23-6:30 My
    '23
LaMarr, B.   My screen lovers.   Photop 24-6:63 N '23
Doughtery, J.   Why I quit being Mr. Barbara LaMarr.
    Photop 26-5:28 O '24
York, C.   Can Barbara come back?   Photop 29-2:28 Ja
    '26
St. Johns, A. R.   Hail and farewell.   Photop 29-5:41 Ap
    '26
Collins, F. L.   Four women who suffered.   Good H 95:
    40 Jl '32
Uselton, R. A.   Barbara LaMarr, inc. filmog.   Films
    In Review 15-6:352 Je/Jl '64

LAMARR, HEDY
Ecstasy to Algiers.   Newsweek 12:27 Jl 11 '38
Hamilton, S.   Hedy wine.   Photop 52-10:23 O '38
Crichton, K.   Escape to Hollywood.   Colliers 102:14 N
    5 '38
Liepmann, H.   Vienna farewell.   Photop 53-4:17 Ap '39
Hayes, B.   Hedy Lamarr vs. Joan Bennett.   Photop 53-
    11:18 N '39
Parsons, L. O.   My fight for Jimmy.   Photop 54-10:19
    O '40
Asher, J.   When G-Girls get together.   Photop 20-3:36
    F '42
Hedy.   Am Mag 133:86 Mr '42
Hedy Lamarr helps to preserve the glow of Stenbeck's
    novel.   Life 12:39 Je 1 '42
West, R.   Right about love.   Photop 21-1:30 Je '42
Proctor, K.   Play truth or consequences with Hedy La-
    marr.   Photop 21-6:45 N '42
Bentley, J.   Hedy over heels in love.   Photop 22-5:30
    Ap '43
Martin, P.   I go shopping with Hedy Lamarr.   Sat Eve
    Post 216:19 F 5 '44
Skolsky, S.   Handbook on Hedy Lamarr.   Photop 24-6:
    36 My '44

Lamarr, H. I, Hedy. Photop 26-4:54 Mr '45
Parsons, L. O. The strange case of Hedy Lamarr.
   Photop 31-4:36 S '47
Graham, S. Can this be love? Photop 32-1:46 D '47
Biographical note. Newsweek 34:71 N 28 '49
Life goes on a Southampton weekend. Life 29:156 S 25 '50
Martin, P. Hedy sells her past. Sat Eve Post 224:32
   S 29 '51
Court denies injunction against Hedy Lamarr book.
   Pub W 190:52 O 10 '66
King, L. L. Poème d'extase. New Repub 155:34 N 26 '66
Ringgold, G. Hedy Lamarr, inc. filmog. Screen Facts
   11:entire issue. n. d.

LAMAS, FERNANDO
Roberts, W. Her heart is showing again. Photop 41-3:58
   Mr '52
Ford, E. The true Turner-Lamas story. Photop 42-4:
   70 O '52
Swanson, P. From Lana to Arleen. Photop 43-5:34 My
   '53
Kingsley, K. Two's company. Photop 44-1:48 Jl '53
At home in the U. S. A. Americas 5:20 O '53
Graham, S. Fernando Lamas--hero or heel? Photop
   45-2:38 F '54
Lamas, F. Who wears the pants? Photop 46-6:42 D '54
People are talking about . . . Vogue 129:136 Ap 1 '57

LAMOUR, DOROTHY
Pringle, H. F. La Belle Lamour. Colliers 100:22 S 25
   '37
Lamour, D. How I saved my marriage. Photop 52-9:
   20 S '38
Bennett, H. Distance ends enchantment. Photop 53-7:
   32 Jl '39
Proctor, K. New kind of love for Lamour. Photop 19-1:
   31 Je '41
Fletcher, A. W. It looks like love. Photop 22-6:25 My
   '43
Hope, B. My favorite sarong. Photop 23-5:46 O '43
Roberts, W. Life with the major's lady. Photop 27-4:
   47 S '45
Biography. Cur Bio '46

LAMPERT, ZOHRA
Mee, C. L. Jr. On stage: Zohra Lampert. Horizon
   4:48 Jl '62

Prideaux, T.   Mute on stage, a beaut at home.   Life
   54:A16 Ap 12 '63
On again and off again Broadway.   Look 27:110a My 21 '63
Higgins, R.   TV gives you plenty of time to get nerves.
   TV Guide 15-33:21 Ag 19 '67

LANCASTER, BURT
   Hellinger, M.   The Swede.   Photop 30-4:48 Mr '47
   Deere, D.   Big guy.   Photop 32-2:42 Ja '48
   Martin, P.   Hollywood hard guy.   Sat Eve Post 221:38 S
      11 '48
   Edwards, R.   Play truth or consequences with Burt Lan-
      caster.   Photop 33-5:50 O '48
   Lancaster, J.   I'll bet on Burt.   Photop 43-1:52 Ja '53
   Biography.   Cur Bio 14:36 Jl '53
      Same.   Cur Bio Yrbk 1953:337 '53
   Jamison, B. B.   From here to maturity.   N. Y. Times
      Mag p20 Ag 23 '53
   Itria, H.   Story of a hard man.   Look 17:92 O 20 '53
   Stronger sex makes strong box office.   Life 36:93 My 31
      '54
   Harvey, E.   Coop gets girl, Burt gets bullet.   Colliers
      134:72 Ag 6 '54
   Waterbury, R.   Soft-hearted menace.   Photop 46-2:38 Ag
      '54
   Morgan, J.   Hecht-Lancaster Productions.   Sight & Sound
      25-1:38 Sum '55
   Shipp, C.   Burt Lancaster.   Cosmop 139:28 Ag '55
   Waterbury, R.   Don't run from yourself.   Photop 49-1:
      45 Ja '56
   Five little Lancasters.   McCalls 83:10 Ap '56
   Muscle man.   Coronet 40:8 Jl '56
   Top branch.   Time 68:74 S 3 '56
   Dance: what it means to me.   Dance Mag 31:26 Je '57
   Please tell us, Mr. Lancaster.   Photop 52-6:30 D '57
   Whitcomb, J.   Redcoats are coming again.   Cosmop 146:
      19 F '59
   Martin, P.   I call on Burt Lancaster.   Sat Eve Post 234:
      32 Je 24 '61
   Lancaster, B.   Hollywood drove me to a double life.
      Films & Filming 8-4:10 Ja '62
   Saga of a strange jailbird.   Life 53:39 Ag 24 '62
   Biography.   Am Ann 1962:423 '62
   Alexander, S.   Will the real Burt Lancaster please stand
      up?   Life 55:80 S 6 '63
   Schuster, M.   Burt Lancaster, inc. filmog.   Films In
      Review 20-7:393 Ag/S '69

LANCHESTER, ELSA
Charles Laughton and I.   Atlan 161:157 F; 332 Mr; 532
Ap '38
Edgerton, G.   How the Charles Laughtons live in Blooms-
bury.   Arts & Dec 48:6 S '38
Roberts, K.   Great man's wife.   Colliers 103:19 Mr 4 '39
Elsa's gazebo.   Time 51:78 My 24 '48
Life visits the Laughtons.   Life 26:109 Ja 24 '49
Coronets to Charles Laughton and Elsa Lanchester.
Coronet 26:10 S '49
Biography.   Cur Bio My '50
Same.   Cur Bio Yrbk 1950:316 '51
New pitch in the Persian room.   Time 56:65 N 6 '50
Swisher, V. H.   Isadora Duncan had nothing to pass on
to the future; says a defiant pupil named Elsa Lan-
chester.   Dance Mag 40:52 S '66

LANDAU, MARTIN
Conversations with the Landaus.   TV Guide 16-18:29 My
4 '68
Hanley, P.   His gamble with his life and wife.   Photop
73-5:69 My '68
Ephron, N.   Marriage: impossible?   Good H 167:60 N '68

LANDI, ELISSA
Granddaughter of an empress.   Photop 40-4:28 S '31
They stand out from the crowd.   Lit Digest 118:10 Ag 11
'34
Royce, J.   Does music help the actor?   Etude 63:504 S
'45
Obit.   Newsweek 32:57 N 1 '48
Time 52-88 N 1 '48
Pub W 154:2286 D 4 '48
Wilson Lib Bul 23:282 D '48

LANDIS, CAROLE
Carole Landis does not want to be a ping girl.   Life 8:
94 Je 17 '40
Ping.   Am Mag 131:82 Ja '41
Crichton, K.   Determined lady.   Colliers 107:12 My 10
'41
Dudley, F.   How to be happy while drafted.   Photop 20-
6:36 My '42
Man upstairs.   Am Mag 134:52 O '42
Ping girl weds Eagle.   Life 14:32 F 1 '43
Pyle, E.   Four good soldiers.   Sr Schol 42:2 Mr 29 '43
Landis, C.   My wartime honeymoon.   Photop 23-1:22

Je '43

I want to go back.   Womans H C 70:10 Jl '43

Four jills in a jeep.   Sat Eve Post 216:14 D 18; 24 D
   25 '43; 24 Ja 1; 24 Ja 8; 26 Ja 15 '44

Baskette, K.   War wife, Hollywood style.   Am Mag 137:
   26 Mr '44

NG, baby?   Newsweek 24:57 O 16 '44

Landis, C.   Don't marry a stranger.   Photop 26-2:36 Ja
   '45

Obit.   Newsweek 32:60 Jl 12 '48

Casualty in Hollywood.   Time 52:26 Jl 19 '48

Ross, D.   The true story of my sister.   Photop 33-6:32
   N '48

Reichenthal, C.   Carole Landis.   Films In Review 16-5:
   323 My '65

Zucker, P.   Filmography.   Films In Review 16-6:397
   Je/Jl '65

LANDIS, CULLEN
   Winship, M.   The curly kid.   Photop 19-5:60 Ap '21

LANDON, MICHAEL
   Ardmore, J.   Adorable?   That's the story of my life.
      Photop 59-2:56 F '61
   Sands, A.   I cried when my son was born.   Photop 66-4:
      63 O '64
   Tusher, B.   Mixed marriage made me a man.   Photop
      67-4:54 Ap '65
   Lewis, R. W.   Bonanza.   Sat Eve Post 238:84 D 4 '65
   Ardmore, J.   My kids' problem--me.   Photop 69-5:41
      My '66
   Resnick, S.   They lose a baby.   Photop 76-1:4 Jl '69

LANE, ADELE
   Willis, R.   Adele Lane, pretty and proud and petite.
      Photop 6-3:67 Ag '14

LANE, ALLAN
   Cocchi, J.   The films of Allan Lane, a checklist.
      Screen Facts 19:50 n. d.

LANE, CHARLES
   Once a grouch, always a grouch.   TV Guide 13-12:12 Mr
      20 '65

LANE, JACKIE
   Person of promise.   Films & Filming 3-12:19 S '57

LANE, LOLA
Cranford, R. That Mulligan spirit. Photop 38-2:70 Jl
'30
Crichton, K. Young and lively. Colliers 101:36 F 12 '38

LANE, PRISCILLA
Crichton, K. Young and lively. Colliers 101:36 F 12 '38
Sobol, L. Golden girl. Photop 52-12:22 D '38
Hoping you are the same. Photop 53-8:60 Ag '39
Palmborg, R. P. No secret marriage this time. Photop
19-6:28 N '41
Priscilla Lane--in person. TV Guide 6-47:16 N 22 '58

LANE, ROSEMARY
Crichton, K. Young and lively. Colliers 101:36 F 12 '38

LANGDON, HARRY
North, J. It's no joke to be funny. Photop 28-1:86 Je
'25
Albert, K. What happened to Harry Langdon. Photop
41-3:40 F '32
Agee, J. Baby. Life 27:80 S 5 '49

LANGE, HOPE
Right place at the right time. TV Guide 6-23:20 Je 7 '58
Christian, F. Young family in Hollywood. Cosmop 145:
57 S '58
Smith, K. We used to call Hope hopeless. Photop 54-
5:38 N '58
Gehman, R. Movieland marriage with a mission.
Coronet 46:38 My '59
Ardmore, J. K. New billing: the four Murrays.
Parents Mag 34:50 Je '59
Rowland, T. When's the marriage? Photop 59-5:56 My
'61
DeRoos, R. Sometimes she'll have a cigar. TV Guide
16-43:24 O 26 '68

LANGFORD, FRANCES
I saw him fighting for you. Am Mag 137:17 Ja '44
G. I. nightingale. Time 43:88 F 28 '44
Langford, F. What I notice about men. TV Guide 5-6:4
F 8 '52
Frances Langford presents. TV Guide 7-11:6 Mr 14 '59

LANSBURY, ANGELA
Arvad, I. English with blonde accent. Photop 28-5:56

Ap '46

Bundle from Britain. Am Mag 142:123 Ag '46

On the move. TV Guide 2-30:12 Jl 24 '54

At home with Angela Lansbury. Theatre 3-2:24 F '61

Garvin, R. Angela Lansbury, inc. filmog. Films In
Review 14-2:123 F '63

No shame for Mame. Newsweek 67:89 Je 6 '66

Hallowell, J. Smashing new dame to play Mame. Life
60:88 Je 17 '66

Hallowell, J. How the angels smile on Angela. Life
60:92B Je 17 '66

Biography. Cur Bio 28:21 S '67

Same. Cur Bio Yrbk 1967:237 '68

Burrows, R. To star in the fashionable dream. After
Dark 11-1:42 My '69

LANSING, JOI

Good luck girl. TV Guide 5-27:24 Jl 6 '57

LANSING, ROBERT

Lewis, J. D. The general died at dusk. TV Guide 13-
20:24 My 15 '65

LANZA, MARIO

Whitney, D. Celluloid Caruso? Colliers 124:46 S 3 '49

Hollywood musical presents much publicized young tenor.
Mus Am 69:24 O '49

Cooke, J. F. I learned to sing by accident. Etude 67:
9 D '49

Cooke, J. F. My first big opportunity. Etude 68:17 Ja
'50

Lucy Lanza. Newsweek 37:84 Mr 5 '51

New idol. Time 57:92 Mr 19 '51

Million-dollar voice. Time 58:60 Ag 6 '51

Steele, J. Encore! Photop 40-2:62 Ag '51

Zeitlin, I. The Mario Lanza story. Photop 40-3:36 S '51

Hopper, H. Is Mario Lanza Hollywood's biggest headache? Photop 41-1:30 Ja '52

Zeitlin, I. In the name of love. Photop 41-3:39 Mr '52

Hopper, H. The truth about the Kathryn Grayson-Mario
Lanza feud. Photop 40-4:40 Ap '52

Lanza, M. I wouldn't be single again. Photop 42-3:46
S '52

Armstrong, G. The truth behind the Mario Lanza blow-
up. Photop 42-6:42 D '52

Hopper, H. Mario Lanza answers back. Photop 44-3:
48 S '53

Comeback for Lanza. Time 64:80 O 11 '54
New Lanza. Newsweek 47:116 Ap 9 '56
Brown, R. W. Tenor will out. Sat R 39:34 S 29 '56
Obit. Illus Lond N 235:453 O 17 '59
   Newsweek 54:84 O 19 '59
   Time 74:104 O 19 '59
   Mus Am 79:33 N 1 '59
   Am Ann 1960:855 '60
   Brit Bk Yr 1960:511 '60
   Screen World 11:220 '60
Lyle, J. The man who destroyed himself. Photop 57-1:
   30 Ja '60
Kolodin, I. On first hearing Lanza in recital. Sat R
   44:47 Ap 15 '61
Curreri, J. Great Mario. Opera News 26:32 Ap 21 '62
Cocozza, M. L. Mario Lanza lives! Photop 62-6:21 D
   '62

LA ROCQUE, ROD
Smith, A. The bloom of the oats. Photop 16-6:63 N '19
Lieber, E. Vilma and Rod. Photop 42-2:34 Jl '32

LA ROY, RITA
Albert, A. The tragic story of a beauty. Photop 38-6:
   39 N '30

LA RUE, JACK
Biery, R. I'm right, you're wrong. Photop 43-6:45 My
   '33
Biery, R. & Packer, E. Jack LaRue's big secret.
   Photop 44-3:28 Ag '33
Maxwell, V. Is the jinx of "trigger" still on? Photop
   44-6:72 N '33
LaRue, J. as told to Frank Stein. Additional light on
   "lights out." TV Guide 3-1:8 Ja 7 '50
Where are they now? Newsweek 64:18 D 14 '64

LAUGHTON, CHARLES
Shackleton, E. English stage album. Theatre Arts 15:
   769 S '31
Barry, B. Such a naughty Nero. Photop 43-3:47 F '33
Bahn, C. B. Jannings-Laughton duel? Cinema Digest
   3-5:9 Ap 7 '39
Rankin, R. A son of freedom. Photop 46-5:50 O '34
Reynolds, Q. Meet an actor. Colliers 95:9 F 2 '35
Johnston, A. Charles Laughton, a versatile performer.
   Womans H C 62:11 Mr '35

Van Doren, M. When acting counts. Nation 141:658 D
    4 '35
McAllister, A. The secret behind Laughton's acting.
    Photop 49-2:36 F '36
Lejeune, C. A. Laughton on the lot. Liv Age 351:232 N
    '36
Ferguson, O. Laughton of the movies. New Repub 89:
    218 D 16 '36
Lanchester, E. Charles Laughton and I. Atlan 161:157
    F; 332 Mr; 532 Ap '38
Edgerton, G. How the Charles Laughtons live in Blooms-
    bury. Arts & Dec 48:6 S '38
Call me up; selling war bonds. Newsweek 20:92 O 12 '42
One-man sales force. Time 40:64 O 12 '42
Charles Laughton in the movie Captain Kidd. Life 19:62
    N 5 '45
Muir, F. Actor discovers the Bible. Sat Eve Post N
    24 '45
Experimental payoff. Newsweek 30:60 D 29 '47
Biography. Cur Bio N '48
    Same. Cur Bio Yrbk 1948:368 '49
Life visits the Laughtons. Life 26:109 Ja 24 '49
Poylack, T. Taught by the ancients. Art Digest 23:10
    F 15 '49
Miller, A. Laughton, art lover. Art Digest 23:9 F 15
    '49
Halferty, G. Actor finds work. C S Mon Mag p6 Jl 23
    '49
Coronets to Charles Laughton and Elsa Lanchester.
    Coronet 26:10 S '49
Do you read the Bible? Am Mag 148:117 N '49
Storytelling. Atlan 185:71 Je '50
Spotlight on the Bible. Coronet 28:8 Ag '50
Gordon, R. Legitimate Laughton: Charles Laughton
    players company. Theatre Arts 34:30 N '50
Read aloud, it's fun. Read Digest 58:19 Ja '51
Four Hollywood veterans go to hell on Broadway.
    Life 31:46 N 5 '51
Charles Laughton inspires local reading clubs. Pub W
    161:139 Ja 12 '52
How Mr. Laughton became the devil. N. Y. Times Mag
    p21 Mr 23 '52
Happy ham. Time 59:62 Mr 31 '52
Four-star chat. New Yorker 28:26 Ap 19 '52
Only fabulous country. Life 33:66 Jl 7 '52
Johnson, G. When Laughton reads the Bible. Coronet
    32:92 Ag '52

Harvey, E.   John Brown's body hits the road.   Colliers
  130:24 D 6 '52
For TV listeners.   Time 61:68 Ja 12 '53
Laughton's lectern.   Newsweek 41:70 Ja 12 '53
Four from Hollywood.   TV Guide 6-4:10 Ja 23 '53
Brown, J. M.   Marching on; Laughton production of John
  Brown's body.   Sat R 36:34 Mr 14 '53
How to enjoy your food.   Look 17:109 O 6 '53
What I live for.   Good H 140:16 F '55
Personality of the month.   Plays & Players 5-10:3 Jl '58
Mehling, H.   Living legends.   Todays Health 37:4 Je '59
Storm inside.   Time 74:53 Ag 31 '59
Personality of the month.   Films & Filming 5-12:5 S '59
Charles Laughton Christmas reader.   Good H 151:49 D '60
Obit.   Newsweek 60:56 D 31 '62
   Illus Lond N 241:1064 D 29 '62
   Am Ann 1963:386 '63
   Brit Bk Yr 1963:872 '63
   Cur Bio 24:19 Ja '63
   Cur Bio Yrbk 1963:235 '64
   Screen World 14:222 '63
McVay, D.   Intolerant giant.   Films & Filming 9-6:20
   Mr '63
Vermilye, J.   Charles Laughton, inc. filmog.   Films In
   Review 14-5:257 My '63
Charles Laughton.   Film 35:22 Spg '63
Plagemann, B.   My most unforgettable character.   Read
   Digest 91:127 D '67

LAUREL, STAN
   Where are they now?   Newsweek 50:18 Jl 15 '57
   Verb, B.   Laurel without Hardy.   Films In Review 10-2:
     153 F '59
   Obit.   Time 85:77 Mr 5 '65
     Illus Lond N 246:25 Mr 6 '65
     Newsweek 65:63 Mr 8 '65
     Screen World 17:238 '66
   (See also: LAUREL AND HARDY)

LAUREL & HARDY
   (Stan Laurel, Oliver Hardy)
   Spensley, D.   Those two goofy guys.   Photop 38-2:72 Jl
     '30
   Hurley, J.   Laurel and Hardy editorialized.   Cinema
     Digest 1-6:8 Jl 25 '32
   Moak, E. R.   Tear-stained laughter.   Photop 44-1:40
     Je '33

Robinson, D.   The lighter people.   Sight & Sound 24-1:
   39 Jl/S '54
No laughing matter.   TV Guide 3-17:14 Ap 23 '55
Durgnat, R.   Mr. Laurel and Mr. Hardy.   Films & Film-
   ing 12-2:14 N '65
Laurel and Hardy cult.   Time 90:74 Jl 14 '67
Everson, W. K.   The crazy world of Laurel and Hardy.
   Take One 1-9:16 n. d.
(See also: HARDY, OLIVER; LAUREL, STAN)

LAURIE, PIPER
Every youngster's dream.   Am Mag 150:62 N '50
Riley, V.   Piper calls the tune.   Photop 42-3:50 S '52
Waterbury, R.   Is love for Laurie?   Photop 43-1:50 Ja
   '53
Hubler, R. G.   Pretty Piper picks up a peck of pretty
   profits.   Colliers 131:56 Je 20 '53
Waterbury, R.   Piper, Photoplay and Rick.   Photop 44-2:
   40 Ag '53
Bailey, C.   She's a natural.   Photop 44-5:44 N '53
Laurie, P.   Don't twist cupid's arm.   Photop 45-6:70
   Je '54
Oppenheimer, P.   The things mom never said.   Photop
   46-4:66 O '54
Laurie, P.   When a guy meets an old-fashioned doll.
   Photop 48-1:32 Jl '55
Holland, J.   The men in her life.   Photop 48-5:63 N '55
Abramson, M.   Starlet who became an actress.   Coronet
   44:130 My '58
A tough customer.   TV Guide 7-26:12 Je 27 '59

LAVI, DALIAH
Lavi, c'est la vie.   Look 26:50 My 8 '62
O'Brien, E.   Daliah Lavi.   Vogue 144:130 N 15 '64
Miller, E.   Lord Jim in a jungle paradise.   Seventeen
   23:220 N '64

LAW, JOHN PHILLIP
Miller, E.   I dig acting!   Seventeen 27:142 Mr '68
Koldys, M.   John Phillip Law, inc. filmog.   Films In
   Review 20-7:449 Ag/S '69

LAWFORD, PETER
Arnold, M.   British-on the beam.   Photop 27-6:36 N '45
Steele, J. H.   Portrait of Peter Lawford.   Photop 28-4:
   39 Mr '46
Ormiston, R.   The P. Q. of Pete.   Photop 29-1:48 Je '46

Perkins, L.   Photolife of Peter Lawford.   Photop 29-3:
   56 Ag '46
Kilgallen, D.   All bores barred.   Photop 30-1:43 D '46
Sammis, F. R.   Life at the Lawfords.   Photop 30-6:33
   My '47
Harris, E.   Two men in Manhattan.   Photop 31-2:54 Jl
   '47
Graham, S.   Accidentally yours.   Photop 31-3:40 Ag '47
Lawford, P.   Hollywood's ten best dates.   Photop 32-5:
   36 Ap '48
Sharpe, H.   That Lawford touch.   Photop 33-4:60 S '48
Edwards, R.   Play truth or consequences with Peter Law-
   ford.   Photop 33-6:48 N '48
Arnold, M.   Bond St. bebop.   Photop 34-5:65 Ap '49
Howe, H.   Ace of hearts.   Photop 36-1:42 Je '49
Waterbury, R.   Wouldn't it be romantic?   Photop 38-2:
   46 Ag '50
Zeitlin, I.   Corrections, please.   Photop 39-4:48 Ap '51
A bachelor named Phoebe.   TV Guide 2-48:5 N 27 '54
Wood, C.   TV personalities biographical sketchbook.
   TV Personalities p132 '54
The return of "The thin man."   TV Guide 5-43:8 O 26 '57
Cohen, M.   What do you give your in-laws when they move
   into a new house?   Photop 59-2:38 F '61
Brother-in-law.   Newsweek 57:98 Mr 6 '61
Markel, H.   Many lives of Peter Lawford.   Good H 154:
   45 F '62
Lawford, P. ed by V. Scott.   White House is still wonder-
   ing what to do with me.   McCalls 90:68 Ja '63
Barred from 117 E 72nd.   Newsweek 63:44 Ap 20 '64

LAWRENCE, BARBARA
Wheeler, L.   A room of her own.   Photop 39-1:50 Ja '51

LAWRENCE, CAROL
Mlle merit awards.   Mlle 46:69 Ja '58
No. 1 student, now no. 1 grad.   Life 49:73 O 17 '60
Triple threat.   Newsweek 57:90 Ap 10 '61
Biography.   Cur Bio 22:10 N '61
   Same.   Cur Bio Yrbk 1961:257 '62
Joel, L.   Vital performing energy.   Dance Mag 35:30 D
   '61
Person of promise.   Films & Filming 8-6:29 Mr '62
Poirier, N.   Lawrence of Illinois.   Sat Eve Post 237:72
   Mr 21 '64
Terry, W.   Dancing on the ladder of success.   Sat R
   51:60 D 7 '68

LAWRENCE, FLORENCE
   "Rosy Flo" Lawrence.   Photop 4-4:53 S '13
   Florence Lawrence--the star who "came back." Photop
      5-2:71 Ja '14
   Lawrence, F. with Monte Katterjohn.   Growing up with
      the movies.   Photop 6-6:28 N; 7-1:91 D '14; 7-2:95 Ja;
      7-3:142 F '15
   St. Johns, A. R.   The return of Florence Lawrence.
      Photop 19-6:32 My '21
   Obit.   Newsweek 13:4 Ja 9 '39

LEARN, BESSIE
   Craig, J.   The 'bantam champ' of leading women.
      Photop 9-2:89 Ja '16

LEBEDEFF, IVAN
   Ogden, E.   The most disliked man in Hollywood.   Photop
      38-4:73 S '30
   Lang, H.   He is the real thing.   Photop 40-6:57 N '31
   Obit.   Wilson Lib Bul 27:684 My '53
      Screen World 5:208 '54

LEDERER, FRANCIS
   Young, S.   Largely Mr. Lederer.   New Repub 73:99 D 7
      '32
   Men fading out of the play.   Lit Digest 114:14 D 24 '32
   Kennedy, J. B.   Matinee idol.   Colliers 91:15 Mr 18 '33
   Pacifist.   Sr Schol 25:26 N 10 '34
   Fox film star turns preview party into peace rally.
      Newsweek 6:17 S 21 '35
   Mullen, S. M.   Personality plus purposefulness; intv.
      Sr Schol 27:26 N 9 '35
   Vose, C.   "Excuse me, but aren't you crazy?" Photop
      50-4:21 O '36

LEDERER, GRETCHEN
   Obit.   Screen World 7:225 '56

LEE, ANNA
   Crichton, K.   Lady makes good.   Colliers 108:14 N 29 '41
   Dudley, F.   The beautiful British.   Photop 22-6:50 My '43
   Preacher's daughter.   Am Mag 135:106 Je '43

LEE, CANADA
   Biography.   Cur Bio D '44
   Obit.   Newsweek 39:75 My 19 '52
      Time 59:96 My 19 '52

Cur Bio 13:26 Je '52
Cur Bio Yrbk 1952:339 '53

LEE, CAROLYN
Hamman, M.   Normal little girl in the movies.
   Good H.   112:11 Je '41
Carolyn Lee, 7, marches into stardom.   Life 11:98 N 17
   '41

LEE, CHRISTOPHER
Nolan, J. E.   Five TV heavies.   Film Fan Mo 92:15 F
   '69

LEE, FRANKIE
Copeland, G.   Good boy, bad boy.   Photop 17-2:63 Ja '20

LEE, GYPSY ROSE
Crichton, K.   Strip to fame.   Colliers 98:13 D 19 '36
Richmond, J.   Gypsy Rose Lee, striptease intellectual.
   Am Mer 52:36 Ja '41
McEvoy, J. P.   More tease than strip.   Read Digest
   39:71 Jl '41
G-string murders.   Life 11:110 O 6 '41
Miss Gypsy Rose Lee, author, weds Broadway actor.
   Life 13:41 S 14 '42
Gypsy Rose Lee, general collector.   Hobbies 47:6 O '42
My burlesque customers.   Am Mer 55:548 N '42
Lauterback, R. E.   Gypsy Rose Lee combines a public
   body with a private mind.   Life 13:92 D 14 '42
Mother and the Knights of Pythias.   New Yorker 19:20
   Ap 10 '43
Just like children leading normal lives; autobiography.
   New Yorker 19:20 Jl 3 '43
Mother and the man named Gordon; autobiography.
   New Yorker 19:26 N 20 '43
How two trees and a tradition grew into a home.   House
   & Gard 84:66 D '43
Biography.   Cur Bio '43
Vanishing stripteaser.   Time 52:42 O 4 '48
Gypsy joins the carny.   Life 26:141 Je 6 '49
Fighting the blacklist, Red channels.   New Repub 123:8
   O 2 '50
Dolbier, M.   Gypsy.   N. Y. Her Trib Bk R p2 Ap 28 '57
Men laugh hardest with women in the audience.   News-
   week 49:114 Ap 29 '57
Stranded in Kansas City.   Harper 214:44 Ap '57
Churchill, A.   Struggles of Gypsy.   Sat R 40:21 My 25 '57

Yarling, B.   Ecdysiast's memoir.   New Repub 136:24
   My 27 '57
Scrapbook views of a smart stripper.   Life 42:103 My 27
   '57
Up the runway to Minsky's.   Harper 214:44 My '57
Pickrel, P.   Ex-newsboy.   Harper 214:79 Je '57
Fuller, J. G.   Trade winds.   Sat R 40:6 Ag 17 '57
Tips by an improbable pro.   Life 46:108 Je 29 '59
Richards, S.   A visit with Gypsy Rose Lee.   Theatre 2-
   1:22 Ja '60
Balliett, W.   Off Broadway.   New Yorker 37:118 My 20
   '61
Cut short.   Time 86:38 Ag 27 '65
Hamilton, J.   Gypsy Rose Lee: dowager stripper.
   Look 30:58 F 22 '66

LEE, JANE
   Obit.   Screen World 9:223 '58

LEE, LILA
   Shorey, J.   Do you believe in fairies?   Photop 14-4:47
      S '18
   Yost, R. M.   Happy endings.   Photop 18-3:33 Ag '20
   St. Johns, A. R.   A game girl.   Photop 21-2:71 Ja '22
   Albert, K.   Cuddles grows up.   Photop 36-4:36 S '29

LEIGH, JANET
   St. Johns, E.   Cinderella in pigtails.   Photop 32-2:66 Ja
      '48
   Fascinating.   Am Mag 145:103 Ja '48
   Morrison, Mrs. F.   She's magic.   Photop 33-3:58 F '49
   Colby, A.   She's younger than springtime.   Photop 36-6:
      58 N '49
   Leigh, J.   Love comes more than once.   Photop 37-2:60
      F '50
   Curtis, T.   Across a crowded room.   Photop 39-2:38 F
      '51
   Janet Leigh.   Life 30:43 F 26 '51
   New life begins for Janet Leigh.   Life 30:53 Je 25 '51
   Janet's and Tony's home sweet home.   Photop 40-5:54 N
      '51
   Waterbury, R.   Their rules for romance.   Photop 40-6:
      39 D '51
   Martin, P.   Perils of being a young movie star.   Sat
      Eve Post 224:22 F 9 '52
   Curtis, T.   Our first year.   Photop 41-6:56 Je '52
   Lewis, J.   I'm in love with my best friend's wife.

Photop 42-2:58 Ag '52

Brown, F.   The threat to the Tony Curtis-Janet Leigh
marriage.   Photop 43-2:48 F '53

Waterbury, R.   Happiness quiz.   Photop 43-5:48 My '53

Parsons, L. O.   It's tough to stay married in Hollywood.
Cosmop 135:8 Ag '53

Swanson, P.   No sad songs.   Photop 44-4:54 O '53

King and queen of hearts.   Look 18:50 F 23 '54

Leigh, J.   Spoil the brute.   Photop 45-2:50 F '54

Corwin, J.   Love those in-laws.   Photop 45-4:66 Ap '54

Emmett, R.   The secret life of Janet Leigh.   Photop
45-6:62 Je '54

Arnold, M.   When love is enough.   Photop 46-4:58 O '54

Leigh, J.   Imagine me, shy.   Photop 46-6:38 D '54

Edwards, R.   Hey there, you with the stars in your eyes.
Photop 47-1:52 Ja '55

Steele, J. H.   What's the difference.   Photop 47-3:49 Mr
'55

Hollywood talent in trade.   Life 38:57 Ap 4 '55

Hall, G.   Some wives have secrets.   Photop 47-5:46 My
'55

Jones, M. W.   Having wonderful time.   Photop 48-6:58
D '55

Swanson, P.   Janet Leigh: she held faith in her hand.
Photop 49-5:52 My '56

Janet Leigh lights up Africa.   Look 20:28 Je 12 '56

Debut: Janet Leigh's baby.   Look 20:20 N 13 '56

Parisian picnic.   Look 19:90 N 29 '56

Meltsir, A.   Once upon a time.   Photop 50-6:60 D '56

Phillips, D.   Are you retiring?   Photop 52-2:54 Ag '57

Leigh, J.   Wish you were here.   Photop 52-4:68 O '57

Divas, G.   I've never had a birthday party.   Photop 54-
5:56 N '58

Day, D.   I won't break these resolutions.   Photop 55-2:
48 F '59

Downs, R.   There will be no divorce.   Photop 57-1:50
Ja '60

Ardmore, J.   Would he marry you all over again?
Photop 58-2:46 Ag '60

A quiet afternoon with Janet and Tony.   Photop 58-4:54
O '60

Dinter, C.   Mommy, what church does Santa Claus go to?
Photop 59-1:32 Ja '61

Day, D.   Janet, don't let your castles crumble.   Photop
60-2:48 Ag '61

It's time you opened your eyes.   Photop 60-4:36 O '61

Wall, T.   The last goodbye.   Photop 60-5:50 N '61

Reynolds, L.   Why I'm in third place.   Photop 61-3:60
   Mr '62
Janet tells: why I left Tony.   Photop 61-6:18 Je '62
Janet, the belle of the brawl.   Life 53:39 Ag 10 '62
Sinatra-Leigh: what gives?   Photop 62-5:48 N '62
Janet Leigh's new life.   Photop 62-6:28 D '62

LEIGH, VIVIEN
   Waterbury, R.   A love worth fighting for.   Photop 53-
      12:18 D '39
   Pringle, H. F.   Finished at last; inside story of the film-
      ing of Gone with the wind.   Ladies Home J 57:25 Ja
      '40
   Gable, C. as told to Ruth Waterbury.   Vivien Leigh,
      Rhett Butler and I.   Photop 54-2:12 F '40
   Busch, N. F.   Laurence et Vivien.   Life 8:74 My 20 '40
   Woolf, S. J.   Juliet, not Scarlett; Vivien Leigh talks of
      two great roles and compares them.   N. Y. Times Mag
      p9 Je 9 '40
   Harris, R.   Star-cross'd lovers.   Photop 54-10:28 O '40
   Cerf, B.   Trade winds; how the role of Scarlett O'Hara
      finally was filled.   Sat R 28:22 Je 16 '45
   Stokes, S.   Oliviers.   Theatre Arts 29:711 D '45
   Biography.   Cur Bio Jl '46
      Same.   Cur Bio Yrbk 1946:340 '47
   Cleopatra at home.   Newsweek 28:77 Ag 26 '46
   Harris, R.   A knight and his lady.   Photop 29-5:36 O '46
   Hill, G.   Oliviers in Hollywood.   N. Y. Times Mag p24
      O 22 '50
   Watts, S.   Enter the Oliviers diffidently.   N. Y. Times
      Mag p15 D 16 '51
   Newman, J. L.   Cleopatra and friends.   Colliers 128:21
      D 22 '51
   Encrusted.   New Yorker 28:24 Mr 22 '52
   Nathan, G. J.   Two Cleopatras.   Theatre Arts 36:18 Mr
      '52
   Gehman, R.   Oliviers live their own love story.   Coronet
      33:131 Ja '53
   Spoon and plums.   Plays & Players 1-2:4 N '53
   Baker, F.   Oliviers.   Sat R 36:46 D 5 '53
   Biography.   Am Ann 1953:401 '53
   Biography.   Colliers Yrbk 1953:425 '53
   Shakespeare by the Oliviers.   N. Y. Times Mag p16 Jl 10
      '55
   Olivier as Titus.   N. Y. Times Mag p20 S 4 '55
   More than beauty.   Plays & Players 3-1:12 O '55
   Panter-Downes, M.   Letter from London; campaign to

save St. James'. New Yorker 33:91 Ag 17 '57
Personality of the month. Plays & Players 4-11:3 Ag '57
Miss Leigh's lament. Theatre Arts 41:13 S '57
Barker, F. G. Mistress of comedy. Plays & Players
　7-1:7 O '59
Talk with a star. Newsweek 55:54 My 2 '60
Gelman, M. Vivien Leigh. Theatre 2-5:15 My '60
Williams, T. Five fiery ladies. Life 50:86 F 3 '61
Muzhikal. Time 81:46 Mr 29 '63
Bowers, R. L. Vivien Leigh, inc. filmog. Films In
　Review 16-7:403 Ag/S '65
Obit. Time 90:88 Jl 14 '67
　Newsweek 70:82 Jl 17 '67
　Life 63:32 Jl 21 '67
　Brit Bk Yr 1968:594 '68
　Cur Bio 28:44 O '67
　Cur Bio Yrbk 1967:479 '68
　Screen World 19:235 '68
Trewin, J. C. Vivien Leigh. Plays & Players 14-12:38
　S '67
Arkadin. Film clips. Sight & Sound 36-4:208 Aut '67

LEIGHTON, MARGARET
Biography. Cur Bio 18:24 Mr '57
　Same. Cur Bio Yrbk 1957:319 '58
Personality of the month. Plays & Players 7-4:5 Ja '60
Pumphrey, A. Portrait of a gazelle. Theatre Arts 47:16
　F '63
Biography. Am Ann 1963:391 '63

LEMMON, JACK
Man named Lemmon refuses to change his name for show
　business. TV Guide 5-39:12 S 26 '52
Biographical note. Newsweek 44:98 N 8 '54
O'Leary, D. It should happen to Lemmon. Photop 47-5:
　59 My '55
Hopper, H. Young men of Hollywood. Coronet 38:58 Jl
　'55
Deane, P. He inherited the mirth. Photop 48-3:48 S '55
Lemmon, C. I fainted when he kissed me. Photop 49-5:
　50 My '56
Waterbury, R. What ever happened to that nice couple
　next door? Photop 51-3:42 Mr '57
Likeable Lemmon. Coronet 41:12 Mr '57
Talk with a star. Newsweek 53:113 Ap 6 '59
Hubler, R. G. Sweet slice of Lemmon. Coronet 46:
　134 O '59

Martin, P. I call on Jack Lemmon. Sat Eve Post 232:
38 Ap 16 '60
Talk with a twosome. Newsweek 55:110 Je 20 '60
Stang, J. Mr. Lemmon comes to Broadway. N.Y.
Times Mag p80 O 9 '60
Tornabene, L. L. Lunch date with Jack Lemmon.
Cosmop 149:22 D '60
Biography. Cur Bio 22:32 F '61
Same. Cur Bio Yrbk 1961:266 '62
Bester, A. All-American boy. Holiday 30:87 Jl '61
Bunzel, P. Does everybody here like Jack? Life 54:
103 Mr 22 '63
Davidson, M. Under the Lemmon skin. Ladies Home J
80:115 S '63
Lemmon, R. Go find something wrong with him. Sat Eve
Post 238:68 Ja 16 '65
Farr, F. ed. by M. Davidson. My husband, Jack Lem-
mon. Good H 160:58 Ap '65
Crossard, C. Jack Lemmon: most serious funnyman in
the flicks; intv. Look 21:66 F 7 '67
Redbook dialogue. Redbook 130:50 D '67

LENNON, JOHN
Nichols, L. Writing Beatle. N.Y. Times Bk R p8 Ap
12 '64
All my own work. Time 83:E7 My 1 '64
Schickele, P. About the awful; the writing Beatle.
Nation 198:588 Je 8 '64
Biography. Cur Bio 26:19 D '65
Same. Cur Bio Yrbk 1965:255 '65
According to John; remark about Christianity. Time 88:
38 Ag 12 '66
Davis, T. N. Of many things; Beatle John Lennon's
statement. America 115:164 Ag 20 '66
Gross, L. John Lennon: Beatle on his own. Look 30:
59 D 13 '66
Bascombe, L. You took my husband. Photop 72-6:37 D
'67
Beatle in the raw. Newsweek 72:102 N 25 '68
Harrow, S. He expects a love child. Photop 75-1:50 Ja
'69
Cott, J. John Lennon talks. Vogue 153:170 Mr 1 '69
Rollin, B. Top pop merger: Lennon/Ono inc. Look 33:
36 Mr 18 '69
Sander, E. John and Yoko Ono Lennon: give peace a
chance. Sat R 52:46 Je 28 '69
(See also: BEATLES)

LENYA, LOTTE
Return to Germany. Newsweek 46:53 D 26 '55
That was a time. Theatre Arts 40:78 My '56
Home-coming. Theatre Arts 41:12 O '57
Echo from Berlin. Time 72:42 Ag 11 '58
Biography. Cur Bio 20:18 Je '59
   Same. Cur Bio Yrbk 1959:254 '60
Weill parade. Newsweek 55:89 F 8 '60
Kroegler, H. Lotte Lenya and Seven deadly sins in
   Frankfurt. Dance Mag 34:12 Jl '60
Kupferberg, H. They shall have music. Atlan 209:113
   My '62
Helm, E. Lenya. Mus Am 82:22 My '62
On Brecht on Brecht. New Yorker 38:25 Je 16 '62
Beams, D. Lotte Lenya. Theatre Arts 46:10 Je '62
Lotte Lenya. Plays & Players 10-1:7 O '62
Kolodin, I. Music to my ears; evening of Kur Weill at
   Carnegie Hall. Sat R 48:38 Ja 23 '65
Reed, R. Lady known as Lenya. N.Y. Times Mag p128
   N 20 '66
Flagler, J. M. Where the pre-Nazis play. Look 31:72
   Mr 7 '67
Weaver, N. Lenya, whatever you do is epic enough for
   me. After Dark 11-3:32 My '69

LEONARD, MARION
Obit. Screen World 8:225 '57

LEONARD, SHELDON
Hano, A. Sometimes right, sometimes wrong but never
   in doubt. TV Guide 12-33:22 Ag 15 '64
Leonard, S. Having a wonderful time. TV Guide 13-30:
   6 Jl 24 '65
Punk who made good. Time 86:75 N 19 '65
Barthel, J. What a TV producer produces. N.Y. Times
   Mag p38 N 21 '65

LESLIE, GLADYS
Howe, H. A truly ingenuous ingenue. Photop 14-2:27
   Jl '18

LESLIE, JOAN
Crichton, K. Strenuous life. Colliers 107:13 Je 28 '41
Hall, G. The love of three sisters. Photop 19-5:40
   O '41
Seventeen. Am Mag 133:77 Ap '42
Joan Leslie shines brightly as a full-fledged movie star.

Life 13:75 O 26 '42
Leslie, J. I'm not a dull girl! Photop 24-1:44 D '43
Roberts, W. She's like this. Photop 28-5:44 Ap '46
Reichenthal, C. Joan Leslie, inc. filmog. Films In
    Review 15-5:319 My '64

LESLIE, LILIE
    Bacon, G. V. Lilie, the love-pirate, intv. Photop 7-6:
        135 My '15

LEVANT, OSCAR
    Music in aspic. Harper 179:527 O '39
    Koussevitsky, Toscanini, Stokowski. Harper 179:589 N
        '39
    Audacious Oscar. Newsweek 15:46 Ja 15 '40
    Jack-of-all-trades. Time 35:36 Ja 15 '40
    Burnham, P. Shop talk. Commonweal 31:309 Ja 26 '40
    Musical know it all. Life 8:55 F 5 '40
    I like music books; intv. Pub W 137:883 F 24 '40
    Music at home. Good H 110:34 Mr; 63 Ap '40
    Heylbut, R. Odyssey of Oscar Levant; autobiography.
        Etude 58:316 My '40
    Biography. Cur Bio '40
    Smith, F. J. Smattering of Oscar Levant. Sr Schol 38:
        20 My 5 '41
    Scratching the surface. Sat R 30:sup14 Ag 30; 50 S 27
        '47
    Zolotow, M. Lucky Oscar, sour genius of the keyboard.
        Sat Eve Post 223:24 O 21 '50
    Biography. Cur Bio O '52
        Same. Cur Bio Yrbk 1952:53
    Battling Levant. Newsweek 41:95 Mr 23 '53
    His bite is worse than his bark. TV Guide 4-19:14 My
        12 '56
    Frenzied road back. Time 71:48 My 5 '58
    Why Levant played. Newsweek 51:69 Je 16 '58
    Forgive me if I've been rude. TV Guide 6-27:10 Jl 5 '58
    Oscar writhes again. Time 72:52 Jl 7 '58
    Gehman, R. Oscar: the despotic neurotic. Coronet 45:
        114 N '58
    Muggeridge, M. Books. Esquire 64:26 O '65
    Fadiman, C. Anatomizing Oscar: a friend looks at
        Levant. Holiday 38:27 N '65

LEVENE, SAM
    They stand out from the crowd. Lit Digest 119:26 Ap 27
        '35

Reynolds, Q. Kid brother. Colliers 100:58 O 30 '37

Millstein, G. Acting? My aching back! Theatre Arts
43:20 Je '59

Shrugging Sam. Newsweek 60:60 D 17 '62

LEWIS, DIANA

Waterbury, R. The third Mrs. Powell. Photop 54-3:
18 Mr '40

Hamilton, S. Second year. Photop 19-2:30 Jl '41

LEWIS, JERRY

Lewis, Mrs. J. I married a madman! Am Mag 153:22
Ja '52

Lewis, J. I'm in love with my best friend's wife.
Photop 42-2:58 Ag '52

Lewis, Mrs. J. How I trained my husband. Photop 43-
3:52 Mr '53

Kass, R. Jerry Lewis analyzed. Films In Review 4-3:
119 Mr '53

Clouse, B. Jerry Lewis, movie maker; hints to fellow
amateurs. Photography 33:87 D '53

Jerry's jitterbug. Look 18:107 Mr 9 '54

Taurog, N. It really happened. Photop 45-4:36 Ap '54

Rogow, L. Making sows' ears from silk purses. Sat R
37:35 Jl 31 '54

Wood, C. TV personalities biographical sketchbook.
TV Personalities p64 '56

The birth of Jerry Lewis' new career. TV Guide 5-3:17
Ja 12 '57

Davidson, B. I've always been scared. Look 21:51 F 5
'57

Eustis, H. McCalls visits. McCalls 84:22 Mr '57

Thomas, B. Has Jerry fooled the critics? Photop 52-3:
62 S '57

Hoffman, J. Hollywood's funniest feud is on. Photop
53-6:42 Je '58

Hoffman, J. I'm not Jerry Lee Lewis. Photop 54-4:
29 O '58

Taves, I. Always in a crowd--always alone. Look 22:
83 D 23 '58

Talk with a star. Newsweek 52:64 D 29 '58

Phillips, D. Jerry Lewis helps answer a little boy's
prayer. Photop 55-1:42 Ja '59

Hoffman, J. Jerry Lewis: this thermometer tastes awful. Photop 55-3:50 Mr '59

Wolters, L. Jerry Lewis: what makes him tick?
Todays Health 37:24 Je '59

School for comedy. TV Guide 7-35:14 Ag 29 '59
The day the undertaker called--for me. Photop 57-3:36
    Mr '60
Exit Jerry, enter Danny. Newsweek 56:69 S 5 '60
Lewis, C. I always play with daddy. Photop 58-3:58 S
    '60
Jean, G. Nobody knows about me and Jerry. Photop
    59-2:54 F '61
Triple-decker bachelor's paradise for Jerry Lewis.
    Life 50:12 Mr 3 '61
Jerry Lewis spoofs the world's great lovers. Look 25:
    51 My 9 '61
Miller, E. Frantic world of Jerry Lewis. Seventeen 20:
    100 Je '61
Ardmore, J. L. I'm nutty about my kids; intv. Parents
    Mag 36:48 Jl '61
Bogdanovich, P. Mr. Lewis is a pussycat. Esquire 58:
    136 N '62
Biography. Cur Bio 23:10 N '62
    Same. Cur Bio Yrbk 1962:252 '63
Gehman, R. That kid. TV Guide 11-24:20 Je 15 '63
Linn, E. Search for Jerry Lewis. Sat Eve Post 236:83
    O 12 '63
Gehman, R. What happened to Jerry Lewis. TV Guide
    11-50:18 D 14 '63
Hill, L. "Nutty professor" contest winners. Photop 65-
    1:84 Ja '64
Public loves him. Newsweek 63:92 F 17 '64
Taylor, J. R. Jerry Lewis. Sight & Sound 34:82 Spg '65
Alpert, H. France is mad for . . . Jerry Lewis?
    N. Y. Times Mag p28 F 27 '66
Schickel, R. Jerry Lewis retrieves a lost ideal. Life 61:
    10 Jl 15 '66
His threatened marriage. Photop 73-4:60 Ap '68
Behn, A. Big daddy. Photop 75-5:56 My '69
(See also: MARTIN AND LEWIS)

LEWIS, MITCHELL
    St. Johns, A. R. Trapping a vagabond. Photop 16-1:81
        Je '19
    Obit. Screen World 8:223 '57

LEWIS, RALPH
    Ralph Lewis. Film Culture 36:42 Spg/Sum '65

LEWIS, SHELDON
    Obit. Screen World 10:223 '59

LIGHTNER, WINNIE
Earle, E. Winnie wows 'em. Photop 37-4:71 Mr '30
Shepard, R. The tomboy of the talkies. Photop 39-3:57
   F '31

LILLIE, BEA
Sproehnle, K. Beatrice Lillie and Lady Peal, a double
   role. Pict R 27:2 Ap '26
Don't be silly; autobiography. Colliers 77:10 Je 12 '26
Young, S. Beatrice Lillie. New Repub 50:169 Mr 30 '27
Adams, M. Beatrice Lillie, comedienne; intv. Womans
   J 14:15 F '29
Should a husband eat breakfast alone? Colliers 83:22 F
   23 '29
Ross, I. Happy hostess. Ladies Home J 52:15 O '35
Queen Bea recaptures Broadway. Lit Digest 120:18 N 2
   '35
Pic-ings. Pict R 37:34 Mr '36
Nathan, G. J. Lillie the Lulu. Newsweek 13:29 Ja 30
   '29
Eustis, M. High jinks at the Music box. Theatre Arts
   23:115 F '39
Minton, R. Queen Bea. Colliers 104:21 O 21 '39
Hayes, H. Enter, a great lady. Read Digest 44:70 Mr
   '44
Woolf, S. J. Bea Lillie's recipe for laughter. N. Y.
   Times Mag p13 N 26 '44
Lillie, 1945. New Yorker 20:15 Ja 20 '45
Biography. Cur Bio F '45
Heggie, B. Hit on the head with a wand. Sat Eve Post
   217:22 My 26 '45
Loners, Lady Peel, and a lady peeler. Theatre Arts 36:
   17 Ag '52
Evening with Bea Lillie. N. Y. Times Mag p54 S 21 '52
Evening with Bea Lillie. New Yorker 28:60 O 11 '52
Evening with Bea Lillie. Newsweek 40:88 O 13 '52
Evening with Bea Lillie. Time 60:57 O 13 '52
Marshall, M. Drama. Nation 175:365 O 18 '52
Evening with Bea Lillie. Life 33:61 O 20 '52
Hayes, R. Evening with Bea Lillie. Commonweal 57:
   62 O 24 '52
Brown, J. M. Seeing things. Sat R 35:26 O 25 '52
Miss Lillie. New Yorker 28:34 N 15 '52
Wyatt, E. V. Bea Lillie with Reginald Gardiner. Cath
   World 176:148 N '52
Nathan, G. J. Evening with Bea Lillie. Theatre Arts
   36:28 D '52

Abramson, M. Queen Bea of comedy. Coronet 34:87 Je
     '53
Old hands across the sea. Life 37:121 D 6 '54
Panter-Downes, M. Letter from London. New Yorker
     30:63 D 25 '54
Barker, R. The perfect Bea. Plays & Players 2-4:11
     Ja '55
Kolodin, I. Queen Bea. Sat R 39:47 F 25 '56
Tynan, K. Lady is a clown. Holiday 20:96 S '56
Personality of the month. Plays & Players 5-1:3 S '58
Pearly hoop of an early hoopster. Life 45:18 N 10 '58
Miss Lillie. New Yorker 35:26 F 13 '60
Prideaux, T. Consider the Lillie, fresher than ever.
     Life 56:9 My 1 '64
Coward, N. Old friend gives the low down on Lillie.
     Life 56:129 My 15 '64
Fleming, S. Notes from our correspondents. Hi Fi 14:
     12 Jl '64
Biography. Cur Bio 25:41 S '64
     Same. Cur Bio Yrbk 1964:255 '64

LINDEN, ERIC
     Baskette, K. Life begins for Eric Linden. Photop 49-3:
     60 Mr '36

LINDER, MAX
     Max Linder--the Charlie Chaplin deluxe. Everybodys 36:
     253 F '17
     Spears, J. Max Linder, inc. filmog. Films In Review
     16-5:272 My '65

LINDFORS, VIVECA
     Postwar Garbo. Time 47:35 Ap 22 '46
     Dark and silent. Am Mag 145:111 Ap '48
     Sad short story of Viveca Lindfors. Life 26:76 F 14 '49
     Stockholm to Hollywood to Broadway. Theatre Arts 36:
     15 D '52
     Three stars brighter than ever. Vogue 125:89 Ap 15 '55
     Biography. Cur Bio 16:25 Ap '55
          Same. Cur Bio Yrbk 1955:363 '56
     Who's who cooks. Good H 146:10 Ap '58
     McClelland, D. Waste. Films In Review 13-2:125 F '62
     Actress prepares. Newsweek 59:64 Mr 12 '62
     Jungstedt, T. Swedish filmography. Films In Review
     13-6:381 Je/Jl '62
     McClelland, D. Viveca Lindfors, inc. filmog. Screen
     Facts 20:1 n.d.

LINDSAY, MARGARET
  Rhea, M. Doing anything tonight? Photop 18-2:30 Ja '41

LISI, VIRNA
  Name is Virna Lisi. Life 56:94A Je 5 '64
  Sunniness on sight: Virna Lisi. Vogue 145:156 Ap 1 '65
  La Lisi. Time 85:47 Ap 2 '65
  Hamilton, J. Virna Lisi: experiment in star making.
    Look 29:60 My 18 '65

LITTLEFIELD, LUCIEN
  Rubber makeup gives actor many faces. Pop Sci 132:58
    Mr '38
  Jacobs, J. Lucien Littlefield. Films In Review 11-7:
    442 Ag/S '60
  Obit. Screen World 13:222 '62

LIVINGSTON, MARGARET
  Busby, M. A vamp steps out. Photop 37-5:58 Ap '30
  Mended hearts incorporated. Today Health 36:31 F '58

LLOYD, DORIS
  Obit. Screen World 20:236 '69

LLOYD, HAROLD
  Leigh, A. Specs without glass. Photop 17-2:68 Ja '20
  Mullett, M. B. Movie star who knows what makes you
    laugh. Am Mag 94:36 Jl '22
  St. Johns, A. R. What about Harold Lloyd. Photop 22-
    3:21 Ag '22
  Safety first stuff in Safety last. Lit Digest 78:43 Jl 14
    '23
  St. Johns, A. R. How Lloyd made "Safety last."
    Photop 24-2:33 Jl '23
  Harold Lloyd is the one white cow in the Hollywood colony,
    he's not conceited. Sunset 51:15 Ag '23
  The autobiography of Harold Lloyd. Photop 25-6:32 My;
    26-1:43 Je; 26-2:56 Jl '24
  Kennedy, J. B. It pays to be snappy; intv. Colliers 79:
    12 Je 11 '27
  Hardships of fun making; autobiography. Ladies Home J
    45:19 F '28
  Stout, W. ed. American comedy; autobiography. Sat Eve
    Post 200:6 Mr 24; 18 Mr 31: 27 Ap 7; 29 Ap 14; 26
    Ap 21; 38 Ap 28 '28
  Fame and fortune from a pair of goggles. Lit Digest
    99:34 O 6 '28

Lloydian laughs by proxy. Newsweek 17:62 Mr 17 '41
Marshall, J. Back to the mines. Colliers 117:58 Je 1
    '46
Shriner. New Yorker 25:18 Jl 2 '49
World of Hiram Abif. Time 54:13 Jl 25 '49
Agee, J. Boy. Life 27:78 S 5 '49
Alpert, H. Middle years of Harold Diddlebock. Sat R
    33:26 N 4 '50
It's tremendous. Time 61:64 Ja 19 '53
Peck, S. Then and now. N. Y. Times Mag p78 My 10
    '53
Hochman, L. My adventures in stereo. Photography
    34:52 Ap '54
Grafton, S. Harold Lloyd. Good H 140:54 My '55
Film pioneers' roll of their living immortals. Life 40:
    118 Ja 23 '56
Meeting with Harold Lloyd. Sight & Sound 28-1:4 Win
    '58/'59
Speedy. New Yorker 38:29 My 26 '62
All-American fall guy. Newsweek 59:98 Je 4 '62
Friedman, A. B. Interview. Film Q. 15-4:7 Sum '62
Garringer, N. E. Harold Lloyd, inc. filmog. Films In
    Review 13-7:407 Ag/S '62
Lloyd, H. The funny side of life. Films & Filming 10-
    4:19 Ja '64

LOCKHART, GENE
    They stand out from the crowd. Lit Digest 118:12 N 24
    '34
    Biography. Cur Bio My '50
        Same. Cur Bio Yrbk 1950:346 '51
    Obit. Time 69:88 Ap 8 '57
        Am Ann 1958:539 '58
        Cur Bio 18:51 Je '57
        Cur Bio Yrbk 1957:330 '58
        Screen World 9:225 '58
    He lived by his convictions. America 97:32 Ap 13 '57

LOCKHART, JUNE
    Ingenue. New Yorker 23:27 N 22 '47
    Wildman, H. H. It shouldn't happen to . . . N. Y. Times
        Mag p26 N 23 '47
    Star is born. Life 23:59 N 24 '47
    Encyclopedia with curves. TV Guide 2-35:13 Ag 28 '54
    Wood, C. TV personalities biographical sketchbook.
        TV Personalities p111 '54
    A busy June. TV Guide 6-6:17 F 8 '58

Lassie's third lass.   TV Guide 6-32:17 Ag 9 '58

Nichols, M.   Lockhart and her Lassie.   Coronet 45:14 Ap '59

This is Lassie's mother?   TV Guide 8-18:17 Ap 30 '60

Durslag, M.   Now she's the fur-bearing animal.   TV Guide 13-45:35 N 6 '65

Wasserman, J. L.   Now they allow her a kiss or two. TV Guide 17-30:18 Jl 26 '69

LOCKWOOD, GARY
Wedding bells for Tuesday.   Photop 60-4:24 O '61

Ardmore, J.   My nights are all Tuesday.   Photop 61-1: 32 Ja '62

Dinter, C.   If they're in love.   Photop 62-3:55 S '62

Still he's a very likable fellow.   TV Guide 12-9:22 F 29 '64

Miller, E.   You get what you go after.   Seventeen 26: 142 F '67

LOCKWOOD, HAROLD
Willis, R.   Harold Lockwood--athlete.   Photop 6-5:142 O '14

Henderson, M.   A star of stars.   Feature Movie 5-1:61 Ja '16

Pike, C.   It never can happen again.   Photop 13-3:61 F '18

Obit.   Photop 15-2:51 Ja '19

LOCKWOOD, MARGARET
Shopgirl's dream; Britain's most popular cinemactress. Time 51:94 My 24 '48

Biography.   Cur Bio S '48
   Same revised.   Cur Bio Yrbk 1948:382 '49

The good lady.   Plays & Players 2-4:5 Ja '55

Where are they now?   Newsweek 67:14 Ja 24 '66

LODER, JOHN
Bentley, J.   Hedy over heels in love.   Photop 22-5:30 Ap '43

LOFF, JEANETTE
Howe, H.   The all star blonde.   Photop 35-6:37 My '29

LOGAN, ELLA
Obit.   Time 93:100 My 9 '69
   Newsweek 73:69 My 12 '69

LOLLOBRIGIDA, GINA
Sexy Signore. Life 31:64 S 3 '51
Bogart, H. Beat the devil. Look 17:128 S 22 '53
D'Alessandro, A. Italian movie stars. Cosmop 136:47
    F '54
Hollywood on the Tiber. Time 64:54 Ag 16 '54
That certain something. Newsweek 44:85 O 4 '54
Speaking of pictures. Life 37:18 N 15 '54
Gina. Look 18:37 N 30 '54
Harvey, E. Lollobrigida: pin-up or paesana? Colliers
    135:29 Ja 21 '55
Italian movie star visits us. McCalls 82:6 Ja '55
Angell, R. Gina. Holiday 17:90 F '55
Leapin' Gina. Life 39:173 O 24 '55
Kurnitz, H. Antic arts. Holiday 19:65 F '56
Gina joins the circus. Look 20:56 My 15 '56
Cook your way into a man's heart; with recipes. Look
    21:70 Mr 19 '57
Bow to beauty. Life 44:30 F 17 '58
Mama Gina and Milko. Life 45:118 O 20 '58
Morton, F. Gina Lollobrigida. Holiday 25:111 Je '59
Whitcomb, J. Gina as Sheba. Cosmop 147:12 Ag '59
Gina plays the Queen of Sheba. Life 47:123 O 5 '59
In the new world, a new life for Gina. Life 49:69 Ag 8
    '60
Johnson, R. Saga of a siren. Sat Eve Post 233:18 Ag
    13 '60
Biography. Cur Bio 21:29 S '60
    Same. Cur Bio Yrbk 1960:235 '61
Anderson, N. Must we always live among strangers.
    Photop 58-6:64 D '60
Gehman, R. Gina. Good H 152:76 F '61
Redbook dialogue. Redbook 121:58 S '63
Levine, I. R. Lollo on TV. TV Guide 17-39:13 S 27 '69

LOM, HERBERT
Milson, S. He chose slow way to success. Films &
    Filming 2-10:10 Jl '56
Lom, H. Hollywood as I saw it. Films & Filming 5-
    11:8 Ag '59

LOMBARD, CAROLE
Hunt, J. L. How Carole Lombard plans a party. Photop
    47-3:67 F '35
Seymore, H. Carole Lombard tells "How I live by a
    man's code." Photop 51-6:12 Je '37
Bentley, J. She gets away with murder. Photop 52-3:

27 Mr '38
Doherty, E.   Can the Gable-Lombard love story have a
  happy ending?   Photop 52-5:18 My '38
Baral, R.   Blonde beauty grows up.   Photop 53-5:34 My
  '39
Binyon, C.   Subject: Lombard.   Photop 54-1:17 Ja '40
Crichton, K.   Fun in flickers.   Colliers 105:11 F 24 '40
Pringle, H. F.   Mr. and Mrs. Clark Gable.   Ladies
  Home J 57:20 My '40
Fletcher, A. W.   How Clark and Carole Lombard live.
  Photop 54-10:30 O '40
Death on Table Rock.   Newsweek 19:26 Ja 26 '42
End of a mission.   Time 39:17 Ja 26 '42
Obit.   Life 12:25 Ja 26 '42
  Time 39:76 Ja 26 '42
  Cur Bio '42
Waterbury, R.   What the loss of Carole Lombard means
  to Clark Gable.   Photop 20-5:28 Ap '42
Carole Lombard's greatest wish.   Photop 20-5:30 Ap '42
McCarthy, J.   Five wives of Clark Gable.   Look 19:103
  O 18 '55
Dickens, H.   Carole Lombard, inc. filmog.   Films In
  Review 12-2:70 F '61
Garceau J. & Cocke, I.   Dear Mr. Gable.   Ladies Home
  J 78:25 Jl; 42 Ag; 66 S '61
Samuels, C.   Clark Gable and the women who loved him;
  excerpt from The King; the story of Clark Gable.
  Good H 153:68 N '61

LONDON, JULIE
  Julie London.   Life 22:87 F 24 '47
  Sweet and sultry.   Am Mag 146:105 S '48
  Small voice makes big stir.   Life 42:75 F 18 '57
  Martin, P.   I call on Julie London.   Sat Eve Post 230:
    24 Ag 17 '57
  Shiffman, B. E.   A right to sing the blues.   Photop 52-6:
    38 D '57
  Ardmore, J. K.   Private blues of Julie London.   Coronet
    44:61 Je '58
  Girl with two new careers.   Look 22:85 S 16 '58
  Biography.   Cur Bio 21:23 My '60
    Same.   Cur Bio Yrbk 1960:237 '61
  Like a lioness on a leash.   TV Guide 9-28:17 Jl 15 '61
  Cohen, J.   Filmography.   Films In Review 20-3:188 Mr
    '64

LONG, RICHARD
  Gregory, J. Death of a man's heart. Photop 60-3:50 S '61
  Whitney, D. Richard the good. TV Guide 16-29:22 Jl 20
    '68

LONG, WALTER
  Walter the wicked. Photop 12-2:67 Jl '17

LOO, RICHARD
  Seeley, W. Richard Loo, inc. filmog. Films In Review
    13-4:249 Ap '62

LOPEZ, PERRY
  Emmett, R. Bronx block buster. Photop 49-6:44 Je '56

LORD, JACK
  Person of promise. Films & Filming 2-10:9 Jl '56
  Gill, A. Big, big, big! TV Guide 10-46:15 N 17 '62
  Ardmore, J. I'd be a bum without her. Photop 64-4:
    52 O '63
  Raddatz, L. How an ex-rodeo rider went west to enjoy
    the good life as a Hawaiian cop. TV Guide 17-1:14 Ja
    4 '69

LOREN, SOPHIA
  Italy's Sophia Loren. Newsweek 46:53 Ag 15 '55
  Saga of Sophia. Life 39:42 Ag 22 '55
  Harvey, E. Sophia in Sorrento. Colliers 136:36 S 16 '55
  New pictures. Time 67:94 F 6 '56
  Clark, H. Limelights and footlights. Theatre Arts 40:11
    Mr '56
  Reese, J. From starvation to stardom. Sat Eve Post
    229:24 O 20 '56
  Rich and famous at twenty-two. Look 20:107 D 25 '56
  Joel, J. Movie star as flamenco dancer. Dance Mag
    31:10 Ja '57
  Nichols, M. Sophia Loren: spaghetti-inspired sex appeal.
    Coronet 41:38 F '57
  Lane, J. F. Neapolitan gold. Films & Filming 3-7:9 Ap
    '57
  Sophia at the peak of her busy career. Life 42:137 My 6
    '57
  Wilkes, E. Hollywood says benovenuto Sophia. Photop
    52-1:17 Jl '57
  Americanization of Sophia Loren. Look 21:92 Ag 6 '57
  Archerd, A. Photoplay visits a movie set. Photop 52-
    4:73 O '57

Lewis, J. I have loved only once. Photop 53-1:23 Ja '58
Whitcomb, J. Sophia Loren in America. Cosmop 144:76
   F '58
Neapolitan maid in Manhattan. Life 44:113 Je 23 '58
In love with whom? Newsweek 52:76 Jl 28 '58
People are talking about . . . Vogue 132:118 S 15 '58
Gay Sophia gets her man. Life 45:56 O 13 '58
Biography. Cur Bio Mr '59
   Same. Cur Bio Yrbk 1959:266 '60
One-gal galaxy. Life 46:12 Ap 27 '59
Bester, A. Dilemma of Sophia Loren. Holiday 26:87 S
   '59
Culver, M. Threatened. Photop 56-5:77 N '59
People are talking about . . . Vogue 135:110 Ja 1 '60
Kauffmann, S. Stars in their courses. New Repub 143:
   19 O 3 '60
Royal time for lovely Sophia. Life 49:129 N 14 '60
Sophia Loren: photographic dossier. Vogue 137:122 My
   '61
Hamblin, D. J. Che gioia, la vita: whatajoy is life.
   Life 51:50 Ag 11 '61
Much woman. Time 79:78 Ap 6 '62
Sent for one. Time 79:79 Ap 20 '62
York, C. Sophia faces jail. Photop 62-3:14 S '62
Moravia, A. This is your life. Show 2-9:55 S '62
Ponti, C. At home with Sophia. Show 2-9:56 S '62
DeSica, V. DeSica on Sophia Loren. Vogue 140:102 N
   1 '62
Nolan, J. E. Sophia Loren, inc. filmog. Films In Re-
   view 13-10:633 D '62
Sophia Loren does her Easter shopping. Look 27:121 Ap
   23 '63
At last I have my baby. Photop 63-5:32 My '63
Wyndham, F. Sophia Loren: the strength of love.
   Vogue 142:172 O 1 '63
Biography. Am Ann 1963:398 '63
If my baby is illegal. Photop 65-1:33 Ja '64
Hamill, P. First I am a woman. Sat Eve Post 237:60
   F 15 '64
My country or my baby. Photop 65-4:45 Ap '64
When stripping, look into a man's eyes. Life 56:56 Ap
   10 '64
Loren, S. Three Sophias for the price of one. Life
   56:49 Ap 10 '64
Ghedini, F. Secrets of Sophia. McCalls 91:98 Ag '64
Hamblin, D. J. Carlo and Sophia. Life 57:80 S 18 '64
LoBello, N. A reporter visits Sophia Loren as the

movie star tours Rome to make a TV special.   TV
Guide 12-39:15 S 26 '64
Concubinage Italian style.   Time 85:56 F 19 '65
Random, E.   The truth about my heart attack.   Photop
67-4:60 Ap '65
Viva Sophia.   Christian Cent 82:695 My 26 '65
Shenker, I.   Name is Ponti, not Loren.   N.Y. Times
Mag p32 Je 6 '65
Hamblin, D. J.   Bigamy Italian style.   Life 59:52A Jl 23
'65
Chamber, G.   Saint?   Photop 68-2:56 Ag '65
Haranis, C.   Sinner?   Photop 68-2:58 Ag '65
Sophia Loren writes about Sophia Loren.   Ladies Home J
83:73 Mr; 84 Ap '66
Sophia plays a museum.   N.Y. Times Mag p38 My 15 '66
Real treasure.   Newsweek 67:92 Je 6 '66
Menen, A.   Sophia Loren: on women who are bored and
boring.   McCalls 94:54 Ja '67
Sophia Loren talks to women who want to be beautiful;
intv.   Redbook 129:68 Je '67
Camber, G.   Adopts baby.   Photop 71-6:64 Je '67
Ghedini, F.   Sophia Loren talks about sorrow of losing
her baby.   Ladies Home J. 84:68 S '67
Cheever, J.   Sophia, Sophia, Sophia.   Sat Eve Post 240:
33 O 21 '67
Manasse, S.   I already have a baby.   Photop 74-1:64 Jl
'68
Harrow, S.   Desperate to save unborn baby.   Photop 74-
5:54 N '68
Barry, J.   Sophia Loren's baby: the doctor who made it
possible.   McCalls 96:124 Ap '69
Blum, S.   Sophia Loren and Carlo Ponti talk about their
new baby.   Redbook 133:81 My '69
Ellis, E.   Her gypsy baby.   Photop 76-1:49 Jl '69
A star is born--at last.   Life 67-5:44 Ag 1 '69

LORNE, MARION
Bless you, Mrs. Gurney.   Look 18:100 O 5 '54
Wood, C.   TV Personalities biographical sketchbook.
TV Personalities p118 '57

LORRE, PETER
Reynolds, Q.   Reluctant menace.   Colliers 97:16 Ja 18
'36
Season's first guests.   Theatre Arts 20:822 O '36
He's only human.   TV Guide 5-44:28 N 2 '57
Luft, H. G.   Peter Lorre, inc. filmog.   Films In Review

11-5:278 My '60
Obit. Time 83:84 Ap 3 '64
Newsweek 63:59 Ap 6 '64
Illus Lond N 244:537 Ap 4 '64
Screen World 16:223 '65
Dyer, P. J. Fugitive from murder. Sight & Sound 33-
2:125 Sum '64

LORRING, JOAN
Wood, C. TV personalities biographical sketchbook.
TV Personalities p148 '54

LOUISE, ANITA
Martin, M. Anita Louise and mother love. Photop 50-
2:48 Ag '36
Loretta and I are both hams. TV Guide 6-29:17 Jl 19
'58

LOUISE, TINA
Tina. Colliers 137:90 Ap 27 '56
It's time for Tina. Look 22:60 My 27 '58

LOVE, BESSIE
Sayford, I. S. Just a little love. Photop 10-3:123 Ag '16
St. Johns, I. The little brown wren. Photop 27-2:56
Ja '25
Howe, H. The girl who talked back. Photop 35-6:60 My
'29
Dunham, H. Bessie Love, inc. filmog. Films In Review
10-2:86 F '59
Bessie Love on working behind the camera. Films &
Filming 8-10:16 Jl '62
Love, B. Jokers mild. Films & Filming 12-11:21 Ag
'66

LOVE, MONTAGU
Bartlett, R. Speaking of Love. Photop 15-2:71 Ja '19

LOVEJOY, FRANK
Wood, C. TV personalities biographical sketchbook.
TV Personalities p60 '56
Obit. Screen World 14:225 '63

LOWE, EDMUND
Tully, M. Why I'm going to marry. Photop 28-3:78
Ag '25
Albert, K. How to manage six famous wives. Photop

38-2:68 Jl '30

LOWERY, ROBERT
  Wood, C. TV personalities biographical sketchbook.
  TV Personalities p105 '57

LOY, MYRNA
  Colman, R. The siren from Montana. Photop 36-4:63
  S '29
  North, J. No more Chinese, Myrna? Photop 43-5:53
  Ap '33
  Baker, K. Working girl. Photop 45-3:70 F '34
  They stand out from the crowd. Lit Digest 118:11 Jl 28
  '34
  Condon, F. Giggle, giggle, little star. Colliers 94:17
  D 22 '34
  Johnston, A. From Asia to America in 100 reels.
  Womans H C 62:12 My '35
  Star mutinies. Newsweek 6:29 Ag 24 '35
  Manners, D. I know Myrna Loy--but not very well.
  Photop 48-3:30 Ag '35
  Manners, D. At last, the heart-stirring love story of
  Myrna Loy. Photop 50-2:12 Ag '36
  Harrington, L. The marriage code of Myrna Loy.
  Photop 51-5:36 My '37
  Miller, L. R. Times change: women never; intv. C S
  Mon Mag p4 Je 2 '37
  He's a tough guy. Pict R 38:24 Je '37
  Powell, W. She's a softie. Pict R 38:25 Je '37
  Willson, D. The revealing true story of Myrna Loy.
  Photop 52-5:16 My; 52-6:64 Je; 52-7:66 Jl '38
  Waterbury, R. Symphony in serenity. Photop 53-2:26
  F '39
  Powell, W. Myrna. Photop 54-2:21 F '40
  Owens, E. Why the perfect wife's marriage failed.
  Photop 18-3:52 F '41
  Hamilton, S. Goodby again. Photop 21-1:32 Je '42
  Fletcher, A. W. Mr. & Mrs. John Hertz, Jr. Photop
  21:4:67 S '42
  Grant, C. She's my dream wife. Photop 33-3:50 Ag '48
  Biography. Cur Bio O '50
  Same. Cur Bio Yrbk 1950:356 '51
  Ringgold, G. Myrna Loy, inc. filmog. Films In Re-
  view 14-2:69 F '63
  Hemming, R. We're not second-class citizens or sad
  sacks. Sr Schol 93:13 O 25 '68

LUCAS, WILFRED
Aye, J. Messrs Wilfred Lucas. Photop 10-1:97 Je '16

LUGOSI, BELA
What one monster could do. TV Guide 1-20:A6 Ag 14 '53
Cured. Newsweek 46:45 Ag 8 '55
Obit. Newsweek 48:75 Ag 27 '56
    Time 68:72 Ag 27 '56
    Brit Bk Yr 1957:577 '57
    Screen World 8:225 '57
Koffenberger, W. M. Jr. Filmography. Films In Review
    15-8:512 O '64
Everson, W. K. Frankenstein, Dracula, Karloff and
    Lugosi. Screen Facts 7:38 n. d.

LUKAS, PAUL
Busby, M. Lukas masters the microphone. Photop 39-1:
    65 D '30
Rankin, R. Paul goes American and how. Photop 44-1:
    56 Je '33
Reformed villain. New Yorker 17:10 My 10 '41
Bits to big time. Time 42:96 S 6 '43
Matthews, F. B. He calls her "Daisy." Photop 24-1:50
    D '43
Poling, J. Smile when you call Merman madam.
    Colliers 126:22 O 21 '50

LUND, JOHN
Schallert, E. Listen, it's John Lund. Photop 30-1:62 D
    '46
Deere, D. If you were the house guest of John Lund.
    Photop 30-5:58 Ap '47
Lund, J. Get me! Photop 31-5:38 O '47
Arnold, M. The lion in Lund. Photop 34-3:50 F '49
Small, C. Johnny's our boy. Colliers 124:24 Jl 23 '49

LUNDIGAN, WILLIAM
Mrs. Lundigan's anniversary hats. McCalls 82:8 S '55
Traveling trademarks. Coronet 40:118 Je '56
TV's traveling-est salesman. TV Guide 4-29:17 Jl 21 '56
Whitcomb, J. Star salesman for Climax! Cosmop 141:
    86 D '56
Wood, C. TV personalities biographical sketchbook.
    TV Personalities p157 '56
Goodman, W. Social science on Madison Avenue.
    Commentary 23:374 Ap '57
Hoover, G. F. Chrysler's man Lundigan. Sales Mgt.

80:39 Mr 7 '58

LUPINO, IDA

Small, F.   It was hate at first sight.   Photop 50-4:66
O '36
Crichton, K.   Career girl.   Colliers 99:20 Je 26 '37
Rhea, M.   The lady has character.   Photop 54-8:31 Ag '40
How Mr. and Mrs. Hayward live.   Photop 20-1:48 D '41
Sharpe, H.   Ida, the mad Lupino.   Photop 20-2:52 Ja;
20-3:50 F '42
Lupino, I. to Dorothy Haas.   Wives should have war
dates.   Photop 22-4:40 Mr '43
Biography.   Cur Bio '43
Perkins, D. W.   Perpetual emotion.   Am Mag 138:28 S '44
Lupino, I.   My fight for life.   Photop 28-3:58 F '46
Lupino, I.   New faces in new places.   Films In Review
1-9:17 D '50
Holiday awards for 1950.   Holiday 9:79 Ja '51
Hill, G.   Hollywood's beautiful bulldozer.   Colliers 127:
18 My 12 '51
A fourth for TV.   TV Guide 3-49:16 D 3 '55
Bartlett, M.   Howard Duffs set their own stage.   Am
Home 56:72 N '56
Mr. Duff and Ida.   TV Guide 5-22:17 Je 1 '57
Wood, C.   TV personalities biographical sketchbook.
TV Personalities p16 '57
Vermilye, J.   Ida Lupino, inc. filmog.   Films In Review
10-5:266 My '59
Mother Lupino.   Time 81:42 F 8 '63
Nolan, J. E.   Ida Lupino.   Films in Review 16-1:61 Ja
'65
Whitney, D.   Follow Mother, here we go Kiddies.
TV Guide 14-41:14 O 8 '66

LYNDE, PAUL

Nervous Nellie of the networks.   TV Guide 11-28:20 Jl
18 '63
Wilkie, J.   That what's-his-name is a very funny fellow.
TV Guide 17-29:15 Jl 19 '69

LYNLEY, CAROL

Success story at fifteen.   Life 42:128 Ap 22 '57
Christy, G.   Shall we tell them all about us?   Photop
54-4:34 O '58
Nice kids in tale of trouble.   Life 47:69 Ag 24 '59
Christy, G.   First love is . . .   Photop 56-4:34 O '59
Person of promise.   Films & Filming 6-1:17 O '59

Johnson, A. What girls don't understand about boys and vice versa. Photop 56-6:44 D '59

Cohen, M. I know they're talking about me behind my back. Photop 58-3:34 S '60

Draper, D. Love is a simple thing, but . . . Photop 59-3:38 Mr '61

Dean, B. Can a jinx strike twice? Photop 59-4:62 Ap '61

Corbin, J. Little girl, you've had a busy day. Photop 62-3:37 S '62

Goodbye age of innocence. Life 54:41 My 3 '63

Gregory, J. I'm not an unfit mother. Photop 64-1:45 Jl '63

Jenkins, D. The single-minded quest of Carol Lynley. TV Guide 11-31:26 Ag 3 '63

Lewis, R. W. Fair young Hollywood girls. Sat Eve Post 236:22 S 7 '63

Gregory, J. My baby taught me love. Photop 65-4:61 Ap '64

LYNN, DIANA

Diana Lynn plays her first big role. Life 17:65 O 23 '44

Kimbrough, E. Her heart is gay. Photop 26-3:45 F '45

Smarty. Am Mag 139:130 Ap '45

Beatty, J. Her heart was young and brave. Am Mag 141:44 Je '46

Pine, H. Diamond on her finger. Photop 29-5:31 O '46

Lynn, D. My teenage mistakes. Photop 33-5:62 O '48

Dreier, H. The lost cost of happiness. Photop 37-1:58 Ja '50

TV leading ladies. Life 32:143 My 5 '52

Biography. Cur Bio 14:14 N '53

  Same. Cur Bio Yrbk 1953:379 '53

Shrinking tigress. TV Guide 7-34:24 Ag 22 '59

Garvin, R. Filmography. Films In Review 19-1:64 Ja '68

LYNN, JEFFREY

Franchey, J. R. Life of Lynn. Photop 18-3:32 Ja '41

LYNN, SHARON

Ogden, E. The dunce's cap. Photop 37-6:39 My '30

Obit. Screen World 15:223 '64

LYON, BEN

St. Johns, A. R. Hollywood's new heartbreaker. Photop 27-2:42 Ja '25

Lang, H.   Bebe and Ben.   Photop 38-2:73 Jl '30
Busby, M.   A great come-back.   Photop 38-4:41 S '30
Whitney, P. D.   Then and now.   N.Y. Time Mag p22
   F 28 '54

LYON, SUE
Nymphet found.   Time 76:92 O 10 '60
Hamilton, J.   Sue Lyon: star of the year's most contro-
   versial movie.   Look 26:48 Jl 17 '62
Ellis, F.   Why Lolita gets what she wants.   Photop 65-
   3:28 Mr '64
Sanders, A.   My husband married Lolita.   Photop 66-
   2:58 Ag '64
Rivers, N.   The wedding smile turned sour.   Photop 67-
   1:26 Ja '65

LYTELL, BERT
Valentine, S.   Lytell: Chapter two.   Photop 22-2:25 Jl
   '22
Obit.   Newsweek 44:78 O 11 '54
   Time 64:112 O 11 '54
   Screen World 6:224 '55
   Am Ann 1955:438 '55
   Brit Bk Yr 1955:579 '55
Biography.   NCAB 43:160 '61

LYTELL, WILFRED
Obit.   Screen World 6:224 '55

LYTTON, L. ROGERS
Craig, G.   He hates his success.   Photop 11-5:97 Ap '17

MAC ARTHUR, JAMES
Meet my Helen Hayes; ed by S. Fields. McCalls 83:40 F '56
Carson, E. Heritage of love. Photop 51-1:50 Ja '57
In a star's steps. Life 42:63 Ap 8 '57
Christy, G. Shall we tell them all about us? Photop 54-4:34 O '58
Person of promise. Films & Filming 5-1:17 O '58
My mother, Helen Hayes; ed by A. Whitman. Good H 154:68 F '62

MAC BRIDE, DONALD
Obit. Screen World 9:225 '58

MAC DERMOTT, MARC
Briscoe, J. Why film favorites forsook the footlights. Photop 6-5:123 O '14
Frederick, J. S. Marc MacDermott: Movie '49er. Photop 12-5:104 O '17

MAC DONALD, JEANETTE
Hall, L. The prima donna and the old man. Photop 39-3:63 F '31
Denton, F. Up the ladder with Jeanette. Photop 43-1:77 D '32
Jeanette MacDonald. Cinema Digest 3-6:11 Ap 24 '33
Shawell, J. Girl who plays queens. Pict R 38:22 S '33
Taviner, R. How to be naughty but nice. Photop 46-4:35 S '34
Manners, D. The romantic love story of Jeanette Mac Donald and Gene Raymond. Photop 50-5:22 N '36
Smalley, J. An open letter to Jeanette MacDonald. Photop 51-2:24 F '37
Beatty, J. Girl who sang in the bathtub. Am Mag 124:32 Jl '37
Hayes, B. The secret Gene Raymond kept from Jeanette MacDonald. Photop 51-9:15 S '37
Laine, J. Operetta and the sound film. Etude 59:359 Je '38
Waterbury, R. Marriage is a laughing matter. Photop 52-8:22 Ag '38
Eddy, N. Jeanette. Photop 54-6:22 Je '40
No royal road to song. Bet Hom & Gard 20:27 S '41

Taylor, F. J.   Hollywood cliff gardeners: Jeanette Mac
   Donald and Gene Raymond.   Bet Hom & Gard 20:26 S
   '41
Hollywood halo.   Am Mag 133:132 F '42
Zeitlin, I.   Jeanette sends her man to war.   Photop 21-
   1:62 Je '42
Eddy, N.   What I don't like about Jeanette.   Photop 21-
   3:54 Ag '42
Hollywood Juliet.   Time 44:50 N 13 '44
MacDonald in opera.   Life 17:39 N 20 '44
Heylbut, R.   If you hope for a film career.   Etude 71:19
   N '53
Obit.   Illus Lond N 246:27 Ja 23 '65
   Newsweek 65:63 Ja 25 '65
   Time 85:72 Ja '65
   Screen World 17:238 '66
Funeral of the year.   Newsweek 65:22 F 1 '65
Bodeen, D.   Jeanette MacDonald, inc. filmog.   Films In
   Review 16-3:129 Mr '65

MAC DONALD, KATHERINE
   McGaffey, K.   Consider Katherine.   Photop 14-6:45 N '18
   Regis, J.   Beauty her great handicap.   Photop 18-1:34 Je
      '20
   Obit.   Screen World 8:225 '57

MAC DONALD, RAY
   Obit.   Screen World 11:223 '60

MAC FARLAND, SPANKY
   Crichton, K.   Actor at 8.   Colliers 98:22 N 21 '36

MAC GRAW, ALI
   New Princess.   Newsweek 73:108 My 5 '69
   Girl who has everything--just about.   Time 93:102 My 9
      '69
   One film turns life upside down for the new star named
      Ali.   Life 66:46 Je 20 '69

MACK, HELEN
   Hunt, J. L.   Not a minute of childhood.   Photop 46-5:38
      O '34

MACKAILL, DOROTHY
   Sewell, J.   A Cockney beauty.   Photop 24-3:51 Ag '23
   Burton, S.   Second thoughts on matrimony.   Photop 37-
      4:43 Mr '30

MAC LAINE, SHIRLEY

I predict these will be the bright new stars of 1955.
  Look 19:17 Ja 11 '55
Shirley on way up.   Life 38:102 Mr 14 '55
Lucky understudy.   Look 19:90 Ap 19 '55
Fleming, T. J.   Multimillion Monroe doctrine.   Cosmop
  139:58 Jl '55
Mundy, J.   Sweet, hot and sassy.   Photop 48-6:57 D '55
Phillips, D.   When Shirley MacLaine blows a fuse.
  Photop 49-5:58 My '56
Person of promise.   Films & Filming 2-9:18 Je '56
Real pixie.   TV Guide 5-30:28 Jl 27 '57
Maynard, J.   Westward-ha!   Photop 52-1:64 Jl '57
Mama is a madcap.   Look 21:123 D 10 '57
Portrait of a remarkable square.   TV Guide 6-32:24 Ag 9
  '58
Talk with a star.   Newsweek 52:91 Ag 18 '58
Phillips, D.   Love has Shirley up a tree.   Photop 54-4:
  58 O '58
Fun of being look-alikes.   Life 46:12 F 9 '59
Nichols, M.   MacLaine on the move.   Coronet 45:10 Ap
  '59
Ring-a-ding girl.   Time 73:66 Je 22 '59
Harris, E.   Free spirit.   Look 23:55 S 15 '59
Advance notice.   Vogue 134:143 S 15 '59
Whitcomb, J.   Shirley MacLaine, sassy and off-beat.
  Cosmop 147:24 S '59
Shirley's spoof party.   Life 47:167 D 7 '59
Biography.   Cur Bio 20:7 D '59
    Same.   Cur Bio Yrbk 1959:277 '60
Cry, laugh, cry, laugh.   Newsweek 56:72 S 5 '60
Johnson, A.   Conversation with Shirley MacLaine.   Dance
  Mag 34:44 S '60
Mr. Parker's geisha.   Time 77:51 Ja 27 '61
East-West twain find a meeting in MacLaine.   Life 50:91
  F 17 '61
Martin, P.   I call on Shirley MacLaine.   Sat Eve Post
  234:26 Ap 22 '61
Barber, R.   Hollywood's most unconventional mother.
  Redbook 117:32 Jl '61
Four for posterity.   Look 26:83 Ja 16 '62
Bean, R.   The two faces of Shirley; intv.   Films &
  Filming 8-5:11 F '62
Weaver, J. D.   Queen of kooks.   Holiday 32:93 Jl '62
Stand, L.   Shirley MacLaine you never knew.   Good H
  155:72 S '62
Roddy, J.   New style star tries a rough role.   Look 27:

61 Ja 29 '63
Surprising spin for Shirley. Life 54:62A Je 21 '63
I lived with street walkers. Photop 64-2:62 Ag '63
Davidson, M. Shirley MacLaine sounds off. Sat Eve
    Post 236:30 N 30 '63
Garth, D. Boy meets girl. Seventeen 23:79 Ja '64
Jenkins, D. In an epic movie, one dame beats another.
    Sports Illus 21:50 Jl 20 '64
Haranis, C. The day she was arrested. Photop 67-2:21
    F '65
Redbook dialogue. Redbook 127:52 My '66
Hamilton, J. Shirley MacLaine as Sweet Charity.
    Look 32:56 Jl 9 '68
Hockstein, R. Crusades and capers of Shirley MacLaine.
    Good H 168:52 Je '69

MAC LANE, BARTON
    What happens to old heavies? TV Guide 9-15:28 Ap 15
    '61

MAC LAREN, MARY
    Kingsley, G. Sweet sobber of the celluloid. Photop 11-
        3:27 F '17
    Anderson, L. C. An everyday Diana. Photop 17-1:56
        D '19
    Shirley, L. Sadder but wiser. Photop 34-1:39 Je '28
    MacLaren, M. I was once a star. Photop 43-3:60 F '33

MAC LEAN, DOUGLAS
    Spensley, D. The businessman--comedian. Photop 30-6:
        72 N '26

MAC MAHON, ALINE
    Crichton, K. Queen of parts. Colliers 93:13 Je 23 '34
    Stein, J. Aline MacMahon, inc. filmog. Films In Re-
        view 16-10:616 D '65

MAC MURRAY, FRED
    Hunt, J. L. Love comes first for Fred MacMurray.
        Photop 48-4:29 S '35
    Crichton, K. Star without limousine. Colliers 97:16 Je
        20 '36
    Hunt, J. L. They budgeted everything but love. Photop
        50-5:30 N '36
    Sharpe, H. New day for Fred MacMurray. Photop 52-
        6:27 Je '38
    Binyon, C. "Long shot" MacMurray. Photop 53-5:20

My '39

Steele, J. H.   Portrait of a right guy.   Photop 22-3:34
F '43

Amory, C.   Hollywood's ho-hum boy.   Sat Eve Post 217:
17 Mr 3 '45

Waterbury, R.   The saga of Frederick and Lilly.   Photop
26-6:46 My '45

Shearer, M.   How to live up to a good old tradition;
Fred MacMurray home, Brentwood, Calif.   House B
88:62 Jl '46

Howe, H.   Laziest man in town.   Photop 32-1:64 D '47

Senseney, D.   The day fate smiled.   Photop 46-1:44 Jl
'54

Saga of a saxophone player.   TV Guide 8-46:17 N 12 '60

MacMurray, F.   I've been lucky; as told to Pete Martin.
Sat Eve Post 235:36 F 24 '62

The big lug has something.   TV Guide 11-33:15 Ag 17 '63

Hano, A.   Ben-Hur in the suburbs.   TV Guide 12-30:24
Jl 25 '64

He likes to cook.   Bet Hom & Gard 43:30 Ap '65

Whitney, D.   The anatomy of success.   TV Guide 13-31:
15 Jl 31 '65

Biography.   Cur Bio 28:23 F '67
Same.   Cur Bio Yrbk 1967:273 '68

Barthal, J.   Fred MacMurray at 60.   TV Guide 16-40:
26 O 5 '68

MACNEE, PATRICK
The Edwardian in Malibu.   TV Guide 16-46:18 N 16 '68

MAC RAE, GORDON
Languor, curls and tonsils; crooners.   Time 50:83 S 15
'47

MacRae for Martin.   Newsweek 31:45 Mr 1 '48

Walker, H. L.   He says it with music.   Photop 37-1:48
Ja '50

MacRae, S.   My guiding star.   Photop 39-4:46 Ap '51

Maxwell, E.   That old MacRae magic.   Photop 40-4:46
O '51

P. S. I got the job.   Am Mag 153:102 Mr '52

MacRae, G.   Listen, Kate.   Photop 43-4:76 Ap '53

Return to youth.   TV Guide 3-25:15 Je 18 '55

MacRae's beautiful mornin'.   Look 19:38 D 27 '55

MacRae, G.   Ready, able and praying.   Photop 49-4:48
Ap '58

Keeping it in the clan.   TV Guide 4-28:4 Jl 14 '56

Wood, C.   TV personalities biographical sketchbook.

TV Personalities p109 '56

Liston, J.   At home with Gordon MacRae.   Am Home 64: 12 Ja '61

Family fling by the MacRaes.   Life 50:122 Je 9 '61

MACREADY, GEORGE

Heffer, B. J.   George Macready, inc. filmog.   Films In Review 19-6:390 Je/Jl '68

MADISON, CLEO

Willis, R.   Cleo Madison--the vivacious beauty of the 101-Bison pictures.   Photop 5-2:47 Ja '14

Madison, C.   When Cleo Madison was afraid.   Photop 7-3:38 F '15

Henry, W. M.   Cleo, the craftswoman.   Photop 9-2:109 Ja '16

St. Johns, I.   Former top-notcher comes back.   Photop 26-6:59 N '24

Obit.   Screen World 16:224 '65

MADISON, GUY

Walker, H. L.   With a Guy--Madison.   Photop 27-5:36 O '45

Mann, A.   Glamor Guy.   Colliers 117:24 Ap 6 '46

Scott, D.   Tall and tawny.   Photop 28-5:64 Ap '46

Russell, G.   My kind of Guy!   Photop 29-3:41 Ag '46

Sharpe, H.   A Guy named Bob.   Photop 29-6:52 N '46

Madison, G.   Bachelors, Ltd.   Photop 30-4:38 Mr '47

Deere, D.   The lie.   Photop 31-2:46 Jl '47

Hamilton, S.   Open letter to Guy and Gail.   Photop 31-6:66 N '47

Connolly, M.   That Guy--Madison.   Photop 44-4:50 O '53

I'm living my life backwards.   Look 17:80 D 1 '53

Hubler, R. G.   He came in the back door to stardom. Sat Eve Post 226:38 D 12 '53

Swanson, P.   The story of Guy Madison's heartbreak marriage.   Photop 45-3:42 Mr '54

Jacobi, E.   He stuck to his guns.   Photop 46-6:36 D '54

Madison, S. C.   I'm in love with a wonderful Guy. Photop 47-3:54 Mr '55

Hopper, H.   Young men of Hollywood.   Coronet 38:53 Jl '55

Arnold, M.   The dividends of courage.   Photop 48-5:38 N '55

Arnold, M.   The story of a happy Guy Madison.   Photop 49-5:46 My '56

Wood, C.   TV personalities biographical sketchbook.

TV Personalities p58 '56

MAGNANI, ANNA
  Cianfarra, J.   Tigress of Italy's screen.   N. Y. Times
    Mag p28 O 16 '49
  Kobler, J.   Tempest on the Tiber.   Life 28:115 F 13 '50
  Sexy signore.   Life 31:62 S 3 '51
  Knight, A.   Star turn.   Sat R 36:29 Mr 21 '53
  Anna in Harlem.   New Yorker 29:21 Ap 25 '53
  D'Allessandro, A.   Italian movie stars.   Cosmop 136:45
    F '54
  Magnificent drab.   Life 39:139 N 28 '55
  Knight, A.   Magnificent Magnani.   Sat R 38:25 D 10 '55
  World's greatest actress.   Time 66:94 D 19 '55
  Magnificant Magnani.   Newsweek 46:65 D 26 '55
  Hartung, P. T.   Anna Magnani's magnificent performance.
    Woman H C 82:12 D '55
  Magnetic Magnani.   Coronet 39:8 D '55
  Parsons, L. O.   Magnificent Magnani.   Cosmop 139:74
    D '55
  Biography.   Cur Bio 17:35 Ap '56
    Same.   Cur Bio Yrbk 1956:400 '57
  Barzini, L.   Italy's greatest actress.   Harper 215:52 S
    '57
  Biography.   Colliers Yrbk 1957:705 '57
  Hartung, P. T.   Magnificent, magnanimous Magnani.
    Commonweal 67:383 Ja 10 '58
  Williams, T.   Five fiery ladies.   Life 50:84 F 3 '61
  Whitehall, R.   Anna Magnani.   Films & Filming 7-10:15
    Jl '61
  Anna is everything!   Newsweek 65:81 Je 7 '65

MAHARIS, GEORGE
  Rough road.   Newsweek 57:60 Ja 2 '61
  In the driver's seat.   TV Guide 9-7:17 F 18 '61
  Maharis, G.   Hi there, I'm a single man.   Photop 59-6:
    40 Je '61
  Dinter, C.   Love is a hit on the head.   Photop 60-4:46
    O '61
  Denis, P.   Let's face it--I'm different.   Photop 61-1:48
    Ja '62
  Carpozi, G. Jr.   Why they arrested me.   Photop 61-2:
    30 F '62
  Gehman, R.   He's always racing his motor.   TV Guide
    10-15:5 Ap 14; 10-16:17 Ap 21 '62
  Wall, T.   Get me my pants.   Photop 62-2:46 Ag '62
  Richards, J.   Pinup #11.   Photop 62-5:59 N '62

Somers, A. My mother steals. Photop 62-6:33 D '62
Crash on route 66. Photop 63-2:36 F '63
George Maharis' life story. Photop 63-3:32 Mr '63
Ormond, E. Married woman keeps him single. Photop
    63-6:36 Je '63
Camber, G. Accused of wife stealing. Photop 65-2:64
    F '64
Waterbury, R. Our love story. Photop 66-4:68 O '64

MAHONEY, JOCK
Jocko the gymnast. TV Guide 7-11:24 Mr 14 '59

MAIN, MARJORIE
Wilson, L. & McClure, D. Ma and Pa Kettle--Hollywood
    goldmine. Colliers 128:22 D 8 '51
Biography. Cur Bio 12:24 O '51
    Same. Cur Bio Yrbk 1951:397 '52
Wilson, N. H. The Kettles. Films In Review 5-10:524
    D '54
Moshier, W. F. Marjorie Main, inc. filmog. Films In
    Review 17-2:96 F '66

MAISON, EDNA
Richards, W. Carmen Edna Maisonave. Photop 6-3:79
    Ag '14
Dorsey, E. T. Versatile Edna Maison. Feature Movie
    4-1:5 O 10 '15

MALDEN, KARL
Malden, K. My friend Brando. Photop 46-3:61 S '54
Biography. Cur Bio 18:33 Ap '57
    Same. Cur Bio Yrbk 1957:349 '58
Broadway star and Hollywood director. Theatre Arts
    41:69 O '57
Malden, K. The two faces of Brando. Films & Filming
    5-11:7 Ag '59
Interview with Karl Malden. Kaleidoscope 3-1:4 n. d.

MALLORY, PATRICIA
Obit. Screen World 10:223 '59

MALONE, DOROTHY
Hall, G. What really goes on with Scott Brady and
    Dorothy Malone? Photop 42-2:54 Ag '52
Who is Dorothy Malone? Photop 52-1:52 Jl '57
Posner, C. The strange case of Dorothy Malone.
    Photop 53-1:24 Ja '58

Johnson, M. The day Dorothy's secret prayer was answered. Photop 56-4:47 O '59

Hollywood's strangest divorce. Photop 67-2:44 F '65

Her address is Peyton Place. TV Guide 13-12:22 Mr 20 '65

Hobson, D. Dorothy Malone: the actress and the woman. TV Guide 15-10:20 Mr 11 '67

Hart, M. I pray my daughters marry young. Photop 73-4:52 Ap '68

Parish, J. R. Jr. Dorothy Malone, inc. filmog. Film Fan Mo 85-6:27 Jl/Ag '68

Waterbury, R. How she lost her man. Photop 75-1:52 Ja '69

Riley, N. Six days later, I said yes. Photop 76-1:74 Jl '69

MANGANO, SILVANA
Candide. Most beautiful woman in the world. U. N. World 4:26 D '50

Sexy signore. Life 31:2 S 3 '51

Which is glamour? Colliers 131:34 Ja 3 '53

Two ways to be a woman. Colliers 132:52 O 30 '53

D'Alessandro, A. Italian movie stars. Cosmop 136:46 F '54

Kinney, N. McCalls visits. McCalls 85:14 F '58

MANNERS, DAVID
Lang, H. Manners--he has them. Photop 40-5:65 O '31

MANNING, IRENE
They waited three years for Irene. Am Mag 134:94 O '42

Salesmanship in singing. Etude 64:135 Mr '46

MANNING, MILDRED
Frederick, J. S. An ingenue who won't ingenue. Photop 12-4:35 S '17

MANSFIELD, JAYNE
Jayne Mansfield is a basic blonde. Life 39:101 N 21 '55

Havemann, E. Star's legend in the making. Life 40:178 Ap 23 '56

Waiting for Eddie. TV Guide 4-25:6 Je 23 '56

Obstacle course. Theatre Arts 40:14 N '56

Maynard, J. All she want to be is a move star. Photop 51-2:50 F '57

Lane, L. Eeeny, meeny, miny, mo, who will be the first to go? Photop 51-3:38 Mr '57

Donovan, R.   She will do anything for publicity.   Sat Eve
    Post Je 1 '57
Hamilton, S.   Which is for real?   Photop 52-2:58 Ag '57
Bester, A.   Jayne Mansfield: whistle stop.   Holiday 22:
    129 D '57
Weller, H.   Will success spoil Jayne Mansfield?   Photop
    52-6:28 D '57
Jayne is wed under glass.   Life 44:37 Ja 27 '58
Hamilton, S.   Love was never like this.   Photop 53-2:47
    F '58
Hurst, T.   Got a pink sofa you'd like to get rid of?
    Photop 55-1:44 Ja '59
Lost at sea.   Newsweek 59:54 F 19 '62
Hoffman, J.   An incredible interview.   Photop 64-6:54
    D '63
McClure, M.   Defense of Jayne Mansfield.   Film Culture
    32:24 Spg '64
Obit.   Newsweek 70:98 Jl 10 '67
    Time 90:79 Jl 7 '67
    Screen World 19:236 '68
Gowland, P.   Jayne loved photographers.   Pop Phot 61:66
    D '67

MANSFIELD, MARTHA
    Evans, D.   Making over Martha.   Photop 18-2:29 Jl '20

MARA, ADELE
    She's a barber?   TV Guide 7-40:21 O 3 '59

MARAIS, JEAN
    Curtiss, T. G.   Film idol Jean Marais crashes the
        Comedie-Française.   Theatre Arts 36:23 Ap '52
    Biography.   Cur Bio 23:23 Ap '62
        Same.   Cur Bio Yrbk 1962:285 '63

MARCH, FREDRIC
    Merton, P.   Fred marches on.   Photop 38-1:86 Je '30
    Kahn, J. M.   Wandering with the Marches.   Photop 41-1:
        52 D '31
    Bickel, M. D.   The baby of the family.   Photop 42-2:50
        Jl '32
    March, F. as told to Cromwell MacKechnic; intv.
        Photop 45-2:30 Ja '34
    March, F.   Leaves of absence.   Photop 47-4:56 Mr '35
    Hayes, B.   March versus stage.   Photop 52-3:22 Mr '38
    Biography.   Cur Bio '43
    On location for 200 years!   Fredric March home, New

Milford, Conn. Am Home 31:14 Mr '44
Isaacs, H. R. Two girls and Fredric March. Theatre
   Arts 28:243 Ap '44
Funke, L. Broadway husband and wife teams. N. Y.
   Times Mag p19 Ja 12 '47
Funke, L. Broadway stars--ten years ago and today.
   N. Y. Times Mag p24 Ap 20 '47
March story. Newsweek 35:49 Ja 2 '50
Papa Christmas. Am Mag 160:88 D '55
Tozzi, R. Fredric March, inc. filmog. Films In Re-
   view 9-10:545 D '58
Bitlisian, P. Fredric March. Films In Review 10-3:
   190 Mr '59
New image of Bryan. Life 49:77 S 26 '60
Talk with the star. Newsweek 58:62 S 4 '61
Gehman, R. Theatre Arts gallery. Theatre Arts 45:
   15 D '61

MARCH, HAL
Man behind the $64,000 question. Look 19:56 S 20 '55
Could you answer the $64,000 question? Am Mag 160:
   21 D '55
Hal March . . . he got a $64,000 break. Look 20:57
   S 18 '56
Wood, C. TV personalities biographical sketchbook.
   TV Personalities p43 '56
March, H. $64,000 and I. Sat Eve Post 230:19 N 30
   '57
Where are they now? Newsweek 68:20 N 7 '66

MARGO
Crichton, K. Girl with one name. Colliers 92:28 N 30
   '35
Reed, E. Some actors, season of 1935-36. Theatre
   Arts 20:444 Je '36
Virtue of night clubs. Time 63:47 My 3 '54
New husband and wife hit. Look 18:74 Jl 13 '54

MARGOLIN, JANET
People on the way up. Sat Eve Post 234:33 D 23 '61
Miller, E. Father calls me a rebel. Seventeen 23:108
   D '64

MARIS, MONA
Albert, K. Deeds and dreams. Photop 38-5:58 O '30
Cousin. Am Mag 132:70 Ag '41

MARKEY, ENID
   Boone, A. Re-discovering an ingenue. Photop 16-4:54
     S '19
   Dear Mr. Woods: have talent, am here. Theatre Arts
     43:77 S '59
   A new sister act. TV Guide 9-2:12 Ja 14 '61

MARLOW, LUCY
   People of promise. Films & Filming 3-3:16 D '56

MARSH, MAE
   Brooke, F. Two snapshots of Mae Marsh. Photop 7-1:
     101 D '14
   Bruce, R. The girl on the cover; intv. Photop 8-2:57
     Jl '15
   Bartlett, R. There were two little girls named Mary.
     Photop 11-4:36 Mr '17
   Evans, D. Will Mae Marsh come back? Photop 23-4:
     28 Mr '23
   Film pioneers' roll of living immortals. Life 40:120 Ja
     23 '56
   Dunham, H. Mae Marsh, inc. filmog. Films In Review
     9-6:306 Je/Jl '58
   Dunham, H. Mae Marsh since '32. Films In Review
     10-3:190 Mr '59
   Loos, A. Vachel, Mae and I. Sat R 44:5 Ag 26 '61
   50 years of tears. Show 2-12:138 D '62
   Sterne, H. On Mae Marsh. Film Culture 36:47 Spg/Sum
     '65
   Kael, P. Current cinema. New Yorker 44:102 F 24 '68
   Obit. Newsweek 71:93 F 26 '68
     Time 91:73 F 23 '68
     Screen World 20:237 '69

MARSHAL, ALAN
   Surmelian, L. He calls her "Binks." Photop 24-1:51
     D '43
   Obit. Screen World 13:225 '62

MARSHALL, BRENDA
   Crichton, K. Bashful Brenda. Colliers 107:13 F 15 '41
   Ford, G. My pals, Brenda and Bill. Photop 21-1:52
     Je '42
   Rice, B. Star's preference in toby mugs. Hobbies 48:
     66 Ap '43
   Personal appearance. Am Mag 135:58 Je '43
   Marshall, B. What loneliness has taught me. Photop

23-2:44 Jl '43
Asher, J.   Happiness is a thing called Bill.   Photop 31-
5:48 O '47
Howe, H.   Dear Husband.   Photop 38-4:36 O '50

MARSHALL, E. G.
That actor feller.   TV Guide 6-9:22 Mr 1 '58
The man nobody knows.   TV Guide 9-44:17 N 4 '61
Kelly, V.   Defenders: TV and the law.   Look 26:86 D
4 '62
Defender.   Newsweek 62:56 D 16 '63
Wanted: more hot issues.   TV Guide 12-34:15 Ag 22 '64

MARSHALL, HERBERT
Rankin, R.   Actresses clamor for this man!   Photop 46-
2:33 Jl '34
Wiles, O.   What it's like to work with Garbo.   Photop
46-6:43 N '34
Manners, D.   Romance and Herbert Marshall.   Photop
51-5:28 My '37
Personalities.   U. N.   Bul 2:176 F 25 '47
Oldest actor in the world.   Theatre Arts 31:39 O '47
Where are they now?   Newsweek 67:14 Ja 24 '66
Obit.   Newsweek 67:61 Ja 31 '66
Time 87:72 Ja 28 '66
Brit Bk Yr 1967:596 '67
Screen World 18:237 '67
Hughes, A. H.   Filmography.   Films In Review 17-4:260
Ap '66
Mandelbaum, H. I.   Herbert Marshall, inc. filmog.
Films In Review 20-3:190 Mr '69

MARSHALL, TULLY
Handy, T. B.   Everyone's ag'in him.   Photop 16-3:100
Ag '19
Obit.   Cur Bio '43
Gray, B.   Tully Marshall, inc. filmog.   Films In Re-
view 18-9:596 N '66

MARTEN, HELEN
Brandon, F. M.   An eclair beauty.   Photop 4-3:62 Ag '13
Condon, M.   Helen Marten, her work and her play.
Photop 6-1:115 Je '14

MARTIN, CHRIS-PIN
Condon, F.   El Comico.   Colliers 105:11 Je 22 '40
Bloom, M. T.   Hollywood's good samaritan.   Am Mag

148:24 N '49

MARTIN, DEAN
   Martin, Mrs. D.   How I trained my husband.   Photop 43-
      3:52 Mr '53
   Arnold, M.   The more the merrier.   Photop 45-1:38 Ja
      '54
   Taurog, N.   It really happened.   Photop 45-4:36 Ap '54
   Wood, C.   TV personalities biographical sketchbook.
      TV Personalities p64 '56
   I'm tired of being the heavy.   TV Guide 5-15:17 Ap 13 '57
   Make-a-million Martin.   Life 45:109 D 22 '58
   $1 million a year.   Newsweek 53:94 F 9 '59
   Dean Martin, the man behind the myths.   Look 24:53 N 8
      '60
   Martin, P.   I call on Dean Martin.   Sat Eve Post 234:
      16 Ap 29 '61
   Gordon, S.   Dino goes dramatic.   Look 27:89 Ap 9 '63
   Biography.   Cur Bio 25:19 N '64
      Same.   Cur Bio Yrbk 1964:280 '64
   Fessier, M.   Why he drinks on stage!   Photop 66-6:62
      D '64
   Condon, M.   They remember Dino.   TV Guide 13-38:8
      S 18 '65
   Old moderately.   Time 87:60 Mr 11 '66
   Rollin, B.   Dean Martin cools it, and makes it.   Look
      30:54 My 17 '66
   Durslag, M.   TV's most engaging fraud.   TV Guide 14-
      14:10 Ap 2 '66
   Raddatz, L.   It's 2 o'clock and nobody's opened the pea-
      nut butter yet.   TV Guide 15-7:15 F 18 '67
   Funny-side up.   Newsweek 69:97 Mr 20 '67
   Williamson, B.   Dino's breezy way to easy money; Dean
      Martin show.   Life 62:18 My 26 '67
   Dinter, C.   Why I don't like my wife.   Photop 71-6:41 Je
      '67
   Thomas, B.   Is there a real Dean Martin?   Good H 165:
      96 N '67
   Fallaci, O.   Dean Martin talks about his drinking, the
      Mafia, Frank Sinatra, women, Bobby Kennedy; intv.
      Look 31:78 D 26 '67
   TV Christmas with the Martins and the Sinatras.   Look
      31:76 D 26 '67
   His last call to his father.   Photop 72-6:32 D '67
   O'Brien, F.   What they do to daughters.   Photop 73-3:41
      Mr '68
   Morris, A.   Embarrassed to be Dean's son.   Photop 73-

4:37 Ap '68
O'Brien, F.   All about their children .   Photop 74-1:50
   Jl '68
Hobson, D.   This man earns more money in a year than
   anyone in the history of show business.   TV Guide 16-
   39:20 S 28 '68
Martin, J. B. ed by V. Scott.   Improbable private life of
   Mrs. Dean Martin; intv.   Ladies Home J 85:97 N '68
Bascombe, L.   I bore my husband.   Photop 75-2:68 F '69
Storrick, B. E.   His other women.   Photop 75-3:56 Mr '69
(See also: MARTIN AND LEWIS)

MARTIN, DEWEY
Harbert, R.   Assignment in Hollywood.   Good H 136:17
   F '53
Bailey, C.   His lady is lucky.   Photop 44-6:62 D '53
Oppenheimer, P. J.   Dewey Martin is the darndest.
   Photop 49-3:47 Mr '56

MARTIN, MARY
Texas town hails its favorite daughter on her cinema de-
   but.   Life 8:24 Ja 8 '40
Mary Martin plays Cindy Lou and sings a song in Kiss the
   boys goodbye.   Life 10:81 My 26 '41
I sing for Bing.   Am Mag 135:44 Ap '43
   Same.   Read Digest 42:34 Je '43
Venus scores season's first hit.   Newsweek 22:86 O 18
   '43
One touch of Venus.   Life 15:61 O 25 '43
Mary Martin's dress.   Life 15:57 N 22 '43
Perkins, J.   Mary Martin.   Life 15:98 D 27 '43
Biography.   Cur Bio '44
One touch of Martin; New York apartment.   House & Gard
   88:62 Ag '45
Crichton, K.   Mary had a little talent.   Colliers 117:16
   Mr 2 '46
Fun on an island.   Newsweek 33:78 Ap 11 '49
Mary Martin curls her own.   Womans H C 76:133 S '49
My year of South Pacific.   Read Digest 56:25 Je '50
Amos, W.   Day in the life of Mary Martin.   Am Mag 149:
   42 Je '50
Hammond, H.   Uncontrary Mary Martin.   House & Gard
   98:38 Jl '50
Long, Long ago.   Theatre Arts 34:39 S '50
That's my boy; Mary Martin and son.   Time 56:57 D 18
   '50
Christmas belle.   Theatre Arts 35:20 Ja '51

Mary Martin's other life.   Coronet 30:111 My '51
Benchley, N.   Off stage.   Theatre Arts 35:46 S '51
Evening with Martin enchants Londoners.   Life 31:50 N
    19 '51
Dempsey, D.   That man.   N.Y. Times Bk R p8 D 9 '51
Peck, S.   She washed that girl right outa her hair.
    N.Y. Times Mag p19 S 20 '56
Martin, Boyer and Kind sir: a powerful box-office team.
    Newsweek 42:56 N 9 '53
No more shampoos for Nellie.   Colliers 132:32 N 13 '53
Mary Martin's own scrapbook.   Vogue 122:98 D '53
Plimmer, C. & Plimmer, D.   Her heart belongs to
    Broadway.   Coronet 35:68 Mr '54
There is nothing like a frame.   House & Gard 106:48 Ag
    '54
Neverland to Broadway.   Life 37:109 N 8 '54
Brown, J. M.   With the greatest of ease.   Sat R 37:29 N
    20 '54
Mary Martin sings Peter Pan.   Look 18:54 D 14 '54
Halliday, H.   My mother, Mary Martin; as told to S.
    Fields.   McCalls 82:46 Mr '55
Two stars float a TV show.   Life 39:172 O 17 '55
Martin, M.   Lights in the Halliday home.   Coronet 39:
    126 N '55
Heller dances, so does ma.   N.Y. Times Mag p42 D 11
    '55
Hopper, H.   Mary Martin I know.   Womans H C 83:22
    Ja '56
McCarthy, J.   Her heart belongs to fory million people.
    Cosmop 140:26 Ja '56
Mary Martin and the shape.   McCalls 83:44 Mr '56
Miss Martin, I presume?   Newsweek 48:85 Ag 13 '56
Dizzy broad.   Time 68:83 N 5 '56
Biography.   Colliers Yrbk 1956:529 '56
Mary Martin and Richard Halliday, pioneering in central
    Brazil.   Vogue 129:142 Ja 1 '57
Martin, M.   My mother-in-law and me.   Good H 144:102
    Je '57
Bull wins, man loses, Martin reacts.   Look 21:26 Jl 9 '57
Horseback, piggyback.   Life 43:124 D 9 '57
My favorite Christmas present.   McCalls 85:6 D '57
Biography.   Mus Am 78:4 Jl '58
Lansdale, N.   Mary Martin: 1958-59.   Theatre Arts 42:
    17 S '58
Martin, M. & Halliday, R.   We did it and we're glad.
    Good H 148:56 Ja '59
Martin, P.   I call on Mary Martin.   Sat Eve Post 231:

32 Mr 28 '59
120 minutes of Mary. Newsweek 53:68 Mr 30 '59
Frazier, G. Sight and sound. McCalls 86:6 Ap '59
Rice, C. D. Everybody sing! Read Digest 74:207 Ap '59
Trapp family and Mary. Life 47:87 S 21 '59
Offstage talk. Newsweek 54:102 N 30 '59
Nichols, M. Rx for hit: Mary, music, kids. Coronet
    47:16 Mr '60
Mary Martin's other talent. Good H 150:259 My '60
Martin, M. Best advice I ever had. Read Digest 76:49
    Je '60
Liston, J. At home with Mary Martin. Am Home 64:18
    Ag '61
Mary Martin. Esquire 57:58 Mr '62
Weir, H. H. My mother Mary Martin. Good H 156:54
    Ja '63
Kelly, V. Mary Martin: perpetual motion. Look 27:66
    S 10 '63
Alexander, S. Broadway show in a theater of war.
    Life 59:30 O 22 '65
Hello, Dolly, and hellish ambush. Life 59:32 O 22 '65
Paar, J. Mary Martin. McCalls 94:101 O '66
My ranch in Brazil. Esquire 69:105 Ap '68

MARTIN, ROSS
A Latin from Manhattan. TV Guide 8-21:10 My 21 '60
Raddatz, L. The wild, wild man from the wild, wild
    west. TV Guide 14-21:15 My 21 '66

MARTIN, TONY
Parsons, L. O. Intermission for romance. Photop 28-6:
    30 My '46
Dreier, H. Hobby house. Photop 37-4:58 Ap '50
Martin on top. Newsweek 35:84 Je 12 '50
Kass, R. Film and TV. Cath World 179:223 Je '54
Tony Martin's a lucky guy. Womans H C 81:67 S '54
Wheatland, C. M. & Sharpe, E. Young Hollywood at
    home. Ladies Home J 74:70 Je '57

MARTIN, VIVIAN
Vivacious Vivian. Cosmop 55:413 Ag '13
MacGaffey, K. It should have been different. Photop
    12-3:95 Ag '17
Alexander, S. Ingenue from the eyes down. Photop 17-1:
    108 D '19

MARTIN AND LEWIS
  (Dean Martin & Jerry Lewis)
  New voices, old gags. Newsweek 33:61 Ap 18 '49
  Talk of show business. Time 53:57 My 23 '49
  The riot started in Atlantic City. TV Guide 3-45:8 N11 '50
  Davidson, B. Anything for a laugh. Colliers 127:30 F
    10 '51
  Jeffers, W. Investigating Martin and Lewis. TV Guide
    4-25:24 Je 23 '51
  Hard work. Time 58:82 Jl 23 '51
  Free show; Paramount Theatre. New Yorker 27:16 Jl 28
    '51
  Crackpots hit jackpot. Life 31:57 Ag 13 '51
  Edwards, J. Martin and Lewis: tops in comedy. Coro-
    net 31:85 F '52
  Martin and Lewis marathon. TV Guide 5-11:6 Mr 14 '52
  Funny men Dean Martin and Jerry Lewis. Sight & Sound
    22-1:30 Jl/S '52
  Zeitlin, I. Behind the riot act. Photop 42-3:56 S '52
  Armstrong, G. Time to part? Photop 43-5:31 My '53
  Martin and Lewis' backyard movies. TV Guide 1-10:4
    Je 5 '53
  Bailey, C. Mayhem, unlimited. Photop 44-4:46 O '53
  Arnold, M. Are Martin and Lewis breaking up? Photop
    46-1:50 Jl '54
  It's not love, Chum. Newsweek 46:81 Ag 15 '55
  Arnold, M. Are they heading for the big split-up?
    Photop 48-3:31 S '55
  Zolotow, M. Martin and Lewis feud. Cosmop 139:62 O
    '55
  To the rescue. Time 67:74 Ja 9 '56
  (See also: LEWIS, JERRY; MARTIN, DEAN)

MARTINDEL, EDWARD
  Obit. Screen World 7:225 '56

MARTINELLI, ELSA
  Nichols, M. Foreign accent in starlets. Coronet 40:54
    Ag '56
  Newest eyeful from Italy. Life 43:115 N 25 '57
  Talese, G. Accommodation, Italian style. Esquire 59:
    88 F '63

MARVIN, LEE
  Man in a strait jacket. TV Guide 7-6:17 F 7 '59
  Assorted blasts from an angry man. TV Guide 7-40:17
    O 3 '59

Man for vicaries. Time 85:58 Je 4 '65

Drunkest gun in the West. Life 58:121 Je 11 '65

Schwartz, W. Lee Marvin, inc. filmog. Films In Review 17-6:384 Je/Jl '66

Biography. Cur Bio 27:32 S '66

  Same. Cur Bio Yrbk 1966:265 '67

Redbook dialogue. Redbook 130:74 N '67

Kluge, P. F. Old foes with a new view of war. Life 65:52 S 27 '68

Barthel, J. He's way up on top, baby! TV Guide 16-39: 15 S 28 '68

MARX, CHICO

  Obit. Illus Lond N 239:683 O 21 '61

    Newsweek 58:68 O 23 '61

    Time 78:88 O 20 '61

    Cur Bio 22:7 D '61

    Cur Bio Yrbk 1961:300 '62

    Am Ann 1962:855 '62

    Screen World 13:225 '62

  (See also: MARX BROTHERS)

MARX, GROUCHO

  My poor wife! Colliers 86:15 D 20 '30

  Bad days are good memories. Sat Eve Post 204:12 Ag 29 '31

  Many happy returns. Sat R 25:14 Ja 24 '42

  Philippic. Sat R 28:20 D 22 '45

  How to be a spy. Life 20:65 Ap 1 '46

  Which is Groucho? Life 24:100 F 2 '48

  Master Marx. Newsweek 33:53 My 2 '49

  What comes naturally. Time 54:69 N 7 '49

  Groucho's garland of gags. Life 27:139 N 21 '49

  Hot out of Vassar. Time My 1 '50

  Groucho rides again. Newsweek 35:56 My 15 '50

  Rosten, L. Groucho--the man from Marx. Read Digest 56:5 My '50

  Groucho marks up a hit. TV Guide 4-2:8 Ja 13 '51

  Marx, H. My brother, Groucho. Coronet 29:130 F '51

  Groucho the great. TV Guide 4-23:20 Je 9 '51

  Marx, A. Groucho is my pop. Colliers 128:13 O 13 '51

  Personality. Time 58:29 D 31 '51

  Perelman, S. J. Weekend with Groucho Marx. Holiday 11:59 Ap '52

  Marx, G. How I pick my contestants. TV Guide 5-18: 4 My 2 '52

  Does Groucho Marx really ad lib? TV Guide 5-29:4 Jl

18 '52

Tein, P. Why Groucho is turning copy writer.   Ptr Ink
240:40 Jl 18 '52

Groucho Marx says.   Coronet 32:61 Jl '52

Groucho plays it straight.   Theatre Arts 36:15 S '52

Ace, G. Groucho Marx vs. the people.   Sat R 35:28 S
27; 32 O 11 '52

Fenneman talks back.   TV Guide 6-9:4 F 27 '53

What's wrong with the Giants?   Colliers 132:13 Jl 18 '53

Groucho bets on people.   TV Guide 1-17:5 Jl 24 '53

The truth about Groucho's ad libs.   TV Guide 2-12:5 Mr
19 '54

Marx, A. My old man, Groucho.   Sat Eve Post 227:19
S 18; 22 S 25 ; 36 O 2; 38 O 9; 42 O 16; 25 O 23;
36 O 30; 30 N 6 '54

Wood, C. TV personalities biographical sketchbook.
TV Personalities p104 '54

Gibbons, T. Groucho Marx.   Film 4:22 Mr '55

I could never grow a moustache.   Coronet 37:126 Mr '55

The Marx man's targets.   TV Guide 3-35:4 Ag 27 '55

Groucho and his gang.   TV Guide 4-51:8 D 22 '56

Everybody's a critic.   TV Guide 5-17:20 Ap 27 '57

Martin, P. I call on Groucho.   Sat Eve Post 229:31 My
25 '57

Eells, G. Secret of Groucho.   Look 21:28 Jl 9 '57

Stupider the better.   Newsweek 50:52 S 2 '57

Rosten, L. Lunar world of Groucho Marx.   Harper 216:
31 Je '58

When I was young and charming; reminiscences of twenty
years ago.   Sat Eve Post 201:58 Je 22 '59

Marx, G. Groucho and me, abridged.   McCalls 86:44
Je '59

Best of the best; excerpt from Groucho and me.   Vogue
134:115 N 1 '59

Groucho tackles 'The Mikado.'   TV Guide 8-17:12 Ap 23
'60

Lord high Groucho.   Newsweek 55:80 My 2 '60

Fuller, J. G. Trade winds.   Sat R 47:8 F 8 '64

Zimmerman, P. D. Epistles of Groucho.   Newsweek 69:
93A Ap 3 '67

Nolan, M. Marxisms.   Reporter 37:61 Jl 13 '67

Groucho writes.   Take One 1:11 n. d.

(See also: MARX BROTHERS)

MARX, HARPO

Harpo goes straight.   TV Guide 8-51:28 D 17 '50

Marx, H. My brother Groucho.   Coronet 29:130 F '51

Harpo leers, frowns and speaks.   Life 50:65 My 19 '61
Marx, H. with R. Barber.   Harpo speaks!; abridged.
   McCalls 88:76 My '61
Harpo in toyland.   N. Y. Times Mag p82 N 5 '61
Harpo tells a story; excerpt from Harpo speaks! ed. by
   R. Barber.   Read Digest 80:143:6 F '62
Harpo.   Life 57:45 O 9 '64
Quiet one.   Newsweek 64:81 O 12 '64
Obit.   Time 84:82 O 9 '64
   Illus Lond N 245:565 O 10 '64
   Pub W 186:37 O 19 '64
   Cur Bio 25:22 N '64
   Cur Bio Yrbk 1964:282 '64
   Screen World 16:|224 '65
Sherman, A.   Gift of laughter.   Read Digest 87:82 O '65
(See also: MARX BROTHERS)

MARX BROTHERS
   (Chico, Groucho, Harpo, Zeppo)
Wollcott, A.   Mother of the two-a-day.   Sat Eve Post
   197:42 Je 20 '25
Kennedy, J. B.   Slapstick stuff.   Colliers 78:28 Jl 10 '26
Seldes, G.   Markert and the Marxes.   New Repub 56:351
   N 14 '28
Hamilton, S.   The nuttiest quartette in the world.   Photop
   42-2:27 Jl '32
Marx brothers abroad.   Liv Age 343:371 D '32
Chavance, L.   Four Marx brothers as seen by a French-
   man.   Canad Forum 13:175 F '33
Night at the opera will win converts to Marxism.   News-
   week 6:29 N 23 '35
Ferguson, O.   Marxian epileptic: Night at the opera.
   New Repub 85:130 D 11 '35
Shammis, E. R.   Those mad Marx hares.   Photop 49-2:
   26 F '36
Johnston, A.   Marx brothers; scientific side of lunacy.
   Womans H C 63:12 S '36
   Same abridged.   Read Digest 29:49 O '36
Baskette, K.   Hoodlums at home.   Photop 51-7:38 Jl '37
Seton, M.   S. Dali + 3 Marxes = .   Theatre Arts 23:
   734 O '39
Marshall, J.   Marx menace.   Colliers 117:24 Mr 16 '46
Marx, A.   Marx cousins.   Time 47:6 Ap 1 '46
Biography.   Cur Bio 9:37 My '48
   Same, revised.   Cur Bio Yrbk 1948:425 '49
Kurnitz, H.   Return of the Marx brothers.   Holiday 21:
   95 Ja '57

Marx brothers now.   Newsweek 51:104 Mr 17 '58
Perelman, S. J.   The winsome foursome. Show 1-2:34
 N '61
Kroll, J.   Sam's sons.   Newsweek 72:116 N 25 '68
(See also: MARX, CHICO; MARX, GROUCHO; MARX,
 HARPO)

MASINA, GIULIETTA
Sad and saucy star.   Life 41:48 Ag 6 '56
Nichols, M. Foreign accent in starlets.   Coronet 40:53
 Ag '56
Hatch, R.   Films.   Nation 185:396 N 23 '57
That round-eyed girl.   Newsweek 50:99 D 9 '57
People are talking about . . .   Vogue 131:56 Ja 15 '58
Biography.   Cur Bio 19:22 Ap '58
 Same.   Cur Bio Yrbk 1958:275 '58
Ross, L.   Profiles: F. Fellini.   New Yorker 41:63 O 30
 '65
Lyon, N.   Second fame: good food.   Vogue 147:152 Ja
 1 '66
Davis, M. S.   First the pasta, then the play.
 N. Y. Times Mag p10 Ja 2 '66

MASKELL, VIRGINIA
Coulson, A. A.   Letter, inc. filmog. 19-10:659 D '68
Obit.   Screen World 20:237 '69

MASON, JAMES
Two new stars embellish British film on psychiatry.
 Life 20:65 Ja 28 '46
Wild, R.   One-man invasion.   Photop 29-4:54 S '46
Winslow, T. S.   British idyl.   Photop 30-1:50 D '46
Osborne, J.   James Mason.   Life 22:33 Ja 6 '47
Villain turns hero-worshiper.   N. Y. Times Mag p20
 My 27 '47
Biography.   Cur Bio 8:39 My '47
 Same revised.   Cur Bio Yrbk 1947:429 '48
In praise of cats.   N. Y. Times Mag p16 S 28 '47
Eythe, W.   I meet the menace.   Photop 31-4:48 S '47
Mr. Mason names six best actresses.   N. Y. Times Mag
 p17 N 30 '47
Long, J.   Mean and lovely.   Am Mag 143 Vacation no:
 44 '47
Hubler, R. G.   He makes Hollywood mad.   Sat Eve Post
 227:32 Je 25 '55
Marks, R. W.   L'enfant terrible.   Colliers 138:92 S 28
 '56

Arkadin. Film clips. Sight & Sound 33-3:140 Sum '64

MASON, SHIRLEY
  Boone, A. Surely, Shirley--surely. Photop 14-6:42 N
    '18
  Tully, J. The girl who kept step. Photop 29-2:63 Ja '26

MASSEY, ILONA
  Ducas, D. Lady says no. Colliers 101:11 Je 18 '38
  Fletcher, A. W. This woman has loved! Photop 54-3:
    12 Mr '40; 54-4:70 Ap '40

MASSEY, RAYMOND
  Young, S. Hamlet, Broadhurst theatre, New York, Nov.
    5, 1931. New Repub 69:44 N 25 '31
  Massey into Lincoln. Colliers 103:11 F 18 '39
  Copies. Am Mag 127:92 Mr '39
  Free men are not ersatz people. Survey 79:227 S '43
  Stephen Benet's radio artistry. Sat R 28:24 Ap 14 '45
  Biography. Cur Bio 7:33 F '46
    Same revised. Cur Bio Yrbk 1946:381 '47
  My current reading. Sat R 30:10 D 13 '47
  Wood, C. TV personalities biographical sketchbook.
    TV Personalities p82 '56
  He made them forget Barrymore. TV Guide 10-24:10 Je
    16 '62
  Stein, J. Raymond Massey, inc. filmog. Films In Re-
    view 13-7:389 Ag/S '63

MASTROIANNI, MARCELLO
  Talk with a star. Newsweek 59:96 F 19 '62
  Everymantis. Time 80:71 O 5 '62
  Peck, S. Leading men, European style. N. Y. Times
    Mag p106 N 18 '62
  New veers. Vogue 141:116 Ja 1 '63
  Hamblin, D. J. Symbol of something for all the girls.
    Life 54:79 Ja 18 '63
  Biography. Cur Bio 24:26 Je '63
    Same. Cur Bio Yrbk 1963:260 '64
  Fellini, F. What Fellini thinks Mastroianni thinks about
    women. Vogue 142:50 Ag 15 '63
  Newman, D. Ciao, Marcello. Esquire 60:110 N '63
  Socialist Savonarola. Time 83:95 My 1 '64
  Bocca, G. Marcello Mastroianni: reluctant lover.
    McCalls 91:64 My '64
  Lawrenson, H. Marcello Mastroianni: Latin lover, new
    style. Look 28:26 Ag 11 '64

Bimonte, R.   Art of anti-acting.   Reporter 31:49 O 22 '64
Menen, A.   Actor, Italian style.   Holiday 37:95 Ja '65
Italy for Barbra Streisand.   Esquire 63:68 F '65
Redbook dialogue: Barbra Streisand and Marcello Mas-
    troianni.   Redbook 125:50 Jl '65
Barzini, L.   Mastroianni the man, the actor, the reluc-
    tant lover.   Vogue 146:96 O 15 '65
Shenker, I.   Man who made apathy irresistable.   N. Y.
    Times Mag p54 D 12 '65
Chamberlin, A.   Great undashing lover of our time.
    Sat Eve Post 239:81 Ag 13 '66
Royce, A.   Marriage Italian style.   Photop 73-2:33 F '68
Fellini, F.   Marcello at home: is he?   Vogue 152:134
    N 15 '68
Hamilton, J.   Faye and the Italian.   Look 33:44 Ja 21 '69
Brandt, S.   In love with Mastroianni.   Photop 75-1:39 Ja
    '69

MATTHAU, WALTER
Misleading man.   Theatre Arts 37:15 Mr '53
Dubivsky, B.   Up and coming.   N. Y. Times Mag p65 O
    18 '53
Ross, L.   Player.   New Yorker 37:98 N 4 '61
Gill, A.   The boy from the cold-water flat has made it.
    TV Guide 12-24:16 Je 13 '64
That wonderful what's-his-name.   Time 85:52 Mr 26 '65
Biography.   Cur Bio 27:26 Je '66
    Same.   Cur Bio Yrbk 1966:267 '67
Moore, G.   Unmasking the great putty face; intv.   Life
    62:37 Mr 3 '67
Jennings, C. R.   Matthau in full flower.   Esquire 70:
    192 D '68
Lear, M. W.   Walter Matthau: juiciest actor in the west;
    intv.   Redbook 132:69 Ja '69

MATTHEWS, JESSIE
Pringle, H. F.   John Bull's girl.   Colliers 98:48 O 31 '36
Rhea, M.   The star whom money doesn't tempt.   Photop
    51-10:30 O '37
Roman, R. C.   Jessie Matthews.   Dance Mag 40:66 S '66

MATURE, VICTOR
Coughlan, R.   New matinee idol.   Life 10:65 Ap 7 '41
Franchey, J. R.   Life owes you nothing.   Photop 20-5:
    52 Ap; 20-6:56 My '42
Othman, F. C.   Gall is a wonderful thing.   Sat Eve Post
    215:24 Jl 18 '42

Waterbury, R.   The romance Hollywood doesn't like.
Photop 21-6:28 N '42
Mature, M.   Why I'm not divorcing Victor Mature.
Photop 22-2:23 Ja '43
Addison, R.   When Rita Hayworth said goodby to Victor
Mature.   Photop 22-4:47 Mr '43
Addison, R.   Breakup--the truth about Rita Hayworth and
Victor Mature.   Photop 23-3:28 Ag '43
So your man came back.   Photop 24-2:30 Ja '44
Sammis, F. R.   Here is a sailor!   Photop 27-6:27 N '45
Parsons, L. O.   Smoke screen.   Photop 28-4:30 Mr '46
Fink, H.   I was there.   Photop 32-1:52 D '47
Arnold, M.   Mature mood.   Photop 32-2:58 Ja '48
Mature, D. B.   The man that I married.   Photop 33-1:
40 Je '48
Ott, B.   Tough softie.   Photop 47-1:50 Ja '50
Maynard, J.   The Victor Mature view.   Photop 37-2:54
F '50
Biography.   Cur Bio 12:33 D '51
Same.   Cur Bio Yrbk 1951:416 '52

MAUCH TWINS
(Billy and Bobby)
Mauch twins and Mark Twain.   Time 29:25 My 3 '37
Beatty, J.   It's a toss-up.   Am Mag 123:20 Je '37
Sinclair, L.   Double trouble.   Photop 51-9:22 S '37

MAUREY, NICOLE
Rita, Marlene and the farmer's daughter.   Life 35:65 Ag
3 '53

MAURICE, MARY
Meloney, Mrs. W. B.   Mother of the movies.   Delin 87:
9 Ag '15
Bartlett, R.   Madonna of the movies.   Photop 9-4:49 Mr
'16

MAXWELL, MARILYN
Taunted tiger mars Marilyn.   Life 37:22 S 6 '54

MAY, DORIS
Jordan, J.   Love and company.   Photop 20-6:47 N '22

MAY, EDNA
Blum, D.   Ten beauties of the American stage.   Theatre
Arts 36:68 S '52

MAY, ELAINE
    Watt, D.   Tables for two.   New Yorker 33:46 D 21 '57
    Success story.   Newsweek 51:64 Ja 27 '58
    People are talking about.   Vogue 131:91 Ap 1 '58
    Fresh eggheads.   Time 71:53 Je 2 '58
    Scott, J. A.   How to be a success in show business.
        Cosmop 145:68 N '58
    Cotler, G.   For the love of Mike and Elaine.   N.Y.
        Times Mag p71 My 24 '59
    TV gets laughs from its griefs.   Life 48:106 F 15 '60
    Mirror to our madness.   Look 24:46 Je 21 '60
    Two characters in search . . .   Time 76:61 S 26 '60
    McCarten, J.   Theatre.   New Yorker 36:74 O 15 '60
    Evening with Mike Nichols and Elaine May.   Time 76:73
        O 24 '60
    Brustein, R.   Comedians from the underground.
        New Repub 143:28 O 31 '60
    Nichols, May and horses.   New Yorker 36:44 N 12 '60
    Fun with human foibles.   Life 49:65 N 21 '60
    Evening with Mike Nichols and Elaine May.   Theatre Arts
        44:12 D '60
    Nichols, M.   Entertainment of the month.   Coronet 52:22
        F '61
    Markel, H.   Mike Nichols and Elaine May.   Redbook
        116:32 F '61
    Comics Nichols and May take a long, hard look at the art
        of conversation.   Liv for Young Hom 14:88 Mr '61
    Biography.   Cur Bio 22:34 Mr '61
        Same.   Cur Bio Yrbk 1961:300 '62
    Rice, R.   Tilted insight.   New Yorker 37:47 Ap 15 '61
    Nichols, M.   Broadway's top comedy team takes up bowl-
        ing.   Good H 152:32 My '61
    Nichols, M.   Elaine May.   McCalls 94:98 O '66
    Thompson, T.   Whatever happened to Elaine May?   Life
        63:54 Jl 28 '67

MAY, NINA
    Howe, H.   A jungle Lorelei.   Photop 36-2:36 Jl '29

MAYNARD, KEN
    Spensley, D.   Young Lochinvar Maynard.   Photop 30-5:
        84 O '26
    Three R's of the range.   St N 63:16 Mr '36

MAYO, EDNA
    Thein, M.   A chat with the girl on the cover.   Feature
        Movie 1-2:5 Ap 1 '15

Craig, J.   The girl on the cover.   Photop 9-5:36 Ap '16

MAYO, FRANK
   Obit.   Screen World 15:223 '64

MAYO, VIRGINIA
   Build your home now.   Am Home 36:30 Je '46
   Colby, A.   Summer performance.   Photop 31-2:66 Jl '47
   Best year of her life.   Am Mag 145:103 Ag '48
   Mayo, V.   The transformation of Sis Jones.   Photop 37-
      5:52 My '50
   O'Shea, M.   Mrs. Whistle Bait.   Photop 42-5:66 N '52
   Leon, R.   Oh, Baby!   Photop 44-3:46 S '53
   Noel, T.   Becoming a father's no joke.   Photop 45-2:44
      F '54
   Jeffers, D.   There's a girl called Virginia.   Photop 47-
      2:34 F '55

MC AVOY, MAY
   Evans, D.   Waiting for fame.   Photop 19-3:64 F '21
   Sangster, M. E.   The enchanted princess.   Photop 25-5:
      55 Ap '24
   Bodeen, D.   May McAvoy, inc. filmog.   Films In Review
      19-8:482 O '68

MC BAIN, DIANE
   Exiled to Siberia.   TV Guide 8-50:28 D 10 '60
   Johnson, M.   Girls say I'm fast.   Photop 60-3:60 S '61
   McBain, D.   I fell for a married man.   Photop 61-3:36
      Mr '62

MC CALLISTER, LON
   Hamilton, S.   "California" coming up.   Photop 23-6:54
      N '43
   Delehanty, T.   The Mick of McCallister.   Photop 24-5:34
      Ap '44
   McCallister, L.   My G. I. dates.   Photop 26-2:48 Ja '45
   McCallister, L.   A letter to my mother.   Photop 26-6:
      32 My '45
   McCallister, L.   You may never come back.   Photop
      28-5:54 Ap '46
   Maddox, B.   Lines on Lon.   Photop 32-1:58 D '47

MC CALLUM, DAVID
   The greatest thing since peanut butter and jelly.   TV
      Guide 13-16:6 Ap 17 '65
   Brossard, C.   U. N. C. L. E.'s Illya; new kind of TV idol.

Look 29:79 Jl 27 '65
Kessner, J.   His wild days, his lonely nights.   Photop
    68-2:39 Jl '65
Who would you run to?   Photop 68:2:39 Ag '65
Miller, E.   Spy who'd rather not be known.   Seventeen
    24:116 S '65
Wolfe, B.   Man called I-L-L-Y-A.   N. Y. Times Mag
    p56 O 24 '65
Illya goes home to the heather.   Life 60:45 Ap 29 '66
My husband David . . .   TV Guide 14-23:24 Je 4 '66
Byrnes, A.   Love sales on.   Photop 72-2:66 Ag '67
York, C.   His wedding to Kathy Carpenter.   Photop 72-6:
    6 D '67

MC CAMBRIDGE, MERCEDES
Radio star shows her versatility.   Life 21:55 S 23 '46
Hill, G.   Tough as a kitten.   Colliers 126:23 S 9 '50
They come from Chicago.   Theatre Arts 35:45 Jl '51
Dynamite in skirts.   TV Guide 5-26:12 Je 29 '57
Wood, C.   TV personalities biographical sketchbook.
    TV Personalities p48 '57
Campaigner.   Time 83:56 Ja 31 '65
Biography.   Cur Bio 25:22 Je '64
    Same.   Cur Bio Yrbk 1964:262 '64
Hagen, R.   Mercedes McCambridge, inc. filmog.   Films
    In Review 16-5:292 My '65

MC CARTNEY, PAUL
Jacobs, A.   Beatle Paul is my brother.   Photop 66-3:57
    S '64
Hirschler, Z.   Paul tells the truth.   Photop 68-1:70 Jl
    '65
Biography.   Cur Bio 27:32 N '66
    Same.   Cur Bio Yrbk 1966:251 '67
(See also: THE BEATLES)

MC CLURE, DOUG
He started with soapsuds.   TV Guide 8-30:28 Jl 23 '60
Ardmore, J.   Private life of a private eye.   Photop 59-
    4:40 Ap '61
Pretty boy or actor?   TV Guide 9-36:17 S 9 '61
Dern, M.   Is it true blonde cowboys have more fun?
    TV Guide 12-29:6 Jl 18 '64
Discriminating against dames.   Photop 76-6:48 D '69

MC CORMACK, PATTY
Schumach, M.   Private lives of child thespians.   N. Y.

Times Mag p22 Ja 16 '55
Person of promise. Films & Filming 8-1:25 O '61

MC COY, TIM
Thomas, A. Tim McCoy, inc. filmog. Films In Review
19-4:218 Ap '68

MC CRACKEN, JOAN
Joan McCracken is in new show. Life 17:78 O 2 '44
Biography. Cur Bio Je '45
Porter, A. Girl who fell up. Colliers 118:20 Jl 20 '46
Raher, D. New York's Peter Pan. Plays & Players 1-
2:22 N '53
Obit. Cur Bio 23:24 Ja '62
Cur Bio Yrbk 1962:278 '63
Time 78:78 N 10 '61

MC CREA, JODY
McCrea, J. We and our boys live country style; ed by
J. Morris. Parents Mag 25:40 Ap '50
A family affair. TV Guide 8-2:12 Ja 9 '60

MC CREA, JOEL
Wilkinson, L. A. What makes love tick? Photop 52-12:
28 D '38
McCrea, J. My friend Coop. Photop 53-10:20 O '39
Teacher's pet; autobiography. Am Mag 135:54 F '43
Dudley, F. McCrea Inc. Photop 25-2:52 Jl '44
McCrea, J. We and our boys live country style; ed by
J. Morris. Parents Mag 25:40 Ap '50
Nugent, F. S. Good ol' Joel. Colliers 128:30 S 15 '51
A family affair. TV Guide 8-2:12 Ja 9 '60

MC DANIEL, HATTIE
Biography. Cur Bio '40
Egg fry. Time 50:102 D 1 '47
Obit. Newsweek 40:71 N 3 '52
Time 60:98 N 3 '52
Cur Bio 13:25 D '52
Cur Bio Yrbk 1952:370 '53
Am Ann 1953:414 '53

MC DONALD, MARIE
Scheuer, P. K. Miss McDonald has a form. Colliers
114:14 S 30 '44
Star of India. Am Mag 138:64 O '44
Fletcher, A. W. Every time I leave you. Photop 27-1:

47 Je '45
New clothes horse. Life 22:133 Ap 21 '47
McDonald, M. I learned about men. Photop 32-2:40 Ja
'48
Vanishing lady re-enacts her story. Life 42:117 Ja 21 '57
Obit. Time 86:100 O 29 '65
    Newsweek 66:65 N 1 '65
    Screen World 17:239 '66

MC DOWALL, RODDY
    Zeitlin, I. Awf'ly nice. Photop 22-1:49 D '42
    McDowall, R. This is our job. Photop 24-3:64 F '44
    Nichols, M. Child stars who came back. Coronet 43:
    82 Mr '58
    Eleven fine actors get their dream roles. Life 44:76 Ap
    14 '58
    Biography. Cur Bio 22:25 Ap '61
    Same. Cur Bio Yrbk 1961:280 '62
    Living for today. Newsweek 66:98 N 29 '65

MC ENERY, PETER
    Tomorrow's lead. Plays & Players 8-3:22 D '60

MC FARLAND, OLIVE
    Person of promise. Films & Filming 5-6:26 Mr '59

MC GAVIN, DARREN
    Who's who in the cast. TV Guide 4-51:15 D 21 '51
    Traveling under a full head of steam. TV Guide 8-23:17
    Je 4 '60
    Diehl, D. Old take me-or-leave-me McGavin. TV Guide
    17-3:10 Ja 18 '69
    Sherwood, D. His bitter custody fight. Photop 75-5:62
    My '69

MC GIVER, JOHN
    Old McGiver had a farm. TV Guide 12-35:26 Ag 29 '64

MC GOOHAN, PATRICK
    Tomorrow's lead. Plays & Players 2-8:20 My '55
    Musel, R. James Bond is no hero to him. TV Guide
    14-20:10 My 14 '66
    Barthal, J. An enigma comes to American TV. TV
    Guide 16-21:22 My 25 '68
    Private I. Time 91:65 Je 21 '68
    Shayon, R. L. Orwellian necessities. Sat R 51:54 S 7
    '68

MC GRAW, CHARLES
Wood, C.   TV personalities biographical sketchbook.
TV Personalities p74 '56

MC GREGOR, MALCOLM
Winship, M.   Yale to Hollywood.   Photop 23-1:33 D '22
Howe, H.   What chance has a man in pictures?   Photop
25-2:57 Ja '24

MC GUIRE, DOROTHY
Berch, B.   They call her Mac.   Colliers 108:13 Jl 19 '41
Hellman, G. T.   Actress fits her part so well it is hard
to tell where McGuire ends and Claudia begins.   Life
11:118 N 17 '41
Biography.   Cur Bio '41
Plain girl.   Am Mag 136:122 S '43
Walker, H. L.   The magic of McGuire.   Photop 27-1:34
Je '45
Shipp, C.   Nebraska natural.   Photop 28-1:46 Je '46
Till the end of time.   Life 21:61 Jl 15 '46
Clemens, P.   Dorothy McGuire; a portrait.   Life 21:7 S
2 '46
First ladies.   Coronet 25:16 D '48
Speaking of pictures.   Life 26:18 Mr 14 '49
Star's maternity dresses.   Life 34:53 Je 22 '53
Parish, J. R. & Ringgold, G.   Dorothy McGuire, inc.
filmog.   Films In Review 15-8:466 O '64

MC HUGH, FRANK
Crichton, K.   Out of character.   Colliers 95:30 Mr 23
'35

MC INTIRE, JOHN
Now meet the new wagon master.   TV Guide 9-25:21 Je
24 '61
He's at home on the range.   TV Guide 10-14:22 Ap 7 '62

MC INTYRE, FRANK
Bartlett, R.   A lot to laugh at.   Photop 15-4:74 Mr '19
Biography.   NCAB 38:388 '53

MC KENNA, SIOBHAN
Siobhan of Galway.   New Yorker 31:38 S 17 '55
Lansdale, N.   Joan of London.   Theatre Arts 39:70 S '55
Season's dazzlers.   Vogue 126:116 N 1 '55
Bit o' magic from Ireland.   Look 20:52 Ap 3 '56
Irish star in a U. S. triumph.   Life 40:71 My 21 '56

MacVeagh, A.   St. Joan in Cambridge.   Mlle 43:318 Ag
'56
New Saint Joan.   N. Y. Times Mag p62 S 2 '56
Siobhan shows U. S. her Joan.   Life 41:59 S 10 '56
Hewes, H.   Joan of Galway.   Sat R 39:24 S 15 '56
Gibbs, W.   Joan on Twelfth St.   New Yorker 32:96 S 22
'56
Old play in Manhattan.   Time 68:78 S 24 '56
Something.   Newsweek 48:102 S 24 '56
In search of St. Joan in Ireland.   Life 41:90 O 15 '56
Saint Bernard's Siobhan.   Theatre Arts 40:15 O '56
Ryan, T. C.   Siobhan of Arc.   Colliers 138:42 N 9 '56
Siobhan McKenna and her family.   Vogue 128:104 N 15 '56
Biography.   Cur Bio 17:18 N '56
  Same.   Cur Bio Yrbk 1956:392 '57
Shanley, J. P.   Television: on Person to person program.
America 96:280 D 1 '56
Beckley, P. V.   Spell caster.   Sr Schol 70:6 F 1 '57
Shaw and the actor.   Theatre Arts 41:30 Mr '57
Hewes, H.   Master Hamlet and Saint Viola.   Sat R 40:
26 Jl 20 '57
Bonnie colleen.   Newsweek 53:80 F 9 '59
Going her way.   Time 73:61 F 9 '59
Hyde, H. M.   Siobhan and the BBC.   Spectator (Lond)
202:658 My 8 '59
It's mostly a theatre bird I am.   TV Guide 8-8:24 F 20
'60
Verdi vs. Shakespeare: excerpt from radio broadcast.
Theatre Arts 44:38 Mr '60

MC LAGLEN, VICTOR
Tully, J.   A whale of a man.   Photop 46-1:28 Je '34
Ramsey, W.   The man who plays The informer.   Photop
48-4:65 S '35
Reynolds, Q.   Luck in strange places.   Colliers 96:19 N
16 '35
Johnston, A.   Victor McLaglen, master of the light house.
Womans H C 63:20 N '36
Luck o' gold; autobiography.   Am Mag 135:56 My '43
Obit.   Newsweek 54:79 N 16 '59
  Time 74:93 N 16 '59
  Illus Lond N 235:661 N 14 '59
  Am Ann 1960:856 '60
  Brit Bk Yr 1960:511 '60
  Screen World 11:223 '60
Roman, R. C.   Victor McLaglen.   Films In Review 11-
1:55 Ja '60

MC LEOD, CATHERINE
Hall, G.   On the dot.   Photop 31-6:76 N '47

MC MAHON, HORACE
New cop on the beat.   TV Guide 7-13:20 Mr 28 '59
Gehman, R.   The squire of residual manor.   TV Guide
    10-51:18 D 22 '62

MC NAMARA, MAGGIE
Jacobi, E.   The jig's up, Maggie!   Photop 47-4:42 Ap '55

MC QUEEN, BUTTERFLY
What they are doing now.   Show 4-4:116 Ap '64

MC QUEEN, STEVE
So he got a horse.   TV Guide 7-22:12 My 30 '59
Hoffman, J.   We're trapped.   Photop 56-5:45 N '59
Nichols, M.   Ex-beatnik on the range.   Coronet 48:15 S
    '60
Rugged, tormented, thrill happy.   Look 24:47 O 11 '60
Johnson, R.   TV's angry young star.   Sat Eve Post
    234:26 Ja 14 '61
Miller, E.   Keep it cool.   Seventeen 21:92 D '62
Mild one.   Time 81:48 Je 28 '63
Bunzel, P.   Bad boy's breakout.   Life 55:62 Jl 12 '63
Larkin, L.   A rage to live and love.   Photop 64-6:60
    D '63
Real McQueen.   Newsweek 63:42 Ja 6 '64
Kessner, J.   I live in a McQueen world.   Photop 65-2:59
    F '64
Havemann, E.   Twenty-four hours in the life of Steve
    McQueen.   McCalls 91:138 Ap '64
Agustus, A.   I searched for my father.   Photop 66-2:33
    Ag '64
McQueen, S.   Star among fast friends.   Sports Illus 25:
    34 Ag 8 '66
Rudeen, K.   I still get goose pimples.   Sports Illus 25:
    39 Ag 8 '66
Biography.   Cur Bio 27:18 O '66
Same.   Cur Bio Yrbk 1966:256 '67
Motorcycles: what I like in a bike, and why.   Pop Sci
    189:76 N '66
Armbrister, T.   Loser makes it big.   Sat Eve Post 240:
    26 Ja 14 '67
Conroy, F.   Short, bumpy ride with Steve McQueen.
    Esquire 67:108 Je '67
Robbins, F.   How he made his wife happy.   Photop 74-

1:44 Jl '68
Why he's scared to death.   Photop 75-2:74 F '69
Ardmore, J.   I never thought we'd last.   Photop 75-5:66
  My '69

MEADOWS, AUDREY
  Second bananas.   Look 17:17 My 5 '53
  McCarthy, J.   Meadows sisters and how they grew.
    Cosmop 136:25 Mr '54
  Steadfast sister act.   Life 37:57 Jl 5 '54
  Long, J.   Sisters with a secret.   Am Mag 160:20 S '55
  Wood, C.   TV personalities biographical sketchbook.
    TV Personalities p11 '56
  Biography.   Cur Bio 19:27 My '58
  Same.   Cur Bio Yrbk 1958:278 '58

MEADOWS, JAYNE
  McCarthy, J.   Meadows sisters and how they grew.
    Cosmop 136:25 Mr '54
  Steadfast sister act.   Life 37:57 Jl 5 '54
  French, M. G.   Husbands of four beautiful women tell us
    why she goods good to me.   McCalls 82:105 Ag '55
  Long, J.   Sisters with a secret.   Am Mag 160:20 S '55
  Wood, C.   TV personalities biographical sketchbook.
    TV Personalities p93 '56
  Meadows, J.   Seven men in my life; as told to L. Berg-
    quist.   Look 22:26 Mr 4 '58
  Biography.   Cur Bio 19:29 My '58
    Same.   Cur Bio Yrbk 1958:280 '58
  Allen, S.   Conquest of Jayne Mansfield.   Look 23:57 Ap
    14 '59

MEDINA, PATRICIA
  An actress in spite of herself.   TV Guide 7-35:24 Ag 29
    '59

MEEK, DONALD
  Mullett, M. B.   Donald Meek's ladder to fame has had
    758 steps.   Am Mag 98:34 O '24
  Obit.   Newsweek 28:61 D 2 '46
  McClure, A.   The unsung heroes: Donald Meek.
    Film Fan Mo 92:19 F '69

MEEKER, RALPH
  Raher, D.   New York's matinee idol.   Plays & Players
    1-1:9 O '53

MEI, TSEN
    Evans, D.   A new China doll.   Photop 15-3:41 F '19

MEIGHAN, THOMAS
    Craig, J.   The chap the camera chased.   Photop 12-3:
        67 Ag '17
    Owen, K.   Not so darn ugly.   Photop 16-5:68 O '19
    Meighan, T.   Confessions of a caveman.   Photop 18-4:45
        S '20
    Meighan, T.   Temperament.   Photop 20-4:100 S '21
    Howe, H.   The man who gets what he wants.   Photop
        24-2:37 Jl 23
    Ade, G.   Talks about Tom.   Photop 25-4:42 Mr '24
    Tarkington, B.   What Tom's pal thinks of him.   Photop
        26-3:47 Ag '24
    Harding, A.   What Thomas Meighan is like in real life;
        intv.   Am Mag 99:16 Ap '25
    Hero's life is not an easy one.   Colliers 76:12 Ag 22 '25
    Smith, A.   He knows all the champs.   Photop 32-5:30 O
        '27
    Shakleton, W. D.   Tom Meighan is restless.   Photop 47-
        2:83 Ja '35

MENJOU, ADOLPHE
    Waterbury, R.   Why women like sophisticated men.
        Photop 29-6:32 My '26
    Lang, H.   Adolphe comes home!   Photop 38-2:35 Jl '30
    Hall, L.   Let's give 'Dolphe a hand.   Photop 43-5:67 Ap
        '33
    Reynolds, Q.   Father was right.   Colliers 101:11 Je 25
        '38
    Henderson, J.   The three careers of Adolphe Menjou.
        Photop 52-8:18 Ag '38
    I'm a pigeon at golf.   Am Mag 144:46 N '47
    Menjou, A.   It took nine tailors; an autobiography with
        M. M. Musselman; abridged.   Read Digest 52:143 F '48
    Biography.   Cur Bio 9:41 Je '48
        Same revised.   Cur Bio Yrbk 1948:440 '49
    Four from Hollywood.   TV Guide 6-4:11 Ja 23 '53
    Wood, C.   TV personalities biographical sketchbook.
        TV Personalities p20 '57
    Menjou, A.   Man of two worlds and 250 movies.   Films
        & Filming 7-11:8 Ag '61
    Obit.   Time 82:94 N 8 '63
        Illus Lond N 243:783 N 9 '63
        Newsweek 62:84 N 11 '63
        Nat R 15:440 N 19 '63

Am Ann 1964:742 '64
Brit Bk Yr 1964:631 '64
Cur Bio 25:25 Ja '64
Cur Bio Yrbk 1964:289 '64
Screen World 15:223 '64

MERCER, BERYL
Obit. Newsweek 14:37 Ag 7 '39

MERCER, FRANCES
Chierchetti, D. Film Fan Monthly interviews Frances
Mercer. Film Fan Mo 85-6:24 Jl/Ag '68

MERCHANT, VIVIEN
Mrs. Pinter. Time 89:78 F 10 '67

MERCOURI, MELINA
Her name means honey. Life 49:73 S 19 '60
Grenier, C. Mercouri rises. N.Y. Times Mag p90 S
25 '60
Nichols, M. Greece's gifted gypsy. Coronet 49:10 Ap
'61
Greek goddess. Newsweek 58:102 S 11 '61
Melina gives all or nothing. Life 51:121 O 6 '61
Schoenbrun, D. Melina Mercouri on love; intv. Esquire
57:62 Ap '62
Mercouri, a blaze in white. Vogue 140:104 N 15 '62
Ginna, R. E. Melina Mercouri. Sat Eve Post 236:24 My
25 '63
Knowles, J. Melina the Greek. Holiday 35:101 Ja '64
Melina Mercouri and Salvador Dali. Redbook 124:52 F '65
Biography. Cur Bio 26:25 Jl '65
Same. Cur Bio Yrbk 1965:289 '65
Duras, M. People are talking about. Vogue 147:108 Ap
15 '66
Melina Mercouri. Vogue 148:114 N 15 '66
Hallowell, J. Taming Melina to be a hoofer. Life 61:52
D 2 '66
Hamilton, J. Melina Mercouri rehearses Never on Sunday
for Broadway. Look 31:66 Ja 24 '67
Hicklin, R. View from the road; dances of Illya darling.
Dance Mag 41:24 Mr '67
Melina. Life 62:48 Je 30 '67
Fallaci, O. I was born Greek, I will die Greek; intv.
Look 31:72 S 5 '67

MEREDITH, BURGESS
Reed, E. Roster of new faces. Theatre Arts 18:64 Ja '34
Reed, E. Personae gratae. Theatre Arts 20:51 Ja '36
Eustis, M. Actor attacks his part. Theatre Arts 21:
227 Mr '37
Roberts, K. Fired to fame. Colliers 99:24 Ap 11 '37
Sugrue, T. Farewell to youth; intv. Am Mag 124:32
Ag '37
Biographical note. Sr Schol 31:22E Ja 22 '38
Biography. Cur Bio '40
Addison, R. Paulette's in love. Photop 22-3:66 F '43
Waterbury, R. Exclusive on Paulette Goddard and Bur-
gess Meredith. Photop 25-3:62 Ag '44
Leonard, H. Present and accounted for. Sight & Sound
15-59:88 Aut '46
Meredith, B. This is my wife. Photop 29-5:62 O '46
Wood, C. TV personalities biographical sketchbook.
TV Personalities p46 '54
Four-faced Hamlet; Baylor university. Life 40:97 Je 11
'56
Macrobiotics. New Yorker 38:22 Ag 25 '62
Film Fan Monthly interviews Burgess Meredith. Film
Fan Mo 80:3 F '68

MERKEL, UNA
North, J. Two ladies who make you laugh. Photop 40-3:
66 Ag '31
Hamilton, S. She want to be funny. Photop 42-1:40 Je
'32
Hill, M. I think women are swell says Una Merkel.
Photop 48-4:49 S '35
Crichton, K. Something to fight about. Colliers 101:17
Ap 2 '38

MERMAN, ETHEL
Crichton, K. Singing Merman. Colliers 95:15 F 16 '35
Life and times. Time 36:65 O 28 '40
Biography. Cur Bio '41
Annie scores a bull's eye. Newsweek 27:84 My 27 '46
Woolf, S. J. Sharpshooting singer from Astoria. N. Y.
Times Mag p22 Je 2 '46
Brown, J. M. La Merman. Sat R 29:30 Je 15 '46
What comes naturally. New Yorker 22:20 Je 22 '46
Gibbs, W. Ethel Merman, queen of musical comedy.
Life 21:84 Jl 8 '46
Porter, A. Sureshot Merman. Colliers 118:20 Ag 10 '46
Gibbs, W. Ethel Merman, queen of musical comedy;

abridged.   Read Digest 49:84 O '46
Manning, M.   You can't tell some people there is no
    Santa Claus!   Am Home 37:26 D '46
Female of the species.   Time 54:48 Ag 15 '49
Merman's adventure.   Newsweek 34:50 Ag 15 '49
Hostess with the mostes'.   Life 29:92 S 18 '50
Millstein, G.   Madam Ambassador from and to Broadway.
    N.Y. Times Mag p24 O 1 '50
Poling, J.   Smile when you call Merman madam.
    Colliers 126:22 O 21 '50
Brown, J. M.   With the mostes' on the ball.   Sat R 33:
    42 O 28 '50
Biographical note.   Time 61:110 Mr 23 '53
Anything goes again.   Life 36:91 Mr 15 '54
Merman-Martin book.   Sat Eve Post 227:104 F 12 '55
Merman, E. as told to Pete Martin.   That's the kind of
    dame I am.   Sat Eve Post 227:17 F 12; 20 F 19; 22 F
    26; 32 Mr 5; 30 Mr 12; 30 Mr 19; 36 Mr 26 '55
Biography.   Cur Bio 16:39 My '55
Rogow, L.   Brassy dame.   Sat R 38:27 Jl 2 '55
Gibbs, W.   Ethel is back.   New Yorker 32:54 D 22 '56
Ethel Merman and her magic.   Newsweek 48:35 D 31 '56
Biography.   Cur Bio Yrbk 1955:412 '56
Merman and company come to town.   Theatre Arts 41:72
    F '57
Keating, J.   Marathon named Merman.   Theatre Arts
    44:62 S '60
O. K. , O. K. , let's go.   Newsweek 56:40 D 26 '60
Delicious, delectable, de-lovely.   Time 82:78 N 22 '63
Now: Mermania.   Newsweek 63:48 Mr 2 '64
Prideaux, T.   At 78, Berlin gives Annie a new show-
    stopper and is pleased with himself.   Life 60:47 Je 10
    '66
Efron, E.   Doin' what comes natur'lly.   TV Guide 15-
    11:10 Mr 18 '67

MERRILL, DINA
    Living graciously on a whirlwind schedule.   Womans H C
        83:40 Jl '56
    Rich rebel.   TV Guide 5-43:14 O 26 '57
    People are talking about.   Vogue 133:41 Ja 15 '59
    Post-um deb.   Newsweek 54:78 Ag 31 '59
    Lerman, L.   New Grace Kellys.   Mlle 50:56 D '59
    Triple-threat girl in fashion gallery.   Life 48:56 Ja 11
        '60
    Taves, I.   Rich girl who made good.   Good H 151:62
        Ag '60

Nichols, M. Heiress with a legacy of pep. Coronet
  48:14 O '60
Leave the dollar sign off my name. TV Guide 10-23:15
  Je 9 '62

MERRILL, GARY
  Wilson, L. That old magic. Photop 39-3:38 Mr '51
  Zeitlin, I. The present is perfect. Photop 42-4:58 O '52
  Two-by-two across the U.S.A. Life 47:61 D 21 '59
  Reynolds, L. I'll run away . . . I'll elope. Photop 60-
    4:48 O '61

MESTAYER, HARRY
  Hobart, P. A chat with the man on the cover. Feature
    Movie 1-4:5 My 5 '15

METHOD, MAYO
  Delehanty, T. The battling Bogarts. Photop 22-4:30
    Mr '43
  Bogart, M. M. Bogie--over there. Photop 24-6:28 My
    '44
  Parsons, L. O. The bewildering Bogarts. Photop 26-3:
    28 F '45

MICHAEL, GERTRUDE
  Schwartz, W. Gertrude Michael, inc. filmog. Films In
    Review 16-5:326 My '65
  Obit. Screen World 17:239 '66

MICHAELS, DOLORES
  Person of promise. Films & Filming 4-7:17 Ap '58

MICHELENA, BEATRIZ
  The girl on the cover. Photop 7-3:43 F '15

MIDDLETON, CHARLES B.
  Rudikoff, J. R. Charles B. Middleton, inc. filmog.
    Films In Review 17-6:389 Je/Jl '66

MIFUNE, TOSHIRO
  LaBadie, D. W. Japan's top sword. Show 3-5:79 My '63
  Grossman, A. N. Mifune in Los Angeles. Films In
    Review 16-5:321 My '65
  Wright, I. The Hero as hero. Sight & Sound 36-1:16
    Win '66/67
  Lerman, L. International movie report. Mlle 64:116 F
    '67

Kluge, P. F. Old foes with a new view of war. Life
    65:52 S 27 '68
Guy, R. Interview. Cinema 5-1:28 n. d.

MILAN, LITA
    Milan--a young Magnani? Look 22:106 Ap 15 '58

MILES, SARAH
    Minx's progress. Time 78:41 D 22 '61

MILES, VERA
    Hitchcock discovers a new star. Look 20:27 Ag 7 '56
    Marks, R. W. Hitchcock's new star. McCalls 84:10
        My '57
    Clement, C. I walked away from fear. Photop 52-3:58
        S '57
    Lerman, L. New Grace Kellys. Mlle 50:54 D '59

MILFORD, BLISS
    Briscoe, A. Why they forsook footlights for filmdom.
        Photop 7-1:130 D '14

MILLAND, RAY
    Haywood, E. Ray Milland's forgotten year. Photop 50-
        5:45 N '36
    Rhea, M. Rover boy in Hollywood. Photop 52-9:67 S '38
    Asher, J. Ray of light on Milland. Photop 54-10:27 O
        '40
    Wood, V. Don't forget romance. Photop 20-6:50 My '42
    Asher, J. Portrait of an individualist. Photop 23-6:
        48 N '43
    When I missed the bus. Am Mag 138:64 N '44
    Parsons, L. O. The truth about the Ray Millands.
        Photop 27-4:32 S '45
    Biography. Cur Bio F '46
        Same. Cur Bio Yrbk 1946:394 '47
    Jensen, O. Lost weekend hangover. Life 20:17 Mr 11
        '46
    Shipp, C. When the man is Milland. Photop 28-5:50 Ap
        '46
    Asher, J. Beachcomber deluxe. Photop 29-5:64 O '46
    Milland, R. Thrill of my life. Photop 30-6:64 My '47
    Jumpy. Am Mag 143:73 Vacation no. '47
    Wood, C. TV personalities biographical sketchbook.
        TV Personalities p109 '54
    This private eye can read. TV Guide 7-23:8 Je 6 '59
    He boasts a craftsman's pride. TV Guide 8-23:12 Je 4 '60

Maltin, L.   Ray Milland, inc. filmog.   Film Fan Mo 85-
  86:3 Jl/Ag '68

MILLER, ANN
  Crichton, K.   Shake a leg.   Colliers 104:18 N 4 '39
  Ann Miller, 18, dances like a Texas whirlwind.   Life
    11:41 S 8 '41
  Deere, D.   Ann-thology on Ann Miller.   Photop 25-4:47
    S '44
  Riley, V.   Glad hands.   Photop 38-6:58 D '50
  Newsmakers.   Newsweek 73:67 Je 9 '69
  Johnson, D.   I'm like a cat with nine lives.   After Dark
    11-6:52 O '69

MILLER, DENNY
  On-the-job (wagon) training.   TV Guide 10-21:3 My 26 '62

MILLER, PATSY
  St. Johns, A. R.   Presenting Patsy.   Photop 22-5:34 O
    '22

MILLS, HAYLEY
  Mills family's merry mime.   Life 48:12 Je 13 '60
  If you can, you have to.   Seventeen 20:84 Ja '61
  Moskin, J. R.   English pixie chases stardom.   Look 25:
    87 Ag 1 '61
  Spotlight.   Life 51:113 O 27 '61
  Star at 15.   N. Y. Times Mag p21 Ja 7 '62
  Rand, F.   What's her secret?   Photop 61-2:62 F '62
  Markel, H.   Remarkable Hayley Mills.   Good H 154:35
    My '62
  Martin, P.   Backstage with Hayley Mills.   Sat Eve Post
    235:20 Jl 28 '62
  Fisher, G. & Fisher, H.   World's favorite teenager:
    Hayley Mills.   Ladies Home J 79:45 D '62
  Joya, M.   Little girl, we like you.   Photop 63-3:48 Mr
    '63
  Biography.   Cur Bio 24:20 Ap '63
  Same.   Cur Bio Yrbk 1963:268 '64
  Robbins, F.   Love is just around the corner.   Photop
    64-2:36 Ag '63
  Ronan, M.   Chip off the old block.   Sr Schol 82:10 O 25
    '63
  Miller, E.   I'm growing up!   Seventeen 23:70 Ja '64
  Tornabene, L.   Hayley Mills grows up.   Good H 158:34
    Je '64
  Father and daughter talk about fame, families, love and

growing up. Redbook 123:54 Ag '64
Corbin, J. The day Hayley got kissed. Photop 66-2:49
   Ag '64
Somers, A. The night she becomes a woman. Photop
   68-1:60 Jl '65
Hayley at twenty-one. Time 90:51 Jl 28 '67
Sherwood, D. She's named "Other woman." Photop 73-
   1:68 Ja '68
Hamilton, J. Hayley Mills; intv. Look 32:100 My 28 '68
(See also: MILLS FAMILY)

MILLS, JOHN
Johnson, I. Mills. Films & Filming 8-9:22 Je '62
Mills of the week. Newsweek 60:58 S 24 '62
Biography. Cur Bio 24:26 My '63
Same. Cur Bio Yrbk 1963:270 '64
Father and daughter talk about fame, families, love and
   growing up. Redbook 123:54 Ag '64
People are talking about John Mills; like Henry the Eighth
   in mufti. Vogue 145:150 Mr 1 '65
Morton, F. El Morocco. Holiday 39:78 F '66
(See also: MILLS FAMILY)

MILLS, JULIET
Harrity, R. Young lady away from home. Cosmop 148:
   8 My '60
(See also: MILLS FAMILY)

MILLS FAMILY
Haranis, C. The whole bloomin' bunch. Photop 62-2:64
   Ag '62
Mills, J. The Mills family presents. Films & Filming
   12-6:31 Mr '66
(See also: MILLS, HAYLEY; MILLS, JOHN; MILLS,
   JULIET)

MILNER, MARTIN
Rough road. Newsweek 57:60 Ja 2 '61
Goodwin, F. Behind the wheel again. TV Guide 16-47:
   14 N 23 '68

MIMIEUX, YVETTE
Hamilton, J. Hollywood's little princess. Look 24:78
   F 16 '60
Blonde called Me-me-oh. Life 48:85 My 9 '60
More with dreamy Mimieux. Life 51:65 S 22 '61
Talk with a star. Newsweek 59:87 F 12 '62

Miller, E.   Yvette sizes herself up.   Seventeen 21:196
    Ag '62
Unlikely myth.   Time 81:38 Mr 29 '63
Lewis, R. W.   Fair young Hollywood girls.   Sat Eve
    Post 236:25 S 7 '63
She sure doesn't look sick.   Life 55:119 O 25 '63
This is Yvette Mimieux.   Esquire 61:102 My '64
Cooper, C.   Follow a star.   Seventeen 24:77 Ja '65

MINEO, SAL
Meyerson, E.   Man that Sal Mineo's the most!   Photop
    50-2:42 Ag '56
Lane, L.   Why the rebel craze is here to stay.   Photop
    50-5:56 N '56
18 is a crucial age.   TV Guide 5-20:28 My 18 '57
Nichols, M.   Busted beak that flew to fame.   Coronet
    42:10 Ag '57
Mineo, Mrs. J.   What's happened to my son Sal?
    Photop 51-2:36 Ag '57
Mineo, S.   The king and me.   Photop 52-4:54 O '57
Abramson, M.   Bronx boy with box office.   Coronet 43:
    31 F '58
Teens' new thrill.   Photop 54-2:37 Ag '58
Me and the other kids feel saddest at Christmas.   Photop
    55-1:37 Ja '59
Jennings, D.   Boy called Sal.   Sat Eve Post 232:24 O
    31 '59
Mineo, S.   Why I'm sure there is a God.   Photop 56-6:
    56 D '59
Harris, B.   What makes a fellow call again?   Photop
    57-5:40 My '60
Cook, G.   Three Days to grow up.   Photop 60-1:48 Jl '61
Carpozi, G. Jr.   Is he too fast?   Photop 61-2:50 F '62
Lewis, S.   Sal Mineo: rebel with a cause.   After Dark
    11-1:22 My '69

MINNELLI, LIZA
Maxwell, E.   Liza, Liza, smile at me.   Photop 30-6:40
    My '47
Parsons, L. O.   Spotlight on Liza.   Photop 34-5:44 Ap '49
Judy's daughter bows in.   Look 27:51 My 21 '63
Poirier, N.   Momma's girl.   Sat Eve Post 236:30 O 5 '63
Second generation--Garland style.   Sr Schol 84:14 Ja 31
    '64
Triumph of Judy's Liza.   Life 58:82 My 28 '65
Newton, D. & Benton, R.   Follow the yellow-brick super-
    highway.   TV Guide 13-48:12 N 27 '65

Return to Oz. Newsweek 67:88 F 28 '66
Davidson, M. My mom and I; intv. Good H 167:72 Jl
'68

MINTER, MARY MILES
Thrall, C. M. Queen Mary. Photop 8-6:96 N '15
Sheldon, L. Into the mill of the movies. Delin 89:8
Jl '16
It's always swingtime in this clime. Photop 11-2:123 Ja
'17
Peltret, E. The golden girl of the west. Photop 13-3:
16 F '18
Denton, F. The lonely princess. Photop 18-1:45 Je '20
Dixon, J. What happened to Mary? Photop 33-3:29 F
'28
District attorney exonerates Mary Miles Minter of Taylor
death. Lit Digest 123:10 F 13 '37
Ames, A. & Bodeen, D. Mary Miles Minter, inc. filmog.
Films In Review 20-8:490 O '69

MIRANDA, CARMEN
Pringle, H. F. Rolling up from Rio. Colliers 104:23
Ag 12 '39
Biography. Cur Bio '41
Obit. Newsweek 46:63 Ag 15 '55
Time 66:73 Ag 15 '55
Brit Bk Yr 1956:516 '56
Cur Bio 16:58 O '55
Cur Bio Yrbk 1955:421 '56
Screen World 7:225 '56

MITCHELL, CAMERON
Raddatz, L. Everybody on the show hates me. TV
Guide 16-17:14 Ap 27 '68

MITCHELL, GRANT
Obit. Newsweek 49:78 My 13 '57
Time 69:102 My 13 '57
Am Ann 1958:540 '58
Screen World 9:225 '58

MITCHELL, JAMES
Goodman, S. James Mitchell. Dance Mag 29:36 Ag '55

MITCHELL, MILLARD
Obit. Time 62:97 O 26 '53
Screen World 5:208 '54

MITCHELL, RHEA
    Obit. Screen World 9:225 '58

MITCHELL, THOMAS
    Oh, Thomas! TV Guide 5-23:28 Je 8 '57
    Mr. Mitchell goes to England. TV Guide 7-7:20 F 14 '59
    Obit. Newsweek 60:41 D 31 '62
        Time 80:48 D 28 '62
        Am Ann 1963:762 '63
        Brit Bk Yr 1963:874 '63
        Screen World 14:225 '63
    Gray, B. Thomas Mitchell, inc. filmog. Films In Re-
        view 16-2:122 F '63

MITCHUM, JAMES
    Terry, P. Dad always gets the girl. Photop 65-5:51
        My '64

MITCHUM, ROBERT
    Harris, E. Man with the immoral face. Photop 28-1:
        48 D '45
    Shipp, C. Off-trail hombre. Photop 28-3:46 F '46
    Scott, D. The man from rising sun. Photop 29-6:68 N
        '46
    Winslow, T. S. Mitchum-free style. Photop 31-4:50 S
        '47
    Shipp, C. Movie menace. Colliers 121:13 F 21 '48
    Waterbury, R. He's murder! Photop 32-5:60 Ap '48
    Crisis in Hollywood. Time 52:100 S 13 '48
    Fletcher, A. W. The strange case of Robert Mitchum.
        Photop 33-6:52 N '48
    Muir, F. What now for Mitchum? Photop 34-5:31 Ap
        '49
    Mitchum, R. Do I get another chance? Photop 34-6:42
        My '49
    Downing, H. What you don't know about Mitchum.
        Photop 43-4:42 Ap '53
    Hunt, J. Why can't Mitchum behave? Photop 45-3:50
        Mr '54
    Mitchum, D. My Bob--our man behind the mask.
        Photop 46-6:40 D '54
    Kramer, S. Into surgery for: Not as a stranger.
        Colliers 135:78 F 4 '55
    Phillips, D. Mitchum revealed: Not as a stranger.
        Photop 48-1:49 Jl '55
    Parsons, L. O. Hollywood's determined rebel. Cosmop
        139:16 Jl '55

Albright, D.   Robert Mitchum: the man who dared to sue.   Photop 49-1:36 Ja '56

Meyerson, E.   The richest bum in town.   Photop 50-6: 58 D '56

Robert Mitchum as is.   Newsweek 54:79 S 7 '59

Davidson, B.   Many moods of Robert Mitchum.   Sat Eve Post 235:57 Ag 25 '62

Ringgold, G.   Robert Mitchum, inc. filmog.   Films In Review 15-5:257 My '64

Terry, P.   Dad always gets the girl.   Photop 65-5:51 My '64

Lawrenson, H.   Man who never got to speak for National youth day.   Esquire 61:82 My '64

Wood, A.   I can't go home again.   Photop 73-5:37 My '68

Waiting for a poisoned peanut.   Time 92:54 Ag 16 '68

Whitney, D.   Old rumple eyes sits for a portrait.   TV Guide 17-23:36 Je 7 '69

MIX, TOM

Mix, T.   My shadow and I.   Feature Movie 1-3:53 Ap 15 '15

Thein, M.   A short biography.   Feature Movie 3-2:46 Ag 25 '15

Roberts, P. M.   The cowboy Beau Brummel.   Feature Movie 5-2:56 Mr '16

Introducing Tom Mix.   Photop 10-4:33 S '16

Mix, T.   My life story.   Photop 27-3:47 F; 27-4:64 Mr; 27-5:52 Ap '25

Mix, T.   Sure, you can make money in California, but try and keep it.   Photop 30-4:34 S '26

How I was roped for the pictures.   Ladies Home J 44: 14 Mr '27

Mix, T.   Wanted, dead or alive--Edmund Hoyle.   Photop 33-1:38 D '27

Mix, T.   Making a million.   Photop 33-6:70 My; 34-1: 70 Je '28

Mix, T.   The loves of Tim Mix.   Photop 35-4:30 Mr '29

Mix, T.   When I faced death.   Photop 41-4:56 Mr '32

Obit.   Newsweek 16:6 O 21 '40
    Cur Bio '40

King, T.   Tom Mix.   Films In Review 5-8:446 O '54

Mitchell, G. & Everson, W. K.   Tom Mix.   Films In Review 8-8:387 O '57

Biography.   DAB sup2:462 '58

MOBLEY, MARY ANN

Waiting for Mary Ann.   Life 45:157 O 20 '58

Be our guest, Miss America . . . for a while. TV
     Guide 8-17:24 Ap 23 '60
Whitney, D. Miss America 8 years later. TV Guide
     15-51:12 D 23 '67
Anderson, N. Her wedding to Gary Collins. Photop 73-
     3:72 Mr '68
Terry, P. Miss America . . . Photop 75-3:44 Mr '69

MONROE, MARILYN

Monroe, M. Make it for keeps. Photop 40-1:37 Jl '51
Cahn, R. 1951 model blonde. Colliers 128:15 S 8 '51
Hollywood topic A-plus. Life 32:101 Ap 7 '52
Monroe, M. Temptations of a bachelor girl. Photop
     41-4:44 Ap '52
He's her Joe. Photop 42-1:37 Jl '52
Something for the boys. Time 60:88 Ag 11 '52
Johnson, G. Story behind Marilyn Monroe. Coronet
     32:83 O '52
Monroe, M. I want women to like me. Photop 42-5:
     58 N '52
Marilyn Monroe tells the truth to Hedda Hopper. Photop
     43-1:36 Ja '53
Go easy. Time 61:102 F 23 '53
Dougherty, J. Marilyn Monroe was my wife. Photop 43-
     3:46 Mr '53
Heilbroner, R. L. Marilyn Monroe. Cosmop 134:38 My
     '53
Gentlemen prefer Monroe. Colliers 131:16 Je 27 '53
Halsman, P. Shooting Marilyn. Photography 32:66 Je '53
Johnson, H. Hollywood vs. Marilyn Monroe. Photop 44-
     1:42 Jl '53
Alpert, H. Bumps and grinds. Sat R 36:27 Ag 1 '53
Florea, J. Marilyn on the rocks. Colliers 132:54 O 16
     '53
Monroe, M. My beauty secrets. Photop 44-4:34 O '53
Armstrong, G. The private life of Joe and Marilyn.
     Photop 44-6:40 D '53
Merger of two worlds. Life 36:32 Ja 25 '54
Storybook romance. Time 63:108 Ja 25 '54
Mr. and Mrs. Joe DiMaggio. Newsweek 43:44 Ja 25 '54
Smith, S. On the spot with Marilyn Monroe. Photop 45-
     1:30 Ja '54
Walker. Time 63:32 F 15 '54
This is competition. Newsweek 43:32 Mr 1 '54
Pin-up takes shape. Life 36:28 Mr 1 '54
Corwin, J. Orphan in ermine. Photop 45-3:60 Mr '54
Ford, E. Journey into paradise. Photop 45-4:56 Ap '54

Skolsky, S.   Marilyn Monroe's honeymoon whirl.   Photop
   45-5:37 My '54
Cahn, R.   Marilyn Monroe hits a new high.   Colliers
   134:98 Jl 9 '54
Skolsky, S.   260,000 minutes of marriage.   Photop 46-2:
   32 Ag '54
Marilyn on the town.   Life 37:71 S 27 '54
Monroe scene; shooting of a scene for The seven year itch.
   America 92:3 O 2 '54
Last scene: exit unhappily.   Life 37:53 O 18 '54
Out at home.   Time 64:47 O 18 '54
Parting.   Newsweek 44:32 O 18 '54
Moore, I.   If Marilyn has a little girl.   Photop 46-4:74
   O '54
Life goes to a select supper for Marilyn.   Life 37:162
   N 29 '54
Dostoevsky blues.   Time 65:75 Ja 24 '55
Kutner, N.   Don't blame yourself, Marilyn.   Photop 47-1:
   42 Ja '55
Anderson, L.   The girl you know as Marilyn.   Photop
   47-1:44 Ja '55
Ten years of Monroe.   Photop 47-4:63 Ap '55
Bolstad, H.   Marilyn in the house.   Photop 48-3:46 S '55
Winner.   Time 67:96 Ja 16 '56
Who would resist?   Time 67:62 Ja 30 '56
Co-stars.   Time 67:94 F 20 '56
Zolotow, M.   Will failure spur George Axelrod?   Theatre
   Arts 40:31 Mr '56
To Aristophanes and back.   Time 67:74 My 14 '56
Martin, P.   New Marilyn Monroe.   Sat Eve Post 228:25
   My 5; 28 My 12; 42 My 19 '56
Wilson, E.   The things she said to me.   Photop 49-5:37
   My '56
Engagement party.   Newsweek 48:21 Jl 2 '56
People.   Time 68:36 Jl 9 '56
Wedding wine for Marilyn.   Life 41:113 Jl 16 '56
Conquest.   Time 68:50 Jl 30 '56
That old Monroe magic.   Colliers 138:28 Ag 3 '56
Will acting spoil Mrs. Miller?   Sat Eve Post 229:96 Ag
   18 '56
Cute little trick.   Sat R 39:26 Ag 18 '56
Hutchens, J. K.   Leave that Miss Monroe alone, please.
   N. Y. Her Trib Bk R p2 Ag 19 '56
Unveiling of the new Monroe.   Life 41:79 Ag 27 '56
Girl who became Marilyn Monroe.   Read Digest 69:17 Ag
   '56
Knight, A.   Speaking of artists.   Sat R 39:37 S 15 '56

Baker, P.   The Monroe doctrine.   Films & Filming 2-12:
   12 S '56
Olivier and Monroe.   Look 20:44 O 3 '56
Manning, D.   The woman and the legend.   Photop 50-4:
   58 O '56
For art's sake.   Newsweek 48:80 N 19 '56
Obstacle course.   Theatre Arts 40:14 N '56
Farrell, J. T.   Waif to woman.   Coronet 41:65 Ja '57
Lane, L.   Eeny, meeny, miny, mo, who will be the first
   to go?   Photop 51-3:38 Mr '57
Executive sweet.   Time 69:94 Ap 29 '57
Unlikely pair make great match.   Life 42:80 Je 3 '57
Talk with a show girl.   Newsweek 49:111 Je 17 '57
Joyce, A.   Marilyn at the crossroads.   Photop 52-1:44
   Jl '57
Marilyn's new life.   Look 21:110 O 1 '57
Biography.   Colliers Yrbk 1957:708 '57
Miller, A.   My wife Marilyn.   Life 45:143 D 22 '58
Fabled enchantresses.   Life 45:138 D 22 '58
Harris, R.   The empty crib in the nursery.   Photop 54-
   6:24 D '58
Whitcomb, J.   New Marilyn Monroe.   Cosmop 146:68 Mr
   '59
Walk like this, Marilyn.   Life 46:101 Ap 20 '59
Heat wave.   New Yorker 35:17 My 30 '59
Biography.   Cur Bio 20:37 Jl '59
   Same.   Cur Bio Yrbk 1959:303 '60
Michaels, E.   What was Marilyn Monroe doing at 685
   Third Ave. ?   Photop 56-2:34 Ag '59
Dinter, C.   What she couldn't tell the doctor.   Photop
   56-4:42 O '59
Zolotow, M.   Marilyn Monroe; abridged.   McCalls 87:
   76 Ap '60
Marilyn meets Montand.   Look 24:91 Jl 5 '60
Marilyn and the mustangs.   Time 76:56 Ag 8 '60
Zeitlin, D.   Marilyn's movie lover.   Life 49:64 Ag 15 '60
Mathison, R.   Who's a misfit?   Newsweek 56:102 S 12 '60
Kauffmann, S.   Stars in their courses.   New Repub 143:
   19 O 3 '60
Constellation is born.   Newsweek 56:90 O 31 '60
Behind the Yves Montand, Marilyn Monroe, Arthur Miller
   triangle.   Photop 58-4:32 O '60
Out of the fish bowl.   Newsweek 56:37 N 21 '60
Popsie and poopsie.   Time 76:61 N 21 '60
End of famous marriage.   Life 49:88A N 21 '60
Nichols, L.   M. M. goldrush.   N. Y. Times Bk R p 8
   D 18 '60

Whitcomb, J.   Marilyn Monroe--the sex symbol versus
the good wife.   Cosmop 149:53 D '60
Divorce!   Photop 58-6:70 D '60
Weatherby, W. J.   Misfits; epic or requiem?   Sat R 44:
26 F 4 '61
Marilyn's new role.   Time 77:39 F 17 '61
Mosaic of Marilyn; with comments by five men close to
her.   Coronet 49:58 F '61
Peabody, M.   The woman Arthur Miller went to when he
walked out on Marilyn Monroe.   Photop 59-2:67 F '61
McIntyre, A. T.   Making the Misfits; or, Waiting for
Monroe.   Esquire 55:74 Mr '61
Corbin, J.   Will she break Joe's heart again.   Photop
59-4:42 Ap '61
Dean, B.   Marilyn's secret marriage plans.   Photop 59-
5:27 My '61
Tracy, J.   Is it a thing--or is it a fling?   Photop 30-3:
42 S '61
Hamilton, J.   Four for posterity.   Look 26:82 Ja 16 '62
Waterbury, R.   Why they keep it a secret.   Photop 61-1:
60 Ja '62
They fired Marilyn: her dip lives on.   Life 52:87 Je 22
'62
Meryman, R.   Marilyn lets down her hair about being
famous.   Life 53:21 Ag 3 '62
Obit.   Spectator (Lond) 209:181 Ag 10 '62
Illus Lond N 241:223 Ag 11 '62
Christian Cent 79:977 Ag 15 '62
America 107:610 Ag 18 '62
Nation 195:70 Ag 25 '62
Nat R 13:130 Ag 28 '62
Cur Bio 23:45 O '62
Cur Bio Yrbk 1962:302 '63
Am Ann 1963:446 '63
Screen World 14:225 '63
Early, too early, for once.   Newsweek 60:40 Ag 13 '62
Meryman, R.   Last long talk with a lonely girl.   Life
53:32 Ag 17 '62
Remember Marilyn.   Life 53:63 Ag 17 '62
Thrilled with guilt.   Time 80:50 Ag 17 '62
I love you . . . I love you.   Newsweek 60:30 Ag 20 '62
Levy, A.   Marilyn Monroe: a good long look at myself.
Redbook 119:40 Ag '62
Marilyn Monroe.   Vogue 140:190 S 1 '62
Jacobs, J.   Goodby Galatea.   Reporter 27:42 S 27 '62
Rowland, T.   Marilyn poses nude again.   Photop 62-2:
45 S '62

Meryman, R. What it was like to be Marilyn Monroe.
Read Digest 81:67 O '62

Roman, R. C. Marilyn Monroe, inc. filmog. Films In
Review 13-8:449 O '62

Odets, C. To whom it may concern. Show 2-10:67 O '62

Marilyn Monroe. Film 34:11 Win '62

End as a woman? Newsweek 60:67 N 19 '62

Mailer, N. Big Bite. Esquire 58:134 N '62

A final tribute. Photop 62-5:36 N '62

DeBlasio, E. We find her father and sister. Photop
62-6:14 D '62

Front Page. Sight & Sound 31:159 '62

Growing cult of Marilyn. Life 54:89 Ja 25 '63

Schreiber, F. R. Remembrance of Marilyn. Good H 156:
30 Ja '63

Fenin, G. Marilyn Monroe. Films & Filming 9-4:23 Ja
'63

Trilling, D. Marilyn Monroe. Redbook 120:54 F '63

Hoffman, J. We grant her last wish. Photop 63-2:59
F '63

Lyle, J. I love you darling. Photop 63-2:57 F '63

Marilyn, my Marilyn. Time 81:47 My 31 '63

Exploiters. Newsweek 61:105 Je 10 '63

DeBlasio, E. Love letters could have saved her. Photop
63-6:28 Je '63

Donalson, M. Her killer's still at large. Photop 64-2:
52 Ag '63

Sandburg, C. Tribute to Marilyn from a friend. Look
26:90 S 11 '63

Meltsir, A. Life after death. Photop 64-3:40 S '63

Preston, W. Her mother escapes mental hospital. Photop
64-4:42 O '63

Mythraker. Newsweek 62:102 D 2 '63

Luce, C. B. What really killed Marilyn? Life 57:68 Ag
7 '64

Same abridged. Read Digest 85:218 N '64

Losers. Newsweek 66:67 Jl 5 '65

Marilyn Monroe versus Uncle Sam; financial career.
Sat Eve Post 238:88 Jl 31 '65

Hattersley, R. Marilyn Monroe; intvs. with six famous
photographers. Pop Phot 58:104 Ja '66

Meryman, R. Behind the myth the face of Norma Jean.
Life 61:49 N 4 '66

Homebody. Newsweek 68:63 N 28 '66

Lerman, L. Marilyn; peek-preview of Homage of Marilyn
Monroe. Mlle 65:74 Jl '67

Rosten, N. Dear Marilyn. McCalls 94:74 Ag '67

Guiles, F. L. Norma Jean; excerpt. Ladies Home J
    84:171 N '67
Guiles, F. L. Marilyn Monroe, the untold story of her
    last years; excerpt from Norma Jean. Good H 159:63
    Jl '69

MONTALBAN, RICARDO
    Arnold, M. Carpet slipper romeo. Photop 36-5:44 O '49
    Montalban changes personality. Life 27:94 N 21 '49
    Lane, K. The guy's a doll. Photop 39-5:56 My '51
    Morris, J. K. ed. This I have learned as a son and a
        father. Parents Mag 28:42 F '53
    Zegri, A. Spanish Americans invade Broadway.
        Americas 10:26 N '58

MONTAND, YVES
    Billard, G. Rough stuff from the song man. Films &
        Filming 2-11:13 Ag '56
    Schneider, P. E. Formidable M. Montand. N. Y. Times
        Mag p76 S 13 '59
    M. Montand. New Yorker 35:33 S 26 '59
    Explosive Frenchman. Newsweek 54:75 S 28 '59
    Tynan, K. Theatre: one man show. New Yorker 35:94
        O 3 '59
    Troubadour from France. Time 74:51 O 5 '59
    Controlled disarmament. Sat R 42:33 O 10 '59
    Clurman, H. Theatre. Reporter 21:218 O 15 '59
    Hayes, R. Stage. Commonweal 71:75 O 16 '59
    Hentoff, N. Daily nothings of Yves Montand. Reporter
        21:35 O 29 '59
    Women like them. Vogue 134:110 N 15 '59
    Bergquist, L. Simone Signoret: sex appeal grown up.
        Look 24:84 Ja 19 '60
    How pink the stars? Newsweek 55:30 Ap 18 '60
    Gordan, S. Marilyn meets Montand. Look 24:91 Jl 5 '60
    Biography. Cur Bio 21:27 Jl '60
        Same. Cur Bio Yrbk 1960:278 '61
    Zeitlin, D. Marilyn's movie lover. Life 49:64 Ag 15 '60
    Behind the Yves Montand, Marilyn Monroe, Arthur Miller
        triangle. Photop 58-4:32 O '60
    People are talking about. Vogue 136:151 O 1 '60
    Evening with Yves Montand. Time 78:44 N 3 '61
    Evening with Yves Montand. Newsweek 58:69 N 6 '61
    That old ooh-la-la. Show 1-2:82 N '61
    Evening with Yves Montand. Theatre Arts 46:15 Ja '62
    Dictionary of love. McCalls 89:74 Je '62

MONTEZ, MARIA
Crichton, K. Born to act. Colliers 109:17 Ap 4 '42
Tropical. Am Mag 133:76 Je '42
Crichton, K. It's simple if you've got what it takes!
    Read Digest 41:17 Jl '42
In Arabian nights she does the dance of the single veil.
    Life 13:69 S 28 '42
Sprague, D. Lush, Latin and lethal. Photop 23-1:41 Je
    '43
Montez, M. The man I love. Photop 23-6:52 N '43
Martin, P. Dominican dynamite. Sat Eve Post 218:29
    Jl 28 '45
Hall, G. Reunion of Maria Montez and Jean Pierre Au-
    mont. Photop 27-2:27 Jl '45
Scott, D Mythical Maria Montez. Photop 28-2:44 Ja '46
Marshall, J. Strange embarrasment of Madame Aumont.
    Colliers 119:12 Je 28 '47
Montez, M. This is my husband. Photop 31-3:64 Ag '47
Obit. Newsweek 38:63 S 17 '51
    Time 58:91 S 17 '51
    France Illus 7:287a S 22 '51
Smith, J. The perfect filmic appositeness of Maria Mon-
    tez. Film Culture 27:28 Win '62/63
Dickens, H. Maria Montez, inc. filmog. Films In Re-
    view 14-1:59 Ja '63
Smith, J. The memoirs of Maria Montez. Film Culture
    31:3 Win '63/64
Vermilye, J. Maria Montez, inc. filmog. Screen Facts
    13:1 n. d.

MONTGOMERY, GEORGE
Jefferson, S. Surprise romance. Photop 20-1:44 D '41
West, R. Right about love. Photop 21-1:30 Je '42
Crichton, K. Pride and the clan. Colliers 110:14 Jl 25
    '42
Jefferson, S. Gay romance. Photop 23-4:38 S '43
Campbell, K. Dinah Shore and George Montgomery: San
    Fernando Valley home. Am Home 38:18 S '47
My hobby is my house. Womans H C 76:64 F '49
Shore, D. How I met my husband. McCalls 85:100 Ap
    '58
Schroeder, C. Dinah Shore: how a good wife failed.
    Good H 154:78 Ap '62

MONTGOMERY, ROBERT
Earle, E. He wanted to write the worst way. Photop
    37-5:66 Ap '30

Kahn, J. M.   He kept on working.   Photop 40-3:51 Ag '31

Hamilton, S.   This is Bob Montgomery.   Photop 42-6:75
    N '32

Baskette, K.   The midnight ride of Robert Montgomery.
    Photop 49-1:74 Ja '36

Johnston, A.   Starring as a side line.   Womans H C 63:
    18 Je '36

Hamilton, S.   Bob Montgomery--unhappy playboy.   Photop
    50-4:24 D '36

Ferguson, O.   Montgomery in the movies.   New Repub
    91:102 Je 2 '37

Reynolds, Q.   Man with a union card.   Colliers 103:22
    Ap 1 '39

Heyn, E. V.   Why Bob Montgomery went to war.   Photop
    54-8:19 Ag '40

Leonard, H.   Present and accounted for.   Sight & Sound
    15-59:88 Aut '46

President of film actors' union condemns the strike.
    Life 21:32 O 14 '46

Lightman, H. A.   Revolution with a camera.   Colliers
    118:22 N 9 '46

Biography.   Cur Bio Ja '48

Sightless.   Am Mag 145:19 Mr '48

Frazier, G.   Nobody pushes Bob around.   Colliers 123:
    25 Je 4 '49

No crystal ball.   Time 54:85 S 19 '49

Commentator Montgomery.   Newsweek 34:57 S 26 '49

Biography.   Cur Bio Yrbk 1948:457 '49

Carson, S.   On the air: television on its own.   New
    Repub 122:28 F 13 '50

Robert Montgomery presents.   TV Guide 3-12:8 Mr 25 '50

Gentleman producer.   Newsweek 36:58 S 25 '50

Martin, P.   Fightin' Bob--the Hollywood crusader.   Sat
    Eve Post 223:40 O 7 '50

What Robert Montgomery brings to TV.   TV Guide 3:42
    12 O 21 '50

Heads new drama committee.   Recreation 45:169 Je '51

Frazier, G.   Man nobody slows.   Holiday 11:80 F '52

Cattle quiz.   Newsweek 39:108 Ap 21 '52

Montgomery hour: stockholders meeting, R. H. Macy &
    Co.   Time 60:105 N 24 '52

Like dad, like daughter.   TV Guide 1-17:8 Jl 24 '53

White House assist; television problems.   Newsweek 43:
    51 Ja 18 '54

Man of many parts.   TV Guide 2-5:15 Ja 29 '54

Robert Montgomery presents President as a pro.   Life
    36:28 Ap 19 '54

People of the week.   U.S. News 37:14 S 3 '54
Boal, S.   Robert Montgomery presents.   Coronet 36:83
   S '54
The producer and the president.   TV Guide 2-44:5 O 30
   '54
Wood, C.   TV personalities biographical sketchbook.
   TV Personalities p50 '54
Behind each Eisenhower speech: men who do the writing.
   U.S. News 38:12 Ja 7 '55
Challenge of our times.   Theatre Arts 39:30 F '55
People of the week.   U.S. News 39:16 N 25 '55
Gehman, R.   He produces the President.   Good H 141:
   64 N '55
TVs not what it used to be.   TV Guide 3-51:13 D 17 '55
Drury, M.   Many talents of Robert Montgomery.   Womans
   H C 82:80 D '55
Montgomery's secret weapon.   TV Guide 4-46:20 N 17 '56
Goodbys to standbys.   Newsweek 50:80 Jl 8 '57
Where are they now?   Newsweek 59:14 Ja 29 '62
Where are they now?   Newsweek 71:20 My 20 '68

MOORE, COLLEEN
   Boone, A.   One's blue and one's brown.   Photop 15-3:50
      F '19
   Howe, H.   A Hollywood girl.   Photop 22-3:47 Ag '22
   Spensley, D.   The Cinderella girl.   Photop 30-3:30 Ag '26
   Harding, A.   Be prepared for the best, it may come your
      way; intv.   Am Mag 103:18 Ja '27
   My career and my doll's house.   Ladies Home J 44:14 Ag
      '27
   Tully, J.   Colleen Moore.   Pict R 29:2 D '27
   Piano study as a hobby.   Musician 38:2 D 16 '33
   Miss Moore starts her little house on charity trip.
      Newsweek 5:25 Ap 13 '35
   Spears, J.   Colleen Moore, inc. filmog.   Films In Review
      13-7:403 Ag/S '63
   Wicked stepmother.   Good H 166:34 Je '68

MOORE, CONSTANCE
   McClelland, D.   Constance Moore, inc. filmog.   Films In
      Review 18-10:663 D '67

MOORE, DICKIE
   Deek man.   Time 76:82 N 21 '60
   Where are they now?   Newsweek 66:16 N 29 '65

MOORE, MARY TYLER
  Who is that cutie playing his wife?   TV Guide 10-22:10 Je
    2 '62
  Gordon, S.   America's favorite TV wife.   Look 28:M9
    Ap 21 '64
  Gehman, R.   Laura Petrie is Mary Tyler Moore, or is
    she?   TV Guide 12-21:18 My 23 '64
  Tornabene, L.   Tomorrow's stars.   Good H 160:20 Mr '65
  How to succeed though married.   Time 85:62 Ap 9 '65
  Personality girl.   Newsweek 68:78 Ag 1 '66
  Bowers, J.   From TV to Tiffany's in one wild leap.
    Sat Eve Post 239:97 N 19 '66
  Gussow, M.   Holly go quickly.   Newsweek 68:45 D 26 '66
  Hockstein, R.   Mary Tyler Moore bounces back.   Good H
    164:61 Ap '67

MOORE, MATT
  Obit.   Screen World 12:222 '61

MOORE, ROGER
  Moore, R.   One night on Broadway.   Plays & Players 3-
    12:9 S '56
  Gautschy, D.   The case of the ghost who couldn't swim.
    Photop 58-1:62 Jl '60
  White sheep of the mavericks.   TV Guide 8-41:10 O 8 '60
  Higgins, R.   Then the studios found I couldn't act very
    well.   TV Guide 15-31:12 Ag 5 '67

MOORE, TERRY
  Johnson, H.   Highflying Terry.   Photop 43-3:72 Mr '53
  Life goes for a romp on the beach with Terry Moore.
    Life 35:94 Jl 6 '53
  Ott, B.   If this isn't love.   Photop 44-1:34 Jl '53
  Moore, T.   He's my kind of guy.   Photop 44-2:32 Ag '53
  Moore, T.   Teenage marriage is a mistake.   Photop 45-
    1:46 Ja '54
  On stardom's stairway.   Coronet 35:42 Ja '54
  Fusses over ladies and a ladies' man.   Life 36:24 Ja 11
    '54
  Koford, L.   Terry and her gang.   Photop 45-3:58 Mr '54
  Parsons, L. O.   Young girl in a rush.   Cosmop 136:19
    My '54
  Arnold, M.   Terry can take it.   Photop 45-6:52 Je '54
  Moore, T.   How's your social rating.   Photop 46-1:12
    Jl '54
  Edwards, R.   Non-stop Terry.   Photop 46-2:44 Ag '54
  Hall, G.   What is this thing called love?   Photop 48-1:

46 Jl '55
Koford, L. W. My darling, daring daughter. Photop
48-3:42 S '55
Wilson, E. Why I did not. Photop 50-5:54 N '56
And then the bottom fell out. TV Guide 11-1:3 Ja 5 '63

MOORE, TOM
Johnson, J. Clan Moore. Photop 15-1:27 D '18
Obit. Newsweek 45:66 F 21 '55
   Screen World 7:226 '56

MOORE, VICTOR
Crichton, K. He makes anything go. Colliers 96:44 D
21 '35
Beatty, J. Gentle Victor. Am Mag 124:42 O '37
Gilder, R. Song and dance. Theatre Arts 23:6 Ja '39
One-minute interviews. Am Mag 129:130 Mr '40
Woolf, S. J. Throttlebottom discusses the vice presi-
dency. N. Y. Times Mag p13 F 16 '41
Some film actors who have made themselves known this
year. Theatre Arts 26:188 Mr '42
Funke, L. B. Victor Moore, or forty years a timid man.
N. Y. Times Mag p12 Ja 6 '46
Victor Moore. Time 47:43 My 27 '46
Speaking of pictures. Life 22:12 Je 9 '47
Where are they now? Newsweek 48:24 N 12 '56
Obit. Time 80:44 Ag 3 '62
   Life 53:25 Ag 3 '62
   Newsweek 60:72 Ag 6 '62
   Am Ann 1963:762 '63
   Brit Bk Yr 1963:874 '63
   Screen World 14:225 '63

MOOREHEAD, AGNES
Sorry, wrong number; Agnes Moorehead stars in repeat
performance of radio melodrama. Life 19:91 S 24 '45
Right number Agnes. Newsweek 29:54 F 3 '47
Moorehead's makeup. Life 22:143 Je 9 '47
Four Hollywood veterans go to hell on Broadway.
Life 31:46 N 5 '51
Four-star chat. New Yorker 28:26 Ap 19 '52
Biography. Cur Bio 13:36 Je '52
   Same. Cur Bio Yrbk 1952:437 '53
People of talent. Sight & Sound 25-2:84 Aut '55
Whitney, D. The strength of an amazon . . . the guile
of a general . . . the hide of a crocodile. TV Guide
13-29:22 Jl 17 '65

Bowers, R. L.   Agnes Moorehead, inc. filmog.   Films
In Review 17-5:293 My '66

MORAN, DOLORES
Moran, D.   Hold his hands!   Photop 25-4:54 S '44
No time to retire.   Am Mag 149:103 Je '50

MORAN, POLLY
Severance, C.   Polly of the laughs.   Photop 10-4:99 S '16
Evans, D.   She knocks 'em dead.   Photop 23-2:51 Ja '23
York, C.   50 years of "IT"   Photop 37-2:54 Ja '30
Busby, M.   Three's a crowd.   Photop 38-1:77 Je '30
Obit.   Newsweek 39:53 F 4 '52
Time 59:70 F 4 '52

MOREAU, JEANNE
France's Bette Davis.   Newsweek 55:100 F 15 '60
People are talking about . . .   Vogue 140:153 S 15 '62
Stanbrook, A.   The star they couldn't photograph.   Films
& Filming 9-5:10 F '63
Making the most of love.   Time 85:78 Mr 5 '65
Collins, L. & Zapierre, D.   Name is Moreau (not Bardot).
N. Y. Times Mag p46 Mr 21 '65
Les girls in Mexico.   Life 58:53 Ap 2 '65
Jennings, C. R.   Jeanne Moreau: death, suffering, love.
Sat Eve Post 238:86 Ap 10 '65
Broussard, C.   On the set with Moreau and Bardot.
Look 29:64 My 4 '65
Duras, M.   Jeanne Moreau.   Vogue 146:100 N 15 '65
Biography.   Brit Bk Yr 1966:142 '66
Biography.   Cur Bio 27:24 D '66
same.   Cur Bio Yrbk 1966:283 '67
Liber, N.   Moreau, she lives to love; intv.   Life 62:39
Ja 20 '67
Arkadin.   Film clips.   Sight & Sound 36-3:155 Sum '67

MORENO, ANTONIO
Jordan, J.   Confessions of a modern Don Juan.   Photop
19-6:46 My '21
Howe, H.   Mrs. Coolidge knew him when.   Photop 30-2:
35 Jl '26
Bodeen, D.   Antonio Moreno, inc. filmog.   Films In Re-
view 18-6:325 Je/Jl '67
Obit.   Screen World 19:237 '68

MORENO, RITA
Satirist of sex.   Life 36:65 Mr 1 '54

Phillips, D.   Barefoot girl with chic.   Photop 49-4:58
   Ap '56
It's hard to be a lady.   Look 20:41 S 4 '56
Jacobi, E.   Hep-cat sage hen.   Photop 50-3:46 S '56
Weaver, J. D.   Hollywood's most outspoken actress.
   Holiday 30:119 N '61
Bermel, A.   Getting out from under an image.   Harper
   230:38 Ap '65

MOREY, HARRY T.
   Morey, H. T.   A movie villain's confession.   Photop 7-1:
      68 D '14

MORGAN, DENNIS
   Steele, J. H.   Portrait of a young man on the way up.
      Photop 20-5:36 Ap '42
   Harris, E.   If you were Dennis Morgan's house guest.
      Photop 25-3:56 Ag '43
   Quinn, M.   Just because--Dennis Morgan.   Photop 25-5:
      49 O '44
   Dawson, T.   A man and his dream.   Photop 27-2:45 Jl
      '45
   Arnold, M.   Badger boy.   Photop 28-3:36 F '46
   Deere, D.   Tent show.   Photop 30-2:42 Ja '47
   Morgan, D.   My handicap--Jack Carson.   Photop 30-5:54
      Ap '47

MORGAN, FRANK
   Actor and Angostura official.   Newsweek 3:28 Mr 24 '34
   Beatty, J.   Mr. Wuppermann wows 'em.   Am Mag 134:
      40 O '42
   Wappermann boy.   Time 43:72 Ja 17 '44
   Obit.   Newsweek 34:64 S 26 '49
      Time 54:94 S 26 '49
   McDonald, R.   Frank Morgan.   Films In Review 20-7:
      454 Ag/S '69

MORGAN, HARRY
   Don't remind him of his wife's people.   TV Guide 5-11:14
      Mr 16 '57
   Wood, C.   TV personalities biographical sketchbook.
      TV Personalities p129 '57
   Fessier, M. Jr.   You ought to see what they've got Harry
      doing now.   TV Guide 15-18:29 My 6 '67

MORGAN, MICHELE
   Hollywood remodels this French actress to make an Amer-

ican movie star.   Life 11:84 N 3 '41
Crichton, K.   Paris model.   Colliers 109:21 F 21 '42
Some film actors who have made themselves known this
    year.   Theatre Arts 26:188 Mr '42
Rhea, M.   Strangers in arms.   Photop 20-4:44 Mr '42
Mike.   Am Mag 133:81 My '42
Mulvey, K.   Keeping up with Hollywood.   Womans H C
    69:32 N '42

MORGAN, RALPH
    Obit.   Time 67:88 Je 25 '56
    Screen World 8:225 '57

MORISON, PATRICIA
    Crichton, K.   Pretty Pat.   Colliers 107:15 F 1 '41
    Downes, B.   Singing shrew.   Colliers 123:24 Ja 15 '49
    Sheveloff, S.   Patricia Morison filmography.   Films In
        Review 17-4:262 Ap '66
    Rode, D.   Patricia Morison, inc. filmog.   Films In Re-
        view 19-6:391 Je/Jl '68

MORLEY, KAREN
    Biery, R.   She sat on the floor.   Photop 42-5:40 O '32

MORLEY, ROBERT
    Roberts, K.   Least effort.   Colliers 102:11 D 17 '38
    Eustis, M.   Footlight parade.   Theatre Arts 23:719 O '39
    Stokes, S.   Robert Morley.   Theatre Arts 26:778 D '42
    Brown, J. M.   Actors' theatre.   Sat R 31:26 O 16 '48
    About the authors.   Theatre Arts 33:58 S '49
    Actor of personality.   Plays & Players 1-7:4 Ap '54
    Jangled by the jingles.   Newsweek 54:104 D 7 '59
    Morley, R.   In who's who of the critics.   Films & Film-
        ing 8-8:15 My '62
    Biography.   Cur Bio 24:24 N '63
        Same.   Cur Bio Yrbk 1963:277 '64
    Morley view of sport.   Sports Illus 22:52 Ap 26 '65
    Morley, R.   I hate acting.   Films & Filming 11-10:5 Jl
        '65
    Redbook dialogue: Mary Hemingway and Robert Morley.
        Redbook 126:62 N '65
    Morley, R.   On tour and all that.   Plays & Players 14-5:
        70 F '67
    Morley, R. & Stokes, S.   Backstage with Shakespeare,
        Morley and Bogart; excerpt from Robert Morley: a
        reluctant autobiography.   Atlan 219:58 Ap '67
    Weeks, E.   Enter laughing.   Atlan 219:126 Je '67

MORRIS, CHESTER
    Hamilton, S. You can't live on promises. Photop 42-3:
        77 Ag '32
    McAllister, A. The Chester Morris plan. Photop 48-7:
        74 D '35
    There's magic up your sleeve. Pop Mech 88:137 O '47

MORRIS, WAYNE
    Bailey, K. The kid speaks his mind about marriage.
        Photop 52-5:23 My '38
    Morris, Mrs. W. My husband is home. Photop 26-5:32
        Ap '45
    Obit. Newsweek 54:85 S 28 '59
        Time 74:92 S 28 '59
        Screen World 11:223 '60

MORROW, JO
    Person of promise. Films & Filming 6-4:10 Ja '60
    Jo Morrow: I'm an up-and-coming new face. Look 24:
        90 Mr 1 '60

MORROW, VIC
    Dern, M. The sergeant's private war. TV Guide 13-40:
        30 O 2 '65

MORSE, ROBERT
    Anderson, D. Show stopper. Theatre Arts 42:67 O '58
    Talk with the star. Newsweek 58:62 O 23 '61
    I believe in you. Time 78:78 N 17 '61
    How to succeed on Broadway. Newsweek 58:50 N 27 '61
    Robert Morse: starry-eyed star of How to succeed.
        Look 25:111 D 5 '61
    Brown, W. F. How to succeed at Christmas without real-
        ly crying. Vogue 138:102 D '61
    Lerman, L. Mlle presents Robert Morse in the lover
        boys. Mlle 54:101 F '62
    Rich, royal way of King Saud. Life 53:21 N 30 '62
    Biography. Cur Bio 23:26 N '62
        Same Cur Bio Yrbk 1962: 304 '63
    Efron, E. He's a puzzlement. TV Guide 16-49:21 D 7
        '68

MOSTEL, ZERO
    Funnymen in the money. Newsweek 20:74 Ag 17 '42
    Crichton, K. Podden the expression. Colliers 110:78 S
        19 '42
    Butterfield, R. Zero Mostel is a funny man with method

in his madness. Life 14:61 Ja 18 '43
Biography. Cur Bio '43
Zero Mostel shows what waiters must forget. Life 19:
  14 O 15 '45
Zero televised. Life 25:76 N 22 '48
Movie fan. Colliers 123:58 F 19 '49
Card trick. Colliers 123:63 Ap 9 '49
Slater, B. Interview. TV Guide 2-53:24 D 31 '49
Ross, L. Player. New Yorker 37:72 O 28 '61
Wilner, N. Zero. Esquire 57:94 F '62
Talk with the star. Newsweek 59:85 My 21 '62
Zero's a bust. Look 26:70e My 22 '62
Meehan, T. Actor comedian painter litterateur . . . they
  all add up to Zero. Horizon 4:50 My '62
Millstein, G. Funny man happened. N. Y. Times Mag
  p40 Je 3 '62
Biography. Am Ann 1962:500 '62
Foster, H. G. Infinite Zero. Holiday 33:131 Mr '63
Biography. Cur Bio 25:26 N '63
Same. Cur Bio Yrbk 1963:286 '64
Infinite Zero. Newsweek 63:51 Ja 13 '64
Hail the conquering Zero. Newsweek 64:94 O 19 '64
Hamblin, D. J. Big mouth + massive wit + soul of a
  daffodil = Zero. Life 57:108 D 4 '64
Mostel revisited. New Yorker 40:25 Ja 2 '65
Musel, R. It all adds up to Zero. TV Guide 15-17:16
  Ap 29 '67
Zero in Dallas. Newsweek 71:87 Ap 1 '68
Newsmakers. Newsweek 73:58 My 12 '69

MOWBRAY, ALAN
  Con man with a conscience. TV Guide 2-12:17 Mr 19 '54
  The little bit of rogue in all of us. TV Guide 8-24:8 Je
    11 '60
  Obit. Time 93:90 Ap 4 '69

MULHALL, JACK
  Elliott, M. The youngest grand old man. Photop 38-6:
    71 N '30

MULHARE, EDWARD
  Edward Mulhare. Vogue 129:90 Mr 15 '57

MUNI, PAUL
  Burton, S. Don't call me Lon Chaney. Photop 37-2:78
    Ja '30
  Skolsky, S. "Scarface." Photop 42-1:27 Je '32

North, J.   Only Muni can do it.   Photop 43-3:35 F '33
Rankin, R.   What's this Muni mystery.   Photop 45-4:45
   Mr '34
Rankin, R.   The disappearing Muni.   Photop 48-3:65 Ag
   '35
Golding, L.   The true Paul Muni.   Photop 49-6:28 Je '36
Biographical sketch.   Newsweek 10:19 Ag 14 '37
Prestige picture.   Time 30:34 Ag 16 '37
Master character actor.   Sr Schol 31:39 S 18 '37
Dieterle, W.   The Paul Muni I know.   Cinema Arts 1-3:
   68 S '37
Clausen, B. C.   Moment in the conscience of man.
   Christian Cent 54:1484 D 1 '37
Beatty, J.   Man who is always somebody else.   Am Mag
   125:42 F '38
Zeitlin, I.   Mr. Muni at home.   Photop 53-3:26 Mr '39
Eustis, M.   Paul Muni: a profile and a self portrait.
   Theatre Arts 24:194 Mr '40
Biography.   Cur Bio '44
Schumach, M.   Muni's second fling with fame.   N.Y.
   Times Mag p17 My 22 '55
Biography.   Am Ann 1957:524 '57
Grand hotel in song.   Newsweek 52:82 Jl 21 '58
Personality of the month.   Films & Filming 6-9:3 Je '60
Funke, L. & Booth, J. E.   Actor's method: his life.
   N.Y. Times Mag p40 O 1 '61
Jacobs, J.   Paul Muni, inc. filmog.   Films In Review
   12-9:527 N '61
Mr. Paul Muni.   Newsweek 70:72 S 4 '67
Luft, H. G.   Letter.   Films In Review 18-7:520 O '67
Obit.   Brit Bk Yr 1968:596 '68
   Cur Bio 28:47 N '67
   Cur Bio Yrbk 1967:480 '68
   Screen World 19:237 '68

MUNRO, JANET
   British girl in an Irish role.   Look 22:40 Jl 22 '58
   Person of promise.   Films & Filming 5-2:17 N '58

MUNSHIN, JULES
   Breit, H.   Epistolarian.   N.Y. Times Bk R p8 Je 23 '57
   At home with the Lunts.   Theatre Arts 45:23 Ap '61

MUNSON, ONA
   Obit.   Time 65:78 F 21 '55
      Screen World 7:226 '56

MURPHY, AUDIE
Most decorated soldier comes home to the little town of
Farmersville, Texas.   Life 19:94 Jl 16 '45
Boyles, C. S. Jr.   Audie is home.   Sat Eve Post 218:6
S 15 '45
Hero and actress.   Life 23:106 N 17 '47
Proctor, K.   Love is young.   Photop 32-5:52 Ap '48
Murphy, A.   Why I'm not afraid to marry Wanda Hendrix.
Photop 34-2:24 Ja '49
Hero from Texas.   Newsweek 33:20 F 28 '49
Hendrix, W.   Hero's wife.   Photop 36-7:30 D '49
Medal of honor.   Life 30:75 Ja 29 '51
Zeitlin, I.   Lonely Joe.   Photop 39-1:34 Ja '51
Arnold, M.   His love wears wings.   Photop 39-5:54 My
'51
Murphy, A.   Forever, Audie Murphy.   Photop 40-2:42 Ag
'51
Burns, C.   Audie gets his "man."   Photop 42-2:60 Ag '52
Hubler, R.   He doesn't want to be a star.   Sat Eve Post
225:35 Ap 18 '53
McNeill, D.   Surprise for a hero.   Coronet 34:29 Jl '53
Gould, H.   Deep in the heart of Hollywood.   Photop 44-2:
64 Ag '53
Edwards, R.   This is your life, Audie Murphy.   Photop
45-6:56 Je '54
War hero turned actor acts himself as hero.   Life 39:67
Jl 4 '55
Role for a hero: most decorated soldier of World War II.
Am Mag 160:50 Ag '55
Hubler, R. G.   Audie Murphy: the man behind the medals.
Coronet 38:65 Ag '55
Soldier relives Anzio.   Colliers 136:72 S 2 '55
Arnold, M.   The personal war of Audie Murphy.   Photop
48-4:60 O '55
Riley, V.   Journey into light.   Photop 51-2:56 F '57
Elsenberg, H.   A father's prayers for his sons.   Photop
53-2:62 F '58
Audie isn't exactly shouting for joy.   TV Guide 9-30:28
Jl 29 '61

MURPHY, EDNA
Stanley, M.   Says she'll never marry an actor.   Photop
27-4:49 Mr '25

MURPHY, GEORGE
Murphy, G.   My friend Fred.   Photop 54-3:22 Mr '40
Chute, M.   Dance if you're blue.   Photop 19-5:44 O '41

Cosby, V. Gentleman of courage. Photop 21-6:50 N '42
English, R. Hollywood's Yankee-Doodle-Dandy. Sat Eve
  Post 228:28 Jl 2 '55
Wood, C. TV personalities biographical sketchbook.
  TV Personalities p24 '56
NAVA convention spotlights. Educ Screen 42:352 Jl '63
Hollywood pavilion. New Yorker 39:26 D 28 '63
Trombley, W. New role for legendary George. Sat Eve
  Post 237:22 My 30 '64
Who is the good guy? Time 84:34 O 16 '64
Just call him Senator. Time 84:42 N 13 '64
How Murphy upset Salinger. U.S. News 57:19 N 16 '64
Alexander, S. My technicolor senator. Life 57:30 D 4
  '64
Gold, H. Nobody's mad at Murphy. N.Y. Times Mag
  p42 D 13 '64
Biography. Cur Bio 26:25 D '65
  Same. Cur Bio Yrbk 1965:296 '65
Sutton, H. George Murphy; the old soft shoe. Sat R 50:
  25 S 23 '67
Senator Murphy digs the facts. Nation 205:517 N 20 '67

MURPHY, MARY
  On stardom's stairway. Coronet 35:56 Ja '54

MURRAY, CHARLIE
  Murray, C. If I say it myself. Photop 12-5:21 O '17
  Obit. Cur Bio '41

MURRAY, DON
  DeRoulf, P. Love on the run. Photop 50-5:70 N '56
  Hanson, E. Good boy. Photop 51-1:20 Ja '57
  Film's fast-rising star. Life 42:82 Ap 29 '57
  Person of promise. Films & Filming 3-7:19 Ap '57
  Nichols, M. Don Murray: versatile idealist. Coronet
    42:8 Jl '57
  Please take me as I am. Photop 52-3:54 S '57
  Hopper, H. Actor with a mission. Look 21:99 D 10 '57
  Joyce, A. I worked--and God rewarded me. Photop 53-
    1:37 Ja '58
  Shayon, L. Help. Sat R 41:72 Ja 11 '58
  Christian, F. Young family in Hollywood. Cosmop 145:
    57 S '58
  Brown, J. He used to call Don "Mitzy." Photop 54-5:
    39 N '58
  Gehman, R. Movieland marriage with a mission.
    Coronet 45:38 My '59

Ardmore, J. K.   New billing: the four Murrays.
Parents Mag 34:50 Je '59
Biography.   Cur Bio 20:28 S '59
Same.   Cur Bio Yrbk 1959:315 '60
Corbin, J.   Never fall in love with a married man.
Photop 59-5:32 My '61
Conviction convention: Don Murray and Walter Wood de-
bate American and European cinema today.   Films &
Filming 7-12:8 S '61
How can a square fit into the Hollywood circle?   TV
Guide 17-32:25 Ag 9 '69

MURRAY, JAMES
Schonert, V. L.   James Murray, inc. filmog.   Films In
Review 19-10:618 D '68

MURRAY, JAN
Borscht boys.   Newsweek 36:54 Ag 21 '50
Wood, C.   TV personalities biographical sketchbook.
TV Personalities p17 '54

MURRAY, MAE
Sayford, I. S.   Talking all around Mae Murray.   Photop
10-5:38 O '16
Corliss, A.   Motoring with Mae.   Photop 11-4:29 Mr '17
Evans, D.   The truth about Mae Murray.   Photop 18-3:
40 Ag '20
Morgan, M.   Secrets of Mae Murray's success.   Photop
21-2:31 Ja '22
St. Johns, A. R.   Mae Murray--a study in contradictions.
Photop 26-2:43 Jl '24
Obit.   Screen World 17:239 '66

MYERS, CARMEL
Porter, V. H.   And the elephant beckoned "Come on,
come on."   Photop 14-1:32 Je '18
North, G.   The girl who cried.   Photop 18-2:36 Jl '20
From siren to saleswoman.   Show 2-10:140 O '62

NADER, GEORGE
  Allen, D. He's George. Photop 47-6:41 Je '55
  Waterbury, R. Don't kid yourself. Photop 48-6:53 D '55
  Rush, B. George Nader and the marriage question.
    Photop 49-5:40 My '56
  Nader, G. Tell a guy he's wonderful. Photop 50-4:68
    O '56
  Maynard, J. Alas, he's no hero to his cat. Photop 51-
    4:48 Ap '57
  Nader, G. Sr. My first and last words on George.
    Photop 52-2:42 Ag '57
  Nader, G. Are you the girl I'm looking for? Photop
    54-1:40 Jl '58
  Ellery Queen--30 years later. TV Guide 6-48:12 N 29
    '58
  George Nader answers the 4,688 girls who said yes.
    Photop 54-5:40 N '58

NAGEL, ANN
  Obit. Screen World 18:238 '67

NAGEL, CONRAD
  Allison, D. Conrad in quest of age. Photop 16-2:67
    Jl '19
  Boone, A. A nice boy, etc. Photop 19-3:38 F '21
  Larkin, M. Conrad in quest of a voice. Photop 35-2:
    58 Ja '29
  Albert, K. The strange case of Conrad Nagel. Photop
    38-4:63 S '30
  Ruthie goes to the movies. Ladies Home J 49:11 S '32
  Wood, C. TV personalities biographical sketchbook.
    TV Personalities p71 '56

NAISH, J. CARROLL
  Whitney, D. What a character actor! Colliers 125:30
    Je 10 '50
  Biographical note. Time 58:84 O 29 '51
  Luigi and TV. Newsweek 40:69 O 6 '52
  Biography. Cur Bio 18:33 Ja '57
    Same. Cur Bio Yrbk 1957:396 '58

NALDI, NITA
  Winship, M. Madame Manhattan. Photop 22-2:42 Jl '22
  Naldi, N. What men have told me about other women.

Photop 25-5:28 Ap '24
Rag and a bone and a hank of hair.   Theatre Arts 36:17
    O '52
Talese, G. J.   Then and now.   N. Y.   Times Mag p20 O
    16 '55
Obit.   Newsweek 57:65 F 27 '61
    Time 77:52 F 24 '61
    Brit Bk Yr 1962:512 '62
    Screen World 13:225 '62

NANSEN, BETTY
The "idol of Europe" arrives.   Photop 7-4:87 Mr '15
The Vikingess.   Photop 9-1:115 D '15

NASH, JOHNNY
Nash, J.   My way to escape.   Films & Filming 5-12:7
    S '57

NATWICK, MILDRED
Reed, E.   New faces: 1935.   Theatre Arts 19:277 Ap '35
Reed, E.   Personae gratae.   Theatre Arts 20:49 Ja '36
Grand old lady.   New Yorker 17:16 N 29 '41
Pringle, H. F.   Girl grows younger.   Colliers 109:23
    Ja 24 '42

NAZIMOVA, ALLA
Saint-Gaudens, H.   Russian players.   Critic 48:318 Ap
    '06
Interpretation of Ibsen.   Cur Lit 42:60 Ja '07
Acting and English of Nazimova.   Harper 51:240 F 16 '07
Estimate.   Nation 84:367 Ap 18 '07
Forman, H. J.   New Histrionic genius and her art.
    Harper 51:576 Ap 20 '07
Dale, A.   Nazimova and some others.   Cosmop 42:674
    Ap '07
Webber, J. E.   Acting of Nazimova.   Canad Mag 29:129
    Je '07
Ibsen's woman.   Ind 63:909 O 17 '07
Sholl, A. M.   Madama Nazimova--a comparison.   Lippinc
    80:684 N '07
Transformation of Nazimova.   Cur Lit 43:671 D '07
Comment on Nazimova.   Putnams 3:500 Ja '08
Ruhl, A.   Nazimova again.   Colliers 45:34 My 7 '10
Hamilton, C.   Ibsen once again; Nazimova's revival.
    Bookm 47:426 Je '18
Raftery, H.   Elsie or Alla?   Photop 14-2:22 Jl '18
Fredericks, E.   The real Nazimova.   Photop 17-3:55 F '20

An open letter to Mme. Nazimova. Photop 20-3:31 Ag '21
Howe, H. A misunderstood woman. Photop 21-5:24 Ap
   '22
Mullett, M. B. How a dull, fat girl became a great ac-
   tress. Am Mag 93:18 Ap '22
Craven, T. Salome and the cinema. New Repub 33:225
   Ja 24 '23
Howe, H. The daring of Salome. Photop 23-4:35 Mr '23
Roberts, K. Artists don't need ruffles. Colliers 90:9
   D 10 '32
Bamberger, T. Nazimova goes a-trouping. Delin 128:64
   Ap '36
Vernon, G. Mme. Nazimova as Hedda Gabler. Common-
   weal 25:134 N 27 '36
Eustis, M. Actor attacks his part. Theatre Arts 20:950
   D '36
Exit Alla, with flowers. Newsweek 26:83 Jl 23 '45
Phalen, K. Alla Nazimova. Commonweal 42:381 Ag 3 '45
Wyatt, E. V. America's loss. Cath World 162:69 O '45
Kirkland, A. Woman from Yalta. Theatre Arts 33:28 D
   '49
Biography. NCAB 36:415 '50
Ashby, C. Alla Nazimova and the advent of the new acting
   in America. Q. J. Speech Ed 45:182 Ap '59
Robinson, D. Players' witness: notes on some early act-
   ing performances preserved in the National film ar-
   chive. Sight & Sound 29:150 Sum '60

NEAGLE, ANNA

Seafarer. Am Mag 118:44 D '34
Biographical sketch. Time 26:35 Jl 1 '35
Crichton, K. Choice for a queen. Colliers 101:13 F 5 '38
First lady of British screen. Life 8:59 Ap 8 '40
Rhea, M. Anna Neagle's London diary. Photop 21-4:44
   S '42
Biography. Cur Bio N '45
Neagle, A. Anna Neagle on producing. Films In Review
   8-8:423 O '57
Coulson, A. A. Anna Neagle, inc. filmog. Films In
   Review 18-3:149 Mr '67

NEAL, PATRICIA

Blue grass belle. Am Mag 147:95 F '49
Hopper, H. Patricia Neal's heartbreak. Photop 42-2:42
   Ag '52
Neal, P. What Kazan did for me. Films & Filming
   4-1:9 O '57

Gregory, J. Heartbreak! Photop 63-4:49 Ap '63
Kiss kiss. Time 83:57 Mr 20 '64
Patrick, S. Patricia Neal, inc. filmog. Films In Re-
view 15-3:188 Mr '64
Biography. Cur Bio 25:43 S '64
Same. Cur Bio Yrbk 1964:314 '64
Arkadin. Film clips. Sight & Sound 32-4:191 Aut '64
Road back. Time 85:37 Mr 26 '65
Personalities of the week. Illus Lond N 246:18 My 29 '65
Her best performance. Newsweek 65:55 My 31 '65
Personalities of the week. Illus Lond N 247:19 Ag 14 '65
Frank, S. Patricia Neal; a woman's fight to live.
Good H 161:65 Ag '65
Dahl, R. My wife, Patricia Neal. Ladies Home J 82:53
S '65
Farrell, B. Gallant fight of Pat Neal. Life 59:92 O 22
'65
Personalities of the week. Illus Lond N 248:15 Ap 2 '66
Gift of love. McCalls 94:72 D '66
People. Time 89:43 Mr 17 '67
Newsmakers. Newsweek 69:60 Mr 20 '67
Farrell, B. Pat Neal makes a radiant return. Life
62:119 Ap 7 '67
DeBlasio, E. We saw her come back to life. Photop
71-54 Je '67
Frank, S. Patricia Neal: suddenly I wanted to live.
Good H 165:70 Jl '67
Newsmakers. Newsweek 71:57 F 12 '68
Movie star again. Good H 167:19 Jl '68
Lemon, R. Patricia Neal: a star is born. Sat Eve
Post 241:45 O 5 '68
Redbook dialogue. Redbook 132:80 N '68
Zimmermann, G. Does everybody love Patricia Neal?
Oh, yes! Look 33:82 F 18 '69

NEDELL, BERNARD
Barbour, A. G. Bernard Nedell. Screen Facts 7:28 n. d.

NEFF, HILDEGARDE
Lerman, L. Something to talk about. Mlle 40:86 Ja '55
Harvey, E. New Ninotchka. Colliers 135:84 F 18 '55
George, M. Hildegarde Neff. Films In Review 6-9:445
N '55
Knef. Newsweek 67:115 My 16 '66

NEGRI, POLA
Vinder, M. She delivered the goods. Photop 21-6:20

My '22

Howe, H.   The real Pola Negri; intv.   Photop 22-6:59
   N '22

Jordan, J.   You can't hurry Pola.   Photop 23-4:63 Mr '23

Howe, H.   The loves of Pola Negri.   Photop 24-6:36 N
   '23

The autobiography of Pola Negri.   Photop 25-2:32 Ja; 25-
   3:50 F; 25-4:56 Mr; 25-5:38 Ap '24

St. Johns, I.   How Pola was tamed.   Photop 29-2:53 Ja
   '26

York, C.   He who got slapped and why.   Photop 30-2:
   78 Jl '26

Hall, L.   The passing of Pola.   Photop 35-1:29 D '28

Hamilton, S.   Ach! That Pola.   Photop 41-2:40 Ja '32

Pinchot, A.   Not in the picture.   Delin 128:19 My '36

New picture.   Time 42:48 Jl 26 '43

Remember?   Am Mag 137:130 Je '44

Askew, E.   Pola Negri.   Films In Review 12-10:636 D
   '61

Liebling, A. J.   Reporter at large.   New Yorker 39:97
   Ja 11 '64

Bodeen, D. & Ringgold, G.   Pola Negri, inc. filmog.
   Screen Facts 3-3:1 n. d.

NEILAN, MARSHALL
   Obit.   Newsweek 52:66 N 10 '58
        Time 72:88 N 10 '58

NELSON, BARRY
   Wood, C.   TV personalities biographical sketchbook.
      TV Personalities p146 '54

NELSON, DAVID
   Like Ozzie, like son.   TV Guide 1-34:10 N 20 '53
   Wood, C.   TV personalities biographical sketchbook.
      TV Personalities p99 '56
   Just like the kids next door?   TV Guide 6-52:17 D 27 '58
   Borie, M.   Dave and Rick Nelson in Dave's new home.
      Photop 55-3:60 Mr '59
   Borie, M.   Honeymoon.   Photop 60-1:20 Jl '61
   (See also: NELSON, HARRIET; NELSON, OZZIE;
      NELSON, RICKY; NELSON FAMILY)

NELSON, GENE
   Dancer acts out bedtime story.   Life 27:14 Ag 15 '49
   Nelson, Mrs. G.   How I pursued my husband.   Photop
      40-1:40 Jl '51

Nelson, M.   I married a serviceman.   Photop 41-2:46
F '52

Knight, A.   Gene Nelson, Agnes DeMille and Oklahoma!
Dance Mag 29:28 Jl '55

Gene Nelson: working in Hollywood.   Dance Mag 30:24
My '56

NELSON, HARRIET
(Also known as Harriet Hilliard)

Herrod, V. & Monze, M. E.   Ozzie and Harriet make an
old-fashioned home in Hollywood.   Am Home 35:27 Ap
'46

Biography.   Cur Bio 10:40 My '49
Same.   Cur Bio Yrbk 1949:451 '50

Shipp, C.   My heart belongs to my three sons.   Womans
H C 80:42 Je '53

Wood, C.   TV personalities biographical sketchbook.
TV Personalities p97 '56

Gordon, S.   Men in my life.   Look 22:41 N 11 '58

(See also: NELSON, DAVID; NELSON, OZZIE; NELSON,
RICKY; NELSON FAMILY)

NELSON, LORI

Nelson, Mrs. L.   Tomboys make wonderful ladies.
Photop 46-5:52 N '54

Noel, T.   Demure dynamo.   Photop 48-1:98 Jl '55

The lady takes a walk.   TV Guide 7-22:24 My 30 '59

NELSON, OZZIE

Herrod, V. & Monze, M. E.   Ozzie and Harriet make an
old-fashioned home in Hollywood.   Am Home 35:27 Ap
'46

Nelson touch.   Newsweek 29:67 Ap 28 '47

Full Nelson.   Time 51:73 F 16 '48

Biography.   Cur Bio 10:40 My '49
Same.   Cur Bio Yrbk 1949:451 '50

Greatest guy in the world.   Coronet 26:102 Jl '49

Life of the party.   McCalls 83:16 D '55

Wood, C.   TV personalities biographical sketchbook.
TV Personalities p97 '56

Old '21-job' Ozzie.   TV Guide 10-33:15 Ag 18 '62

(See also: NELSON, DAVID; NELSON, HARRIET;
NELSON, RICKY; NELSON FAMILY)

NELSON, RICK

TV's youngest comic.   TV Guide 1-7:8 My 15 '53

Wood, C.   TV personalities biographical sketchbook.

TV Personalities p100 '56
What makes Ricky tick?   TV Guide 5-52:17 D 28 '57
Stern, D. A day with Rick Nelson.   Photop 53-1:40 Ja
'58
Borie, M. Luck: everything happens to me.   Photop 53-
5:53 My '58
Scott, J. A. How to be a success in show business.
Cosmop 145:69 N '58
Teenager rocks teenagers.   Life 45:123 D 1 '58
Just like the kids next door?   TV Guide 6-52:17 D 27 '58
Borie, M. Dave and Rick Nelson in Dave's new home.
Photop 55-3:60 Mr '59
Nelson, R. Were you the girl in the gingham dress.
Photop 55-6:54 Je '59
Sheeley, S. What makes a nice boy change like that?
Photop 57-1:48 Ja '60
Marsh, B. Rick, why dare death?   Photop 58-5:38 N '60
Borie, M. When you pray, you have to believe God lis-
tens. Photop 59-3:56 Mr '61
Tusher, B. I dig my brother's wife.   Photop 60-3:32 S
'61
Roberts, J. Introducing Tracy.   Photop 66-3:44 S '64
(See also: NELSON, DAVID; NELSON, HARRIET;
NELSON, OZZIE; NELSON FAMILY)

NELSON FAMILY
The nation's second best-known family.   TV Guide 9-30:
14 Jl 29 '61
Normality and $300,000.   Newsweek 40:66 N 17 '52
Ozzie and Harriet's daring new program.   TV Guide 5-
52:8 D 26 '52
Ozzie and Harriet's Ricky and David.   Look 17:77 My 19
'53
Great competitor.   Time 62:62 D 14 '53
Dalmas, H. Ozzie, Harriet and family.   Coronet 36:74
Jl '54
Stump, A. Meet Hollywood's most exciting family.
Am Mag 160:24 O '55
One family's triumph.   Newsweek 50:62 Ag 26 '57
Hostick, K. Saluting the lovable Nelson family.
Hobbies 63:24 Mr '58
Scott, V. A nice normal family.   TV Guide 11-38:10 S
21 '63
(See also: NELSON, DAVID; NELSON, HARRIET;
NELSON, OZZIE; NELSON, RICKY)

NESBITT, CATHLEEN
    Biography. Cur Bio 17:39 N '56
      Same. Cur Bio Yrbk 1956:459 '57
    Never toss a tomato at a lady. TV Guide 12-43:26 O 24
      '64

NESBITT, MIRIAM
    Briscoe, J. Why film favorites forsook the footlights.
      Photop 6-4:70 S '14

NESTELL, BILL
    Obit. Screen World 18:238 '67

NEVILLE, JOHN
    Youth at the Old Vic. Plays & Players 2-7:10 Ap '55
    Gibbs, W. Theatre; Old Vic company. New Yorker 32:
      71 N 3 '56

NEWLEY, ANTHONY
    People are talking about . . . Vogue 140:106 O 15 '62
    Busy comic kingpin. Life 53:117 N 30 '62
    Oulahan, R. All-purpose cockney. Life 55:55 N 29 '63
    Poppy cocky. Time 85:83 My 28 '65
    Biography. Cur Bio 27:22 O '66
      Same. Cur Bio Yrbk 1966:294 '67
    Miller, E. Anthony Newley: inside out. Seventeen 26:
      124 O '67

NEWMAN, PAUL
    Embattled actor ages fast. Life 39:147 O 31 '55
    Maas, P. Newman scores K. O. Colliers 138:46 Jl 20
      '56
    Parmeter, A. Somebody up there likes him. Photop 50-
      2:46 Ag '56
    Lane, L. Why the rebel craze is here to stay. Photop
      50-5:56 N '56
    Joyce, A. The honeymoon is over. Photop 54-1:59 Jl
      '58
    Here's what we, your hometown folks, feel about you,
      Paul Newman. Photop 55-4:50 Ap '59
    People are talking about . . . Vogue 133:122 My '59
    Bester, A. Solemn lovers. Holiday 26:91 Jl '59
    Biography. Cur Bio 20:39 N '59
      Same. Cur Bio Yrbk 1959:321 '60
    Nichols, M. Flexible perfectionist. Coronet 52:18 F '61
    Miller, E. Jamming on the left bank. Seventeen 20:
      210 Ag '61

Kauffmann, S.   Talent of Paul Newman.   New Repub 145:
    28 O 9 '61
Britten, R.   A love letter from Joanne.   Photop 61-2:66
    F '62
Woods, M.   That blond stripper in his life.   Photop 62-
    5:51 N '62
Bunzel, P.   Western non-hero named Hud.   Life 55:45
    Jl 5 '63
Robbins, F.   I want to kill my husband.   Photop 64-3:48
    S '63
Schroeder, M.   Two days in a nudist colony.   Photop 64-
    5:58 N '63
Baskette, K.   Love story for adults only.   Photop 66-3:
    68 S '64
Eyles, A.   The other Brando.   Films & Filming 11-4:7
    Ja '65
Lyon, N.   Second fame: good food.   Vogue 146:144 Ag 1
    '65
Bean, R.   Success begins at forty.   Films & Filming
    12-4:5 Ja '66
Stern, S.   Paul Newman.   McCalls 94:106 O '66
Lewis, R. W.   Paul Newman makes a western.   N. Y.
    Times Mag p38 N 6 '66
Cool Hand Paul.   Newsweek 69:95 Ja 23 '67
Nelson, W.   Strange actions when he drinks.   Photop 71-
    6:49 Je '67
Wilson, J.   What if my eyes turned brown?   Sat Eve
    Post 241:26 F 24 '68
Johns, C.   Marriage American style.   Photop 73-2:33 F
    '68
Steinem, G.   Paul Newman: the trouble with being too
    good-looking.   Ladies Home J 85:99 Ap '68
Gardiner, H.   We solve his biggest problem.   Photop
    74-1:69 Jl '68
Kerr, M.   Love affair with a baby sitter.   Photop 74-2:
    35 Ag '68
Joanne and Paul--and Rachel.   Life 65:47 O 18 '68
Davidson, M.   Joanne Woodward tells all about Paul New-
    man; intv.   Good H 168:72 F '69
Sin makes marriage survive.   Photop 75-5:60 My '69
A delicate problem.   Photop 75-6:33 Je '69
Bondurant, B.   How we turned Paul Newman into a win-
    ning driver.   Pop Sci 194:51 Je '69
Times they're not married.   Photop 76-2:47 Ag '69

NEWMAR, JULIE
    Big girl on the marriage-go-round.   Look 22:112 D 9 '58

Millstein, G. Quantities of qualities.   N. Y. Times Mag
  p29 F 8 '59
Lithe, limber, long-legged, lovely.   Life 49:59 N 7 '60
Electronic tomato.   Time 84:81 D 4 '64

NEWTON, ROBERT
  Are English amateurs growing up?   Theatre Arts 17:819
    O '33
  Obit.   Time 67:104 Ap 2 '56
    Illus Lond N 228:241 Ap 7 '56
    Screen World 8:225 '57

NEWTON, THEODORE
  Obit.   Screen World 15:224 '64

NEY, RICHARD
  Emerson, B.   Secret romance.   Photop 21-3:26 Ag '42
  Jefferson, S.   Navy lady.   Photop 23-5:29 O '43
  Ney sayer.   Newsweek 67:87 Ap 4 '66

NICHOLS, BARBARA
  TV's answer to Marilyn Monroe.   TV Guide 3-33:10 Ag
    13 '55
  Dumb blonde? Don't bet on it.   TV Guide 8-30:24 Jl 23
    '60

NICHOLSON, JACK
  Weaver, N.   I have the blood of kings in my veins, is my
    point of view.   After Dark 11-6:38 O '69

NIELSEN, ASTA
  Winge, J. H.   Asta Nielsen.   Sight & Sound 19-2:58 Ap
    '50
  Luft, H. G.   Asta Nielsen.   Films In Review 7-1:19 Ja
    '56
  In the picture.   Sight & Sound 30-1:15 Win '60/61

NIELSEN, LESLIE
  Who's who in the cast.   TV Guide 3-42:16 O 21 '50
  Prowling the wilds of Los Angeles.   TV Guide 10-16:22
    Ap 21 '62

NILSSON, ANNA Q.
  O'Reilly, E.   Anna misplaced, intv.   Photop 18-6:44 N
    '20
  St. Johns, A. R.   At last--the blonde vampire.   Photop
    27-4:42 Mr '25

Mahlon, M. On with the pants. Photop 30-2:63 Jl '26

NIVEN, DAVID
   Reynolds, Q. Charming young man. Colliers 101:23 Ja
     8 '38
   Hamilton, S. Rover boy with sex appeal. Photop 53-9:
     22 S; 53-10:68 O '39
   Soldier of good fortune. New Yorker 21:18 Ja 12 '46
   Nichols, M. Unique non-stuffed shirt. Coronet 41:8 D
     '56
   Wood, C. TV personalities biographical sketchbook.
     TV Personalities p146 '56
   Biography. Cur Bio 18:34 Mr '57
     Same. Cur Bio Yrbk 1957:405 '58
   The Frenchman, the Yankee and the Canny Scot. TV
     Guide 5-15:28 Ap 13 '57
   Inside I was a seething mass. . . TV Guide 6-8:20 F
     22 '58
   Hubler, R. G. Hollywood's most irresistible scoundrel.
     McCalls 85:43 My '58
   Niven, D. I'm always surprising myself; as told to D.
     Jennings. Sat Eve Post 231:11 Jl 19; 26 Jl 26; 30 Ag
     2 '58
   Talk with David Niven. Newsweek 52:80 D 22 '58
   Lunch with David Niven. TV Guide 7-15:12 Ap 11 '59
   Fraser, P. C. David Niven puzzles me. Good H 148:32
     Ap '59
   Allen, A. The wacky life of an English gentleman.
     Photop 56-1:69 Jl '59
   Biography. Am Ann 1960:547 '60
   Niven, D. In who's who of the critics. Films & Filming
     8-8:16 My '62
   Niven, D. Wagging tales. Photop 63-2:76 F '63
   Whitney, D. The "Rogue" that got away. TV Guide 12-
     41:15 O 10 '64
   Thomas, A. David Niven, inc. filmog. Films In Review
     20-2:92 F '69

NIXON, MARIAN
   Fiddler, J. M. Marian and Janet. Photop 42-2:73 Jl '32

NIXON, MARNI
   Instant voice. Time 83:81 F 7 '64

NOLAN, LLOYD
   Sprague, D. Beloved lug. Photop 21-5:47 O '42
   That new Martin Kane. TV Guide 4-42:8 O 19 '51

Queeg. New Yorker 30:23 F 27 '54
Spotlighted at Sardi's. Theatre Arts 38:65 O '54
Capt. Queeg's poison is actor Nolan's meat. Theatre
    Arts 39:58 Ja '55
Biography. Cur Bio 17:43 N '56
    Same. Cur Bio Yrbk 1956:465 '57
deRoos, R. The unforgettable man from many forgettable
    movies is proving unforgettable again. TV Guide 17-51:
    16 D 20 '69

NOONAN, TOMMY
    Obit. Screen World 20:238 '69

NORMAND, MABEL
    Quirk, J. R.   The girl on the cover; intv.   Photop 8-3:
        39 Ag '15
    Bartlett, R. Why aren't we killed? Photop 9-5:81 Ap '16
    Bartlett, R. Would you ever suspect it? Photop 14-3:
        43 Ag '18
    Anthony, N. Imaginery interviews. Photop 18-6:56 N '20
    St. Johns, A. R. Hello Mabel! Photop 20-3:24 Ag '21
    St. Johns, A. R. The butterfly man and the little clown.
        Photop 36-2:38 Jl '29
    Quirk, J. R. Mabel Normand says goodbye. Photop 37-
        6:36 My '30
    Collins, F. L. Four women who suffered. Good H 95:
        194 Jl '32

NORTH, SHEREE
    She shimmied her way to success. Cosmop 135:98 S '53
    Sheree's jitterbug. Look 18:107 Mr 9 '54
    Harvey, E. Match for Marilyn. Colliers 133:30 Ap 16
        '54
    Sheree goes in for Marilyn. Life 38:65 Mr 21 '55
    Fleming, T. J. Multimillion Monroe doctrine. Cosmop
        139:56 Jl '55
    Which way North? Look 19:41 S 20 '55
    Allen, D. 1955 Sexation. Photop 48-3:52 S '55
    North, S. Poverty's child. Photop 50-2:40 Ag '56

NORTHRUP, HARRY S.
    Briscoe, J. Why film favorites forsook the footlights.
        Photop 6-4:70 S '14

NORTON, BARRY
    Obit. Screen World 8:225 '57

NORTON, JACK
  Obit. Newsweek 52:64 O 27 '58
    Time 72:85 O 27 '58

NOVAK, JANE
  Winship, M. That chin. Photop 21-2:58 Ja '22

NOVAK, KIM
  Kim kids questionnaire. Life 36:59 Jl 28 '54
  Parmeter, L. Don't be a teenage misfit. Photop 47-1:
    48 Ja '55
  Kim for success. Vogue 125:109 Ap 1 '55
  On her way up. Look 19:62 My 31 '55
  Multimillion Monroe doctrine. Cosmop 139:56 Jl '55
  Waterbury, R. How to be good and popular. Photop 48-
    2:45 Ag '55
  Kim and friends. Am Mag 160:49 S '55
  Limke, H. Faith began with a wishing tree. Photop 48-
    5:49 N '55
  Courts and contracts. Newsweek 47:40 Ja 9 '56
  Maddox, T. Kim Novak--stabbed by scandal. Photop
    49-2:54 F '56
  Kim Novak moves uncertainly in new world of movie fame.
    Life 40:149 Mr 5 '56
  Wilson, E. She ain't fooling, men! Photop 49-3:53 Mr
    '56
  Lavender blonde. Coronet 40:6 Je '56
  Lerman, L. Prettiest girl in town. Mlle 43:77 Je '56
  Allen, D. Kim Novak found someone new. Photop 50-1:
    42 Jl '56
  Kim Novak. Colliers 138:22 Ag 17 '56
  Jennings, D. Hollywood's melancholy blonde. Sat Eve
    Post 229:38 O 6 '56
  Scullin, G. The girl with the lavender life. Photop
    50-5:43 N '56
  Vamp of the '20's is recreated. Life 42:121 Mr 11 '57
  Lane, L. Eeny, meeny, miny, mo, who will be the first
    to go. Photop 51-3:38 Mr '57
  Arnold, M. Fame cloaks the lonely heart. Photop 51-4:
    41 Ap '57
  Hubler, R. G. Glamor queen in a quandary. Coronet 41:
    45 Ap '57
  Biography. Cur Bio 18:36 Ap '57
    Same. Cur Bio Yrbk 1957:412 '58
  Johnson, H. What makes her a star. Photop 51-6:54 Je
    '57
  Star is made. Time 70:52 Jl 29 '57

Arnold, M.   Why I worry about Kim.   Photop 52-3:44 S
   '57
People are talking about.   Vogue 130:76 O 15 '57
Whitcomb, J.   Kim Novak's move to No. 1.   Cosmop 143:
   84 O '57
Kim on Kim: a girl's got to fight.   Newsweek 50:120 N
   11 '57
Star who wants to be an actress.   Look 21:38 N 12 '57
Kasell, N.   Is Kim getting married?   Photop 52-5:51 N
   '57
Scott, D.   I believed, and God blessed me.   Photop 53-1:
   34 Ja '58
Real nice party group.   Life 44:153 My 26 '58
Allen, D.   I used to be in love.   Photop 54-1:34 Jl '58
Flight from sexy?   Newsweek 53:100 F 16 '59
Arnold, M.   Everybody's laughing at me.   Photop 55-2:
   38 F '59
For Kim: Cary? or Mario?   Life 46:28 Je 1 '59
Toutkoushian, F.   Come over . . . I'm having a party.
   Photop 55-6:66 Je '59
Christy, G.   The one thing I could never tell my father.
   Photop 56-5:60 N '59
Talk with a star.   Newsweek 56:85 Jl 4 '60
Ardmore, J.   Kim Novak's struggle to understand herself.
   Cosmop 149:49 N '60
Christy, G.   Kim Novak: why I'm afraid of marriage.
   Ladies Home J 79:41 My '62
Willoughby, B.   Kim the killer.   Look 26:68 Ag 28 '62
Carpozi, G.   Kim in the Kremlin.   Photop 62-3:30 S '62
Bester, A.   Hollywood's number one spinster.   Holiday
   32:83 S '62
Douglas, D.   Look what she brought from Paris!   Photop
   63-3:34 Mr '63
I said "yes" too soon.   Photop 64-6:18 D '63
Kim Novak in her hideaway by the sea.   Life 56:108 Ap
   17 '64
Marriot, J.   Where she hides from love.   Photop 65-4:
   50 Ap '64
Scott, V.   Kim Novak vs. the code.   Sat Eve Post 237:
   16 S 5 '64
Arnold, M.   The operation she's afraid of.   Photop 67-1:
   46 Ja '65

NOVARRO, RAMON
   Howe, H.   What are matinee idols made of?   Photop 23-5:
      41 Ap '23
   Howe, H.   A prediction.   Photop 25-6:51 My '24

Howe, H. Ramon Novarro in Europe. Photop 27-5:58
   Ap '25
Reyes, M. Ramon's ancestors greeted the Mayflower.
   Photop 28-5:46 O '25
Albert, K. The volunteer grandma. Photop 37-5:35 Ap
   '30
Wheelright, R. When Nordic met Latin. Photop 41-3:45
   F '32
Albert, K. What's all this chatter about Novarro?
   Photop 42-6:49 N '32
Quirk, M. A. Fulfillment of a wink. Photop 43-5:58 Ap
   '33
Krehm, W. Where is Ramon Novarro? Sat Eve Post
   216:85 Ja 15 '44
Where are they now? Newsweek 70:16 N 6 '67
Bodeen, D. Ramon Novarro, inc. filmog. Films In Re-
   view 18-9:528 N '67
Obit. Newsweek 72:97 N 11 '68
   Time 92:75 N 15 '68
   Screen World 20:238 '69

NOVELLO, IVOR
   Tipperary's rival; Ivor Novello's Keep the home fires
      burning. Lit Digest 52:821 Mr 25 '16
   Evans, D. Introducing Ivor Novello. Photop 23-5:31 Ap
      '23
   Stokes, S. English spotlight. Theatre Arts 30:673 N '46
   Romance in London. Time 50:64 O 6 '47
   Hassall, C. Ivor Novello: an appreciation. Spectator
      185:306 Mr 9 '51
   British lose an idol. Life 30:46 Mr 26 '51
   Obit. Illus Lond N 218:363 Mr 10 '51
      Mus Am 71:38 Mr '51
      Newsweek 37:65 Mr 19 '51
      Time 57:103 Mr 19 '51
   Welsh profile. Time 58:108 S 10 '51

NUYEN, FRANCE
   Elements of new trend. Life 44:61 Ja 27 '58
   Millstein, G. World of France Nuyen. N.Y. Times Mag
      p12 O 5 '58
   Young star rises as Suzie Wong. Life 45:95 O 6 '58
   Moody actress's story. Life 45:98 O 6 '58
   Whitcomb, J. New Suzie Wong. Cosmop 148:10 Je '60
   Refugee from a cookie shop. TV Guide 9-15:24 Ap 15
      '61
   People are talking about . . . Vogue 139:91 Mr 15 '62

OAKIE, JACK

Jennings, T. He's Oakie! Photop 37-6:45 My '30
Kennedy, J. B. Jack of parts; intv. Colliers 86:35 Jl 5 '30
Hamilton, S. The tooth will tell. Photop 44-1:62 Je '33
Hamilton, S. Look out, Jack, for "Ma." Photop 45-2:45 Ja '34
Hunt, J. L. Why Jack Oakie has changed. Photop 48-5: 65 O '35
Oakie, J. Through thick and thin. Photop 52-11:18 N '38
Hamilton, S. Oakie--on the spot. Photop 19-4:48 S '41
When Lucy was a bit player . . . TV Guide 12-9:5 F 29 '64
Where are they now? Newsweek 68:10 Jl 4 '66

OBERON, MERLE

Harrison, H. Why Merle clicked. Photop 48-1:65 Je '35
Roberts, K. She acts natural. Colliers 97:17 Mr 7 '36
Reeve, W. The exclusive inside story of Merle Oberon's $123,000 damage suit. Photop 50-1:21 Jl '36
Crichton, K. Boss's wife. Colliers 108:18 S 13 '41
Biography. Cur Bio '41
Not a creature was stirring. Am Mag 133:22 Ja '42
First lady of Hollywood. Am Mag 137:126 Ap '44
Merle Oberon as George Sand. Life 18:68 F 5 '45
Waterbury, R. The lady and the camerman. Photop 27-3:27 Ag '45
Maxwell, E. Ill fated love story. Photop 37-5:62 My '50
Harvey, E. Napoleon Brando. Colliers 134:108 O 29 '54
Children are to enjoy. Vogue 142:94 Ag 15 '63
Travel. Vogue 149:43 Ja 15 '67
Kirkland, S. In a swinging resort the star is Merle Oberon. Life 62:62A Ja 27 '67
In Acapulco: a pavilion by the sea. House & Gard 131:98 Ja '67
Benson, E. Merle Oberon, inc. filmog. Film Fan Mo 79:3 Ja '68
Suzy. Ahhh! Capulco; or, who's afraid of Merle Oberon? Harper Baz 101:1011 Jl '68

O'BRIAN, HUGH

Keeping a bead on the buck. TV Guide 5-6:17 F 9 '57
Earp's other life. Life 42:115 Je 10 '57

Martin, P.   I call on Wyatt Earp.   Sat Eve Post 229:
28 Je 15 '57
Barrett, M. & Bourgin, S.   Just wild about westerns.
Newsweek 50:51 Jl 22 '57
Hugh O'Brian: Mr. Wyatt Earp.   Look 21:42 Ag 6 '57
Stern, D.   The return of Hugh O'Brian.   Photop 52-6:48
D '57
Wood, C.   TV personalities biographical sketchbook.
TV Personalities p30 '57
The man behind the gun.   TV Guide 6-15:8 Ap 12 '58
Love: what is love?   Photop 53-5:61 My '58
Biography.   Cur Bio 19:29 Jl '58
Same.   Cur Bio Yrbk 1958:315 '58
The marshal meets his match.   TV Guide 6-31:17 Ag 2
'58
Christy, G.   When there is no happy ending.   Photop 56-
2:48 Ag '59
Gust, J.   A heart in exile.   Photop 59-2:42 F '61
Britten, R.   Marriage for Hugh and Soraya? Photop 60-
2:62 Ag '61

O'BRIEN, EDMOND
Wheels of fortune.   N.Y. Times Mag p60 D 14 '47
Edmond O'Brien defends Hollywood actors.   Threatre 2-8:
16 Ag '60
The case of O'Brien vs. O'Brien.   TV Guide 10-43:15 O
27 '62

O'BRIEN, EUGENE
Davis, H. R.   Letter, inc. filmog.   Films In Review 17-
7:458 Ag/S '66
Obit.   Screen World 18:238 '67

O'BRIEN, GEORGE
St. Johns, I.   The catch of Hollywood.   Photop 27-4:48
Mr '25
Martin, D.   George O'Brien, inc. filmog.   Films In Re-
view 13-9:541 N '62

O'BRIEN, MARGARET
Jefferson, S.   Junior Miss miracle.   Photop 23-3:53 Ag
'43
At the age of seven one of Hollywood's most gifted ac-
tresses.   Life 16:87 Ap 3 '44
Essay on Margaret O'Brien.   Photop 24-6:46 My '44
Markel, H.   She might be your child.   N.Y. Times Mag
p16 O 1 '44

Agee, J.   Child actress.   Nation 159:670 N 25 '49
Three little movie girls.   Life 18:71 F 26 '45
Fletcher, A. W.   Junior pin-up.   Photop 26-6:54 My '45
Hecht, A. B.   Education for Margaret.   Womans H C 72:
   22 Ag '45
Busch, N. F.   Margaret O'Brien.   Life 19:106 D 10 '45
   Same abridged.   Read Digest 48:37 F '46
Beatty, J.   Maggie was a cover girl.   Am Mag 141:44
   Mr '46
Happiest days of my life.   Womans H C 73:30 Ag '46
Waterbury, R.   Maggie's dreamy.   Photop 30-3:50 F '47
Speaking of pictures.   Life 22:24 Ap 7 '47
Howe, H.   Did I say candy?   Photop 31-6:52 N '47
Frazier, G.   Princess Margaret of Hollywood.   Colliers
   123:18 Ja 29 '49
O'Brien, G.   My little girl is Margaret O'Brien.
   Parents Mag 24:24 Je '49
O'Brien, M.   My mother understands.   Photop 36-1:64
   Je '49
Van Ryan, F.   Case of Margaret O'Brien.   Good H 136:
   15 Ap '53
Margaret O'Brien grows up.   Colliers 132:31 S 4 '53
Grown-up graduation.   Newsweek 45:42 Je 27 '55
Parsons, L. O.   Adult Margaret O'Brien.   Cosmop 140:
   24 Ja '56
Today she is a woman.   TV Guide 5-44:12 N 2 '57
Nichols, M.   Child stars who came back.   Coronet 43:84
   Mr '58
Gamin gets glamor.   Life 44:91 My 19 '58
Condon, L.   Who can I turn to now that I'm all alone.
   Photop 54-6:59 D '58
Bester, A.   Princess of pretend.   Holiday 25:111 Mr '59
Ardmore, J.   I miss my mother most of all now.   Photop
   56-3:28 S '59
Where are they now?   Newsweek 70:20 S 25 '67

O'BRIEN, PAT
   O'Brien, P.   A harp in Honolulu.   Photop 44-3:43 Ag '33
   Lane, J.   He failed for a million.   Photop 47-3:43 F '35
   Peterson, E. T.   Human side of Hollywood he-men.   Bet
      Hom & Gard 17:22 My '39
   Luck of the Irish.   Am Mag 133:28 Je '42
   Tracy, S.   Dress suit.   Am Mag 134:52 D '42
   H-A-double R-I-G-A-N.   TV Guide 8-52:17 D 24 '60
   Liston, J.   At home with Pat O'Brien.   Am Home 64:17
      Jl '61
   Biography.   Cur Bio 27:30 Mr '66

Same.   Cur Bio Yrbk 1966:296 '67

O'CONNOR, DONALD
  O'Liam, D.   He's hep!   Photop 23-2:58 Jl '43
  Hamilton, S.   Mr. O'Connor in love.   Photop 24-5:32 Ap
    '44
  O'Connor, D.   We saved our marriage.   Photop 37-6:66 Je
    '50
  Who's who in the cast.   TV Guide 5-5:34 F 1 '52
  Hubler, R. G.   Truly a trouper.   Colliers 129:30 Ap 26
    '52
  Swanson, P.   Singin' in the sun.   Photop 42-1:50 Jl '52
  O'Connor the comer.   Newsweek 41:60 Mr 16 '53
  Song and dance man.   Time 61:50 Mr 16 '53
  Old time song and dance man, age 27.   TV Guide 1-9:13
    My 29 '53
  Wilkie, J.   Too busy for the blues.   Photop 44-2:42 Ag
    '53
  Knight, A.   Introducing the new O'Connor.   Dance Mag
    27:38 O '53
  Wood, C.   TV personalities biographical sketchbook.
    TV Personalities p128 '54
  Parsons, L. O.   Never off stage.   Cosmop 138:12 Ja '55
  Biography.   Cur Bio 16:46 My '55
    Same.   Cur Bio Yrbk 1955:457 '56
  Old comic and pupil.   Life 42:91 My 6 '57
  Marill, A. H.   Donald O'Connor, inc. filmog.   Screen
    Facts 18:1 n. d.

O'CONNOR, UNA
  Taviner, R.   The little maid of "Cavalcade."   Photop 44-
    1:71 Je '33
  Obit.   Time 73:98 F 16 '59
    Am Ann 160:857 '60
    Screen World 11:223 '60

O'DAY, DAWN
  (See SHIRLEY, ANNE)

O'DONNELL, CATHY
  Crichton, K.   Girl with a poetic touch.   Colliers 122:71
    O 30 '48
  'Bama beauty.   Am Mag 148:110 O '49

O'HARA, MAUREEN
  Roberts, K.   Serene Maureen.   Colliers 104:11 O 7 '39
  Irish.   Am Mag 133:79 Mr '42

Albert, D.   I want to be loved.   Photop 20-5:41 Ap '42
O'Hara, M.   What marriage has taught me.   Photop 22-5:
40 Ap '43
O'Hara, M.   I'm waiting for my baby.   Photop 25-1:55
Je '44
O'Hara, M.   Temptations of a girl who waits.   Photop
27-2:47 Jl '45
Maddox, B.   Oh, O'Hara!   Photop 29-3:46 Ag '46
Graham, S.   Will and me.   Photop 31-1:42 Je '47
Howe, H.   Star spangled Colleen.   Photop 32-3:52 F '48
Edwards, R.   Play truth or consequences with Maureen
O'Hara.   Photop 33-4:54 S '48
Hall, G.   She knows where she's going!   Photop 42-6:68
D '52
Biography.   Cur Bio 14:40 F '53
Same.   Cur Bio Yrbk 1953:462 '53

OHMART, CAROL
Svelte sphinx in Malibu sands.   Life 39:41 Jl 4 '55
Slater, L.   Star comes to life.   Newsweek 46:78 Jl 11 '55
Person of promise.   Films & Filming 2-7:10 Ap '56

O'KALEMO, HELEN
Martin, M.   She is also called 'the versatile Miss Lind-
roth.'   Photop 6-4:129 S '14

O'KEEFE, DENNIS
Deere, D.   Sentimental Celt.   Photop 26-5:55 Ap '45
Dreier, H.   A house with growing plans.   Photop 36-5:58
O '49
Role I liked best.   Sat Eve Post 223:58 Ag 26 '50
Next week we've got to get organized.   TV Guide 7-51:8
D 19 '59
Obit.   Newsweek 72:69 S 16 '68
Time 92:66 S 13 '68
Screen World 20:238 '69

OLAND, WARNER
Bartlett, R.   A high brow villain from the arctic circle.
Photop 13-3:99 F '18
Rankin, R.   The most of every moment.   Photop 49-1:
60 Ja '36
Obit.   Newsweek 12:4 Ag 15 '38

OLIVER, EDNA MAY
Lang, H.   Two ladies who make you laugh.   Photop 40-3:
67 Ag '31

Crichton, K. She acts by the clock. Colliers 97:17 Ap
   25 '36
Brown, W. Edna May Oliver's home is just like her.
   Bet Hom & Gard 19:38 D '40
Obit. Newsweek 20:8 N 16 '42
   Time 40:62 N 16 '42
   Cur Bio '43
Jacobs, J. Edna May Oliver, inc. filmog. Films In
   Review 13-1:57 Ja '62

OLIVER, SUSAN
The girl with the balalaika. TV Guide 8-35:28 Ag 27 '60

OLIVIER, LAURENCE
Crichton, K. Hollywood doesn't count. Colliers 103:15
   Je 10 '39
Waterbury, R. A love worth fighting for. Photop 53-12:
   18 D '39
Harris, R. Star-cross'd lovers. Photop 54-10:28 O '40
Stokes, S. Oliviers. Theatre Arts 29:711 D '45
Masterpiece: Olivier's Henry V. Time 47:56 Ap 8 '46
Schwarz, D. Present and future of Shakespeare. N.Y.
   Times Mag p22 My 12 '46
Brown, J. M. Seeing things. Sat R 29:46 Je 8 '46
Biography. Cur Bio 7:28 Je '46
   Same. Cur Bio Yrbk 1946:433 '47
Laurence Olivier and wife Vivien Leigh. Time 48:40 Jl
   1 '46
Olivier's Lear. Time 48:56 O 7 '46
Olivier as Henry V. Sr Schol 49:6T O 14 '46
Harris, R. A knight and his lady. Photop 29-5:36 O '46
Stokes, S. English spotlight; Old Vic production of King
   Lear. Theatre Arts 30:702 D '46
Knighted. Newsweek 29:52 Je 23 '47
Made a knight by George VI. Time 49:40 Je 23 '47
Olivier as Hamlet. N.Y. Times Mag p15 Ag 10 '47
Speaking of pictures. Life 23:18 N 24 '47
Olivier's Hamlet. Time 51:54 Je 28 '48
Kobler, J. Sir Laurence Olivier. Life 25:129 O 18 '48
Lejeune, C. A. "The Bard" competes with "the body."
   N.Y. Times Mag p24 D 12 '48
Cobb, J. Promise and the achievement. Theatre Arts
   33:95 Je '49
Hill, G. Oliviers in Hollywood. N.Y. Times Mag p24
   O 22 '50
Watts, S. Enter the Oliviers (diffidently). N.Y. Times
   Mag p15 D 16 '51

Newman, J. L. Cleopatra and friends. Colliers 128:21
D 22 '51

Morehouse, W. King of the thespians. Am Mer 74:116
Ja '52

Hewes, H. Olivier and his green umbrellas. Sat R 35:
29 Mr 8 '52

Encrusted. New Yorker 28:24 Mr 22 '52

Nathan, G. J. Two Cleopatras. Theatre Arts 36:18 Mr
'52

Gehman, R. Oliviers live their own love story. Coronet
33:131 Ja '53

Bentley, E. I hear Olivier singing. New Repub 128:20
Jl 20 '53

Knight, A. Sir Laurenc's opus 3: Beggar's opera.
Sat R 36:28 Ag 15 '53

Peck, S. Now Olivier acts a Shakespeare villain;
Richard III on the screen. N.Y. Times Mag p24 Ja
30 '55

Blakelock, D. Larry the lamb. Plays & Players 2-6:
8 Mr '55

Heroic hypnotist. Plays & Players 2-9:9 Je '55

Shakespeare by the Oliviers. N.Y. Times Mag p16 Jl 10
'55

Olivier as Titus. N.Y. Times Mag p20 S 4 '55

Panter-Downes, M. Letter from London; Richard III.
New Yorker 31:49 D 31 '55

Co-stars. Time 67:94 F 20 '56

Peck, S. Sir Laurence again widens his range. N.Y.
Times Mag p28 F 26 '56

Knight, A., Hewes, H., Seldes, G. Sir Laurence and the
Bard. Sat R 39:26 Mr 10 '56

New pictures. Time 67:112 Mr 12 '56

Sir Laurence Olivier; triumph in Shakespeare's great year.
Newsweek 47:105 Mr 19 '56

At home and abroad with Richard III. Theatre Arts 40:22
Mr '56

Amour and the man. Sat R 39:29 O 13 '56

Harvey, E. TV imports. Colliers 136:37 O 14 '56

Olivier and Monroe. Look 20:44 O 30 '56

Knightly entertainer. Plays & Players 4-8:5 My '57

Unlikely pair make great match. Life 42:80 Je 3 '57

Supreme player of many parts. Illus Lond N 231:37 Jl
6 '57

Barker, F. G. Knight at the music hall. Plays & Players
5-1:7 O '57

Case of TV fright. Newsweek 52:84 D 1 '58

First knight. Time 74:70 Jl 20 '59

Hewes, H.   Gems from Coriolanus.   Sat R 42:26 Jl 25
    '59
$100,000 TV debut for Olivier.   Life 47:55 N 2 '59
Gelman, M.   Sir Laurence Olivier.   Theatre 2-2:17 F '60
Bester, A.   Sir Larry.   Holiday 27:119 F '60
Knight, A.   Many faces of Sir Laurence.   Sat R 43:31 O
    1 '60
Olivier--from holy man to hoofer.   Life 49:95 O 24 '60
Garbo chill.   Newsweek 57:79 Ja 16 '61
Pryce-Jones, A.   Sir Laurence & Larry.   Theatre Arts
    45:14 F '61
Hewes, H.   Awake at the switch.   Sat R 44:26 My 27 '61
Clurman, H.   Theatre.   Nation 192:467 My 27 '61
Herndon, B.   The power and the glory.   TV Guide 9-43:
    17 O 28 '61
Robin, A.   Living legends.   Todays Health 40:84 Ja '62
Laurence Olivier.   Plays & Players 9-10:7 Jl '62
McVay, D.   Hamlet to clown.   Films & Filming 8-12:16
    S '62
Panter-Downes, M.   Letter from London.   New Yorker
    38:80 D 22 '62
Brien, A.   Openings: London.   Theatre Arts 46:57 D '62
Definitive Moor.   Time 83:80 My 1 '64
Tynan, K.   In his talent, Shakespeare summoned up.
    Life 56:101 My 1 '64
The great Sir Laurence.   Life 56:80A My 1 '64
Trewin, J. C.   Laurence Olivier: a profile.   Plays &
    Players 11-8:8 My '64
Panter-Downes, M.   Letter from London.   New Yorker
    40:98 Je 13 '64
Rogoff, G.   Olivier's Othello, coiling power and wounded
    majesty.   Hi Fi 14:34 D '64
Personalities of the week.   Illus Lond N 247:12 Jl 17 '65
Kallet, N.   Olivier and the Moor.   Holiday 39:143 Ap '66
Tynan, K.   The actor and the moor.   Plays & Players
    13-11:47 Ag '66
Coward, N.   Laurence Olivier.   McCalls 94:103 O '66
Tynan, K.   Actor; intv.   Tulane Drama R 11:71 Win '66
Tynan, K.   Shakespeare and Laurence Olivier; intv.
    World Theatre 16:67 Ja '67
Panter-Downes, M.   Letter from London; performance of
    Strindberg's Dance of death at the Old Vic.   New
    Yorker 43:158 Ap 15 '67
Clurman, H.   Theatre in Europe.   Nation 204:797 Je 19
    '67
Hewes, H.   Olivier triumphant.   Sat R 50:36 Jl 1 '67
Best of breed.   Time 90:64 N 3 '67

Hart, H.   Laurence Olivier.   Films In Review 18-10:593
  D '67
Roman, R. C.   Laurence Olivier filmography.   Films In
  Review 18-10:610 D '67
Miller, E.   Hollywood scene.   Seventeen 27:48 Ag '68

OLSEN, MORONI
  Obit.   Screen World 6:224 '55

O'MALLEY, PAT
  Obit.   Screen World 18:238 '67

O'NEAL, FREDERICK
  Biography.   Cur Bio 7:32 N '46
    Same.   Cur Bio Yrbk 1946:438 '47
  Cartwright, M.   No type casting--Frederick O'Neal
    scores again.   Negro Hist Bul 18:3 O '54
  Actors' new boss.   Ebony 19:58 Je '64

O'NEIL, NANCE
  Obit.   Screen World 17:240 '66

O'NEILL, HENRY
  Obit.   Screen World 13:225 '62

O'SHEA, MICHAEL
  O'Shea, M.   Mrs. whistle bait.   Photop 42-5:66 N '52
  Drama for winter vacationists.   Theatre Arts 36:77 D '52
  Leon, R.   Oh baby!   Photop 44-3:46 S '53
  Noel, T.   Becoming a father's no joke.   Photop 45-2:44
    F '54
  Wood, C.   TV personalities biographical sketchbook.
    TV Personalities p15 '56

O'SULLIVAN, MAUREEN
  Hartley, K.   They waited two long years for love.
    Photop 50-6:32 D '36
  Hayes, B. A.   What I plan for my son in today's troubled
    world.   Photop 54-1:67 Ja '40
  Grafton, S.   Some people have to grow up twice.   Good H
    140:62 Ja '55
  Girl from Roscommon.   New Yorker 38:23 D 22 '62
  Efron, E.   New girl on 'Today.'   TV Guide 12-20:24 My
    16 '64
  Block, J. L.   Many lives of Maureen O'Sullivan.   Good H
    161:28 N '65

O'TOOLE, PETER
Hewes, H.   Bloodless revolution.   Sat R 43:43 S 17 '60
Soft sell.   Theatre Arts 45:9 N '61
Lawrence of Leeds.   Time 80:63 O 19 '62
People are talking about.   Vogue 140:122 N 15 '62
Miller, E.   Go at the world! Seventeen 21:124 N '62
Talk with a star.   Newsweek 60:64 D 24 '62
Armbrister, T.   Oscar winner? Sat Eve Post 236:26 Mr
     9 '63
Armbrister, T.   O'Toole of Arabia.   Sat Eve Post 236:23
     Mr 9 '63
Peter O'Toole.   Plays & Players 10-6:11 Mr '63
Marowitz, C.   Peter O'Toole: an impression.   Plays &
     Players 10-7:18 Ap '63
Talese, G.   O'Toole on the Ould Sod.   Esquire 60:77 Ag
     '63
Peter O'Toole and Rebecca West.   Redbook 122:56 Mr '64
Asher, E.   A reasonable man.   Photop 66-2:71 Ag '64
Miller, E.   Lord Jim in a jungle paradise.   Seventeen
     23:132 N '64
Lord Jim.   Life 58:85 Ja 22 '65
Leduc, V.   Steal-scening with Hepburn and O'Toole.
     Vogue 147:172 Ap 1 '66
Hamill, P.   New roughneck breed of ladies' men. Good H
     165:94 O '67
Biography.   Cur Bio 29:33 S '68
Same.   Cur Bio Yrbk 1968:295 '69

OUSPENSKAYA, MARIA
Obit.   Newsweek 34:61 D 12 '49
     Time 54:85 D 12 '49
Dickens, H.   Maria Ouspenskaya, inc. filmog.   Screen
     Facts 4:45 n.d.

OVERMAN, LYNN
Obit.   Cur Bio '43

OWEN, REGINALD
Tragedy, comedy and farce.   Drama 15:49 D '24

OWEN, SEENA
"Owen" or "Auen."   Photop 9-4:142 Mr '16
Evans, D.   The camera is cruel to her.   Photop 17-6:69
     My '20
St. Johns, A. R.   Do you believe in dimples.   Photop 20-
     1:57 Je '21
Obit.   Screen World 18:238 '67

PAGE, ANITA
Busby, M. Dating Anita. Photop 37-3:65 F '30

PAGE, GERALDINE
Spotlight. Theatre Arts 36:29 Jl '52
Edge of greatness. Life 33:107 S 8 '52
Geraldine Page. Time 61:48 F 2 '53
How it would be. New Yorker 28:24 F 7 '53
Geraldine Page. Vogue 121:136 Mr 1 '53
Stardom for Page. Life 34:67 Mr 2 '53
White, S. Ave atque vale. Look 17:20 Mr 24 '53
Carroll, J. Geraldine Page; irony of a legend. Theatre
    Arts 37:18 Ap '53
Nathan, G. J. Miss Page. Theatre Arts 37:26 Ap '53
Biography. Cur Bio 14:49 N '53
    Same. Cur Bio Yrbk 1953:468 '53
Tune-up time for rising stars. Life 36:65 Ja 25 '54
Four young stars; will they be great? Vogue 123:111 Ap
    1 '54
Love walks in on Lizzie. Life 37:143 N 15 '54
Peanut butter sandwiches and dreams. Mlle 40:206 Ap '55
Millstein, G. Portrait of Miss Page on and off stage.
    N. Y. Times Mag p 15 Mr 29 '59
Williams, T. Five fiery ladies. Life 50:86 F 3 '61
Ross, L. Profile; intv. New Yorker 37:62 N 4 '61
Golden age of Geraldine Page. Life 52:96 Ja 26 '62
Baldwin, J. Bird of light. Show 2-2:88 F '62
Talk with a star. Newsweek 59:86 Ap 2 '62
Arkadin. Film Clips. Sight & Sound 31-3:141 Sum '62
Geraldine Page. Film 32:10 Sum '62
Davidson, B. Geraldine Page; diamond who likes it rough.
    Sat Eve Post 235:30 N 17 '62
Out of the mold. Time 82:64 Jl 5 '63
Letter to a star. Newsweek 64:92 N 30 '64

PAGET, DEBRA
Russell, J. Mama's girl. Photop 41-1:32 Ja '52
Dudley, F. Debra and her answer man. Photop 44-1:70
    Jl '53
Arnold, M. Half saint--half siren. Photop 51-3:50 Mr
    '57
A yound lady of decorum. TV Guide 5-23:24 Je 8 '57
Arnold, M. The strange truth about Debra's rushed mar-
    riage and hushed divorce. Photop 54-1:31 Jl '58

PAIGE, JANIS
Marshall, J. Girl we'd most. Colliers 121:48 Mr 27 '48
Anderson, D. Show stopper. Theatre Arts 36:46 Ja '52
Zolotow, M. Everything but a man. Cosmop 139:118 S
  '55
She's sitting prettier. TV Guide 4-4:13 Ja 28 '56
Wood, C. TV personalities biographical sketchbook.
  TV Personalities p14 '56
Biography. Cur Bio 20:30 Ja '59
  Cur Bio Yrbk 1959:341 '60
Janis comes over loud and clear. TV Guide 10-30:12 Jl
  28 '62
Poirier, N. Jubilant Janis is back on Broadway.
  Sat Eve Post 236:35 N 9 '63
McClelland, D. Janis Paige, inc. filmog. Films In
  Review 17-1:61 Ja '66

PAIGE, ROBERT
Wood, C. TV personalities biographical sketchbook.
  TV Personalities p93 '57

PAIVA, NESTOR
Obit. Screen World 18:239 '67

PALANCE, JACK
Man and menace. Colliers 132:20 Jl 18 '53
Hubler, R. G. Hollywood's frightening lover. Sat Eve
  Post 227:32 N 13 '54
Tormented poet turned tormented actor. TV Guide 5-25:
  20 Je 22 '57
He has learned to count to 10. TV Guide 12-17:8 Ap 25
  '64

PALLETTE, EUGENE
Hollywood's No. 1 hide-out; Eugene Pallette's wilderness
  paradise in Oregon. Sat Eve Post 215:24 D 12 '42
Obit. Newsweek 44:81 S 13 '54
  Time 64:104 S 13 '54
  Screen World 6:224 '55
Jones, J. Eugene Pallette, inc. filmog. Films In Review
  18-9:588 N '67

PALMER, BETSY
Wood, C. TV personalities biographical sketchbook.
  TV Personalities p37 '57
People of promise. Films & Filming 4-6:17 Mr '58
She's got a secret. Newsweek 52:71 S 22 '58

Scott, M. Petsy Palmer. Cosmop 146:44 Ja '59
Van Slingerland, P. Betsy Palmer: child of TV.
    Look 23:73 Mr 3 '59
I've got a secret's two great assets. TV Guide 10-33:18
    Ag 18 '62

PALMER, LILLI
    American women are lucky. Am Home 38:27 O '47
    Maxwell, E. Rex and his queen. Photop 32-3:60 F '48
    New team. New Yorker 26:14 D 30 '50
    Ladies' night. Time 57:46 Ja 15 '51
    Palmer chase. Newsweek 37:54 Ja 29 '51
    Hamburger, P. Television: Miss Lilli. New Yorker 26:
        72 F 3 '51
    Lilli's new idea. TV Guide 4-7:9 F 17 '51
    Biography. Cur Bio My '51
        Same. Cur Bio Yrbk 1951:471 '52
    Frazier, G. Lilli Palmer's secret. Holiday 10:91 N '51
    Life is better after 30. TV Guide 1-22:17 S 4 '53
    Miller, F. I learned America's secret. Nations Bus 42:
        68 Jl '54

PANGBORN, FRANKLYN
    Obit. Time 72:64 Ag 4 '58
        Screen World 10:223 '59
        Am Ann 1959:517 '59

PANZER, PAUL
    Obit. Newsweek 52:61 Ag 25 '58
        Screen World 10:223 '59

PAPAS, IRENE
    New Electra. N. Y. Times Mag p92 N 25 '62

PARKER, ELEANOR
    Eleanor Parker plays Bette Davis role. Life 18:37 Ap 30
        '45
    Irwin, L. Shy girl with nerve. Photop 27-1:59 Je '45
    Asher, J. Miss paradox. Photop 28-3:34 F '46
    Parker's progress. Photop 32-5:70 Ap '48
    Parsons, L. O. Interrupted melody. Cosmop 138:18 Ap
        '55
    Downing, H. Changeable lady. Photop 47-4:53 Ap '55
    McClelland, D. Eleanor Parker, inc. filmog. Films In
        Review 13-3:135 Mr '62
    McClelland, D. Eleanor Parker on TV. Films In Re-
        view 16-8:526 O '65

PARKER, FESS
King of the wild frontier. TV Guide 3-18:5 Ap 30 '55
Meet Davy Crockett. Look 19:36 Jl 26 '55
Parsons, L. O. Hollywood frontier. Cosmop 139:16 Ag '55
Allen, D. Date bait for a guy like me. Photop 49-1:53 Ja '56
Wood, C. TV personalities biographical sketchbook. TV Personalities p116 '56
Westheimer, D. The senator's mighty sharp. TV Guide 10-52:15 D 29 '62
Amory, C. Celebrity register. McCalls 90:144 Jl '63
Hano, A. Out of the moth balls came the coonskin cap. TV Guide 12-52:12 D 26 '64
Whitney, D. Old Dan'l on the Santa Barbara frontier. TV Guide 16-19: 24 My 11 '68
Gardiner, H. From Boone to tycoon! Photop 74-2:52 Ag '68

PARKER, JEAN
Proctor, K. They thought they would keep their marriage a secret. Photop 50-1:54 Jl '36

PARKER, SUZY
Model into photographer: Suzy Parker at twenty-one. Vogue 124:142 Ag 1 '54
American girl makes good in Paris. Look 19:98 F 8 '55
People are talking about. Vogue 130:100 Ag 1 '57
All the U. S. will soon know Suzy. Life 43:94 S 23 '57
Gordon, S. If you knew Suzy. Look 21:115 O 15 '57
Bachelor girl. Time 71:16 Je 23 '58
About Suzy. Newsweek 51:26 Je 23 '58
Bergquist, L. Strange case of Suzy Parker. Look 22:26 Ag 19 '58
Cozy chat with a beauty. Newsweek 53:105 Je 15 '59
Gay soaking for Suzy. Life 47:53 Jl 20 '59
Gehman, R. Lives of Suzy Parker. Cosmop 147:86 N '59
Girl next door; intv. Newsweek 55:114 Je 6 '60
Morgan, T. B. World's most beautiful woman. Redbook 117:38 Ag '61
Amory, C. Celebrity register. McCalls 90:144 Jl '63

PARKER, WILLARD
Wood, C. TV personalities biographical sketchbook. TV Personalities p104 '57

PARKS, LARRY
  Skolsky, S.   The Parks story.   Photop 30-3:66 F '47
  Deere, D.   Almost down to earth.   Photop 30-6:54 My '47
  Parsons, L. O.   The Larry Parks puzzle.   Photop 31-5:
    30 O '47
  Parks, L.   I believe.   Photop 32-3:44 F '48
  Downing, H.   Journey from fear.   Photop 33-2:68 Jl '48
  Garrett, B.   I'm just wild about Larry Parks.   Photop
    33-5:48 O '48
  Parks, L.   Happy am I.   Photop 34-3:40 F '49
  Scott, D.   Larry Parks sings again.   Photop 37-2:44 F
    '50; 38-4:46 O '50
  Parks, L.   Isn't it wonderful.   Photop 37-2:44 F '50
  Command performance.   Time 57:94 Ap 2 '51
  Larry Parks in red face.   Newsweek 37:21 Ap 2 '51

PARKS, MICHAEL
  Man who plays Adam.   Life 57:69 N 27 '64
  Miller, E.   Who's Michael Parks?   Seventeen 25:174 S
    '66
  Prelutsky, B.   The angriest young man on two wheels has
    turned the corner.   TV Guide 17-50:30 D 13 '69

PARRISH, HELEN
  Obit.   Screen World 11:224 '60

PATRICK, GAIL
  Crichton, K.   Ex leopard lady.   Collier 101:11 My 7 '38
  Langley, K.   Fun land for tiny tots.   C S Mon Mag p4
    D 24 '49
  The case of the businesslike beauty.   TV Guide 6-25:17
    Je 21 '58

PATRICK, LEE
  Wood, C.   TV personalities biographical sketchbook.
    TV Personalities p73 '54

PATRICK, NIGEL
  Knickerbocker glory.   Plays & Players 2-10:9 Jl '55

PATTERSON, ELIZABETH
  Obit.   Screen World 18:238 '67

PAVAN, MARISA
  Watson, E. M. D.   Italy's twin sisters.   Cosmop 137:28
    S '54
  Balling, F. D.   Imported glamour, Italian style.   Photop

48-6:48 D '55
Allen, D. La bella rosa. Photop 49-3:60 Mr '56
Downing, H. The wonderful world of Marisa Pavan.
  Photop 49-6:40 Je '56
Jones, M. W. An afternoon with Madame Aumont.
  Photop 52-2:38 Ag '57

PAXINOU, KATINA
Free theatre for a free people. Theatre Arts 26:117 F
  '42
Crichton, K. Corinthian Pilar. Colliers 112:50 Jl 24
  '43
Biography. Cur Bio '43
Greek goddess in Hollywood. Am Mag 137:104 Ja '44
Shaw, A. Katina Paxinou, actress and patriot. Ind
  Woman 23:135 My '44

PAYNE, JOHN
Berch, B. Romance--as planned. Photop 19-4:32 S '41
Hamilton, S. Love, honor and goodbye. Photop 20-5:31
  Ap '42
Trotter, M. You belong together. Photop 21-1:39 Je '42
Sharpe, H. Bewildered knight. Photop 21-5:28 O; 21-6:
  56 N '42
Emerson, B. Heart affair. Photop 22-2:20 Ja '43
Payne, J. A letter to my mother. Photop 23-1:19 Je '43
Waterbury, R. The difference is you. Photop 26-4:32
  Mr '45
Payne, J. An ex-G. I. challenges American women.
  Photop 26-4:33 Mr '45
Sharpe, H. Triangle. Photop 28-5:58 Ap '46
Arnold, M. Take-off. Photop 29-5:41 O '46
I learned about flying from that! Flying 41:52 Jl '47
A dark horse. TV Guide 5-32:8 Ag 10 '57
How to be a TV cowboy. TV Guide 6-3:28 Ja 18 '58
Rough but Payne-less. TV Guide 7-10:8 Mr 7 '59

PAYTON, BARBARA
Obit. Screen World 19:237 '68

PEARCE, ALICE
Minx with three minks. Newsweek 30:76 O 6 '47
Wildman, H. H. Sutton place pixie. N. Y. Times Mag
  p28 N 2 '47
Watt, D. Tables for two. New Yorker 33:103 Mr 16 '57
Finally the center of attention. TV Guide 13-52:12 D 25
  '65

Obit. Newsweek 67:93 Mr 14 '66
Screen World 18:238 '67

PEARSON, BEATRICE
Crichton, K. Colliers movies. Colliers 122:82 N 20 '48

PEARSON, VIRGINIA
Pike, C. Virginia from Kentucky. Photop 13-4:16 Mr '18
Obit. Screen World 10:223 '59

PECK, GREGORY
Star in the Keys of the kingdom. Life 18:60 Ja 15 '45
Smith, D. The key to Gregory Peck. Photop 26-5:47
Ap '45
Martin, P. Phantom star. Sat Eve Post 218:14 S 22 '45
Waterbury, R. These are the days of Gregory Peck.
Photop 27-4:40 S; 27-5:60 O '45
Porter, A. Mr. Peck's good boy. Colliers 116:27 D 15
'45
Peck, G. I'm like this. Photop 28-1:36 D '45
Peck, G. Ingrid, spellbinder. Photop 28-4:32 Mr '46
Peck, G. It's like this to be Mrs. Gregory Peck.
Photop 28-6:42 My '46
Summer theatre. Life 21:81 Ag 5 '46
Deere, D. Dark hour. Photop 29-3:44 Ag '46
Pierson, N. Two sons has Gregory Peck. Photop 30-2:
50 Ja '47
Tobey, K. My pal Gregory Peck. Photop 30-5:38 Ap '47
Lowrance, D. The affairs of Peck. Photop 31-2:40 Jl
'47
Biography. Cur Bio Jl '47
Same, revised. Cur Bio Yrbk 1947:503 '48
Perkins, S. Photolife of Gregory Peck. Photop 31-6:60
N '47
Gentleman's agreement. Life 23:95 D 1 '47
Leading man. Time 51:52 Ja 12 '48
Howe, H. Everything but ulcers. Photop 32-4:64 Mr '48
Parsons, L. O. The Gregory Peck marriage puzzles me.
Photop 34-6:54 My '49
Peck, G. Jenny and Miss Jones. Photop 36-1:44 Je '49
Downing, H. Restless heart. Photop 36-5:52 O '49
Peck, G. as told to Morris, J. Peck and sons. Parents
Mag 26:44 Jl '51
Zeitlin, I. A Tobey and a Peck. Photop 41-4:58 Ap '52
Parsons, L. O. Gregory Peck, phantom star. Cosmop
138:22 F '55
Harris, R.. Gregory Peck: saint or sinner? Photop 48-

3:68 S '55

Suiting up as a suburbanite; film version of Man in the gray flannel suit. Life 39:135 N 7 '55

Hubler, R. G. Sensitively rugged Mr. Peck. Coronet 39:104 Mr '56

Tall, dark and dignified. Look 20:81 Jl 24 '56

Peck, incorporated. Newsweek 50:114 O 21 '57

Slater, L. McCalls visits. McCalls 85:8 Jl '58

Nichols, M. Disquieted quiet man. Coronet 50:12 Je '61

Scott, V. Gregory. McCalls 90:104 S '63

Biography. Am Ann 1964:449 '64

Block, J. L. Gregory Peck turns crusader. Good H 162:70 My '66

Stein, J. Gregory Peck, inc. filmog. Films In Review 18-3:129 Mr '67

Kaleidoscope interviews Gregory Peck. Kaleidoscope 2-3:4 n. d.

PEIL, EDWARD J.
Obit. Screen World 10:225 '59

PELLICER, PINA
Obit. Screen World 16:224 '65

PENDLETON, NAT
Obit. Screen World 19:237 '68

PENNER, JOE
Martin, M. Hollywood buys a duck. Photop 46-4:71 S '34

Wanna buy a duck? Sat Eve Post 207:30 N 10 '34

Babcock, M. And so you think he's funny. Photop 48-6: 32 N '35

Obit. Time 37:76 Ja 20 '41

Cur Bio '41

PENNICK, JACK
Gray, B. Jack Pennick, inc. filmog. Films In Review 16-1:60 Ja '65

PEPPARD, GEORGE
Miller, E. George Peppard; a personality in spite of himself. Seventeen 22:128 N '63

Wall, T. The girl who paid for his love. Photop 66-6:60 D '64

Anderson, G. Fight that saved our lives. Photop 68-1:40 Jl '65

Biography. Cur Bio 26:27 D '65

Same. Cur Bio Yrbk 1965:319 '65

PEPPER, BARBARA
  Limbacher, J. L. The unsung heroes: Barbara Pepper,
    inc. filmog. Film Fan Mo 99:22 S '69
  Barbara Pepper; letters. Film Fan Mo 101:9 N '69

PERCY, EILEEN
  Owen, K. Eileen from the Emerald Isle. Photop 13-3:
    77 F '18

PERKINS, ANTHONY
  (See PERKINS, TONY)

PERKINS, MILLIE
  Hollywood's Anne Frank. Newsweek 51:100 Je 16 '58
  Slater, L. McCalls visits. McCalls 85:6 Jl '58
  Shy unknown becomes a star. Life 46:121 Ap 6 '59
  Ardmore, J. She no longer has to pretend. Photop 56-
    6:64 D '59
  Blake, E. Why Millie had to settle for a runaway mar-
    riage. Photop 58-1:54 Jl '60

PERKINS, TONY
  Twenty-four year-old copy of Cooper. Life 41:59 Jl 16 '56
  Ott, B. You'd take him home to mother. Photop 50-5:
    46 N '56
  Lane, L. Little boy. Photop 51-1:22 Ja '57
  Hyams, J. Barefoot boy with cheek? Photop 51-4:44 Ap
    '57
  Personality of the month. Films & Filming 3-7:3 Ap '57
  Perkins, T. To you from Tony: Sa-wad-du. Photop 51-
    6:66 Je '57
  Perkins, T. Siam by streetcar and sampan. Photop 52-
    1:50 Jl '57
  Phillips, D. Manuscript released to editor. Photop 52-3:
    40 S '57
  Archerd, A. Photoplay visits a movie set. Photop 52-4:
    73 O '57
  Goldsmith, B. L. Tony Perkins, Hollywood's wonder boy.
    McCalls 85:70 O '57
  Going around in circles. Photop 52-5:62 N '57
  Hubler, R. G. Lonely ladder. Coronet 43:37 N '57
  New play in Manhattan. Time 70:72 D 9 '57
  Stage struck. New Yorker 33:20 D 28 '57
  Perkins, Mrs. O. He still baffles me. Photop 53-2:
    35 F '58

Tony Perkins: shooting star. Newsweek 51:47 Mr 3 '58
Ashton, S. Tony and an old pocket watch. Photop 53-
3:54 Mr '58
Eleven fine actors get their dream roles. Life 44:76 Ap
14 '58
Knowles, J. Actor of the year. Holiday 23:111 My '58
Lonely Tony Perkins. Look 22:47 Je 24 '58
Asher, J. Wanted: a wife. Photop 54-2:64 Ag '58
Levin, R. J. Tony Perkins, the quiet rebel. Good H
149:88 N '59
Johnson, R. Lonely Tony Perkins. Sat Eve Post 232:25
Ja 9 '60
People are talking about. Vogue 135:94 Mr 15 '60
Richards, S. A visit with Tony Perkins. Theatre 2-5:
22 My '60
What makes a woman interesting? Photop 58-2:60 Ag '60
Biography. Cur Bio 21:36 S '60
Same. Cur Bio Yrbk 1960:316 '61
Miller, E. Hollywood scene. Seventeen 20:16 My '61
Talk with a star. Newsweek 58:72 Jl 3 '61
Ross, L. Profile; intv. New Yorker 37:83 N 4 '61
Talk with a star. Newsweek 60:87 O 29 '62
Bean, R. Pinning down the quicksilver. Films & Film-
ing 11-10:44 Jl '65

PERREAU, GIGI
Chandler, D. Bringing up a movie moppet. Colliers 124:
17 Ag 13 '49
Harbert, H. Assignment in Hollywood. Good H 137:126
D '53
Dowager at 21. TV Guide 10-7:8 F 17 '62

PERSOFF, NEHEMIAH
Bald or bearded. TV Guide 8-22:28 My 28 '60

PETERS, BROCK
Brock Peters. Ebony 18:106 Je '63

PETERS, HOUSE
Corliss, A. They won't let him be bad. Photop 10-3:131
Ag '16
Copeland, G. A genial crab. Photop 17-3:57 F '20
Obit. Screen World 19:237 '68

PETERS, JEAN
Co-ed from Ohio. Am Mag 143:117 Vacation No. 1947
Hollywood's new generation. Life 24:96 My 24 '48

Wallace, R. Halfway to Heaven. Photop 33-6:56 N '48
Harris, E. Girl who didn't go Hollywood. Colliers 124:
    18 N 5 '49
Hopper, H. Hollywood's mystery girl. Photop 41-3:50
    Mr '52
New star over Hollywood. Coronet 31:14 Ap '52
Hall, G. The mysterious Miss Peters. Photop 46-4:50
    O '54
Meyer, J. Jean Peters, inc. filmog. Films In Review
    15-3:183 Mr '64
Lyons, D. L. America's richest wife. Ladies Home J
    85:100 N '68

PETERS, SUSAN
    We call on a new star. Am Mag 135:120 Mr '43
    Sharpe, H. M. Susie cues. Photop 23-6:55 N '43
    Bentley, J. Out of this dream. Photop 24-3:67 F '44
    Parsons, L. O. Courage is a girl named Susan. Photop
        26-6:28 My '45
    Peters, S. My Hollywood friends. Photop 28-1:30 D '45;
        28-2:34 Ja; 28-3:48 F; 28-4:52 Mr; 28-6:62 My '46;
        30-3:74 F '47
    Peters, S. My Hollywood friends gave a baby shower.
        Photop 29-3:30 Ag '46
    Peters, S. Easy does it. Photop 31-3:56 Ag '47
    Crippled star acts. Life 23:89 S 8 '47
    Girl can go places without legs. Am Mag 144:42 D '47
    Quine, R. The bravest girl in town. Photop 32-5:38 Ap
        '48
    Peters, S. The children's hour. Photop 32-6:44 My '48
    Peters, S. Valentine story. Photop 34-3:38 F '49
    Obit. Newsweek 40:71 N 3 '52
        Time 60:98 N 3 '52

PETERSON, DOROTHY
    Talbot, R. So Hollywood got her. Photop 43-4:72 Mr '33

PETROVA, OLGA
    Serverance, C. Our lady of troubles. Photop 10-5:56 O
        '16
    Mullett, M. B. Ugly duckling who became the white pea-
        cock; intv. Am Mag 98:34 D '24

PHILBIN, MARY
    St. Johns, I. The girl on the cover. Photop 26-5:39 O
        '24
    Smith, A. Mary herself. Photop 30-6:30 N '26

PHILIPE, GERARD
Obit. Illus Lond N 235:813 D 5 '59
Time 74:76 D 7 '59
Am Ann 1960:858 '60
Screen World 11:224 '60
Philipe, A. No longer than a sigh; excerpt. Ladies Home
J 81:64 S '64

PHILLIPS, AUGUSTUS
Briscoe, J. Why film favorites forsook the footlights.
Photop 6-6:124 N '14

PHILLIPS, NORMA
A sweet girl graduate from musical comedy. Photop
4-5:48 O '13

PIAZZA, BEN
Nichols, L. Actor-author. N.Y. Times Bk R p8 Ag 9
'64

PICKFORD, MARY
Actress from the movies. Cosmop 55:265 Jl '13
Kegler, E. The charm of wistfulness; an intv. Photop
4-3:34 Ag '13
Smith, F. J. Maude Adams of the movies. Am Mag
77:64 Ap '14
Synon, K. The unspoiled Mary Pickford. Photop 4-4:35
S '14
Best-known girl in America; what it means to be a movie
actress. Ladies Home J 32:9 Ja '15
Wright, E. A weekend with Mary Pickford; intv. Photop
7-4:101 Mr '15
Edwards, L. The incomprable Mary. Feature Movie 4-
1:5 O 10 '15
Johnson, J. Mary Pickford; biography. Photop 8-6:53 N
'15
Belasco, D. When Mary Pickford came to me. Photop
9-1:27 D '15
Johnson, J. Mary Pickford--herself and her career.
Photop 9-2:37 Ja '16
Johnson, J. Mary Pickford: Herself and her career.
Photop 9-3:49 F '16
Two most popular women in America. Everybodys 34:
782 Je '16
Lindsay, V. Queen of my people. New Repub 11:280 Jl
7 '17
Ranck, E. Mary Pickford--whose real name is Gladys

Smith.   Am Mag 85:34 My '18
Same.   Cur Opinion 64:392 Je '18
Evans, D. Mary Pickford, the girl.   Photop 14-2:90 Jl
    '18
Bartlett, R. Mary the well beloved.   Photop 17-5:28 Ap
    '20
Woollcott, A. Strenuous honeymoon.   Everybody's 43:36
    N '20
St. Johns, A. R. Why does the world love Mary? Photop
    21-1:50 D '21
Greatest business in the world.   Colliers 69:7 Je 10 '22
Mullett, M. B. Mary Pickford describes her most thrill-
    ing experience.   Am Mag 95:34 My '23
My own story.   Ladies Home J 40:6 Jl; 16 Ag; 9 S '23
Howe, H. Mary Pickford's favorite stars and films.
    Photop 25-2:28 Ja '24
Pickford, M. as told to R. Birdwell. When I am old.
    Photop 27-3:52 F '25
Pickford, M. Mary is looking for pictures.   Photop
    28-1:39 Je '25
Quirk, J. R. The public just won't let Mary Pickford
    grow up.   Photop 28-4:36 S '25
Why I have not bobbed mine.   Pict R 28:9 Ap '27
London, M. Mary Pickford, a closeup.   Overland 86:72
    Mr '28
St. Johns, A. R. Why Mary Pickford bobbed her hair.
    Photop 34-4:32 S '28
When Mary Pickford was the girl with the curls. Lit
    Digest 99:58 N 3 '28
Collins, F. L. Mary Pickford's successors.   Womans
    H C 56:24 F '29
Ambassadors.   Sat Eve Post 203:6 Ag 23 '30
Hall, L. How about Mary and Doug?   Photop 38-3:42 Ag
    '30
MacCulloch, C. Stay away from Hollywood.   Good H 91:
    36 O '30
Albert, K. Mary Pickford denies all.   Photop 39-2:60
    Ja '31
Going back to the stage.   Pict R 32:16 Mr '31
Biery, R. As Mary faces forty.   Photop 39-6:66 My '31
Larkin, M. Mary returns to herself.   Photop 43-4:62
    Mr '33
Spencer, H. E. Mary Pickford.   Cinema Digest 3-3:13
    Ap 3 '33
Melcher, E. Mary Pickford and "Peter Pan." Cinema
    Digest 3-6:10 Ap 24 '33
Collins, F. L. Where are those second Mary Pickfords?

Good H 96:20 Ap '33

What religion means to me. Forum 90:67 Ag '33

Foster, A. So comes the end of the rainbow trail. Photop 44-4:28 S '33

Shawell, J. Mary Pickford's empty arms. Pict R 35: 18 Ja '34

She tunes in on God, a 24-hour station. Newsweek 4:37 N 10 '34

Sangster, M. E. Mary Pickford's search for happiness. Photop 47-3:34 F '35

Mercer, J. The Fairbanks' social war is on. Photop 50-2:22 Ag '36

To lead drive on polio. Ind Woman 23:30 Ja '44

Biography. Cur Bio Ap '45

A must do for January. Ind Woman 25:26 Ja '46

Life visits Pickfair. Life 23:158 N 17 '47

Mary's mighty megaphone. Life 34:45 Ap 13 '53

My whole life. McCalls 81:29 Mr; 50 Ap; 44 My; 43 Je '54

Schwartz, D. Mary Pickford: the little girl in curls. New Repub 132:17 Je 6 '55

Churchill, A. Sweetheart and the silver. Sat R 38:19 Je 11 '55

Nichols, L. Talk with Mary Pickford. N. Y. Times Bk R p9 Je 12 '55

Film pioneers' roll of their living immortals. Life 40: 116 Ja 23 '56

Wistful reunion at Pickfair. Life 40:163 Ap 16 '56

Greatest stars. Cosmop 141:28 O '56

Mayer, A. L. The origins of United Artists. Films In Review 10-7:390 Ag/S '59

Spears, J. Mary Pickford's directors. Films In Review 17-2:71 F '66

Where are they now? Newsweek 70:16 N 6 '67

PIDGEON, WALTER

Hughes, M. He has the girls gasping. Photop 38-1:65 Je '30

Winter, E. Design for serenity. Photop 54-8:26 Ag '40

Baskette, K. This is Pidge. Photop 20-6:42 My '42

Biography. Cur Bio '42

Beatty, J. Hollywood hermit. Am Mag 135:36 Mr '43

Hamilton, S. Walter Pidgeon on the spot. Photop 22-5: 36 Ap '43

Chapman, J. Perennial Pidgeon. Photop 25-4:40 S '44

Howe, H. Pidgeon--pirate and diplomat. Photop 27-5: 52 O '45

Steele, J. H.   Portrait of a Royal Canadian.   Photop 30-
    1:68 D '46
Strip please.   Am Mag 144:19 N '47
Garson, G.   That prize Pidgeon.   Photop 34-4:62 Mr '49
Walter Pidgeon and Cordelia Drexel Biddle.   Vogue 128:
    148 N 1 '56
Hudson, R.   Walter Pidgeon, inc. filmog.   Films In Re-
    view 11-8:509 O '60

PIERLOT, FRANCIS
    Obit.   Screen World 7:226 '56

PITTS, ZASU
    Cohn, A. A.   Eliza + Susan = Zasu.   Photop 15-5:64 Ap
        '19
    Spensley, D.   The hands speak.   Photop 30-4:46 S '26
    Condon, F.   From Eliza and Susan.   Sat Eve Post 204:24
        Ap 30 '32
    Hamilton, S.   Zasu, a good samaritan.   Photop 43-3:78
        F '33
    Crichton, W.   Mr. Woodall's wife.   Colliers 97:26 Je 6
        '36
    Manning, M.   Cooking fool is Zasu!   Intv.   Am Home 32:
        92 Je '44
    Recognition.   Am Mag 138:64 D '44
    The hands have it.   TV Guide 5-14:14 Ap 6 '57
    Wood, C.   TV personalities biographical sketchbook.
        TV Personalities p26 '57
    Gray, B.   Letter, inc. filmog.   Films In Review 13-7:
        441 Ag/S '63
    Obit.   Time 81:65 Je 14 '63
        Newsweek 61:63 Je 17 '63
        Screen World 15:223 '64
        Am Ann 1964:743 '64
        Brit Bk Yr 1964:632 '64

PLATT, EDWARD
    Sorry about that.   TV Guide 15-34:8 Ag 26 '67

PLATT, MARC
    Marc Platt: guest from the west.   Dance Mag 36:36 Ap
        '62

PLEASENCE, DONALD
    British invasion.   Time 78:64 D 15 '61
    People are talking about . . .   Vogue 139:38 Ja 15 '62
    Pleasence, D.   Taking the pick.   Films & Filming 8-11:

11 Ag '62
Act of atonement.   Time 92:65 O 4 '68
Donald Pleasence, the fantastical Man in the glass booth.
   Vogue 152:94 O 15 '68
Prideaux, T.   One of the ten best ever.   Life 65:77 N 1
   '68
Biography.   Cur Bio 30:36 Je '69

PLESHETTE, SUZANNE
   She starts bells a-ringing.   TV Guide 10-1:26 Ja 6 '62
   Gordon, S.   Swinging Suzy.   Look 26:102 O 23 '62
   Somers, A.   Love is a violent argument.   Photop 63-2:
      71 F '63
   Somers, A.   The big rumor--they're married.   Photop
      63-3:62 Mr '63
   Robbins, F.   She wants to go all the way.   Photop 63-6:
      32 Je '63
   Lewis, R. W.   Fair young Hollywood girls.   Sat Eve Post
      236:26 S 7 '63
   Ormandy, E.   When we're getting married.   Photop 64-
      4:45 O '63
   Suzanne finally said "yes."   Photop 65-2:38 F '64
   Gregory, J.   With this kiss.   Photop 65-3:6 Mr '64
   Miller, E.   Straight from the shoulder.   Seventeen 23:
      140 My '64
   How marriage changed us.   Photop 65-6:33 Je '64
   Honeymoon killed by love.   Photop 66-4:54 O '64
   All about that nude love scene.   Photop 66-5:50 N '64

PLUMMER, CHRISTOPHER
   Theatre Arts gallery.   Theatre Arts 40:32 Je '56
   Biography.   Cur Bio 17:55 Jl '56
      Same.   Cur Bio Yrbk 1956:494 '57
   Hewes, H.   Edinburgh 1956.   Sat R 39:39 O 6 '56
   Hewes, H.   Master Hamlet and Saint Viola.   Sat R 40:26
      Jl 20 '57
   Hewes, H.   Plummer's summer.   Sat R 41:28 Jl 12 '58
   So nice for an egotist.   Newsweek 57:55 Ja 16 '61
   Roberts, P.   Star of three Stratfords.   Plays & Players
      8-12:6 S '61

PODESTA, ROSANNA
   Speaking of pictures; Italian actress demonstrates plot of
      her first starring movie.   Life 35:26 S 14 '53
   D'Alessandro, A.   Italian movie stars.   Cosmop 136:44
      F '54

POITIER, SIDNEY
  Person of promise. Films & Filming 3-6:19 Mr '57
  Talk with a star. Newsweek 49:115 My 13 '57
  Sidney Poitier: Negro actor. Look 22:83 O 28 '58
  Pryor, T. M. Defiant one becomes a star. N.Y. Times
    Mag p27 Ja 25 '59
  Prideaux, T. Poitier's search for the right corner.
    Life 46:140 Ap 27 '59
  Biography. Cur Bio 20:33 My '59
    Same. Cur Bio Yrbk 1959:364 '60
  Nichols, M. Self-made powerhouse. Coronet 46:14 Jl '59
  Poitier, S. They call me a do-it-yourself man. Films
    & Filming 5-12:7 S '59
  Dig? Newsweek 56:114 S 19 '60
  Poitier, S. Thinking of corruption. Films & Filming 7-
    11:7 Ag '61
  Funke, L. & Booth, J. E. Actor's method; his life.
    N.Y. Times Mag p49 O 1 '61
  Morton, F. Audacity of Sidney Poitier. Holiday 31:103
    Je '62
  Lilies of the field. Ebony 18:55 O '63
  Berg, G. Oscar-bound pace-setter. Sr Schol 84:20 Mr
    20 '64
  Top actor of the year. Ebony 19:123 Mr '64
  Wailing for them all. Time 83:52 Ap 24 '64
  Poirier, N. Sidney Poirier's long journey. Sat Eve
    Post 237:26 Je 20 '64
  Braithwaite, E. R. Teacher in slum school. Sr Schol
    90:sup6 Ap 7 '67
  To sir, with love. Ebony 22:68 Ap '67
  Newsmakers. Newsweek 70:46 Jl 2 '67
  Sanders, C. L. Sidney Poitier; the man behind the super-
    star. Ebony 23:172 Ap '68
  Greenfeld, J. What's the secret of Sidney Poitier's
    zooming appeal? Good H 166:92 My '68
  Baldwin, J. Sidney Poitier. Look 32:50 Jl 23 '68
  Terry, P. Linda's love for Sidney Poitier. Photop 74-
    6:38 D '68

POLLARD, HARRY
  Barry, R. H. Harry Pollard: writer, director, actor.
    Photop 6-1:80 Je '14

POLLARD, MICHAEL J.
  Miller, E. Hail the underground hero! Seventeen 27:150
    S '68

POLO, EDDIE
Hair-raising act.   Life 24:142 Ap 12 '48
Obit.   Screen World 13:225 '62

PORTMAN, ERIC
Tables have turned.   Plays & Players 2-1:12 O '54
Biography.   Cur Bio 18:36 Mr '57
    Same.   Cur Bio Yrbk 1957:432 '58
Portman minus grease paint.   Theatre Arts 41:12 Ag '57
Touch of the actor.   Theatre Arts 42:56 D '58
Eric Portman.   Plays & Players 12-11:7 Ag '65

POWELL, DAVID
Flanner, J.   The male background.   Photop 19-1:33 D '20

POWELL, DICK
Harper, S.   Would you girls marry Dick Powell?   Photop
    46-1:48 Je '34
Ramsey, W.   Dick Powell admits he's in love.   Photop
    49-5:21 My '36
Ramsey, W.   Dick Powell lost his voice, and discovered
    his own soul.   Photop 50-1:34 Jl '36
Mook, S. R.   The Dick Powells' hectic honeymoon.   Photop
    51-1:21 Ja '37
Crichton, K.   Double star; story of Dick Powell and Joan
    Blondell.   Colliers 99:22 F 20 '37
Pine, D.   Breakup.   Photop 24-5:65 Ap '44
Waterbury, R.   They're Mr. and Mrs. Dick Powell.
    Photop 27-6:32 N '45
St. Johns, E.   Corner on happiness.   Photop 28-6:38 My
    '46
Downing, H.   Dick Powell.   Photop 32-1:56 D '47
Biography.   Cur Bio F '48
    Same revised.   Cur Bio Yrbk 1948:502 '49
Allyson, J.   Lady with a past.   Photop 36-1:46 Je '49
Powell, D.   Mr. and Mrs. Mike.   Photop 36-4:50 S '49
Dreier, H.   Welcome home.   Photop 37-5:60 My '50
Arnold, M.   The best years of our lives.   Photop 38-1:
    44 Jl '50
Arnold, M.   The happy heart.   Photop 38-5:36 N '50
Engstead, J.   I was there.   Photop 38-6:36 D '50
Martin, P.   Hollywood's child bride.   Sat Eve Post 223:
    34 Ja 20 '51
Zeitlin, I.   Hollywood's first family.   Photop 40-5:46 N
    '51
Powell's progress.   Life 34:62 Je 8 '53
Backstage mutiny; Caine mutiny courtmartial.   Newsweek

43:83 Ja 25 '54

Voight, R. D.   June Allyson says: Our adopted child
  taught us family love.   Womans H C 81:18 F '54

Another project for Powell.   TV Guide 2-40:10 O 2 '53

Ott, B.   Rumor's targets.   Photop 48-6:50 D '55

Man in the middle.   TV Guide 5-7:4 F 16 '57

Too many bears.   Outdoor Life 119:48 F '57

Harrison, J.   The three weeks we'd like to forget.
  Photop 52-1:48 Jl '57

Allyson, J.   Let's be frank about me.   Sat Eve Post
  230:17 D 14; 20 D 21 '57

Wood, C.   TV personalities biographical sketchbook.
  TV Personalities p121 '57

We start with the character.   TV Guide 7-17:8 Ap 25 '59

Tornabene, L.   Lunch date with Dick Powell.   Cosmop
  150:11 Ja '61

Thomas, A.   Dick Powell.   Films In Review 12-5:267 My
  '61

Roman, R. C.   An index of Dick Powell's films.   Films
  In Review 12-5:27 My '61

J. Pierpont Powell.   Time 79:40 Ja 5 '62

Davidson, B.   Deadeye Dick from Little Rock.   TV Guide
  10-12:6 Mr 24; 10-13:22 Mr 31; 10-14:15 Ap 7 '62

Torre, M.   Much-mended marriage of Dick Powell and
  June Allyson.   McCalls 89:94 Je '62

James, E. H.   Boss is his brightest star.   Television
  19:50 S '62

Obit.   Broadcasting 64:74 Ja 7 '63
  Time Ja 11 '63
  Illus Lond N 242:63 Ja 12 '63
  Newsweek 61:49 Ja 14 '63
  Cur Bio 24:31 F '63
  Cur Bio Yrbk 1963:343 '64
  Am Ann 1964:743 '64
  Brit Bk Yr 1964:632 '64
  Screen World 15:224 '64

O'Hara, J.   Egos and actors.   Holiday 40:34 O '66

POWELL, ELEANOR

Reeves, M. W.   The glorifying of Eleanor Powell.   Photop
  48-7:70 D '35

Timid.   Am Mag 121:55 Ja '36

Kutner, N.   You can't dance on a dime.   Pict R 37:10
  Ap '36

Fletcher, A. W.   The real story of Eleanor Powell's
  collapse.   Photop 49-5:30 My '36

Small, F.   Three cornered love.   Photop 51-3:34 Mr '37

Cummings, M.   To Ellie with love.   Photop 22-2:26 Ja
   '43
Cummings, M.   Order of the wedding day.   Photop 24-2:
   24 Ja '44
Biography.   NCAB curG:403 '46
Asher, J.   We have home.   Photop 31-4:42 S '47
Coons, R.   '49 Fords.   Photop 36-4:62 S '49
Corwin, J.   Secrets behind Hollywood heartbreaks.
   Photop 42-5:48 N '52
Ford, E. P.   For the love of Pete.   Photop 46-4:64 O '54
Ardmore, J. K.   At home with the Glenn Fords.   Parents
   Mag 30:50 N '55
Itria, H.   McCalls visits Eleanor Powell's TV Sunday
   school.   McCalls 84:4 D '56
Downing, H.   Last interview.   Photop 56-2:56 Ag '59
Eleanor comes back dancing.   Life 50:59 Mr 24 '61
Duncan, D.   Dance with the noise.   Dance Mag 35:42 Ag
   '61
Kahn, R.   Eleanor Powell's comeback.   Good H 153:32
   O '61
Werner, C. L.   Letter.   Films In Review 17-9:599 N '66

POWELL, JANE
   Perkins, J.   Jane Powell.   Life 21:91 S 9 '46
   Arnold, M.   Little Miss Portland.   Photop 30-1:36 Ja '47
   Howe, H.   'N' everything nice.   Photop 32-1:50 Je '48
   Steffen, G.   It happened on ice.   Photop 34-6:44 My '49
   Mulvey, K.   Spring shower.   Photop 36-1:56 Je '49
   Taylor, E.   The luckiest girl in town.   Photop 37-2:40 F
      '50
   Powell, J.   Marriage is like this.   Photop 38-1:52 Jl '50
   Wheeler, L.   Happiness house.   Photop 39-2:60 F '51
   Steffen, G.   I love Janie Powell.   Photop 40-3:50 S '51
   Arnold, M.   I was there.   Photop 40-5:62 N '51
   Bolstad, H.   Backstage baby.   Photop 41-1:38 Ja '52
   Brigham, R.   Her heart knows.   Photop 41-4:50 Ap '52
   Dudley, F.   Room for one more.   Photop 42-5:38 N '52
   Corwin, J.   Mother's day.   Photop 43-2:76 F '53
   Ford, E.   Will maturity end Jane's appeal.   Photop 43-3:
      36 Mr '53
   Rogers, M.   Love that Jane.   Photop 43-6:50 Je '53
   Ford, E.   Marriage at the crossroads.   Photop 44-1:31
      Jl '53
   Graham, S.   The truth about Jane Powell's marriage.
      Photop 44-2:36 Ag '53
   Waterbury, R.   Love is a course in wisdom.   Photop 46-
      5:60 N '54

Waterbury, R.   Little girl no longer lost.   Photop 47-6:
  48 Je '55
Arnold, M.   So happy she can't stand it.   Photop 48-1:61
  Jl '55
Jane Powell tries on a hairdo.   McCalls 82:20 S '55
Clement, C.   Can this be Jane Powell?   Photop 52-5:64
  N '57
Taub, P.   What's a bunny?   Photop 53-5:37 My '58
Aldrich, H. K.   Letter, inc. filmog.   Films In Review
  20-6:392 Je/Jl '69

POWELL, WILLIAM
  Spensley, D.   Bold but not brazen.   Photop 30-3:47 Ag '26
  Spensley, D.   Not guilty.   Photop 35-4:54 Mr '29
  Ross, L.   The villain unmasked.   Photop 37-3:67 F '30
  Busby, M.   "Willy" to his mother.   Photop 39-2:65 Ja '31
  Fiddler, J. M.   Bill Powell exposed.   Photop 42-5:46 O
    '32
  Collins, F.   The confidential history of Bill Powell.
    Photop 49-3:14 Mr; 49-4:76 Ap '36
  Pettit, G.   The thin man's here again.   Photop 51-1:32 Ja
    '37
  She's a softie.   Pict R 38:25 Je '37
  Loy, M.   He's a tough guy.   Pict R 38:24 Je '37
  Waterbury, R.   A new day for Bill Powell.   Photop 52-
    6:26 Je '38
  Castle, M.   And then there were three.   Photop 52-7:18
    Jl '38
  Waterbury, R.   What pain can teach you.   Photop 53-10:
    30 O '39
  Loy, M.   Bill.   Photop 54-2:20 F '40
  Waterbury, R.   The third Mrs. Powell.   Photop 54-3:18
    Mr '40
  Reynolds, Q.   Smoothie.   Colliers 105:15 My 11 '40
  Hamilton, S.   Second year.   Photop 19-2:30 Jl '41
  Eddy, D.   It pays to be a poser.   Am Mag 132:20 Ag '41
  Marshall, J.   Life with Mr. Powell.   Colliers 120:38 Ag
    16 '47
  Biography.   Cur Bio O '47
    Same revised.   Cur Bio Yrbk 1947:525 '48
  Powell, B. Jr.   Life with my father.   Photop 32-1:60
    D '47
  Jacobs, J.   William Powell, inc. filmog.   Films In Re-
    view 9-9:497 N '58
  How not to die of cancer.   Time 81:54 My 10 '63

POWER, TYRONE
    Biographical sketch. Time 29:57 Mr 8 '37
    Sharpe, H. Life story of a problem child. Photop 51-7:
        29 Jl; 51-8:58 Ag; 51-9:56 S '37
    Hayes, B. How Tyrone Power won the lonely heart of
        Janet Gaynor. Photop 52-1:14 Ja '38
    Waterbury, R. Even his best friends don't know him.
        Photop 52-12:26 D '38
    Waterbury, R. Tyrone Power's own story of his South
        American trip. Photop 53-3:17 Mr '39
    Reid, S. Mrs. Tyrone Power. Photop 53-8:24 Ag '39
    St. Johns, A. R. Tyrone learns from Clark. Photop 53-
        9:18 S '39
    Waterbury, R. Don, Alice and Ty. Photop 54-4:14 Ap ₊0
    How I got even. Am Mag 131:122 F '41
    Hall, G. The Tyrone Powers fight it out! Photop 19-2:
        38 Jl '41
    Tyrone Power home, Brentwood. House B 86:64 My '44
    St. Johns, A. R. Return of the Marine. Photop 28-6:32
        My; 29-1:60 Je '46
    Mamlok, M. The inner Power. Photop 30-1:56 D '46
    Power, T. Saludos Amigos. Photop 30-3:72 F '47
    Hamilton, S. Ty Power talks it over. Photop 30-4:53
        Mr '47
    Parsons, L. O. Lana and Ty. Photop 31-1:32 Je '47
    Fink, H. I was there. Photop 31-3:36 Ag '47
    St. Johns, E. Take-off. Photop 32-4:48 Mr '48
    Schroeder, C. Jigsaw romance. Photop 32-6:48 My '48
    Fink, H. I was there. Photop 33-3:46 Ag '48
    Parsons, L. O. I'm going to marry Tyrone Power.
        Photop 33-4:36 S '48
    Maxwell, E. Power's progress. Photop 34-2:38 Ja '49
    And circuses. Time 53:18 F 7 '49
    Tyrone and Linda get married. Life 26:32 F 7 '49
    Viva Ty! Viva Linda! Newsweek 33:34 F 7 '49
    Non-Catholic marriage is no marriage. Christian Cent
        66:165 F 9 '49
    One foot from eternity. Flying 44:33 My '49
    Christian, L. How lucky can you be? Photop 36-6:36 N
        '49
    Biography. Cur Bio D '50
        Same. Cur Bio Yrbk 1950:463 '51
    Harvey, E. John Brown's body hits the road. Colliers
        130:24 D 6 '52
    Harris, R. The Power and the glory. Photop 48-1:34 Jl
        '55
    Barker, F. G. Power the peacemaker. Plays & Players

4-2:5 N '56

Eleven fine actors get their dream roles.   Life 44:76 Ap 14 '58

Obit.   Newsweek 52:88 N 24 '58
  Time 72:83 N 24 '58
  Screen World 10:225 '59
  Cur Bio 20:35 Ja '59
  Cur Bio Yrbk 1959:367 '60
  Colls Yrbk 1959:707 '59
  Am Ann 1959:606 '59
  Brit Bk Yr 1959:515 '59
  Illus Lond N 233:905 N 22 '58

Dashing actor's last duel.   Life 45:44 D 1 '58

He was a beautiful man.   Time 72:57 D 1 '58

Last rites in Hollywood.   Newsweek 52:21 D 1 '58

Roman, R. C.   Tyrone Power, inc. filmog.   Films In Review 10-1:5 Ja '59

Dinter, C.   Will Tyrone Power's last prayer be answered?   Photop 55-2:34 F '59

Williams, J.   His little boy's terrible loss.   Photop 63-6:30 Je '63

POWERS, MALA
  One in 300.   Am Mag 151:58 F '51
  Arnold, M.   I prayed--and God heard me.   Photop 53-1:38 Ja '58

POWERS, STEFANIE
  Sanders, A.   I want to be a mother.   Photop 65-6:66 Je '64
  Mothner, I.   Stefanie Powers: the U. N. C. L. E. doll.   Look 30:42 O 18 '66

PRENTISS, PAULA
  Talk with a newcomer.   Newsweek 57:84 Ja 23 '61
  Show business.   Time 78:45 Jl 28 '61
  Perils of Paula.   Look 25:82 S 12 '61
  Schickel, R.   1962: the year of Paula Prentiss.   Show 2-1:52 Ja '62
  Miller, E.   Growing pains in Hollywood.   Seventeen 21:126 Mr '62
  Meltsir, A.   Passion's for the birds!   Photop 61-4:33 Ap '62
  Person of promise.   Films & Filming 8-10:54 Jl '62
  Benjamin, D.   I married a ten year old.   Photop 62-3:33 S '62
  Marco, B.   Fly around the world.   Photop 63-4:52 Ap '63

Garner, A. Put glamour in your lunchbox. Photop 63-
   5:64 My '63
Grove, G. Paula Prentiss. Sat Eve Post 237:68 F 8 '64
Preston, W. Life with Dick is swinging, but . . .
   Photop 73-3:35 Mr '68

PRESLE, MICHELINE
   Davidson, B. Romance at 20 paces. Colliers 125:30
      Je 17 '50

PRESLEY, ELVIS
   Beware Elvis Presley. America 95:294 Je 23 '56
   Howling hillbilly success. Life 40:64 Ap 30 '56
   Hillbilly on a pedestal. Newsweek 47:82 My 14 '56
   Teeners' hero. Time 67:53 My 14 '56
   Lardner, J. Devitalizing Elvis. Newsweek 48:59 Jl 16
      '56
   Elvis Presley, he can't be, but he is. Look 20:82 Ag 7
      '56
   Elvis, a different kind of idol. Life 41:101 Ag 27 '56
   Inextinguishable. Newsweek 48:68 Ag 27 '56
   Discussion. Life 41:19 S 17 '56
   Brown, C. Craze called Elvis. Coronet 40:153 S '56
   Mud on the stars. Newsweek 48:58 O 8 '56
   Ryan, T. C. Rock 'n' roll battle: Boone vs. Presley.
      Colliers 138:109 O 26 '56
   Sharnik, J. War of the generations. House & Gard 110:
      40 O '56
   Morrison, C. Great Elvis Presley industry. Look 20:
      98 N 13 '56
   Lane, L. Why the rebel craze is here to stay. Photop
      50-5:56 N '56
   Face is familiar. Look 20:130 D 11 '56
   Weales, G. Movies: the crazy, mixed-up kids take over.
      Reporter 15:40 D 13 '56
   Winn, J. Star is born. New Repub 135:22 D 24 '56
   Condon, E. What is an Elvis Presley? Cosmop 141:54
      D '56
   Archerd, A. Presley takes Hollywood. Photop 50-6:42
      D '56
   Wilson, E. Lover boy. Photop 51-1:24 Ja '57
   Presley spells profit. Newsweek 49:84 F 18 '57
   Combat the menace. Time 69:58 Ap 29 '57
   Mr. Harper. Elvis, the indigenous. Harper 214:86 Ap
      '57
   Linely and shook up. Time 69:101 My 27 '57
   Larkin, L. F. God is my refuge. Photop 52-1:62 Jl '57

Hurwitz, A. Elvis Presley and art. School Arts 57:17
S '57

Rock is solid. Time 70:48 N 4 '57

Joyce, A. Elvis--why can't he get married? Photop 52-
5:56 N '57

Biography. Colliers Yrbk 1957:711 '57

Baxter, J. & Baxter, A. Man in the blue suede shoes.
Harper 216:45 Ja '58

Private Presley's debut. Life 44:117 Ap 7 '58

Hart, D. Private note to Elvis. Photop 54-2:56 Ag '58

Farewell squeal for Elvis. Life 45:77 O 6 '58

Lewis, J. Please don't forget me while I'm gone.
Photop 54-4:41 O '58

O'Donnell, M. Why did my mother have to die? Photop
54-5:43 N '58

Elvis and the frauleins. Look 22:113 D 23 '58

Hoffman, J. Dad, let's make this the Christmas mom
would have wanted. Photop 55-1:40 Ja '59

Beurgin, M. Elvis kissed me. Photop 55-3:54 Mr '59

Fuel, A. P. Elvis elopes. Photop 55-5:38 My '59

Clark, D. Who'll top Elvis this year? Photop 55-6:38 Je
'59

Sheeley, S. Our love song. Photop 55-6:52 Je '59

Etter, B. You can spend 30,400 seconds with him.
Photop 56-3:50 S '59

Biography. Cur Bio 20:33 S '59

Same. Cur Bio Yrbk 1959:371 '60

Farewell to Priscilla, hello to U.S.A. Life 48:97 Mr 14
'60

Presley, E. Why I've changed. Photop 57-4:42 Ap '60

Elvis comes marching home. TV Guide 8-19:10 My 7 '60

Idols team up on TV. Life 48:103 My 16 '60

Man who sold parsley. Time 75:61 My 16 '60

Is this a new Presley? Newsweek 55:91 My 30 '60

Willert, P. Elvis, did your kiss mean anything at all?
Photop 57-6:50 Je '60

Anderson, N. Photoplay calls Elvis. Photop 57-6:54 Je
'60

Wood, J. I wouldn't do nothing to hurt my boy Elvis.
Photop 58-1:26 Jl '60

Dean, R. Can Tuesday hold on to Elvis. Photop 58-3:
32 S '60

Rock-a-bye for Presley. Life 49:121 O 10 '60

Whitcomb, J. Elvis and Juliet. Cosmop 149:12 O '60

Fowler, J. Is my face red! Photop 58-4:30 O '60

Montel, C. Elvis, what are you scared of? Photop 58-
5:28 N '60

York, C.   The girl Elvis tries to hide.   Photop 59-5:18
   My '61
Gregory, J.   If only mom had lived.   Photop 60-4:64 O
   '61
Presley, E.   Witness for the defense.   Music J 19:31 O
   '61
Howard, E.   Is this Mrs. Elvis Presley?   Photop 60-5:
   45 N '61
Anderson, N.   Goodbye my lover.   Photop 61-4:36 Ap '62
Lee, J.   The pinup to end all pinups.   Photop 62-2:61 Ag
   '62
Anderson, N.   Cheatin' woman.   Photop 62-5:54 N '62
Wall, T.   Elvis threatened with murder.   Photop 63-1:
   39 Ja '63
Scott, V.   Elvis: ten million dollars later.   McCalls
   90:90 F '63
Farmer, P.   Elvis at home.   New Statesm 65:373 Mr 15
   '63
Gideon, N.   As you've never seen him.   Photop 63-5:29
   My '63
Wheaton, T.   Errand of death.   Photop 63-6:45 Je '63
Anderson, N.   Did he give her the brushoff?   Photop 64-
   4:32 O '63
Grant, C.   Elvis secretly engaged.   Photop 65-1:27 Ja '64
Terry, P.   We say Elvis is married.   Photop 65-2:62 F
   '64
Terry, P.   Why he hides behind his boys.   Photop 66-1:
   33 Jl '64
Dean, S.   The truth about those parties.   Photop 66-4:37
   O '64
Forever Elvis.   Time 85:61 My 7 '65
Jennings, C. R.   There'll always be an Elvis.   Sat Eve
   Post 238:76 S 11 '65
Terry, P.   Elvis to wed!   Photop 69-5:50 My '66
Bean, R.   The changing face of Elvis.   Films & Filming
   12-11:51 Ag '66
Story behind the brawl.   Photop 73-1:46 Ja '68
Miron, C.   Commandments for his baby.   Photop 73-2:
   49 F '68
Booth, S.   Hound dog to the manner born.   Esquire 69:
   106 F '68
Fox, M.   Scoop baby photos!   Photop 73-4:4 Ap '68
Valentine, L.   The birth of Lisa Presley.   Photop 73-5:
   49 My '68
Anderson, N.   All about his mixed marriage.   Photop 74-
   2:30 Ag '68
Reynolds, L.   He breaks first love tie.   Photop 75-1:32

Ja '69
Green, J. The pelvis returns. Photop 75-2:66 F '69
How his marriage works. Photop 75-6:68 Je '69
Webb, M. Family can't escape women. Photop 76-2:42
   Ag '69
Reynolds, L. Those backstage kisses. Photop 76-5:33 N
   '69

PRESNELL, HARVE
Dawes, A. Pin-up #22. Photop 66-5:49 N '64

PRESTON, ROBERT
New tricks. New Yorker 33:24 Ja 11 '58
Success story of the year. Look 22:53 Mr 4 '58
Pied Piper of Broadway. Time 72:42 Jl 21 '58
Hage, G. S. Happiest actor on Broadway. Sat Eve Post
   231:32 D 6 '58
Biography. Cur Bio 19:8 D '58
   Same. Cur Bio Yrbk 1958:341 '58
Miller, E. Star of a musical make-merry. Seventeen
   21:86 Je '62
Millstein, G. That brassy music man returns to Broad-
   way as poor Richard. Sat Eve Post 237:86 O 17 '64
Hemming, R. Interview. Sr Schol 86:21 Mr 4 '65
The music man hits a patriotic note. TV Guide 13-34:
   15 Ag 21 '65
Peper, W. Robert Preston, inc. filmog. Films In Re-
   view 19-3:129 Mr '68

PREVOST, MARIE
Jordan, J. She laughed 'til she cried. Photop 20-2:26
   Jl '21
Smith, F. J. The perfect understanding. Photop 22-4:
   24 S '22
York, C. The girl on the cover. Photop 28-4:82 S '25

PRICE, VINCENT
Role I liked best. Sat Eve Post 219:58 Jl 13 '46
Sheridan, M. All actors are bums. Photop 29-2:64 Jl
   '46
Biography. Cur Bio 17:55 N '56
   Same. Cur Bio Yrbk 1956:502 '57
How to buy a painting. Good H 147:55 Ag '58
Washburn, G. B. International jury of award. Carnegie
   Mag 32:304 N '58
Back from the dead. Newsweek 59:80 Ja 22 '62
Kent, N. Editorial; Sears Roebuck's plan to sell original

art. Am Artist 26:3 N '62

At Sears, art conquers. Bsns W p28 D 1 '62

Bargain debasement? original art for Sears Roebuck.
Time 81:62 Ja 25 '63

Brossard, C. Vincent Price: king of the horror movies.
Look 27:66a Ap 23 '63

Gilpin, L. Comfortable clutter of an actor in love with
the arts. House B 105:153 Ap '63

Nolan, J. E. The Price is right. Films In Review 15-
3:189 Mr '64

Price, V. Mean, moody and magnificent. Films &
Filming 11-6:5 Mr '65

Vincent Price: he likes what he knows; intv. Design
67:18 Ja '66

Talent for Christmas. House & Gard 132:136 D '67

Marill, A. H. Vincent Price, inc. filmog. Films In
Review 20-5:276 My '69

PRINGLE, AILEEN
Winship, M. The tiger queen. Photop 25-2:45 Ja '24
Albert, K. What do you mean--intellectual? Photop
35-2:56 Ja '29

PROUTY, JED
Obit. Time 67:95 My 21 '56
Screen World 8:226 '57

PROVINE, DOROTHY
Barrett, P. Just building castles in the sand. Photop
57-6:64 Je '60
Dorothy Provine: TV acclaim for a twenties type.
Look 25:38 Ja 31 '61
Girl on the red swing. Time 77:53 My 19 '61
Richards, J. This feud's for real. Photop 30-3:30 S '61

PROVOST, JON
Big changeover for Lassie. Life 43:75 N 25 '57

PROWSE, JULIET
Wolfson, S. New girl on the set. Dance Mag 34:40 Mr
'60
Nicest yet. Time 75:49 Je 20 '60
Whitcomb, J. Elvis and Juliet. Cosmop 149:12 O '60
Montel, C. Elvis, what are you scared of? Photop 58-
5:28 N '60
Adams, C. Prowess of Prowse. Coronet 50:133 O '61
High-kicking Juliet for Frank Sinatra. Life 52:40B

Ja 19 '62
Skolsky, S. Why they must marry. Photop 61-4:41 Ap
   '62
Gideon, N. Wedding bells won't jingle-o. Photop 61-
   5:6 My '62
Williams, M. Juliet Prowse in New York. Dance Mag
   36:17 N '62
Lewis, R. W. America's leggiest international incident.
   TV Guide 13-49:20 D 4 '65

PRUD'HOMME, CAMERON
   Obit. Screen World 19:237 '68

PURDOM, EDMUND
   Hollywood's new glamour boy. Look 18:51 Je 1 '54
   Buckley, M. Getting to know Purdom. Photop 46-5:50
      N '54
   Downing, H. Purdom--man on a tightrope. Photop 47-1:
      30 Ja '55
   Hubler, R. G. Hollywood's impudent newcomer. Sat Eve
      Post 227:26 Ja 8 '55

PURVIANCE, EDNA
   Blackwood, J. H. The star soubrette. Photop 9-1:42 D
      '15
   Awstruck, W. Interviewing Edna. Photop 10-4:71 S '16
   St. Johns, A. R. Hollywood heroes! Photop 16-1:35 Je
      '19
   St. Johns, A. R. Hollywood's mystery woman. Photop
      25-3:32 F '24
   Obit. Newsweek 51:71 Ja 27 '58
      Illus Lond N 232:151 Ja 25 '58
      Screen World 10:225 '59
   Kornick, M. Edna Olga Purviance, inc. filmog.
      Films In Review 9-3:156 Mr '58

QUALE, ANTHONY
    Personality of the month. Plays & Players 1-8:3 My '54
    Stratford's big boss. Plays & Players 1-11:8 Ag '54
    Stratford quiz. Plays & Players 3-1:8 O '55
    Quale, A. Society and the actor. Films & Filming 3-
      10:6 Jl '57

QUALEN, JOHN
    McClure, A. The unsung heroes: John Qualen. Film
      Fan Mo 81:22 Mr '68
    Beaver, J. Letter, inc. filmog. Films In Review 19-4:
      256 Ap '68

QUIGLEY, JUANITA
    Reid, S. Precocity plus! Photop 53-2:65 F '39

QUINE, RICHARD
    Bentley, J. Out of this dream. Photop 24-3:67 F '44
    Parsons, L. O. Courage is a girl named Susan. Photop
      26-6:28 My '45
    Quine, R. The bravest girl in town. Photop 32-5:38 Ap
      '48
    Richard Quine. Film 31:7 Spg '62

QUINN, ANTHONY
    Man in need of a shave. Time 68:46 D 31 '56
    Triumph's not enough. Newsweek 49:112 My 6 '57
    Biography. Cur Bio 18:13 D '57
      Same. Cur Bio Yrbk 1957:440 '58
    Nichols, M. No time for ulcers. Coronet 45:14 Mr '59
    Harris, E. Improbable Anthony Quinn. Good H 150:68
      F '60
    Quinn, A. The actor and his mask. Films & Filming
      6-12:7 S '60
    Johnson, I. Anthony Quinn. Films & Filming 8-5:13 F
      '62
    Bester, A. Anthony Quinn: virility and violence. Holiday
      31:123 My '62
    Mr. Quinn. N. Y. Times Mag p104 S 23 '62
    Schaap, D. Anthony Quinn, unsettled star. Sat Eve Post
      235:20 O 13 '62
    In total demand. Time 80:43 D 21 '62
    Bunzel, P. Quinn. Life 54:63 F 1 '63

Redbook dialogue: Anthony Quinn and Harry Belafonte.
    Redbook 120:54 Mr '63
Anthony Quinn's love child.   Photop 64-3:46 S '63
Graham, S.   I must be free.   Photop 64-6:58 D '63
Hamilton, J.   Visit.   Look 28:52 Je 16 '64
Lawrenson, H.   Life and suspiciously hard times of
    Anthony Quinn.   Esquire 66:93 O '66
Musel, R.   A man for the new season.   TV Guide 16-38:
    41 S 21 '68
Marill, A. H.   Anthony Quinn, inc. filmog.   Films In
    Review 19-8:465 O '68
Tornabene, L.   Walking with Anthony Quinn; intv.   Mc
    Calls 96:60 Mr '69
Simons, M.   Loving world of Anthony Quinn.   Look 33:
    48 Ap 1 '69
Mexican-Americans: the nation's best kept secret.
    Sr Schol 94:12 Ap 18 '69

RAFFERTY, FRANCES
Daughter of the bride. TV Guide 3-40:20 O 1 '55
Wood, C. TV personalities biographical sketchbook.
TV Personalities p127 '56

RAFT, GEORGE
Hughes, A. That "second Valentino" curse. Photop 42-3:27 Ag '32
Baker, K. Gentleman George. Photop 45-6:31 My '34
Taviner, R. A sucker for a sob story. Photop 51-1:74
Ja '37
Hartley, K. Why George Raft settled that contract fight.
Photop 51-3:36 Mr '37
Churchill, E. Him Georgie--the life story of a mystery
man. Photop 52-1:20 Ja; 52-2:68 F '38
Durant, J. Tough on and off; movies professional tough
guys. Colliers 106:24 Ag 31 '40
Stein, H. The women in my life. Photop 19-2:66 Jl '41
St. Johns, A. R. What you don't know about the Betty
Grable-George Raft romance. Photop 22-5:26 Ap '43
Raft, G. as told to D. Jennings. Out of my past. Sat
Eve Post 230:23 S 21; 44 S 28; 28 O 5; 30 O 12; 36 O
19 '57
Raft, G. You've got to be tough with Hollywood. Films
& Filming 8-10:15 Jl '62

RAGLAND, "RAGS"
Obit. Newsweek 28:48 S 2 '46
Time 48:70 S 2 '46
Cur Bio 7:43 O '46
Cur Bio Yrbk 1946:497 '47

RAIMU
Priestley, J. B. Raimu. New Statesm 32:227 S 28 '46
Same. Theatre Arts 31:64 Ja '47
Obit. Newsweek 28:52 S 30 '46
Time 48:84 S 30 '46
Cur Bio 7:36 N '46
Cur Bio Yrbk 1946:497 '47
Jaconson, H. L. Homage to Raimu. Hollywood Q 3-2:
169 Win '47

RAINER, LUISE
  Baskette, K. Know Luise Rainer. Photop 48-5:44 O '35
  Crichton, K. Girl who hates movies. Colliers 97:36 My
    23 '36
  Fletcher, A. W. The tempestuous life story of Luise
    Rainer. Photop 50-1:24 Jl; 50-2:74 Ag '36
  Hall, L. The romantic story of Luise Rainer's surprise
    marriage. Photop 51-3:50 Mr '37
  Hamilton, S. What's happened to Rainer? Photop 52-6:
    22 Je '38
  Daugherty, F. Luise Rainer in a new role. C S Mon
    Mag p4 Ag 24 '38
  Thank offering; Shaw's Saint Joan. Time 35:68 Mr 18 '40
  Bronner, E. Luise Rainer. Films In Review 6-8:390
    O '55
  Where are they now? Newsweek 61:20 Ap 15 '63

RAINES, ELLA
  Million-dollar baby. Am Mag 136:126 D '43
  Pretty young star. Life 16:63 F 28 '44
  Greggory, D. Sensation from Seattle. Photop 24-6:59 My
    '44
  Holiday with Ella Raines. Life 19:76 Jl 30 '45
  Ella Raines' Rx for TV. TV Guide 2-29:13 Jl 17 '54
  Wood, C. TV personalities biographical sketchbook.
    TV Personalities p118 '56
  Rode, D. Ella Raines, inc. filmog. Films In Review
    17-1:62 Ja '67

RAINS, CLAUDE
  Roberts, K. Plow and the star. Colliers 102:13 N '38
  Biography. Cur Bio 10:40 N '49
    Same. Cur Bio Yrbk 1949:495 '50
  Gratified old revolutionary. New Yorker 27:25 F 17 '51
  Unlikely idol. TV Guide 6-12:17 Mr 22 '58
  Stein, J. Claude Rains, inc. filmog. Films In Review
    14-9:513 N '63
· Obit. Newsweek 69:103 Je 12 '67
    Time 89:96 Je 9 '67
    Cur Bio 28:47 Jl '67
    Cur Bio Yrbk 1967:481 '68
    Brit Bk Yr 1968:597 '68
    Screen World 19:238 '68
  Malton, L. Claude Rains 1890-1967. Film Fan Mo 72:
    14 Jl '67

RALL, TOMMY
  Goodman, S. Tommy Rall. Dance Mag 33:51 My '59

RALSTON, ESTHER
  Prosser, C. S. Just a small town girl. Photop 33-5:58
    Ap '28
  Tully, J. Esther Ralston. Pict R 29:6 Jl '28
  Hughes, M. Gone--another ingenue. Photop 39-2:41 Ja '31
  I wore thousand-dollar dresses. TV Guide 10-33:26 Ag
    18 '62

RALSTON, JOBYNA
  St. Johns, A. R. Betty and Jobyna. Photop 26-6:52 N
    '23
  Howe, H. The discovery of Jobyna Ralston. Photop 26-
    3:52 Ag '24
  Obit. Screen World 19:238 '68

RALSTON, VERA HRUBA
  Scott, D. Memory wears carnations. Photop 34-6:72 My
    '49
  Chill in Hollywood. Newsweek 48:116 N 12 '56
  Meyer, J. Vera Hruba Ralston, inc. filmog. 83:3 My
    '68

RAMBEAU, MARJORIE
  She was the Bernhardt of the Klondike. Photop 11-5:85 Ap
    '17
  Bartlett, R. A northern star. Photop 15-5:72 Ap '19
  Seamy side of life won't hurt you. Am Mag 90:36 Jl '20
  Patterson, A. How a stage or screen career can be made
    happy. Photop 19-3:32 F '21
  Ogden, E. A great trouper comes to town. Photop 39-2:
    59 Ja '31

RANDALL, TONY
  Person of promise. Films & Filming 3-10:15 Jl '57
  Talk with the star. Newsweek 51:66 F 17 '58
  Spoofing the sponsors. TV Guide 7-7:12 F 14 '59
  Randall, T. Just like money in the bank. TV Guide 8-
    27:5 Jl 2 '60
  Biography. Cur Bio 22:41 Ja '61
    Same. Cur Bio Yrbk 1961:380 '62
  Hoffman, J. It was a tough fight, folks . . . but I lost.
    Photop 59-5:70 My '61
  Funnyman changes faces. Life 55:139 O 18 '63

RATHBONE, BASIL
  Baskette, K. Love life of a villain. Photop 52-8:15 Ag
    '38
  Daugherty, F. Baker Street regulars; Rathbone and Bruce
    make pictures based on Dyle stories and fill in the times
    between with radio program. C S Mon Mag p7 Ag 19
    '44
  Art lover. Am Mag 140:64 S '45
  How do you look to your audience? Etude 69:16 Mr '51
  Biography. Cur Bio 12:52 Mr '51
    Same. Cur Bio Yrbk 1951:506 '52
  Theatre Arts album. Theatre Arts 37:76 O '53
  Hudson, R. Basil Rathbone. Films In Review 11-6:380
    Je/Jl '60
  Obit. Newsweek 70:49 Jl 31 '67
    Time 90:67 Jl 28 '67
    Cur Bio 28:45 O '67
    Cur Bio Yrbk 1967:482 '68
    Brit Bk Yr 1968:597 '68
    Screen World 19:238 '68

RATOFF, GREGORY
  Obit. Illus Lond N 237:1154 D 24 '60
    Newsweek 56:41 D 26 '60
    Time 76:49 D 26 '60
    Opera News 25:34 F 4 '61
    Cur Bio 22:42 F '61
    Cur Bio Yrbk 1961:384 '62
    Am Ann 1961:848 '61
    Brit Bk Yr 1961:519 '61
    Screen World 12:225 '61

RAWLINSON, HERBERT
  Willis, R. Herbert Rawlinson--of the Jack London Players.
    Photop 5-2:48 Ja '14
  Obit. Screen World 5:208 '54

RAY, ALDO
  Biographical note. Newsweek 39:110 Mr 24 '52
  Cahn, R. Rugged Romeo. Colliers 129:20 Ap 19 '52
  Meltsir, A. The boy who swallowed a dream. Photop
    47-6:46 Je '55
  Hopper, H. Young men of Hollywood. Coronet 38:57 Jl
    '55
  Phillips, D. Who's no angel? Photop 48-5:52 N '55
  People of talent. Sight & Sound 25-3:141 Win '55/56

RAY, CHARLES
  Martin, M. The young and debonair Charles Ray.
    Photop 6-5:46 O '14
  The biography of Charles Ray. Feature Movie 2-7:44
    Jl 10 '15
  O'Hara, K. Ince's new wonder boy. Photop 9-2:106 Ja
    '16
  Obit. Newsweek 22:10 D 6 '43
    Time 42:76 D 6 '43
    Cur Bio '44
  Bodeen, D. Charles Ray, inc. filmog. Films In Re-
    view 19-9:548 N '68

RAYE, MARTHA
  Hartley, K. Ultra violent Raye. Photop 51-1:44 Ja '37
  Crichton, K. Girl with a voice. Colliers 99:15 My 1
    '37
  Churchill, E. Behind Martha Raye's divorce. Photop
    51-11:23 N '37
  Pyle, E. Four good soldiers. Sr Schol 42:2 Mr 29 '43
  Who's who in the cast. TV Guide 5-21:12 My 23 '52
  Gould, J. TV's top comediennes. N. Y. Times Mag p16
    D 27 '53
  Raucous rowdy Raye. TV Guide 2-3:15 Ja 15 '54
  At home, she's quieter. Look 18:81 F 9 '54
  Day's work. Time 63:70 Mr 1 '54
  Muggs and Cupid put the bite on Martha in a busy week.
    Life 36:133 My 3 '54
  Wood, C. TV personalities biographical sketchbook.
    TV Personalities p54 '54
  Graziano, R. The Rock and the Heart. TV Guide 3-5:
    20 Ja 29 '55
  TV's no. 1 female clown. Look 19:112 Mr 22 '55
  Martha Raye in focus. TV Guide 3-48:5 N 26 '55
  Biography. Cur Bio 24:35 Jl '63
    Same. Cur Bio Yrbk 1963:356 '64

RAYMOND, GARY
  Raddatz, L. More British than big ben. TV Guide 15-
    30:15 Jl 29 '67

RAYMOND, GENE
  Russell, A. Gene Raymond is really a lone wolf.
    Photop 49-5:60 My '36
  Manners, D. The romantic love story of Jeanette Mac
    Donald and Gene Raymond. Photop 50-5:22 N '36
  Hayes, B. The secrete Gene Raymond kept from Jean-

ette MacDonald. Photop 51-9:15 S '37

Waterbury, R. Marriage is a laughing matter. Photop
52-8:22 Ag '38

Maddox, B. The man Hollywood couldn't beat. Photop
18-4:49 Mr '41

Taylor, F. J. Hollywood cliff gardeners: Jeanette Mac
Donald and Gene Raymond. Bet Hom & Gard 20:26 S
'41

Zeitlin, I. Jeanette sends her man to war. Photop 21-1:
62 Je '42

RAYMOND, PAULA
What's the verdict? Am Mag 149:105 Ap '50

READ, LILLIAN
The tiny star of a mighty picture. Photop 10-6:105 N '16

REAGAN, RONALD
Zeitlin, I. Love among the Reagans. Photop 20-2:30 Ja
'42

Reagan, R. How to make yourself important. Photop 21-
3:44 Ag '42

Parsons, L. O. This is the truth about Janie and Ronnie.
Photop 26-2:22 Ja '45

Asher, J. We're the Ray-gans. Photop 30-1:52 D '46

Howe, H. St. Joe's Jane. Photop 31-1:60 Je '47

Hall, G. Those fightin' Reagans. Photop 32-3:37 F '48

Parsons, L. O. Last call for happiness. Photop 32-5:40
Ap '48

Arnold, H. "Dutch." Photop 33-1:72 Je '48

Edwards, R. Play truth or consequences with Ronald
Reagan. Photop 34-2:52 Ja '49

Biography. Cur Bio 10:39 D '49

Same. Cur Bio Yrbk 1949:502 '50

Irresponsible press of Hollywood. Time 57:56 F 26 '51

Wood, C. TV personalities biographical sketchbook.
TV Personalities p126 '54

Don't envy the actor. TV Guide 5-15:6 Ap 13 '57

Hey Ronnie--did the guy get the girl? TV Guide 6-47:17
N 22 '58

Too many people. Time 77:19 Ap 21 '61

No place for a ho-hum attitude. TV Guide 9-21:8 My 27
'61

Encroaching control; keep government poor and remain
free. Vital Speeches 27:677 S 1 '61

Republican party and the conservative movement. Nat R
16:1055 D 1 '64

Alexander, S. My technicolor senator. Life 57:30 D 4
  '64
Will he size up? Newsweek 65:18 Je 7 '65
Stage to Sacramento? Time 86:13 Jl 30 '65
Alexander, S. Ronald Regan for governor? Life 59:22
  Ag 13 '65
Down with plinkers. Am For 71:4 Ag '65
Moment of truth. Vital Speeches 31:681 S 1 '65
Reagan rides East. Newsweek 66:42 O 11 '65
Litwak, L. E. Ronald Reagan story; or, Tom Sawyer en-
  ters politics. N. Y. Times Mag p46 N 14 '65
Alsop, S. Good guy. Sat Eve Post 238:18 N 20 '65
Buckley, W. F. Jr. How is Ronald Regan doing? Nat R
  18:17 Ja 11 '66
New role for Reagan. Time 87:28 Ja 14 '56
Enter Ronald Reagan. Newsweek 67:31 Ja 17 '66
Oulahan, R. & Lambert, W. Real Ronald Reagan stands
  up. Life 60:71 Ja 21 '66
Brown vs. Reagan. New Repub 154:7 Ja 22 '66
Murray, J. Ronald Reagan to the rescue! Esquire 65:
  76 F '66
Reagan in the wilderness. Newsweek 67:30 Mr 28 '66
Parkinson's law. Time 87:20 My 27 '66
Phelan, J. Can Reagan win California? Sat Eve Post
  239:89 Je 4 '66
Up from Death Valley. Time 87:24 Je 17 '66
Conservative tide. Newsweek 67:31 Je 20 '66
People of the week. U. S. News 60:19 Je 20 '66
Why Republican hopes are rising. U. S. News 60:31 Je 20
  '66
Trek to the East. Newsweek 67:32 Je 27 '66
People of the week. U. S. News 60:19 Je 27 '66
Ryskind, M. Reagan saga. Nat R 18:616 Je 28 '66
Clinton, F. Ronald Reagan: a light in the West. Nat R
  18:613 Je 28 '66
Reagan for president? New Repub 155:4 Jl 2 '66
Grandpa vs. The Dude. Newsweek 68:61 Ag 22 '66
Reagan campaign purring. Nat R 18:818 Ag 23 '66
Atlantic report. Atlan 218:22 Ag '66
Duscha, J. Will California stand Pat? Reporter 35:40 S
  22 '66
Ronald for real. Time 88:31 O 7 '66
Bonfante, J. Reagan vs. Brown; see how they run. Life
  61:43 O 14 '66
Langguth, J. Pat Brown vs. Ronnie Reagan: political fun
  and games, in California. N. Y. Time Mag p27 O 16
  '66

Hill, G. Barbecues and other trivia. Nation 203:377 O
    17 '66
Once and future governor? Christian Cent 83:1323 O 26
    '66
Just folks. Newsweek 68:41 O 31 '66
McWilliams, C. Reagan vs. Brown: how to succeed with
    the backlash. Nation 203:438 O 31 '66
Ryskind, M. California: the final battle? Nat R 18:
    1094 N 1 '66
Roddy, J. Ronnie to the rescue. Look 30:51 N 1 '66
People feel they've been regimented; intv. U. S. News 61:
    55 N 21 '66
People of the week. U. S. News 61:26 N 21 '56
Giant rocks block road for Reagan. Bsns W p70 N 26 '66
Weaver, W. Jr. Four hearties of the good ship G. O. P.
    N. Y. Times Mag p150 N 27 '66
Citizen politician. Sr Schol 89:20 D 2 '66
Greenberg, D. S. Berkeley: new crisis breaks out on
    California campus. Science 154:1304 D 9 '66
Gold, H. Notes from the land of political pop. N. Y.
    Times Mag p48 D 11 '66
Action on the set. Time 88:73 D 16 '66
Story of Ronald Reagan--governor of nation's biggest state.
    U. S. News 62:20 Ja 2 '67
Take two. Newsweek 69:21 Ja 9 '67
Battle over budget. Time 89:64 Ja 20 '67
Showmanship in Sacramento. Nation 204:100 Ja 23 '67
Stith, R. As Berkeley awaits Ronald Reagan. Common-
    weal 85:443 Ja 27 '67
Failure of a peacemaker: California's board of regents
    dismiss Kerr. Time 89:60 Ja 27 '67
Reagan uses his broom. Bsns W p38 Ja 28 '67
Wounded are many. Newsweek 69:87 Ja 30 '67
Duscha, J. What Reagan hath wrought. New Repub 156:
    10 F 4 '67
Star is born. Newsweek 69:39 F 6 '67
Reagan's lesson. Nation 204:166 F 6 '67
Berkeley story: facts on a big university. U. S. News
    62:54 F 6 '67
Happy 50. 4th! Time 89:24 F 17 '67
California's Kerr ousted. Sr Schol 90:13 F 17 '67
Tragedy at Cal: a fiscal and presidential crisis. Time
    89:44 F 24 '67
Reagan retreats. Newsweek 69:80 F 27 '67
Biography. Cur Bio 28:35 F '67
Krebs, A. V. Ronald Reagan, governor. Commonweal
    85:639 Mr 10 '67

Langer, E.   Report from California: the governor and the
   university.   Science 155:1220 Mr 10 '67
In the black, with crust.   Time 89:24 Mr 17 '67
Trombley, W.   Three Rs in California: Reagan, the
   Regents, and the right.   Sat R 50:47 Mr 18 '67
On the run.   Newsweek 69:28 Mr 20 '67
Brodie, F. M.   Ronald Reagan plays surgeon.   Reporter
   36:11 Ap 6 '67
Who is Ronald Reagan?   Read Digest 90:102 Ap '67
Hunter, J. F.   Ronald Reagan, inc. filmog.   Films In Re-
   view 18-4:207 Ap '67
The governor and the university: discussion.   Science 156:
   581 My 5 '67
Welcome to the fraternity.   Time 89:30 My 19 '67
Ronald Reagan: rising star in the West?   Newsweek 69:
   27 My 22 '67
Ronnie-Bobby show.   Newsweek 69:26 My 29 '67
Brandon, H.   California notebook.   Sat R 50:10 Je 3 '67
Rosin, A. & Simmons, R. H.   Governor Reagan's slightest
   vestige.   New Repub 156:10 Je 24 '67
Wright, A.   Governor talks of sport.   Sports Illus 26:40 Je
   26 '67
Evans, R. & Novak, R.   Now that Reagan is governor,
   how's he doing?   Sat Eve Post 240:40 Jl 1 '67
Kopkind, A.   Reagan, ex-radical.   New Repub 157:17 Jl
   15 '67
Boxer Reagan of California.   New Repub 157:4 Jl 22 '67
Making of a candidate; a look at the Reagan boom.   U. S.
   News 63:53 Jl 24 '67
Buckley, W. F. Jr.   Reagan in the State house.   Nat R 19:
   787 Jl 25 '67
Reichley, A. J.   Ronald Reagan faces life.   Fortune 76:
   98 Jl '67
Fast start.   Time 90:17 Ag 11 '67
Has Reagan mastered his role?   Bsns W p100 Ag 12 '67
Brandon, H.   Reagan on the rise?   Sat R 50:12 Ag 12 '67
Looking stronger for '68:   Reagan.   U. S. News 63:13 Ag
   14 '67
Getting out of the shade.   Newsweek 70:23 Ag 14 '67
Craig, J. B.   Matter of principle.   Am For 73:9 Ag '67
Ronald Reagan in the limelight.   U. S. News 63:52 S 18
   '67
Kerby, P.   Revolt against the poor.   Nation 205:262 S 25
   '67
Homecoming day.   Newsweek 70:27 O 9 '67
Now Reagan tries a cross-country tour.   U. S. News 63:
   20 O 9 '67

Reagan's road show. Time 90:28 O 13 '67

Rockefeller, Romney, Reagan: what kind of governors; a
study of the record. U. S. News 63:54 O 30 '67

Harris, E. What is Nancy Reagan really like? Look 31:
40 O 31 '67

Right to fulfillment. Time 90:57 N 3 '67

Trillin, C. U. S. letter: McFarland. New Yorker 43:
173 N 4 '67

Credibility in Sacramento. Time 90:27 N 10 '67

Spots on Mr. Clean. Newsweek 70:34 N 13 '67

Young Easterner with style. Time 90:25 N 24 '67

Pearson vs. Reagan. Newsweek 70:88 N 27 '67

Buckley, W. F. Jr. Reagan: a relaxing view. Nat R
19:1319 N 28 '67

Riots, Reagan and Rockefeller. Nations Bus 55:80 N '67

Duscha, J. Not great, not brilliant, but a good show.
N. Y. Times Mag p28 D 10 '67

Chubbmanship. Time 90:25 D 15 '67

Most happy fellow. Newsweek 70:35 D 18 '67

Tailored press. Nation 205:676 D 25 '67

Reagan's work. Nat R 19:1415 D 26 '67

Arlen, M. J. Air. New Yorker 43:59 D 30 '67

Biography. Brit Bk Yr 1967:163 '67

Reagan takes a look ahead; and explains some '67 deci-
sions. U. S. News 64:11 Ja 8 '68

Davidson, M. What eighteen smart women think of Ronald Reagan. Good H 166:78 Ja '68

Politics' golden boy? intv. Nations Bus 56:44 Ja '68

Governor Reagan's reckless remarks; park and recreation
profession and homosexuals. Parks & Rec 3:19 Ja '68

Rae, D. W. & Lupsha, P. A. Politics of theatre: Reagan
at Yale; role of Chubb fellow. New Repub 158:11 F 3
'68

Reagan as Janus. New Repub 158:8 F 10 '68

Creative society; address January 17, 1968. Vital Speeches 34:266 F 19 '68

Fleming, K. Reagan for president? Newsweek 71:24 F
26 '68

Leary, M. E. Report: California. Atlan 221:22 F '68

Reagan talks of the issues and his plans; intv. U. S. News
64:56 Mr 25 '68

Miles, M. Reagan and the respectable right. New Repub
158:25 Ap 20 '68

Hart, J. Nervous view of Ronald Reagan; with reply. Nat
R 20:444 My 7 '68

Meyer, F. S. Why I am for Reagan. New Repub 158:17
My 11 '68

Nixon's steppingstones, Reagan's TV show.   Time 91:27
  My 24 '68
Reagan on film: a campaign asset.   U.S. News 64:16 My
  27 '68
Dream or nightmare.   Reporter 38:7 My 30 '68
Sounding the south.   Time 91:12 My 31 '68
Kaufman, R. W.   Ronald Reagan: a Republican Messiah?
  N. Am R 5:8 Mr; 10 My '68
Want to hear a plot? involving Ronald Reagan?   Nat R
  20:534 Je 4 '68
Goetz, R.   Reagan and the poor.   Christian Cent 85:776
  Je 12 '68
Buckley, W. F. Jr.   Reagan, Rockefeller.   Nat R 20:624
  Je 18 '68
What Ronald Reagan is saying.   Nat R 20:594 Je 18 '68
Katcher, L.   Political pragmatism.   Sat R 51:27 Je 29 '68
California's sick campuses.   Nation 207:6 Jl 8 '68
Star, J.   What about Ronald Reagan?   Look 32:80 Jl 23
  '68
Not so favorite son.   Time 92:24 Jl 26 '68
Nixon and the veepstakes.   Newsweek 72:19 Ag 5 '68
Convention countdown.   Newsweek 72:18 Ag 12 '68
Once and future candidates.   Time 92:21 Ag 16 '68
Boffey, P. M.   California: Reagan and the mental health
  controversy.   Science 161:1226 S 20; 161:1329 S 27 '68
Cleaver, E.   Introduction to selections from the biography
  of Huey P. Newton, with an aside to Ronald Reagan.
  Ramp Mag 7:22 O 26 '68
Freedom vs. anarchy on campus; warning from Governor
  Reagan; excerpts from address December 8, 1968.
  U.S. News 65:47 D 30 '68
Biography.   Cur Bio Yrbk 1967:338 '68
Reagan on the rise.   Newsweek 73:41 My 5 '69

REARDON, MILDRED
  Corliss, A. & Bartlett, R.   They both came back.   Photop
    17-5:32 Ap '20

REDFORD, ROBERT
  Meehan, T.   Between actors.   Show 4-11:28 D '64
  Miller, E.   Reflections of a secret soldier of fortune.
    Seventeen 25:126 F '66

REDGRAVE, LYNN
  Chelminski, R.   Lynn, the reluctant Redgrave; intv.
    Life 61:61 N 18 '66
  People are talking about . . .   Vogue 149:91 Ja 1 '67

Lerman, L.   International movie report.   Mlle 64:116 F
   '67
Jennings, C. R.   Gaucherie, grace, gall and gaiety.
   TV Guide 15-52:26 D 30 '67
Miller, E.   Beaut of a British bird.   Seventeen 26:99 D
   '67
(See also: REDGRAVE FAMILY)

REDGRAVE, MICHAEL
   Dukes, A.   Three English actors.   Theatre Arts 23:405
      Je '39
   Brown, J. M.   When the hurly-burly's done; Michael Red-
      grave's current Macbeth.   Sat R 31:42 Ap 17 '48
   Allen, P.   A very good Hamlet by Mr. Redgrave.   C S
      Mon Mag p4 F 25 '50
   Biography.   Cur Bio 11:46 F '50
   Same.   Cur Bio Yrbk 1950:478 '51
   His roles fit like a glove.   Plays & Players 1-2:4 N '53
   Redgrave, M.   I am not a camera.   Sight & Sound 24-3:
      132 Ja/Mr '55
   Giraudoux's choice.   Plays & Players 2-10:9 Jl '55
   Lerman, L.   Male attraction.   Mlle 42:152 F '56
   Matter of mood; excerpt from Actor's ways and means.
      Theatre Arts 40:21 Mr '56
   Michael Redgrave.   Vogue 128:151 N 1 '56
   Personality of the month.   Plays & Players 5-9:3 Je '58
   Redgrave reflects.   Plays & Players 5-10:5 Jl '58
   Personality of the month.   Plays & Players 6-12:5 S '59
   Ross, L.   Player.   New Yorker 37:73 O 21 '61
   Kitchin, L.   Michael Redgrave: a profile.   Plays &
      Players 11-5:14 F '64
   Trussler, S.   The Guildford adventure.   Plays & Players
      12-9:12 Je '65
   (See also: REDGRAVE FAMILY)

REDGRAVE, VANESSA
   Spotlight.   Life 51:114 O 27 '61
   Shorter, E.   Vanessa Redgrave: a profile.   Plays &
      Players 11-7:10 Ap '64
   Laerte's daughter.   Time 87:82 My 27 '66
   Hicks, J.   Shakespearean turned sexpot.   Life 61:79 Jl 1
      '66
   Biography.   Cur Bio 27:31 D '66
   Same.   Cur Bio Yrbk 1966:324 '67
   Blackmon, R.   Vanessa Redgrave.   Vogue 149:68 F 15 '67
   Hamilton, J.   Variety of Vanessa.   Look 31:46 My 2 '67
   Ronan, M.   Vanessa, the innest Redgrave; intv. Sr Schol

91:17 O 19 '67

West, A. Vanessa Redgrave takes on Isadora. Vogue
150:108 N 15 '67

Biography. Brit Bk Yr 1967:163 '67

Maclain, J. & Sylvia, K. Isadora: a remarkable film
reincarnation. Dance Mag 42:43 F '68

Meehan, T. Super girl. Sat Eve Post 241:25 Mr 9 '68

Hamilton, J. Immortal Isadora. Look 32:70 D 10 '68

Morris, J. Baby--yes! Husband--no! Photop 75-6:71 Je
'69

(See also: REDGRAVE FAMILY)

REDGRAVE FAMILY

First family. Newsweek 67:102 My 23 '66

Birds of a father. Time 89:80 Mr 17 '67

Eckman, F. M. Redgraves talk about their children.
McCalls 94:87 S '67

Graham, J. Those astonishing Redgraves. Good H 166
Ja '68

(See also: REDGRAVE, LYNN; REDGRAVE, MICHAEL;
REDGRAVE, VANESSA)

REED, DONNA

Holliday, K. Farmer's daughter. Colliers 109:13 Je 27
'42

Homespun. Am Mag 134:71 S '42

Donna Reed. Life 20:133 Ja 10 '46

Donna Reed: James Stewart's new leading lady. Life 20:
133 Je 10 '46

Howe, H. Wonderful life of Donna. Photop 31-2:64 Jl '47

Hall, G. What is this thing called love? Photop 48-1:46
Jl '55

Goldsmith, B. My most wonderful time of day. Womans
H C 83:18 F '56

Just what the doctor ordered. TV Guide 6-50:8 D 13 '58

Never argue with a woman. TV Guide 7-32:8 Ag 8 '59

Nichols, M. Farmer's daughter. Coronet 47:14 F '60

Christy, G. It's worth fighting to save a marriage. Photop 57-2:54 F '60

No prima donna. TV Guide 8-13:24 Mr 26 '60

The farmer's daughter who went to town. TV Guide 9-18:
12 My 6 '61

From eternity to here. Newsweek 58:75 Jl 31 '61

Wheeling and dealing--Hollywood style. TV Guide 10-29:
19 Jl 21 '62

What greater service? NEA J 52:29 Ja '63

Freeman, D. Donna Reed; fire and ice. Sat Eve Post 237:

22 Mr 28 '64
Peters, A.   Real life for the doctor's wife.   Todays
    Health 42:24 Je '64
Dern, M.   Sweet, sincere and solvent.   TV Guide 12-25:
    10 Je 20 '64

REED, FLORENCE
    Mullett, M. B.   Florence Reed has made herself what
        she preferred not to be.   Am Mag 102:180 '26
    Obit.   Screen World 19:238 '68

REEVES, GEORGE
    Obit.   Brit Bk Yr 1960:513 '60
        Screen World 11:224 '60

REEVES, STEVE
    A. A. U. 's ideal man.   Life 23:42 Jl 14 '47
    All muscle.   Time 74:32 Jl 27 '59
    Mighty profits of Hercules.   Life 47:76 Ag 10 '59
    Matter over mind.   Newsweek 56:86 Ag 29 '60

REICHER, FRANK
    Obit.   Screen World 17:240 '66

REID, ELLIOTT
    Anderson, D.   Elliott Reid, show stopper.   Theatre Arts
        35:55 N '51

REID, PEGGY
    "Pretty Peggy" Reid.   Photop 4-4:47 S '13

REID, WALLACE
    Carr, A.   Wallace Reid.   Feature Movie 2-7:48 Jl 10 '15
    York, S.   Wally the wonderful.   Photop 9-4:76 Mr '16
    McGaffey, K.   Wandering with Wally.   Photop 14-1:59 Je
        '18
    Reid, W.   How to hold your wife.   Photop 19-2:28 Ja '21
    Reid, Mrs. W.   Getting back at friend husband.   Photop
        20-6:   N '22
    The unhappy ending of Wally Reid's life story.   Photop 23-
        4:36 Mr '23
    Reid, D. D.   The real Wally.   Photop 27-4:58 Mr '25
    Amour and the man.   Sat R 39:29 O 13 '56
    Bodeen, D.   Wallace Reid, inc. filmog.   Films In Re-
        view 17-4:205 Ap '66

REMICK, LEE
  Star by instinct.   Look 23:120 O 13 '59
  New Grace Kellys.   Mlle 50:57 D '59
  Girl with a lilt in her eyes.   Life 48:101 Je 6 '60
  Nichols, M.   Southern broad from Boston.   Coronet 48:
    14 Ag '60
  Whitcomb, J.   Lee Remick--the winsome witch.   Cosmop
    149:10 S '60
  Doomed by a wiggle.   TV Guide 9-10:8 Mr 11 '61
  People are talking about . . .   Vogue 137:58 Ap 15 '61
  Onceness in a while.   Newsweek 59:56 Ja 15 '62
  Davidson, B.   Double image of Lee Remick.   Sat Eve
    Post 236:38 My 18 '63
  Miller, E.   Two ways to skin a cat.   Seventeen 22:136
    My '63
  Chapman, D.   Lee Remick soars in a sightless role.
    Look 30:112 My 17 '66
  Biography.   Cur Bio 27:29 O '66
    Same.   Cur Bio Yrbk 1966:327 '67
  Actress Lee Remick's second talent: decorating.
    Good H 164:100 Ja '67

RENALDO, DUNCAN
  The Cisco's kids.   TV Guide 3-33:20 Ag 13 '55
  Wood, C.   TV personalities biographical sketchbook.
    TV Personalities p11 '57
  Riggan, B.   /Damn the crocodiles, keep the cameras roll-
    ing!   Am Heritage 19:38 Je '68

RENNIE, MICHAEL
  People are talking about . . .   Vogue 137:125 My '61
  Debonair, distinguished and dangerous.   TV Guide 9-41:
    17 O 14 '61

REVERE, ANNE
  Downing, H.   Star without glamor.   Colliers 116:77 O 20 '45
  McClelland, D.   Anne Revere.   Film Fan Mo 96:18 Je '69

REY, ALEJANDRO
  Goodwin, F.   The flying Argentine.   TV Guide 16-27:12
    Jl 6 '68

REYNOLDS: ADELINE DeWALT
  Taylor, F. J.   Granny storms Hollywood.   Ind Woman 22:
    210 Jl '43
    Same abridged, with title 83-year-old granny, idol of
    Hollywood.   Read Digest 43:44 Ag '43

Walworth, D.   Heart that did not break.   Read Digest
55:35 D '49
Obit.   Time 78:65 Ag 25 '61
Screen World 13:225 '62

REYNOLDS, BURT
Jenkins, D.   The blacksmith who really makes sparks
fly.   TV Guide 11-21:15 My 25 '63

REYNOLDS, DEBBIE
Out of the doghouse.   Am Mag 150:61 D '50
Speaking of pictures.   Life 30:12 F 26 '51
Riley, V.   Paint a pretty picture.   Photop 39-2:54 F '51
Arnold, M.   Li'l lightnin' bug.   Photop 40-1:44 Jl '51
Wagner, R.   Debbie's dateline.   Photop 42-2:40 Ag '52
Reynolds, D.   Boys are here to stay.   Photop 42-2:40
Ag '52
Zeitlin, I.   Split personality.   Photop 43-1:48 Ja '53
Goode, B. & Goode, B. M.   Debbie comes of age.   Photop
43-5:46 My '53
Reynolds, B.   I never knew Debbie.   Photop 44-2:44 Ag
'53
Angeli, P.   Saludos Amiga!   Photop 44-3:38 S '53
Thomas, B.   Debbie's hopeless.   Photop 44-6:56 D '53
On stardom's stairway.   Coronet 35:54 Ja '54
Hunter, T.   Why Debbie's my ideal.   Photop 45-2:40
F '54
Reynolds, D.   Look at me now.   Photop 45-3:38 Mr '54
Reynolds, M.   My girl, Debbie.   Photop 46-1:66 Jl '54
Parsons, L. O.   Cosmopolitan movie citations.   Cosmop
137:22 Jl '54
Teenage tizzy.   Life 37:185 S 13 '54
Edwards, R.   Gayer than laughter is she.   Photop 46-5:
64 N '54
Debbie and Eddie announce it.   Life 37:45 N 8 '54
Chapman, P.   A wonderful thing happened today.   Photop
47-1:26 Ja '55
Debbie and Eddie.   Look 19:22 F 22 '55
Johnson, J.   Hi Debbie, I'm talking about you.   Photop
47-3:36 Mr '55
And it comes out here.   Am Mag 159:49 Ap '55
Block, M.   Getting in step for marriage.   Photop 47-5:
43 My '55
Reynolds, D.   I've never been in love before.   Womans
H C 82:42 Je '55
The marriage the whole world waited for.   Photop 48-1:
56 Jl '55

Debbie's ring on at last.   Life 39:59 O 10 '55
Arnold, M.   A dream come true.   Photop 48-6:42 D '55
No time is their time.   Look 20:105 Mr 6 '56
Cohen, M. A.   A guy and his dungaree doll.   Photop 49-
  4:60 Ap '56
Arnold, M.   Love and marriage.   Photop 49-6:48 Je '56
Wheatland, C. M. & Sharpe, E.   Young Hollywood at
  home.   Ladies Home J 73:88 N '56
Eisenberg, H.   Why Eddie Fisher almost left Debbie
  Reynolds waiting.   Photop 51-2:46 F '57
Scott, D.   Love and marriage and a baby carriage.
  Photop 51-4:52 Ap '57
Thompson, E.   No marriage stories for us.   Photop 52-
  3:52 S '57
Girl and a ballad.   Newsweek 50:96 S 23 '57
Debbie Reynolds.   Cosmop 143:79 N '57
Confess, or take the consequences.   Photop 53-1:45 Ja '58
Pollock, L.   The story Debbie wanted told.   Photop 54-2:
  51 Ag '58
Just friends.   Time 72:44 S 22 '58
Tale of Debbie, Eddie and the widow Todd.   Life 45:39 S
  22 '58
That's show biz.   Newsweek 52:77 S 22 '58
Lyle, J.   Why Debbie and Eddie are leaving Hollywood.
  Photop 54-3:53 S '58
Debbie back with a bounce.   Life 45:145 N 17 '58
Reich, I.   We'd never be happier than we were last year.
  Photop 54-6:32 D '58
Pollock, L.   Tragic triangle.   Photop 54-6:34 D '58
Dinter, C.   Is daddy going to be with us all the time?
  Photop 55-1:59 Ja '59
Hawley, E.   We spend the day with Debbie Reynolds.
  Photop 55-2:40 F '59
Gehman, R.   Debbie Reynolds: her story.   McCalls 86:
  49 Mr '59
Debbie comes up dancing.   Life 46:67 Mr 30 '59
Fast divorce OK by Debbie.   Life 46:41 Ap 13 '59
Life of the senses.   Time 73:65 Ap 13 '59
Larner, P.   What I found out from Debbie.   Photop 55-4:
  36 Ap '59
Talk with a star.   Newsweek 53:90 Je 22 '59
Rowland, R.   I wish them happiness.   Photop 56-2:27 Ag
  '59
Has Debbie gotten over Eddie?   Photop 56-5:37 N '59
Culver, M.   What did Debbie feel when Liz and Eddie
  walked in?   Photop 57-1:20 Ja '60
Reynolds, D. as told to J. Ardmore.   If I had it to do

over again. Ladies Home J 77:52 F '60

Day, D. Much of what I tried to do in marriage was
wrong. Photop 57-2:40 F '60

Martin, P. I call on Debbie Reynolds. Sat Eve Post
232:28 Mr 26 '60

Don't be the girl in the comic valentine. Photop 57-3:
24 Mr '60

Whitcomb, J. Box office darling. Cosmop 148:22 Ap '60

Sturies, S. Come on in the party's for you. Photop 57-
4:54 Ap '60

Hamilton, S. Exclusive interview with Debbie Reynolds.
Photop 57-5:71 My '60

Dean, R. Behind Debbie's marriage fears. Photop 57-6:
33 Je '60

What Glenn Ford's hiding from Debbie. Photop 58-1:42
Jl '60

Stump, A. Debbie Reynolds: now I'm a happy cynic.
Coronet 48:79 Jl '60

Blake, E. Is Debbie settling for less than love. Photop
58-2:34 Ag '60

Johnson, M. Why Debbie must keep her real love out of
the family picture. Photop 58-3:25 S '60

The $300,000 come on. TV Guide 8-43:19 O 22 '60

Is Debbie planning to call off her wedding now? Photop
58-5:25 N '60

Ardmore, J. Glenn, will you marry Debbie? Photop 58-
5:26 N '60

Liz and Eddie's wedding gift to Debbie. Photop 58-6:14
D '60

Ardmore, J. Wouldn't you like to help Debbie smile
again? Photop 59-1:54 Ja '61

Ardmore, J. The bride--her private life. Photop 59-5:
52 My '61

Debbie Reynolds and Billy Graham talk frankly about love
and faith. Read Digest 117:34 My '61

Dean, B. Eddie's back in Debbie's life. Photop 60-1:44
Jl '61

Schroeder, C. Don't let gossip hurt you. Good H 153:70
S '61

Why I'm afraid to have another baby. Photop 60-5:40 N
'61

Haranis, C. The life he still shares with Debbie. Photop
60-6:28 D '61

Reynolds, D. Should married women date? Photop 61-3:
34 Mr '62

Robbins, F. What I tell my children. Photop 61-4:43
Ap '62

Ardmore, J.   I'll just have to have twins.   Photop 61-5:
   13 My '62
Debbie's big fear--Eddie.   Photop 62-2:20 Ag '62
Spencer, F.   Fight over Todd's religion!   Photop 62-3:
   25 S '62
Ardmore, J.   Debbie loses her baby.   Photop 62-4:8 O
   '62
How to be very, very popular; excerpt from If I knew
   then.   Seventeen 21:148 N '62
Camber, G.   The woman who . . .   Photop 63-4:29 Ap
   '63
Somers, A.   Together--for children's sake.   Photop 63-
   5:40 My '63
Ormond, E.   A new baby for Debbie.   Photop 64-1:51
   Jl '63
Carpozi, G.   Can she have another baby?   Photop 64-3:
   50 S '63
Becket, B.   Debbie adopting baby?   Photop 65-1:37 Ja
   '64
Wayne, D.   The night the stars prayed.   Photop 65-2:
   70 F '64
Ellis, F.   She talks about the racial crisis.   Photop 65-
   5:58 My '64
They couldn't sink Debbie either.   Life 56:108 Je 19 '64
Hello Debbie.   Newsweek 63:87 Je 29 '64
Miller, E.   Debbie does it!   Seventeen 23:80 Jl '64
Ellis, F.   My church called me a sinner.   Photop 66-1:
   43 Jl '64
Lewis, R. W.   Unsinkable Debbie Reynolds.   Sat Eve
   Post 237:74 Ag 22 '64
Baird, S.   My children kept me from dying.   Photop 66-
   5:64 N '64
Biography.   Cur Bio 25:8 D '64
   Same.   Cur Bio Yrbk 1964:368 '64
York, C.   Debbie flips over Burton.   Photop 67-1:8 Ja
   '65
White, R.   A doctor's warning to her.   Photop 68-2:67
   Ag '65
Henry, L.   Don't marry again.   Photop 76-2:58 Ag '69
Debbie Reynolds comes to grips with TV comedy.   TV
   Guide 17-42:19 O 18 '65
Terrorized in her home.   Photop 76-6:33 D '69

REYNOLDS, JOYCE
   Exuberant 19-year-old plays a 16-year-old in Janie.
      Life 17:59 Ag 21 '44
   Proctor, K.   Don't be a Junior Miss.   Photop 26-3:52

F '45

Fergus, D.   Filmography.   Films In Review 18-6:384 Je/
Jl '67

REYNOLDS, MARJORIE
Crichton, K.   Marjorie's horse comes in.   Colliers 110:
20 N 7 '42
She took off her spurs and danced with Astaire.   Am Mag
135:100 Ja '43
Riley's wife.   TV Guide 1-32:15 N 6 '53

REYNOLDS, VERA
St. Johns, I.   A surf board flapper.   Photop 26-4:65 S
'24
Obit.   Screen World 14:226 '63

RHUE, MADLYN
Allergic to cactus.   TV Guide 9-24:22 Je 17 '61

RICH, IRENE
Winship, M.   Raising Riches.   Photop 19-1:32 D '20
Voils, J. W.   I'm in New York.   Pict R 39:61 D '37

RICH, LILLIAN
Obit.   Screen World 6:225 '55

RICH, VIVIAN
Bagg, H.   Many sided Vivian Rich.   Photop 6-6:51 N '14
Thein, M.   A chat with the girl on the cover.   Feature
Movie 2-7:7 Jl 10 '15

RICHARDS, ADDISON
Obit.   Screen World 16:225 '65

RICHARDS, ANN
Eddy, D.   It can't happen, but it did!   Am Mag 136:36
O '43
McClelland, D.   Ann Richards, inc. filmog.   Screen Facts
13:49 n. d.

RICHARDSON, RALPH
Hobson, H.   Day dawns for the actor.   C S Mon Mag p6
Mr 31 '37
Dukes, A.   Three English actors.   Theatre Arts 23:405 Je
'39
Sinner and saint.   Time 46:64 D 31 '45
Clurman, H.   Theatre: London completed.   New Repub

123:21 Jl 3 '50
Biography.   Cur Bio 11:43 N '50
   Same.   Cur Bio Yrbk 1950:490 '51
Bevan, I.   Ralph Richardson: self-made star.   Theatre
   Arts 36:27 Je '52
Personality of the month.   Plays & Players 1-5:3 F '54
Richardson, R.   Sir Alexander Korda.   Sight & Sound 25-
   4:214 Spg '56
Barker, F. G.   No fun for Falstaff.   Plays & Players
   44:5 O '56
Return of Sir Ralph.   N. Y. Times Mag p58 Ja 6 '57
Pumphrey, A.   Tale of two knights.   Theatre Arts 47:18
   Ja '63
Trewin, J. C.   Ralph Richardson.   Plays & Players 13-4:
   7 Ja '66
Coulson, A. A.   Ralph Richardson, inc. filmog.   Films In
   Review 20-8:457 O '69

RICHMAN, MARK
   He has come up with the right prescription.   TV Guide
      10-5:15 F 3 '62

RIDGELEY, JOHN
   Obit.   Screen World 20:239 '69

RIGG, DIANA
   Good-chap sexuality.   Newsweek 67:94 Ap 4 '66
   Musel, R.   En garde!   TV Guide 15-3:19 Ja 21 '67
   Musel, R.   She's Miss Rigg of St. John's Wood, now.
      TV Guide 16-31:16 Ag 3 '68

RISDON, ELIZABETH
   Obit.   Screen World 10:225 '59

RITTER, THELMA
   Connell, E. T.   Housewife who became a movie star.
      Am Mag 152:116 Jl '51
   Hughes, C.   Thelma Ritter's road to stardom.   Coronet
      30:85 S '51
   Talk with a star.   Newsweek 49:70 My 27 '57
   Nice pair in town.   New Yorker 33:20 Jl 6 '57
   Biography.   Cur Bio 18:20 D '57
      Same.   Cur Bio Yrbk 1957:467 '58
   Bester, A.   Saddest comedienne.   Holiday 27:115 Mr '60
   Obit.   Time 93:80 F 14 '69
      Newsweek 73:93 F 17 '69

RITZ, AL
    Obit.   Time 86:78 D 31 '65
        Newsweek 67:37 Ja 3 '66
        Screen World 17:240 '66
    (See also: RITZ BROTHERS)

RITZ, HARRY
    (See: RITZ BROTHERS)

RITZ, JIMMY
    (See: RITZ BROTHERS)

RITZ BROTHERS
    (Al, Harry, Jimmy)
    Condon, F.   Triple hysterics.   Colliers 99:13 F 27 '37
    Wright, J.   Three damp fools.   Photop 52-4:32 Ap '38
    (See also: RITZ, AL)

RIVA, EMMANUELE
    Emmanuele Riva.   Film 33:11 Aut '62
    New veers.   Vogue 141:114 Ja 1 '63

ROBARDS, JASON SR.
    Talk with two players.   Newsweek 52:63 D 15 '58
    Ross, L.   Player.   New Yorker 37:72 N 4 '61
    Obit.   Newsweek 61:70 Ap 15 '63
        Screen World 15:224 '64

ROBARDS, JASON JR.
    Eleven fine actors get their dream roles.   Life 44:76 Ap
        14 '58
    Hewes, H.   Plummer's summer.   Sat R 41:28 Jl 12 '58
    Talk with two players.   Newsweek 52:63 D 14 '58
    One rail.   New Yorker 34:20 Ja 3 '59
    Nichols, M.   Robards' rocky road.   Coronet 45:10 My '59
    What the stars say.   Mlle 49:30 Je '59
    Sound and fury.   Time 74:40 Ag 10 '59
    Biography.   Cur Bio 20:38 O '59
        Same.   Cur Bio Yrbk 1959:387 '60
    Re Robards.   Theatre Arts 43:85 N '59
    Keating, J.   Jason Robards Jr.   Theatre Arts 44:10 Ap
        '60
    Talk with the star.   Newsweek 59:100 Ap 16 '62
    Efron, E.   His very bearing speaks tragedy.   TV Guide
        12-5:16 F 1 '64
    Thompson, T.   Send the script to Jason.   Life 60:83 F
        25 '66

ROBERTS, ALLENE
Sweet and sultry. Am Mag 146:105 S '48
Arnold, M. Sitting on top of the world. Photop 36-7:
48 D '49

ROBERTS, RACHEL
Tomorrow's lead. Plays & Players 1-7:19 Ap '54
Rex Harrison and his own fair lady. Look 27:72 Je 18 '63
Hamilton, J. Rich, restless life of Rex Harrison.
Look 29:62 N 2 '65

ROBERTS, THEODORE
Owen, K. Grand duke of Hollywood; intv. Photop 8-4:
38 S '15
Kennedy, J. B. Old man of the movies; intv. Colliers
82:14 S 15 '28
Collins, F. L. Motion picture role of honor. Good H
95:62 Ag '32

ROBERTSON, CLIFF
Maddox, T. Adventure loving man. Photop 50-2:60 Ag
'56
Quirk, L. J. The magic of love. Photop 52-5:60 N '57
The man who will play the president. TV Guide 10-34:8
Ag 25 '62
Davidson, B. President Kennedy casts a movie. Sat Eve
Post 235:26 S 8 '62
He likes to cook: Clif Robertson, the movies' JFK.
Bet Hom & Gard 41:78 Mr '63
Reische, D. Hollywood's JFK. Sr Schol 82:19 Ap 24 '63
Twenty years after: PT 109. Life 54:98 My 17 '63
Kelly, V. He needed the President for his breakthrough.
Look 27:52 Je 18 '63
Meltsir, A. JFK is taking over my life. Photop 64-2:
57 Ag '63
Terry, P. His escape from the 20th Century. Photop
65-6:34 Je '64
Hemming, H. Lively arts. Sr Schol 90:26 Ap 28 '67
Hart, H. Cliff Robertson, inc. filmog. Films In Re-
view 20-3:553 Mr '69

ROBERTSON, DALE
Arnold, M. I was there. Photop 40-3:52 S '51
Zeitlin, I. The faith of Dale Robertson. Photop 41-5:
44 My '52
Robertson, J. Dale's little dividend. Photop 42-1:54 Jl
'52

Townsend, P.   Father's day.   Photop 42-5:70 N '52

Armstrong, G.   Can Dale Robertson save his marriage.
Photop 43-1:64 Ja '53

Ford, E.   Terrific trio.   Photop 43-4:32 Ap '53

Arnold, M.   Stop telling lies about us.   Photop 43-6:44
Je '53

Corwin, J.   Life begins with marriage.   Photop 44-3:
60 S '53

Arnold, M.   I want a divorce.   Photop 47-2:38 F '55

Fighting for honest westerns.   TV Guide 5-28:29 Jl 20
'57

Wood, C.   TV personalities biographical sketchbook.
TV Personalities p45 '57

Looking a gift horse in the mouth.   TV Guide 6-29:20
Jl 19 '58

TV's real cowboy.   Life 45:90 D 22 '58

A horseman who became an actor.   TV Actor 7-43:17 O
24 '59

Borie, M.   Oh my God, I can't see.   Photop 59-1:42
Ja '61

Fox, W. P. Jr.   The man from Harrah says "howdy."
TV Guide 15-5:21 F 4 '67

ROBINSON, EDWARD G.

Hall, L.   What? No guns?   Photop 39-5:56 Ap '31

Kennedy, J. B.   Tough as velvet.   Colliers 89:21 Ja 2
'32

Kropotkin, A.   An actor with strange ideas.   Photop 48-3:
72 Ag '35

Actor-collector.   Lit Digest 123:27 Ja 9 '37

Proctor, K.   Robinson and company.   Photop 52-10:26 O
'38

Ducas, D. & Brown, A.   Men mix it.   Colliers 104:18 S
2 '39

Baker, G.   Here's my favorite; intv.   Scholastic 40:21
Mr 16 '42

Millier, A.   Living art radio program; intv.   Mag Art
35:256 N '42

Othman, F. C.   Arts is a tough racket, pal.   Sat Eve
Post 217:26 Jl 1 '44

Biography.   Cur Bio 11:44 Ja '50
Same.   Cur Bio Yrbk 1950:497 '51

Collectors at work.   Time 57:48 F 5 '51

Return of Robinson.   Life 40:99 F 27 '56

Highest bidder.   Newsweek 49:85 F 4 '57

Big deal.   Time 69:77 Mr 4 '57

Robinson to Niarchos.   Life 42:107 Ap 15 '57

Eyles, A.   Edward G. Robinson.   Films & Filming 10-
    4:12 Ja '64
Roman, R. C.   Edward G. Robinson, inc. filmog.   Films
    In Review 17-7:419 Ag/S '66

ROBSON, FLORA
    Biography.   Cur Bio 12:41 Ja '51
        Same.   Cur Bio Yrbk 1951:528 '52
    From tears to laughter.   Plays & Players 2-6:5 Mr '55
    Personality of the month.   Plays & Players 6-3:3 D '58

ROBSON, MAY
    Croy, H.   Women capture screen honors for 1933.   Lit
        Digest 116:42 N 4 '33
    Condon, F.   Lady who tells her age.   Colliers 95:19 Ja
        26 '35
    Rankin, R.   Salute May Robson!   Photop 47-2:67 Ja '35
    Williams, W.   Only families with children need apply;
        May Robson builds houses with yards.   C S Mon Mag
        p4 D 30 '39
    Rhea, M.   Lesson in living.   Photop 54-12:28 D '40
    Obit.   Time 40:58 N 2 '42
        Cur Bio '42

ROGERS, BUDDY (CHARLES)
    Ingram, A.   Buddy conquers Broadway.   Photop 38-1:88
        Je '30
    York, C.   Am I an actor?   Photop 40-1:65 Ja '31
    Carroll, L.   What really happened to Buddy Rogers.
        Photop 41-4:30 Mr '32
    Life visits Pickfair.   Life 23:158 N 17 '47

ROGERS, GINGER
    Reeve, W.   The private life of Ginger Rogers.   Photop
        48-3:26 Ag '35
    Holdom, C.   One step at a time.   C S Mon Mag p3 Mr
        4 '36
    How I came to be a dancer.   St N 63:10 Mr '36
    Reeves, M. W.   Ginger Rogers' rules for slaying the stag
        line.   Photop 49-5:52 My '36
    Early, D.   Lew Ayres' own story of the breakup of his
        and Ginger Rogers' marriage.   Photop 50-1:22 Jl '36
    Hamilton, S.   Freedom is glorifying Ginger.   Photop 50-
        3:22 S '36
    Dancing with Astaire and Rogers.   Lit Digest 122:20 D
        12 '36
    Proctor, K.   Ginger was threatened with death.   Photop

51-2:21 F '37

Portman, D.   Ginger's having wonderful time.   Photop 52-
3:18 Mr '38

Rogers, G.   Love story.   Photop 52-8:16 Ag '38

Dancing girl.   Time 33:49 Ap 10 '39

Rogers, L.   Why not be somebody?   Photop 53-5:17 My
'39

Hartley, K.   Play truth or consequences with Ginger
Rogers.   Photop 53-7:22 Jl '39

Waterbury, R.   The marriage plans of Ginger Rogers and
Howard Hughes.   Photop 54-6:18 Je '40

Business girl makes good.   Ind Woman 20:97 Ap '41

Jefferson, S.   Surprise romance.   Photop 20-1:44 D '41

Biography.   Cur Bio '41

She adds new chapter to her success story.   Life 12:60
Mr 2 '42

Jefferson, S.   Mrs. G. Briggs.   Photop 22-5:25 Ap '43

Fink, H.   Scoop!   Ginger Rogers' hideaway honeymoon.
Photop 23-3:55 Ag '43

Woolf, S. J.   Highest paid move actress; intv.   N.Y.
Times Mag p18 D 5 '43

Skolsky, S.   The gist of Ginger Rogers.   Photop 24-5:42
Ap '44

Schallert, E.   Wartime wife.   Photop 26-6:45 My '45

Arnold, M.   Two on leave.   Photop 27-5:27 O '45

Shipp, C.   How to dance like four antelopes.   Colliers
123:14 Ja 8 '49

Arnold, M.   Roger!   Photop 36-3:36 Ag '49

Oldtime champ at the Charleston.   Life 28:32 Ap 3 '50

Busch, N.   New Ginger on Broadway.   Colliers 128:28 S
29 '51

Dressed to kill.   Life 31:87 N 5 '51

Hawkins, W.   Return to Broadway.   Theatre Arts 35:54 N
'51

Ford, E.   Love set.   Photop 43-5:70 My '53

Miss Rogers consents.   TV Guide 2-42:5 O 16 '54

Hamburger, P.   Television; Noel Coward sketches on Tonight at 8:30.   New Yorker 30:96 N 30 '54

Ginger and old dad.   Newsweek 52:62 S 15 '58

By Ginger.   TV Guide 6-41:17 O 11 '58

Famous pair's new partners.   Life 45:44 O 20 '58

Backstage with Ginger.   TV Guide 7-7:8 F 14 '49

Fraser, P. C.   Ginger Rogers puzzles me.   Good H 148:
32 Mr '59

Haines, A. B.   Her school was the stage.   Dance Mag 37:
32 N '63

Dickens, H.   Ginger Rogers, inc. filmog.   Films In Re-

Review 17-3:129 Mr '66
Ginger Rogers film festival.   Film Society R p7 D '66
Ginger peachy.   Time 89:78 F 10 '67
Biography.   Cur Bio 28:38 D '67
    Same.   Cur Bio Yrbk 1967:345 '68

ROGERS, JEAN
    Reynolds, Q.   Hollywood sweepstakes.   Colliers 102:20
        D 24 '38

ROGERS, PAUL
    Personality of the month.   Plays & Players 2-3:5 D '54
    Biography.   Cur Bio 21:40 Mr '60
        Same.   Cur Bio Yrbk 1960:344 '61

ROGERS, ROY
    Cowboy with sex appeal.   Photop 19-6:64 N '41
    Tully, T.   Keep punchin'.   Photop 21-4:51 S '42
    King of the cowboys.   Newsweek 21:74 Mr 8 '43
    Smith, H. A.   King of the cowboys.   Life 15:47 Jl 12 '43
    Delehanty, T.   Cowboy in the velvet.   Photop 25-6:47 N
        '44
    Horse laugh.   Am Mag 139:64 My '45
    Martin, P.   Cincinnati cowboy.   Sat Eve Post 217:26 Je
        9 '45
    Greenbaum, L.   Sinatra in a sombrero.   N.Y. Times Mag
        p42 N 4 '45
    Arnold, M.   Buckeye buckaroo.   Photop 29-6:45 N '46
    Parsons, L. O.   Roy rides alone.   Photop 30-5:32 Ap '47
    Dusek, J.   I was there.   Photop 32-2:54 Ja '48
    Biography.   Cur Bio 9:48 Mr '48
        Same.   Cur Bio 1949:531 '49
    Reid, A.   Hero on horseback.   Colliers 122:27 Jl 24 '48
    Don't shoot, ma!   Am Mag 148:28 Ag '49
    Here comes Roy Rogers.   TV Guide 4-52:8 D 28 '51
    Kingsley, K.   With open hearts.   Photop 43-2:82 F '53
    Roy Rogers is big business.   TV Guide 1-6:8 My 8 '53
    Stump, A.   Meet the Roy Rogers family.   Am Mag 156:
        38 Ag '53
    Children made Roy king of the cowboys.   TV Guide 2-29:
        5 Jl 17 '54
    Wood, C.   TV personalities biographical sketchbook.
        TV Personalities p137 '54
    Valentry, D.   Man, a horse and a guitar.   Am Mer 80:
        131 Ja '55
    Man and wife.   Time 65:55 Mr 7 '55
    Meanwhile, back at their ranches.   TV Guide 7-32:17 Ag

8 '59

Davidson, M.   Are they going to be headed off at the
pass.   TV Guide 10-49:10 D 8 '62

Baskette, K.   Gift of Debbie.   Good H 160:93 Mr '65

Anderson, W. E. A.   Roy Rogers goes north.   Outdoor
Life 137:52 Ap '66

Cocchi, J.   Filmography.   Screen Facts 5:48 n. d.

ROGERS, WILL

Metcalfe, L.   All sweet and pretty.   Photop 16-2:59 Jl '19

Martin, G.   Wit of Will Rogers.   Am Mag 88:34 N '19
Same abridged.   Lit Digest 63:60 N 15 '19

Will Rogers as our Aristophanes.   Lit Digest 75:29 D 16
'22

Will Rogers, cowboy comedian.   Cur Opinion 74:103 Ja
'23

Etiquette as lassoed by Will Rogers.   Lit Digest 79:46 O
6 '23

Will Rogers ropes the Digest poll.   Lit Digest 83:42 N 15
'24

Scallan, R. O.   Ride 'em, author!   intv.   Colliers 74:8
D 13 '24

Tittle, W.   Glimpses of interesting Americans.   Cent 110:
317 Jl '25

Will Rogers weighs up the new Ford.   Lit Digest 87:78 N
7 '25

Will Rogers in London.   Lit Digest 90:22 Ag 28 '26

Will Rogers: solitary.   Lit Digest 92:29 Ja 15 '27

Duck, Al!   Here's another open letter.   Sat Eve Post 200:
3 O 29 '27

Rogers, W.   Will Rogers says.   Photop 32-6:35 N '27

Bucking a head wind.   Sat Eve Post 200:6 Ja 28 '28

Van Doren, D.   Will Rogers, the bunkless candidate.
Nation 127:314 O 3 '28

There is life in the old gal yet.   Sat Eve Post 201:6 Ja
19 '29

Lardner, R.   With rope and gun; or, Up from the ranch.
Colliers 83:13 F 2 '29

Mr. Toastmaster and Democrats.   Sat Eve Post 201:3 Mr
30 '29

Hoofing kid from Claremore.   Am Mag 107:34 Ap '29

Coolidge.   Am Mag 107:20 Je '29

How to be funny.   Am Mag 108:61 S '29

Clancy, C. S.   Aviation's patron saint.   Sci Am 141:283
O '29

Grand champion.   Am Mag 108:34 D '29

Corn whiskey, courage and commerce.   Am Mag 109:69

My '30

Will Rogers at the microphone. World's Work 59:17 Je
'30

World's best loser. Am Mag 101:30 S '30

Beatty, J. Betty holds the reins. Am Mag 110:60 O '30

Pringle, H. F. King Babbitt's court jester. Outlook 157:
494 Ap 8 '31

Wisdom of a modest humorist. Christian Cent 48:764 Je
10 '31

Will of the people. Colliers 88:35 Jl 4 '31

Bacon and beans and limousines; radio address for the
President's Committee on unemployment relief. Survey
67:185 N 15 '31

Letters of a self-made diplomat to Senator Borah. Sat
Eve Post. 204-6 F 27; 8 Mr 5; 8 Mr 12; 6 Mr 19;
21 Ap '32

Letter to the Philippines. Sat Eve Post 204:6 Ap 30 '32

King, Will. Commonweal 17:173 D 14 '32

Baskette, K. "I'll be at Doc Law's." Photop 45-2:31 Ja
'34

New Ah wilderness cast headed by Will Rogers. Newsweek
3:23 My 12 '34

Kent, G. The mammy and daddy of us all. Photop 45-6:
32 My '34

Cobb, I. Another Will Rogers. Photop 47-4:34 Mr '35

On the current screen. Lit Digest 119:34 Ap 20 '35

Obit. Pub W 128:514 Ag 24 '35

Rogers conquered the world with humor. Lit Digest 120:
8 Ag 24 '35

Two great men die. Newsweek 6:18 Ag 24 '35

Death in the Arctic. Time 26:32 Ag 26 '35

Cowboy philosopher. New Repub 84:62 Ag 28 '35

Where the loss of Will Rogers may be most deeply felt.
Christian Cent 52:1075 Ag 28 '35

Rogers and Post. Commonweal 22:416 Ag 30 '35

Homespun philosophers. Sat R 12:8 Ag 31 '35

Time's up folks, s'long! Musician 40:11 Ag '35

Taviner, R. On the set with Will Rogers. Photop 48-3:
36 Ag '35

Ferguson, O. Two show figures. New Repub 84:104 S
4 '35

Rogers fans want their idol kept immortal on screen.
Newsweek 6:28 S 14 '35

Will Rogers. Survey 71:274 S '35

Last film role as trainer in In old Kentucky. Lit Digest
120:24 N 30 '35

Will Rogers library, Claremore, Oklahoma. Lib J 62:

310 Ap 1 '37

20,000 dedicate memorial to America's favorite son.
  Newsweek 12:15 N 14 '38

Rogers, B. B.   Uncle Clem's boy.   Sat Eve Post 213:9
  O 5; 28 O 12; 24 O 19; 26 O 26; 22 N 2; 24 N 9; 34
  N 16; 24 N 30 '40

Will Rogers shrine in California; ranch home in Santa
  Monica.   Hobbies 46:32 Ap '41

Cerf, B.   He made his country laugh.   Good H 125:40 N
  '47

Fort Worth unveils Will Rogers statue.   Am City 62:89
  D '47

Biography.   NCAB 33:2 '47

Will Rogers stamp.   Sr Schol 53:29 O 27 '48

Butterfield, R.   Legend of Will Rogers.   Life 27:78 Jl 18
  '49

Winterich, J. T.   Simon-pure Rogersana.   Sat R 32:19 O
  15 '49

Butterfield, R.   Legend of Will Rogers, abridged.   Read
  Digest 55:31 N '49

Will's playmates.   Life 28:25 Ja 23 '50

Will Rogers: American legend.   Coronet 27:133 Ja '50

Our country is richer because of their lives.   Instructor
  59:23 My '50

Myers, D.   Will Rogers' home town.   Holiday 9:73 Ap '51

Bridges, S. R.   I managed presidents; as told to K. Singer.   S. Atlan Q 50:313 Jl '51

Best of Will Rogers' political wisecracks; excerpt from
  How we elect our presidents.   Colliers 129:18 Ja 26 '52

Debus, A. G.   Recordings of Will Rogers.   Hobbies 60:
  30 Ja '56

Maheffey, J. Q.   How Will Rogers changed my life.
  Read Digest 69:143 Ag '56

Cantor, E.   Most unforgettable character I've met.
  Read Digest 76:179 Mr '60

Will Rogers: wise words and (wise) cracks.   N. Y. Times
  Mag p35 Ag 7 '60

Amory, C.   America's most complete human document.
  Sat R 45:14 Ag 25 '62

I never met a man I didn't like.   Sr Schol 89:3 N 4 '66

ROLAND, GILBERT
  Ten things that make my heart beat faster.   Good H 142:
    202 Ap '56

ROLAND, RUTH
  Groves, G.   A real vaudeville equilibrist.   Photop 15-5:

66 Ap '19
St. Johns, A. R.   Just a good business man.   Photop
   22-3:49 Ag '22
Geltzer, G.   Ruth Roland.   Films In Review 11-9:537 N
   '60
Smith, F. L.   Ruth Roland.   Films In Review 11-10:628
   D '60

ROMAN, RUTH
   Lovely Ruth.   Am Mag 148:109 N '49
   Rapid rise of Ruth Roman.   Life 28:51 My 1 '50
   Hopper, H.   The sexiest girl in town.   Photop 38-3:34
      S '50
   Second self.   Am Mag 150:112 O '50
   Kantor, S.   Roman history.   Photop 39-1:36 Ja '51
   Hine, A.   People and prospects.   Holiday 9:21 F '51
   Blades of terror.   Coronet 29:90 F '51
   Hill, G.   Hollywood's Roman candle.   Colliers 127:26 Mr
      17 '51
   Roman, R.   Miracle in Boston.   Photop 40-1:51 Jl '51
   Aldrich, H. K.   Film listing.   Films In Review 20-7:455
      Ag /S '69

ROMERO, CESAR
   Proctor, K.   Hail, Cesar!   Photop 49-6:36 Je '36
   Romero, C.   What's wrong with dancing?   Photop 53-11:
      20 N '39
   Hall, G.   Empty bridal suite.   Photop 19-1:36 Je '41
   Peters, S.   My Hollywood friends.   Photop 28-6:62 My '46
   Wood, C.   TV personalities biographical sketchbook.
      TV Personalities p14 '57
   See, C.   He tells it like it was.   TV Guide 16-50:18 D
      14 '68

ROONEY, MICKEY
   Baskette, K.   Mickey, the McCoy.   Photop 52-10:71 O '38
   Mickey's old man.   Time 34:46 Ag 28 '39
   Waterbury, R.   How Andy Hardy reformed Mickey Rooney.
      Photop 54-1:8 Ja '40
   America's favorite movie actor steals the show at Presi-
      dent's birthday ball.   Life 8:19 F 12 '40
   Success story.   Time 35:84 Mr 18 '40
   MacKaye, M.   Mighty atoms of Hollywood.   Ladies Home
      J 57:19 S '40
   Brady, T.   No. 1 boy of filmdom.   N. Y. Times Mag p8
      Ja 12 '41
   Hamilton, S.   Mickey Rooney picks a wife.   Photop 20-4:

26 Mr '42

Van Ryn, F. Alias Andy Hardy. Read Digest 40:47 Ap
'42

Kahn, E. J. Jr. Andy Hardy comes to camp. New
Yorker 18:55 Je 13 '42

Hamilton, S. Heartbreak for Mickey Rooney. Photop 22-
1:28 D '42

Biography. Cur Bio '42

Picture of the week. Life 20:37 Ap 29 '46

Frank, S. Hollywood's fabulous brat. Sat Eve Post 220:
40 D 6 '47

Shorty. Time 51:63 Ap 5 '48

Jacobi, F. Jr. Alias. New Yorker 25:92 My 7 '49

Parsons, L. O. Cosmopolitan movie citations. Cosmop
136:6 Je '54

TV's Mickey Rooney. TV Guide 2-36:4 S 4 '54

Rooney rumpus. Newsweek 44:38 S 6 '54

Andy Hardy grows up. TV Guide 5-19:8 My 11 '57

Rooney on the run. Newsweek 49:107 My 13 '57

Harris, E. Remarkable comeback of Mickey Rooney.
McCalls 84:52 S '57

Ups and downs of Mickey Rooney. Look 21:152 D 10 '57

Wood, C. TV personalities biographical sketchbook.
TV Personalities p146 '57

Pollock, L. I'm going to quit acting. Photop 53-3:39 Mr
'58

Slipped Mickey. Time 74:70 D 14 '59

Judy and Mickey reunited. Life 55:47 Jl 19 '63

Raddatz, L. A driving and driven little man. TV Guide
11-33:5 Ag 17 '63

Biography. Cur Bio 26:33 S '65
Same. Cur Bio Yrbk 1965:346 '65

Rooney, M. I. E. an autobiography; excerpts. Look 29:
133 O 19 '65

Epstein, J. After Andy Hardy. Commentary 43:94 Mr
'67

ROSAY, FRANÇOISE
Parisian stage celebrates return of a favorite. Theatre
Arts 29:675 D '45
Mme Rosay. New Yorker 36:25 F 11 '61

ROSENBLOOM, MAXIE
Reynolds, Q. Sing, champ, sing. Colliers 93:20 Je 2
'34
Crichton, K. Who's a bum? Colliers 103:13 F 18 '39

ROSS, KATHARINE
  DePaolo, R.   Sudden stardom of the graduate girl.   Life
    64:54A Mr 1 '68
  Champlin, C.   It's all slightly frightening and it's not
    going to last.   McCalls 95:88 Ap '68
  Ehrlich, H.   Katharine Ross; the elegant tomboy.   Look
    33:33 Je 10 '69
  Furth, G.   Katharine Ross: post graduate.   After Dark
    11-4:42 Ag '69

ROSS, SHIRLEY
  Reynolds, Q.   Hollywood sweepstakes.   Colliers 102:21
    D 24 '38

ROSSI-DRAGO, ELEANORA
  Which is glamour?   Colliers 131:34 Ja 3 '53

ROWLANDS, GENA
  Broadway love story.   Look 21:62 Je 11 '57
  Picture of a picture.   TV Guide 9-38:20 S 23 '61
  She was too much of a good thing.   TV Guide 10-7:15 F 17 '62

RUBENS, ALMA
  Gray, J. A.   The girl on the cover.   Photop 13-3:93 F '18
  Howe, H.   Meet the duchess!   Photop 24-2:39 Jl '23
  Quirk, J. R.   Hollywood's greatest true love story.   Photop
    37-5:38 Ap '30
  Collins, F. L.   Four women who suffered.   Good H 95:
    193 Jl '32

RUGGLES, CHARLIE
  Kennedy, J. B.   Rolling stone.   Colliers 88:14 D 12 '31
  Page, A.   He wields the scissors.   Photop 43-5:48 Ap '33
  Lynn, H.   Mama loves papa.   Photop 44-4:40 S '33
  Hamilton, S.   We want a divorce.   Photop 47-3:46 F '35
  Morehouse, W.   Charlie comes home.   Theatre Arts 43:
    56 Jl '59
  Couple of agile codgers.   Life 49:61 O 17 '60
  About a veteran.   Newsweek 57:100 My 29 '61

RUICK, BARBARA
  Ford, E.   Elopement.   Photop 44-5:80 N '53

RULE, JANICE
  First steps up a familiar ladder.   Life 30:78 Ja 8 '51
  Biographical sketch.   Theatre Arts 37:28 O '53
  Realism is a nasty word.   TV Guide 8-44:24 O 29 '60

Jennings, C. R. Golden Rule. Sat Eve Post 237:72 Je
13 '64

RUMAN, SIG
Obit. Time 89:90 F 24 '67
Screen World 19:239 '68
Heffer, B. J. Letter, inc. filmog. Films In Review 20-
6:388 Je/Jl '69

RUSH, BARBARA
Rogers, M. The dangerous years. Photop 42-6:44 D '52
Leon, R. Hunters' paradise. Photop 44-5:60 N '53
Hunter, J. So nice to come home to. Photop 45-3:46 Mr
'54
Johnson, H. Barbara's shining hour. Photop 46-3:51 S
'54
Rush, B. George Nader and the marriage question.
Photop 49-5:40 My '56
Rush, B. Brando--the young lion. Films & Filming 4-
6:10 Mr '58
Miss Barbara Rush dialectician. TV Guide 7-6:20 F 7 '59
Hobson, D. No tears for Miss Rush. TV Guide 16-45:
18 N 9 '68

RUSSELL, GAIL
Eaton, H. Gingham girl with sequins. Photop 27-1:58
Je '45
Hamilton, S. Our Gail is growing up. Photop 28-4:64
Mr '46
Russell, G. My kind of Guy. Photop 29-3:41 Ag '46
Hamilton, S. Open letter to Gail Russell. Photop 31-6:
66 N '47
Swanson, P. The story of Guy Madison's heartbreak mar-
riage. Photop 45-3:42 Mr '54
Waterbury, R. Gail Russell: a woman reborn. Photop
49-3:48 Mr '56
Vermilye, J. Gail Russell; inc. filmog. Films In Re-
view 12-8:499 O '61
Obit. Screen World 13:226 '62

RUSSELL, JANE
1941's best new star prospect. Life 10:42 Ja 20 '41
Tomboy. Am Mag 131:75 Ap '41
Jane Russell can be seen everywhere but in a movie.
Life 12:8 Ap 13 '42
Emerson, B. Heart affair. Photop 22-2:20 Ja '43
Reid, A. Jane does a movie. Colliers 115:70 Ja 13 '45

Bob Waterfield, actress Jane Russell's husband.   Life
   19:49 D 17 '45
This week: Jane Russell.   Time 47:98 Mr 25 '46
Sammis, F. R.   The case against The outlaw.   Photop
   29-4:34 S '46
Maxwell, E.   The girl in The outlaw.   Photop 29-4:37 S
   '46
Jane Russell story.   Coronet 27:107 Mr '50
Zeitlin, I.   Just plain Jane.   Photop 38-3:48 S '50
Wheeler, L.   Skytop house.   Photop 41-1:50 Ja '52
Maxwell, E.   Jane Russell's fight for her British Tommy.
   Photop 42-3:36 S '52
Fusses over ladies and a ladies' man.   Life 36:24 Ja 11
   '54
Leon, R.   Handle with care.   Photop 45-1:26 Ja '54
Ott, B.   Jane Russell's happiest year.   Photop 45-6:64
   Je '54
St. Johns, E.   Do Lord . . . do Lord!   Cosmop 137:270
   '54
Russell, J.   Gentlemen prefer brains.   Photop 46-6:58
   D '54
Trouble over torsos; picture advertising Underwater and
   underwater cover for Colliers.   Life 38:38 Mr 7 '55
Phillips, D.   Move over for Jane Russell.   Photop 47-6:
   67 Je '55
Downing, H.   Happy-go-lucky firebrand.   Photop 48-6:62
   D '55
Wise, E.   The terrible tempered temptress.   Photop 49-
   6:62 Je '56
Phillips, D.   The shape they're in.   Photop 52-5:44 N '57
Hagen, R.   Jane Russell, inc. filmog.   Films In Review
   14-4:226 Ap '63
Where are they now?   Newsweek 70:22 N 13 '67

RUSSELL, JOHN
   Don't be a villain they warned him.   TV Guide 6-28:28 Jl
      12 '58
   He had all the expressions of a rock.   TV Guide 7-30:17
      Jl 25 '59

RUSSELL, ROSALIND
   Biographical sketch.   Time 26:54 N 4 '35
   Pinchot, A.   Hard-working debutante.   Photop 50-2:58
      Ag '36
   Pringle, H. F.   Girl who bluffed.   Colliers 99:25 Ja 16
      '37
   Baskette, K.   Rahs for Roz!   Photop 53-10:70 O '39

Shadow.   Am Mag 130:90 N '40

Sharpe, H.   Roz the reckless.   Photop 18-5:34 Ap; 18-6:
58 My '41

Baskette, K.   Hollywood madcap.   Am Mag 132:20 O '41

Albert, D.   Who said women aren't men's equals.   Photop
21-5:38 O '42

Steele, J. H   Portrait of a best dressed woman.   Photop
22-5:49 Ap '43

Biography.   Cur Bio '43

Pierson, L. R.   She had to be me.   Photop 27-1:42 Je
'45

Russell, R.   Sister Kenny, the woman I know.   Photop
30-1:72 D '46

Berch, B.   Laugh-long friends.   Photop 36-3:60 Ag '49

Rosalind Russell shows six slips that spoil the picture.
McCalls 80:36 Ja '53

Roz romps around Wonderful town.   Life 34:134 Mr 16
'53

Millstein, G.   When you are a star you glow.   N. Y.
Times Mag p22 Mr 29 '53

Comic spirit.   Time Mr 30 '53

Show stopper.   Theatre Arts 37:16 My '53

What I've learned about men.   Am Mag 156:18 Ag '53

Scheff, A.   Land, ham and platter; Barter theatre award.
Theatre Arts 37:84 Ag '53

Come back, all is forgiven.   Theatre Arts 37:22 S '53

What I've learned about men, abridged.   Read Digest 63:
27 N '53

Medal for Freddie.   Coronet 38:108 Jl '55

Kinney, H.   Visit with Rosalind Russell.   McCalls 82:6
S '55

Hubler, R. G.   Perils of Rosalind Russell.   Sat Eve Post
228:39 O 1 '55

Best advice I ever had.   Read Digest 68:173 F '56

Markel, H.   Visit with breathless Rosalind Russell.
N. Y. Times Mag p17 O 28 '56

Wise, wacky Auntie Mame.   Life 41:129 N 12 '56

Banton, T.   Amusing fashions from Auntie Mame.
Theatre Arts 41:70 F '57

Wenning, T. H.   This is the busiest star at her busiest.
Newsweek 49:67 My 13 '57

Wonderful wizardry of Roz.   Look 21:68 My 28 '57

My favorite Christmas present.   McCalls 85:10 D '57

Rosalind Russell.   TV Guide 6-48:8 N 29 '58

Rollicking Roz all over the place.   Life 45:103 D 1 '58

Whitcomb, J.   Auntie Roz.   Cosmop 145:16 D '58

I'm glad I didn't marry young; ed by L. David.   Read

Digest 74:75 F '59
Boy who got away. Seventeen 20:106 Je '61
Hyams, J. Rosalind Russell. Theatre Arts 45:20 Je '61
Russell, R. Kind of gal I am. Sat Eve Post 235:26 S
    29; 36 O 6; 72 O 13 '62
Eimeri, S. Can women be funny? Mlle 56:150 N '62
Indestructible Roz. Life 59:109 S 10 '65
Dear, dear teenagers. Seventeen 24:156 N '65
Frank Sinatra's $25,000 weekend. Ladies Home J 84:48
    Ja '67

RUSSELL, WILLIAM
Wood, C. TV personalities biographical sketchbook.
    TV Personalities p154 '57

RUTHERFORD, ANN
Girl friend. Am Mag 132:84 N '41
Brown, H. W. Strictly sentimental; home of Ann Ruther-
    ford. Bet Hom & Gard 20:32 N '41
Former Polly Benedict. Good H 147:44 N '58

RUTHERFORD, MARGARET
Anderson, D. Tea and crumpets with Margaret Ruther-
    ford. Theatre Arts 38:74 Ja '54
Personality of the month. Plays & Players 4-3:3 D '56
First rehearsal. New Yorker 36:21 S 3 '60
Smith, M. A visit with Margaret Rutherford. Theatre
    2-10:18 O '60
Mrs. John Bull ltd. Time 81:72 My 24 '63
Old girl still kicks up. Life 55:56 O 4 '63
Biography. Cur Bio 25:30 Ja '64
    Same. Cur Bio Yrbk 1964:383 '64
Princess Margaret. Newsweek 64:90A S 14 '64
Musel, R. The great ghost hunt of '64. TV Guide 12-
    47:22 N 21 '64
Margaret Rutherford goes after England's ghosts. Travel
    123:45 F '65

RYAN, EDDIE
Harris, E. Rooting for Eddie Ryan. Photop 26-3:51 F
    '45

RYAN, PEGGY
Jefferson, S. Irrepressible Ryan. Photop 24-4:58 Mr '44

RYAN, ROBERT
Dudley, F. Romancing with Ryan. Photop 24-5:50 Ap '44

Engelsman, N.   Backstage with us Ryans.   Parents Mag
    29:48 S '54
People of talent.   Sight & Sound 25-1:37 Sum '55
Nichols, M.   Robert Ryan--hero and heel.   Coronet 47:
    16 Ja '60
Personality of the month.   Films & Filming 7-10:5 Jl '61
Biography.   Cur Bio 24:14 D '63
    Cur Bio Yrbk 1963:365 '64
Stein, J.   Robert Ryan, inc. filmog.   Films In Review
    19-1:9 Ja '68

RYDER, ALFRED
    Business as usual.   Theatre Arts 44:2 N '60

SABU
Story of Sabu: from elephant boy to screen star.
Sr Schol 33:30 S 24 '38
Roberts, K. Civilizing Sabu of India. Photop 53-1:24
Ja '39
Bacon, R. L. Jungle-book boy. St N 66:23 Mr '39
Sabu and Lady. Sr Schol 40:2 F 9 '42
Obit. Time 82:94 D 13 '63
Illus Lond N 243:1001 D 14 '63
Newsweek 62:60 D 16 '63
Screen World 15:224 '64
Farewell little master of the universe. Kaleidoscope 2-
1:14 n. d.

ST. CLAIR, MALCOLM
Waterbury, R. Sex--with a sense of humor. Photop 30-
4:42 S '26

SAINT, EVA MARIE
Havemann, E. Breaking into television. Life 27:93 S
19b '49
Harvey, E. Saint on the waterfront. Colliers 133:86 Mr
19 '54
Love and gore on the docks. Life 37:45 Jl 19 '54
New star from Greenwich Village. Newsweek 44:78 Ag 2
'54
Bountiful, Broadway and Brando. TV Guide 2-15:8 Ap 9
'54
Mlle. merit awards. Mlle 40:63 Ja '55
Gehman, R. Eva Marie Saint--a new kind of star.
Cosmop 138:58 Mr '55
Biography. Cur Bio 16:54 Je '55
Same. Cur Bio Yrbk 1955:524 '56
Saint on a spree. Look 20:87 F 7 '56
Wood, C. TV personalities biographical sketchbook.
TV Personalities p67 '56
Ardmore, J. K. Making time for Darrell. Parents Mag
32:47 Je '57
Nichols, M. Willowy and willful. Coronet 42:8 O '57
Can actors be parents? Look 22:41 Ap 1 '58
Whitcomb, J. Saga of Exodus. Cosmop 149:12 N '60

ST. JOHN, AL
Obit. Screen World 15:224 '64

ST. JOHN, JILL
  March, B. Once upon a time. Photop 57-2:62 F '60
  Smoking toad. Time 82:47 S 27 '63
  Jill, the beautiful kook. Life 55:123 N 8 '63
  Lewis, R. W. Hollywood's carefree child. Sat Eve Post
    237:32 My 9 '64
  Raddatz, L. I was a woman at 6. TV Guide 12-40:12
    O 3 '64

SAKALL, S. Z.
  Obit. Time 65:78 F 21 '55
  Screen World 7:226 '56

SALE, CHIC
  Kelly, F. C. Chic Sale makes us laugh at ourselves.
    Am Mag 96:36 Jl '23
  Kennedy, J. B. We're all hicks; intv. Colliers 79:16 Mr
    19 '27
  Barry, B. Ah, there? It's Chic himself. Photop 43-1:
    76 D '32
  Obit. Pub W 130:2374 D 19 '36
  Hutchens, J. K. Note from Parnassus. N. Y. Herald
    T Bk R p2 D 19 '54

SALE, VIRGINIA
  Wren, S. Second Sale. Life 10:138 Je 9 '41

SALES, SOUPY
  Simple Simon pieman. Time 85:52 Ap 23 '65
  Schmidt, S. Prize always went to someone who sang
    Aida. Life 58:56 My 14 '65
  Man who is also a mouse. Life 58:49 My 14 '65
  Smith, W. J. Sales and the mouse. Commonweal 82:446
    Je 25 '65
  Miller, E. New York scene. Seventeen 24:30 S '65
  Biography. Cur Bio 28:26 Ja '67
    Same. Cur Bio Yrbk 1967:370 '68
  Hewes, H. Sales tacks. Sat R 50:51 F 11 '67
  Braun, S. Transmogrification of Soupy Sales. Esquire
    68:104 O '67

SALISBURY, MONROE
  Corliss, A. A good Indian but a live one. Photop 13-3:
    81 F '18

SALVATORI, RENATO
  Person of promise. Films & Filming 5-7:10 Ap '59

SANDERS, GEORGE
  Hall, G. George Sanders puts women in their place.
    Photop 21-1:36 Je '42
  Biographical sketch. Time 40:98 O 19 '42
  Riley, N. Sneers for Mr. Sanders. Colliers 110:21 N
    14 '42
  Foster, C. The strictly private life of George Sanders.
    Photop 23-4:53 S '43
  Biography. Cur Bio '43
  Sanders, G. Crime on my hands. Photop 25-6:34 N '44
  Eaton, H. Too well remembered. Photop 31-2:34 Jl '47
  Martin, P. He sneered his way to stardom. Sat Eve
    Post 224:32 Ag 18 '51
  Unfortunately one has to work. TV Guide 5-32:17 Ag 10
    '57
  Wood, C. TV personalities biographical sketchbook.
    TV Personalities p112 '57
  Actor with notions. Newsweek 55:101 Mr 28 '60
  Content with mediocrity. Time 75:49 Mr 28 '60
  Sanders, G. Memoirs of a professional cad; excerpt.
    Good H 150:63 Ap '60
  There's a lot to like about women. Good H 152:84 Ap '61

SANDS, DIANA
  Biography. Time 83:96 Je 5 '64
  Caston, S. Diana Sands: notes on a Broadway pussycat.
    Look 29:38 F 9 '65
  Owl and the pussycat. Ebony 20:98 F '65
  Wolff, A. Passion of Diana Sands. Look 32:71 Ja 9 '68

SANDS, JOHNNY
  Sands, J. Story of last year's winner. Photop 38-2:45
    Ag '50

SANDS, TOMMY
  He rocked 'em in his first role. TV Guide 5-16:22 Ap 20
    '57
  Teenage crush. Time 69:46 My 13 '57
  Storm over Sands. Life 42:92 Je 3 '57

SAUNDERS, JACKIE
  Corliss, A. The girl on the cover. Photop 12-3:92 Ag
    '17
  Evans, D. Grand crossing impressions. Photop 13-4:
    36 Mr '18

SAUNDERS, MARY JANE
New marker.   Am Mag 147:113 Je '49

SAVAGE, ANN
McClelland, D.   Ann Savage, the perfect vixen, inc.
filmog.   Film Fan Mo 101:21 N '69

SAVALAS, TELLY
Raddatz, L.   Get me Savalas.   TV Guide 15-40:30 O 7
'67

SAXON, JOHN
Churchill, R. & Churchill, B.   We made him a star.
Photop 52-4:47 O '57
Downing, H.   You can't go home again.   Photop 53-4:78
Ap '58
Johnson, H.   Johnny lives with us.   Photop 54-4:51 O '58
Borie, M.   Why Johnny doesn't go for Sandra.   Photop
54-5:59 N '58
Christy, G.   The day Johnny Saxon cried.   Photop 55-3:
46 Mr '59
Anderson, N.   Boy is he stuck on himself.   Photop 56-5:
49 N '59
Nichols, M.   Sinvasion.   Coronet 48:14 My '60
Lee, E.   Why I can't marry Vicki Thal.   Photop 58-2:8
Ag '60

SCALA, GIA
Arnold, M.   Child of sorrow.   Photop 53-2:60 F '58
Lyle, J.   Gia Scala tries to take her own life.   Photop
54-5:54 N '58

SCARDON, PAUL
Obit.   Screen World 6:225 '55

SCHELL, MARIA
Honeyed newcomer.   Newsweek 50:100 Jl 15 '57
Tears pay off for Maria.   Life 43:99 Jl 15 '57
Golden look.   Time 70:40 D 30 '57
Slater, L.   McCalls visits.   McCalls 85:6 Mr '58
There is always the challenge.   TV Guide 7-19:12 My 9
'59
Stepping into big shoes.   Newsweek 55:78 Ap 18 '60
Miller, E.   Oh, for the life of an actress.   Seventeen
20:104 Mr '61
Biography.   Cur Bio 22:40 Je '61
Same.   Cur Bio Yrbk 1961:411 '62

Redbook dialogue. Redbook 117:46 Jl '61
Ross, L. Player. New Yorker 37:100 O 28 '61
Meltsir, A. Ocean of death. Photop 67-2:52 F '65

SCHELL, MAXIMILIAN
  Maximilian Schell. Theatre 2-10:46 O '60
  Other Schell. Time 79:48 Ja 19 '62
  Miller, E. Actor, actor burning bright. Seventeen 21:
    136 Ap '62
  Skolsky, S. Maximilian. Photop 61-4:56 Ap '62
  Academy Award winner. Look 26:144 My 22 '62
  Biography. Cur Bio 23:15 D '62
    Same. Cur Bio Yrbk 1962:373 '63
  Biography. Am Ann 1963:591 '63
  Hoffman, J. The kiss that brought the cops. Photop 65-
    2:72 F '64
  Schell's Hamlet. Newsweek 72:90 Ag 19 '68

SCHILDKRAUT, JOSEPH
  Evans, D. The future great actor. Photop 20-6:22 N '22
  Larkin, M. What is it? Photop 36-1:34 Je '29
  Biography. Cur Bio 17:52 Ap '56
    Same. Cur Bio Yrbk 1956:550 '57
  Obit. Time 83:68 Ja 31 '64
    Newsweek 63:53 F 3 '64
    Cur Bio 25:29 Mr '64
    Cur Bio Yrbk 1964:391 '64
    Screen World 16:225 '65

SCHNEIDER, JAMES
  Obit. Screen World 19:239 '68

SCHNEIDER, ROMY
  Star. Newsweek 51:106 F 10 '58
  Hamilton, J. Romy Schneider: she gave up royalty to be-
    come a woman. Look 26:38 S 11 '62
  Jades' apprentice. Time 80:38 D 14 '62
  Lovely Romy goes home. Life 54:45 Je 14 '63
  Jennings, C. R. Romy Schneider. Sat Eve Post 236:36
    N 23 '63
  Talese, G. Arrivederci, Romy. Esquire 60:112 N '63
  Biography. Cur Bio 26:30 Ja '65
    Same. Cur Bio Yrbk 1965:369 '65
  Tornabene, L. Tomorrow's stars. Good H 160:24 Mr '65

SCOFIELD, PAUL
  Cobb, J. Promise and the achievement. Theatre Arts

33:4 Je '49
Hobson, H. Paul Scofield: a rising actor. C S Mon
    Mag p15 Jl 8 '50
His name remains in lights. Plays & Players 2-4:5 Ja
    '55
Personality of the month. Plays & Players 3-3:5 D '55
Whittaker, H. England's great young virtuoso actor.
    Show 1-2:70 N '61
Pumphrey, A. Scofield. Theatre Arts 45:15 N '61
Man for all styles of acting. N.Y. Times Mag p35 D 3
    '61
Talk with a star. Newsweek 58:78 D 4 '61
British invasion. Time 78:64 D 15 '61
This season's man. New Yorker 38:26 Mr 24 '62
Biography. Cur Bio 23:35 Mr '62
    Same. Cur Bio Yrbk 1962:379 '63
Paul Scofield. Plays & Players 10-3:17 D '62
Barnes, C. The faces of Scofield. Plays & Players 10-
    4:15 Ja '63
Biography. Am Ann 1963:591 '63
Introverted Englishman. Time 89:68 Ja 6 '67
Biography. Brit Bk Yr 1968:161 '68

SCOTT, GEORGE C.
Talk with a star. Newsweek 55:60 Ja 11 '60
Harrity, R. Make-believe murder. Cosmop 148:14 Mr
    '60
Balch, J. George C. Scott. Theatre Arts 44:10 Je '60
Heavy star. Time 79:59 F 23 '62
Talk with actor Scott. Newsweek 60:52 Jl 2 '62
Don Quixote on Broadway. Look 26:87 N 6 '62
Davidson, B. Great Scott. Sat Eve Post 236:88 N 16 '63
Schickel, R. I've been just as obnoxious as humanly pos-
    sible. TV Guide 11-48:16 N 30 '63
Efron, E. Who killed Neil Brock? TV Guide 12-13:7 Mr
    28 '64
The show is over, but the actor is still fuming. TV
    Guide 12-29:18 Jl 18 '64
Sorry about that. Esquire 64:208 D '65
Risk actor cuts loose. Life 64:37 Mr 8 '68

SCOTT, LIZABETH
Marshall, J. Not like the movies. Colliers 116:59 Ag 18 '45
Shipp, C. She's impact. Photop 28-2:56 Ja '46
Deere, D. Saga of Liz. Photop 28-5:48 Ap '46
Campbell, K. Intensely, Lizabeth Scott. Photop 29-6:43
    N '46

Perkins, L. Photolife of Lizabeth Scott. Photop 31-2:
58 Jl '47
Scott, L. Don't misunderstand me. Photop 32-2:34 Ja
'48
Lancaster, B. Golden Lizzie. Photop 32-6:42 My '48

SCOTT, MARTHA
Tributary to professional. Theatre Arts 22:529 Jl '38
Reynolds, Q. Hollywood sweepstakes. Colliers 102:21
D 24 '38
Typical small-town girl. Life 8:56 My 27 '40
Hilton, J. Martha knows best. Photop 54-11:18 N '40
Crichton, K. Great Scott. Colliers 106:12 D 7 '40
Greene, J. D. Girl next door. Am Mag 130:11 D '40
Waterbury, R. I'm going to be somebody. Photop 19-3:
38 Ag; 19-4:56 S '41
Stage reclaims its own. Theatre Arts 38:30 Mr '54

SCOTT, PIPPA
Mother was an actress. TV Guide 8-14:28 Ap 2 '60

SCOTT, RANDOLPH
Grant, E. The rise of Randolph Scott. Photop 48-2:39
Jl '35
Franchey, J. R. You can't count him out! Photop 19-6:
52 N '41
Steele, J. H. Portrait of an easy listener. Photop 24-4:
51 Mr '44
Groat, R. F. Randolph Scott, inc. filmog. Films In Re-
view 18-10:663 D '67

SCOTT, ZACHARY
Asher, J. The name is Zach Scott. Photop 28-4:56 Mr
'46
Dreier, H. The house that Zach built. Photop 36-4:52
S '49
Obit. Time 86:104 O 15 '65
Newsweek 66:79 O 18 '65
Screen World 17:241 '66

SCOURBY, ALEXANDER
Biography. Cur Bio 26:37 Jl '65
Same. Cur Bio Yrbk 1965:378 '65
Voice from Brooklyn. Time 91:58 Mr 15 '68

SEARL, JACKIE
Smile when you call him 'Curly.' TV Guide 10-32:20

Ag 11 '62

SEARS, HEATHER
Ott, B. Here's Heather.   Photop 53-2:36 F '58

SEBASTIAN, DOROTHY
Albert, K. Little Alabam.   Photop 36-2:29 Jl '29
Obit.   Time 69:106 Ap 22 '57
   Screen World 9:225 '58

SEBERG, JEAN
Dragnet for new Saint Joan.   Life 41:119 O 29 '56
A Jean becomes a Joan.   Life 41:120 O 29 '56
Jean becomes Joan.   Look 21:104 Mr 5 '57
St. Joan really burns.   Life 42:138 Mr 11 '57
Millstein, G. Evolution of a new Saint Joan. N. Y.
   Times Mag p28 Ap 7 '57
Eustis, H. McCalls visits Saint Joan.   McCalls 84:10
   Ap '57
Galbreth, W. H. Jean Seberg pays tribute to her teachers
   for her success.   Midland Sch 71:15 My '57
Ott, B. The trials of Jean.   Photop 51-6:50 Je '57
Ott, B. Sprite with spunk.   Photop 52-6:33 D '57
Nichols, M. Bobby sox to hard knocks.   Coronet 43:12
   F '58
Seberg, J. We fell in love on a Saturday night.   Photop
   54-2:61 Ag '58
Film Cinderella's Iowa wedding.   Life 45:131 S 22 '58
Johns, C. Ooh! I want everyone to know I got my wish.
   Photop 54-6:39 D '58
Missing Miss Seberg.   Newsweek 56:84 O 3 '60
Ginna, R. E. Jean Seberg.   Horizon 4:81 My '62
Roddy, J. Restyling of Jean Seberg.   Look 26:45 Jl 3 '62
Miller, E. Jean Seberg revisited.   Seventeen 22:130 Mr
   '63
Innocence abroad.   Newsweek 61:94 My 6 '63
Hamill, P. Jean Seberg.   Sat Eve Post 236:22 Je 15 '63
Under the locusts; Lilith on location.   New Yorker 39:23
   Ag 17 '63
LaBadie, D. W. Everybody's Galatea.   Show 3-8:76 Ag
   '63
Biography.   Cur Bio 27:32 Ap '66
   Same.   Cur Bio Yrbk 1966:360 '67
Roman, M. Lively arts; intv.   Sr Schol 93:23 N 15 '68
Nymphs in a home movie.   Time 92:110 D 6 '68

SEDGWICK, JOSIE
  Cole, J. Twixt Josephine and Joe. Photop 14-3:42 Ag '18

SEGAL, GEORGE
  Guerin, A. Happy to be a king.   Life 59:141 N 19 '65

SEGAL, VIVIENNE
  Where are they now?   Newsweek 58:12 N 27 '61

SELLERS, PETER
  Personality of the month.   Films & Filming 5-8:5 My '59
  Waggoner, W. H.   Arrival of Sellers.   N. Y. Times Mag
    p64 Mr 27 '60
  Sellers, P. A serious look at laughter.   Films & Film-
    ing 6-6:7 Mr '60
  Zinsser, W. K. Young man riding high.   Life 48:63 Je
    20 '60
  Talk with a star.   Newsweek 55:113 My 9 '60
  People are talking about. . . Vogue 135:107 Je '60
  Biography.   Cur Bio 21:24 D '60
    Same.   Cur Bio Yrbk 1960:371 '61
  Tynan, K. Nondescript genius.   Holiday 29:127 Je '61
  Sellers season.   N. Y. Times Mag p80 Ap 1 '62
  Shy man.   Time 79:74 Ap 27 '62
  Sellers, P. In who's who of the critics.   Films & Film-
    ing 8-8:17 My '62
  People are talking about. . . Vogue 140:189 S 1 '62
  McVay, D. One man band.   Films & Filming 9-8:44 My
    '63
  Lewis, F. Ubiquitous, multifarious Sellers.   N. Y.
    Times Mag p20 Je 23 '63
  Krantz, J. This man says he's Peter Sellers.   McCalls
    90:42 Ag '63
  World of Sellers.   Newsweek 62:90 S 9 '63
  Miller, E. Which one's real? Seventeen 22:48 N '63
  Redbook dialogue: Peter Sellers and Carol Burnett.
    Redbook 122:60 D '63
  Brossard, C. Weird world of Peter Sellers.   Look 28:
    M5 Ja 28 '64
  Alexander, S. Sellers' last role--almost.   Life 57:27
    Jl 31 '64
  Ardmore, J. His bride's deathwatch.   Photop 66-1:46 Jl
    '64
  Peter Sellers talks to teens.   Seventeen 23:92 Jl '64
  Come on out, Pete.   Newsweek 64:98 N 2 '64
  Fawcett, I. Now I'm having a baby.   Photop 67-1:51 Ja
    '65

Champlin, C.   Peter's $3 million party.   Life 64:60A
   Mr 15 '68

SENNETT, MACK
   Lindsay, F.   Movie spirit of the Keystone comedies.
     Sunset 39:34 D '17
   Wagner, R.   Dean of custard college; intv.   Colliers 80:
     8 O 29; 13 N 5 '27
   Beatty, J.   Anything for a laugh; intv.   Am Mag 111:40
     Ja '31
   Inside story told by Mack Sennett's rise to fame.   News-
     week 4:26 O 27 '34
   Pie in art.   Nation 139:524 N 7 '34
   Fowler, G.   Father Goose; the story of Mack Sennett.
     Sat R 11:270 N 10 '34
   Custard-pie classics.   N. Y. Times Mag p28 Je 8 '47
   Agee, J.   Comedy's greatest era.   Life 27:70 S 5 '49
   Pryor, T. M.   Then and now.   N. Y. Times Mag p27 F
     22 '53
   Custard pies.   Newsweek 44:106 D 6 '54
   Knight, A.   Era of the great comedians.   Sat R 37:20
     D 18 '54
   Seldes, G.   Memoirs of a pie-throwing man.   New Repub
     131:20 D 20 '54
   Mack Sennett's at it.   Newsweek 52:90 O 6 '58
   Galaxy of present-day stars in a classic Mack Sennett
     chase.   Life 45:148 D 22 '58
   Obit.   Illus Lond N 237:859 N 12 '60
     Newsweek 56:28 N 14 '60
     Time 76:104 N 14 '60
     Am Ann 1961:663 '61
     Brit Bk Yr 1961:520 '61
     Screen World 12:225 '61
   Giroux, R.   Mack Sennett.   Films In Review 19-10:593 D
     '68; 20-1:1 Ja '69

SERNAS, JACQUES
   The Hollywood story.   Photop 51-4:62 Ap '57

SEVERN, BILLY
   Film-star family.   Life 22:133 Mr 10 '47

SEYMOUR, ANNE
   Actress Anne Seymour collects angels.   Am Home 59:34
     D '57

SEYMOUR, CLARINE
  Robbins, E. M. Two strange women. Photop 16-3:86 Ag '19
  Shannon, B. An unfinished story. Photop 18-2:81 Jl '20

SEYMOUR, DAN
  Wood, C. TV personalities biographical sketchbook.
  TV Personalities p75 '56

SHAIFFER, HOWARD CHARLES "TINY"
  Obit. Screen World 19:239 '68

SHANNON, PEGGY
  Kish, F. Peggy from Pine Bluff. Photop 43-1:69 D '32
  Obit. Cur Bio '41

SHARIF, OMAR
  Arabian knight. Time 81:66 F 1 '63
  Tornabene, L. Tomorrow's stars. Good H 160:24 Mr
    '65
  Random, E. I'm what's happening, baby! Photop 73-5:
    66 My '68
  His illegitimate child. Photop 75-1:37 Ja '69
  Tornabene, L. Walking with Omar Sharif. McCalls 96:
    42 Ap '69

SHATNER, WILLIAM
  Fessier, M. Jr. No one ever upsets the star. TV Guide
    14-42:30 O 15 '66
  His marriage problems. Photop 72-2:14 Ag '67
  Bowen, T. The day I knew I could kill. Photop 72-6:17
    D '67
  Higgins, R. The intergalactic golden boy. Photop 16-25:
    12 Je 22 '68
  Was this divorce necessary? Photop 74-1:48 Jl '68

SHAW, MONTAGUE
  Obit. Screen World 20:239 '69

SHAW, OSCAR
  Leamy, H. Five o'clock boy. Colliers 81:16 My 5 '28
  Obit. Screen World 19:239 '68

SHAW, VICTORIA
  Three miffed misses frame frustration. Life 40:22 Ap
    23 '56
  Ott, B. Crazy kid makes good. Photop 50-2:54 Ag '56
  Whitcomb, J. Speed record for stardom. Cosmop 143:

19 Ag '57
Borie, M. Did I remember to tell you I love you?
Photop 56-2:50 Ag '59
Christy, G. 48 hours to live. Photop 56-4:32 O '59
Smith, R. Why do you love me? Photop 57-3:26 Mr '60
Anderson, N. Breakdown. Photop 59-3:36 Mr '61
Hollywood love triangle. Photop 66-5:60 N '64

SHAW, WINI
Hagen, R. Wini Shaw, intv., inc. filmog. Screen Facts
17:28 n. d.

SHAWN, DICK
One of the better unknowns. Look 18:47 O 19 '54
People on the way up. Sat Eve Post 235:28 Ap 28 '62

SHEARER, MOIRA
Pin-up ballerina. Time 52:46 Jl 5 '48
Biography. Cur Bio 11:51 Ja '50
Same. Cur Bio Yrbk 1950:530 '51
Again it is Shearer. N. Y. Times Mag p22 Ap 1 '51
Many Moiras. N. Y. Times Mag p46 Jl 25 '54
Clarke, M. Moira Shearer: dancer into actress. Dance
Mag 30:16 My '56
Belle that helped toll defeat for Tories. Life 44:40 F 24
'48
Return, the rapture. Newsweek 56:80 Jl 11 '60
Barnes, C. Moira Shearer today. Dance Mag 36:48 My
'62
Newsmakers. Newsweek 71:36 Ja 1 '68

SHEARER, NORMA
Howe, H. What is Norma Shearer's charm for men?
Photop 28-1:72 Je '25
Robertson, W. S. Canada's own film star. Canad Mag
66:8 N '26
Ogden, E. Will Norma Shearer retire? Photop 38-3:47
Ag '30
Hamilton, S. Telling on Norma. Photop 41-4:54 Mr '32
Shirley, L. Why Norma Shearer says let the honeymoon
wait. Photop 43-3:50 F '33
Schallert, E. Norma's love comes first. Photop 43-6:
31 My '33
Maxwell, V. It's a grand adventure. Photop 44-5:75 O
'33
Lee, B. The real first lady of films. Photop 46-1:28
Jl '34

Shawell, J. Norma Shearer's perfect marriage. Pict R
  36:4 O '34
Rankin, R. Let's be civilized about sex. Photop 47-1:
  45 D '34
Willson, D. Lady you know. Delin 126:50 Ap '35
I'm tame as a lion; autobiography. Am Mag 120:58 Jl '35
Manners, D. How Norma Shearer faces the future.
  Photop 50-6:36 D '36
Hayes, B. The man who guides Norma Shearer's father-
  less children. Photop 51-11:20 N '37
Baskette, K. A queen comes back. Photop 52-7:30 Jl
  '38
Willson, D. Norma Shearer returns; story of her part in
  Marie Antoinette. Good H 107:64 Ag '38
Willson, D. Norma Shearer's handful of memories.
  Photop 52-10:32 O '38
Hartley, K. Play truth or consequences with Norma
  Shearer. Photop 53-11:68 N '39
Jacobs, J. Norma Shearer; inc. filmog. Films In Re-
  view 11-7:390 Ag/S '60

SHEERER, WILL E.
  Brandon, F. M. Character actor supreme. Photop 4-4:
    45 S '13

SHEFFIELD, REGINALD
  Obit. Screen World 9:226 '58

SHERIDAN, ANN
  Seymore, H. Young love--Hollywood style. Photop 51-
    3:45 Mr '37
  Rankin, R. From ranch to riches. Photop 53-6:16 Je
    '39
  Crichton, K. Easy, thar, with our Clara Lou. Colliers
    104:18 Jl 22 '39
  Brent, G. Ann. Photop 54-9:19 S '40
  Blake, A. What Ann Sheridan learned in exile. Photop
    19-1:42 Je '41
  Cheatham, M. George Brent tells: why Ann Sheridan
    and I won't marry. Photop 19-4:30 S '41
  Hall, G. Ann Sheridan's surprise marriage. Photop 20-
    4:28 Mr '42
  Mulvey, K. Real Sheridan. Womans H C 69:40 My '42
  Jefferson, S. Why Ann Sheridan and George Brent have
    separated. Photop 22-1:68 D '42
  Gwynne, A. & Sheridan, A. Uniform Date-iquette.
    Photop 23-3:36 Ag '43

Skolsky, S. "Annie" to all. Photop 23-6:36 N '43
Fletcher, A. W. Gay companions. Photop 24-4:27 Mr
'44
Marshall, J. Sheridan's ride. Colliers 120:26 Jl 19 '47
Howe, H. Sheridan preferred. Photop 31-5:58 O '47
Legacy. Newsweek 46:44 Ag 8 '55
Higgins, R. The oomph girl is 51. TV Guide 14-21:24
My 21 '66
Obit. Time 89:70 Ja 27 '67
Illus Lond N 250:12 Ja 28 '67
Newsweek 69:100 Ja 30 '67
Brit Bk Yr 1968:598 '68
Screen World 19:229 '68
Hagen, R. Ann Sheridan; inc. filmography; intv. Screen
Facts 14:entire issue n. d.

SHERMAN, LOWELL
Jamison, J. Does wickedness pay? Photop 39-3:33 F '31

SHERWOOD, MADELEINE
Whitney, D. It's not precisely Tennessee Williams.
TV Guide 17-18:24 My 3 '69

SHIELDS, ARTHUR
Playboy of the western world. New Yorker 25:21 F 18 '50

SHIRLEY, ANNE
(Also known as Dawn O'Day)
One of the few child stars who made adult comeback.
Life 8:77 My 8 '40
Berch, B. Romance--as planned. Photop 19-4:32 S '41
Crichton, K. Anne the angel. Colliers 109:18 Ja 17 '42
Hamilton, S. Love, honor and goodbye. Photop 20-5:31
Ap '42
Trotter, M. You belong together. Photop 21-1:39 Je '42
Fletcher, A. W. Deal yourself in on life. Photop 24-2:
40 Ja '44
Hine, A. Some of the newer Hollywood columnists are
improving the gossip--and the grammar--of the old
hands. Holiday 5:8 Ap '49

SHORE, DINAH
Noodler. Am Mag 131:83 Je '41
Dynamic Dinah. Time 40:65 O 19 '42
Biography. Cur Bio '42
Beatty, J. Hot whispers. Am Mag 135:132 Ap '43
Dinah for Shore. Newsweek 24:102 O 16 '44

Is there anything finer? Newsweek 29:72 Je 30 '47
Campbell, K. Dinah Shore and George Montgomery; San
    Fernando Valley home. Am Home 38:18 S '47
Montgomery, G. My hobby is my home. Womans H C
    76:64 F '49
Tables for two. New Yorker 25:69 F 4 '50
Johnson, G. Dinah Shore story. Coronet 33:92 N '52
Dinah's showcaser. Newsweek 40:54 D 8 '52
Lindsay, C. H. She's still winning her fight for happi-
    ness. Womans H C 80:32 F '53
Dinah Shore's TV art. Look 17:44 D 15 '53
Everybody loves Dinah. Womans H C 81:129 Ap '54
Montgomery, M. My mother and Dinah Shore; as told
    to M. L. Runbeck. Good H 138:56 My '54
Wood, C. TV personalities biographical sketchbook.
    TV Personalities p77 '54
Morehead, A. For fifteen years nobody finer. Cosmop
    139:44 Ag '55
Sharpshooting star. Newsweek 49:102 Ap 1 '57
Dinah goes glamorous. Look 21:145 Ap 30 '57
Rock beat. Dance Mag 31:58 Ag '57
Is there anyone finah? Time 70:60 D 16 '57
Martin, P. I call on Dinah Shore. Sat Eve Post 230:26
    O 19 '57
Shore, D. How I met my husband. McCalls 85:100 Ap
    '58
Cerf, P. Dinah Shore puzzles me. Good H 148:32 My
    '59
Hubler, R. G. Indestructible Dinah. Coronet 47:143 N
    '59
Tornabene, L. Miss Shore's TV wardrobe. Cosmop 147:
    60 N '59
Dual lives of Dinah. Life 48:73 F 1 '60
Eels, G. Dinah Shore. Look 24:90 D 6 '60
Schroeder, C. Dinah Shore: how a good wife failed.
    Good H 154:79 Ap '62
Biography. Cur Bio 27:36 D '66
    Same. Cur Bio Yrbk 1966:376 '67

SHORT, GERTRUDE
    Obit. Screen World 20:239 '69

SIDNEY, SYLVIA
    Melcher, E. Sylvia Sidney. Cinema Digest 1-11:10 O
        3 '32
    Maxwell, V. I'd never let my daughter be a star.
        Photop 45-6:60 My '32

Hamman, M.   Their lucky break.   Pict R 38:64 D '36
Albert, D.   No more impulses.   Photop 51-7:82 Jl '37
Roberts, K.   Tears by Sylvia.   Colliers 100:11 N 6 '37
Martin, F.   Portrait of Sylvia Sidney.   Life 19:61 S 10
    '45
Springer, J.   Sylvia Sidney, inc. filmog.   Films In Re-
    view 17-1:6 Ja '66

SIGNORET, SIMONE
    French star wins room at top.   Life 46:93 Je 22 '59
    Explosive Frenchman.   Newsweek 54:75 S 28 '59
    Berquist, L.   Simone Signoret: sex appeal grown up.
        Look 24:85 Ja 19 '60
    People are talking about . . .   Vogue 135:137 Mr 1 '60
    Subtle poison.   Time 75:44 Ap 4 '60
    How pink the stars.   Newsweek 55:30 Ap 18 '60
    Simone Signoret's moment of suspense.   Life 48:99 Ap 18
        '60
    Tozzi, R.   Simone Signoret.   Films In Review 11-5:310
        My '60
    Berquist, L.   Lives and loves of Simone Signoret.   Look
        24:66 Ag 30 '60
    Biography.   Cur Bio 21:26 D '60
    Same.   Cur Bio Yrbk 1960:381 '61
    Ross, L.   Player.   New Yorker 37:89 N 4 '61
    Biography.   Am Ann 1961:665 '61
    Redbook dialogue.   Redbook 118:50 Mr '62
    Simone Signoret on being under a director's spell.
        Films & Filming 8-9:11 Je '62
    A noted French actress looks at TV.   TV Guide 13-47:16
        N 20 '65
    Weinraub, B.   You can see that I'm not 20 years old.
        Sat Eve Post 240:39 F 25 '67

SILVERS, PHIL
    Top banana.   Newsweek 38:92 N 12 '51
    Clurman, H.   Punch and Judy.   New Repub 125:21 N 26
        '51
    Top banana.   Life 31:75 D 3 '51
    Gehman, R. B.   Comic's comic.   Theatre Arts 35:36 D
        '51
    Frank, S.   Refugee from burlesque.   Sat Eve Post 224:
        40 Mr 15 '52
    No sad sack, he.   TV Guide 3-44:4 O 29 '55
    At ease, men!   TV Guide 4-8:13 F 25 '56
    Goldberg, T.   Top banana to top kick.   Cosmop 140:
        123 F '56

He aims to please. Look 20:70 Ap ა '56
Samuels, C. Phil Silvers: TV's melancholy madcap.
   Coronet 39:133 Ap '56
Drury, M. Backstage with Phil Silvers. Colliers 137:
   40 My 11 '56
Bester, A. Meet the real Sergeant Bilko. Holiday 20:
   141 N '56
Wood, C. TV personalities biographical sketchbook.
   TV Personalities p129 '56
The reformation of Phil Silvers. TV Guide 5-33:17 Ag
   17 '57
Martin, P. I call on Phil Silvers. Sat Eve Post 230:
   28 S 7 '57
Biography. Cur Bio 18:29 D '57
   Same. Cur Bio Yrbk 1957:504 '58
Phil's happy gagmen. Newsweek 51:53 Ap 28 '58
Paul, D. Ooh what she said! ooh what he answered.
   Photop 54-1:52 Jl '58
Taps for Sergeant Bilko. TV Guide 7-20:5 My 16 '59
Just Polly and me. TV Guide 8-41:12 O 8 '60
Gehman, R. The scamp. TV Guide 11-40:10 O 5; 11-
   41:22 O 12 '63
Gillespie, A. Frenzied world of Phil Silvers. Good H
   158:30 Ja '64
Higgins, R. "The scamp" grows up. TV Guide 15-14:14
   Ap 8 '67

SIM, ALASTAIR
   Alpert, H. Our Mr. Sim Sat R 34:38 D 1 '51

SIMMONS, JEAN
   Olivier's Hamlet. Time 51:54 Je 28 '48
   Britain's busiest actress. Life 29:87 O 9 '50
   Waterbury, R. A toast to love. Photop 39-4:42 Ap '51
   Biography. Cur Bio 13:50 F '52
      Same. Cur Bio Yrbk 1952:542 '53
   Zeitlin, I. Trouble in paradise? Photop 42-6:38 D '52
   Murray, M. Why the Stewart Granger marriage won't
      fail. Photop 43-5:56 My '53
   Actress Simmons. Look 17:153 D 15 '53
   Howe, H. He kissed her--if only he hadn't. Photop 45-
      5:59 My '54
   Hopper, H. Happiness is a state of mind. Photop 46-
      1:42 Jl '54
   Jacobi, E. Sweet stuff. Photop 47-1:34 Ja '55
   Phillips, D. A doll's life with a guy. Photop 48-3:59
      S '55

Jean Simmons becomes a star.   Look 19:82 N 29 '55
Waterbury, R.   Confession of a husband in love.   Photop
    49-2:67 F '56
Manning, D.   They're expecting a living doll.   Photop 50-
    1:44 Jl '56
Reich, I.   Nothing in common.   Photop 55-2:50 F '29
Nichols, M.   Elmer Gantry comes to the screen.   Cosmop
    148:78 Mr '60
Nichols, M.   Blue jeans Simmons.   Coronet 48:18 My '60
Jennings, C. R.   Jean Simmons: the mouse becomes a
    cat.   Sat Eve Post 238:77 Ag 28 '65

SIMMS, GINNY
    Mulvey, K.   They all go for the farmer's daughter.
        Am Mag 136:28 N '43
    Where are they now?   Newsweek 69:22 Ap 17 '67

SIMON, SIMONE
    Smalley, J.   Simone Simon--pronounced problem child.
        Photop 51-1:22 Ja '36
    New French star stirs Hollywood.   Lit Digest 122:20 Ag
        29 '36
    Crichton, K.   Temper from Paris.   Colliers 99:11 Ap 3
        '37
    Smith, A. H.   Ditto ditto.   Cinema Arts 1-3:18 S '37

SIMPSON, RUSSELL
    Obit.   Screen World 11:224 '60

SINATRA, FRANK
    He can't read a note but he's dethroning Bing.   Newsweek
        21:62 Mr 22 '43
    Henderson, H. & Shaw, S.   Gift to the girls.   Colliers
        111:69 Ap 17 '43
    Frazier, G.   Frank Sinatra rose through voice that makes
        women swoon.   Life 14:55 My 3 '43
    That old sweet song.   Time 42:76 Jl 5 '43
    Swoon song.   Newsweek 22:80 Ag 16 '43
    Swooner-crooner.   Life 15:127 Ag 23 '43
    Long, J.   Sweet dreams and dynamite.   Am Mag 136:41
        S '43
    Parsons, L.   Fabulous Frank Sinatra.   Photop 23-6:28 N
        '43
    The voice.   Newsweek 22:94 D 20 '43
    Biography.   Cur Bio '43
    Sinatra, N.   It isn't all roses.   Photop 25-2:32 Jl '44
    Bliven, B.   Voice and the kids; phenomenon of mass

hysteria seen only two or three times in a century.
New Repub 111:592 N 6 '44

Sinatra, F.   If my daughter were 17.   Photop 25-6:32 N
'44

Bliven, B.   Voice and the kids; abridged.   Read Digest
46:12 Ja '45

Gould, L.   You and Frank Sinatra.   Photop 26-4:48 Mr
'45

La voce and the U. S. A.   Newsweek 26:90 Jl 23 '45

Sinatra, F.   I want to talk to you.   Photop 27-3:30 Ag;
27-4:49 S; 27-5:32 O '45

What's this about races?   Sr Schol 47:23 S 17 '45

Frank Sinatra in Gary.   Life 19:45 N 12 '45

Harris, E.   If you were Frank Sinatra's house guest.
Photop 28-2:58 Ja '46

Refuge from bobby-soxers.   Time 47:45 Ap 22 '46

Busted.   Newsweek 27:60 Ap 22 '46

Cartwright, H.   Revealing Mr. Sinatra.   Photop 28-6:70
My '46

Wittels, D. G.   Star-spangled octopus; how MCA acquired
Frank Sinatra.   Sat Eve Post 219:20 Ag 24 '46

Kahn, E. J Jr.   Phenomenon.   New Yorker 22:36 O 26;
37 N 2; 36 N 9 '46

Frankie's Robert soxers.   Newsweek 28:61 D 23 '46

Letter of the week.   New Repub 116:3 Ja 6 '47

Hamilton, S.   Happy New Year, Nancy Sinatra.   Photop
30-2:25 Ja '47

Words and music.   Time 49:44 Ap 21 '47

Parsons, L. O.   What's wrong with Sinatra?   Photop 30-
6:34 My '47

Harris, E.   Two men in Manhattan.   Photop 31-2:54 Jl
'47

Sold, American.   Newsweek 34:54 S 19 '49

Whimpering in the dark?   Time 56:47 Jl 31 '50

Sinatra, F.   I learned about TV the hard way.   TV Guide
4-21:16 My 26 '51

Maxwell, E.   The Gardner-Sinatra jigsaw.   Photop 40-1:
48 Jl '51

Mortimer, L.   Frank Sinatra confidential; gangsters in
the nightclubs.   Am Mer 73:29 Ag '51

Well, said Frankie, we finally made it.   Life 31:49 N 19
'51

Hopper, H.   Why Nancy Sinatra gave Frankie his freedom.
Photop 40-5:42 N '51

Fink, H.   I was there.   Photop 40-6:66 D '51

Warren, J.   New name for happiness.   Photop 41-2:45
F '52

Clarke, S. Why they are the battling Sinatras. Photop
    41-6:38 Je '52
From here to eternity. Colliers 132:28 Ag 7 '53
Corwin, J. Cease fire! Photop 44-6:33 D '53
Arnold, M. Lonesome on top of the world. Photop 45-2:
    58 F '54
Wilson, E. Stranger to happiness. . . Photop 54-4:44
    Ap '54
Back on top. Time 63:72 My 10 '54
Can Sinatra make good on TV? TV Guide 2-20:5 My 14
    '54
Wells, E. Rise and fall and rise again of Frank Sinatra.
    Good H 139:56 Ag '54
Touchy theme for Frank. Life 37:134 O 25 '54
Edwards, R. The pied piper of Hoboken. Photop 46-4:52
    O '54
Pops tops. Time 64:40 D 27 '54
U. S. star goes down under. Time 65:38 F 7 '55
I love secretaries! Coronet 37:38 Ap '55
Kid from Hoboken. Time 66:52 Ag 29 '55
Frankie says: TV racket's too tough! TV Guide 3-38:5
    S 17 '55
That guy Sinatra. Coronet 39:6 N '55
Sinatra, N. Jr. I swoon for Frank Sinatra. Photop 49-
    2:65 F '56
St. Johns, A. R. Nine lives of Frank Sinatra. Cosmop
    140:82 My '56
Weinman, M. High jinks in High society. Colliers 137:
    32 Je 8 '56
Taves, I. Frank Sinatra. Womans H C 83:38 My; 34 Je
    '56
Paramount piper. New Yorker 32:23 Ag 25 '56
Bolstad, H. The truth about Frank Sinatra's gang.
    Photop 50-3:54 S '56
Pryor, T. M. Rise, fall and rise of Frank Sinatra.
    N. Y. Times Mag p17 F 10 '57
Davidson, B. Life story of Frank Sinatra. Look 21:37
    My 14; 123 My 28; 84 Je 11 '57
Davidson, B. Talent, tantrams and torment. Look 21:36
    My 14 '57
Voice and payola. Time 70:76 S 9 '57
Solid-gold Sinatra. Newsweek 50:70 O 21 '57
Shanley, J. P. Television; special program on behalf of
    the Edsel car. America 98:118 O 26 '57
Lardner, J. Air. New Yorker 33:114 N 2 '57
Fulford, R. Sinatra with sweetening. New Repub 137:
    22 N 18 '57

Steele, J. H.   The man nobody knows.   Photop 52-5:68
  N '57
Harris, R.   The big rumor.   Photop 52-6:21 D '57
Wood, C.   TV personalities biographical sketchbook.
  TV Personalities p41 '57
Speaker: Frank Sinatra.   Subject: what is a woman?
  Photop 53-1:28 Ja '58
What's happening to Sinatra?   TV Guide 6-6:8 F 8 '58
Frankie in Madison.   Time 72:64 Ag 25 '58
With Sinatra in London.   Newsweek 52:48 N 3 '58
Bee volant.   Time 72:55 N 10 '58
Talk with a star.   Newsweek 54:84 Jl 6 '59
Idols team up on TV.   Life 48:103 My 16 '60
Gehman, R.   Enigma of Frank Sinatra.   Good H 151:60
  Jl '60
Biography.   Cur Bio 21:26 O '60
  Same.   Cur Bio Yrbk 1960:384 '61
Tracy, J.   Is it a thing--or is it a fling?   Photop 60-3:
  42 S '61
Hollywood set and the Kennedy family.   U. S. News 51:60
  O 16 '61
President's week.   Time 79:48 Ja 19 '62
Skolsky, S.   Why they must marry.   Photop 61-4:41 Ap
  '62
Innocent abroad.   Time 79:53 My 18 '62
Gideon, N.   Wedding bells won't jingle-o.   Photop 61-5:
  6 My '62
Sinatra-Leight: what gives?   Photop 62-5:48 N '62
Somers, A.   If Frank Sinatra were your father.   Photop
  63-4:32 Ap '63
Slobber, slobber.   Newsweek 62:96 S 23 '63
Oulahan, R. & Thompson, A. . . . and Sinatra tangles
  with the law.   Life 55:93 S 27 '63
Chairman of the board.   Newsweek 62:60 O 28 '63
Anthony, T.   Son defends his tie to gangsters.   Photop
  64-6:52 D '63
Robbins, F.   Nobody has a family like mine.   Photop 65-
  2:46 F '64
Carpozi, G.   Nightmare of being his son.   Photop 65-3:
  59 Mr '64
Newman, D.   Where the king of the world goes.   Esquire
  61:120 Ap '64
King of the birds.   Time 83:48 My 22 '64
Christy, G.   Frankie's kids.   Good H 158:80 Je '64
New role for Sinatra-san.   Life 57:80 Jl 3 '64
Richards, J.   The night he was arrested.   Photop 66-6:
  13 D '64

York, C. Sinatra to marry Mia Farrow. Photop 67-2:
14 F '65

Sinatra, F. Me and my music. Life 58:86 Ap 23 '65

Chairman of the board. Time 86:62 Jl 16 '65

Evelyn, M. Idol remembered. Esquire 64:84 Jl '65

Thompson, T. Seagoing soap opera of Sinatra. Life
59:34B Ag 20 '65

Voyage of the Southern Breeze. Time 86:64 Ag 20 '65

At sea with Sinatra. Newsweek 66:71 Ag 23 '65

Sinatra: where the action is. Newsweek 66:39 S 6 '65

No news is good news. Newsweek 66:88 N 29 '65

Bryson, J. Sinatra at fifty. Look 29:61 D 14 '65

Talese, G. Frank Sinatra has a cold. Esquire 65:89
Ap '66

Raddatz, L. The time of his life. TV Guide 14-20:15
My 14 '66

Somers, A. He's gotta marry her now. Photop 69-5:37
My '66

Fun couples. Newsweek 68:58 Jl 25 '66

Mia to Mrs. in four minutes. Life 61:46A Jl 29 '66

Ace, G. Boy meets girl. Sat R 49:6 Ag 13 '66

Scott, V. Nancy Sinatra talks about life with father.
Ladies Home J 83:83 S '66

Korall, B. Measure of Sinatra. Sat R 49:58 O 15 '66

Ferrer, J. M. 3rd. Sinatra special that's very. Life 61:
24 D 9 '66

Russell, R. Frank Sinatra's $25,000 weekend. Ladies
Home J 84:48 Ja '67

Scott, V. Mia Farrow's swinging life with Frank Sinatra.
Ladies Home J 84:84 My '67

Lees, G. Performance and the pair. Hi Fi 17:95 My '67

Action in Las Vegas. Time 90:101 S 22 '67

Render unto Caesars. Newsweek 70:32 S 25 '67

Hamilton, J. Working Sinatras. Look 31:86 O 31 '67

Newsmakers. Newsweek 70:52 D 4 '67

Martin, D. ed by O. Fallaci. Dean Martin talks about
his drinking, the Mafia, Frank Sinatra, women, Bobby
Kennedy. Look 31:78 D 26 '67

TV Christmas with the Martins and the Sinatras. Look
31:76 D 26 '67

Kerr, D. Why his pals wouldn't help him. Photop 72-6:
40 D '67

York, C. Why he was glad to let Mia go. Photop 73-
2:50 F '68

Ehrlich, H. Sinatra's English import. Look 32:71 Mr 19
'68

O'Brien, F. What they do to daughters. Photop 73-3:41

Mr '68

O'Brien, F. How she begged Sinatra. Photop 73-4:50
Ap '68

O'Brien, F. All about their children. Photop 74-1:50
Jl '68

Newquist, R. Sinatra power. McCalls 95:79 Jl '68

Hobson, D. How Sinatra did his thing. TV Guide 16-
47:29 N 23 '68

Korall, B. Sinatra syndrome. Sat R 52:47 F 8 '69

SINGLETON, PENNY

Brown, H. W. This is Blondie's home. Bet Hom &
Gard 19:32 Je '41

Blondie. Am Mag 141:145 Ap '46

Porter, A. Blondie's gold mine. Colliers 118:81 N 16
'46

SKELTON, RED

Jefferson, S. The Skelton in Hollywood's closet.
Photop 21-2:38 Jl '42

Proctor, K. Play truth or consequences with Red Skelton. Photop 24-2:38 Ja '44

Biography. Cur Bio 8:46 N '47

Same revised. Cur Bio Yrbk 1947:580 '48

Arnold, M. Clown in civvies. Photop 32-3:66 F '48

Shearer, L. Is he a big laugh! Colliers 125:22 Ap 15
'50

Rubber face on TV. Life 31:71 O 22 '51

The secret of Skelton's success. TV Guide 5-2:8 Ja 11
'52

Clown of the year. Newsweek 39:56 Mr 17 '52

Chassier, R. Helter Skelton. Colliers 129:26 Mr 29 '52

Arnold, M. Clown with wings. Photop 41-5:39 My '52

Skelton's troubles. TV Guide 5-48:10 D 5 '52

Skelton tries again. TV Guide 1-27:5 O 2 '53

Wood, C. TV personalities biographical sketchbook.
TV Personalities p74 '54

Right up there. TV Guide 4-17:5 Ap 28 '56

Abramson, M. Red Skelton story. Cosmop 141:88 S '56

Still fighting for laughs. Look 21:57 Ap 2 '57

A comedian faces a tragedy. TV Guide 5-24:20 Je 15 '57

What makes a clown? TV Guide 7-4:17 Ja 24 '59

Brossard, C. Red Skelton: what keeps him going?
Look 23:34 O 13 '59

Giddy heights. Newsweek 54:58 D 28 '59

Wolters, L. Red Skelton: America's most durable
clown. Todays Health 37:23 D '59

It hasn't all been laughs.   TV Guide 8-8:17 F 20 '60
Sixth sense only.   Time 76:65 O 3 '60
Invincible Red.   Life 50:109 Ap 21 '61
DeRoos, R.   Television's greatest clown.   TV Guide 9-
   41:12 O 14; 9-42:26 O 21 '61
Jennings, D.   Sad and lonely clown.   Sat Eve Post 235:
   50 Je 2 '62
Whitney, D.   The weekly ordeal of Red Skelton.   TV
   Guide 11-16:15 Ap 20; 11-17:15 Ap 27 '63
Busch, N. F.   Red Skelton, television's clown prince.
   Red Digest 86:145 Mr '65
Searle, R.   Portrait of a clown.   TV Guide 13-42:20 O
   16 '65
Whitney, D.   A clown is a warrior who fights gloom.
   TV Guide 14-34:16 Ag 20 '66
Wynn, E.   Red Skelton.   McCalls 94:101 O '66
Davidson, B.   I'm nuts and I know it.   Sat Eve Post
   240:66 Je 17 '67

SKIPWORTH, ALLISON
   Obit.   Newsweek 40:59 Jl 14 '52
     Am Ann 1953:627 '53

SLEZAK, WALTER
   Theatre Arts gallery.   Theatre Arts 37:22 Ag '53
   Slezak, W.   Slezaks, father and son; intv. ed. by B.
     Paige.   Etude 72:17 Mr '54
   Biography.   Cur Bio 16:52 Mr '55
   News: three sizes in spring chickens.   Look 19:92 My
     31 '55
   Ten things that make my heart beat faster.   Good H 142:
     160 Ja '56
   Biography.   Cur Bio Yrbk 1955:556 '56
   Miniature of papa.   Theatre Arts 41:77 Ap '57
   Talk with a star.   Newsweek 49:106 My 6 '57
   Dinner by male.   Am Home 58:8 Jl '57
   Actor sings--at last.   Newsweek 54:98 D 7 '59
   Heavyweight of the acting game.   TV Guide 8-26:12 Je
     25 '60
   Chitchat with the host.   Newsweek 56:82 Jl 11 '60
   Slezak, W.   What time's the next swan?; excerpt.
     Theatre Arts 46:62 O '62
 · He likes to cook.   Bet Hom & Gard 42:106 O '64

SLOANE, EVERETT
   Biography.   Cur Bio 18:49 Ja '57
     Same.   Cur Bio Yrbk 1957:516 '58

Versatile villain. Newsweek 50:78 N 18 '57
Beacon in a sea of mediocrity. TV Guide 9-13:17 Ap 1
   '61
Everett Sloane. Films 37:13 Aut '63
Obit. Newsweek 66:59 Ag 16 '65
   Cur Bio 26:40 O '65
   Cur Bio Yrbk 1965:390 '65
   Screen World 17:241 '66
Coulson, A. A. Everett Sloane, inc. filmog. Films In
   Review 16-9:591 N '65

SMITH, ALEXIS
Timid. Am Mag 133:70 F '42
Crichton, K. Leggy blonde. Colliers 110:18 D 5 '42
Raymond, M. American original. Photop 23-5:58 O '43
Ballerina Smith. Life 15:76 D 13 '43
Walker, H. L. Priority on paradise. Photop 25-4:65
   S '44
Garvin, R. Alexis Smith, inc. filmog. Films In Review
   14-1:62 Ja '63

SMITH, C. AUBREY
A regular toff. Photop 11-3:29 F '17
Miller, L. R. Man of parts. C S Mon Mag p4 Ja 12 '38
Obit. Time 52:57 D 27 '48
   Cur Bio 10:52 Ja '49
   Cur Bio Yrbk 1949:574 '50
Jones, K. D. C. Aubrey Smith. Films In Review 19-6:
   387 Je/Jl '68

SMITH, MAGGIE
Maggie Smith. Time 82:78 N 22 '63
Peter, J. Maggie Smith: a profile. Plays & Players
   12-3:12 D '64

SMITH, ROGER
Coach Cagney and the private eye. TV Guide 7-27:20
   Jl 4 '59
Borie, M. Did I remember to tell you I love you?
   Photop 56-2:50 Ag '59
Christy, G. 48 hours to live. Photop 56-4:32 O '59
Davidson, B. Five hours from death. Look 24:70 Mr 1
   '60
Smith, R. Why do you love me? Photop 57-3:26 Mr '60
Hamilton, S. A secret that can only be whispered.
   Photop 57-6:40 Je '60
Anderson, N. Breakdown. Photop 59-3:36 Mr '61

Gehman, R.   The man who got the breaks.   TV Guide
    9-13:8 Ap 1; 9-14:24 Ap 8 '61
Smith, R.   I won't fight.   Photop 65-5:39 My '64
Hollywood love triangle.   Photop 66-5:60 N '64
Reynolds, L.   How she got Roger Smith.   Photop 72-2:
    58 Ag '67

SNOW, MARGUERITE
Briscoe, J.   Why film favorites forsook the footlights.
    Photop 6-6:124 N '14
Franklin, W.   That Snow-Cruze lady; intv.   Photop 8-5:
    33 O '15
Bartlett, R.   She never worked with Griffith.   Photop
    14-4:69 S '18
Kornick, M.   Marguerite Snow.   Films In Review 9-6:
    346 Je/Jl '58
Obit.   Screen World 10:225 '59

SOKOLOFF, VLADIMIR
Ross, L.   Player.   New Yorker 37:118 O 21 '61

SOMMER, ELKE
The girl in the picture.   Films & Filming 6-7:31 Ap '60
Elke's big blitz on Hollywood.   Life 54:74 My 31 '63
Packaged tomato.   Time 82:58 Jl 12 '63
Gordon, S.   Elke Sommer, the movies' new wonder child.
    Look 27:71 O 22 '63
Hyams, J.   Season of Sommer.   Sat Eve Post 237:70 Ap
    18 '64
Tornabene, L.   Tomorrow's stars.   Good H 160:24 Mr
    '65

SONDERGAARD, GALE
Crichton, K.   No intermission.   Colliers 100:11 O 16 '37
Courage in action.   Nation 183:233 S 22 '56

SOO, JACK
This actor is no Oriental Uncle Tom.   TV Guide 13-13:
    10 Mr 27 '65

SORDI, ALBERTO
Mazzetti, L.   People of talent.   Sight & Sound 26-1:51
    Sum '56

SOTHERN, ANN
Curtis, A.   Marriage is no gamble when it's love.
    Photop 51-4:34 Ap '37

Asher, J.   Languid lady.   Photop 53-10:32 O '39
Rhea, M.   Maisie's remedies for heartaches.   Photop
    19-1:34 Je '41
Crichton, K.   Amazing Maisie.   Colliers 108:23 Jl 12 '41
Asher, J.   When girls get together.   Photop 20-3:36 F
    '42
Burton, J.   Goodby to marriage, hello to romance.
    Photop 21-2:65 Jl '42
Day with a star.   Am Mag 135:110 F '43
Walker, H. L.   Talk about romance.   Photop 22-3:48 F
    '43
Walker, H. L.   Sterling wedding pattern.   Photop 23-3:
    30 Ag '43
Sothern, A.   What kind of woman will your man come
    home to?   Photop 25-6:44 N '44
Parsons, L. O.   It's still the Sterlings.   Photop 29-2:56
    Jl '46
Waterbury, R.   Star in your home.   Photop 36-2:62 Jl
    '49
Sympathetic Susie; Private secretary.   Time 61:62 Ap 20
    '53
Gould, J.   TV's top comediennes.   N. Y. Times Mag p16
    D 27 '53
So who's a private secretary?   TV Guide 2-8:15 F 19 '54
Singing secretary.   TV Guide 2-38:20 S 18 '54
TV personalities biographical sketchbook.
    TV Personalities p17 '54
It's her turn to be boss.   TV Guide 4-9:20 Mr 3 '56
Biography.   Cur Bio 17:39 D '56
    Same.   Cur Bio Yrbk 1956:595 '57
Everything is in limbo.   TV Guide 5-29:20 Jl 20 '57
Always Ann.   TV Guide 6-42:17 O 18 '58
Madam presents.   TV Guide 7-12:12 Mr 21 '59
Hubler, R. G.   Belle named Sothern.   Coronet 46:91 Je
    '59
Eells, G.   Ann Sothern helps her daughter grow up.
    Look 25:131 Ap 25 '61
Briggs, C.   Filmography.   Films In Review 13-7:44 Ag/
    S '63
All she ever heard while she was growing up is how beau-
    tiful she was; intv.   Esquire 67:78 Ja '67

SPAAK, CATHERINE
    Hamill, P.   Stardom and boredom of Catherine Spaak.
    Sat Eve Post 237:58 My 2 '64

SPAIN, FAY
Person of promise.   Films & Filming 5-11:17 Ag '59

SPARKS, NED
Appreciation.   Am Mag 137:60 Je '44
Obit.   Newsweek 49:80 Ap 15 '57
Time 69:114 Ap 15 '57
Illus Lond N 230:595 Ap 13 '57
Screen World 9:226 '58

STACK, ROBERT
Stack, R.   I'm no Cinderella boy.   Photop 20-4:41 Mr
'42
Hawkins, M.   The case of the missing phonograph.
Photop 27-4:64 S '45
Stack, R.   Duke--prince among men.   Photop 47-4:54
Ap '55
The surprised Mr. Stack.   TV Guide 7-49:6 D 5 '59
Nichols, M.   Spotlight on Stack.   Coronet 48:15 Je '60
Martin, P.   I call on Mr. Untouchable.   Sat Eve Post
233:38 Jl 9 '60
How The untouchables hypoed TV's crime wave.   Look
20:35 S 27 '60
Tusher, W.   You can stay in love.   Photop 58-5:30 N '60
Gehman, R.   What took him so long?   TV Guide 9-45:
10 N 11; 9-46:15 N 18 '61
Liston, J.   At home with Robert Stack.   Am Home 65:10
Mr '62
Whitney, D.   The unlikely story of The untouchables.
TV Guide 10-32:8 Ag 11 '62
O'Brien, F.   Protected from killing self.   Photop 75-1:
60 Ja '69
Waterbury, R.   What his wife knew.   Photop 75-3:33 Mr
'69

STAMP, TERENCE
Person of promise.   Films & Filming 7-11:21 Ag '61

STANDER, LIONEL
Crichton, K.   Hard and bright.   Colliers 100:63 S 11 '37
Name is familiar; big-name fellow traveler.   Time 61:25
My 18 '53
Lawrenson, H.   Who is the world's foremost actor?
Esquire 68:180 D '67

STANDING, GUY
Davenport, W.   Regular guy.   Colliers 95:19 Ja 5 '35

Ulman, W. A. Jr.   The trackwalker who was knighted.
   Photop 48-2:67 Jl '35
Schwartz, W.   Filmography.   Films In Review 17-10:
   672 D '66

STANLEY, KIM
   Hewes, H.   Goon girl.   Sat R 36:53 Ap 11 '53
   Biographical note.   Time 64:56 N 8 '54
   Kim for success.   Vogue 125:108 Ap 1 '55
   Biography.   Cur Bio 16:55 My '55
      Same.   Cur Bio Yrbk 1955:569 '56
   TV saddens a 'Young pro.'   TV Guide 3-42:20 O 15 '55
   Girl on your set.   Newsweek 49:106 Je 17 '57
   How to pose for a pin-up picture.   McCalls 85:22 Mr '58
   One touch of . . .   Time 73:45 Ap 6 '59
   Millstein, G.   Theatre Arts gallery.   Theatre Arts 43:
      14 N '59
   Gelman, M.   Kim Stanley.   Theatre 2-9:13 S '60
   Talk with the star.   Newsweek 57:69 Ap 17 '61
   Ross, L.   Player.   New Yorker 37:59 O 21 '61
   Lukas, M.   Kim Stanley.   Show 3-7:64 Jl '63

STANWYCK, BARBARA
   Albert, K.   She has Hollywood's number.   Photop 40-1:
      69 Je '31
   St. Johns, A. R.   The story behind the Stanwyck-Fay
      breakup.   Photop 49-1:21 Ja '36
   Stevens, G.   Dinner for one, please, Johns.   Photop
      49-6:24 Je '36
   Ramsey, W.   Some call it love.   Photop 50-2:28 Ag '36
   Ramsey, W.   Barbara Stanwyck tells why she won't
      marry Robert Taylor.   Photop 51-4:24 Ap '37
   Willson, D.   Barbara--for her own sake.   Photop 51-12:
      68 D '37
   Stanwyck, B.   Can Hollywood mothers be good mothers?
      Photop 54-6:17 Je '40
   Rhea, M.   The law of averages.   Photop 18-4:32 Mr '41
   To my lady of courage.   Photop 19-6:54 N '41
   Stanwyck, B.   Don't be afraid.   Photop 24-1:34 D '43
   Lent, L.   When you're cozy, waiting is easier.   House
      B 87:100 O '45
   Biography.   Cur Bio 8:48 Jl '47
      Same revised.   Cur Bio Yrbak 1947:607 '48
   Deere, D.   Date with Bob and the Queen.   Photop 31-4:
      52 S '47
   Benny, J.   La belle Babs.   Photop 32-5:42 Ap '48
   Stanwyck, B.   Moving days.   Photop 34-2:32 Ja '49

Biographical note. Theatre Arts 35:36 Ag '51

Nugent, F. S. Stanwyck. Colliers 130:16 Jl 12 '52

Waterbury, R. Secrets behind Hollywood heartbreaks.
Photop 42-5:44 N '52

Nobody knows Barbara Stanwyck as I do; ed. by M. L.
Runbeck. Good H 139:48 Jl '54

Hall, G. The poison gas of gossip. Photop 49-6:72 Je
'56

Raring to go. TV Guide 6-47:28 N 22 '58

Stanwyck, the frustrated stunt woman. TV Guide 9-3:17
Ja 21 '61

Ringgold, G. Barbara Stanwyck, inc. filmog. Films In
Review 14-10:577 D '63

Whitney, D. The Queen goes west. TV Guide 14-9:6
F 26 '66

Elliot, R. The man who took her son's love. Photop
72-2:47 Ag '67

Kessner, J. Men who make life worthwhile. Photop 73-
3:38 Mr '68

Tildesly, A. Is she husband hunting? Photop 76-5:44 N
'69

STAPLETON, MAUREEN

New star. New Yorker 27:19 F 24 '51

Biography. Cur Bio 20:36 My '59

Same. Cur Bio Yrbk 1959:424 '60

Richards, S. A visit with Maureen Stapleton. Theatre
2-3:22 Mr '60

Millstein, G. Theatre Arts gallery. Theatre Arts 44:10
Jl '60

Ross, L. Player. New Yorker 37:120 O 28 '61

Stahl, B. A prisoner of emotion. TV Guide 11-27:26
Jl 6 '63

STARKE, PAULINE

Craig, M. Snub nose--freckle face. Photop 16-6:36 N
'19

Kelly, J. The girl without "it." Photop 28-3:72 Ag '25

Herzog, D. Yep--it's the same gal. Photop 30-2:46
Jl '26

French, J. The ugly duckling who became a great beauty.
Photop 38-1:44 Je '30

STARR, RINGO

Alexander, S. Ringo, Ringo, let down your hair. Life
59:28 S 10 '65

Deardorff, R. Ringo Starr: domesticated Beatle.

Redbook 125:60 S '65
Biography.   Cur Bio 26:38 D '65
  Same.   Cur Bio Yrbk 1965:404 '65
Hicks, J.   Is that you in there, Ringo?   Life 66:59 Je
  13 '69
(See also: BEATLES)

STEELE, BARBARA
Lovely loiterer in London.   Life 45:85 D 1 '58
Person of promise.   Films & Filming 5-5:28 F '59

STEELE, TOMMY
Piltdown poppa.   Time 70:48 D 30 '57
Boy of Bermondsey.   New Yorker 41:32 Je 12 '65
Cockney star bounces in.   Life 59:45 Jl 2 '65
Miller, E.   Tommy Steele.   Seventeen 26:78 Jl '67

STEELE, VERNON
Obit.   Screen World 7:226 '56

STEIGER, ROD
Another Paul Muni?   Newsweek 47:124 My 14 '56
Mosby, A.   Weeper.   Colliers 137:103 My 25 '56
Steiger, R.   The truth about the method.   Films & Film-
  ing 3-7:7 Ap '57
Hubler, R. G.   I'm a weeper no more.   Coronet 45:96
  Ap '59
Jennings, D.   Case of the angry actor.   Sat Eve Post
  232:39 F 20 '60
Ross, L.   Player.   New Yorker 37:90 O 28 '61
Steiger, the Pawnbroker.   Newsweek 62:75 D 23 '63
Biography.   Cur Bio 26:39 Je '65
  Same.   Cur Bio Yrbk 1965:407 '65
Beauty and the beast.   Life 59:45 O 29 '65
No way to treat a lady.   Time 91:98 Mr 29 '68
Antic arts; an actor comments.   Holiday 43:83 Je '68
Paum, P.   Oscar winner; intv.   Sr Schol 93:21 O 11 '68

STEN, ANNA
Crichton, K.   Kid from the Ukraine.   Colliers 93:32 Mr
  31 '34
Lynn, H.   Anna Sten the million dollar gamble.   Photop
  45-5:40 Ap '34
Auburn, M.   What is this woman.   Photop 47-1:49 D '34
What they are doing now.   Show 3-12:164 D '63

STEPHENSON, HENRY
    Obit. Newsweek 47:73 My 7 '56
        Time 67:106 My 7 '56
        Screen World 8:225 '57

STEPHENSON, JAMES
    Zeitlin, I. The last hours of James Stephenson.
        Photop 19-5:65 O '41
    Obit. Cur. Bio '41

STERLING, JAN
    Brady, T. F. That Sterling character. Colliers 127:20
        My 26 '51
    Hine, A. Three smart blondes. Holiday 10:6 S '51
    Douglas, P. Take my wife. Photop 41-2:58 F '52
    Aldrich, H. K. Filmography. Films In Review 20-7:
        455 Ag/S '69

STERLING, ROBERT
    Walker, H. L. Bob Sterling--next for fame. Photop
        20-3:46 F '42
    Burton, J. Goodby to marriage, hello to romance.
        Photop 21-2:65 Jl '42
    Walker, H. L. Talk about romance. Photop 22-3:48 F
        '43
    Walker, H. L. Sterling wedding pattern. Photop 23-3:
        30 Ag '43
    Parsons, L. O. It's still the Sterlings. Photop 29-2:
        56 Jl '46
    Inventive mind. Time 53:59 Ap 11 '49
    Wood, C. TV personalities biographical sketchbook.
        TV Personalities p157 '54

STEVENS, CONNIE
    A girl should meet a guy halfway. Photop 56-2:38 Ag '59
    Connie Stevens spoofs the gimmick girls. Look 24:44 Mr
        29 '60
    Tusher, B. To me she was a stranger. Photop 57-4:66
        Ap '60
    Anderson, N. Will he still want to marry me? Photop
        48-1:58 Jl '60
    Borie, M. How can I tell if I'm really in love. Photop
        58-4:34 O '60
    Barrett, R. What gives? Photop 59-1:44 Ja '61
    Gautschy, D. Nobody can stop us now. Photop 59-4:32
        Ap '61
    Clarke, G. The girl I didn't marry. Photop 59-6:19

Je '61

Richards, J.   The feud's for real.   Photop 60-3:30 S '61

Britten, R.   The nuttiest date I ever had.   Photop 60-3:
48 S '61

Connie comes out swinging.   TV Guide 10-16:12 Ap 21 '62

Connie and Glenn run to Paris.   Photop 61-4:60 Ap '62

Corbin, J.   Connie and Glenn to marry, if . . .   Photop
61-5:26 My '62

The perfect couple--on screen.   TV Guide 10-35:15 S 1
'62

Friedman, F.   Girl with the glass heart.   Photop 62-3:
56 S; 62-4:46 O '62

She knows what she wants.   Look 26:586 D 18 '62

Friedman, F.   I thought my life was over.   Photop 62-6:
48 D '62

Ardmore, J.   Connie weds Gary.   Photop 63-3:16 Mr '63

Kesner, J.   Why Gary and I fight.   Photop 63-4:41 Ap
'63

Arnold, M.   Why Connie and I fight.   Photop 63-4:41
Ap '63

Beck, M.   The lie I've lived.   Photop 64-1:54 Jl '63

Anderson, N.   Did he give her the brushoff?   Photop
64-4:32 O '63

We'd better get married.   Photop 64-5:17 N '63

Ardmore, J.   What Jim Stacy has.   Photop 64-6:43 D '63

Hopper, H.   Connie's wedding to Jim Stacy.   Photop 65-
1:47 Ja '64

Waterbury, R.   The honeymoon that didn't work.   Photop
65-2:76 F '64

Stacy, J.   Marriage isn't all candlelight.   Photop 66-3:
64 S '64

Gareth, A.   God gave me nine children.   Photop 67-4:
36 Ap '65

Hurley, W.   The tenth we're going to adopt.   Photop 67-
4:38 Ap '65

Lewis, R. W.   An apple bloosom with the wham of a
bulldozer.   TV Guide 13-16:16 My 1 '65

Williams, C.   I've surrendered everything.   Photop 68-
2:60 Ag '65

Gardiner, H.   Her shocking pregnancy.   Photop 72-6:29
D '67

York, C.   1st photos: Their secret baby.   Photop 73-1:8
Ja '68

Wells, V.   How she'll tell baby about Eddie.   Photop
73-1:48 Ja '68

Smith, M.   The wedding that wasn't.   Photop 73-3:57
Mr '68

Foxx, M.   How Eddie Fisher humiliates her.   Photop
   73-5:58 My '68
Berger, C.   She walks out on Eddie Fisher.   Photop
   74-2:48 Ag '68
Holloway, J.   Why he always leaves her.   Photop 75-2:
   58 F '69
Gambino, R.   I'll lose Eddie if . . .   Photop 75-3:51
   Mr '69
Wood, S.   She sees ex-husband.   Photop 75-5:48 My '69
Tolley, N.   His divorce--her pregnancy?   Photop 76-1:
   63 Jl '69

STEVENS, CRAIG
   Have Gunn, will unravel.   TV Guide 7-1:17 Ja 3 '59
   These Gunns for hire.   Time 74:50 O 26 '59
   Stevens, C.   Hunting another kind of prey.   TV Guide
      14-4:15 Ja 22 '66

STEVENS, INGER
   O'Donnell, M.   The nightmare I can't forget.   Photop
      54-2:41 Ag '58
   Michaels, E.   No one to turn to.   Photop 55-4:52 Ap '59
   Everything but the tears.   TV Guide 10-36:8 S 8 '62
   DeRoos, R.   Sometimes I just want to go awwrrk.   TV
      Guide 11-39:15 S 28 '63
   Lewis, R. W.   Inger Stevens.   Sat Eve Post 237:20 Ja
      4 '64
   Dawes, A.   Pinup #21.   Photop 66-4:65 O '64
   Ryder, E.   When it's right to have an affair.   Photop
      66-6:64 D '64
   DeRoos, R.   Dear Inger.   TV Guide 13-5:15 Ja 30 '65

STEVENS, MARK
   Asher, J.   Mark against time.   Photop 29-4:48 S '46
   Shipp, C.   Even Steven.   Photop 30-5:66 Ap '47
   Graham, S.   Can this be love?   Photop 32-1:46 D '47
   Cigaret smoking made him an able Kane.   TV Guide 2-
      19:15 My 7 '54
   Martin Kane in 'Big Town.'   TV Guide 2-41:13 O 9 '54
   Wood, C.   TV personalities biographical sketchbook.
      TV Personalities p122 '54
   'Big Town's' big boss.   TV Guide 3-41:8 O 8 '55

STEVENS, STELLA
   Person of promise.   Films & Filming 8-3:27 D '61
   Stella Stevens.   Film 31:4 Spg '62
   Lewis, R. W.   Fair young Hollywood girls.   Sat Eve

Post 236:24 S 7 '63
She hopes the prescription works.   TV Guide 12-39:10
    S 26 '64
McGinniss, J.   Success is a relative thing.   TV Guide
    17-6:26 F 8 '69

STEWART, ANITA
    Johnson, J.   Anita: a star-in-law; intv.   Photop 7-5:
        50 Ap '15
    Johnson, J.   Girl on the cover; intv.   Photop 8-4:53 S
        '15
    Denton, F.   Anita's war garden.   Photop 14-5:83 O '18
    St. Johns, A. R.   A pair of queens.   Photop 16-4:81 S
        '19
    Obit.   Time 77:88 My 12 '61
        Screen World 13:226 '62
    Bodeen, D.   Anita Stewart, inc. filmog.   Films In Re-
        view 19-3:145 Mr '68

STEWART, ELAINE
    Starlet goes home to Jersey.   Life 34:166 Mr 23 '53
    Policeman's daughter.   Look 17:47 Ap 7 '53
    Zolotow, M.   Her favorite star|is herself.   Sat Eve Post
        226:26 S 5 '53
    On stardom's stairway.   Coronet 35:41 Ja '54
    Meltsir, A.   Better to be certain than sorry.   Photop
        45-4:52 Ap '54
    Waterbury, R.   Boudoir secrets.   Photop 45-6:68 Je '54

STEWART, JAMES
    Reed, E.   New faces: 1935.   Theatre Arts 19:276 Ap
        '35
    Reeve, W.   Introducing James Stewart.   Photop 50-2:21
        Ag '36
    Small, F.   Three cornered love.   Photop 51-3:34 Mr '37
    Crichton, K.   Blade of Beverly Hills.   Colliers 100:26
        O 9 '37
    Proctor, K.   Through thick and thin.   Photop 52-11:19
        N '38
    Morse, W. Jr.   Lackadaisical Lothario.   Photop 53-7:
        16 Jl; 53-8:62 Ag; 53-9:68 S '39
    Morse, W. Jr.   We have a wonderful time together.
        Photop 54-4:64 Ap '40
    Morse, W. Jr.   The draft--and Jim Stewart: The real
        story.   Photop 19-1:50 Je '41
    Biography.   Cur Bio '41
    Mr. Smith goes to town.   Time 44:60 Jl 24 '44

Life comes home with James Stewart.   Life 19:126 S
  24 '45
MacGregor, L. Col. James Stewart. Photop 27-5:30
  O '45
Lay, B. Jr. Jimmy Stewart's finest performance.
  Sat Eve Post 218:18 D 8; D 15 '45
Stewart touch. Newsweek 28:72 D 30 '46
Wechsberg, J. Target: Hollywood. Colliers 119:13 Ap
  5 '47
What became of Jimmy? Life 22:138 Ap 14 '47
Heggie, B. Penrod in Hollywood. Womans H C 74:34
  Ap '47
Skolsky, S. The squire of Vinegar Hill. Photop 30-5:
  46 Ap '47
Peters, S. Easy does it. Photop 31-3:56 Ag '47
Foster, I. W. American as apple pie. C S Mon Mag
  p5 O 25 '47
James Stewart is married at last. Life 27:22 Ag 22 '49
Arnold, M. Kiss the girls goodbye. Photop 36-4:40 S
  '49
McKee, B. Happy hobos. Photop 37-3:38 Mr '50
Jimmy Stewart hits the jackpot. Life 29:109 D 4 '50
Stewart, Mrs. J. I'm in love with a wonderful guy.
  Photop 39-2:50 F '51
Martin, P. Shyest guy in Hollywood. Sat Eve Post
  224:42 S 15 '51
Weinman, M. Jimmy's twins. Colliers 129:47 My 17
  '52
Alvin, J. Jimmy Stewart tells what he wants for his
  family. Parents Mag 27:38 Jl '52
Glenn Miller story. Look 18:84 Ja 26 '54
Jimmy Stewart shows off his twins. McCalls 81:10 Ja '54
Parsons, L. O. Hollywood's nicest star. Cosmop 136:
  10 F '54
Dudley, F. The case of the vanquished bachelor. Photop
  47-2:61 F '55
James Stewart--highest paid actor. Look 19:94 Jl 26 '55
Innocent goes abroad. Life 39:50 S 5 '55
Maynard, J. Jimmy on the Q. T. Photop 48-4:70 O '55
Stewart, J. Lucky to be Lindy; with J. Laitin. Colliers
  137:30 Mr '56
Hume, R. Small-talk star. Films & Filming 2-10:4 Jl
  '56
Maynard, J. "Slim" Pickin'. Photop 50-2:56 Ag '56
Direct hit. Time 70:16 S 2 '57
No star for Jimmy. Newsweek 50:20 S 2 '57
One star for Jimmy? Newsweek 53:35 F 23 '59

Lady balks again. Newsweek 53:37 Mr 23 '59
Star for a star but . . . Newsweek 54:22 Jl 27b '59
Cindy's fella. TV Guide 7-50:12 D 12 '59
Davidson, M. Jimmy Stewart's instant kitchen. Ladies
  Home J 77:80 My '60
Biography. Cur Bio 21:31 D '60
  Same. Cur Bio Yrbk 1960:399 '61
Biography. NCAB cur I:44 '60
Stewart, J. Jimmy Stewart, as told to P. Martin.
  Sat Eve Post 234:13 F 11; 22 F 18; 22 F 25; 30 Mr
  4; 36 Mr 11 '61
Coddled commandos. Newsweek 63:28 F 10 '64
Stewart, J. This was my father. McCalls 91:130 My '64
Sweigart, W. R. James Stewart, inc. filmog. Films In
  Review 15-10:585 O '64
Stewart, J. One hat's enough for me. Films & Filming
  12-7:19 Ap '66
Bogdanovich, P. Th' respawnsibility of bein' J...Jimmy
  Stewart, gosh! Esquire 66:104 Jl '66

STEWART, ROY
  St. Johns, A. R. A blue-ribbon baby. Photop 14-4:93
  S '18
  Henderson, F. A college cowboy. Photop 17-1:94 D '19

STICKNEY, DOROTHY
  Steinfel, R. Dynamic Dorothy. Colliers 106:21 N 16 '40
  Actress collects music boxes. Hobbies 47:14 Mr '42
  Biography. Cur Bio '42
  Gleason, C. & Davis, R. Life with mother. Am H 41:
    26 F '49
  Monze, M. E. Star lights. Am Home 45:27 Ja '51
  McCalls visits. McCalls 85:19 N '57
  Summer more. Time 74:44 Jl 13 '59
  Tynan, K. Theatre. New Yorker 36:102 F 20 '60
  Lovely light. Time 75:100 F 22 '60
  Hewes, H. Light is light enough. Sat R 43:27 F 27 '60

STOCKWELL, DEAN
  Phillips, W. Week's preview. Colliers 123:36 Ja 15 '49
  Melick, W. Young rebel. Am Mag 148:50 D '49
  Stockwell, B. It's a boy's world; as told to J. Morris.
    Parents Mag 25:50 D '50
  Steinhauser, I. A handful of quarters. Photop 52-6:27
    D '57
  Christy, G. Exposed. Photop 53-6:40 Je '58
  Hoffman, J. Can Dean Stockwell shake off the Jimmy

Dean jinx?   Photop 54-5:62 N '58
Ardmore, J.   She no longer has to pretend.   Photop 56-6:64 D '59
Stockwell, D.   Believe in the part . . . and see it grow.
Films & Filming 6-7:7 Ap '60
Blake, E.   Why Millie had to settle for a runaway marriage.   Photop 58-1:54 Jl '60

STONE, GEORGE E.
Friend of trees.   Time 37:64 Je 9 '41
Obit.   Screen World 19:239 '68

STONE, LEWIS
Larkin, M.   What is it?   Photop 36-1:34 Je '29
Loring, H.   Stone debunks the actor.   Photop 39-1:75
D '30
Hall, G.   Lewis Stone is really Judge Hardy.   Photop 53-6:20 Je '39
Obit.   Newsweek 42:66 S 21 '53
Time 62:104 S 21 '53
Am Ann 1954:694 '54
Screen World 5:208 '54

STONE, MILBURN
Wood, C.   TV personalities biographical sketchbook.
TV Personalities p24 '56
Nichols, M.   Gunsmoke's dancing doctor.   Coronet 48:18
O '60
Lewis, R. W.   Dodge City's medicine man.   TV Guide
10-47:22 N 24 '62
Phillips, D. & Copeland, B.   Riding high on the waves
of indignation.   TV Guide 13-24:24 Je 12 '65

STONEHOUSE, RUTH
Edwards, L.   The girl on the cover.   Feature Movie 3-3:25 S 10 '15

STORCH, LARRY
Fessier, M. Jr.   The world of Larry Storch.   TV Guide
14-33:15 Ag 13 '66

STOREY, EDITH
Smith, F. J.   The story of Edith Storey.   Photop 12-4:
72 S '17
Johnson, J.   The story of Storey.   Photop 14-6:28 N '18

STORM, GALE
  Who's who in the cast. TV Guide 5-34:37 Ag 22 '52
  The saga of Josephine O. Cottle. TV Guide 1-19:13 Ag
    7 '53
  Gehman, R. Storm behind My little Margie. Cosmop
    135:8 D '53
  Sunny Gale Storm. TV Guide 2-22:15 My 28 '54
  Wood, C. TV personalities biographical sketchbook.
    TV Personalities p67 '54
  Breezing right along. TV Guide 5-26:17 Je 29 '57
  Party line. TV Guide 6-14:12 Ap 5 '58
  McCalls visits. McCalls 85:8 Je '58
  Getting back on course. TV Guide 7-23:24 Je 6 '59
  Storm, G. Can I grow up to be a mommy too. Photop
    56-6:48 D '59

STRASBERG, SUSAN
  Teenage with the magic touch. Look 19:51 Ap 19 '55
  Big picnic for a star. Life 39:129 Jl 11 '55
  Harvey, E. Kansas Picnic. Colliers 136:26 Ag 5 '55
  Acting their age. Vogue 126:154 O 1 '55
  Broadway's big beginning. Life 39:161 O 17 '55
  Rainy day. New Yorker 31:26 O 29 '55
  Most sought after is Susan Strasberg. Life 39:104 N 21
    '55
  This sparkling theatre season. Newsweek 46:53 D 19 '55
  Harris, R. If you knew Susie. Photop 48-6:65 D '55
  Arnow, M. When you take a screen test. Good H 142:
    38 Ja '56
  French, M. G. Susan Strasberg, beautiful teenager.
    McCalls 83:34 Ja '56
  Star. Time 67:67 F 6 '56
  Long, J. Teenage dream comes true. Am Mag 162:22
    Ag '56
  Person of promise. Films & Filming 3-11:16 Ag '57
  Talk with two stars. Newsweek 50:84 N 25 '57
  Who's who cooks. Good H 146:10 F '58
  Susan grows up. Look 22:120 Mr 18 '58
  Eleven fine actors get their dream roles. Life 44:76
    Ap 14 '58
  Biography. Cur Bio 19:40 My '58
    Same. Cur Bio Yrbk 1958:418 '58
  DeRoulf, P. Wake up, little Susie. Photop 54-1:50 Jl
    '58
  Spotlight. Life 51:115 O 27 '61
  Lawrenson, H. The route from Anne Frank to Camille
    is straight down the Appian Way. Show 2-7:69 Jl '62

Hochstein, R. One battle I had to win. Good H 156:88
My '63

STREISAND, BARBRA

Coming star. New Yorker 38:34 My 19 '62
She knows what she means. Time 81:59 Ja 25 '63
Bea, Billie and Barbra. Newsweek 61:79 Je 3 '63
Hamill, P. Goodbye Brooklyn, hello fame. Sat Eve
Post 236:22 Jl 27 '63
Success is a baked potato. Life 55:112 S 20 '63
Miller, E. Barbra Streisand; singing, swinging show
stopper! Seventeen 22:109 O '63
Brossard, C. Barbra Streisand: new singing sensation.
Look 27:M12 N 19 '63
Weidman, J. I remember Barbra. Holiday 34:123 N '63
Playbill. Theatre Arts 47:9 N '63
Individualists: Mlle's annual merit awards. Mlle 58:75
Ja '64
People are talking about. Vogue 143:118 Mr 1 '64
On the Rue Streisand. Time 83:54 Ap 3 '64
Full throttle. Newsweek 63:76 Ap 6 '64
The girl. Time 83:62 Ap 10 '64
Gilman, R. Barbra Streisand: that's enough. Common-
weal 80:147 Ag 24 '64
Alexander, S. Born loser's success and precarious love.
Life 56:52 My 22 '64
Lerman, L. Barbra Streisand show. Mlle 59:158 My '64
Wilson, J. S. Kook from Madagascar. Hi Fi 14:43 My
'64
Biography. Cur Bio 25:40 Je '64
Same. Cur Bio Yrbk 1964:438 '64
Nielsen's newest. Time 84:62 Jl 3 '64
Money girl. Newsweek 64:48 Jl 6 '64
Alexander, S. Born loser's success and precarious love;
abridged. Read Digest 85:51 Ag '64
Wonderful year of Barbra Streisand. Vogue 144:220 D '64
Taylor, C. Follow a star. Seventeen 24:76 Ja '65
Streisand at 23. Time 85:68 Ap 30 '65
Person who changed my life. Seventeen 24:156 Ap '65
Miss Streisand's New York for Marcello Mastroianni.
Esquire 63:56 My '65
Lear, M. W. She is tough, she is earthy, she is kicky.
N. Y. Times Mag p10 Jl 4 '65
Redbook dialogue. Redbook 125:50 Jl '65
We talk to . . . ; intv. Mlle 61:228 Ag '65
Goodbye Jackie, hello Amanda! picking order among the
world's best dressed women. Time 87:56 Ja 21 '66

Not so funny girl. Time 87:56 F 11 '66
Devlin, P. Instant Barbra. Vogue 147:69 Mr 15 '66
Lurie, D. It's scary--it could suddenly all fall apart.
   Life 60:95 Mr 18 '66
Barbra. Newsweek 67:92 Mr 28 '66
Girl who catches the light. Vogue 147:144 Ap 1 '66
Morgan, T. B. Superbarbra. Look 30:54 Ap 5 '66
Flip-side Streisand. Time 87:61 Ap 8 '66
Ace, G. Fan letter to Barbra Streisand. Sat R 49:15
   Ap 16 '66
Poifect. Time 88:64 Ag 19 '66
Steinem, G. Brabra Streisand talks about her million
   dollar baby. Ladies Home J 83:64 Ag '66
Robbins, J. Barbra Streisand. McCalls 94:102 O '66
What makes a Barbra special. Bsns W p64 My 20 '67
Efron, E. If her nose had been a half inch shorter . . .
   TV Guide 15-29:10 Jl 22 '67
Mothner, I. Mama Barbra. Look 31:75 Jl 25 '67
Hallowell, G. Funny girl goes west. Life 63:139 S 22
   '67
Funny girl makes a movie. N. Y. Times Mag p34 S 24
   '67
Lear, M. Her name is Barbra. Redbook 130:54 Ja '68
People are talking about . . . Vogue 151:154 Mr 1 '68
Building a dowry for Funny girl. Bsns W p82 S 28 '68
Mothner, I. Barbra; a frantic, brassy, tender Funny
   girl. Look 32:50 O 15 '68
Watt, D. Popular records. New Yorker 44:131 N 16 '68
Barbra Streisand of Hello, Dolly! Vogue 152:210 D '68
Korall, B. Her name is Barbra. Sat R 52:108 Ja 11 '69
Valentine, L. Their songs of love. Photop 75-1:35 Ja
   '69
Ephron, N. Private world of Barbra Streisand. Good H
   168:93 Ap '69
My husband isn't with me. Photop 75-5:33 My '69
Webb, M. Her secret dates with Beatty. Photop 75-6:
   56 Je '69
Adam, C. Her millionaire man. Photop 76-2:66 Ag '69

STRICKLYN, RAY
   Alderson, K. Letter, inc. filmog. Films In Review
      15-1:54 Ja '64

STRITCH, ELAINE
   Anderson, D. Show stopper. Theatre Arts 36:43 Ap '52
   Wood, C. TV personalities biographical sketchbook.
      TV Personalities p152 '57

She can play without Stritching.   TV Guide 9-14:28 Ap 8
'61

STRONGHEART, CHIEF NIPO
Indian sign for Hollywood.   Am Mag 151:57 Mr '51
Obit.   Screen World 19:239 '68

STUART, GLORIA
Rankin, R.   And was Gloria burned up!   Photop 45-6:34
My '34

STUART, IRIS
St. Johns, I.   Two hands and a face.   Photop 30-6:58
N '26

SULLAVAN, MARGARET
Taviner, R.   She abhors being beautified.   Photop 44-5:
69 O '33
They stand out from the crowd.   Lit Digest 116:9 N 25
'33
Morse, W. Jr.   The lady who laughed at Hollywood.
Photop 45-3:77 F '34
Crichton, K.   She says its spinach.   Colliers 93:22 Mr
17 '34
Making of a movie star.   Am Mag 117:50 My '34
Baskette, K.   Margaret Sullavan wants none of it.
Photop 47-2:28 Ja '35
Stevens, G.   Why I will not remarry Margaret Sullavan.
Photop 49-5:36 My '36
Hamilton, S.   The stormy heart of Margaret Sullavan.
Photop 49-6:30 Je '36
New York's rehearsal club inspires adroit comedy.   News-
week 8:24 O 31 '36
St. Johns, A. R.   The exciting inside story of Margaret
Sullavan's marriage.   Photop 51-2:14 F '37
Sharpe, H.   Beautiful brat.   Photop 52-10:19 O; 52-11:64
N; 52-12:70 D '38
Van Druten, J.   Featuring the voice of the turtle.   The-
atre Arts 28:272 My '44
Biography.   Cur Bio Jl '44
Sullavan without bangs.   Theatre Arts 36:15 N '52
City celebrity in country setting.   Life 34:136 F 16 '53
Stage reclaims its own.   Theatre Arts 38:29 Mr '54
Obit.   Illus Lond N 236:61 Ja 9 '60
Newsweek 55:28 Ja 11 '60
Time 75:66 Ja 11 '60
Cur Bio 21:37 F '60

Cur Bio Yrbk 1960:412 '61
Am Ann 1961:850 '61
Brit Bk Yr 1961:521 '61
Screen World 12:225 '61
Missed cues.   Time 75:55 Ja 18 '60
Keating, J.   Margaret Sullivan.   Theatre Arts 44:26 F
'60
Jacobs, J.   Margaret Sullavan, inc. filmog.   Films In
Review 11-4:193 Ap '60
Biography.   NCAB 44:59 '62

SULLIVAN, BARRY
Shaw, G. B.   Sullivan, Shakespeare and Shaw.   Atlan
181:56 Mr '48
Biography.   D Aus B 2:390 '49
Rockport opened his eyes, and vice versa.   TV Guide 5-
46:24 N 16 '57
Wood, C.   TV personalities biographical sketchbook.
TV Personalities p19 '57
Seventh son of a seventh gun.   TV Guide 9-34:24 Ag 26
'61

SULLIVAN, FRANCIS L.
Biography.   Cur Bio 16:56 Je '55
Same.   Cur Bio Yrbk 1955:586 '56
Obit.   Illus Lond N 229:938 D 1 '56
Newsweek 48:69 D 3 '56
Time 68:94 D 3 '56
Cur Bio 18:51 Ja '57
Cur Bio Yrbk 1957:540 '58
Screen World 8:226 '57

SUMMERVILLE, SLIM
Jamison, J.   It wasn't the baby's fault.   Photop 44-4:35
S '33
Obit.   Newsweek 27:72 Ja 14 '46
Time 47:73 Ja 14 '46
Cur Bio 7:55 F '46
Cur Bio Yrbk 1946:588 '47

SUTHERLAND, VICTOR
Obit.   Screen World 20:240 '69

SUTTON, GRADY
Maltin, L.   Grady Sutton, inc. filmog.   Film Fan Mo
100:18 O '69

SUTTON, JOHN
  Where is Hollywood? Am Mag 135:56 Mr '43
  Obit. Screen World 15:226 '64

SWAIN, MACK
  West, M. Our Ambrose goes straight. Photop 30-4:41
    S '26

SWANSON, GLORIA
  Evans, D. Don't change your coiffure. Photop 16-3:73
    Ag '19
  Glyn, E. A photobiography of Gloria Swanson. Photop
    20-1:24 Je '21
  Swanson, G. Confessions of a modern woman. Photop
    21-3:20 F '22
  St. Johns, A. R. Gloria! An impression. Photop 24-
    4:28 S '23
  Is woman suffrage failing? Woman Cit 8:8 Mr 22 '24
  Keel, A. C. What next, Gloria? Photop 27-5:32 Ap '25
  Ashley, R. Almost changed the city's name to Swanson,
    West Virginia. Photop 28-6:32 N '26
  Swanson, G. There is no formula for success. Photop
    29-5:32 Ap '26
  Hyland, D. Won by a nose. Photop 34-6:53 N '28
  Kennedy, J. B. Drop that pie! intv. Colliers 83:28 Je
    8 '29
  Albert, K. What next for Gloria? Photop 36-2:64 Jl '29
  Waterbury, R. Gloria, Connie and the Marquis. Photop
    38-3:32 Ag '30
  Lamg, H. So this is Gloria! Photop 38-4:35 S '30
  Biery, R. The troubles of Gloria. Photop 40-1:45 Ja'31
  Hall, L. It's a long way to Tipperary! Photop 41-2:34
    Ja '32
  Gloria Swanson's progeny. Cinema Digest 1-11:11 O 3
    '32
  Biery, R. Gloria's new troubles. Photop 43-4:35 Mr
    '33
  Hall, H. Swanson's swan song? Cinema Digest 3-3:3
    Ap 3 '33
  Maxwell, V. I'm not broke, says Gloria. Photop 44-1:
    36 Je '33
  Mastin, M. The husbands in Gloria's career. Photop
    46-2:40 Jl '34
  Smith, F. J. Why I am going back to the screen. Pho-
    top 51-4:14 Ap '37
  Sullivan, F. Gloria Swanson defends her title. New
    Yorker 16:21 Mr 30 '40

Same, abridged.   Read Digest 37:122 Jl '40
Biographical sketch.   Time 38:84 S 29 '41
Forever Gloria.   Life 28:81 Je 5 '50
Sunset boulevard: Hollywood takes that Gloria Swanson
  makes great.   Newsweek 35:82 Je 26 '50
Frank, S. Grandma Gloria Swanson comes back.   Sat
  Eve Post 223:30 Jl 22; 36 Jl 29 '50
Biographical note.   Time 56:82 Ag 14 '50
Biography.   Cur Bio 11:48 S '50
   Same.   Cur Bio Yrbk 1950:556 '51
Swanson creation.   Newsweek 36:54 O 30 '50
McEvoy, J. P. I remember Gloria.   Read Digest 58:73
  Ja '51
20th century.   Life 30:117 F 19 '51
Swanson, G. My most wonderful experience.   Photop 39-
  2:58 F '51
Mr. Harper. After hours.   Harper 202:102 F '51
Brown, J. M. Gloria rediviva.   Sat R 34:25 Mr 24 '51
Meegan, J. Thirteen twenty-five a week.   Theatre Arts
  35:50 Jl '51
Vegetable and I.   House & Gard 101:126 Ap '52
Birth of a telefilm.   TV Guide 1-8:10 My 22 '53
Why won't men dress properly?   Coronet 35:128 D '53
Should a woman tell the truth about her age?   Read
  Digest 66:91 Ja '55
Film pioneers' roll of their living immortals.   Life 40:
  117 Ja 23 '56
Columnist in bloom.   Newsweek 46:69 O 10 '56
St. Johns, A. R. Why a man gets tired of a woman.
  Photop 59-1:36 Ja '61
A visit with Gloria Swanson.   Theatre 3-6:26 Je '61
Brownlow, K. Gloria Swanson.   Film 41:7 Aut '64
Bodeen, D. Gloria Swanson, inc. filmog.   Films In
  Review 16-4:194 Ap '65
Hollywood sunset.   Esquire 66:76 Ag '66
Taylor, J. R. Show people.   Sight & Sound 37:201 Aut
  '68

SWEET, BLANCHE
  Owen, K. The girl on the cover; intv.   Photop 7-5:89
    Ap '15
  Thein, M. A sweet mystery.   Feature Movie 3-2:24 Ag
    25 '15
  St. Johns, A. R. An impression of Blanche Sweet.
    Photop 26-4:58 S '24
  Bodeen, D. Blanche Sweet, inc. filmog.   Films In Re-
    view 16-9:549 N '65

SWITZER, CARL "ALFALFA"
Kids get older. Newsweek 52:23 F 2 '59
Obit. Newsweek 52:23 F 2 '59
Screen World 11:226 '60

SYDNEY, BASIL
Shakespeare and the modern vogue. Drama 18:165 Mr '28
Obit. Screen World 20:240 '69

SYMS, SYLVIA
Person of promise. Films & Filming 2-12:19 S '56

TALBOT, LYLE
 Hamilton, S. Born to be a villain. Photop 43-4:79 Mr
 '33

TALIAFERRO, MABEL
 Laughter--and tears. Harper 53:23 O 9 '09
 Novels of the theatre. Bookm 30:371 D '09

TALMADGE, CONSTANCE
 Kingsley, G. The wild woman of Babylon. Photop 11-6:
 80 My '17
 Hilliker, K. That imp Constance. Photop 13-5:29 Ap '18
 St. Johns, A. R. Matrimony--and meringue. Photop 16-
 2:80 Jl '19
 Talmadge, C. The most engaged girl in the world.
 Photop 24-5:36 O '23
 Talmadge, C. Why men fall in love with actresses.
 Photop 27-3:32 F '25
 Bodeen, D. Constance Talmadge; inc. filmog. Films In
 Review 18-10:613 D '67

TALMADGE, NORMA
 Vance, E. Norma Talmadge, the adorable. Photop 7-3:
 68 F '15
 Hornblow, A. Jr. Norma Talmadge, intv. Photop 8-3:
 99 Ag '15
 Moody, J. First ladies of the land. Everybodys 40:84
 My '19
 Sumner, K. Great moving up star. Am Mag 93:36 Je
 '22
 St. Johns, A. R. The lady of the vase. Photop 24-3:38
 Ag '23
 Carroll, G. Why. Photop 26-2:72 Jl '24
 I live in the camera. Ladies Home J 42:15 Mr '25
 St. Johns, A. R. Our one and only great actress.
 Photop 29-3:58 F '26
 Close-ups; autobiography. Sat Eve Post 199:6 Mr 12;
 26 Mr 26; 30 Ap 9; 34 My 7; 41 My 21; 43 Je 25 '27
 Melcher, E. Norma Talmadge. Cinema Digest 4-3:14
 My 29 '33
 Film pioneers' role of their living immortals. Life 40:
 120 Ja 23 '56
 Obit. Illus. Lond N 232:29 Ja 4 '58
 Newsweek 51:48 Ja 6 '58

Time 71:72 Ja 6 '58
Am Ann 1958:543 '58
Brit Bk Yr 1958:519 '58
Screen World 9:226 '58
Biography. NCAB 48:92 '65
Spears, J. Norma Talmadge, inc. filmog. Films In
    Review 17-1:16 Ja '67

TALMAN, WILLIAM
    Obit. Time 92:68 S 6 '68
    Newsweek 72:103 S 9 '68
    Screen World 20:240 '69
    Last judgment. Newsweek 72:59 S 23 '68

TAMBLYN, RUSS
    Balling, F. D. Rock 'n' Roll kid. Photop 48-3:40 S '55
    Manning, D. We're not too young to marry. Photop 49-
        2:45 F '56
    Bolstad, H. Two on a marry-go-round. Photop 49-6:38
        Je '56
    Hollywood newlyweds. Look 20:39 O 2 '56
    Tamblyn, R. A lot of love went into our divorce.
        Photop 52-4:51 O '57
    Borie, M. Russ, what's your side of the story?
        Photop 54-3:74 S '58

TAMIROFF, AKIM
    Steele, J. H. Portrait with a Russian accent. Photop
        54-1:24 Ja '40

TANDY, JESSICA
    Porter, A. Tandy arrives in a streetcar. Colliers 121:
        26 Ap 17 '48
    Diesel, L. Round-the-clock with the Cronyns. Theatre
        Arts 36:44 F '52
    Biography. Cur Bio 17:54 Mr '56
        Same. Cur Bio Yrbk 1956:619 '57
    Tynan, K. A for effort, O for obstinacy. New Yorker
        35:82 Ap 25 '59
    Hayes, R. Three for two. Commonweal 70:206 My 22
        '59
    Lefferts, B. Theatre Arts gallery. Theatre Arts 43:
        30 D '59

TANNEN, JULIUS
    Obit. Screen World 17:241 '66

TAPLEY, ROSE
 Briscoe, J. Why film favorites forsook the footlights.
  Photop 6-2:95 Jl '14

TASHMAN, LILYAN
 Tully, M. Why I'm going to marry.   Photop 28-3:78 Ag
  '25
 Spensley, D. 3170 miles from Broadway.   Photop 29-4:
  33 Mr '26
 Albert, K. Connie and Lilyan. Photop 39-6:30 My '31
 Tashman, L. Frolics and follies. Pict R 33:160; 17 N;
  22 D '31
 Tashman, L. Frolics and follies . . . autobiography of
  an American chorus girl. Fashion & Society p22 Ja
  '32
 Obit. Newsweek 3:33 Mr 31 '34
 Sangster, M. E. Cinderella of Broadway.   Photop 46-1:
  43 Je '34

TATE, SHARON
 Bowers, J. Sexy little me. Sat Eve Post 240:26 My 6
  '67
 Rollins, B. Dames in the Valley of the dolls. Look 31:
  54 S 5 '67
 Haspiel, J. Sharon Tate's films. Films In Review 20-
  8:516 O '69
 Hardwicke, T. She handed her killer the weapon.
  Photop 76-5:52 N '69

TATI, JACQUES
 Knight, A. One man's movie. Sat R 37:30 Je 19 '54
 Mr. Hulot. New Yorker 30:20 Jl 17 '54
 Mayer, A. C. The art of Jacques Tati. Q of Film,
  Radio & Television 10-1:19 Fall '55
 Talk with Tati. Newsweek 52:98 N 10 '58
 Torment of Mr. Tati. Life 45:20 N 17 '58
 Biography. Cur Bio 22:44 F '61
  Same. Cur Bio Yrbk 1961:443 '62

TAYLOR, ELIZABETH
 Three little movie girls. Life 18:74 F 26 '45
 Arnold, M. Velvet girl. Photop 26-6:34 My '45
 Howe, H. Little Queen Bess. Photop 28-1:40 D '45
 Taylor, E. My Washington diary. Photop 28-6:58 My '46
 Taylor, E. Nibbles and me. Photop 29-3:32 Ag '46
 Elizabeth Taylor. Life 23:115 Jl 14 '47
 Scott, D. Life with Liz. Photop 31-4:40 S '47

Taylor, S. S.   Liz is growing up.   Photop 33-1:62 Je '48
Griswold, J. B.   Elizabeth grows up.   Am Mag 146:43
   Jl '48
Levison, F.   Elizabeth Taylor.   Life 26:78 F 21 '49
MacGregor, A.   Love and a girl named Liz Taylor.
   Photop 36-1:36 Je '49
Big dig.   Time 54:48 Ap 22 '49
School and sodas.   Time 54:50 Ag 22 '49
Brigham, R.   That young magic.   Photop 36-5:56 O '49
Taylor, F.   My daughter, Elizabeth; ed. by T. Morris
   and J. Morris.   Parents Mag 24:36 O '49
Maxwell, E.   The most exciting girl in Hollywood.
   Photop 37-1:56 Ja '50
Taylor, E.   Elizabeth Taylor.   Life 28:44 F 6 '50
Taylor, E.   The luckiest girl in town.   Photop 37-2:40
   F '50
Parsons, L. O.   Sub-deb or siren?   Photop 37-3:46 Mr
   '50
Wedding in movieland.   Life 28:46 My 22 '50
Jacobs, C. H.   Song for a bride.   Photop 37-6:36 Je '50
Parsons, L. O.   Elizabeth's love story.   Photop 37-6:38
   Je '50
Johnson, V.   Hey, Sugar.   Photop 38-3:46 S '50
Maxwell, E.   Honeymoon unlimited.   Photop 38-4:38 O
   '50
Sullivan, B.   Reunion in Paris.   Photop 38-4:44 O '50
Parsons, L. O.   Liz and Nick speak for themselves.
   Photop 39-1:28 Ja '51
Zeitlin, I.   Liz Taylor--spoiled brat or mixed-up teen-
   ager.   Photop 39-5:40 My '51
Hopper, H.   I know the truth about Liz as a bachelor
   girl.   Photop 40-2:38 Ag '51
Taylor, S.   A mother's view of Liz Taylor.   Photop 40-
   3:46 S '51
Maxwell, E.   That girl behind the headlines.   Photop 41-
   1:44 Ja '52
That old feeling.   Time 59:40 Mr 3 '52
Sakol, J.   Liz and Mike.   Photop 41-5:40 My '52
Sakol, J.   Honeymoon house.   Photop 42-1:48 Jl '52
Biography.   Cur Bio 13:54 Jl '52
   Same.   Cur Bio Yrbk 1952:576 '53
Swanson, P.   She's a new woman.   Photop 42-5:50 N '52
Swanson, P.   Two guys named Mike.   Photop 43-4:46
   Ap '53
Elizabeth Taylor's baby.   Colliers 132:28 Ag 21 '53
Fischler, G.   Home is where her heart is.   Photop 44-
   5:40 N '53

Street, R. Honeymoon with baby. Photop 45-2:56 F '54
Taylor, S. S. Elizabeth, my daughter. Ladies Home J
    71:37 F; 70 Mr; 50 Ap '54
Howe, H. Liz takes a French leave. Photop 45-6:44 Je
    '54
Edwards, R. Queen Liz of Hollywood. Photop 46-6:54
    D '54
Service, F. Vaguely wonderful. Photop 47-2:55 F '55
Elizabeth Taylor and her men. Look 19:26 Je 28 '55
Block, M. The sons in her heaven. Photop 48-2:42 Ag
    '55
Roth, S. H. Two lives of Liz Taylor. Colliers 137:34
    F 3 '56
Harris, E. Men in her life. Look 20:38 Jl 10 '56
Harris, E. Elizabeth Taylor story. Look 20:119 Je 26;
    39 Jl 10; 43 Jl 24 '56
Ott, B. She beat the barrier of beauty. Photop 50-1:
    50 Jl '56
Whitcomb, J. Liz Taylor as Edna Ferber's heroine.
    Cosmop 141:44 Ag '56
Williams, D. Odd man out. Photop 50-5:62 N '56
Mosby, A. Who will be Elizabeth Taylor's next husband?
    Photop 51-1:17 Ja '57
Frank, G. Most beautiful girl in the world. Coronet
    41:118 Mr '57
Picnic at Paradise Lake. Look 21:122 Ap 30 '57
Smith, M. Liz and Mike's madcap marriage. Photop
    51-5:47 My '57
Saxton, A. Liz Taylor's fight for life. Photop 52-4:60
    O '57
Trip Liz had to take. Life 44:30 Mr 31 '58
Wilson, E. Who said the first year was the hardest?
    Photop 53-3:32 Mr '58
Heartache: the fabulous face. Photop 53-5:59 My '58
Goodbye my love. Photop 53-6:33 Je '58
Elizabeth Taylor as Mike Todd saw her. Look 22:58 Jl
    8 '58
Schuyler, D. Garbo visits Liz. Photop 54-2:54 Ag '58
Talk with a star. Newsweek 52:56 S 1 '58
Liz plays Cat on hot tin roof. Life 45:45 S 15 '58
Just friends. Time 72:44 S 22 '58
Tale of Debbie, Eddie and the widow Todd. Life 45:39 S
    22 '58
That's show business. Newsweek 52:77 S 22 '58
From tragedy . . . new fame. Look 22:90 O 14 '58
Reich, I. Mike, those tender things remind me of you.
    Photop 54-5:50 N '58

Graves, J. Why Liz turned to Eddie. Photop 54-6:30
    D '58
Pollock, L. Tragic triangle. Photop 54-6:34 D '58
Gehman, R. Debbie Reynolds; her story. McCalls 86:
    49 Mr '59
Convert in Hollywood. Newsweek 53:36 Ap 6 '59
Convert. Time 73:80 Ap 6 '59
Life of the senses. Time 73:65 Ap 13 '59
Fast divorce OK by Debbie. Life 46:41 Ap 13 '59
Brooks, R. J. What's happening to Liz Taylor now?
    Photop 55-5:48 My '59
Stupp, K. Don't blame Liz. Photop 55-5:60 My '59
Dinter, C. What do Liz and Eddie feel when they look
    at these pictures? Photop 55-6:62 Je '59
Skolsky, S. Please give us another chance. Photop 56-
    2:25 Ag '59
Blake, E. Love in a hurry, love on the run. Photop
    56-3:30 S '59
Photoplay tracks down the truth about their baby. Photop
    56-4:27 O '59
Stupp, K. What's happening to Liz and Eddie? Photop
    56-4:29 O '59
Buchwald, A. First exclusive interview. Photop 56-6:
    40 D '59
Boeth, R. Elizabeth Taylor, aftermath of scandal.
    McCalls 87:37 Ja '60
Culver, M. What did Debbie feel when Liz and Eddie
    walked in? Photop 57-1:20 Ja '60
Adams, M. Why Liz had to leave the party. Photop
    57-3:22 Mr '60
Davidson, B. Elizabeth Taylor; her toughest role--grow-
    ing up. Look 24:68 Ap 12 '60
Dinter, C. Does God always punish? Photop 57-4:34 Ap
    '60
Hoffman, J. How much more can Liz take? Photop 58-
    1:33 Jl '60
Lyle, J. Why Liz and Eddie had to have a second honey-
    moon. Photop 58-2:29 Ag '60
Corbin, J. Was her son told Liz is leaving Eddie?
    Photop 58-4:25 O '60
Bad girls, good heroines. Look 24:84 D 6 '60
Shoot only when covered. Time 76:60 D 12 '60
Liz and Eddie's wedding gift to Debbie. Photop 58-6:14
    D '60
Draper, D. Please Elizabeth, don't let them take the
    children away. Photop 59-1:40 Ja '61
Williams, T. Five fiery ladies. Life 50:88 F 3 '61

Liz Taylor's ordeal. Newsweek 57:92 Mr 20 '61
Pages from an M. D.'s report on Liz's strange illness.
   Photop 59-3:17 Mr '61
Bittersweet Oscar triumph. Life 50:69 Ap 28 '61
Gehman, R. Elizabeth Taylor. Good H 152:64 Ap '61
Levin, R. J. Elizabeth Taylor's fight for survival.
   Redbook 117:47 My '61
Hamilton, J. Elizabeth Taylor talks of living, dying,
   acting, loving. Look 25:29 Ag 15 '61
Rand, F. What Liz knows about love. Photop 60-3:27
   S '61
Liz majeste. Time 78:62 O 6 '61
Liz is back as enchantress of Egypt. Life 51:93 O 6 '61
Star's illness costs insurers $2 million. Bsns W p104
   O 28 '61
Lyle, J. Why Eddie doesn't dare leave Liz alone.
   Photop 60-4:38 O '61
Rowland, T. They tried to murder Elizabeth. Photop
   60-5:29 N '61
Haranis, C. The life he still shares with Debbie.
   Photop 60-6:28 D '61
Elizabeth Taylor as Cleopatra. Vogue 139:40 Ja 15 '62
Hamilton, J. Four for posterity. Look 26:81 Ja 16 '62
Slater, L. Mr. Edwin J. Fisher: older and wiser and
   happier. McCalls 89:74 Ja '62
Hoffman, J. Blackmail. Photop 61-1:34 Ja '62
Elizabeth Taylor and the new Cleopatra look. Look 26:
   86 F 27 '62
Herman, P. Why Liz is gaining weight. Photop 61-2:
   48 F '62
Uneasy lies the head. Time 79:64 Mr 2 '62
Gideon, N. We're adopting two daughters. Photop 61-3:
   54 Mr '62
Poor dear little Cleopatra. Life 52:32 Ap 13 '62
Super snoops. Newsweek 59:66 Ap 16 '62
deBlasio, E. The other man in Liz's life. Photop 61-
   5:48 My '62
Carpozi, G. Their separation. Photop 61-5:50 My '62
York, C. The night they destroyed Eddie. Photop 61-6:
   4 Je '62
Gordon, G. What the world says about Liz. Photop 61-
   6:34 Je '62
Hoffman, J. What psychiatrists say about Liz. Photop
   61-6:38 Je '62
Lyle, J. America's two queens. Photop 61-6:40 Je '62
Martin, H. Love, lust and Liz Taylor. Photop 62-1:41
   Jl '62

Skolsky, S.   Their strange marriage deal.   Photop 62-1:
   45 Jl '62
Oates, F.   He tells everything he saw.   Photop 62-1:77
   Jl '62
Gordon, G.   Eddie exposes Liz.   Photop 62-1:51 Jl '62
Can you forgive Liz?   Photop 62-1:52 Jl '62
Hoffman, J.   The terrible truth about her.   Photop 62-2:
   38 Ag '62
Gordon, G.   Liz begs come back.   Photop 62-2:45 Ag '62
Wolk, Dr.   Why she goes from man to man.   Photop
   62-3:44 S '62
Deardoff, R.   Aftermath of an adoption.   Redbook 119:
   60 O '62
Richards, J.   The shameless lovers.   Photop 62-4:38
   O '62
Hoffman, J.   Wedding bells toll their doom.   Photop 62-
   5:44 N '62
York, C.   Is she crawling back to Eddie.   Photop 62-6:4
   D '62
Davis, D.   Liz loses Burton.   Photop 62-6:46 D '62
Biography.   Am Ann 1962:753 '62
Edwards, D.   Her love deal with the Burtons.   Photop
   63-2:48 F '63
Carpozi, G.   She fights Liz.   Photop 63-3:45 Mr '63
Carpozi, G.   Mob beats up Burton.   Photop 63-4:14 Ap
   '63
Reich, W. T.   Liz Taylor poses nude.   Photop 63-4:36
   Ap '63
Hamilton, J.   Elizabeth Taylor talks about Cleopatra.
   Look 27:41 My 7 '63
Joya, M.   How crippled is she?   Photop 63-5:46 My '63
Wanger, W. & Hyams, J.   Trials an tribulations of an
   epic film.   Sat Eve Post 236:29 Je 1 '63
Carpozi, G.   How Liz forced me to give up.   Photop 63-
   6:4 Je '63
Valentine, L.   How she can be saved.   Photop 63-6:41
   Je '63
Keats to the ducks.   Newsweek 62:77 Jl 15 '63
deBlasio, E.   Liz wedding gown.   Photop 64-1:36 Jl '63
Joya, M.   Sybil's plan to ruin Liz.   Photop 64-2:29 Ag
   '63
deBlasio, E.   What Burton does to Liz.   Photop 64-3:33
   S '63
Ringgold, G.   Elizabeth Taylor, her life story and a com-
   plete index of her films to date.   Film Careers 1-1:
   complete issue.   Fall '63
Musel, R.   Liz looks at London.   TV Guide 11-40:4

O 5 '63

Johnson, P. Dining with Liz. New Statesm 66:524 O 18
'63

Cronin, J. The four-letter word that rules her. Photop
64-4:36 O '63

Hopper, H. Passion and waste. Photop 64-5:41 N '63

Perils of a Mexican divorce. Time 82:34 D 27 '63

Brewer, D. Burton two-timing Liz. Photop 64-6:47 D
'63

I'll never let Eddie take Liza. Photop 65-2:52 F '64

Hammond, J. Liz gets Burton--abuse and all. Photop
65-3:40 Mr '64

Lyle, J. Can Burton hold Liz and his liquor? Photop
65-4:52 Ap '64

Asher, E. Liz in physical agony. Photop 65-5:40 My '64

Carpozi, G. Eddie owns Liz. Photop 65-5:44 My '64

York, C. The night they shared a room with Eddie.
Photop 66-1:20 Jl '64

Hoffman, J. Her honeymoon beating. Photop 66-1:48 Jl
'64

Muhan, T. Success et cetera. Show 4-9:32 O '64

Elkin, S. Miss Taylor and family; an outside view.
Esquire 62:118 N '64

Meryman, R. Elizabeth Taylor; she takes a hard, utterly
frank look at herself: I refuse to cure my public image. Life 57:74 D 18 '64

Somers, A. He offers her another man. Photop 67-1:
23 Ja '65

Hoffman, J. Burton crawls for Liz. Photop 67-2:41 F
'65

Burton, R. Burton writes of Taylor. Vogue 145:128 My
1 '65

Hamilton, J. King and queen. Look 29:26 Mr 9 '65

Hoffman, J. Her nights with Richard. Photop 67-4:41
Ap '65

Hoffman, J. Burton's ruining me with liquor. Photop
68-1:59 Jl '65

Carpozi, G. Eddie won't get Liza. Photop 68-2:36 Ag
'65

Let him . . . be the first to throw a stone. Quotation
from Elizabeth Taylor. Christian Cent 82:1463 N 24
'65

Elizabeth Taylor; excerpts. Ladies Home J 82:79 N '65

Taylor, E. Elizabeth Taylor; informal memoir, excerpts.
Ladies Home J 82:79 N '65

Buchwald, A. Liz and I. Ladies Home J 83:26 Ja '65

Roddy, J. Elizabeth Taylor and Richard Burton: the

night of the brawl.   Look 30:42 F 8 '66

Smith, M.   Burtons play Faustus at Oxford as a favor to
    Richard's old tutor.   Life 60:79 Mr 4 '66

Smith, M.   Liz launches 1,000 ships; Faustus at Oxford.
    Life 60:78 Mr 4 '66

Bawd of Avon.   Time 87:58 Je 3 '66

Thompson, T.   Surprising Liz in a film shocker.   Life
    60:87 Je 10 '66

Braddon, R.   Richard Burton to Liz: I love thee not.
    Sat Eve Post 239:88 D 3 '66

Sage, T.   Who's afraid of Dr. Faustus?   Nat R 18:1319
    D 27 '66

Redfield, W.   Night Elizabeth Taylor said "so what?"
    and Richard Burton kicked the television set in.
    Esquire 67:108 Ja '67

Burton, R.   His Liz: a scheming charmer.   Life 62:78
    F 24 '67

Israel, L.   Rise and fall and rise of Elizabeth Taylor.
    Esquire 67:97 Mr '67

Rasponi, L.   Burtons in Dahomey.   Vogue 149:92 Ap 15
    '67

Garrison, L.   On location with Richard and Elizabeth
    (and 145 friends).   N.Y. Times Mag p30 My 7 '67

On location with Richard and Liz; why they're never dull.
    Look 31:64 Je 27 '67

Happy anniversary, Elizabeth and Richard; tributes from
    their friends.   McCalls 94:68 Je '67

Glenville, P.   Peter Glenville talks about the Burtons.
    Vogue 150:282 S 1 '67

Knight, A.   Liz Taylor festival.   Sat R 50:26 O 28 '67

Valentine, L.   What he gets from liquor.   Photop 72-6:
    46 D '67

Pepper, C. G.   Voyage with the Burtons.   McCalls 95:
    66 Ja '68

Haranis, C.   Her narrow escape from death.   Photop 73-
    1:62 Ja '68

Her secret letter about Eddie.   Photop 73-3:61 Mr '68

Musel, R.   The Burtons turn to TV for fun and profit.
    TV Guide 16-22:16 Je 1 '68

Sheed, W.   Burton and Taylor must go.   Esquire 70:173
    O '68

Jamis, H.   Love nor liquor can help her.   Photop 74-5:
    41 N '68

Carmel, B.   Looks in mirror and weeps.   Photop 74-6:
    52 D '68

Thompson, T.   While Burton romances Rex, Liz weighs
    her power and her fortune.   Life 66:65 Ja 17 '69

Birstein, A. Liz Taylor and Richard Burton; what it's like to be walking investments. Vogue 153:100 F 15 '69

Riley, N. Their shocking love scenes. Photop 75-2:39 F '69

Leiter, N. A psychiatrist's report. Photop 75-2:41 F '69

O'Brien, F. I won't be a puppet. Photop 75-3:40 Mr '69

Perry, A. Talks about father's death. Photop 75-3:43 Mr '69

Lurie, D. Elizabeth Taylor talks about being a mother; intv. Ladies Home J 36:83 Mr '69

Herritt, C. I don't have cancer. Photop 75-5:38 My '69

Howard, E. Goes to hospital alone. Photop 75-6:52 Je '69

Conner, P. A search for a world without pain. Photop 76-1:64 Jl '69

Collins, P. Everyone close to me is dying. Photop 76-6:42 D '69

TAYLOR, ESTELLE
Ludlam, H. ed. Our home in the limelight. Colliers 84: 22 O 12 '29

Obit. Newsweek 51:64 Ap 28 '58
    Time 72:96 Ap 28 '58

TAYLOR, ROBERT
Hunt, J. L. Robert Taylor chooses success. Photop 48-4:28 S '35

Ramsey, W. Some call it love. Photop 50-2:28 Ag '36

Anything can happen in Hollywood; autobiography.
    Ladies Home J 53:8 S '36

Crichton, K. Heart bumper. Colliers 98:55 O 3 '36

Fourth in Motion Picture Herald's list. Time 29:25 Ja 18 '37

Logan, H. B. Jr. Robert Taylor's true love story.
    Photop 51-1:14 Ja '37

St. Johns, A. R. Can Robert Taylor escape Hollywood's love racket? Photop 51-3:24 Mr '37

Ramsey, W. Barbara Stanwyck tells why she won't marry Robert Taylor. Photop 51-4:24 Ap '37

Baldwin, F. Dangers that face Robert Taylor. Photop 51-8:36 Ag '37

Doherty, E. Give Robert Taylor a break. Photop 51-11:18 N '37

Ormiston, R. You have to "play ball." Photop 18-6:70

My '41

Peters, S. My Hollywood friends. Photop 30-3:74 F '47

Deere, D. Date with Bob and the Queen. Photop 31-4:52
S '47

Biography. Cur Bio 13:45 My '52

Same. Cur Bio Yrbk 1952:578 '53

Albert, K. Secrets behind Hollywood heartbreaks.
Photop 42-5:45 N '52

Leon, R. Runaway from romance? Photop 43-4:56 Ap
'53

Dudley, F. It's no secret anymore. Photop 46-2:29 Ag
'54

Parsons, L. O. Robert Taylor, by accident, a star a-
gain. Cosmop 157:26 S '54

Waterbury, R. Their date with destiny. Photop 47-4:
51 Ap '55

Taylor talks turkey. TV Guide 7-41:24 O 10 '59

Hero's a private eye. Newsweek 54:72 O 12 '59

Nichols, M. Taylored design for living. Coronet 48:12
My '60

Tornabene, L. Wives you'd like to know; Mrs. Robert
Taylor. Good H 152:28 Ja '61

Robert Taylor; no more glamour for him. Look 25:99
Mr 28 '61

Pollock, L. Robert Taylor: the man behind the slick
pan. Coronet 49:84 Ap '61

He showed up on her doorstep. TV Guide 9-19:17 My 13
'61

When youth and glamor fade--what then? TV Guide 9-50:
6 D 16 '61

Bowers, R. L. Robert Taylor, inc. filmog. Films In
Review 17-1:1 Ja '67

Taylor, R. The golden age. Films Fan Mo 96:3 Je '69

Obit. Newsweek 73:71 Je 16 '69
Time 93:72 Je 20 '69
Cur Bio 30:46 Jl '69

TAYLOR, ROD

Downing, H. A long way from home. Photop 51-3:56
Mr '57

He came from down under. TV Guide 9-17:17 Ap 29 '61

Ardmore, J. Look who's in the mood for love. Photop
60-1:62 Jl '61

People on the way up. Sat Eve Post 235:26 My 19 '62

Corbin, J. Pin-up #14. Photop 64-2:44 Ag '63

Preston, W. A bachelor's shocking discovery. Photop
64-3:53 S '63

Wilkie, J. Our marriage wasn't made in heaven.
  Photop 65-6:42 Je '64
Terry, P. We are separating. Photop 67-2:12 F '65

TEARLE, CONWAY
  Smith, A. A merry Hamlet. Photop 14-4:37 S '18
  Patterson, A. Being a screen idol's wife. Photop 20-
    3:68 Ag '21
  Obit. Newsweek 12:4 O 10 '38

TELLEGEN, LOU
  Merritt, P. Bread and butter. Everybodys 41:15 S '19

TEMPLE, SHIRLEY
  Shawn, B. Shirley, take a bow. Photop 46-3:69 Ap '34
  They stand out from the crowd. Lit Digest 118:10 Jl
    14 '34
  Just pretending nets Shirley Temple $1,250 a week.
    Newsweek 4:24 Jl 28 '34
  Skinner, R. D. Acting of Shirley Temple. Commonweal
    20:389 Ag 17 '34
  Starlette. Am Mag 118:57 Ag '34
  Shawell, J. Hollywood's Golidlocks. Pict R 36:4 N '34
  Temple, G. Bringing up Shirley. Am Mag 119:26 F '35
  My life and times; autobiography. Pict R 36:7 Ag 10 S
    '35
  St. Johns, A. R. Shirley wants the quintuplets for
    Christmas. Photop 48-7:22 D '35
  Pee Wee's progress. Time 27:36 Ap 27 '36
  Baskette, K. The amazing Temple family. Photop 49-4:
    14 Ap '36
  Cocks, D. Beauty secrets of a star; intv. with Mrs.
    Temple. Pict R 37:65 My '36
  Pee Wee's progress; abridged. Read Digest 28:21 Je '36
  Cleveland, P. S. A toast to Shirley Temple. Photop 51-
    1:71 Ja '37
  Jackson, M. Protecting the future of the greatest little
    star. Photop 51-3:26 Mr '37
  Plush and/roses for Shirley Temple. Lit Digest 123:19
    Jl 10 '37
  Hamilton, S. Myth Shirley Temple. Photop 51-9:38 S
    '37
  Willson, D. The answer to Shirley Temple's future.
    Photop 51-11:24 N '37
  Martin, T. Miracle moppet. Ladies Home J 55:22 F '38
  Brushwork. Time 31:40 My 23 '38
  Baskette, K. A goddess grows up. Photop 52-5:14 My '38

McEvoy, J. P.   Little Miss Miracle.   Sat Eve Post 211:
    10 Jl 9 '38
Shirley Temple at home.   House B 80:26 Ag '38
Shultz, G. D.   Child care and training: Shirley Temple.
    Bet Hom & Gard 17:46 S '38
Foster, C. J.   Mrs. Temple on bringing up Shirley.
    Parents Mag 132:22 O '38
McEvoy, J. P.   Shirley in wonderland.   Womans H C
    65:19 N '38
Shirley Temple's last letter to Santa.   Photop 53-1:9 Ja
    '39
Shirley Temple in the Little princess.   Newsweek 13:32
    Mr 20 '39
Kutner, N.   Box office babies.   Colliers 103:74 Mr 25 '39
McGinnis, E. W.   Little princess.   St N 66:25 Mr '39
McGinnis, E. W.   Little Miss Broadway.   St N 65:40 Jl
    '39
McGinnis, E. W.   Susannah of the mounties.   St N 66:41
    Jl '39
Chase, F.   At last Shirley surrenders to radio.   Radio
    Guide p4 D 29 '39
Little Miss Christmas.   Time 35:31 Ja 1 '40
Condon, F.   No mothers wanted; Shirley Temple's suc-
    cessor has been chosen, so keep the children home.
    Colliers 106:20 Ag 17 '40
Nugent, F. S.   Now it's Miss Temple.   N. Y. Times Mag
    p8 N 2 '41
Shirley as a junior miss.   Newsweek 18:70 D 15 '41
Junior Miss Temple.   Newsweek 19:67 Mr 16 '42
First glamour portraits.   Life 12:8 Mr 30 '42
Whirling Shirley.   Newsweek 19:62 My 25 '42
Service, F.   First kiss--and Miss Temple.   Photop 21-
    1:41 Je '42
Picture story.   N. Y. Times Mag p18 O 3 '43
Life goes to Shirley Temple's birthday party.   Life 16:
    116 My 15 '44
Parsons, L. O.   Shirley--at the turn of the teens.   Photop
    25-1:32 Je '44
Sweet sixteen.   Am Mag 138:122 Jl '44
Shirley visits New York.   Womans H C 71:36 D '44
Markel, H.   Goldilocks grows up, but definitely.   N. Y.
    Times Mag p18 F 11 '45
Janis, E.   Shirley Temple--in short.   Photop 26-4:38 Mr
    '45
Herrod, V.   Etiquette for teenagers; posed by Shirley
    Temple.   Am Hom 33:90 Ap '45
Waterbury, R.   The love story of Shirley Temple and

her sergeant. Photop 27-2:56 Jl '45
And they lived happily. Newsweek 26:32 O 1 '45
Shirley marries. Life 19:45 O 1 '45
Biography. Cur Bio O '45
Waterbury, R. Shirley, Lohengrin and happiness. Photop
    28-1:28 D '45
Arnold, M. Super matron. Photop 28-5:39 Ap '46
Shipp, C. Big girl. Photop 29-4:56 S '46
Ten years of Temple. Life 21:66 N 25 '46
Agar, S. T. Ten rules for a happy honeymoon. Photop
    31-1:34 Je '47
Temple, S. The Shirley I know. Photop 31-6:64 N '47
Miller, L. Shirley Temple expects. Womans H C 75:4
    F '48
Temple, S. For my baby. Photop 32-4:44 Mr '48
Parsons, L. O. The Temple lullaby. Photop 33-3:33 Ap
    '48
Shirley Temple's baby. Life 24:34 My 31 '48
Temple, S. A letter to my daughter. Photop 34-6:68 My
    '49
McElroy, J. Breakfast in Hollywood. Photop 36-3:58 Ag
    '49
Three little girls grow up. Good H 129:168 S '49
Dignified manner. Time 54:100 O 24 '49
Little Miss Misfire. Newsweek 34:26 O 24 '49
Parsons, L. O. What happened to the Temple marriage.
    Photop 36-7:32 D '49
Maxwell, E. This you must understand. Photop 37-2:34
    F '50
Zeitlin, I. Living is fun! Photop 38-5:38 N '50
Ormiston, R. Hawaiian love song. Photop 39-2:33 F '51
Wheeler, L. The house that grew up. Photop 39-3:56
    Mr '51
Hopper, H. Shirley Temple won't come back. Photop
    42-3:42 S '52
Shirley Temple's favorite role. Colliers 130:60 O 11 '52
Happy home of Shirley Temple Black. Good H 142:100 My
    '56
Black, S. T. Tomorrow I'll be 30. Good H 145:115 N
    '57
Shirley Temple: 20 years later. TV Guide 6-2:24 Ja 11
    '58
Return of the bluebird. Time 71:62 Ja 27 '58
Shirley opens Storybook. Life 44:38 F 3 '58
Press conference. Pub W 173:38 Mr 24 '58
Nichols, M. Child stars who came back. Coronet 43:88
    Mr '58

Pollock, L.   Why Shirley came back.   Photop 53-3:57
   Mr '58
Forever Shirley.   TV Guide 6-18:20 My 3 '58
Bookstores benefit from new career of Shirley Temple.
   Pub W 174:35 D 29 '58
Shirley Temple's scrapbook.   McCalls 86:64 D '58
Ardmore, J.   Mommy did you really know Shirley Temple?
   Photop 57-2:44 F '60
Wolters, L.   Shirley Temple's three careers.   Todays
   Health 38:39 N '60
Still aboard the good ship Lollipop.   TV Guide 8-49:17 D
   3 '60
Temple, S.   Crisis that changed my life.   Redbook 116:
   38 Ja '61
Nichols, M.   Golden girl grows up.   Coronet 49:69 Mr '61
Liston, J.   At home with Shirley Temple.   Am Home 64:
   25 My '61
Burdick, L.   Shirley Temple's films.   Films In Review
   14-5:318 My '63
Temple, S.   Tomorrow I'll be 35.   McCalls 90:83 My
   '63
Jennings, R.   Shirley Temple: her eyes are still danc-
   ing.   Sat Eve Post 238:93 Je 5 '65
Shirley's big daughter.   Life 59:65 Jl 30 '65
Lloyd, J.   Washington report.   Sr Schol 89:sup6 N 18 '66
Sex at the box office.   McCalls 94:45 Ja '67
Holy lollipop!   Newsweek 69:64 Je 19 '67
Shirley runs but not on the Temple ticket.   Life 63:27 S
   8 '67
Mrs. Black for congress.   Time 90:16 S 8 '67
Baby take a bow.   Newsweek 70:21 S 11 '67
People of the week.   U.S. News 63:20 S 11 '67
Eller, J. N.   Politics American style.   America 117:265
   S 16 '67
Berger, A.   Entertainment culture.   Nation 205:228 S 18
   '67
Berger, A.   Politics of entertainment.   Nation 205:422
   O 30 '67
Duscha, J.   How do you fight Shirley Temple?   Reporter
   37:21 N 2 '67
Alexander, S.   Little Shirley Temple lives.   Life 63:17
   N 3 '67
Moms and pops, arise!   Newsweek 70:35 N 6 '67
Mrs. Black and the neighbors.   Time 90:27 N 10 '67
Williams, L.   Little Miss Candidate.   Look 31:86 N 14 '67
Black out.   New Repub.   157:7 N 25 '67
Lollipop.   Newsweek 70:35 N 27 '67

Miscasting of Shirley.   Nation 205:580 D 4 '67
Ringgold, G.   Shirley Temple; inc. filmog.   Screen Facts
    12:1 n. d.

TERRY, ALICE
    Barton, R.   You never know your luck.   Photop 20-5:21
        O '21
    Evans, D.   She wants to be wicked.   Photop 22-1:45 D
        '22
    Johaneson, B.   Alice and Miss Terry.   Photop 25-2:41
        Ja '24
    Howe, H.   When Alice played a German soldier with a
        beard.   Photop 27-3:59 F '25

TERRY, PHILLIP
    Waterbury, R.   Love is laughter.   Photop 21-5:66 O '42
    O'Liam, D.   Solid citizen.   Photop 26-5:54 Ap '45
    Waterbury, R.   Stormy passage for Joan and Phil.
        Photop 28-4:29 Mr '46

TERRY-THOMAS
    Biography.   Cur Bio 22:43 Mr '61
        Same.   Cur Bio Yrbk 1961:451 '62
    Terry-Thomas.   There'll always be a British Cabinet.
        Show 1-1:96 O '61
    Terry-Thomas.   Playing myself and others.   Films &
        Filming 8-3:11 D '61
    Which is the real Hoar-Stevens?   Time 85:61 Je 25 '65
    Raddatz, L.   His gap is his fortune.   TV Guide 14-35:12
        Ag 27 '66

TETZEL, JOAN
    Handsome couple.   Life 24:71 F 16 '48
    Hard time.   Theatre Arts 38:16 F '54

THAXTER, PHYLLIS
    Arvad, I.   That Thaxter girl.   Photop 26-4:45 Mr '45
    Nugent, F.   Maine event.   Photop 28-1:60 D '45
    Phyllis Thaxter, inc. filmog.   Films In Review 14-4:254
        Ap '63

THEBY, ROSEMARY
    Jackson, J.   A chat with Rosemary Theby.   Photop 4-6:
        27 N '13
    Corliss, A.   Once of the "Hey you" squad.   Photop 11-1:
        123 D '16
    Bates, B.   There's no rue about Rosemary.   Photop

18-5:28 O '20

THIESS, URSULA
  Look of sweet irony.   Life 30:71 Je 4 '51
  Leon, R.   Runaway from romance?   Photop 43-4:56 Ap
    '53
  On stardom's stairway.   Coronet 35:48 Ja '54
  Dudley, F.   It's no secret anymore.   Photop 46-2:29
    Ag '54
  Waterbury, R.   Their date with destiny.   Photop 47-4:51
    Ap '55
  Tornabene, L.   Wives you'd like to know: Mrs. Robert
    Taylor.   Good H 152:28 Ja '61
  He showed up on her doorstep.   TV Guide 9-19:17 My 13
    '61

THOMAS, DANNY
  Lewis, L.   Wailing Syrian.   Colliers 117:54 Ap 20 '46
  New ventures.   Time 51:69 Ja 12 '48
  Donovan, R.   Sad and successful.   Colliers 129:24 Je 14
    '52
  Rosten, L.   Danny Thomas--extraordinary Jacobs.   Look
    17:51 N 17 '53
  Shayon, R. L.   TV and radio: Make room for daddy
    starring Danny Thomas.   Sat R 36:34 N 21 '53
  Two-family man; Make room for daddy.   Newsweek 43:
    86 Ap 5 '54
  Wood, C.   TV personalities biographical sketchbook.
    TV Personalities p20 '54
  Trouble: it's wonderful.   Am Mag 160:17 N '55
  Shipp, C.   Danny Thomas . . . he has a wonderful world
    all his own.   Look 21:106 D 24 '57
  Treacle cutter.   Time 71:39 Ap 21 '58
  Martin, P.   I call on Danny Thomas.   Sat Eve Post 231:
    20 Ja 17 '59
  How to sleep nights; ed by J. C. G. Coniff.   Todays
    Health 37:32 Ja '59
  Biography.   Cur Bio 20:39 F '59
    Same.   Cur Bio Yrbk 1959:466 '60
  Nichols, M.   Danny the toothless lion.   Coronet 47:15
    Ap '60
  Thomas, N.   My father, Danny Thomas.   Good H 154:
    36 Mr '62
  Entertainer, two researchers honored by AMA.   Todays
    Health 44:17 Ag '66
  Rollin, B.   Marlo Thomas; That girl is some girl.
    Look 31:124 O 17 '67

THOMAS, OLIVE
  Lloyd, J. A Broadway queen gone west. Photop 13-1:
    60 D '17
  Evans, D. Grand crossings impressions. Photop 14-5:
    58 O '18
  Obit. Era p20 S 15 '20

THOMPSON, HUGH
  Smith, A. The lady? No, the car. Photop 14-4:42 S
    '18

THOMPSON, KAY
  Dizzy-making. Time 50:79 N 10 '47
  New comedienne. Life 24:73 Ja 26 '48
  Clurman, H. Theatre. New Repub 119:28 Jl 19 '48
  Mr. Harper. After hours. Harper 197:117 Jl '48
  Sly, we call it. Time 63:40 F 8 '54
  Kay and Eloise. Am Mag 161:46 Ap '56
  Lindsay, C. McCalls visits Kay Thompson. McCalls
    84:6 Ja '57
  Hurdling a spectacular. Newsweek 50:86 O 14 '57
  Eloise cashes in. Life 43:121 D 9 '57
  Biography. Cur Bio 20:43 Ap '59
    Same. Cur Bio Yrbk 1959:449 '60
  Authors and editors. Pub W 195:13 My 12 '69

THOMPSON, MARSHALL
  Wheeler, L. Bought and planned for. Photop 40-5:60 N
    '51
  Hano, A. The "little fellow" of Daktari. TV Guide 14-
    32:15 Ag 6 '66

THOMSON, FRED
  Tate, L. N. Athlete, preacher, actor. Photop 25-2:58
    Ja '24
  Stone, H. B. Fred Thomson, inc. filmog. Films In Re-
    view 11-6:380 Je/Jl '60

THOMSON, KENNETH
  Eustis, M. Footlight parade. Theatre Arts 23:878 D '39
  Obit. Screen World 19:240 '68

THORBURN, JUNE
  Obit. Screen World 19:240 '68

THORNDIKE, SYBIL
  I look at the audience. Theatre Arts 16:67 Ja '32

Biography.   Cur Bio 14:47 D '53
Same.   Cur Bio Yrbk 1953:621 '53
Barker, F. G.   The vicar's daughter.   Plays & Players
1-4:4 Ja '54
Guthrie, T.   After 20 years--re-enter Dame Sybil.
N.Y. Times Mag p62 Ja 27 '57
Sir Lewis and Dame Sybil.   Vogue 129:60 F 15 '57
Driver, T. F.   Player's the thing; intv.   Christian Cent
74:267 F 27 '57
Team.   New Yorker 33:26 Mr 2 '57

THREE STOOGES
(MOE HOWARD, JOE DE RITA, CURLY HOWARD,
LARRY FINE)
Masters of mayhem.   TV Guide 7-12:20 Mr 21 '59
Refinished antiques: Three Stooges.   Time 73:54 My 4
'59
Give 'em a bop on the casaba.   TV Guide 13-10:19 Mr 6
'65
Maltin, L.   Three Stooges; inc. filmog.   Film Fan Mo
81:16 Mr '68

THULIN, INGRID
Lerman, L.   New Grace Kellys.   Mlle 50:55 D '59
Ingmar's Ingrid.   Time 83:76 F 28 '64

THURMAN, MARY
Yost, R. M. Jr.   Washed into Drama.   Photop 16-2:36 Jl
'19
St. James, A. R.   Mary got her hair wet.   Photop 20-
2:34 Jl '21

TIERNEY, GENE
Debutant makes her entrance in a Broadway success.
Life 8:35 F 19 '40
Pringle, H. F.   Preview of a star.   Colliers 105:22 Je
29 '40
Poetess.   Am Mag 131:90 My '41
Career climaxed by Shanghai gesture.   Life 11:63 N 10
'41
Reid, J.   This is how it really happened.   Photop 20-3:
28 F '42
Skolsky, S.   The "get" girl.   Photop 22-5:32 Ap '43
Tierney, G.   My great adventure.   Photop 25-3:50 Ag '44
Howe, H.   Design for delight.   Photop 30-1:45 D '46
Maxwell, E.   The G. E. T. girl.   Photop 31-2:42 Jl '47
Tierney, P.   I was there.   Photop 31-6:58 N '47

Wheeler, L.   Treasure house.   Photop 38-4:54 O '50
Riley, V.   Sitting pretty.   Photop 39-3:54 Mr '51
Reborn star.   Time 72:77 S 29 '58
Welcome for a troubled beauty.   Life 45:87 S 29 '58
Hoffman, J.   Something terrible's going to happen to me
    again.   Photop 58-4:40 O '60
She was Laura.   Newsweek 71:8 Ja 29 '68

TIERNEY, LAWRENCE
MacGregor, R.   Two brothers.   Photop 41-4:46 Ap '52

TIFFIN, PAMELA
Miller, E.   Pretty brunette and a German brat.   Seven-
    teen 20:112 N '61
People on the way up.   Sat Eve Post 234:24 D 2 '61
Person of promise.   Films & Filming 8-4:21 Ja '62
Pamela's progress.   Esquire 57:92 Ja '62

TINCHER, FAY
Lloyd, J.   Let Fay try it.   Photop 10-1:53 Je '16

TOBEY, KENNETH
Zeitlin, I.   A Tobey and a Peck.   Photop 41-4:58 Ap '52
Wood, C.   TV personalities biographical sketchbook.
    TV Personalities p153 '57

TOBIAS, GEORGE
Hobson, D.   The last of the oldtime bachelors.   TV Guide
    15-20:26 My 20 '67

TOBIN, GENEVIEVE
Halle, L.   Genevieve goes torrid.   Photop 42-1:30 Je '32

TODD, ANN
Ann Todd is best paid British star.   Life 20:68 Ja 28 '46
First Shakespearean part.   Play & Players 2-1:12 O '54

TODD, RICHARD
Arnold, M.   Level-headed Lochinvar.   Photop 37-5:72
    My '50
Biography.   Cur Bio 16:44 D '55
    Same.   Cur Bio Yrbk 1955:610 '56

TODD, THELMA
Carroll, L.   What Hollywood did to a New England school-
    marm.   Photop 41-3:54 F '32
Maltin, L.   The films of Thelma Todd, inc. filmog.

Film Fan Mo 63:3 S '66
Schwartz, W. Filmography. Films In Review 20-2:129
    F '69
Berkow, G. Filmography. Films In Review 20-3:189
    Mr '69

TOLER, SIDNEY
Toler, S. There's an urge in acting. Theatre p37 My
    '30
Obit. Newsweek 29:57 F 24 '47
    Time 49:82 F 24 '47

TONE, FRANCHOT
Young, S. Title to be announced. New Repub 73:16 N
    16 '32
Jamison, J. I'd rather know Joan than anyone else.
    Photop 44-6:38 N '33
Crichton, K. Limelight blues. Colliers 93:15 Je 30 '34
Cummings, M. Franchot Tone--fortune's favorite.
    Photop 48-4:52 S '35
Kingsley, G. Love honor and obey that impulse. Photop
    49-4:36 Ap '36
Manners, D. Second marriage. Photop 49-5:24 My '36
Ramsey, W. The intimate life of a gentleman rebel.
    Photop 51-5:34 My; 51-6:56 Je '37
Young, S. Mr. Tone and Mr. Hemingway. New Repub
    102:408 Mr 25 '40
Biography. Cur Bio '40
Ladies and gentlemen. Time 58:42 N 12 '51
Funke, L. Uncle Vanya from Fourth street to film.
    Theatre Arts 41:28 O '57
A mellow Tone. TV Guide 6-33:28 Ag 16 '58
Who has ever had a better time? TV Guide 14-1:12 Ja
    1 '66
Obit. Time 92:92 S 27 '68
    Newsweek 72:115 S 30 '68
    Cur Bio 29:43 N '68
    Cur Bio Yrbk 1968:463 '69
    Screen World 20:240 '69

TONG, SAMMEE
Obit. Screen World 16:225 '65

TOOMEY, REGIS
Gabriel blow that horn. Am Mer 55:600 N '42
    Same abridged. Read Digest 42:96 Ja '43

TOREN, MARTA
Crichton, K.   Hunting of a Swede.   Colliers 121:26 Je
    19 '48
Marta's eyes on Hollywood.   Life 26:103 Je 13 '49
Obit.   Screen World 9:226 '58
Roman, R. C.   Marta Toren.   Films In Review 10-7:
    444 Ag/S '59

TORRENCE, ERNEST
Kennedy, J. B.   Lank and Ernest.   Colliers 84:18 Ag 24
    '29
Obit.   Etude 51:559 Ag '33

TORRES, RAQUEL
Albert, K.   Right this way please.   Photop 35-1:63 D '28

TOTO
Glazier, T. H.   Toto; portrait of a clown.   Theatre Arts
    23:597 Ag '39
Toto.   Vogue 128:86 Jl '56
Obit.   Screen World 19:240 '68

TOTTER, AUDREY
Soap to cinema.   Am Mag 140:134 O '45
McClelland, D.   Audrey Totter, inc. filmog.   Film Fan
    Mo 91:15 Ja '69

TOWERS, CONSTANCE
Connie Towers.   Look 23:78 Je 9 '59
Nichols, M.   Stardom bound.   Coronet 47:67 Ja '60

TRACY, LEE
Brenton, G.   A very unreliable fellow.   Photop 42-5:59
    O '32
Ergenbright, E. L.   The most startling confession any
    star ever made.   Photop 51-1:24 Ja '37
He becomes Martin Kane the third this week.   TV Guide
    5-21:24 My 23 '52
Only one murder.   Time 60:80 N 3 '52
The private life of a private eye.   TV Guide 6-7:10 F 23
    '53
Lee Tracy vs. Martin Kane.   TV Guide 1-20:13 Ag 14
    '53
Inglis, R. A.   Lee Tracy in TV action; Martin Kane,
    private eye.   Am Mer 77:117 Ag '53
Talk with a star.   Newsweek 55:86 Ap 11 '60
Obit.   Time 92:98 O 25 '68

Newsweek 72:72 O 28 '68
Screen World 20:240 '69
Jacobs, J. Lee Tracy, inc. filmog. Screen Facts 1-
6:1 n. d.

TRACY, SPENCER

Biery, R. Worry! Who, me? Photop 43-1:60 D '32
Sharpe, H. The adventurous life of Spencer Tracy.
Photop 51-2:22 F; 51-3:56 Mr; 51-4:56 Ap '37
Log of We're here. Womans H C 64:13 Ap '37
Hall, G. Spencer Tracy faces forty. Photop 52-3:30
Mr '38
Sullivan, E. Actor's actor. Pict R 39:21 Jl '38
Steele, J. H. Portrait of a man who has what he wants.
Photop 53-5:32 My '39
Rathbone, A. D. Out of Spencer Tracy's yesterdays.
Photop 54-10:58 O '40
Dress suit. Am Mag 134:52 D '42
Tracy, C. E. My kid brother Spence. Photop 23-3:43
Ag '43
Biography. Cur Bio '43
St. Johns, A. R. Man of conflict. Photop 26-3:30 F
'45
My modest friend. Am Mag 139:64 Mr '45
Rugged path. New Yorker 21:24 N 24 '45
Spencer Tracy's return. Life 19:88 D 3 '45
Keethe, L. I call it heart. Photop 33-4:56 S '48
Ironjaw and golden heart. Life 35:108 N 9 '53
Great star ages gracefully. Life 38:77 Ja 31 '53
Senseney, D. The vintage years. Photop 50-3:66 S '56
When co-stars get together. Newsweek 49:118 My 27 '57
Tracy on Tracy. Newsweek 57:80 Ja 9 '61
Cowie, R. Spencer Tracy. Films & Filming 7-9:8 Je
'61
Davidson, B. Spencer Tracy. Look 26:36 Ja 30 '62
Tozzi, R. Spencer Tracy, inc. filmog. Films In Review
17-10:601 D '66
Obit. Time 89:92 Je 16 '67
Newsweek 69:84 Je 19 '67
Cur Bio 28:46 O '67
Cur Bio Yrbk 1967:484 '68
Brit Bk Yr 1968:599 '68
Screen World 19:240 '68
Old Bucko. Newsweek 69:43 Je 19 '67
Kramer, S. He could wither you with a glance. Life
62:69 Je 30 '67
Hamilton, J. Last visit with two undimmed stars.

Look 31:26 Jl 11 '67
Graham, S. Spencer Tracy and Katharine Hepburn.
Ladies Home J 85:94 D '68
Keneas, A. Spence. Newsweek 73:116 Je 9 '69

TRACY, WILLIAM
Obit. Screen World 19:240 '68

TRAVERS, DICK
Craig, J. Travers, Viking of Hudson Bay. Photop 7-5:
118 Ap '15

TRAVERS, HENRY
Young, S. Mr. Henry Travers. New Repub 58:308 My
1 '29

TRAVERSE, MADLAINE
Obit. Screen World 16:226 '65

TREACHER, ARTHUR
Movie butler sells self for war bond drive. Life 17:26
D 18 '44
Forecasts and side glances. Theatre Arts 36:13 Je '52
Four long cool formulas. Esquire 66:84 Jl '66
Efron, E. The magnificently opinionated Victorian insti-
tution. TV Guide 17-49:18 D 6 '69

TREACY, EMERSON
Obit. Screen World 19:240 '68

TREEN, MARY
Wood, C. TV personalities biographical sketchbook.
TV Personalities p15 '54

TREVOR, CLAIRE
Roberts, K. Cashing in on sin. Colliers 104:14 Jl 1 '39
Dreier, H. Star in your home. Photop 36-3:66 Ag '49
Landworthy ways to improve seawrothy living. House &
Gard 121:138 My '62
Hagen, R. Claire Trevor, inc. filmog. Films In Re-
view 14-9:513 N '63

TRINTIGNANT, JEAN-LOUIS
Trintignants together. Vogue 152:102 Ag 1 '68

TROWBRIDGE, CHARLES
Stewart, W. T. Letter. Films In Review 19-4:249 Ap '68

TRUEX, ERNEST
    Nutting, D. A boy who didn't grow up. Photop 15-1:44
        D '18
    Biography. Cur Bio '41
    Truex, S. M. Your truly, the Truexes. TV Guide p12
        D 3 '49

TRYON, GLENN
    Reay, N. The boy from Julietta. Photop 35-1:56 D '28

TUCKER, FORREST
    Raddatz, L. Actors should act like actors. TV Guide
        13-50:22 D 11 '65

TUCKER, GEORGE LOANE
    Saga of Singing Pine. Bet Hom & Gard 15:24 Mr '37

TUFTS, SONNY
    Mulvey, K. Hollywood manhunt. Womans H C 71:10 Ja
        '44
    Lowrance, D. Towheaded Sonny Tufts. Photop 24-5:45
        Ap '44
    Harris, E. If you were the house guest of Sonny Tufts.
        Photop 27-1:50 Je '45

TULLY, TOM
    Wood, C. TV personalities biographical sketchbook.
        TV Personalities p47 '54
    Climbing from the ranks. TV Guide 4-6:13 F 11 '56

TURNER, FLORENCE
    Interview. Motion Picture Herald. 7:187 Jl 23 '10

TURNER, LANA
    Crichton, K. Campus sweetheart. Colliers 105:11 Mr
        23 '40
    Busch, N. Lana Turner sipping a strawberry malt when
        fame walked in to make her the movie sweater girl.
        Life 9:62 D 23 '40
    Lovely Lana and sweet Deanna are belles of birthday ball.
        Life 10:30 F 10 '41
    Some film actors who have made themselves known this
        year. Theatre Arts 26:186 Mr '42
    West, R. The story behind Lana's madcap marriage.
        Photop 21-5:30 O '42
    Hamilton, S. Lana Turner's baby. Photop 22-4:28 Mr
        '43

Biography. Cur Bio '43

Waterbury, R. Lana Turner alone. Photop 25-2:27 '44

Parsons, L. O. Lana talks about Turhan. Photop 26-5:
30 Ap '45

St. Johns, A. R. Lana. Photop 27-4:38 S '45

Parsons, L. O. And so goodbye. Photop 28-3:32 F '46

St. Johns, E. Bringing up Lana. Photop 29-5:54 O '46

Howe, H. Lana--and Howe. Photop 30-3:54 F '47

Parsons, L. O. Lana and Ty. Photop 31-1:32 Je '47

Fink, H. I was there. Photop 31-3:36 Ag '47

Jacobs, C. H. Valentine pinup. Photop 32-3:38 F '48

Turner, L. This is how we made Cass Timberlaine.
Photop 32-4:54 Mr '48

Lana Turner's fourth and positively last time. Life 24:
45 My 10 '48

Albin, J. I remember Lana. Photop 33-1:54 Je '48

Parsons, L. O. I've waited all my life. Photop 33-2:
35 Jl '48

Hamilton, S. Wedding day. Photop 33-2:38 Jl '48

Parsons, L. O. Diamonds and diapers. Photop 34-2:
22 Ja '49

Turner, L. My most exciting story. Photop 34-3:48 F
'49

Colby, A. About face! Photop 38-2:56 Ag '50

Parsons, L. O. The fabulous Mrs. Topping. Photop 38-
5:56 N '50

Life of a sweater girl. Time 58:106 N 26 '51

Turner, L. My private life; as told to C. Shipp.
Womans H C 78:37 D '51

Roberts, W. Her heart is showing again. Photop 41-3:
58 Mr '52

Ford, E. The true Turner-Lamas story. Photop 42-4:
70 O '52

Swanson, P. From Lana to Arlene. Photop 43-5:34 My
'53

Waterbury, R. The lady said yes. Photop 44-6:48 D '53

Whitcomb, J. One hundred pounds of platinum. Cosmop
138:28 Mr '55

Alpert, H. Lana Turner week. Sat R 39:42 Ja 21 '56

Sweater girl Lana's build-up to a tragedy. Life 44:43
Ap 14 '58

Tragic life of a star. Newsweek 51:37 Ap 14 '58

Death on a pink carpet. Time 71:21 Ap 14 '58

Bad and beautiful. Time 71:17 Ap 21 '58

Cheryl--if . . . if. . . if. Newsweek 51:34 Ap 21 '58

Lana's plea for daugher is real-life drama triumph.
Life 44:21 Ap 21 '58

Lewis, J.   The untold story of Lana Turner's shame.
Photop 54-1:44 Jl '58
Divas, G.   Mummy, how can I choose between you and
daddy?   Photop 54-4:43 O '58
Dinter, C.   Thanks for everything--Cheryl.   Photop 55-
5:50 My '59
Harris, B.   Why Lana let them put her daughter away.
Photop 57-6:48 Je '60
Johnson, M.   Lana's flirting with danger again.   Photop
59-1:28 Ja '61
Kerr, M. A.   New husband right for her?   Photop 76-2:
49 Ag '69

TURPIN, BEN
Carr, H. C.   Looking backward with Ben.   Photop 15-1:
60 D '18
Howe, H.   The life tragedy of a Sennett beauty.   Photop
24-6:46 N '23
Clark, N. M.   First fifty years were the hardest for Ben
Turpin.   Am Mag 98:32 N '24
Obit.   Cur Bio '40
Biography.   DAB sup2:672 '58

TUSHINGHAM, RITA
Padded waif.   Time 79:78 Je 8 '62
I don't want to be a woman.   Life 52:47 Je 8 '62
Seay, S.   Rita Tushingham: the face of a new star.
Life 26:72b N 20 '62
People are talking about . . .   Vogue 141:78 F 15 '63
People are talking about . . .   Vogue 146:152 N 1 '65
Biography.   Cur Bio 26:45 O '65
Same.   Cur Bio Yrbk 1965:427 '65
Biography.   Brit Bk Yr 1966:148 '66

TWELVETREES, HELEN
Busby, M.   An evening with Helen.   Photop 38-2:47 Jl '30
Rankin, R.   Design for acting.   Photop 45-2:79 Ja '34
Obit.   Newsweek 51:73 F 24 '58
Time 71:96 F 24 '58
Am Ann 1959:520 '59
Brit Bk Yr 1959:517 '59
Screen World 10:226 '59

TYLER, JUDY
Singing Judy Tyler has robust charm.   Life 39:102 N 21
'55
Obit.   Newsweek 50:71 Jl 15 '57

Screen World 9:226 '58

TYLER, TOM
   Obit.   Screen World 6:225 '55

ULRIC, LENORE
Pollock, A. Girl with a good philosophy of work. Am
Mag 87:53 Mr '19
Hellinger, M. Just try to interview Ulric. Photop 37-
2:76 Ja '30
Kennedy, J. B. Naughty girl. Colliers 87:18 Ja 17 '31
Audiences, after all, are the best critics. Theatre 53:
20 Ja '31

UMEKI, MIYOSHI
Girls on Grant Avenue. Time 72:42 D 22 '58
Nichols, M. Flower drum songstress. Coronet 50:10
O '61
Lots of laughs and seaweed for breakfast. TV Guide 11-
3:22 Ja 19 '63
Durslag, M. She dispenses wisdom and peanut butter
sandwiches. TV Guide 17-51:22 D 20 '69

URE, MARY
Tomorrow's lead. Plays & Players 2-4:21 Ja '55
New beauties in the public eye. Vogue 130:111 D '57
Albert Finney and Mary Ure talk about acting. Sight &
Sound 30-2:56 Spg '61

URECAL, MINERVA
Obit. Screen World 18:240 '67

USTINOV, PETER
Johns, E. A phenomenal exception. Theatre World p33
S '49
Unquenchable Ustinov. Life 34:101 F 2 '53
One-man band. New Statesm 47:407 Mr 27 '54
Runswick, J. Journey with Ustinov. Plays & Players
2-8:21 My '55
Biography. Cur Bio 16:46 D '55
Same. Cur Bio Yrbk 1955:618 '56
Hobson, L. Z. Trade winds. Sat R 39:6 Jl 21 '56
Barker, F. G. Sugar-coated satirist. Plays & Players
3-10:5 Jl '56
People are talking about. Vogue 130:171 O 1 '57
New perspective for playwrights. Theatre Arts 41:21 O
'57
Busting out all over. Time 71:59 Mr 10 '58

Everything's his line. Newsweek 51:80 Mr 10 '58
Stanley, J. P. Television. America 98:733 Mr 22 '58
Eleven fine actors get their dream roles. Life 44:76 Ap
   14 '58
Schickel, R. Country called Ustinov. Look 22:86 Ap 29
   '58
By the beard of the prophet. TV Guide 6-18:12 My 3 '58
Bester, A. Loveable egghead. Holiday 24:99 Jl '58
McCalls visits. McCalls 86:8 N '58
Brandon, H. America's quest for culture; intv. New
   Repub 139:13 D 8 '58
Salute to Ustinov. Christian Cent 76:5 Ja 7 '59
Ustinov, P. Doing it all at once. Films & Filming 6-
   8:5 My '60
Millstein, G. Cartel called Ustinov. N. Y. Times Mag
   p18 Ja 29 '61
Peter, the great showman. Life 50:81 My 19 '61
Bachmann, G. Ustinov; an intv. Film 30:18 Win '61
Peter Ustinov. Film 34:14 Win '62
Alive and kicking. Life 54:53 Ap 19 '63
Ustinov writes of the days when he was a roadster.
   Life 54:56 Ap 19 '63
Peter Ustinov. Plays & Players 11-4:9 Ja '64
Brandon, H. Peter Ustinov speaking. Atlan 214:29 Jl
   '64
Lyon, N. Peter Ustinov: I like what tempts my eye.
   Vogue 144:223 O 1 '64
Art of asking question; adaptation of address. Sat R 48:
   22 D 25 '65
Politics and the arts; excerpt from address. Atlan 218:
   44 Jl '66
Polymorph. Newsweek 68:99 O 10 '66
Higgins, R. Nobody has ever called him dull. TV Guide
   14-45:38 N 5 '66
Atlantic report. Atlan 218:16 N '66
Ustinov. New Yorker 43:23 Jl 15 '67
Luxury. Vogue 150:147 N 1 '67
Art and artlessness. Films & Filming 15-1:4 O '68
Ustinov, P. Extra weight. Sight & Sound 18-71:14 n. d.

VALENTINO, RUDOLPH

Valentino, R. Women and love. Photop 31-4:40 Mr '22

Dorgan, D. A song of hate. Photop 22-2:26 Jl '22

Waterbury, R. Wedded and parted. Photop 23-1:58 D '22

Motion picture novel. Bookm 56:724 F '23

Valentino, R. My life story. Photop 23-3:3 F; 23-4:54 Mr; 23-5:49 Ap '23

Quirk, J. R. Presto chango Valentino. Photop 27-6:36 My '25

Winkler, J. K. I'm tired of being a sheik; intv. Colliers 77:28 Ja 16 '26

York, C. He who got slapped and why. Photop 30-2:78 Jl '26

Valentino. Lit Digest 90:26 S 11 '26

Price, M. A monument to youth and romance. Photop 30-6:44 N '26

Remembering Valentino. Lit Digest 94:23 Ag 20 '27

Moderwell, H. K. When Rudy was a boy. Photop 33-2: 29 Ja '28

Valentino's memory. Photop 38-3:75 Ag '30

Women who enshrine Valentino. Lit Digest 108:19 F 7 '31

The sheik rides again. World Film News 3:156 '38

Webb, S. After 20 years Valentino still wows them. N.Y. Times Mag p24 My 6 '45

Jennings, D. Actors who won't stay dead. Colliers 123: 24 Jl 2 '49

Great lover. Life 28:36 Ja 2 '50

Queen, H. Perfect lover. Coronet 29:66 Ja '51

Huff, T. The career of Rudolph Valentino. Films In Review 3-4:145 Ap '52

No time for Valentino. Newsweek 46:66 S 5 '55

Amour and the man. Sat R 39:29 O 13 '56

Greatest stars. Cosmop 141:29 O '56

Ah, Valentino! N.Y. Times Mag p60 Ap 24 '60

Valentinoville. Newsweek 57:52 Ap 10 '61

Stang, J. Sheik still rides! N.Y. Times Mag p42 N 12 '61

Smith, B. Farewell, great lover. Sat Eve Post 235:66 Ja 20 '62

Marberry, M. M. Overloved one. Am Heritage 16:84 Ag '65

Crane, E. Rudolph Valentino, legend with feet of clay? inc. filmog. Screen Legends 1-3:4 O '65

Bodeen, D. Rudolph Valentino, inc. filmog. Screen
Facts 17:1 n. d.

VALLEE, RUDY
Gellhorn, M. Rudy Vallee, God's gift to the girls.
New Repub 59:310 Ag 7 '29
Shayon, R. L. Rudy Vallee--model 1929. Parade 1:7
Ag '29
Riding the crest. Outlook 153:58 S 11 '29
Kutner, N. Yankee doodle returns to town. Dance Mag
12:23 S '29
New Rudy whose voice is catnip. Lit Digest 103:46 O 19
'29
Vagabond worries. Outlook 154:578 Ap 9 '30
Did college help me? Pict R 31:2 My '30
Remen, N. Rudy still has his "Vagabond dreams."
Photop 45-5:42 Ap '34
I stand by. Pict R 37:20 Ag '36
Arell, R. Flaws that made fortunes. Delin 130:46 Mr
'37
Perennial: his 500th broadcast over NBC finds him going
strong. Newsweek 13:31 My 15 '39
Street, J. The endless Vallee. Radio Guide Jl 21 p2;
Jl 28 p6 '39
Veteran breaks his skein. Newsweek 14:38 Ag 7 '39
As time goes by. Time 49:81 Ap 21 '47
Biography. Cur Bio 8:58 Je '47
Same. Cur Bio Yrbk 1947:652 '48
Vallee comeback. Life 26:91 Mr 21 '49
Dream and the glory. Coronet 38:119 Jl '55
Talk with the stars. Newsweek 58:62 O 23 '61
Scullin, G. How to succeed in show business by being
rediscovered. Sat Eve Post 235:24 Je 23 '62
Vallee, R. Self-portrait. Esquire 58:127 Je '62
Biography. Cur Bio 24:35 Ap '63
Same. Cur Bio Yrbk 1963:433 '64
He was grandma's idol. TV Guide 12-34:12 Ag 22 '64
Pitts, M. R. Letter. Films In Review 18-5:318 My '67

VALLI, ALIDA
Loveliest Roman of them all. Am Mag 143:136 Je '47
Valli. Life 23:75 S 22 '47
Crichton, K. Veni, vidi Valli. Colliers 121:30 Ja 3 '48
Sheridan, M. Viva Valli. Photop 32-3:46 F '48
Howe, H. Valli of enchantment. Photop 33-4:58 S '48

VALLI, VIRGINIA
   Ludwig, F. A.   From stenography to stardom.   Photop
      13-3:30 F '18
   Jordan, J.   An old fashioned girl.   Photop 22-4:37 S '22
   Evers, P. J.   The emancipation of Virginia.   Photop 27-
      1:41 D '24
   Obit.   Screen World 20:241 '69

VANCE, VIVIAN
   Lucy's neighbors.   TV Guide 6-12:4 Mr 20 '53
   They love Lucy.   Am Mag 155:55 Je '53
   The Mertzes, and how they got that way.   TV Guide 2-52:
      5 D 25 '54
   Maynard, J.   I don't run away any more.   McCalls 82:
      36 My '55
   Wood, C.   TV personalities biographical sketchbook.
      TV Personalities p142 '57
   Hockstein, R.   TV's favorite comedy team breaks up.
      Good H 161:30 O '65

VAN CLEEF, LEE
   Beaver, J.   Letter, inc. filmog.   Films In Review 19-4:
      256 Ap '68
   Hensch, S.   Filmography.   Films In Review 19-7:464
      Ag/S '68

VAN DOREN, MAMIE
   Call me Mamie.   Look 18:73 F 9 '54
   The other Van Doren.   TV Guide 5-15:8 Ap 13 '57
   Go, go, GOP.   Newsweek 62:38 N 11 '63

VAN DYKE, DICK
   Tornebene, L.   Lunch date with Dick Van Dyke.   Cosmop
      149:14 Ag '60
   What's a Dick Van Dyke?   TV Guide 9-49:6 D 9 '61
   People on the way up.   Sat Eve Post 235:25 Jl 28 '62
   Behold a 'supernormal' comedian.   TV Guide 10-49:15
      D 8 '62
   Biography.   Cur Bio 24:39 Mr '63
      Same.   Cur Bio Yrbk 1963:437 '64
   Good scout.   Time 81:54 Je 14 '63
   Jennings, C. R.   Star who thinks he isn't.   Ladies Home
      J 80:78 O '63
   Gordon, S.   Dick Van Dyke: TV family man.   Look 27:
      116 N 5 '63
   Gordon, S.   America's favorite TV wife.   Look 28:M9
      Ap 21 '64

Balling, F. D. His funny, funny world. Photop 65-6:29 Je '64

Fall guy. TV Guide 13-22:10 My 29 '65

Baskette, K. Mr. Marshmellow. Photop 68-1:36 Jl;
68-2:62 Ag '65

Ferrer, J. M. Good show quits while it's ahead. Life
60:15 Je 3 '66

Redbook readers talk with Dick Van Dyke. Redbook 128:
57 N '66

Fennigan, J. Back to television--the hard way. TV
Guide 15-14:10 Ap 8 '67

Gordon, S. Triumph of a square. Look 31:89 Ap 18 '67

Simons, M. Chitty chitty bang bang. Look 32:84 D 24
'68

VAN DYKE, JERRY

People on the way up. Sat Eve Post 235:25 Jl 28 '62

Kid brother. Newsweek Je 24 '63

The other Van Dyke. TV Guide 11-34:12 Ag 24 '63

There's more to his car than keeping up the payments.
TV Guide 14-18:14 Ag 30 '66

VAN FLEET, JO

Smith, M. The two faces of Jo Van Fleet. Theatre 2-
12:28 D '60

VAN VOOREN, MONIQUE

Whitcomb, J. Backstage at the birth of a hit. Cosmop
136:57 Mr '54

Watt, D. Tables for two. New Yorker 33:106 Mr 16 '57

VARDEN, EVELYN

Obit. Time 72:77 Jl 21 '58

Screen World 10:226 '59

VARSI, DIANE

Diane Varsi: the girl who walks alone. Look 22:91 My
13 '58

Arnold, M. Diane Varsi's secret tragedy. Photop 53-5:
41 My; 6:52 Je '58

Nichols, M. Star with a strange horizon. Coronet 44:
14 Jl '58

Laitin, J. Diane Varsi: fawn on a hot tin roof. Coronet
46:139 D '58

Borie, M. I'll never go back to Hollywood. Photop
55-6:71 Je '59

Dean, B. Can a jinx strike twice. Photop 59-4:62 Ap
'61

Hyams, J.   Diane Varsi's escape from success.
    Redbook 116:45 Ap '61
The mystery that still haunts Hollywood.   Photop 59-6:
    70 Je '61

VAUGHN, ROBERT
He prefers politics.   TV Guide 12-8:22 F 22 '64
Bogdanovich, P.   With gun in hand and tongue in cheek.
    TV Guide 12-43:10 O 24 '64
Man inside the man from U. N. C. L. E.   Time 85:68 Ja
    29 '65
Borie, M.   Marriage is a very dull meal.   Photop 67-4:
    32 Ap '65
Freeman, D.   Man from U. N. C. L. E.   Sat Eve Post 238:
    76 Je 19 '65
Who would you run to?   Photop 68-2:39 Ag '65
Amory, C.   First of the month; excerpt from anti-
    Vietnam war speech with interview.   Sat R 50:4 Je 3 '67
Biography.   Cur Bio 28:41 S '67
    Same.   Cur Bio Yrbk 1967:434 '68
Whitney, D.   The other Bobby of American politics.
    TV Guide 16-8:14 F 24 '68

VEIDT, CONRAD
Life mask.   Lit Digest 109:20 My 9 '31
Obit.   Cur Bio '43

VELEZ, LUPE
Albert, K.   A hot baby of Hollywood.   Photop 35-3:36 F
    '29
Busby, M.   Lookee! Lupe! Whoopee!   Photop 37-4:45
    Mr '30
Lawton, B.   Lupe--no change.   Photop 39-1:74 D '30
Biery, R.   The best showman in town.   Photop 40-6:73
    N '31
Condon, F.   Redhead from Mexico.   Sat Eve Post 204:
    26 Ja 2 '32
Dickson, E.   Girl with one talent.   Colliers 89:9 Je 25
    '32
Hamilton, S.   A tornado? No! Lupe and Jimmy.
    Photop 45-1:30 D '33
Hampton, J.   Lupe and Johnny were lovers.   Photop 46-1:
    58 Je '34
Fire is out.   Newsweek 24:32 D 25 '44
Guadaloupe.   Time 44:16 D 25 '44

VENABLE, EVELYN
What are they doing now? Show 2-8:106 Ag '62

VERA-ELLEN
Wilson, L.   Candleflame blonde.   Photop 39-5:42 My '51
Ford, E.   The lady's in love.   Photop 42-6:74 D '52
Carter, J.   Is her love life jinxed?   Photop 44-3:52 S '53
Biography.   Cur Bio 20:42 F '59
Same.   Cur Bio Yrbk 1959:463 '60

VERDON, GWEN
Culver City's loss.   New Yorker 29:24 My 23 '53
New Eve.   Look 17:54 S 8 '53
Roving spotlight.   Dance Mag 27:32 N '53
Devil's disciple.   Time 65:62 Je 13 '55
Beauty and baseball.   Look 19:64 Jl 12 '55
Star's fling at spring.   Life 40:132 Mr 19 '56
Musical comedy.   Theatre Arts 40:26 Ap '56
Hawkins, W.   Something about Gwen Verdon.   Dance Mag
    30:26 Ag '56
Nichols, L.   Gwen Verdon--the town's new girl. N. Y.
    Times Mag p25 My 26 '57
Eleven fine actors get their dream roles.   Life 44:76
    Ap 14 '58
Gwen knocks 'em in the aisles.   Life 46:81 F 23 '59
Biography.   Cur Bio 21:35 O '60
Same.   Cur Bio Yrbk 1960:446 '61
Joel, L.   Gwen Verdon and Bob Fosse.   Dance Mag 35:
    18 Jl '61
Dance Magazine 1961 award winner.   Dance Mag 36:35
    Mr '62
Chayefsky, P.   Dance Magazine awards.   Dance Mag 36:
    71 My '62
Fun on TV.   Dance Mag 38:31 N '64
Thompson, T.   Gwen Verdon all aglow.   Life 60:99 Mr
    25 '66

VIDAL, HENRI
Obit.   Illus Lond N 235:909 D 19 '59
Screen World 11:226 '60

VIDOR, FLORENCE
She was the girl outside, now she's inside.   Photop 12-
    3:28 Ag '17
Jordan, J.   Old lives for new.   Photop 19-5:45 Ap '21
St. Johns, A. R.   Why did the Vidors separate?   Photop
    24-3:28 Ag '23

St. Johns, A. R.   Why has Florence Vidor become the
    toast of Hollywood?   Photop 26-3:63 Ag '24

VITTI, MONICA
    Lucas, C.   Am adventure.   Show 1-1:102 O '61
    Mademoiselle's annual merit awards.   Mlle 54:52 Ja '62
    Platinum bonds.   Newsweek 66:98B S 20 '65
    Walter, E.   Monica Vitti.   Vogue 147:123 F 15 '66
    Monica Vitti; she's not that way at all.   Look 30:83 Je
        14 '66
    Interesting women.   McCalls 96:99 Mr '69

VLADY, MARINA
    Deadly queen.   Time 81:54 Je 14 '63
    Hildenbrand, W.   Marina Vlady--Schauspielerin.   Film
        7-3:12 Mr '69

VON ELTZ, THEODORE
    Obit.   Screen World 16:226 '65

VON FURSTENBERG, BETSY
    She gets away with anything (it says here).   TV Guide
        8-21:12 My 21 '60

VON STROHEIM, ERICH
    Erich von Stroheim plays Field Marshal Rommel.   Life
        14:47 Je 14 '43
    Noble, P.   Stroheim--his work and influence.   Sight &
        Sound 16-64:163 Win '47/48
    Noble, P.   Man you love to hate.   Theatre Arts 34:22 Ja
        '50
    Perelman, S. J.   Cloudland revisited.   New Yorker 28:
        34 S 20 '52
    Jensen, O.   Lunch with Erich von Stroheim.   Vogue
        122:19 O 15 '53
    Stonier, G. W.   Press party.   New Statesm 47:35 Ja 9
        '54
    Reisz, K.   Stroheim in London.   Sight & Sound 23-4:172
        Ap/Je '54
    Obit.   Illus Lond N 230:821 My 18 '57
        Time 69:98 My 27 '57
        Screen World 9:226 '58
        Am Ann 1958:825 '58
    Everson, W. K.   Erich von Stroheim 1885-1957.   Films
        In Review 8-7:305 Ag/S '57
    Mitchell, G.   Stroheim.   Films In Review 8-8:423 O '57
    Marion, D.   Erich von Stroheim: the legend and the

fact. Sight & Sound 31:22 Win '61/62

Pinto, A. Filmography. Films In Review 18-6:374 Je/
Jl '67

VON SYDOW, MAX
Max von Sydow makes a big U.S. debut. Life 58:92 Mr
19 '65
Biography. Cur Bio 28:43 Ap '67

VOSKOVEC, GEORGE
Logan, A. Reporter at large. New Yorker 27:56 My 12
'51
Reunion. New Yorker 39:20 Jl 27 '63

WADSWORTH, WILLIAM
  Briscoe, J. Why film favorites forsook the footlights.
    Photop 6-3:103 Ag '14
  Wadsworth. New Yorker 19:17 Jl 10 '43

WAGNER, ROBERT
  Wagner, R. Debbie's dateline. Photop 42-2:40 Ag '52
  Corwin, J. Can he live down his past? Photop 42-6:52
    D '52
  Wagner, R. The things I've learned. Photop 43-2:40 F
    '53
  Ford, E. Terrific trio. Photop 43-4:32 Ap '53
  Arnold, M. Bachelor on budget. Photop 43-5:42 My '53
  Ott, B. If this isn't love. Photop 44-1:34 Jl '53
  Moore, T. He's my kind of guy. Photop 44-2:32 Ag '53
  Wagner, R. Wish you had a date? Photop 44-5:58 O '53
  Thomas, B. Watch out, Robert Wagner. Photop 44-5:56
    N '53
  Ott, B. Bring him back alive. Photop 45-1:20 Ja '54
  Wagner, R. If you were in love with me. Photop 45-
    5:61 My '54
  Edwards, R. Robert Wagner, Valiant Prince. Photop
    46-1:62 Jl '54
  Wagner, R. Today--I'm living it up! Photop 46-5:44
    N '54
  Block, M. The starting point. Photop 47-4:60 Ap '55
  Wagner, R. Sr. My boy--Bob Wagner. Photop 49-2:49
    F '56
  Nichols, M. Mean for money. Coronet 40:10 S '56
  Arnold, M. He flipped on a dream. Photop 50-4:56 O
    '56
  Maynard, J. Profile in courage. Photop 51-3:58 Mr '57
  Meredith, J. Bob, did you know? Photop 53-3:47 Mr '58
  Borie, M. Why we won't talk about our marriage.
    Photop 53-6:57 Je '58
  Natalie Wood as Bob Wagner sees her. Photop 54-1:54
    Jl '58
  Tornabene, L. Lunch date with Natalie Wood and Bob
    Wagner. Cosmop 149:18 O '60
  Why Natalie and Bob split. Photop 60-3:24 S '61
  Ott, B. Life without Nat--it's a ball. Photop 61-6:24
    Je '62
  Efron, E. The man who seemed to have everything,

until . . . TV Guide 16-26:26 Je 29 '68
Wood, A. The day I woke up blind. Photop 74-1:75 Jl
  '68

WALBROOK, ANTON
  Obit. Newsweek 70:46 Ag 21 '67
  Screen World 19:241 '68
  Davis, H. R. Anton Walbrook, inc. filmog. Films In
  Review 18-10:662 D '67

WALBURN, RAYMOND
  McCabe, R. Raymond Walburn, inc. filmog. Screen
  Facts 16:49 n. d.

WALCAMP, MARIE
  Bell, J. Is it impossible? Marie'll do it. Photop 10-
  6:49 N '16

WALKER, CHERYL
  Stage door canteen girl. Life 14:76 F 22 '43
  Stierhem, E. Special extra. Am Mag 136:28 Jl '43

WALKER, CLINT
  Very tall in the saddle. TV Guide 4-44:21 N 3 '56
  Wood, C. TV personalities biographical sketchbook.
  TV Personalities p73 '56
  Cheyenne's Clint Walker: king-size cowboy. Look 21:147
  My 28 '57
  Hollywood's tallest leading man. McCalls 84:17 Ag '57
  Walker wins war with Warners. TV Guide 7-17:12 Ap 25
  '59
  The cowboys lament. TV Guide 7-47:17 N 21 '59
  Just Clint and the cactus. TV Guide 10-31:12 Ag 4 '62

WALKER, HELEN
  McClelland, D. Helen Walker, inc. filmog. Film Fan
  Mo 81:3 Mr '68
  Obit. Screen World 20:241 '69

WALKER, LILLIAN
  Lillian of the films. Cosmop 56:122 D '13
  Briscoe, J. Why film favorites forsook the footlights.
  Photop 6-3:103 Ag '14

WALKER, NANCY
  Walker, N. Two girls and a friendship. Photop 29-6:50

N '46
Brown, J. M. Look ma. Sat R 31:26 F 21 '48
Broadway cheers new comic star. Life 24:87 F 23 '48
Shane, T. Walker brat. Colliers 121:21 My '48
Out of the basket. New Yorker 31:23 Je 4 '55
Hayes, R. Musical temper. Commonweal 62:329 Jl 1 '55
Triumph for Nancy. Newsweek 46:55 Jl 18 '55
Old plays in Manhattan. Time 67:34 Ja 30 '56
Hayes, R. Stage. Commonweal 63:543 F 24 '56
Bring on the comedians. Theatre Arts 43:58 O '59
Two great comics. Vogue 135:151 F 1 '60
Eimerl, S. Can women be funny? Mlle 56:150 N '62
Biography. Cur Bio 26:40 F '65
Same. Cur Bio Yrbk 1965:441 '65

WALKER, ROBERT DONALD
Robert Donald Walker--hero; intv. Photop 7-4:40 Mr '15

WALKER, ROBERT SR.
Meet two rising stars. Ladies Home J 61:85 Ja '44
Harris, E. The private life of Private Hargrove.
Photop 25-2:60 Jl '44
Parsons, L. O. Bob Walker talks about Jennifer Jones.
Photop 25-6:30 N '44
Delehanty, T. Time for Robert Walker. Photop 27-5:48
O '45
Swanson, P. The Bob Walker story. Photop 36-6:46 N
'49
Obit. Newsweek 38:67 S 10 '51
Time 58:81 S 10 '51
Illus Lond N 219:372 S 8 '51

WALKER, ROBERT JR.
Kessner, G. Double exposure. Photop 65-5:64 My '64

WALLACE, IRENE
Barry, J. Irene Wallace--star of the IMP Co.
Photop 5-1:51 D '13

WALLACE, JEAN
Wilkie, J. Second chance. Photop 43-2:68 F '53

WALLACH, ELI
There's a method to his acting. TV Guide 7-18:26 My 2
'59
Biography. Cur Bio 20:42 My '59
Same. Cur Bio Yrbk 1959:471 '60
At home with Eli Wallach and Anne Jackson. Theatre

3-1:16 Ja '61
Actor's eye on life.   U. S. Camera 24:66 Je '61
Eli Wallach on The misfits.   Film 29:13 Sum '61
Wallach, E.   My strange dilemma.   Films & Filming
    7-11:19 Ag '61
Ross, L.   Player.   New Yorker 37:90 O 21 '61
Talk with the stars.   Newsweek 61:56 F 18 '63
Wallach, E.   In all directions.   Films & Filming 10-8:
    7 My '64
What's with the Wallachs?   At home or on-stage it's Luv.
    Life 58:79 Ja 8 '65
Robinson, D.   Eight famous Americans tell of The day I
    was proudest of my wife; intv.   Good H 167:77 Ag '68

WALLEY, DEBORAH
    Henderson, B.   A girl becomes a woman.   Photop 60-5:
        64 N '61
    Walley-Ashley engagement.   Photop 61-4:29 Ap '62
    Walley-Ashley wedding!   Photop 62-1:14 Jl '61
    Walley, D.   Honeymoon love letter.   Photop 62-2:58 Ag
        '62
    Walley, D.   I'm having a baby.   Photop 63-3:42 Mr '63
    Lyle, J.   The handshake that rocked the beat.   Photop
        64-4:54 O '63
    Whitney, D.   Elvis thought of me as one of the fellows.
        TV Guide 16-49:32 D 7 '68

WALSTON, RAY
    Devil's due.   Theatre Arts 42:11 Ap '58
    Dern, M.   The martian from actors studio.   TV Guide
        12-15:15 Ap 11 '64

WALTERS, POLLY
    Gaines, W. P.   Polly with a future.   Photop 45-5:71 Ap
        '34

WALTHALL, HENRY B.
    Owen, K.   "The little colonel"; intv.   Photop 8-3:27 Ag
        '15
    Jones, G.   The Poe of the screen.   Feature Movie 5-1:
        39 Ja '16
    Mansfield of the movies.   McClure 46:29 Ja '16
    Cohn, A. A.   The reformation of "Wally."   Photop 13-1:
        31 D '17
    Rankin, R.   The little colonel marches back.   Photop
        46-1:70 Je '34
    Griggs, J.   Here was an actor!   Films In Review 3-3:

118 Mr '52
Biography. DAB sup2:693 '58
Henry B. Walthall. Films Culture Spg/Sum '65

WANAMAKER, SAM
Stevens, V. Seven young Broadway artists. Theatre
Arts 31:55 Je '47
Education of a professional. Theatre Arts 34:59 My '50
They come from Chicago. Theatre Arts 35:44 Jl '51
American style. Plays & Players 1-6:4 Mr '54

WARD, FANNIE
Obit. Newsweek 39:53 F 4 '52
Time 59:70 F 4 '52
Illus Lond N 220:184 F 2 '52
Am Ann 1953:758 '53
Youth runs out after 80. Life 32:35 F 11 '52

WARDEN, JACK
Hobson, D. He never loses his cool. TV Guide 14-11:
15 Mr 12 '66

WARNER, H. B.
Evans, D. How to hold a baby. Photop 16-3:67 Ag '19
Mullett, M. B. Actor who wanted to be a surgeon.
Am Mag 96:18 O '23
Obit. Newsweek 53:46 Ja 5 '59
Am Ann 1959:521 '59
Screen World 10:226 '59

WARWICK, ROBERT
Obit. Screen World 16:226 '65

WASHBURN, BRYANT
Bryant Washburn. Feature Movie 1-4:52 My 5 '15
Obit. Screen World 15:226 '64

WATERS, ETHEL
Ethel Waters conquers the devil in Cabin in the sky.
Life 9:63 D 9 '40
Biography. Cur Bio '41
Lewis, T. Theatre. America 82:657 S 23 '50
His eye is on the sparrow; ed. by C. Samuels. Ladies
Home J 67:44 O '50
Smith, W. G. Phylon profile 21: Ethel Waters.
Phylon 11-2:114 '50
Stormy weather. Newsweek 37:92 Mr 5 '51

Where the blues begin. Time 57:104 Mr 12 '51
Breit, H. Talk with Ethel Waters. N.Y. Times Bk R
   p22 Mr 18 '51
Smith, H. It had God in it. Sat R 34:18 Mr 24 '51
Ransey, F. Jr. Lonely life. Nation 172:303 Mr 31 '51
Waters, E. His eye is on the sparrow; excerpt. Atlan
   187:31 Mr '51
Biography. Cur Bio 12:61 Mr '51
   Same. Cur Bio Yrbk 1951:644 '52
Trese, L. J. Books. Commonweal 53:652 Ap 6 '51
Gibbs, W. At home with Ethel Waters. New Yorker 29:
   80 O 3 '53
At home with Ethel Waters. Time 62:78 O 5 '53
At home with Ethel Waters. Newsweek 42:54 O 5 '53
Lewis, T. At home with Ethel Waters. America 90:54
   O 10 '53
Brown, J. M. Still Waters. Sat R 36:30 O 10 '53
Clurman, H. One woman show. Nation 177:298 O 10 '53
Hayes, R. At home with Ethel Waters. Commonweal
   59:38 O 16 '53
Bentley, E. Autumn on Broadway. New Repub 129:20
   O 26 '53
At home with Ethel Waters. Theatre Arts 37:22 N '53
Wyatt, E. V. At home with Ethel Waters. Cath World
   178:148 N '53
Malcolm, D. F. Off Broadway. New Yorker 35:81 Ap 18
   '59
Where are they now? Newsweek 70:14 Jl 17 '67
Ames, M. Ethel Waters, clearly one of the greatest.
   Hi Fi 18:108 Ag '68

WATSON, DEBBIE
   Gordon, S. Debbie Watson: she'll be dangerous at 20.
      Look 30:73 Ja 25 '66
   I like to be me. Seventeen 25:37 Ja '66

WATSON, LUCILE
   Trippingly off the tongue; announcing retirement. Theatre
      Arts 37:16 D '53
   Biography. Cur Bio 14:56 D '53
      Same. Cur Bio Yrbk 1953:645 '53
   Obit. Am Ann 1963:766 '63
      Cur Bio 23:45 S '62
      Cur Bio Yrbk 1962:450 '63

WATSON, MINOR
   Obit. Screen World 17:241 '66

WAYNE, DAVID
  Stevens, V. Seven young Broadway artists. Theatre
    Arts 31:54 Je '47
  Acting for the screen. Theatre Arts 35:7 Ag '51
  Theatre's creative spark vs. Hollywood's deep freeze.
    Theatre Arts 38:26 Ja '54
  Zolotow, M. Mysterious audience. Theatre Arts 38:78
    Je '54
  Problems of performing an older man. Theatre Arts 40:
    64 Je '54
  Biography. Cur Bio 17:57 Je '56
    Same. Cur Bio Yrbk 1956:645 '57
  Wood, C. TV personalities biographical sketchbook.
    TV Personalities p40 '56

WAYNE, JOHN
  Hughes, M. Oh, for a hair cut! Photop 39-1:45 D '30
  Reid, S. "Mother" Wayne. Photop 54-10:26 O '40
  Sharpe, H. John the Duke. Photop 24-2:47 Ja '44
  West, R. Measure of a man. Photop 25-6:58 N '44
  Waterbury, R. Surprise me. Photop 29-1:31 Je '46
  Howe, H. Duke in coonskin. Photop 37-1:54 Ja '50
  Martin, P. Ladies like 'em rugged. Sat Eve Post 223:
    19 D 23 '50
  Ford, J. Man alive! Photop 38-3:42 Mr '51
  Biography. Cur Bio 12:54 F '51
    Same. Cur Bio Yrbk 1951:647 '52
  Wages of virtue. Time 59:64 Mr 3 '52
  Connolly, M. & Ford, E. Secrets behind Hollywood
    heartaches. Photop 42-5:46 N '52
  Itria, H. Big John. Look 17:67 Ag 11 '53
  Armstrong, G. The Duke takes a stand. Photop 44-3:
    33 S '53
  Armstrong, G. The story John Wayne has never told.
    Photop 44-4:38 O '53
  Scott, M. John Wayne. Cosmop 137:26 N '54
  Johnson, G. John Wayne: star of iron. Coronet 37:113
    D '54
  Stack, R. Duke--prince among men. Photop 47-4:54 Ap
    '55
  East and West meet in Wayne. Life 40:161 My 7 '56
  Gray, M. No contract star. Films & Filming 3-6:15 Mr
    '57
  Hoffman, J. Night of terror. Photop 53-5:70 My '58
  Watson, B. Daddy, when will God bring my baby brother?
    Photop 56-4:44 O '59
  Eells, G. Ed Sullivan's changing show. Look 24:67

F 16 '60

Nugent, J. P.   John Wayne's ordeal.   Newsweek 56:107
Jl 25 '60

Hamilton, J.   John Wayne.   Look 24:83 Ag 2 '60

Liston, J.   At home with John Wayne.   Am Home 64:13
Ap '61

Jennings, D.   Woes of a box office king: John Wayne.
Sat Eve Post 235:28 O 27 '62

Dawes, A.   Glamorous grandfather.   Photop 62-6:56 D '62

Morgan, T. B.   God and man in Hollywood.   Esquire
59:74 My '63

Corbin, J.   Big man! big life! big love!   Photop 64-4:
34 O '63

Big John.   Newsweek 65:86 Mr 1 '65

Wayne, J.   How I conquered cancer.   Photop 67-4:63 Ap
'65

John Wayne rides again.   Life 58:69 My 7 '65

Didion, J.   John Wayne, a love song.   Sat Eve Post 238:
76 Ag 14 '65

Tusher, B.   The son who made him cry.   Photop 68-2:
47 Ag '65

Hano, J.   John Wayne: a man in every sense of the
word.   Good H 161:83 O '65

Page, W.   Man's man.   Field & Stream 70:30 Ja '66

Duke at 60.   Time 89:67 Je 9 '67

John Wayne's Green beret.   Nation 205:614 D 11 '67

Barthel, J.   John Wayne, superhawk.   N. Y. Times Mag
p4 D 24 '67

Reply with rejoinder.   N. Y. Times Mag p4 Ja 14 '68

Deedy, J.   News and views; government and in production of The green berets.   Commonweal 88:426 Je 28
'68

Richter, W. D.   Hellfire made to order.   Pop Sci 193:48
D '68

Hall, D. J.   Tall in the saddle.   Films & Filming 16-1:
12 O '69

Thorpe, J.   Playing with death.   Photop 76-6:59 D '69

WAYNE, PAT

Boice, D.   I flipped when he turned out to be my blind
date.   Photop 56-1:54 Jl '59

Dunne, J. G. . . . and then I went home and wrote the
profile.   TV Guide 14-48:30 N 26 '66

WEAVER, DENNIS

Spare your sympathy.   TV Guide 6-4:8 Ja 25 '58

Gunsmoke's Chester.   Look 25:55 S 12 '61

Home, home in the clink.   TV Guide 11-29:6 Jl 20 '63

WEBB, CLIFTON
   Biography.   Cur Bio '43
   Actor vs. gadget.   Life 26:56 Ja 31 '49
   Martin, P.   Hollywood's self-confessed genius.
      Sat Eve Post 221:42 Ap 16 '49
   Bainbridge, J.   Mr. Belvedere and Mr. Webb.   Life 26:
      49 My 30 '49
   Maxwell, E.   The friendliest man in town.   Photop 36-
      3:48 Ag '49
   Parsons, L. O.   Incredible Clifton Webb.   Cosmop 134:
      6 Je '53
   Wood, T.   Clifton Webb: gentleman actor.   Coronet
      36:85 Jl '54
   Obit.   Time 88:110 O 21 '66
      Newsweek 68:83 O 24 '66
      Cur Bio 27:45 D '66
      Cur Bio Yrbk 1966:472 '67
      Screen World 18:241 '67

WEBB, JACK
   Detective story.   Newsweek 39:74 Ja 14 '52
   Crime pays off.   Look 17:88 S 8 '53
   Tregaskis, R.   Cops' favorite make-believe cop.   Sat
      Eve Post 226:24 S 26 '53
   Hubler, R. G.   Jack Webb: the man who makes Dragnet.
      Coronet 34:27 S '53
   Taves, I.   Nobody's man Friday.   McCalls 80:26 S '53
   Jack be nimble!   Time 63:47 Mr 15 '54
   Jack Webb story.   Cosmop 136:127 My '54
   He taught Hollywood a lesson.   TV Guide 2-30:4 Jl 24 '54
   Jack of all trades.   Life 37:50 Ag 30 '54
   Biography.   Cur Bio 16:59 My '55
   Jack Webb gets first 9 mm Smith & Wesson.   Outdoor
      Life 115:27 Je '55
   Jack Webb's "Blues."   TV Guide 3-30:4 Jl 23 '55
   Block, C. B.   Amateur motion-picture making; intv.
      Pop Phot 37:112 O '55
   Biography.   Cur Bio Yrbk 1955:636 '56
   Wood, C.   TV personalities biographical sketchbook.
      TV Personalities p133 '56
   TV's most misunderstood man.   TV Guide 5-12:17 Mr
      23 '57
   Jack Webb revisited.   TV Guide 7-2:10 Ja 10 '59
   No future for Friday?   Newsweek 53:62 F 23 '59
   Jack Webb's blues.   TV Guide 7-18:20 My 2 '59

Webb, J.   Facts about me: as told to D. Jennings.
Sat Eve Post 232:15 S 5; 36 S 12; 38 S 19 '59
Raddatz, L.   Jack Webb revisited.   TV Guide 11-5:15 F
2 '63
Do-it-yourself homicide.   Writer 76:17 O '63
Jack Webb talks about the camera and cameramen.
Am Cinematographer 47-5:318 My '66
Lewis, R. W.   Happiness is a return to the good old
days.   TV Guide 16-42:37 O 19 '68

WEBER, LOIS
Smith, B. H.   Perpetual leading lady.   Sunset 32:634 Mr
'14

WEIDLER, VIRGINIA
Day, L.   Life of an autograph hound.   Photop 23-2:40
Jl '43

WEISSMULLER, JOHNNY
Boy who has broken all swimming records.   Lit Digest
73:57 My 27 '22
Weissmuller, J. & Bush, C. A.   My methods of training.
Sat Eve Post 202:48 Mr 8; 54 Mr 29 '30
Swim, said the doctors, and Johnny swam.   Lit Digest
110:29 Jl 4 '31
Weissmuller swims to films.   Lit Digest 113:18 Ap 16 '32
Albert, K.   Hey! Hey! Here comes Johnny.   Photop 42-
1:28 Je '32
Hampton, J.   Lupe and Johnny were lovers.   Photop 46-
1:58 Je '34
Best advice I ever had.   Read Digest 73:87 Jl '58
Monroe, K.   Johnny Weissmuller was a slow swimmer.
N. Y. Times Mag p32 D 18 '66

WELCH, RAQUEL
Friedman, B. J.   Raquel Welch: the definitive chickie.
Esquire 64:84 O '65
Mad about the girl.   Time 87:80 Je 24 '66
On her way with zap and socko.   Life 61:65 Ag 26 '66
James, H.   What they did to Marilyn.   Photop 71-6:44
Je '67
Hamilton, J.   Raquel.   Look 31:M8 Ag 8 '67
Lewis, R. W.   Sudden stardom of Raquel Welch.   Sat Eve
Post 240:32 N 18 '67
Perfection in an imperfect world.   Esquire 70:48 Ag '68
Larsen, J.   Sea of C cups.   Time 93:92 Ap 4 '69
Hamilton, J. Raquel, Raquel; intv.   Look 33:78 Ap 15 '69

WELD, TUESDAY

My name is Tuesday Weld. Photop 55-3:52 Mr '59
Gordon, S. Tuesday Weld at fifteen, she's past the
awkward age. Look 23:70 My 26 '59
Suddenly it's Tuesday! Coronet 46:133 S '59
Girl called Tuesday. Newsweek 54:76 O 5 '59
Hickman, D. I win Tuesday's loving looks. Photop 56-
5:56 N '59
Tusher, W. Please stop those whispers about me.
Photop 57-3:28 Mr '60
Borie, M. The kids wouldn't let me be friends. Photop
57-6:42 Je '60
Tusher, B. You've made me feel I belong. Photop 58-
2:38 Ag '60
Dean, R. Can Tuesday hold on to Elvis? Photop 58-
3:32 S '60
Douglas, A. Tuesday Weld--the child who acts like a
woman. Cosmop 149:80 N '60
When Tuesday thought nobody was looking. Photop 58-6:
57 D '60
Miller, E. Who is Tuesday Weld? Seventeen 20:115 My
'61
Johnson, M. Living in another woman's shadow. Photop
60-2:36 Ag '61
Wedding bells for Tuesday. Photop 60-4:24 O '61
Ardmore, J. My nights are all Tuesday. Photop 61-1:
32 Ja '62
No, Sir Cedric, she is not a weekday machine tool.
TV Guide 10-27:22 Jl 7 '62
Dinter, C. If they're in love. Photop 62-3:55 S '62
Transformation of Tuesday. Life 55:47 Jl 26 '63
Lewis, R. W. Tuesday past, Tuesday present. Sat Eve
Post 237:28 Ap 11 '64

WELLES, ORSON

Vernon, G. Age twenty-two. Commonweal 26:423 Ag 27
'37
Parker, J. R. Lighted stages: the Mercury rises.
Mag Art 30:619 O '37
Taggard, E. Julius Caesar, 1937 model. Sr Schol 31:
6 D 11 '57
Lindley, D. He has the stage. Colliers 101:14 Ja 29 '38
Marvelous boy. Time 31:27 My 9 '38
Playboy. Am Mag 125:88 Je '38
First person singular: Welles, innovator on stage, ex-
periments on the air. Newsweek 12:25 Jl 11 '38
Panic! This is the Orson Welles broadcast that hoaxed

America.   Radio Guide p2 N 19 '38
Experiment.   Am Mag 126:162 N '38
On staging Shakespeare and on Shakespeare's stage.
   Sr Schol 33:19E Ja 14 '39
Biographical sketch.   Sr Schol 33:21E Ja 14 '39
Orson Welles begins radio book series.   Pub W 135:956
   Mr 4 '39
Chase, F.   He scared us to death!   Radio Guide p15 O
   27 '39
Johnston, A.   Orson Welles.   Sat Eve Post Ja 20 '40
Johnston, A. & Smith, F.   How to raise a child.   Sat
   Eve Post 212:9 Ja 20; 24 Ja 27; 27 F 3 '40
Hearst vs. Orson Welles.   Newsweek 17:62 Ja 20 '41
Sage, M.   Hearst over Hollywood.   New Repub p270
   F 24 '41
Once a child prodigy, he has never quite grown up.
   Life 10:108 My 26 '41
Ferguson, O.   Welles and his wonders.   New Repub 104:
   760 Je 2; 824 Je 16 '41
Man of the moment.   Photop 19-2:26 Jl '41
McEvoy, J. P.   Magic is the world for Orson Welles.
   Read Digest 39:81 D '41
Biography.   Cur Bio '41
Orson's alma mater: Todd school for boys in Woodstock,
   Ill. Time 39:50 Mr 9 '42
Rio party; Orson Welles frolics at famous Mardi gras.
   Life 12:98 My 18 '42
Mulvey, K.   Keeping up with Hollywood.   Womans H C
   69:37 My '42
Welles labors over The magnificent Ambersons and
   emerges with good film but minus RKO job.   Newsweek
   20:56 Jl 20 '42
Welles unlimited.   Newsweek 20:84 N 16 '42
Orson at war.   Time 40:46 N 30 '42
Berch, B.   Orson the great.   N.Y. Times Mag p11 Ag
   29 '43
Denton, J. F. & Crichton, K.   Welles' wonderland.
   Colliers 112:14 S 4 '43
Hopper, H.   Orson Welles--genus genius.   Photop 24-6:
   40 My '44
Dedicated wunderkind.   New Yorker 20:18 Ja 27 '45
Actor turns columnist.   Time 45:68 Ja 29 '45
Wellesapoppin.   Newsweek 27:87 Je 10 '46
Beatty, J.   Big show-off.   Am Mag 143:38 F '47
Murder! Life 25:106 O 11 '48
Houseman, J.   Man from Mars.   Harper 197:74 D '48
Koval, F.   Interview.   Sight & Sound 19-8:314 D '50

James, E. N.　Unprecedented mass panic; the night the
　Martians landed.　Read Digest 58:15 F '51
Kerr, W.　Wonder boy Welles.　Theatre Arts 35:50 S '51
Le gros legume.　New Yorker 29:27 O 24 '53
Orson Welles returns.　Newsweek 42:68 O 26 '53
Hamburger, P.　Television: Omnibus presentation of
　King Lear.　New Yorker 29:103 O 31 '53
Welles, O.　The third audience.　Sight & Sound 23-3:120
　Ja/Mr '54
MacLiammoir, M.　Orson Welles.　Sight & Sound 24-1:
　36 Jl/S '54
Bentley, E.　Theatre; Othello on film.　New Repub 133:
　21 O 3 '55
Harvey, E.　TV imports.　Colliers 136:38 O 14 '55
Winged gorilla.　New Statesm 51:65 Ja 21 '56
Gibbs, W.　Schizo king.　New Yorker 31:89 Ja 21 '56
Old play in Manhattan.　Time 67:80 Ja 23 '56
Orson Welles' Lear.　Newsweek 47:57 Ja 23 '56
Lewis, T.　Theatre; Welles as King Lear.　America 94:
　485 Ja 28 '56
Kurnitz, H.　Antic arts.　Holiday 19:65 Ja '65
Hayes, R.　Citizen Welles.　Commonweal 63:568 Mr 2 '56
Taper, B.　Who's who in the cast.　New Yorker 32:147
　Ap 28 '56
Sacher, S.　New creative writers.　Lib J 82:437 F 1 '57
Return of the prodigy.　Newsweek 49:108 Ap 29 '57
Wood, C.　TV personalities biographical sketchbook.
　TV Personalities p83 '57
Return of awesome Welles.　Life 44:53 F 24 '58
Weales, G.　Movies.　Reporter 18:33 Je 26 '58
Grigs, D.　Conversations at Oxford.　Sight & Sound 29-
　2:82 Apr '60
Campbell, P.　Now, Orson Welles, did I tell you?
　Vogue 136:170 N 1 '60
Tynan, K.　Orson Welles.　Show 1-1:64 O '61
Prodigal revived.　Time 79:30 Je 29 '62
Martinez, E.　The trial of Orson Welles.　Films & Film-
　ing 9-1:12 O '62
Kobler, J.　Citizen Welles rides again.　Sat Eve Post
　235:22 D 8 '62
Macdonald, D.　Orson Welles and his magic steam engine.
　Esquire 60:14 Jl '63
Hatch, R.　Adult prodigy.　Horizon 5:85 Jl '63
Biography.　Cur Bio 26:42 F '65
　Same.　Cur Bio Yrbk 1965:446 '65
Cobos, J. & Rubio, M.　Welles & Falstaff; an interview.
　Sight & Sound 35-4:158 Aut '66

Morgenstern, J. & Sokolov, R.   Falstaff as Orson
   Welles.   Newsweek 69:96 Mr 27 '67
Kael, P.   Orson Welles: there ain't no way.   New
   Repub 156:27 Je 24 '67
Johnson, W.   Orson Welles; of time and loss.   Film Q
   21-1:13 Fall '67
Special report: Orson Welles.   Action 4-3:23 My/Je '69

WERNER, OSKAR
New star--his name is Oskar.   Life 53:33 Jl 30 '65
People are talking about . . . Vogue 146:226 S 1 '65
Miller, E.   Dogs and mice can be movie stars.
   Seventeen 25:112 Je '66
Biography.   Cur Bio 27:40 Je '66
   Same Cur Bio Yrbk 1966:435 '67
Armbrister, T.   A very phony profession.   Sat Eve Post
   239:100 O 8 '66
Bean, R.   Mistress Cinema.   Films & Filming 13-2:19
   N '66
Biography.   Brit Bk Yr 1967:169 '67

WEST, MAE
Young, S.   Diamond Lil.   New Repub. 55:145 Je 27 '28
Sex in the theatre.   Parade 1:12 S '29
Personalities prominent in the press.   Cinema Digest
   1-6:4 Jl 25 '32
Hall, L.   Look out!   Here's Mae West.   Photop 43-2:46
   Ja '33
Patrick, C.   Mae West.   Cinema Digest 3-3:13 Ap 3 '33
Young, S.   Angels and ministers of grace.   New Repub
   77:73 N 29 '33
Croy, H.   Women capture screen honors for 1933.   Lit
   Digest 116:42 N '33
Maxwell, V.   It's the caveman within us calling for Mae.
   Photop 45-1:38 D '33
Baker, K.   War clouds in the West?   Photop 45-1:47 D
   '33
Shawell, J.   Mae West curves herself a career.   Pict R
   35:7 F '34
Kent, G.   The mammy and daddy of us all.   Photop 45-
   6:32 My '34
Condon, F.   Come up and meet Mae West.   Colliers 93:
   26 Je 16 '34
Baskette, K.   Has Mae West gone high hat?   Photop 46-
   2:39 Jl '34
Harrison, H.   The man you want.   Photop 46-4:67 S '34
Brentano, L.   Between covers.   Forum 93:97 F '35

McCarey, L. Mae West can play anything. Photop 48-1:
    30 Je '35
Baskette, K. Mae West talks about her "marriage."
    Photop 48-3:38 Ag '35
Madame Sylvia. Is Mae West skidding on the curves?
    Photop 50-5:48 N '36
Biographical note. Theatre Arts 33:47 Mr '49
America's favorite hussy comes back again as Diamond
    Lil. Life 26:104 My 23 '49
Gabriel, G. W. Westward wow! Theatre Arts 33:26 My
    '49
Brown, J. M. Mae pourquoi. Sat R 32:50 O 8 '49
Return of Mae West; at network radio. Newsweek 35:46
    Ja 16 '50
Nathan, G. J. Monthly critical review. Theatre Arts
    35:20 N '51
TV goes West. Theatre Arts 37:89 O '53
Peeled grape. Time 74:54 S 28 '59
Harrison, H. Sex--I didn't invent it. Photop 59-3:22
    Mr '61
Lapham, L. Let me tell you about Mae West. Sat Eve
    Post 237:76 N 14 '64
Arbus, D. Mae West. Show 5-1:42 Ja '65
Gowland, P. So I went up to see Mae West. Pop Phot
    59:32 Jl '66
Lawrenson, H. Mirror, mirror, on the ceiling: how'm
    I doin'? Esquire 68:72 Jl '67
Biography. Cur Bio 28:40 N '67
Same. Cur Bio Yrbk 1967:455 '68
Meryman, R. Mae West; intv. Life 66:60 Ap 18 '67
Ringgold, G. Mae West, inc. filmog. Screen Facts 7:1
    n. d.

WESTOVER, WINIFRED
Pope, F. She prayed for the part. Photop 36-2:40 Jl '29

WHITE, ALAN
Person of promise. Films & Filming 4-2:12 N '57

WHITE, ALICE
Thornley, G. The disliked girl. Photop 37-1:51 D '29
French, J. Too much sex appeal. Photop 39-1:41 D '30
Hall, L. The story of the girl who fought odds. Photop
    41-6:59 My '32
Mason, S. Alice, please come home. Photop 43-1:35
    D '32
Quirk, M. A. Alice completes her cycle. Photop 43-6:

50 My '33
Minton, E. Alice White. Films In Review 18-5:318 My
'67

WHITE, PEARL
A last word from Crystal's lovely traveler.   Photop 4-5:
46 O '13
Condon, M.   The real perils of Pauline.   Photop 6-5:59
O '14
Bacon, G. V.   The girl on the cover; intv.   Photop 9-2:
52 Ja '16
Eyck, J. T.   Speaking of Pearl.   Photop 12-4:25 S '17
Johnson, J.   The girl on the cover.   Photop 17-5:57 Ap
'20
Mullett, B.   Heroine of a thousand dangerous stunts.
Am Mag 92:32 S '21
Howe, H.   A star in search of her soul.   Photop 24-1:
29 Je '23
Johaneson, B.   Good-by, boys, I'm through.   Photop 25-
5:31 Ap '24
Obit.   Newsweek 12:4 Ag 15 '38
Time 32:21 Ag 15 '38
New movie re-creates the era of Pearl White, the great
serial queen.   Life 21:75 Jl '46
Marshall, J.   Perils of Pearl White.   Colliers 118:72
Jl 6 '46
Tomboys of the screen.   Newsweek 30:92 Jl 7 '47
Stainton, R.   Pearl White in Ithaca.   Films In Review
2-5:19 My '51
Biography.   DAB sup2:710 '58
Davies, W. E.   Truth about Pearl White.   Films In Re-
view 10-9:537 N '59
Smith, F. L.   Letter.   Films In Review 10-10:637 D '59

WHITING, LEONARD
People are talking about . . .   Vogue 150:88 Ag 1 '67
Simons, M.   New Romeo and Juliet.   Look 31:52 O 17
'67
Miller, E.   Love is the sweetest thing.   Seventeen 27:
83 Ja '68
Buckley, P.   Leonard Whiting; a living, breathing cara-
vaggio.   After Dark 11-6:16 O '69

WHITMAN, STUART
Bulldozing his way to an acting career.   TV Guide 5-49:
29 D 7 '57
Person of promise.   Films & Filming 5-10:17 Jl '59

Tusher, B. Love fight of the year. Photop 67-2:50 F '65
Lewis, R. W. Stuart Whitman's "marshal plan." TV
   Guide 15-44:20 N 4 '67

WHITMORE, JAMES
   The legal eagle. TV Guide 8-50:8 D 10 '60
   They appealed to a higher court. TV Guide 10-18:6
      My 5 '62

WHITTY, MAY
   Famous couple. Life 13:90 Ag 31 '42
   Dame May Whitty acts at 80. Life 19:57 O 22 '45
   Biography. Cur Bio D '45
   Obit. Newsweek 31:59 Je 7 '48
      Time 51:95 Je 7 '48
   Biography. DNB 1941-1950:940 '59

WHORF, RICHARD
   Does the summer theatre do its job? Theatre Arts 22:
      446 Je '38
   Some film actors who have made themselves known this
      year. Theatre Arts 26:184 Mr '42
   Shearer, L. One family's formula for the rich, full life.
      House B 94:131 Je '52
   Lavoos, J. Richard Whorf; painter of Americana.
      Am Artist 28:32 Ap '64
   Obit. Time 88:70 D 23 '66
      Newsweek 68:57 D 26 '66
      Screen World 18:241 '67

WIDMARK, RICHARD
   Houghton, N. Tomorrow arrives today. Theatre Arts
      30:82 F '46
   Long voyage north. New Yorker 25:23 F 26 '47
   Widmark the movie villain goes straight. Life 26:81 Mr
      28 '49
   Crichton, K. Young man with a sneer. Colliers 123:
      23 Ap 16 '49
   Howe, H. Drop the gun, Richard. Photop 36-2:54 Jl '49
   Townsend, P. Richard the light hearted. Photop 46-2:
      56 Ag '54
   Old world fans. New Yorker 34:29 My 10 '58
   Widmark, R. Creating without compromise. Films &
      Filming 8-1:7 O '61
   Ross, L. Player. New Yorker 37:60 N 4 '61
   Self-portrait. Esquire 58:142 O '62
   Biography. Cur Bio 24:42 Ap '63

Same.   Cur Bio Yrbk 1963:462 '64

WIECK, DOROTHEA
Taviner, R.   Poor "maedchen."   Photop 44-4:69 S '33
They stand out from the crowd.   Lit Digest 116:10 D
   23 '33

WILBUR, CRANE
Briscoe, J.   Why famous film favorites forsook footlights for filmdom.   Photop 7-1:127 D '14

WILCOX, ROBERT
Obit.   Screen World 7:226 '56

WILCOXON, HENRY
Danard, D.   Henry Wilcoxon, inc. filmog.   Films In
   Review 18-4:254 Ap '67

WILDE, CORNEL
Hamilton, S.   Wilde about love.   Photop 26-1:59 D '44
Walker, H. L.   Gentle swashbuckler.   Photop 27-3:45
   Ag '45
Hamilton, S.   Hungarian rhapsody.   Photop 28-2:40 Ja '46
Arnold, M.   Gypsy cavalier.   Photop 29-1:41 Je '46
Perkins, L.   Photolife of Cornel Wilde.   Photop 29-2:50
   Jl '46
Knight, P.   It's like this to be Mrs. Cornel Wilde.
   Photop 29-4:39 S '46
Deere, D.   If you were the house guest of the Cornel
   Wilde's.   Photop 30-1:46 D '46
Parsons, L. O.   Cornel Wilde talks back.   Photop 30-3:
   48 F '47
Asher, J.   The Wilde affair.   Photop 31-6:42 N '47
Graham, S.   The case of Cornel Wilde.   Photop 32-2:33
   Ja '48
Arden, J.   I was there.   Photop 32-3:56 F '48
Wilkie, J.   Too busy for love.   Photop 43-2:68 F '53

WILDING, MICHAEL
Sakol, J.   Liz and Mike.   Photop 41-5:40 My '52
Sakol, J.   Honeymoon house.   Photop 42-1:48 Jl '52
Swanson, P.   Two guys named Mike.   Photop 43-4:46 Ap
   '53
Street, R.   Honeymoon with baby.   Photop 45-2:56 F '54

WILLES, JEAN
Scornful of the sideburned creeps.   TV Guide 9-16:28 Ap

22 '61

WILLIAM, WARREN
Biery, R. The man who can't talk. Photop 43-3:49 F
  '33
Maddox, B. Don't try to explain Warren William.
  Photop 48-5:37 O '35
Biography. NCAB curG:293 '46
Obit. Newsweek 32:58 O 4 '48
  Time 52:83 O 4 '48

WILLIAMS, BILL
Walker, H. L. That engaging young Bill Williams.
  Photop 28-1:58 D '45
Walker, H. L. Hale to Williams. Photop 29-5:58 O '46
Double feature. Am Mag 146:118 Jl '48
Williams, B. No one else could take her place.
  Photop 37-1:40 Ja '50
The angels rush in. TV Guide 5-30:17 Jl 27 '57
Wood, C. TV personalities biographical sketchbook.
  TV Personalities p66 '57

WILLIAMS, CARA
Gehman, R. The wild, wild world of Cara Williams.
  TV Guide 9-27:12 Jl 8 '61
Raddatz, L. The lady was a poker player. TV Guide
  12-46:15 N 14 '64
Rode, D. Letter, inc. filmog. Films In Review 19-10:
  663 D '68

WILLIAMS, EARLE
Craig, J. Dr. Hero and Mr. Villain. Photop 9-2:116
  Ja '16
Personal correspondence to celebrities. Hobbies 45:30
  '40

WILLIAMS, EMLYN
Season's first guest. Theatre Arts 20:824 O '36
Biography. Cur Bio '41
Stokes, S. Emlyn Williams. Theatre Arts 66:697 N '42
Johns, E. Emlyn Williams--playwright par excellence.
  Theatre World p7 S '43
Hope-Wallace, P. Emlyn Williams, playwright, actor,
  producer. Theatre Arts 32:16 Ja '48
Hobson, H. Mr. Williams melodramatizes a difficult
  theme. C S Mon Mag p7 S 30 '50
Driver, T. F. Chamber drama. Christian Cent 74:1288

O 30 '51
Panter-Downes, M. Letter from London: Emlyn Wil-
liams as Charles Dickens. New Yorker 27:53 D 22 '51
McCarten, J. Theatre: solo with Williams. New
Yorker 27:58 F 16 '52
Emlyn Williams as Charles Dickens. Newsweek 39:92
F 18 '52
Mr. Dickens. Time 59:61 F 18 '52
Brown, J. M. Mr. Dickens read again. Sat R 35:26
F 23 '52
Krutch, J. W. Readings from Dickens. Nation 174:189
F 23 '52
Stage: Williams and Dickens. Commonweal 55:516 F 29
'52
Meet Mr. Dickens. Life 32:77 Mr 3 '52
Beyer, W. H. State of the theatre. Sch & Soc 75:184
Mr 22 '52
Forecasts and side glances: impersonating Charles
Dickens. Theatre Arts 36:13 Mr '52
Biography. Cur Bio 13:55 Ap '52
Same. Cur Bio Yrbk 1952:634 '53
Re-enter Mr. Dickens. Time 61:84 My 4 '53
Tale of 36 characters. Sat R 36:27 My 9 '53
Hayes, R. Bleak house. Commonweal 58:151 My 15 '53
Hoffman, T. Couple of masters. Theatre Arts 37:15 Jl
'53
Wales forever. Plays & Players 3-11:9 Ag '56
Advance notice. Vogue 130:212 S 1 '57
Hewes, H. And death shall have no dominion. Sat R O
19 '57
One man, and funny. Newsweek 50:99 O 21 '57
Recitation in Manhattan. Time 70:56 O 21 '57
Wyatt, E. V. Boy growing up. Cath World 186:228 D '57
Boy growing up; story telling session. Theatre Arts 41:
27 D '57
Personality of the month. Plays & Players 5-7:5 Ap '58
Dickinson, H. Readers or rhapsodes? O. J. Speech Ed
45:258 O '59
Williams, E. They loved each other; excerpt from George;
an early autobiography. Vogue 139:90 F 15 '62
Curtain going up. Time 79:106 Ap 20 '62
Bliven, N. Books. New Yorker 38:210 O 27 '62
My secret scenes off-stage. Travel 122:53 N '64

WILLIAMS, ESTHER
Crichton, K. Big splash. Colliers 110:13 S 26 '42
Hollywood finds starlet swimmer. Life 14:53 Ap 19 '43

Eddy, D.   Girl who always said no.   Am Mag 136:24 S
'43

Holliday, K.   The essence of Esther Williams.   Photop
26-2:41 Ja '45

Marshall, J.   Why drown?   Colliers 116:44 Jl 28 '45

Parsons, L. O.   Thrill of a real romance.   Photop 27-
5:28 O '45

Peters, S.   My Hollywood friends.   Photop 28-2:34 Ja '46

Fink, H.   Honeymoon in Mexico.   Photop 28-4:42 Mr '46

Howe, H.   Fiesta!   Photop 29-2:36 Jl '46

Beatty, J.   Fish out of water.   Am Mag 142:54 Jl '46

Perkins, L.   Photolife of Esther Williams.   Photop 30-
1:58 D '46

Deere, D.   More than ever.   Photop 30-4:46 Mr '47

Graham, S.   Three wishes had Esther.   Photop 31-2:56
Jl '47

Edwards, R.   Play truth or consequences with Esther
Williams.   Photop 33-2:54 Jl '48

Williams, B.   Mother of a star.   Parents Mag 23:38 S
'48

Williams, B.   This one's for laughs.   Photop 33-6:34 N
'48

Gage, B.   Easy to love.   Photop 34-2:26 Ja '49

Steele, J. H   Water color portrait.   Photop 36-1:60 Je
'49

Holliday, K.   Mermaid in waiting.   Photop 36-4:36 S '49

Sellstrom, M. W.   Now they are three.   Photop 37-2:36 F
'50

Gage, B.   Hawaiian lullaby.   Photop 38-2:36 Ag '50

Wernick, R.   Mermaid tycoon.   Life 30:139 Ap 16 '51

Parsons, L. O.   Make her old-fashioned.   Photop 39-4:
50 Ap '51

Wheeler, L.   Esther Williams--R. F. D.   Photop 40-3:54
S '51

Gage, B.   I'm still whistling.   Photop 40-6:64 D '51

Waterbury, R.   Hold your man.   Photop 41-1:36 Ja '52

Graham, S.   Thank heavens I can swim.   Photop 42-2:
62 Ag '52

Mermaid on skis.   Look 17:38 Ap 21 '53

Morris, J.   Esther Williams talks about her marriage.
Photop 43-4:38 Ap '53

Watson, E. W.   Esther Williams paints a flower portrait.
Am Artist 17:32 Je '53

Ott, B.   Everywhere that Esther goes.   Photop 44-3:36
S '53

Enter the heroine on water skis.   Life 36:72 Ja 18 '54

Block, M.   Esther Williams' wonderful Christmas.

Photop 45-1:42 Ja '54
Parsons, L. O. My defense of Esther Williams. Photop
    45-4:46 Ap '54
Parsons, L. O. Mermaid in the money. Cosmop 137:8
    Ag '54
Underwater industry. Look 19:70 F 22 '55
Biography. Cur Bio 16:56 F '55
I'm a lucky woman, all my wishes have come true; ed.
    by J. K. Ardmore. Parents Mag 30:52 Mr '55
Big splash on TV. TV Guide 4-34:9 Ag 25 '56
Biography. Cur Bio Yrbk 1955:651 '56
Venus with arms. TV Guide 5-20:8 My 18 '57
Kreh, B. Navy's war over Esther. Am Mer 87:73 Jl
    '58
Miss Williams takes a dive. TV Guide 8-32:17 Ag 6 '60
Pratt, W. J. Esther Williams, inc. filmog. Screen
    Facts 4-3:5 '69

WILLIAMS, GUINN "BIG BOY"
Obit. Screen World 14:226 '63

WILLIAMS, KATHLYN
Smith, B. H. Nervy movie lady. Sunset 32:1323 Je '14
Williams, K. My experience in the California desert.
    Feature Movie 2-5:7 Je 10 '15
Denton, F. Kathlyn's memory box. Photop 12-6:76 N
    '17
Obit. Screen World 12:226 '61

WILLS, CHILL
Hubler, R. G. Voice of the mule. Colliers 130:54 Jl 5
    '52
He makes sure where that Kodak is at. TV Guide 10-
    17:15 Ap 28 '62
Gray, T. Chill Wills--National General Corp.'s good
    will ambassador. Motion Picture Herald 238-45:40 N
    6 '68

WILSON, LOIS
St. Johns, A. R. Portrait of a lady. Photop 19-5:23 Ap
    '21
Johaneson, B. Must she commit murder? Photop 25-4:
    37 Mr '24

WILSON, MARGERY
Woodside, J. B. She was padded to fame. Photop 13-1:
    83 D '17

They stand out from the crowd. Lit Digest 118:10 D 15
    '34

WILSON, MARIE
    Cummings, M.   Lovely funny face.   Photop 49-6:45 Je
        '36
    Baskette, K.   Love finds a dizzy blonde.   Photop 53-2:
        21 F '39
    Dizzy blonde; My friend Irma.   Time 50:96 O 20 '47
    Crichton, K.   Oh, you beautiful blonde!   Colliers 123:28
        Mr 19 '49
    Irma is a lady.   Life 29:65 Ag 14 '50
    Whitney, D.   My friend Irma is not so dumb.   Coronet
        29:58 N '50
    Wilson, M.   Television, anyone?   TV Guide 4-31:28
        Ag 4 '51
    She made an industry out of ignorance.   TV Guide 5-3:4
        Ja 18 '52
    Fallon, B.   What's it like to be Marie Wilson's husband?
        TV Guide 5-52:7 D 26 '52
    Gould, J.   TV's top comediennes.   N.Y. Times Mag p16
        D 27 '53
    Big-hearted blonde.   TV Guide 2-26:15 Je 25 '54

WINDSOR, MARIE
    When she's bad, she's good.   TV Guide 7-18:28 My 2 '59
    Meyer, J.   Marie Windsor.   Films In Review 13-1:61 Ja
        '62
    Meyer, J.   Marie Windsor, inc. filmog.   Screen Facts
        16:24 n. d.

WING, TOBY
    Where are they now?   Newsweek 68:10 Jl 4 '66

WINNINGER, CHARLES
    Broadway hails Winninger off the Showboat.   Newsweek
        4:22 S 29 '34
    They stand out from the crowd.   Lit Digest 119:10 Ja 5
        '35
    Captain Henry.   Cinema Arts 1-1:38 Je '37
    Obit.   Newsweek 73:91 F 10 '69
        Time 93:70 F 7 '69
    Grant, P.   Letter.   Films In Review 20-3:183 Mr '69

WINSLOW, GEORGE
    Little boy with the big voice.   McCalls 80:15 S '53
    Harbert, R.   Assignment in Hollywood.   Good H 137:126

D '53

WINTERS, GRANT
French, J.   Just a crazy kid.   Photop 37-1:31 D '29
Obit.   Time 73:92 Ap 6 '59
Screen World 11:226 '60

WINTERS, JONATHAN
Wood, C.   TV personalities biographical sketchbook.
TV Personalities p89 '56
Hot Winters.   Newsweek 51:79 F 10 '58
If you're not sick . . .   Time 72:54 O 13 '58
Hamilton, J.   What's so funny?   Look 27:119 Je 18 '63
Winging it.   Newsweek 63:105 My 18 '64
Lear, M. W.   Winging it with Jonathan Winters.   N. Y.
Times Mag p36 Mr 28 '65
Biography.   Cur Bio 26:40 Mr '65
Same.   Cur Bio Yrbk 1965:461 '65
Ace, G.   Jonathan Winters of our discontent.   Sat R
48:14 Ap 24 '65
Berger, T.   Jonathan Winters: always on.   Holiday 38:
101 N '65
Silly putty.   Newsweek 71:50 Ja 15 '68

WINTERS, ROLAND
Wood, C.   TV personalities biographical sketchbook.
TV Personalities p146 '56

WINTERS, SHELLEY
Biographical note.   Time 52:99 O 4 '48
Small, C.   Green-eyed movie madcap.   Colliers 124:46
Jl 30 '49
Done by mirrors.   Life 27:41 S 5 '49
Shelley Winters.   Life 29:95 Ag 7 '50
Winters, S.   You can't help loving that man.   Photop 38-
5:50 N '50
Hine, A.   Lunch with Shelley Winters.   Holiday 9:6 My
'51
Zeitlin, I.   Their love is like this.   Photop 40-2:52 Ag
'51
Perkins, L.   Photolife of Shelley Winters.   Photop 40-6:
52 D '51
Holiday awards for 1951 to movies and movie makers.
Holiday 11:78 Ja '52
Biography.   Cur Bio 13:57 Ap '52
Same.   Cur Bio Yrbk 1952:644 '53
Martin, P.   Hollywood's blonde pop-off.   Sat Eve Post

224:22 Je 28 '52
Maxwell, E.   Latins are lousy lovers.   Photop 42-1:42
    Jl '52
Winters, S.   The man I married.   Photop 43-5:58 My '53
Rogers, M.   Together again.   Photop 44-2:24 Ag '53
Phillips, D.   That do or die doll.   Photop 47-5:61 My '55
Hit and a miss.   Newsweek 46:66 N 21 '55
Shelley Winters.   Vogue 127:124 Ja '56
Taper, B.   Who's who in the cast.   New Yorker 32:147
    Ap 28 '56
That wonderful, deep silence.   Theatre Arts 40:30 Je '56
Mitchell, A.   The losing battle.   Photop 59-1:26 Ja '61
Winters' day at Harvard.   Newsweek 59:77 Mr 5 '62
Davidson, B.   Shelley Winters, headlong talker.   Sat Eve
    Post 235:32 Ag 11 '62
Loneliest years of my life.   Seventeen 21:148 S '62
Funke, L. & Booth, J. E.   Actor's method; his life.
    N.Y. Times Mag p35 O 1 '61
Method madam.   Newsweek 60:61 O 8 '62
The day Shelley Winters returned to her old studio and TV
    in a rented car.   TV Guide 13-27:12 Jl 3 '65

WINTON, JANE
    Obit.   Screen World 11:226 '60

WISEMAN, JOSEPH
    Talk with a villain.   Newsweek 55:113 Ap 18 '60
    Nolan, J. E.   Five TV heavies.   Film Fan Mo 92:15 F
        '69

WITHERS, JANE
    McAllister, A.   She had to be famous.   Photop 48-6:72
        N '35
    Holdom, C.   Little trouper.   C S Mon Mag p3 D 4 '35
    Beatty, J.   Rowdy Jane.   Am Mag 122:22 Ag '36
    Bailey, K.   The reformation of Jane Withers.   Photop
        52-2:25 F '38
    Kutner, N.   Box-office babes.   Colliers 103:74 Mr 25 '39
    Condon, F.   No mothers wanted: Shirley Temple's suc-
        cessor has been chosen, so keep the children home.
        Colliers 106:20 Ag 17 '40
    Bell, L. P.   Her house grows up with Jane; Withers'
        ranch-house transformed into a two-story colonial.
        House B 82:65 N '40
    Waterbury, R.   Hi gang! Come over to Janie's.   Photop
        18-2:22 Ja '41
    Bell, L. P.   Something's doing at Jane's house.   Bet

Hom & Gard 19:36 Mr '41
Mulvey, K.   Keeping up with Hollywood.   Womans H C
   69:16 Ag '42
Ten things that make my heart beat faster.   Good H 141:
   224 S '55
Where are they now?   Newsweek 70:20 S 25 '67

WOLFIT, DONALD
   Lardner, J.   Outbreak of Shakespeare.   New Yorker 23:
      50 Mr 1 '47
   Alas, poor Wolfit.   Newsweek 29:73 Mr 3 '47
   Provincial on Broadway.   Time 49:48 Mr 3 '47
   Krutch, J. W.   Drama.   Nation 164:283 Mr 8 '47
   Woe is Wolfit.   Newsweek 29:82 Mr 10 '47
   Phelan, K.   Donald Wolfit's London company.   Common-
      weal 45:539 Mr 14 '47
   Wolfit, D.   Words and music.   Play & Players 2-7:5
      Ap '55
   Forster, P.   Donning the purple.   Drama 39:29 Win '55
   Barker, F. G.   Lone Wolfit.   Plays & Players 4-6:13 Mr
      '57
   Personality of the month.   Plays & Players 6-2:3 N '58
   Brahms, C.   Sufficient magic.   Plays & Players 7-2:6 N
      '59
   Lambert, J. W.   Lone Wolfit.   Plays & Players 11-4:10
      Ja '64
   Biography.   Cur Bio 26:43 Mr '65
   Same.   Cur Bio Yrbk 1965:464 '65
   Obit.   Cur Bio 29:45 Ap '68
      Cur Bio Yrbk 1968:464 '69
      Screen World 20:241 '69

WOLHEIM, LOUIS
   Lang, H.   Gr-r-r-r-r!   Photop 39-2:66 Ja '31
   The hard boiled samaritan.   Photop 39-6:71 My '31

WONG, ANNA MAY
   Winship, M.   The China doll.   Photop 24-1:35 Je '23
   Sparks, B. N.   Where East meets West.   Photop 26-1:55
      Je '24
   Wong, A. M.   The Chinese theatre, Los Angeles.   Era
      p9 F 27 '29
   Johns, E.   Aesthetic aid from China.   Theatre World p24
      Jl '44
   Obit.   Time 77:78 F 10 '61
      Newsweek 57:68 F 13 '61
      Screen World 13:226 '62

Doerr, C. J.   Letter.   Films In Review 19-10:660 D '68

WOOD, NATALIE
New movie moppet.   Life 19:87 N 26 '45
Wood, N.   You haven't heard the half about Jimmy.
    Photop 48-5:55 N '55
Ott, B.   Junior femme fatale.   Photop 49-6:35 Je '56
Wood, N.   Aloha means goodbye.   Photop 50-3:62 S '56
Lane, L.   Diary of a lady on the loose.   Photop 50-6:48
    D '56
Strange doings of actress at practice.   Life 42:97 Ja 28
    '57
Natalie Wood: teenage tiger.   Look 21:96 Je 25 '57
Robinson, M. & Christian, F.   For fun, I work.   Cosmop
    142:47 Je '57
Gehman, R.   Don't sell Natalie short.   Photop 51-2:52
    Ag; 51-3:60 S '57
Meredith, J.   Bob, did you know?   Photop 53-3:47 Mr
    '58
Borie, M.   Why we won't talk about our marriage.
    Photop 53-6:57 Je '58
Natalie Wood as Bob Wagner sees her.   Photop 54-1:54
    Jl '58
Wood, L. L.   All Nat talks about is pots and pans and
    Bob.   Photop 55-2:52 F '59
Meltsir, A.   Taming of the shrewd.   Coronet 47:127 F
    '60
Tornabene, L.   Lunch date with Natalie Wood and Bob
    Wagner.   Cosmop 149:18 O '60
Beauty and violence.   Look 25:105 Ap 11 '61
Up from Happyland.   Time S 22 '61
Why Natalie and Bob split.   Photop 60-3:24 S '61
About the star.   Newsweek 58:102 O 23 '61
Wall, T.   The Natalie Wood story.   Photop 61-1:24 Ja '62
Movie star into actress: the story of Natalie Wood.
    Newsweek 59:54 F 26 '62
Hoffman, J.   Wedding bells for Natalie.   Photop 61-2:58
    F '62
Magaro, R.   Her sister's side of the story.   Photop 61-
    3:59 Mr '62
Kempton, M.   Is this the girl next door?   Show 2-3:50
    Mr '62
Davidson, B.   Hollywood throwback.   Sat Eve Post 235:
    32 Ap 7 '62
Biography.   Cur Bio 23:45 Ap '62
    Same.   Cur Bio Yrbk 1962:472 '63
But for Natalie no nonsense.   Life 52:88 Je 15 '62

Wood, Peggy

691

Pope, E. What Hollywood does to women. Good H 154:
32 Je '62
Rivkin, A. & Kerr, L. Hello, Natalie Wood! Vogue 139:
88 Je '62
Crowley, W. Their biggest problem is . . . Photop 61-
6:21 Je '62
Somers, A. Are they fighting over Warren. Photop 62-
1:29 Jl '62
Natalie strips down! Photop 62-2:36 Ag '62
Natalie warms up for a take-off. Life 53:101 N 2 '62
Carpozi, G. Good imitation of marriage. Photop 62-6:
52 D '62
Field, E. How she tried to save her sister. Photop 63-
5:42 My '63
Zimmermann, G. Natalie Wood: child of change. Look
27:91 Ag 13 '63
Is the party over? Photop 64-3:64 S '63
Bascombe, L. On the rebound. Photop 64-5:42 N '63
Born to be a star. Life 55:182 D 20 '63
Lyle, J. Natalie's becoming a stepmother. Photop 65-
1:59 Ja '64
Baxter, R. Boys meets girl. Seventeen 23:76 Ja '64
Daly, S. Has she turned her back on men? Photop 67-2:
64 F '65
The man she will marry. Photop 68-1:18 Jl '65

WOOD, PEGGY
How? I don't know. Woman Cit 9:10 My 16 '25
Musical comedy or drama? Drama 16:6 O '25
Mullett, M. P. Peggy Wood seems like such a nice girl;
intv. Am Mag 102:36 Ag '26
Splendid gypsy. Sat Eve Post 200:12 S 3 '27
Immortal gypsy. Sat Eve Post 200:9 F 18 '28
Noah's folly was remembered by Peggy Wood. Outlook
149:70 My 9 '28
Beginners, please! Sat Eve Post 200:10 Je 23 '28
Forty weeks. Sat Eve Post 201:22 S 15 '28
Ladies and ticket buyers. Sat Eve Post 201:10 D 1 '28
See and hear. Sat Eve Post 202:20 Jl 20 '29
Queues and cues. Sat Eve Post 203:5 Ag 30 '30
House in London. Sat Eve Post 203:14 Mr 7 '31
Glasses aren't so bad. Am Mag 114:51 D '32
Skin-deep. Ladies Home J 50:30 N '32
Long way from home; foreword. Harper 186:84 D '42
Biography. Cur Bio '42
Actors speak louder than words. Colliers 113:74 Ap 8 '44
"Mama." TV Guide 2-34:16 Ag 20 '49

Clemenko, H.   The armchair spectator meets Peggy Wood.
   TV Guide 5-19:4 My 9 '52
The real "Mama."   TV Guide 1-27:15 O 2 '53
Biography.   Cur Bio 14:60 D '53
   Same.   Cur Bio Yrbk 1953:659 '53
Six most successful women.   Womans H C 81:20 Ja '54
Wood, C.   TV personalities biographical sketchbook.
   TV Personalities p76 '54
Mama's preserves.   Ladies Home J 73:130 S '56
Mama's soups.   Ladies Home J 74:82 Ja '57
Wood, P.   The festivals--Europe 1960.   Equity 45-11:4
   D '60
Circle of light.   Opera News 30:8 F 19 '66
Wood, P.   The theatre at the crossroads.   N. Y. State
   Community Theatre Journal 6-2:4 n. d.

WOODRUFF, ELEANOR
   Briscoe, J.   Why film favorites forsook the footlights.
      Photop 5-5:123 O '14
   Deuch, E. A.   Eleanor Woodruff.   Feature Movie 4-1:
      40 O 10 '15

WOODS, DONALD
   Wood, C.   TV personalities biographical sketchbook.
      TV Personalities p85 '54

WOODWARD, JOANNE
   She's all right . . . if you like talent.   TV Guide 4-45:
      24 N 10 '56
   Larkin, L.   Million dollar rebel.   Photop 52-2:44 Ag '57
   Tension and triumph for a young actress.   Life 44:81 Ap
      7 '58
   Knight, A.   Truth and illumination.   Sat R 41:43 Ap 12
      '58
   Anderson, N.   I don't want to be an actress.   Photop
      53-4:40 Ap '58
   Biography.   Cur Bio 19:43 Je '58
      Same.   Cur Bio Yrbk 1958:481 '58
   Joyce, A.   The honeymoon is over.   Photop 54-1:59 Jl
      '58
   Dance training for Oscar winner.   Dance Mag 32:32 Jl
      '58
   Kinney, H.   McCalls visits.   McCalls 85:16 S '58
   Markel, H.   Joanne Woodward: the adamant Eve.
      Coronet 45:54 Mr '59
   Prensky, B.   Joanne Woodward's my baby sitter.
      Photop 55-3:48 Mr '59

Anderson, N. Do you sometimes believe in fate?
    Photop 56-1:58 Jl '59
Bester, A. Solemn lovers. Holiday 26:91 Jl '59
Hamilton, J. Joanne Woodward: the fugitive kid.
    Look 23:121 D 8 '59
Biography. Am Ann 1959:833 '59
Lemon, R. Glamour girls off-duty. Newsweek 55:61 Ja
    4 '60
I love learning to cook: ed. by J. Anderson. Ladies
    Home J 77:72 Ag '60
Britten, R. A love letter from Joanne. Photop 61-2:66
    F '62
Dickert, L. Star without an image. Sat Eve Post 235:
    20 S 15 '62
Woods, M. That blond stripper in his life. Photop 62-
    5:51 N '62
Bunzel, P. There's method in Newmans' marriage.
    Life 55:50 Jl 5 '63
Robbins, F. I want to kill my husband. Photop 64-3:48
    S '63
Baskette, K. Love story for adults only. Photop 66-3:
    68 S '64
Lyon, N. Second fame: good food. Vogue 146:144 Ag 1
    '65
Joanne and Paul--and Rachel. Life 65:47 O 18 '68
Davidson, M. Joanne Woodward tells all about Paul New-
    man; intv. Good H 168:72 F '69
Sin makes marriage survive. Photop 75-5:60 My '69
A delicate problem. Photop 75-6:33 Je '69
Times they're not married. Photop 76-2:47 Ag '69
I can't be jealous anymore. Photop 76-6:55 D '69

WOOLLEY, MONTY
    Biography. Cur Bio '40
    St. Monty. New Yorker 18:16 D 19 '42
    Orthman, F. C. Beard that talks like a man. Sat Eve
        Post 216:12 S 4 '43
    Cerf, B. Trade Winds. Sat R 27:18 My 27 '44
    Obit. Time 81:101 My 17 '63
        Newsweek 61:68 My 20 '63
        Am Ann 1964:746 '64
        Brit Bk Yr 1964:635 '64
        Cur Bio 27:47 Je '63
        Cur Bio Yrbak 1963:476 '64
        Screen World 15:226 '64

694   Motion Picture Performers

WRAY, FAY
    Albert, K. The new Fay Wray? Photop 38-5:6 O '30

WRIGHT, TERESA
    Muriel. Am Mag 132:92 D '41
    Crichton, K. No glamor gal. Colliers 109:13 My 23 '42
    Quietly but steadily she grows to stardom. Life 13:41
        Jl 20 '42
    Baskette, K. That's Wright. Photop 22-2:44 Ja '43
    Biography. Cur Bio '43
    Walker, H. L. The best years of her life. Photop 31-5:
        44 O '47
    Phillips, W. Week's preview. Colliers 122:46 D 11 '48

WYATT, JANE
    Speeder. Am Mag 119:41 Mr '35
    Taviner, R. Even blue blood couldn't stop Jane Wyatt.
        Photop 51-4:36 Ap '37
    Fun in bedlam; autobiography. Am Mag 135:50 F '43
    Wood, C. TV personalities biographical sketchbook.
        TV Personalities p135 '54
    Who needs the social register? TV Guide 3-46:15 N 12 '55
    O'Hara, J. Appointment with O'Hara. Colliers 137:6 Je
        22 '56
    Biography. Cur Bio 18:57 My '57
    Same. Cur Bio Yrbk 1957:598 '58
    Jane Wyatt's triple threats. Good H 149:48 O '59

WYCHERLY, MARGARET
    Obit. Time 67:83 Je 18 '56
        Screen World 8:226 '57

WYMAN, JANE
    Zeitlin, I. Love among the Reagans. Photop 20-2:30 Ja
        '42
    Wyman, J. Our child must not hate. Photop 24-6:34 My
        '44
    Parsons, L. O. This is the truth about Jane and Ronnie.
        Photop 26-2:22 Ja '45
    Asher, J. We're the Ray-gans. Photop 30-1:52 D '46
    Howe, H. St. Joe's Jane. Photop 31-1:60 Je '47
    Hall, G. Those fightin' Reagans. Photop 32-3:37 F '48
    Parsons, L. O. Last call for happiness. Photop 32-5:
        40 Ap '48
    Crichton, K. Week's preview. Colliers 122:74 O 2 '48
    Wyman, J. Why I've changed. Photop 33-5:36 O '48
    Memorable make-believe. Coronet 25:22 N '48

Biography. Cur Bio 10:56 Mr '49
Same. Cur Bio Yrbk 1949:647 '50
Waterbury, R. This is a love story. Photop 34-4:64
  Mr '49
Howe, H. Two worlds of Janie Wyman. Photop 34-6:
  50 My '49
Wilson, L. The searching heart. Photop 37-5:50 My
  '50
English, Z. Jane's other life. Photop 38-5:62 N '50
Zeitlin, I. In the cool, cool Jane Wyman way. Photop
  41-1:52 Ja '52
Townsend, P. Torch song. Photop 42-1:40 Jl '52
Jane Wyman dances the zambesi. Colliers 131:20 Ja 10
  '53
Hollywood takes care of its own. McCalls 80:98 Ja '53
Waterbury, R. So they were married. Photop 43-2:38
  F '53
Ardmore, J. Close harmony. Photop 45-2:60 F '54
Hubler, R. G. Calamity Jane Wyman. Coronet 39:92
  Ja '56
Mitchell, A. Is love really better the second time a-
  round? Photop 60-1:73 Jl '61
McClelland, D. Jane Wyman, inc. filmog. Films In
  Review 18-5:312 My '67

WYMORE, PATRICE
  Graham, S. She can handle him. Photop 42-3:68 S '52
  Soap opera actress with a soap opera life. TV Guide
    14-13:12 Mr 26 '66

WYNN, ED
  Kennedy, J. B. Perfect fool. Colliers 81:19 Mr 3 '28
  Krutch, J. W. Fools. Nation 133:582 N 25 '31
  Krutch, J. W. Laughing gases. Nation 145:697 D 18 '37
  I'm a fool about my boy. Am Mag 122:28 O '38
  Ed Wynn is at his barmy best in new Broadway hit Boys
    and girls together. Life 9:57 O 7 '40
  Krutch, J. W. Fool made perfect. Nation 151:345 O 12
    '40
  Smith, B. It's no fun to be funny. Am Mag 131:20 F '41
  Woolf, S. J. How to hatch a joke. N.Y. Times Mag p12
    Jl 5 '42
  King bubbles. Newsweek 24:86 Ag 21 '44
  These pictures show Ed Wynn's nonsensical inventions.
    Life 17:12 S 18 '44
  Nice man. Time 44:81 S 25 '44
  Biography. Cur Bio Ja '45

Nichols, L.   Lament for the age of clowns.   N.Y. Times
    Mag p12 F 1 '48
Sayre, J.   August clown.   Life 25:65 Jl 26 '48
Wynn's bid.   Newsweek 34:54 O 3 '49
Hill, G.   It's Ed Wynn again--in video.   Colliers 124:
    22 O 15 '49
Something old, something new.   Time 54:77 O 17 '49
Wynn takes on TV.   Life 27:74 O 17 '49
Colton, H. E.   Ed Wynn conquers his fourth medium.
    N. Y. Times Mag p20 O 23 '49
Wynn, E.   Laughter on the cable.   TV Guide p8 N 26 '49
Perfect fool.   Coronet 27:6 F '50
McEvoy, J. P.   Secrets of a perfect fool.   Read Digest
    59:99 S '51
Lords of laughter.   Coronet 30:69 O '51
New Ed Wynn.   Newsweek 49:73 Ap 15 '57
Nichols, L.   Ed Wynn: up and coming actor.   N. Y.
    Times Mag p14 My 12 '57
Wainwright, L. S.   Warm father and son story about the
    Wynns.   Life 42:96 Je 17 '57
Whitcomb, J.   Life begins at seventy.   Cosmop 144:74
    Ja '58
Comfortable as an old shoe.   TV Guide 6-51:17 D 20 '58
Wynn, E.   People I have laughed with.   Good H 148:47
    Ja '59
Reese, J.   Grand old man's new career.   Sat Eve Post
    231:24 Ap 4 '59
Wynn, K.   Fool for a father; excerpt from Ed Wynn's
    son.   McCalls 86:32 Ag '59
Perfect fool's son.   Newsweek 54:118 O 12 '59
He changed his clothes.   TV Guide 8-15:12 Ap 9 '60
First time.   Time 88:37 Jl 1 '66
Mahoney, S.   Master of foolishness.   Life 61:89 Jl 1 '66
Obit.   Newsweek 67:83 Je 27 '66
    Time 88:76 Jl 1 '66
    Brit Bk Yr 1967:601 '67
    Cur Bio 27:45 Jl '66
    Cur Bio Yrbk 1966:473 '67
    Screen World 18:241 '67

WYNN, KEENAN
    Proctor, K.   Play truth or consequences with Keenan
        Wynn.   Photop 28-1:56 D '45
    Jefferson, S. & Pritchett, F.   The Van Johnson, Evie
        and Keenan Wynn triangle.   Photop 30-4:34 Mr '47
    Martin, P.   It's tough to have a famous father.
        Sat Eve Post 219:20 My 3 '47

Wainwright, L. S. Warm father and son story about the
    Wynns. Life 42:96 Je 17 '57
He doesn't get splashed anymore.   TV Guide 6-14:22 Ap
    5 '58
Wynn, K.   Fool for a father; excerpt from Ed Wynn's
    son.   McCalls 86:32 Ag '59
Perfect fool's son.   Newsweek 54:118 O 12 '59

WYNN, MAY
    Fashions to flickers.   Am Mag 159:44 Ja '55

WYNTER, DANA
    Girl Britain lost.   Look 18:42 Ap 20 '54
    Too-hidden talent.   Theatre Arts 39:15 Ag '55
    Bolstad, H. Wynter wonder.   Photop 49-2:62 F '56
    Wynter in California.   Look 20:62 Ap 3 '56
    Harris, R. Wynter victorious.   Photop 50-3:18 S '56
    Britain's loveliest export.   TV Guide 5-36:24 S 7 '57
    Phillips, D. Framed! Photop 55-2:62 F '59
    Musel, R. Taking a camera tour of Europe.   TV Guide
        14-39:32 S 24 '66
    Brown, I. Dana Wynter.   Plays & Players 15-7:56 Ap
        '68

WYNYARD, DIANA
    Melcher, E. Screen sensations of the year.   Cinema
        Digest 3-5:9 Ap 7 '33
    Craig, D. If you've wondered about Diana.   Photop 43-
        5:38 Ap '33
    Pringle, H. F. She who gets slapped.   Colliers 92:24 Jl
        1 '33
    Feminine grace.   Plays & Players 1-8:4 My '54
    Diana Wynyard--the art of wearing well.   Vogue 136:111
        Ag 1 '60
    Obit.   Time 83:102 My 22 '64
        Illus Lond N 244:829 My 23 '64
        Newsweek 63:75 My 25 '64
        Screen World 16:226 '65

YAMAGUCHI, SHIRLEY
  Everywhere is human. New Yorker 27:15 S 1 '51
  Isamu-san and Shirley too. Time 60:76 N 3 '52
  Biographical note. Newsweek 39:90 F 11 '52
  Charmer's confession. Newsweek 45:60 Ja 3 '55
  And she can cook, too. Am Mag 160:48 O '55

YORK, DICK
  Efron, E. He's almost invisible in the glare of success.
  TV Guide 13-22:19 My 29 '65

YORK, MICHAEL
  Miller, E. I've come to conquer you! Seventeen 28:
  168 Ap '69

YORK, SUSANNAH
  Britain's dewy dazzler. Life 51:53 Jl 7 '61
  Show business. Time 58:45 Jl 28 '61
  Talk with a star. Newsweek 58:106 N 13 '61
  Ginna, R. E. On screen. Horizon 4:115 N '61
  Lawrenson, H. Susannah York. Show 2-1:68 Ja '62
  Susannah York: England's offbeat star. Look 27:78 F
  26 '63
  Miller, E. Enthusiastic actors dig a classic! Seven-
  teen 22:114 F '63
  Notes and comment. New Yorker 40:31 Je 6 '64

YOUNG, CLARA KIMBALL
  Katterjohn, M. M. Clara Kimball Young. Photop 6-5:
  750 '14
  Baker, C. A chat with Clara Kimball Young. Photop
  7-6:63 My '15
  Young, C. K. The technique of lovers. Photop 17-4:
  39 My '20
  Foster, D. Welcome home, Clara! Photop 39-2:82 Ja
  '31
  Davis, H. R. Clara Kimball Young. Films In Review
  12-7:419 Ag/S '61
  Obit. Newsweek 56:90 O 24 '60
    Brit Bk Yr 1961:522 '61
    Screen World 12:226 '61
  Various letters. Films In Review 12-8:505 O '61

YOUNG, GIG
French, W. F. Gig-Young mariner. Photop 23-2:50 Jl '43

Efron, E. Meet the real Gig Young. TV Guide 13-24: 15 Je 12 '65

YOUNG, LORETTA
Grant, J. The beauty who cannot stay in love. Photop 48-4:26 S '35

Manners, D. Fame, fortune and fatigue. Photop 49-1: 32 Ja '36

A visit with Loretta Young. Photop 50-5:8 N '36

Sharpe, H. Born for romance. Photop 52-7:14 Jl; 52-8:60 Ag; 52-9:68 S '38

Ormiston, R. The tragic role Loretta Young played in the Buckner case. Photop 53-9:20 S '39

Crichton, K. Young idea. Colliers 104:13 N 18 '39

Gilmore, H. Loretta really talks. Photop 19-2:33 Jl '41

Young, L. Forget those fears. Photop 22-3:43 F '43

Young, L. Put ruffles in your life. Photop 25-2:56 Jl '44

Young, L. Because you're brave enough. Photop 27-6: 52 N '45

Marshall, J. Reasonable Miss Young. Colliers 120:48 D 27 '47

Innocent abroad. Life 24:39 F 16 '48

Biography. Cur Bio 9:56 Mr '48

Same. Cur Bio Yrbk 1948:699 '49

Maxwell, E. The Young idea. Photop 32-6:50 My '48

Young, L. I remember Irene Dunne. Photop 33-3:36 Ag '48

Young, L. Winning smile. Am Mag 146:96 O '48

Loretta Young in The accused. Coronet 25:22 F '49

Birch, B. Laugh-long friends. Photop 36-3:60 Ag '49

Biographical note. Theatre Arts 35:38 Ag '51

"The Queen" stakes her crown on television. TV Guide 1-36:15 D 4 '53

Klass, R. Film and TV. Cath World 179:65 Ap '54

Wood, C. TV personalities biographical sketchbook. TV Personalities p84 '54

Loretta and her man. TV Guide 3-1:13 Ja 1 '55

Grafton, S. Loretta Young story. Good H 140:65 Mr '55

Back in working clothes. TV Guide 4-2:14 Ja 14 '56

Ten things that make my heart beat faster. Good H 142: 144 F '56

Good men are hard to find. TV Guide 4-45:9 N 10 '56

Loretta's gowns. TV Guide 5-16:8 Ap 20 '57
I'm still a ham. TV Guide 5-42:8 O 19 '57
Loretta lost an argument. TV Guide 6-45:17 N 8 '58
No shrieks, no screams. Newsweek 52:58 D 8 '58
Just take it out of my salary. TV Guide 7-20:17 My 16
    '59
Television's number one messenger girl. TV Guide 7-
    52:13 D 26 '59
Jennings, D. Indestructible glamour girl. Sat Eve Post
    232:20 My 28 '60
Dinter, C. When everyone you love has left you.
    Photop 58-3:28 S '60
How does Loretta do it? TV Guide 8-45:17 N 5 '60
Young, L. Things I had to learn; abridged. Ladies
    Home J 78:52 Ap '61
Efron, E. The legend of Loretta. TV Guide 10-42:16
    O 20 '62
Wilkie, J. Loretta Young: the steel butterfly. Good H
    156:78 Je '63
Unforgettable Sister Winifred. Read Digest 88:173 Mr '66
Bowers, R. L. Loretta Young, inc. filmog. Films In
    Review 20-4:193 Ap '69

YOUNG, ROBERT
    Churchill, E. Sellers of romance. Photop 43-6:40 My
        '33
    Mastin, M. I want to be a clown. Photop 48-2:48 Jl '35
    Zeitlin, I. Dear ol' mother-in-law o' mine. Photop
        52-7:28 Jl '38
    Young, R. as told to Gladys Hall. I waited eleven years.
        Photop 20-5:64 Ap '42
    Young, R. My first fan. Am Mag 134:37 S '42
    Harris, E. If you were Bob Young's house guest.
        Photop 27-4:62 S '45
    Pretty daughter is like a melody. Parents Mag 22:148 Je
        '47
    Taxi to fame. Am Mag 149:70 Je '50
    Morris, J. We have four daughters. Parents Mag 25:
        40 Jl '50
    Biography. Cur Bio 11:56 Jl '50
        Same. Cur Bio Yrbk 1950:632 '51
    Family spirit. TV Guide 2-52:17 D 25 '54
    Wood, C. TV personalities biographical sketchbook.
        TV Personalities p43 '54
    P.S. -- We want 'Father.' TV Guide 3-36:20 S 3 '55
    Rhodes, K. Father of two families. Cosmop 140:124
        Ap '56

Father does know best.   TV Guide 4-24:9 Je 16 '56
It's not always father.   TV Guide 5-7:17 F 16 '57
Eddy, B.   Private life of a perfect papa.   Sat Eve Post
    229:29 Ap 27 '57
Father still has his day.   TV Guide 6-24:18 Je 14 '58
The penalty of being 'father.'   TV Guide 7-25:24 Je 20
    '59
deRoos, R.   Life as father really leads it.   TV Guide
    10-2:22 Ja 13; 10-3:18 Ja 20 '62
How I won the war of the sexes by losing every battle.
    Good H 154:44 Ja '62

YOUNG, ROLAND
    Audience can do no wrong.   Scrib M 77:453 My '25
    Jamison, J.   Roland and the ladies.   Photop 43-4:47 Mr
        '33
    Hamilton, S.   Young in heart.   Photop 53-8:20 Ag '39
    Lone star razzle dazzle.   Nation 152:722 Je 21 '41
    Obit.   Time 61:99 Je 15 '53
        Newsweek 41:70 Je 15 '53
        Am Ann 1954:791 '54
        Brit Bk Yr 1954:538 '54
        Screen World 5:209 '54
    Biography.   NCAB 40:247 '55

YURKA, BLANCHE
    Morrow, A.   Secret of fine plays.   Woman Cit ns 10:17
        Ja '26
    Row, A. W.   Star who is a luminary.   Poet Lore 39:132
        Mr '28
    Row, A. W.   Pilgrimage to stardom.   Drama 18:196 Ap
        '28
    Young man, go on the stage!   Theatre 53:50 F '31
    Skinner, R. D.   Sophocles Electra.   Commonweal 15:357
        Ja 27 '32
    Second act: Utah.   Theatre Arts 32:56 Je '48
    Schuster, M.   Blanche Yurka; intv. inc. filmog.   Film
        Fan Mo 102:14 D '69

ZETTERLING, MAI
Zetterling, M.   Some notes on acting.   Sight & Sound
   21-2:83 O/D '51
Lerman, L.   International movie report.   Mlle 64:116
   F '67

ZIMBALIST, EFREM JR.
Making a TV idol.   Newsweek 53:90 F 16 '59
Playing quite a different tune.   TV Guide 7-14:17 Ap 4
   '59
March, B.   Life does not end with death.   Photop 56-3:
   40 S '59
Biography.   Cur Bio 21:44 F '60
Same.   Cur Bio Yrbk 1960:474 '61
Zimbalist is a realist.   TV Guide 8-15:17 Ap 9 '60
Allen, A.   Can any wife ever be sure?   Photop 57-5:54
   My '60
Nichols, M.   Trapped by success.   Coronet 50:12 S '61
Durslag, M.   He's left with the grandmothers.   TV
   Guide 10-23:22 Je 9 '62
Mr. Zimbalist goes to Washington.   TV Guide 15-27:6
   Jl 8 '67
Monte, D.   Why ex-wife lives with him.   Photop 75-3:64
   Mr '69

ZORINA, VERA
Roberts, K.   Industrious butterfly.   Colliers 101:15 Mr
   12 '38
Torchy.   Am Mag 130:86 N '40
Biography.   Cur Bio '41
Helen of Troy; Zorina returns to ballet in a made-over
   myth.   Life 14:86 Ap 19 '43
Mother Zorina leaps.   Life 23:65 Jl 14 '47
Harvey, E.   Slaughter off-stage.   Colliers 134:98 O 15
   '54
Native dancer does not retire.   Theatre Arts 38:73 N '54
Zorina as narrator.   Dance Mag 32:36 Ap '58
Zorina, V.   The inward and outward eye.   Dance Mag
   33-12:69 D '59
Where are they now?   Newsweek 58:12 N 27 '61
Martin, G.   Practical streak; intv.   Opera News 32:14 S 23
   S 23 '67
Zorina.   Newsweek 70:90 O 9 '67

702

Reference